For

Gerard R

Joseph Petelo
July 4, 1995

Pete #695

NEVER PLAN TOMORROW

by

Joseph A. Petak

NEVER

PLAN

TOMORROW

THE SAGA OF THE BATAAN DEATH MARCH AND BATTLE OF CORREGIDOR SURVIVORS 1942 - 1945

JOSEPH A. PETAK

AQUATAUR

PRINTED BY DELTA LITHOGRAPH COMPANY
a Bertelsmann company
Valencia, CA

AQUATAUR
Box 5163
Fullerton, California 92635

Library of Congress Cataloging in Publication Data

Petak, A. Joseph
Never Plan Tomorrow

1. World War, 1941-1945 --Prisoners and prisons, Japanese. 2. World War, 1941-1945--Atrocities. 3. Prisoners of War--United States. 4. Prisoners of war--Pacific Area 5. Philippines--Corregidor. 6. Philippines--Bataan. 7. Philippines--Cabanatuan. 8. Prison ships--Japanese. 9. POWs, American, Manchuria.

Library of Congress Catalog Card Number: 91-78112

ISBN 0-9631609-6-6

Printed in the United States of America

First Edition

1 2 3 4 5 6 7 8 9 10

Book Design by Joseph A. Petak

Table of Contents

DEDICATION

This book is dedicated to my cousin, John S. Urban (1559) who died in Taiwan in October, 1942, and, to my comrades of Bataan and Corregidor. To Walt Macarovich (634), Bart Pinson (438). And to Felix Kozakevitch (660) and John Fleming (692).

ACKNOWLEDGEMENT

Special thanks are due to my wife Margaret and son Chris.

Many thanks to Sol Fromer (659) and Arthur Beale (1987).

The roster would not have been possible without the data provided by John C. Ward (602) and Colonel Fortier.

HISTORY OF NEVER PLAN TOMORROW

The original manuscript was written in 1947 as a psychiatric aid due to problems I had after the war. It was written using diaries and other references. The manuscript was stored for many years and was resurrected in 1989. A complete rewrite was performed to make a readable book.

The intent for publication at this time is to provide the story of the men who were in Mukden, Manchuria, since no other known book has been published. And to provide a roster, as a ready reference for all of the guys that were. It is also intended to provide the true story of the freeing of the American, British, Australian, New Zealand, Canadian and Dutch that were with us in Mukden. There are references in General Wainwright's book and in some other books that have various versions of the freeing of the POWs in Mukden. Believe me, the version that is documented here is the way it really happened.

General Jonathan Wainwright

This photograph was taken on Corregidor, outside of the North entrance to Malinta Tunnel, in March of 1942 by the author, a Combat Photographer of the 228th Signal Section.

The General refused to be photographed without his helmet because he had just had a field haircut. He had just received his third star, March 20, 1942.

THE WEATHER
Yesterday's Max.: 94.0 C. or
94.9 F. at 3:35 P. M. Min.:
36.1 C. or 78 F. at 6:05 A. M.

The Tribune

5 Centavos
4 Pages

YEAR XVIII   MANILA, PHILIPPINES, FRIDAY, MAY 8, 1942   NUMBER

CORREGIDOR FALLS

General Wainwright Orders Entire USAFFE to Surrender

Troops Must Disarm, Give Up in 4 Days

Instructions To Officers, Men Read Over Radio

By Ernesto del Rosario and A. J. Malay of the Tribune Staff

Complete and immediate surrender of all the remaining Filipino forces still operating in different parts of the Philippines to the Japanese Imperial Forces was ordered by Lieutenant General Jonathan M. Wainwright, captured commander-in-chief of the USAFFE forces in the Philippines, in a radio broadcast over station KZRH in Manila at 11:40 last night.

Gen. Wainwright, who was captured by the Japanese forces together with his staff with the fall of Corregidor, personally broadcast the order which was addressed to the commanders of the USAFFE troops in three sectors of operations, to all American and Filipino soldiers and officers and to "every Filipino and American in the Philippines."

The USAFFE commanders ordered to surrender are General William F. Sharp, Jr., commanding the Fil-American troops in the Visayas and Mindanao; Colonel J. P. Horan, commanding the troops in the Mountain Province; and Colonel Guillermo Nakar, commanding in Cagayan.

General Wainwright instructed each one of them to assemble their respective troops at designated points of assembly and to present themselves at likewise designated Japanese headquarters to notify the latter of the surrender. Commanding officers of USAFFE troops other than those under these three commanders were instructed to likewise follow the order.

Members of General Wainwright's staff will personally deliver copies of the detailed orders
(Continued on page 4)

Mayor Guinto Urges People To Welcome Commander-in-Chief

Mayor of Greater Manila, Leon G. Guinto yesterday made an appeal to the public to decorate their houses today and take part in the public reception that will be accorded the Commander-in-Chief of the Imperial Japanese Forces and his staff when they enter triumphantly the city after defeating the enemy forces in Bataan and Corregidor.

The triumphal entrance of the Commander-in-Chief and his staff will start from the Bonifacio monument in Balintawak, passing through Rizal Avenue, the Sta. Cruz bridge, up to the official residence of the Commander-in-Chief at the Luneta.

The mayor in his appeal to the public asked everybody to go out and join the big reception that will be accorded the Commander-in-Chief. He also asked that everybody should decorate his home with the Japanese flag. The time for the public reception will be announced by Radio and newspaper.

ORDERING the remaining USAFFE forces throughout the Philippines to surrender is Lt. General Jonathan M. Wainwright, left, commanding general of the American and Philippine Forces. The order was given over the radio last night. A Japanese Army officer is seated at the right.

PNB Emergency Notes Banned

The commander-in-chief of the Imperial Japanese Forces yesterday issued a proclamation and a military ordinance declaring the Philippine National Bank Emergency Circulation Notes issued in the Visayan provinces at the direction of the USAFFE as enemy military notes and as having no monetary value, and prohibiting punishment for any person circulating or accepting the said emergency notes.

The USAFFE since last January ordered the different branches and agencies of the Philippine National Bank in the Visayan provinces to issue these notes for use in the "purchase of military supplies and of creating economic confusion and disturbance."
(Continued on page 5)

People Asked To Display Nippon Flag

With the fall of Corregidor, all Japanese, Filipino and third party foreigners living in Manila and other occupied areas are urged to display the Japanese flag at their homes in celebration of the great Japanese victory.

The public buildings as well as electric posts in important streets in city are now decorated with the flag of the Rising Sun.

The flags will remain in display until after an official celebration is held in the near future.

The department of the interior yesterday received orders from the Executive Commission to raise the Japanese flag on the flagpoles and decorate all government buildings with banners as a part of the celebration of the fall of Corregidor. The flag celebration will continue until further notice.

San Francisco Has Raid Alert

LISBON, May 8 (Domei).—Another air-raid warning was sounded over San Francisco and its vicinity last night, lasting 27 minutes, according to an American radiocast.

The report said all radio stations in the area went off the air. However, a blackout was
(Continued on page 2)

Eye-Witness Tells of "Fall"

Mr. Shibata, of the Propaganda Corps, who was with the first troops that landed in Corregidor Island, arrived in Manila last night bringing the first eye-witness account of the battle for the possession of the fortress.

His account follows:

At the first landing which was effected at 11:15 p. m. on May 5 we rest stiff enemy resistance but we pierced through their lines. Soon afterwards, a second landing unit followed us and by early next morning we occupied
(Continued on page 4)

Army Spokesman Says Fall Of Corregidor Significant

A spokesman of the Imperial Japanese Forces in the Philippines declared yesterday that the fall of Corregidor is a turning point in the life of the Filipinos as the people can now work in earnest for the establishment of a New Philippines.

The statement of the spokesman follows:

"The fall of Corregidor means the total collapse of the Fil-American forces in the Philippines and the end of American oppression and exploitation which the Filipino people have endured for more than 40 years.

With the loss of her Asiatic Fleet and of the USAFFE army, the United States has been driven out of the Philippines, which she planned to use as a base to invade the rest of East Asia under the banner of democracy. And now the so-called ABCD defense line is broken.

Taking advantage of the resistance offered by the small remnants of the USAFFE troops in Corregidor, American propaganda has been trying to mislead the people of the Philippines. However, the fall of Corregidor has blasted this propaganda and opened the eyes of the Filipinos to the real situation.

The fall of Corregidor is indeed a turning point in the life of the Filipinos for the people can now redouble their efforts and work in earnest for the establishment of a New Philippines.

Japan Forces Occupy Entire Stronghold

Tokyo Imperial Headquarters Makes Announcement

TOKYO, May 7 (Domei).—Imperial Headquarters announced this afternoon that Japanese army-land-navy forces succeeded in landing on Corregidor Island in the face of enemy fire at 11:15 o'clock last Tuesday night, May 5, and by 8 o'clock in the morning of Thursday, May 7, had completely occupied Corregidor and other forts on the other islands in Manila Bay.

Headquarters of the Japanese Expeditionary Forces in the Philippines announced at 5 o'clock this afternoon, May 7, that all the fortified islands at the entrance of Manila Bay, including Corregidor, were occupied at 8 o'clock this morning. The fortified islands include Corregidor, Fraile, Caballo, Carabao and La Monja.

Complete occupation of the fortified islands came scarcely two days after the first landing. followed by swift liquidation of enemy resistance on the islands' fortress and the capture of Lt. Gen. Jonathan Wainwright, commander of the Fil-American forces in the Philippines.

Wainwright Surrenders

FROM A BASE ACROSS CORREGIDOR, May 7 (Domei).—Lieutenant General Jonathan Wainwright, unable to further resist the deadly Japanese assault, individually offered to surrender at 11:00 o'clock last night at the post of Malinta Hill, when the vanguard of the Japanese
(Continued on page 4)

The Tribune of Manila carried the story of the fall of Corregidor on the 8th of May, 1942.

VI

Garcia-Guidote Wedding Rites Yesterday

MISS Rosalinda Guidote, daughter of Dr. and Mrs. José Guidote, was married to Dr. Paulino Garcia yesterday morning in a ceremony which took place at 7:15 at the Apostolic Delegation, Mrs. Esperanza L. Osmeña and the bride's father were the sponsors.

The only other attendants were Miss Fe Cu Unjieng and Teddy Evangelista as well sponsors. The church rites over, the couple and their guests, numbering about eighty, had breakfast at The Aristocrat on the Boulevard.

The bride wore a lace wedding terno with touches of gold and silver embroidery. Her long veil was of sheer tulle, worn very simply over a becoming coiffure featuring a pompon of white flowers behind each ear. Instead of flowers, she carried a prayerbook.

Mrs. Isabel Padua sang Ave Maria and Agnus Dei during the ceremony, with Jose Colayco playing the accompaniment on the harmonium.

A PARTY to celebrate the birthday of Dr. Salvador Samson, will be given this afternoon by Mrs. Samson. Mr. and Mrs. Manuel Buencamino and Zacarias Nuguid.

Personal

WE'VE been paying our respects to old magazines and clippings... and .. and ourselves possessed of o' bits of wisdom ...epicurean, horticultural, fashionable... it seems that in the 18th century housewives in some parts of this great, wide world e..ved beer at breakfast... they simmered beer in a brass kettle, crumbling in crusts of brown bread sweetened with molasses ...this was known as "Whistlebelly Vengeance" ... as we haven't tried it ourself we "can't say if this was the inspiration for the discovery hereto-aefter... another writes that "in the summer we can afford to be divinely silly about food because we can eat all we want so we don't wast anything"...

and did you know that phlox is supposed to be the poor man's plant... because he doesn't have to wait three years to get his money's worth... that myrtus are the diplomats of the phlox world because they are very good mixers... we end this paragraph to duly record the fact that a bed was found recently in which the entire roof was a sheet of mirror... such is (was) vanity indeed...

SOME brides come late, some come promptly to their weddings ...Pacita Resurreccion was late to hers yesterday... and so had to wait until the next mass... dogs have their share of the limelight on the boulevard... where everyone still goes ... the other afternoon there was a dachshund on a leash held by one one who looked like Mrs. Leticia Vizgel-mann-Smith ... Miss Manuela Gay for one, subscribes to the popularity or sapatillas for streetwear... she always has a pair in leather to match her crisp-look-ing ternos... some one tells us that anahaw fans are being painted red, or blue, or green, etc... and that you see them in church even...

Metropolitan Chess Next Week

The 1942 Metropolitan chess tournament will get underway next week at the St. Rita's Hall clubroom on Taft Avenue, under the auspices of the Knights of Columbus, Manila Council No. 1000. Strong contestants like R. H. Lopez, V.T. Barcenilla, Dr. Arce, Avecilla, and others, are expected to join the championship.

This year's tourney will be governed by the International Rules of Chess. A registration fee of one peso will be charged each entry. Valuable prizes are at stake.

Entries are received by the K of C secretary, St. Rita's Hall Taft Avenue, or by telephone, 2-06-21. Contestants may also communicate with Prof. Nicolas Zafra, chairman of the K of C chess committee, or with Prof. I. Amado, president of the Philippine Chess Club, for the details.

BIKE CONTEST ENTRY CLOSES TOMORROW

The entry book for the bicycle stunt contest, announced recently will close tomorrow, Saturday. The competition is billed on Sunday.

Several entries have already been received, but more are expected to register. Those desiring to take part may submit their names at Munson Bike Market, 1504 Gral. Luna, Paco.

K OF C LEAGUE

The Jugglers decisively defeated the Poison A. C. in the Knights of Columbus senior-junior game yesterday afternoon in the K of C gymnasium. The final score was 77, 38.

In the novices group Jinkirian trounced Busy 5, 39-21, while Sphinx subdued the Nitehawks, 36-32.

KZRH

Short Wave: 9.930 kc.; 31.18 m.
6.140 kc.; 48.47 m.
Long Wave: 636.9 kc.; 495 m.
Friday - May 8, 1942
Call Sign

Time	
3:00 a.m.—Sign On	
4:00 a.m.—News in English.	
4:10 a.m.—Nora Hispania.	
8:15 a.m.—Famous Artists Program.	
8:45 a.m.—Children's Hour.	
9:00 a.m.—Xmisty Tunes.	
10:00 Noon—(Time Signal)	

Court Calendar

COURT OF FIRST INSTANCE OF MANILA
May 8, 1942

(Court calendar listings — various case entries by Judge)

San Francisco Has Raid Alert

(Continued from page 1)

not ordered.

LISBON, May 6 (Domei)—The United States navy department announced that a medium-sized United Nations merchant vessel and a British merchantman had been torpedoed off the Atlantic coast, according to a Washington report.

The report said that the survivors had been landed at an unnamed east coast port.

LISBON, May 6 (Domei).—A British Broadcasting Corporation announcement heard here reported that Royal Air Force during the month of April lost 314 planes in the aerial assaults against Germany, Occupied France and in the Middle East.

TOKYO, May 7 (Domei).—Domei reports that all dockyards in the United States are operating at highest efficiency. American artisans will not be able to make up for the loss of merchant ships being sung every month as Axis submarines, informed shipping circles asserted.

HALIFAX CONFERS WITH ROOSEVELT

LISBON, May 6 (Domei).—Lord Halifax, British ambassador to the United States, called on President Roosevelt and conferred on the British landing in Madagascar, according to Washington dispatches reaching here.

LISBON, May 6 (Domei).—

(radio program listing continues)

Candy Factory Bodega Burned

Fire believed to be of accidental origin started at 2:30 p.m. yesterday in the O'Racca Confectionery Co. at 77 Barraca, Binondo. Property damage mounted to P90,000.

The fire was preceded by an explosion in a padlocked storehouse on the first floor on the south side of the building. Investigation indicated that the blast was due to spontaneous combustion. Inflammable materials for manufacturing candies and biscuits were stored in the bodega. Officials of the firm also expressed the belief that the explosion was accidental, possibly due to the heat.

The candy factory was functioning at the time of the blast, but no one was hurt.

PAPER DISMISSES CORRESPONDENTS

ISTANBUL, May 6 (Domei). It was learned here that the semi-official *Anadolu News Agency* suddenly dismissed 17 Jewish correspondents yesterday upon orders from the government to eliminate all allegedly dangerous elements from the staff.

Considerable interest was caused by the action as it came after alleged anti-German reports by the Agency regarding the evacuation ship Smyrna of 1,862 tons.

CLASS IN JAPANESE

At the United Church, a class in the Japanese language has been going on for several weeks now. The professor in charge is the Rev. Kusana, member of the Religious Section of Japanese Army. The class meets at 5 every Wednesday and Friday afternoon. To enable students who may desire to enroll at this time to catch up with the students now attending the class, Professor Kusana will start half an hour earlier—4:30 p.m., Wednesday and Friday.

Washington reports revealed that Pres. Gen. Manuel Prado of Peru arrived in Maimi late this afternoon. He is expected in Washington tomorrow, it was reported.

Page two of the Tribune.

The Tribune

INDEPENDENT FILIPINO DAILY

Published every morning by the TVT Publishing Corporation, Calle F. Torres, Manila P. O. Box 775. Associate Editor: Jose P. Bautista.

Entered as 2nd class matter April 26, 1926 at the Manila Post Office. Telephone 2-11-24 connecting all departments.

SUBSCRIPTION RATES—Philippines

1 Month	P 1.50
3 Months	4.25
6 Months	8.00
1 Year	15.00
SUNDAY ONLY	
6 Months	P 3.50
1 Year	6.00

ADVERTISING RATES
THE TRIBUNE (Daily)
P2.00 per Col. Inch
SUNDAY TRIBUNE
P2.00 per Col. Inch

Classified Ads

Announcements

LEAVING TOMORROW
May 9th at 9:00 a.m.
Int. Truck for BAGUIO, LA UNION & PANGASINAN via TARLAC. Apply for reservations to L. A. D.
614 Rizal Ave., Tel. 2-62-93
(In front of Dalisay Theater)

SECOND TRIP TO APARRI ON MAY 10TH. APPLY FOR RESERVATION AT 2104 AZCARRAGA, TEL. 2-69-20

IMMEDIATE SAILINGS
Friday, May 8, for Cebu, Bohol and Ilongos via Pulanduta. And Monday, May 11, for Masbate, Samar and Leyte.
T. CLOMA & CO.
2066 Azcarraga (near FEU)

TRIPS TO PANGASINAN
Passengers & cargo truck leaving for Pangasinan via Tarlac passing Villasis, Urdaneta, Sta. Barbara [illegible] San Carlos on Sunday, May 10 & Wednesday, May 13. Passengers with traveling certificates accepted. Apply to Mr. M. S. Flores, 650 Raon, Quiapo, Manila.
Tel. 2-96-34

TRIP TO SINILOAN
via Sta. Cruz and Pagsanjan
Cargoes and passengers accepted
Starting cor. Taft Ave. & Estrada
Sunday, May 10, 9:00 a. m.
For reservation, call Mr. Durias
Tel. 5-69-77

BEST AVAILABLE TRANSPORTATION
Truck Leaving Soon For GERONA, TARLAC. Receiving Cargoes & Passengers via Bulacan and Pampanga Provinces.
For information see:
Mr. U. M. CRESPO, Mgr.
110 Echague, 2nd floor, Lack & Davis Bldg.

TRIP TO PANGASINAN
A big & comfortable PASSENGER BUS is leaving for Urbiztondo via Tarlac, Villasis, Urdaneta, Sta. Barbara, Malasique and San Carlos tomorrow May 9th at 7:00 a.m. For reservation, apply to:
Mr. N. AROMIN
1689 corner Herran-Gen. Luna, Paco
Tel. 5-41-76

WEEKLY TRIP TO BAGUIO
VIA PANGASINAN & LA UNION
Truck leaving Saturday morning. May 9th.
For reservation,
Call at 2290 Azcarraga, Manila
Tel. 2-51-35

VISAYANS
Trip to Samar, Leyte and Capiz leaving definitely, May 11. Two sailboats ready.
BANZAI TRANS
110 Echague
Telephone 2-66-32

For Hire

WE HAVE CARS FOR HIRE BY THE HOUR
Call Tel. 5-69-54
MANILA YELLOW TAXICAB
MABINI

Legal Notice

The undersigned hereby announces his intention to apply to the Office of the City Engineer for a permit to install refrigerating machineries with approximately 3 ½ h.p. for the manufacture of ice-drops at the premises of 1133 G. Tuason, Sampaloc, Manila on or about May 25, 1942.
C. R. MIRANDA

Lost And Found

P50.00 REWARD
Given to anyone who can recover or lead to the recovery of one
"PILOT FIRESTONE" BICYCLE,
which was STOLEN from inside the Post Office Bldg. on May 6th between 10 and 10:15 a. m.
Descriptions: Original paint: blue with white trimmings, latest model, saddle with khaki cover. U. S. Royal Balloon tires.
Informant please call up
Tel. 2-49-78
During office hours
No questions asked.

LOST CHECKS
REWARD
If finder of Checks Nos. A. W. 09027 and A. W. 09029 lost somewhere on Calle Herran on May 6, 1942, will return them to 1212 Herran, substantial reward will be given and no questions asked.

Houses For Rent

(FOR RENT)
Large apartments in concrete bldg., suitable for hotel or boarding-house, ideal location near Luneta & Boulevard 230 M. H. del Pilar. Large bldg. on Taft Ave., No. 1480, ground floor suitable for store or refreshment parlor. Residential houses, rpts. accesories also available.
Apply J. J. REYES
Tel. 2-42-82 548 Rizal Ave.

Wanted To Rent

WANTED
2 Bachelors want to rent a house in or around Ermita or Malate Districts.
Tel. 2-21-54
Between 10:00 and 12:00 A. M. and 3:00 and 5:00 P. M.

Services Offered

SUITE CONSISTING OF LIVING ROOM, 2 BEDROOMS WITH PRIVATE BATH
Completely furnished including Electric refrigerator, Piccolo and linen. Private entrance. Suitable for two bachelors. Very close to transportation facilities. Apply at
1060 PENNSYLVANIA

ATTENTION TO TRUCK AND CAR OWNERS
We adjust carburators for alcohol, general repairs, recharge batteries, upholstery, painting and electric welding.
Rizal Motors and Auto Service
321 Dorotea Jose and Oroquieta
Tel. 2-30-91

We have BUYERS For Your Merchandise
Inquire:
INDUSTRIAL BROKERAGE
122-124 Crystal Arcade
Tel. 2-06-32

MARAMBA & MARAMBA
Consulting Industrial Engineers
Can fix your diesel engines to use coconut oil
Tel. 5-11-37
Office: 48 Lourdes, Pasay

Refrigeration Service and Repair Shop. Reliable service on any kind of refrigerator. Former mechanics of the H. E. Heacock & Co. All jobs guaranteed.
ALL TYPES, MAKES, ALL MODELS, ALL YEARS
Dial—6-79-92

Used Cars, Trucks, Etc.

SLIGHTLY USED 1941 NASH SEDAN AT QUICKEST SATISFACTORY OFFER. MAY BE SEEN AT 2225 O'DONNELL CORNER BATANGAS.

FOR SALE
One Chevrolet 41 passenger truck model 1939. Maybe seen at 384 Lipa, Sampaloc from 9 a.m. to 6 p.m.
No Agents Wanted

FOR SALE

Portable Spray Paint Outfit, complete with Electric Motor and Spray Gun, used 3 months only	P85.00
Corona Zephyr Portable Typewriter, 1941 model, slightly used	P46.00
Boy's Bicycle, new paint	P40.00
Philco Radio, 8 tubes	P80.00
Wardrobe Trunk, medium size, like new	P85.00

425 A. Mabini

Miscellaneous For Sale

FOR SALE VERY CHEAP
Brand new rattan parlor sets with thick beautiful cushions; secondhand narra parlor and dining sets; narra office desks complete with swivel chairs; refrigerators (Universal, Frigidaire, Electrolux); Magic Chef gas range; radio-phonograph combination and radios (Silverton, RCA, Airline and Philco); Delco auto radio; typewriters; cash register; surveyor's leveling compass; coffee percolator; table lamps; electric fans; etc., etc. WANTED TO BUY: trucks, jitneys, automobiles, sewing machines and secondhand furniture.
Phone 2-08-94
1011 Rizal Avenue

THE BEST BEANS
We have received a new shipment of the best red beans, which we offer at P0.85 a kilo. We also offer centrifugal sugar, bags of 63 kilos, at P6.50 and the delicious "LA MARINA" chocolate, which we deliver.
CAMPOS RUEDA HERMANOS, INC.
2206 Azcarraga
Tel. 2-39-44

PARAÑAQUE SALT IN BAGS OF ABOUT 63 KILOS
COMPETITIVE PRICE
INSULAR COMMERCIAL CO.
721 Evangelista
(Near corner Azcarraga)

TODAY
"HOW TO WIN FRIENDS AND INFLUENCE PEOPLE" centers on a single [illegible] your cleanest best. Your wife can help you attain it Very Economically with—

50 bars SAN PABLO (Lute) Soap	P8.00
1 Pint BETZREST BLUING (Tina)	.70
The Weather Man is adamant; so 12 packages of "JELL-O" & "ROYAL" will [illegible]	P3.28

VITAMIN STORE 1035 Rebibid Viejo

"INSULAR" LAUNDRY SOAP
"LUTU" and "HILAW" and "RAINBOW" TOILET SOAP
At exceptional low prices. Special rates for wholesale and agents.
INSULAR COMMERCIAL CO.
721 Evangelista (near corner Azcarraga)

ONE DE VRY AIR CIRCULATOR
on stand
P125.00
Tel. 2-12-83

LEICA & CONTAX CAMERAS
The gentlemen who are interested about these cameras will please answer this advertisement to arrange for appointment to see them. These cameras will be in reserve for you during a few days only. Address: Leica-Contax, c/o Tribune.

Wanted To Buy

WANTED TO BUY SECONDHAND TRUCK TIRES, OLD NEWSPAPERS, AND DARAK IN SACKS.
TEL. 5-57-50

WANTED TO BUY
WE BUY OLD JEWELRY AND ALL KINDS OF GOLD AT REASONABLE PRICE.
ORO AGUILA
205 Plaza Sta. Cruz
2nd Floor Room No. 5

WANTED TO BUY
DUAL-WHEEL TRUCKS; INTERNATIONAL, FARGO, CHEVROLET, FORD, DODGE. MODEL 1939, 1940, 1941, 1942.
MITSUI MINING COMPANY
2nd floor, National City Bank Bldg.
Tel. 2-31-51

WE BUY FOR CASH
Drugs, groceries, toilet articles, etc. We offer good price for shoe leather. Between 9-12 a. m. to 3-6 p. m.
93 Plaza Goiti
ASK FOR ANDRES

POLICE NOTES

WAREHOUSE FIRE — Fire started shortly before 6 p.m. yesterday in a warehouse along the Pasig River near Ayala bridge. The flames ate up bales of abaca in the bodega. With their hoses drawing water from the river and hydrants on Marques de Comillas and Concepcion streets, firemen confined the blaze to the pile of abaca bales. Japanese soldiers helped the firemen.

COOPED AGAIN Patrolman O. Espinosa was patrolling his beat last Wednesday night when he met a man whose face he thougnt was familiar. The cop decided to invite the stranger to the police bertillon. He was right. The man was Sergio Aliño, long wanted on a court warrant.

WHAT MAKES A GOOD DETECTIVE: punctuality in reporting for work, 15 per cent; efficiency and completeness and accuracy on reports submitted, 10 per cent; conduct, 15 per cent; success in daily investigation of cases assigned to him, 25 per cent; personal tact in handling cases assigned to him, 10 per cent; ability and leadership in the execution of orders and in general work, 10 per cent; personal integrity, honesty and trustworthiness, 15 per cent. This is in accordance with the new basis for ascertaining the merit of each detective as ordered by police headquarters.

STATUTORY—The police yesterday arrested 27-year-old Pablo Hamor on complaint of the mother of 13-year-old Felicidad Delfino, of 1447 Int. A. Oroquieta. The charge was statutory offense.

"VANDALS" who desecrate graves and chop down shade trees in the city's cemeteries will be severely dealt with, the police said as they posted more guards at the cemeteries yesterday to curb thefts of gravestones, marble slabs and ornamental objects in mausoleums, and to arrest firewood gatherers who have been wantonly cutting down trees or chopping off tree branches in the cemetery grounds.

GEM THEFT.—The secret service is investigating the theft of jewelry worth P1,970 stolen from the residence of Lourdes Chico at 909 Dakota some time between the night of May 4 and the next morning.

The victim said that the jewels, including diamonds and heirlooms, were in a cardboard box which she placed in her wardrobe drawer before retiring last Monday night.

Wanted To Buy

WANTED TO BUY
Tires and Automobile spare parts. Will pay good prices.
Apply No. 233 David
Tel. No. 2-47-56

WILL PAY GOOD CASH
For Electric Refrigerators, Radios, Phonographs, Pianos, Electric Fans, Furniture, Typewriters and 1 automobile. Write offers to:
"J. P."
c/o The Tribune

CARRETELA
with 2 or 3 big horses used to pulling heavy loads. Carretela must have good axle, strong spring and high rubber tires. Without these requirements, no offer will be considered. Bring or see:
Mr. A. DE CASTRO
Polo, Bulacan, in front of the church

FOR CASH
Men's bicycle, preferably American make with balloon tires. Only new models with original paint will be considered. See:
MR. GOLDAMMER
21 Alhambra, Ermita
during office hours

Wanted Help

WANTED
50 BEAUTIFUL WAITRESSES
GOOD INCOME GUARANTEED
APPLY 10:00 A. M. SUNDAY MORNING
MR. J. YAMAMOTO
319 RONQUILLO

WANTED IMMEDIATELY
10 BEAUTIFUL HOSTESSES
APPLY PERSONALLY AT 442 P. GOMEZ

WANTED HOSTESSES & WAITRESSES IMMEDIATELY
Apply in person, see Miss Sarmiento at 535 P. Paterno.

U. S. Slashes Consumption Of Gas, Oil

LISBON, May 6 (Domei):—It was reported from Washington that the war production board ordered a 50 per cent slash over the normal demand on all deliveries of gasoline, oil and fuel in 17 eastern states and in the District of Columbia effective on May 16.

Deputy Petroleum Coordinator Ralph K. Davies said that the curtailment of gasoline consumption in areas other than the Pacific, the Northwest and Atlantic seaboard may be necessary because of the withdrawal of transportation facilities from those areas in order to relieve the Atlantic coast shortages.

BUENOS AIRES, May 5 (Domei):—The United States treasury department in an effort to check the flow of American silver into Axis hands announced the prohibition hereafter of all shipments of silver to Spain, Portugal, Sweden, France, Turkey and French territories in Africa, according to a report from Washington.

PNB Emergency Notes Banned

(Continued from page 1)

bance."

The proclamation and military ordinance issued by the commander-in-chief are as follows:

Since January, 1942, the Phil. American Army ordered the different branches or agencies of the Philippine National Bank in the Visayan provinces to issue Philippine National Bank Emergency Circulation Notes for the purpose of using them in the purchase of military supplies and of creating economic confusion and disturbance. For this reason, the circulation of said emergency notes is declared illegal and their acceptance absolutely prohibited.

Inasmuch as these emergency notes were issued for the use of the enemy and considering the nature thereof and the purpose for which they were issued, it is hereby proclaimed that these notes are enemy military notes and consequently, they are declared as having no monetary value whatsoever.

Commander-in-Chief
The Imperial Japanese Forces

Military Ordinance No. 5

Within the territories occupied by the Imperial Japanese Forces, the circulation of Philippine National Bank Emergency Circulation Notes issued by the various branches and agencies of the Philippine National Bank in the Visayan provinces is hereby absolutely prohibited.

Any person circulating or accepting the said emergency notes for any purpose whatsoever will be severely punished in accordance with the Military Law.

Commander-in-Chief
The Imperial Japanese Forces

Page three of the Tribune.

Troops Must Disarm, Give...

(Continued from page 1)
to General Sharp, Colonel Horan and Colonel Necar. It states that the order must be complied with within four days after receipt.

All weapons, ammunition, vessels and other war materials must be surrendered to the Japanese forces intact.

Outstanding points in General Wainwright's order follow:

1. To put a stop to the useless sacrifice of human lives, he decided to make an offer of surrender of the fortress of Corregidor and the four harbor forts of Manila to Lieutenant General Masaharu Homma, commander-in-chief of the Japanese Imperial Forces in the Philippines, but the latter would not consider the offer unless all other USAFFE troops still operating in the Philippines also laid down their arms, including the troops under General Sharp in the Visayas and Mindanao, under Colonel Horan in the Mountain Province and Colonel Necar in Cagayan.

2. General Wainwright advised General Sharp that he had resumed direct command of troops in the Visayas and Mindanao and that, accordingly, he was instructing him to surrender.

3. General Wainwright directed himself also to everyone and all those listening to him to advise immediately General Sharp, Colonel Horan and Colonel Necar of the order of surrender in case these officers had not heard him.

4. The order of surrender was issued by General Wainwright by virtue of the authority vested in him by the President of the United States.

5. General Douglas MacArthur, commander-in-chief of the USAFFE, will be notified of the surrender.

6. All USAFFE troops operating in the Philippines will immediately and voluntarily disarm and take the prescribed steps for surrender.

7. It is absolutely prohibited that arms, ammunition, and other equipment or military establishment be destroyed, burned or dispersed. Portable arms must be gathered by the troops at the point of assembly for surrender and delivery to the Japanese forces. Arms and weapons which cannot be moved must be disclosed to the Japanese forces and their location designated to them.

8. Locations of land and water mines must be disclosed to the Japanese forces. Sketches and maps necessary for their location should also be surrendered.

9. Order to cease firing will be given by the commander-in-chief of the Japanese Imperial Forces only once he is satisfied of the faithfulness of the execution of the order for surrender by the USAFFE troops.

10. Implicit obedience to the order was stressed.

Scheduled to speak at 10 o'clock, General Wainwright did not arrive at Station KZRH until one hour later. He was accompanied by six American Army officers. All of them exhibited haggard faces and their clothes were disheveled.

The broadcast was not started until about 11:30 because General Wainwright and his men were first given cold melon and watermelon, iced water, and drinks. As the surrendering officers ate, the speech to be delivered by General Wainwright was the subject of consultation. General Wainwright's orders, which he read over the radio, were first copied.

General Wainwright was introduced by Marcelo S. Victoriano of the KZRH staff. Photographers of the propaganda corps of the Japanese Army, the Domei News Agency, and Tokyo and Manila newspapers, had a veritable holiday snapping pictures of the surrendering general and his staff.

All the officers looked tired, having made the trip from Bataan by motor car. They were taken from Corregidor to Bataan by boat and came to Manila by motor car.

General Wainwright carried a rattan cane. All officers had no neckties but they retained their insignias. They were not communicative the whole time they were in KZRH, taking down notes of General Wainwright's orders.

General Wainwright's speech follows:

"This is Lt. General J. M. Wainwright, with a message for Gen. William F. Sharp, commanding the Mindanao and Visayan Forces. Any one receiving this message, please notify Gen. Sharp immediately.

"By virtue of the authority invested in me by the President of the United States, I, as commanding general of the United States Forces in the Philippines, hereby resume direct command of General Sharp and of all troops under his command.

"I will now give another order. Subject: Surrender. To put a stop to the further useless sacrifice of human lives, I tendered yesterday, May 6, to Lt. Gen. Homma, commanding general of the Imperial Japanese Forces in the Philippines, surrender of the four harbor defense forts. He declined to accept the surrender unless it included the forces under your (General Sharp) command. I left General Homma without any agreement being reached between us. In the name of humanity, I decided to surrender the American and Philippine Forces to the Japanese Imperial Forces. You will of course realize that this decision was forced upon me by circumstances totally beyond my control. Col. Jesse Treywick, you will report the text of this letter to General Sharp.

"These instructions are applicable to General Sharp, Col. Horan, and Col. Nekar. All troops of the American and Philippine armies operating in the Philippines and the harbor defenses of Manila Bay will immediately and voluntarily disarm and take the following steps:

"Troops in Northern Luzon will assemble at Bayombong or Bontoc and the commanding officers will present themselves to the Japanese officer in Baguio.

"Troops in Panay will assemble at the northern environ of Iloilo, while those in Negros will assemble in the vicinity of Bacolod. At any rate, their commanding officers will assemble at Iloilo City.

"Those in Bohol will assemble in the vicinity of Roai, while their commanding officers will assemble in Cebu City.

"Those troops in Leyte and Samar will assemble in the vicinity of Tacloban and Catbalogan, respectively, their commanding officers to assemble in Legaspi.

"Troops in Mindanao will assemble in the vicinity of Iligan, and those in the Malaybalay district or the Agusan basin will assemble in the vicinity of Malaybalay or Butuan.

"Those at places not mentioned above will assemble at the nearest place.

"These orders must be executed faithfully within four days after receipt.

"It is prohibited that arms, materials, vessels, or any other equipment be destroyed, burned or dispersed. Easily movable weapons such as machineguns and small arms, will be gathered in the vicinity of the assembly points.

"Vessels in waters other than Manila Bay shall proceed immediately to Cagayan in Mindanao.

"Defensive installations of all kinds, especially in areas where land or sea mines are laid, will be reported and their positions indicated by sketch.

"Further orders will be issued if necessary.

"The Japanese Army and Navy will not cease their operations unless they fully realize the faithfulness of the execution of these orders, so they must be carried out faithfully otherwise the Japanese Forces will not cease their operations.

Eye-Witness Tells of "Fall"

(Continued from page 1)
what we called the Sakura fortification where we found five underground roads. General Jonathan Wainwright, commander-in-chief of the USAFFE forces, and members of his staff were sheltered in the underground roads. This appeared to be the only place in the island which was not damaged by the Japanese attack on the island.

A furious attack by our troops on the morning of May 6 met with a final resistance by the USAFFE troops defending the Sakura fortification but before 11 o'clock in the morning of the same day the stronghold fell.

There were three heavy artillery batteries defending the fort, namely, the James, Gallery and Wake batteries which consisted of 40 cm. cannons, but all of them were destroyed by the incessant bombing of Japanese planes and were already useless at that time. Our forces continued their attack and by 8 o'clock of May 7 the remnants of the troops defending the batteries were mopped up.

My impression after landing on Corregidor was that the number of American troops defending the island was much bigger than we expected and that the losses of the Japanese forces were extremely small. Corregidor which has been heralded as stronger than Hongkong and Singapore, was taken in less time and with smaller losses than we expected, showing the high spirit of the Japanese soldiers. I was deeply impressed by this thought.

Corregidor Falls

(Continued from page 1)
landing units cornered the general and his staff.

The commander of the Japanese unit immediately took Gen. Wainwright and his staff as prisoners of war, thus making the remaining Fil-American forces in Corregidor leaderless and without any semblance of organization.

Gen. Wainwright was accompanied by his chief-of-staff, Brigadier General Lewis S. Beebe; Colonel John R. Pugh, aide-de-camp; and Majors Thomas Duely and William Lawrence.

Last Report

LISBON, May 6 (Domei).—A report from Washington said that according to the U. S. war department communique issued on Wednesday morning based on "one of the last messages received from Lt. Gen. Jonathan Wainwright prior to the fall of Corregidor," Japanese artillery was firing from many new positions on Corregidor and other island forts throughout May 5 before the Japanese forces effected a successful landing attack.

Gen. Wainwright said that for the fourth successive day, there were 13 separate air attacks on Corregidor. Pointing out that the artillery and air attacks by the Japanese forces were the continuation of operations against the forts which began soon after the fall of Bataan on April 9, Gen. Wainwright said that the attacks increased in intensity as the Japanese forces installed heavy batteries on the slopes of Mount Mariveles in Bataan.

The communique said that beginning on April 29, Japanese military fire became much heavier and from that time until May 5 there was little respite for Corregidor from artillery and air attacks. It said that during the last few days there were many casualties among the Fil-American forces and damage to military installations was severe.

Steel Barges Used

The announcement said that the Japanese landing was preceded by a heavy artillery attack on the beach defenses which swept away barbed wire entanglements and blasted machinegun installations and other centers of resistance. It said that the Japanese forces used a large number of steel barges in the short water trip from the tip of Bataan Peninsula to Corregidor.

BUENOS AIRES, May 6 (Domei).—According to a report from Washington, the U. S. navy department announced that five American auxiliary vessels had been either sunk or scuttled as the final hours of Corregidor Island approached. They were the Taninger, Oahu, Pigeon, Luzon and Quail.

The announcement said that the Luzon and Quail were severely damaged as a result of which the crews sunk them to prevent them from falling into the hands of the Japanese.

Navy Boats Sunk

LISBON, May 6 (Domei).—The United States navy department issued a communique this afternoon revealing that in one of the last messages from Corregidor, Captain Kenneth M. Hoeffel, commander of the naval forces at the island-fortress, reported the following:

The minesweeper "Tanager" and the 450-ton river gunboat "Oahu" had been sunk by Japanese gunfire from Bataan; the minesweeper "Pigeon" had been sunk by bombers, while the 560-ton river gunboat "Luzon" and the minesweeper "Quail" were damaged by gunfire and scuttled by U. S. forces.

The communique said that when Corregidor fell there were approximately 175 officers and 2,100 men of the U. S. Navy, and 70 officers and 1,500 men of the Marine Corps. The communique added that Colonel Samuel L. Howard is the senior officer of the Marine Corps and it is assumed that all these officers and men had been captured.

Caballo Fort Taken

FROM A BASE ACROSS CORREGIDOR, May 7.—Japanese forces landed on the island fortress of Caballo, located southeast of Corregidor, at 12:04 a. m. shortly after midnight on May 7. Caballo Island is one of the island fortresses surrounding Corregidor and is part of the chain of defenses at the entrance of Manila Bay. With the capture of Caballo Island mopping up operations in Corregidor will be facilitated.

NOW SHOWING FIRST RUN PICTURE
IDEAL
First Show 9:20 A. M. 10:45, 12:30, 2:05 3:40 and 5:15 P.M. Matinee Till 12 Noon
BAD LITTLE ANGEL

LIFE AIR CONDITIONED
LAST DAY
FIRST SHOW 9:00 A.M. | 30¢ — 40¢ ALL-DAY
"MY LOVE CAME BACK" with OLIVIA DE HAVILLAND JEFFREY LYNN
TOMORROW
REGELIO DE LA ROSA NORMA BLANCAFLOR in "ANONG GANDA MO"

AVENUE
NOW SHOWING
FIRST SHOW—10 A.M. LAST SHOW—4:20 P.M. MATINEE TILL—12 NOON
Love Drama of a Private Nurse
By author of "The Citadel"
Carole LOMBARD Brian AHERNE · Anne SHIRLEY
VIGIL in the NIGHT
RKO RADIO Picture

CAPITOL
NOW SHOWING
FIRST SHOW: 9:30 A.M. LAST FULL SHOW: 4:30 P.M. MATINEE TILL 12 NOON
Dorothy Lamour—Ray Milland
"HER JUNGLE LOVE"
IN TECHNICOLOR
A PARAMOUNT PICTURE

STATE
NOW SHOWING
By Popular Request
FIRST SHOW—9:30 A.M. LAST SHOW—4:20 P.M. MATINEE TILL 12 NOON
IN TECHNICOLOR!
"WEEK END IN HAVANA"
Alice Faye * John Payne Carmen Miranda * Cesar Romero

LYRIC
NOW SHOWING
FIRST SHOW 9:30 A.M. LAST FULL SHOW 4:30 P.M. MATINEE TILL 12 NOON
A First Run Picture!
"BLUES in the NIGHT"
with PRISCILLA LANE BETTY FIELD LLOYD NOLAN RICHARD WHORF
A Warner Bros. Picture

LIFE AIR CONDITIONED
"ANONG GANDA MO"
FEATURING TOGO AND PUGO
Directed by Dr. Gerardo de Leon

STARTING TOMORROW
Rogelio de la ROSA Norma BLANCAFLOR in

TIMES
TODAY First Show 9:30 A.M. Last Show 4:25 P.M. Matinee Till 12 Noon
A FIRST RUN PICTURE
BACHELOR DADDY
EDWARD EVERETT HORTON DONALD WOODS · RAYMOND WALBURN and BABY SANDY

DALISAY
OPENS TODAY
First Show 9 A.M.—Last Show 4 P.M.
ACUÑA-ZALDARIAGA PROUDLY PRESENTS ARSENIA FRANCISCO ANGEL ESMERALDA YOLANDA MARQUES
"KUNG KITA'Y KAPILING"

STRAND
NOW SHOWING
SHOW STARTS 9:00 A.M.
SAMUEL GOLDWYN THE HURRICANE

METROPOLITAN THEATRE
PRESENTING NOW GRAND STAGE SHOW BY International Revue Co.
HUNGARIAN RHAPSODY
A Beautiful Fantasy Revue
ACCOMPANIED WITH SONGS, DANCES, COMEDIES, ACROBATICS, ETC.
First Show 2 P.M. — Second 4 P.M.
Change of Program every Thursday

RADIO THEATRE Comfortably Cool
OPENS TODAY
FOUR WIVES
Starring Priscilla Lane, Rosemary Lane, Lola Lane, Gail Page, Jeffry Lynn, John Garfield

Page 4 of the Tribune of May 8th, 1942. Note the current movies being shown locally. The Filipinos told of the Japanese soldiers filling the theaters to see the American movies.

Americans that had just been surrendered by General Wainwright. The men are at the West entrance of the Malinta Tunnel on Corregidor. The soldier with the towel around his neck, lower right hand corner, is Corporal John S. Urban. This photograph was captured by the American forces when they overran the Japanese in 1945 when retaking the Philippines.

HEADQUARTERS

UNITED STATES ARMY FORCES IN THE FAR EAST

FORT MILLS, P.I.

January 15, 1942

Subject: MESSAGE FROM GEN. MACARTHUR

TO: ALL UNIT COMMANDERS

The following message from Gen. MacArthur will be read and explained to all troops. Every Company Commander is charged with the personal responsibility for the delivery of this message. Each Headquarters will follow-up to insure reception by every Company or similar Unit.

"Help is on the way from the United States. Thousands of troops and hundreds of planes are being dispatched. The exact time of arrival of reinforcements is unknown as they will have to fight their way through Japanese against them. It is imperative that our troops hold until these reinforcements arrive.

No further retreat is possible. We have more troops in Bataan than the Japanese have thrown against us, our supplies are ample; a determined defense will defeat the enemy's attack.

It is a question now of courage and of determination. Men who run will merely be destroyed but men who fight will save themselves and their country.

I call upon every soldier in Bataan to fight in his assigned position, resisting every attack. This is the only road to salvation. If we fight we will win; if we retreat we will be destroyed.

" MACARTHUR "

By Command of General MacArthur
(Signed)   Carl H. Seals
            Colonel, AGD
            Adjutant General

General MacArthur's Letter. Help is on the way.

COPY

April 12th, 1942

          Lieutenant General Jonathan M. Wainwright, Commanding the United
States Forces in the Philippines, issued the following message to the troops
on Corregidor this morning.

          "Corregidor can and will be held. There can be no question of
surrendering this m ghty fortress to the enemy, it will be defended with
all the resources at our command. Major General George F. Moore, Commanding
General of Fort Mills, is whole-heartedly with me in the unalterable decision
to hold this island together with its auxilliary forts.

          I call upon every person on this fortess - officer, enlisted man,
or civilian - to consider himself from this time onward as a member of this
force as resolved to meet the enemy's challenge each hour of every night and
day. The men who have served here before will remain at their post, while
those who have come from Bataan will be assigned to appropriate tasks and
battle stations. It is essential, above all, that the men who have joined us
from the mainland promptly rid themselves of any defeatist attitude which they
may have and consider themselves as part of this fighting unit.

          Bataan has fallen, but Corregidor will carry on. On this mighty
fortress - a pearl of great price on which the enemy has set covetous eyes -
the spirit of Bataan will continue to live.!"

General Wainwright's Letter after the fall of Bataan.

Epilogue to Bataan and Corregidor.

America had decided to sacrifice the men and women in the Philippine Islands for political reasons.

Bataan was overrun on the 9th of April 1942.

Corregidor was surrendered on May the 6th of 1942, twenty-seven days after the fall of Bataan.

Vivid in the minds of the men and women who were captured on Corregidor were the stories, and the rumors, of the atrocities of the Bataan Death March.

Facing their unknown future, the defenders of Corregidor disappeared from the world as far as their country was concerned. They did not disappear as far as General Homma, their captor, and Premier - General Tojo of Japan were concerned. Tojo had long cherished, and had developed, the capabilities of the War Machine he controlled as the Minister of War. As the Premier of Japan, he approved a plan that centered around the men from Bataan and Corregidor. The Japanese had developed a diabolically clever and cruel scheme to capitalize on th knowledge and skill of the Americans. This scheme involved the building of a huge factory in one of the northernmost reaches of the Empire, Manchuria.

Manchuria had been one of the fruits of a previous coup, a coup that had been a personal involvement for Tojo. Under Tojo and the Japanese militarists, the ambitious development of the resources that had belonged to the Manchu Emperors. This development had been in force ever since Japan had overrun Manchuria. There, in Mukden, renamed by the Japanese, Hoten, was an extremely important segment of the Japanese war machine, the Manchurian Machine, Tool and Die Company. This company was to employ hundreds of machinists. The machinists, Prisoners of War.

It had become apparent that here was an asset to be exploited, the mechanical skills of the westerners. Here was an unexpected bonus. Here, instead of a liability that would drain manpower to guard the wily Americans, was a skilled labor pool, and it was slave labor, regardless of the Geneva Convention. Combined with this group of Americans with men who lived in a technical civilization, were the survivors of Singapore, British, New Zealanders and Australians. Fourteen hundred and eight

Americans and one hundred British, New Zealanders and Australians were the work force.

Starvation was the prime tool, the ultimate weapon, that was used by the barbaric Japanese. Used cruelly, brutally and methodically. Barbarically. If a man didn't work, he didn't eat. The man that didn't eat didn't live long. Work to eat. Work to live. To live was to fight another day. So, the men worked to live. However, the Japanese, for all of their threats, all of their brutality, for all of their savage treatment, found that they had fifteen hundred saboteurs.

To live was still to fight. That was the philosophy, the driving force, the purpose for existence. It was the creed that was adopted and practiced by the men in Mukden. The battleground had shifted from Bataan, from Singapore, from Corregidor, to Mukden Manchuria. The battle continued in the camp and the factories. It was a battle of nightmares, of disease, starvation, freezing subzero winters, suffering and vicious death that was fought for three long miserable years.

The episodes of pathos, of courage, adaptation, and sacrifice, were spiced, at times with humor. This humor, as reflective as it was of the circumstances, was sometimes droll, sometimes grim, but always human, and always relished. And, in between all of this, there was always the man, the individual and his own private battle for life and existence, such as it was.

These are the experiences of these men, " The Expendables".

These Americans were the only American soldiers in history of the United States Militery, who had been declared expendable, were never rescued!

Never Plan Tomorrow

They did not turn their backs in flight,
The Bastards of Bataan.*

* From the poem, The Bastards of Bataan. Authors were a couple of Bastards, and Frank Hewlitt of UP.

PROCLAMATION TO THE DEFENDERS OF CORREGIDOR ISLAND

Bataan Peninsular is about swept away; important points of southern Luzon between Ternate and Nasugbu are in the hands of Japanese Forces and mouth of Manila Bay is under complete control of the Japanese Navy. Hopes for the arrival of reinforcements are quite in vain, The fate of Corregidor Island is sealed.

If you continue to resist the Japanese Forces will by every possible means destroy Corregidor Island and annihilate your forces relentlessly to the last man.

This is your final chance to cease resistance. Further resistance is completely useless.

Your commander will sacrifice every man and in the end will surrender in order to save his life.

You, dear soldiers, take it into consideration and give up your arms and stop resistance at once.

Commander-in-Chief of the
Imperial Japanese Forces

Courtesy of R.A. Brown, Mukden #190
From a copy. He kept it hidden for three years and four months.

XVI

CHAPTER 1 -- THE SIXTH OF MAY

The island was finally quiet.

Quiet except for the muttering and moaning of the men, and the buzzing of the fat blue flies. But it was quiet. War quiet.

The bombs and shells, the ripping explosions, the roaring swishing sounds that preceded death had stopped.

Ever since the fall of Bataan on the ninth of April, there had been bombs, shells, whining shrapnel and roaring airplanes. Blasting, thundering, pounding noise. Night and day there had been noise. Now the noise of war had stopped. The air was hot and thick with the smells of battle. Dried blood, festering wounds, heat, gunpowder, burned wood and hot damp raw earth. Every so often the whisper of a breeze that came in from the sea brought with it the sickening stench of bodies that were rotting in the hot tropic sun.

I looked up at the mouth of Malinta Tunnel. There, the Japs were moving in and out of the tunnel carrying off the booty of their recent victory.

We sat with our backs against the concrete embankment about a hundred yards from the west end of the tunnel. The space along the rails, the road and the rocky slopes were all covered with the Americans who had found shelter in the tunnel only hours before. The Japs had run us out and parked us close at hand. Now we sat and waited.

"The sixth of May." Johnny muttered.

"Yes, the sixth of May," I echoed, "and we still may not see tomorrow." I shivered apprehensively even though the afternoon was very hot. "I guess we can't plan tomorrow."

"What the hell are the bastards going to do with us?" asked a soldier sitting close by.

No one answered him. No one had an answer.

We sat waiting. The Japs came through one at a time, or three or four in a group. They stopped here and there took what they saw or could find on the men. A watch. A ring, a wallet, or the money that a soldier had hidden in hope of buying food or medicine from those fortunate enough to have thought of grabbing anything of value.

As the afternoon wore on, the Japs became more systematic in their searching. They also became more demanding and more brutal in their actions.

One group of five Japs came up from the South dock plundering as

1

they came in our direction. They stopped about thirty feet away. A private with gold buck teeth ordered the Americans around him to their feet. He lined them up, pushing and shoving as the other Japs watched, laughing as he roughed up the beaten soldiers. The Americans who were in the way were either stepped on or shoved aside.

"Kura! Kura!" shouted the little Jap as he lined up the men. His companions started to search the pockets of the dozen men that they had bullied into line. One of the Japs carried a pillowcase that had "U.S. ARMY HOSPITAL" stenciled on it. Everything that was taken from the men was dropped into the makeshift sack. Americans and Filipinos watched and grumbled. An American, who stood about six foot, towered over the small Jap that was searching his pockets. The Jap took the American's cigarettes, watch, ring and money. Then he reached into a pocket and pulled out the man's wallet. The American grabbed for it. The Jap shoved him back. Quickly the American started to swing at the Jap. The Jap stepped back and brought his rifle up to jab with the bayonet. The rifle tangled with two men that stood behind him, blocking the motion of the rifle. The bayonet pointed high into the air. The Jap looked back at the men he had hit. He shoved the butt of the gun into the crotch of the man he had intended to bayonet. The man screamed in pain as he reflexively reached for his crotch. He fell into the Jap, pushing him away, and then he collapsed on the ground at the Jap's feet. The Jap raised his rifle an smashed the butt into the fallen man's back, once, twice, three times, as the man screamed in agony. We rose to our feet collectively, roaring and shouting at the unnecessary brutality.

"Knock it off you bastards."
"You stinking monkeys. Barbarians!"
"You yellow louse."

The captive soldiers crowded in, yelling, shoving and swearing in protest. Japs that were standing guard on the high ground near the tunnel fired their guns into the air. "KURA! KURA!" they shouted as they started toward the milling mass of bodies around the foraging Japs. They cut their way with bayonets to the encircled Japs. Their bayonets were dripping blood as they cut their path. The bayoneted men screamed their pain. More shots. I couldn't tell if they were fired into the air or into the crowd of POWs. More shots continued to ring out sporadically. I squatted and pulled Johnny down to the ground.

"Stay down!" I shouted. "Less chance of being shot down on the ground!"

Others dropped to the ground following our example. Within seconds only the Japs remained standing in the road. Men were piled one on top of the other. The Japs swung their rifles left and right as they worked their way to the looters. There were ten Jap soldiers standing in a tight bunch in the middle of the sprawling Filipinos and Americans. The Jap contingent worked their way to the ruins of the bakery a hundred yards down toward the beach. They continued to strike out with their rifle butts and jabbed with their bayonets as they rushed along the crowded road.

"The rotten stinking yellow cowards. Scum!"

"Pigs."

"Yellow pigs. Animals."

Curses, jeers and cat calls followed the Japs.

I heard someone moaning. "My leg! Oh goddamn my leg!" A group of POWs had formed around a man who lay on the ground a few feet away. Two men picked him up and carried him to the tunnel mouth. Seven other men, holding bleeding wounds followed.

We sat and watched helplessly.

"Bet they don't take care of them." Johnny stated flatly. "Bet they won't let them into the hospital lateral."

"I don't know, they might help them." I was hoping that wording my wish would make it come true. "They might treat them. The nurses and doctors are still in the hospital."

We waited. The sun set low in the west shrouding the mouth of the tunnel in shadow. It was hard to make out what was going on there around the huge iron gate that was used to control access to the tunnel.

Word came as though by telegraph, from one man to another until finally we heard the Japs had taken the wounded men inside. It seemed as though a sigh worked its way through the mass of men. A sigh that signified that maybe there was some hope. If the men had been turned away by the Japs ---. We had seen some of the wounded men that had been turned out of the hospital lateral, and some of the wounded that had been out on the island. The Japs were merciless. There had been no offer of help. It was, to us, inhuman. We couldn't guess why. We had always helped the wounded Jap POW.

Suddenly the tropical sun went down. We sat and waited. The wounded and sick groaned in pain and misery. The others bitched and grumbled.

The Japs came through constantly. They looted and searched without any consideration. Some were more brutal than others.

I fell asleep time after time. Many times I awoke with a start. At these times I jumped to my feet, ready to run, heart pounding furiously, wondering what it was that had awakened me. Then I would settle down, with my back against the low concrete wall, and doze off again. I woke with a sudden fearful feeling, my pulse pounding in my throat. The sound of hell breaking loose had blasted the quiet of the night. Shells exploded with ripping thunderous sounds. Concussion waves bounced around the hills and through the ravines of Corregidor. I flattened to the ground next to Johnny. I saw the narrow crevice between the wall a concrete blockhouse a few feet away. I crawled over bodies and wedged myself into the opening as far as I could. In between the explosions I heard the men shouting in fear and consternation. The shells continued to come in as though being fired from a machine-gun. From my shelter I couldn't make out just where the shells were hitting. The acoustics of the island made them seem to be hitting only a few yards away. The whistling shrapnel filled the night air as though a million bees were flying around.

Suddenly the shelling stopped.

"It's Morrison!"

"They're shelling Morrison." I heard. Morrison was just to the west of our position, not more than a few thousand yards away. A single shell whirred through the night and landed in the ravine between Malinta and Morrison Hill. The big gun on Morrison had never fired a return shot.

"Why the hell are they shelling Morrison?"

"They are still holding out at Morrison."

Machine-gun fire started along in sporadic bursts at short intervals.

"Johnny?" I called. "Johnny? Where are you?" I strained my eyes in the moonless night to see if I could spot my cousin John somewhere in the squash of men on the ground.

"Over here Joe. By the wall."

I reached up to the top of the kiosk, holding the edge I pulled myself up slowly and painfully. I was wedged in tight. My back scraped along the rough concrete wall. My spine caught on a sharp edge. I sucked in my stomach and strained. My legs were numb and cramped. By the time I raised myself from the space I could feel the pins and needles in my feet and legs. My muscles were cramped. I moaned as I straightened out. I took my time and rested until my legs were alive again. My back ached again in the same place it had since the bombing raid on Bataan.

"Boy, you sure have to be scared to squeeze into this hole." The soldier further in the crevice spoke up.

"You ain't alone buster." The other soldier still stuck in the narrow slot groaned. "I'm going to stay right here in the middle of this concrete until they force me out."

I grinned in the darkness. It made me feel better to know that I hadn't been the only one who had been scared.

"Johnny! Where are you?" I craned my neck to look around.

"Over here."

His voice came from my left.

I worked myself over beside him. I stepped around men that were scrunched up in tight little groups. I sat down, wiggling my way to the ground in between them.

"I'm pretty damn hungry. I wonder if there is any way to get some food from the tunnel?" I scratched my brain trying to recall just where the entrance to the Machine Shop Lateral entrance was located. I was sure it was just around the ridge to the west of the main entrance to Malinta.

"You nuts or something?" asked Johnny. "We don't know if we are going to be shot in the morning, and you want to eat. His voice carried the message of his impatience with me as well as his annoyance. "Eat! For cripes sake, all you can think about is eating." And true, I was. The quarter rations for the past months had made all of us twenty or more pounds lighter. I had weighed myself on the scales in the hospital lateral only a few days before I had gone to Bataan. I was down to a hundred and sixty pounds from my normal one hundred and eighty-four. I knew I looked gangly with my six foot three frame.

Johnny who usually weighed in at one hundred and sixty-seven that he bragged about, was down to about a hundred and forty. He was five foot nine, with broad shoulders that made him look chunky. I watched him as he sat back , annoyed. His blonde hair and receding hairline, over a strong jaw reminded me of Gene Raymond. He had had a mild temper, but that seemed to have changed some in the past few months. I put that down to the stress of the war. He was a Slav, as I am.

"Well what the hell else can we do?" I snapped back. "You don't want to try for the boat I have stashed." My voice had a nasty undertone.

"Knock it off!" Johnny snarled. "You know damned well the officers gave strict orders. It would be desertion. Just like the orders on Bataan."

"Yes, but that was different." I argued. "That was only because they figured that escaping on Bataan would cause the Japs to kill the guys they had taken prisoner. There is nothing wrong with escaping from the freaking Japs now!"

"Aw nuts! let's not go through that again." Johnny turned away. "I don't want to hear about it anymore. Anyway, Wainwright went up to the tunnel earlier. Somebody said that he had to surrender to the JAp in charge of the troops."

"Yeah. Did you see him?" I asked.

"Yes," he didn't say anything else. I let it go at that. I settled down with my arms around my legs and my head on my knees buried in my own crazy thoughts. I became aware of the blood seeping from under the handkerchief wrapped around my left palm. I had scraped it somehow and had started it bleeding again. I unwrapped the bloody cloth and examined the shrapnel wound. The ragged piece of metal had stuck out in such a way that it had been easy to remove. It had been a triangle about an inch on each side and about an eighth of an inch in thickness. It had happened on the morning of the sixth. It had been about two in the morning. Somebody said there were a couple of men that had been hit were lying out in the open at the South end of Malinta Tunnel. Several of us had gone out. We didn't find anyone. As we were returning the Japs lobbed in three of the two hundred and forty millimeter mortar shells right smack in front of the mouth of the tunnel. We were lucky. Outside of having our eardrums blasted, I was the only one who had been hit. I pulled out the shrapnel and let the wound bleed to clean it out. I had washed it out when we made it inside. The hospital lateral was full, so they couldn't bandage it. Now it felt hot for some strange reason. I dug into my coveralls pocket for the clean hanky and wrapped it around my palm. Johnny watched. He reached over and tied a knot in the makeshift bandage. I put my head down again and rested.

Sometime later the sound of rifle fire startled me. I raised my head and listened. The firing stopped. I dropped my head and dozed. Dazedly I heard shots on and off through the rest of the night.

The sky was bright in the east over Manila Bay when I awoke. My neck ached. I felt rotten I looked around and stood up stiffly.

"Where the hell do you take a leak around here?" I asked anybody and everybody. I looked around as someone answered.

"Over the bank by the rails. And don't step in the crap."

I turned to see a steady stream of men moving to the bank and back. I made my way to the railroad and joined the others who were relieving themselves. When I finished I returned and sat down beside Johnny.

"There must be some way to get something to eat."

Johnny looked at me as though I were crazy.

"There you go again with your freaking eating." He shook his head in disgust. "Always thinking about some damned food."

"Hell, if we don't eat we won't last long!" I prophesied.

"Look." I pointed to the west side of the slope at the end of the tunnel. "There's the Machine Shop Lateral over there." Johnny, and a couple of the soldiers who were listening to us because they had nothing better to do, looked to where I was pointing. "The small tunnel comes out right behind that shoulder of rock. Maybe we could sneak over there and ---"

"And nuts! We have our damn heads shot off. Can't you ever think like other people?" He shook his head again in frustration as he continued to mumble. "Go ahead! Go ahead and commit suicide! How the hell you've missed having your ass blown off I don't know, but you should quit being stupid!" Johnny raved in annoyance which I interpreted as being more worry than anger. "You'll have your ass scattered all over the damned island. Go ahead! Damn it! You're a jerk. The friggin Japs will probably shoot all of us tonight, but you won't even last that long."

"Holy shit! What the hell wound you up?" I hadn't expected him to spout off at me that way. He got something out of his system.

The men around us watched and listened. Suddenly three or four of them started at once.

"What about the food?"

"What tunnel?" asked a young redheaded Marine.

He was tall and as skinny as the rest of us. He didn't seem to take the sun too well because his face and arms looked red and sunburned. No tan at all. I imaged it was a real problem to him in the tropical sun.

"Come on. I'm with you."

"Let's go!" The redheaded Marine in coveralls said enthusiastically. He stood up and was joined by four more of the men around us. The Marine picked his way to the west side of the hill. The fifty or so yards didn't take long. The Japs on the slope above us didn't seem to mind us moving around. I tagged along behind the redhead.

The verbal busting I had had from Johnny made me sulky and defiant. I didn't feel like sitting there and thinking about it.

There were a few scraggly tree trunks, stripped of all leaves and small branches around the shoulder of rock. Some tattered camouflage netting still hung between the tree trunks and the rock, over the tunnel mouth that came out of the west side of Malinta Hill.

We stopped and looked at the Jap sentries that were spread out around the area. None of them seemed to be the least bit interested in our small group.

"The yellow pricks are up to something." The redheaded Marine spat out. "They ain't paying any attention to us. I don't trust them suckers!" He looked around as though he expected to be shot at any moment.

"Stay here and I'll take a fast looksee." He turned and started around the rise of ground and into the cool dark mouth of the cave-like tunnel about ten feet away. He stopped fast. I saw his hands as they shot into the air above his head. I was ready to duck or run, whichever proved to be the best move. A Jap walked up to him and placed a bayonet against his chest.

"NANDA." The Jap frowned around his glasses. "NANDA." He repeated.

The Marine made a helpless gesture with his raised hands. The bayonet commanded.

"Food. Food. Something to eat."

Red brought his right hand down and close to his mouth. He made scooping motions with it. The Jap smirked his gold teeth at Red and shoved the bayonet. Red gave with it and went backward, flat on the ground.

"Tabemono. Food." I offered.

"Kura." The Jap motioned him back further. The Marine scuttled back on his hands and feet with his butt scraping on the ground.

"Up!" The Jap spoke the word clearly. "Stand up you!" Red stood up and made dusting motions at the seat of his pants.

"I speak English." He looked at me. "You speak Japanese?"

"Only a little."

We stood looking at him. He motioned to all of us. He turned and walked into the tunnel. In what seemed like only seconds he came back with another Jap, this one a sergeant with an issue sword hanging on his belt. I had seen the Jap non-coms on Bataan with their cheese cutters. This on looked like a mean little bastard.

"What are you doing here?" The sergeant asked in passable English.

No one answered. I glanced around at the others. When no one spoke I answered. "We are looking for something to eat."

"You are not supposed to leave the roadway." He gestured to the road. "Why did you leave the road?" He pulled the sword from its scabbard and waved it at waist level.

I looked at the sharp blade and then at the little sergeant.

"I wanted to find some food. I haven't eaten since yesterday morning." I chanced a fast look at Red and the others. They were not going to share my problem. I had spoken up and was now the center of the Jap's attention. I looked back at the Japs, waiting for the next move. The five foot three sergeant looked up at my six foot three and smirked.

"You think you can escape from the Imperial Japanese soldiers?" asked the sergeant.

"No. Of course not." I tried to put conviction in my voice. I wasn't about to tell him that I had already escaped from the Imperial Japanese assholes on Bataan and hadn't been smart enough to keep running in the other direction. "We wanted to see if there was any food in the tunnel." I motioned to the hole in the rock behind them. "I just wanted something to eat. We are all pretty hungry." It was the third time I had mentioned eating in one form or another.

The sergeant turned to the private beside him and sang out a stream of words in Japanese that were too fast for me to catch. The private snickered maliciously.

He turned to me. "If you want something to eat there are some boxes over there. Eat that." The non-com pointed to a stack of boxes about twenty feet further on in the mouth of the tunnel. He smiled as if at some secret joke of his own.

I sighed unconsciously, realizing that I had gotten out of trouble. For some unknown reason I thought of something I had read or heard a long time ago, "What I tell you three times is true."

"Thank you. Arrigato. Thanks." I repeated.

We hurried over to the stacks of cartons. I bellied up one of the cartons, got my hands under it and lifted it so that I carried it with the weight of it against my gut. I turned and walked off with it. The other men each picked up a carton.

"There's plenty of cartons over there. Grab them."

The men on the road scattered over the rocks and holes and headed for the boxes in the tunnel. It seemed as though there was some form of mental telepathy operating. There was a buzzing and scurrying. The roadful of men were making their way to the food. As I hurried off to where Johnny was sitting the cans were coming out of the cartons and were being passed around. Somebody made a grab at my carton and I tore it away viciously. I swung the weight of the box at another eager beaver. "Lay off. I'll knock your head off. Get the hell up there and get your own." I yelled. I elbowed another man as I made my way the last few feet to Johnny's side. Behind me I heard shouting and yelling as the cans of food were passed around. Fights broke out as the men snatched at the cans.

"What is it? What is it? What you got?"

I didn't know what I had because the cartons had no labels and the cans had no labels either. I handed a can to Johnny. I searched the carton for some sign of the contents. I picked up a can and sat on the carton to protect the cans that were left.

"I don't know Johnny, but as soon as I get this GI can opener going I am going to find out." I fumbled in the pocket of my cutup coveralls for one of the standard issue folding can openers that came with the C rations. I worked on the can feverishly.

"Tomatoes! Goddamit! Hell! There is nothing but canned tomatoes." I heard the shouting coming from around the stack of cartons.

The Jap sentries were shouting to one another and laughing.

"Come on. Hurry up!" urged Johnny. " Maybe we got something else."

The can lid lifted as I pried it with my fingers. The tomatoes floated in the watery juice.

"Damn!" Johnny spit out.

"Hell! It's food." I said. I was just as disappointed as he was. "It'll fill the gut until there is something better." I raised the can to my mouth and drank the warm juice. I reached for one of the tomatoes and pushed one drank the warm juice. I reached for one of the tomatoes and pushed one of them into my mouth. I took a bite of the firm flesh. It tasted good, damned good. I drank more of the juice.

"Now if there was some salt this would be great." I smiled as the juice dripped down from my chin.

"Hey! If you don't want the stuff I'll give you ten bucks, American, for a can," offered one of the soldiers who had missed out.

"Naw, I don't want to sell." I answered and continued to eat.

Johnny opened his can and was eating the tomatoes with as much hungry relish as I was for all of his bitching.

"Remember the farm in Jersey? How we used to eat the tomatoes while we were weeding?" He returned to devouring the warm tomatoes. "All I need now is the spaghetti."

"I'll settle for some salt." I answered. "I guess the juice will do in place of water for a while." I drank the rest of the juice.

The skinny soldier that had offered me the ten dollars sat looking at the bill in his hand and at the carton on which I was sitting. I looked at Johnny and then back at the sad looking character. Something went through my mind about how we had already started to look after ourselves and screw the other guy. I shrugged my shoulders in a helpless gesture, more for my own benefit than for Johnny's. "Here, here's a can. Give me the ten."

He grabbed for the can and held his hand out for the opener. He started to gobble the tomatoes hungrily. In two minutes he had nothing but an empty tin can.

"Thanks man. Thanks a lot." He had a big grin on the skinny face that was smeared with juice.

"Forget it." I felt good about what I had done even though I had taken his ten dollars. He wasn't going to buy any beer with it anyway.

"Where to now." Johnny asked. Now that he had a full stomach he was just as curious as the rest of us.

"I don't know." I looked around at the men, the Japanese soldiers, and at the rest of the island speculatively. "I just don't know."

"Think they'll keep us here long?"

"Who knows?" I answered thoughtfully. "I'm wondering just what they intend to do with us. They could have just herded us down around North Dock and shot us. But they didn't just shoot the men on Bataan that I was with. They did kill one hell of a lot on the march to San Fernando." I was not only puzzled, I was worried, and, I couldn't understand why I wasn't afraid.

Slowly the day dragged by. There was nothing but the hot sun in a clear blue sky. Then there was the smell of tomatoes, of men, and the stench of the open latrine areas. There seemed to be no thought of hope, or of any future for any of us. There was no water, and the Japs weren't concerned about feeding us. It was just luck that Johnny and I had the rest of the carton of tomatoes. Each number ten can was a full meal. The tomato juice served in the place of water.

It wasn't long into the afternoon when both Johnny and I developed a problem. Diarrhea. Between runs to the open latrine we had little to talk about that served to cheer us up.

"Damn! What the hell have we got?" Johnny groaned with pain.

"Was that stuff poisoned?"

"Hell no!" I answered with a know-it-all attitude, "It's just the tomatoes. They are nothing but mushy meat and water. I think right now that I would rather go hungry than have the shits!"

I sat by the concrete wall trying to get as comfortable as possible. Between the runs, the rough concrete wall, the hot ground, the hot sun and the buzzing blue ass flies as big as bees, I wasn't doing too well.

"Nuts!" Johnny spat out, "You eat because you're hungry. Then you get diarrhea because you eat. Then you're weak from the runs. So what does it get you?"

I noticed that the line to the latrine wasn't getting any smaller. For lack of anything better to do I stared around at first one thing and then another. There was the tunnel mouth. Then there was Malinta Hill. The South Dock. The railroad bridge over the road. The rails led back into the tunnel. The bombed out store and the bakery.

The bakery!

There were Jap guards on the other end of the bridge. I looked around for the other guards. The Imperial assholes. One on the hill between Malinta and Queens Tunnel. One on the dock. One under the bridge. And another one on the road that led from Southside Dock up past the road to Queen Tunnel, the Navy tunnel.

There were soldiers, American and Filipino, spread out from the tunnel mouth, down across the road, and across from the bakery. But there wasn't anyone around the store or the bakery. An idea started to form. I perked up at the thought of getting to the bakery. Just by chance there might be something there to eat. Bread, old stale bread. Or maybe some flour. Flour, plain flour could stop the runs. It was an old European remedy. You took a couple of tablespoons of flour with a little water to get it down. They said it worked, and I was willing to try it.

"Hey Johnny." I whispered.

"Yeah?"

"I'm going to see if I can make it to the bakery over there. Maybe there is something to eat there." I spoke in a low guarded tone. I was afraid that somebody might hear me and beat me to the bakery.

"WHAT?" He yelled out loud.

"Shush. Damn it. Keep it down. What the hell are you shouting for?" The words gritted out.

"You're going to get into trouble. Can't you sit and wait? Something will happen and you will get other people into trouble. Or shot! Stay here!"

I wasn't at all happy at the response. Inside I burned, but I kept it in.

"I'll be back." I stood up and worked the stiffness out of my back and legs by stretching a few times. "Watch the rest of the cans." Then without waiting I started out. I picked my way through the men sprawled on the road. A half hour of meandering to throw off the Jap guards brought me to the bakery. Some of the men watched me curiously as I had made my way down the road. It was difficult to make up my mind. Either I walked boldly, or, I could make my way to the Jap on the road and somehow get his permission to go into the bakery building. If I walked across boldly I might get shot, or maybe I would be lucky and get away with it by boldness alone.

I looked from one Jap to the other. Finally, after marching them, I decided they wouldn't shoot. I didn't know why I thought so, but I did.

I took a deep breath and stepped out, away from the men, and marched across the road. The Jap on the railroad bridge watched almost curiously. Nothing happened. I looked into the front of the building through the large opening that had been a window at one time. I leaned over the edge to get a better look. All the time I expected to hear a shot, or at least a shout. Still nothing happened. I stepped back from the building and examined it thoroughly. I stole a look at first one Jap and then another. I could hear the men behind me mumbling. They sat and watched. Still nothing happened. I walked in through what had once been a door, turned to face the road and backed into the room. Either the Japs would stop me or they would let me go just to see what the stupid American was up to. I turned and took another shaky step into the building and waited. Nothing happened. Then I quickly walked out of the back of the bombed out building and started to search the bins and ruins of the storage area. Minutes passed and I had no luck. There wasn't a piece of bread, not a crust. No flour. Nothing! I searched through the cabinets and bins, moved aside wood and other debris from the building.

A slight scraping sound made me freeze. I stopped and turned quickly. A grinning gold toothed Jap stood in the doorway, his bayoneted rifle pointing at me.

"Nanda."

I spread my hands, swallowed saliva I didn't know existed, and smiled a sickly smile. Shit.

"I'm looking for something to eat. Pahn. Bread." I gestured with my hands, bringing one up to my mouth and made a circular motion as though pushing something in.

"So so." His bayonet wasn't pointing at me any more. "Kura." It sounded nasty. He motioned for me to move out to where I had come from. I walked toward and past him. When my back was to him I started to sweat. I expected momentarily to feel either the bayonet or the rifle butt. On Bataan, before I had escaped from the column of men that were being marched out of Marveles, there had been a lot of bayonets stuck into the backs of men.

"Kura!"

I jumped forward and looked back over my shoulder.

"KURA!"

I continued to move fast with the freaking Jap scuttling right behind me in his split toe sneakers.

"Stop." He ordered.

I stopped and turned around.

"You go back. Stay there." He pointed with his head to the area occupied by the captives. "Understand?" He asked.

"Yes." I answered readily. I turned fast and walked across the road. Curiosity showed on the faces of the men as I made my way through them. Surprise showed on some, on others there was a look of amazement.

"Well?" Johnny asked .

"No luck. I said disgustedly. "Not a damned thing. Not even a moldy crumb." I sat down next to Johnny and waited.

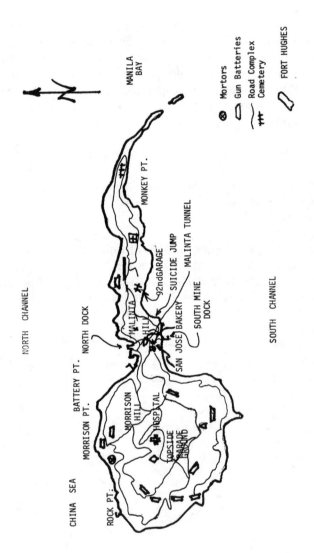

NORTH CHANNEL

CHINA SEA

ROCK PT.

MORRISON PT.

BATTERY PT.

NORTH DOCK

MORRISON HILL

HOSPITAL

TOPSIDE
PARADE
GROUND

MALINTA
HILL

SAN JOSE

BAKERY

92nd GARAGE

SUICIDE JUMP

MALINTA TUNNEL

SOUTH MINE
DOCK

MONKEY PT.

MANILA
BAY

SOUTH CHANNEL

⊗ Mortars

◁ Gun Batteries

Road Complex

⁺⁺⁺ Cemetery

▱ FORT HUGHES

CHAPTER 2 -- 92nd GARAGE

With the waiting, the afternoon, the evening, and then the long night, it seemed like eternity. Morning finally came. The sun climbed into the sky fast.

"Last can of tomatoes." I held the can upside down.

"Just as well. I don't think I could make the crapper many more times." Johnny sounded pooped.

"Yeah. But what do we do for food now?" I looked around wondering. "No more tomatoes. No water. We won't last long in this heat."

It wasn't long before the tropical sun started to blister the island again. The morning passed miserably. A hot afternoon stretched ahead.

About two o'clock, according to somebody's watch, there was a flurry of motion at the south end of the road near the bakery. Japanese soldiers were marching in squads from the North Dock. Their non-coms issued sharp orders as the squads stood at attention. We watched, wondering what this would mean as far as we were concerned. We found out in minutes. The Japs started to move through the POWs.

"Attention! Attention! Line up." A small Japanese sergeant with a sword hanging at his side started shouting. "Line up in a column of fours." He shouted in surprisingly good English. "Move, move move!" He continued to shout. Then he started to shove and push the men. The Jap soldiers followed suit, pushing and shoving. Bayonets and rifle butts soon came into play. A long column started to form up. It extended from the bakery to the mouth of the big tunnel, on the West side of the road. At the tunnel the column doubled back along the East side of the road. Hundreds of men fell into line in the double column. The Japs pushed the Filipinos aside, forming up only the Americans.

"Where to now?" Johnny asked of no one in particular.

"I don't know," I answered, "maybe Middleside or Topside if we go into a barracks. Topside is in better shape." I remembered that my photo forays after the bombings had been at both of the barracks sites as well as the gun emplacements.

"Do you think they'll put us in barracks someplace?" someone else asked. No one answered.

The front of the column started to move along the road. It wasn't in the direction of either Middleside or Topside. The column moved south toward the docks and then east past Queens Tunnel. This was the road that climbed up the South side of Malinta Hill and then away from the

South Dock along the rocky cliff, then turning north to join up with the road that led through Malinta Tunnel at the east end. It then ran along the spine of the island, east to Kindley Field, the airport, and on to the cemetery beyond Monkey Point.

We reached the east side of the Hill where the road was about a hundred feet above the water. Here a low wall had been built along the edge of the road as a safety barrier. The Japs kept on butting and cudgeling the men as we moved along the narrow road. For no apparent reason one of the Japs jabbed a bayonet into the butt of one of the men. The man moaned, but didn't scream. Red blood stained the point of the bayonet. Grinning, with oddly placed gold teeth gleaming, the Jap moved along behind the wounded man and wiped first one side of the bayonet, then the other side on the arm and shoulder of the man.

The Jap private laughed and uttered some unintelligible words as he continued to berate the prisoners.

Suddenly, a very young looking American on the outside of the column broke into a run. He ran to the edge of the road and dove headfirst over the side of the cliff to the water below.

No one stopped.

There was a sickening sound as the body hit rocks below. Then came the sound of rolling stones. Everyone went on, unheeding.

There was a complete lack of emotion, as though everyone was dead, walking zombies. It was scary. There was a void, a fatalistic acceptance of the act of self violence, self destruction. It was as though unconsciously, or perhaps consciously, we recognized our helplessness to provide any assistance, and accepted the fact fatalistically.

One of the Jap guards approached the edge of the cliff and looked down cautiously. He scanned the slope for a few seconds, evidently seeing nothing, he shrugged his shoulders and turning to the men, he grinned maliciously. He shouldered his rifle, mumbled something and moved on.

"Who was it?" I asked the man in front of me.

"I don't know." He trudged on.

"Who was it?" I asked again.

"Don't know. Why worry about it?" Asked the man beside me. "What are you going to do about it? Help him? Hell, just say a friggin prayer."

"What difference does it make who he was?" The man behind me snarled. "He doesn't have any more worries now. He doesn't have to remember yesterday or worry about tomorrow."

I turned my head to look at the instant philosopher and stumbled. The open wound in my leg throbbed from the sudden shock.

Johnny walking beside me, said "They don't care about anybody but themselves. Forget it Joe."

The column continued marching. It wound slowly around the Hill and soon turned east after it passed the officer's quarters.

"Where the hell are we going anyway?"

"Monkey Point." someone offered from somewhere behind us.

"No we're not."

"The officer's quarters."

"Like hell. There ain't enough room there."

"The airfield." A loud voice carried up and down the column. "Kindley Field."

"The 92nd Garage! That's where."

"Hell there isn't that much room there. Not for all of these men!"

Words came from many parts of the column as the men realized what their destination was.

The road branched off from the east end of Malinta Tunnel, off to the left was MacArthur's house. Further on and to the right, south, was a pocket formed by some hills and Malinta Hill. The small bay had a small beach area down below the road. The pocket was on the south side of the island from where Fort Hughes could be seen out in the South Channel.

Slowly the column continued to crawl along the bumpy pockmarked road that led down the steep slope to the natural prison compound formed by the spine of Corregidor, Malinta Hill and further east by Monkey Point. As we passed from the road to the flat concrete the Japs attempted to counted us and moved us on.

This part of the island had served as the airdrome for amphibious aircraft due to its sheltered location. The hangar and sheds, what remained of them, were located on the northeast, along the hill. The concrete extended about six hundred feet west from the hangar toward Malinta, and about four hundred feet from the beach to the spine of the island.

What remained of the hangar was an incredible conglomeration of tin supported by a metal skeleton. The corrugated sheet metal had hardly a square foot that hadn't been perforated by either bullets or shrapnel.

This meager shelter from the sun was immediately pre-empted by the officers without regard for the sick or the wounded among us. It was evidence of the officer's "rights".

Men scrambled for select or seemingly select pieces of the concrete real estate.

Johnny and I found a small space not far from the hangar. We marked off a spot only by occupation and stretched out in the hot sun.

Johnny looked hot, broiled, and generally miserable.

"What do we do for water?" he asked.

"I don't know what we do for drinking water. I haven't anymore in my canteen. But, I sure as hell am going to take a bath in the bay later on. Tell you what. I'll take a bath while you watch my clothes, and I'll watch yours when you wash. Otherwise we'll lose everything."

"OK. Only let's wait until the sun goes down some." He laid down on the concrete buried in his own thoughts.

The men milled around like a bunch of ants trying to find a place to settle down and rest. Some of the men were fortunate enough to have blankets and musette bags with some of their personal belongings. Johnny and I had nothing but our canteens, mess kits, and the meager clothes on our backs. I still had my watch and school ring pinned to the inside of my undershorts.

The sun dropped toward Malinta to our west. We made arrangements with the men next to us to watch our spot for us. We said we would watch their spot for them later. Real estate was hard to come by as the area became jammed with the men being forced in by the Japs. There was little room to walk between the men as we threaded our way to the strip of beach I stripped and removed the messy bandage from my right leg. The shrapnel wound wasn't very big, but it didn't look to good. There was a sickly redness around the gash. The water was warm and refreshing. Taking a bath after weeks of sweat, heat, dirt and battlefield filth, helped to lift my spirits. Johnny took his turn and came out with a more relaxed look. I washed my bandages in the salt water and rewrapped both my hand and my leg.

The Japs didn't provide any food or water. The closest water that I knew of was at Queens Tunnel. Or, it was possible that the water mains to the Officer's Quarters on the top of the hill were still supplying water there. We found some water. A single faucet not far from the bombed out hangars. It must have been for some kind of a water tank that had disappeared some time in recent past. A line formed almost immediately. There must have been three hundred or more men in the line within minutes after the word spread. It took hours to get the water. We spelled each other until we made it to the faucet. We carefully filled our canteens and our canteen cups and made our way back to our spot.

Food. There was plenty of food stored at Cold Storage not far from the North Dock, but the Japs probably wouldn't issue any.

"Notice how quiet it is Johnny?" Again I noticed that there wasn't any gunfire. No artillery. No sound of airplanes or of whistling bombs. None of the terrible sounds of war.

It was a hungry and thirsty night. Sleep came just from utter exhaustion. Some of the old tensions and fears of war were gone to be replaced by new ones.

Morning seemed to come much too suddenly. I went to the beach to wash while Johnny remained at the spot. The water was cold. After I had finished washing I was wide awake and hungry.

Instead of returning to the site with Johnny I made my way to the gate at the main road. The Japs were picking work details. I was picked by a gold toothed Jap and pushed into a detail that was marched out to Monkey Point.

"Do you think there are any Japs that don't have gold teeth?" I asked the man next to me.

"Nah! All of the bastards like gold. I'm going knock out some gold teeth after the war is over." He looked at one of the Japs who had a mouthful. "Bet I could get enough to buy me a new Buick. A convertible. I'll get the sons of bitches when this is over. The yellow shits can't go on winning. Wait and see."

The detail turned out to be one of the rottenest we could imagine. We loaded the bodies of the dead men onto the trucks for burial in one of the mass graves. The bodies were bloating from the heat. Some were dismembered and rotting. No one stopped the Japs from looting the dead. Some of the POWs filched some things when the Japs weren't around.

Millions of flies swarmed around the bodies. They rose in hordes whenever we moved a body. Then they settled on the bodies on the trucks. They crawled all over us as we moved among them. They got into our clothes and around our ears. We swatted at them constantly. The buzzing they generated was incredible. They were the giant blue assed variety that seemed to be more aggressive than any I had encountered before anywhere. The sound was that of death and disease.

The Japs called a lunch break and distributed cans of pineapple and peaches. I shoved the two cans of fruit into my coveralls and tightened the pistol belt to keep them from dropping out. Some generous soul passed around some cigarettes. As I sat smoking I felt better. I had a couple of cans of food that we, Johnny and I, could share for supper. I didn't have any appetite. The dead destroyed that for the moment. After a short rest period the Japs moved us along the ridge to continue the cleanup. I was becoming somewhat inured to our ghoulish task.

A group of four men were ordered into a tunnel on the north beach side of the ridge. There were some bodies strewn about a few yards into the dark hole. The tunnel had been dug in about fifteen feet. The men crawled in, they were there about twenty seconds when a terrific explosion ripped the side of the hill open and collapsed the tunnel.

Everybody dove for the ground and spread out. Japs ran to the site jabbering unintelligibly. We sat on the ground staring. No one moved to the site of the tunnel.

"Booby trapped." said a sailor standing next to me.

"Yeah. Poor bastards. I guess we don't have to worry about burying those guys."

After that the rest of the detail was a harrowing experience. Each moment was again filled with the possibility of death. No one could guess, could know, where there was a mine or a booby trap.

We heard two explosions from along the far end of the island, toward Hooker Point, during the afternoon.

At four o'clock we were marched back to Fly Camp. Another two cans of food were passed out to each of the men who had been on the detail as we were marched through the gate. The men I passed were making nasty remarks about how we smelled as we moved among them. They looked at us as though we had the plague.

"Well screw you too." One of the men on the detail responded to one group. "See how the hell you'd smell if you were hauling dead bodies all afternoon."

I found Johnny at the site. "Come on. Let's go down to the beach so I can wash the smell of death off of me."

"You smell like a latrine." Johnny observed. "Cripes! What the hell did they have you doing?"

"You stink!"

"What did you do? Fall into a slit trench?"

"Come on Johnny." I handed him my wallet, watch and ring, and the prayer book I had found. Then I handed him the four cans.

He stared at the cans. "What's in the cans?"

"Pineapple and peaches. I think one of them is Vienna sausage. But we don't open them until I wash them and me."

We asked Ed and Schwartz to watch our spot. At the beach I took off my shoes and scrubbed them with sand and water. I handed them to Johnny. I didn't want to loose them. I walked into the water with my clothes on until the water was waist deep. I took off my coveralls and washed them. Then I took off my undershirt, shorts and socks and scrubbed them clean of the blood and the stench of death. I washed the leg and hand bandage last. I got into the shorts and put on my shoes. Johnny helped me ring out the coveralls. The wounds felt raw and burned.

We made our way back to our site among the men hearing all kinds of jibes on the way.

Ed, one of the men close by loaned me his blanket while my coveralls dried because the evening breeze was cooling things off.

We ate the sausage and finished off the fruit, sharing it with Ed and Schwartz, the two men we had befriended.

Ed was almost a caricature. He had lost more weight than the rest of us. He had had dysentery and an infected bullet wound that had knocked the crap out of him. He seemed to be about five foot seven. I was almost a head taller than Ed. He couldn't have weighed more than one thirty. He had told us that he had been down to one twenty something when they had discharged him from the island hospital in March. His hair was brown and scraggly since he had not had a haircut from a barber in months. His brown eyes made me think of the big dog that we had had down on Uncle Martin's, Johnny's father's, farm. That dog had the saddest eyes I had ever seen on any living thing. Ed also had bushy eyebrows and a small nose that perked up at the end over a straight upper lip that made him look very young. He said he was twenty-three which made him a year older than me. His frame was small. Altogether it made him look like a kid.

He had buddied up with Schwartz.

They had been on the Rock since the war had started. Both were in the Coast Artillery.

Schwartz was a second hitcher. He said he had liked the first three years in the islands and had re-upped in forty. He was about thirty one or two. He said that he had joined up because he hasn't been able to find a job that was permanent. He had tired of going from one place to another and figured that he had found a home in the Army. He wanted to do his twenty years and retire with a pension. He was just like the rest us, skinny, and beat. He was taller than Johnny by about an inch or more. He weighed in at a guess of maybe a hundred and sixty. Schwartz had mousy blonde hair that was growing out of a field haircut and a raunchy looking start of a beard that grew every which way but straight. His green eyes and dark skin made an odd combination. He never did say whether he was German or Jewish. He was easy going and generous. Too generous I thought. He gave away more than he received. I wondered if he would survive for long in the camps we were no doubt going to if he continued to be so generous. Maybe he would change like the rest of us and survive.

"That sure was a rotten detail today." I told the story of the ghoulish work and the fate of the four men in the tunnel. "If they take out any details tomorrow I'll try to make it to Queens or Bottomside and maybe find some clothes and a musette bag. This stuff we have isn't going to last very long."

"See if you can find some medicine." Johnny sounded worried. "Ed had the GIs. The guys around here with Malaria and dysentery are starting to die. There isn't medicine around, and the Japs don't give a shit if we die."

"Anybody die today?"

"I heard some talk from the officers. They say that about ten are dead."

I looked around. "I wonder how long we stay here?"

Johnny seemed to become more despondent during the next few days. He said his cramps were getting worse and that he felt hot and tired all the time.

The hot sun beat down continuously out of a cloudless sky. There was no shade. The whole place was a concrete oven. Only the millions of big blue green flies were thriving. They bit, they crawled on and into everything, and flew in massive clouds. The constant buzzing they created only died at night, to start at daybreak again.

On Tuesday, it was the twelfth of May, I left the spot early in the morning and headed down toward the beach. The heat had been so bad that even after the night's rest I felt weak and miserable. The bath in the cool water helped me perk up some as I scoured the beach for anything of value that might have washed up during the night. I stopped at the far west end of the beach near the bottom of the hill.

There was a sudden flurry of activity that started among the men a few feet away. At this point there was a steep slope that swept up about a hundred and fifty feet and then leveled off into the road around the hill. There were bomb and shell craters scattered all over. Broken trees and bushes sprinkled the rocky area. Three or four men had started to scramble up the hill. I looked around the top of the slope for the cause of the rush. There, near the top, was a neat stack of boxes. I couldn't imagine what was in them, but I ran and climbed with the rest of them. By the time I reached the top I had outdistanced all but one of the ragged panting pack. I had forgotten about my leg in the anticipation of getting food.

"C rations!" The man ahead of me shouted.

He grabbed for a carton and ripped it open. I looked behind me at the struggling pack of starved men and ran to the cartons. I picked up two of them, one under each arm and started back down the hill.

The hungry pack reached the food, fought and yelled for possession of the cans that spilled from the cartons that had been broken open. Fighting broke out over single cans of food. Street fighting, mean, dirty and rotten, and the determination of hungry men.

Hands grabbed for my two boxes of rations as I ran at breakneck speed down the rough slope to the concrete pad below. I knocked down two, three, four men on my way down. I used the cartons as battering rams, and along with the speed of my descent, and the weight of my body, they made a combination that were deadly in clearing my path. My desperation and the realization that this was food, our food, my food, pushed me down the slope with amazing speed.

The bottom of the hill seemed to come up at me with frightening freight train speed. For a moment it was as though I was going to slam into the dirt, drop my cartons of food, and break my fool neck. Breaking my legs or my neck seemed to be, in that split second, only minor problems. Keeping the food was the most important thing in the world. I wasn't going to lose my food. I saw the mass of men at the bottom of the slope and beyond. Hundreds of men were standing, shouting, cheering us on as they watched the action on the hill. They were egging on the men in their battle for food. Rocks and dirt flew as I came down off of the slope. Men scattered and flew from in front of me. I finally stumbled, my feet coming out from under me after I had cleared the bottom of the hill by about twenty feet. Both of the cartons hit the dirt with me. Men rushed toward me. Whether they intended to help me or to steal my food I didn't know. I snarled and swung the cartons at the hands that reached out. I rose to my feet fast. They pulled their hands back and growled back at me.

Puffing, gasping for breath, I made my way through the crowd of men.

The shouting continued behind me as the action spilled down from the hill out and onto the flat of the clearing. Cans of food were being fought over and bought and sold within minutes.

I had a big shit-eating grin on my face as I greeted Johnny at our spot. "C rations." I grinned.

"You're kidding?" Johnny responded unbelievingly.

"The hell I am!" I retorted. "C rations. Two big cartons of C rations." I was elated.

"Where the hell did they come from?" Johnny grabbed for one of the cartons.

"Up the hill. By the gun emplacement up there. There were cartons of them. But I'll bet there isn't one left up there now."

I sat down opposite Johnny with the two precious cartons between us.

"Let's eat. What would you like for a first course?" I bantered happily, then grimaced in pain as I became aware of the pain in my leg.

"What is the matter?" Johnny asked.

"I just forgot all about my leg during the excitement. Now the damned thing hurts like hell. And my back isn't doing so great either."

"They say you forget about pain when you are excited."

"I sure as hell did. But what the hell, we have some food. I'll go and soak in the bay after we eat."

The men around us stared at us and made nasty remarks about the selfish slobs eating the food that should be shared between everybody. We shared only with Ed and Schwartz. Hogs that we had become. A matter of survival. The food was delicious, even though it was spiced with shitty invectives.

The following week was at least not a hungry one. It was miserable in many other ways. For one thing, the officers were causing a great deal of trouble. They had made deals with the Japs and had an abundant supply of coffee, sugar and chocolate. They were all exempt from work details. The officers even had their water brought to them while the enlisted men, particularly the sick, went without any. This caused a great deal of resentment among the enlisted men. The officers were not in the least concerned in taking care of anyone except themselves. The great leaders were showing their true colors.

One day Provoo showed up. Provoo, an American enlisted man, had joined the Japs. He was in the main tunnel. Provoo was a slim blonde in his mid thirties. He had a face that reminded me of some actor I had seen on a set in Burbank, but I couldn't make the connection. Johnny had been in the Judge Advocate General's Office. Johnny told me that Provoo spoke fluent Japanese. "A hell of a lot better than what you do, that's for sure." I remembered that I had met Provoo before the war in Manila, but it had been only a casual acquaintance.

He was accompanied by a tall soldier, another American whom someone said was a guy named Brown. Provoo provided us with one interesting bit of news. "You are officially Prisoners of War as of the thirteenth of May."

What the hell ever that means, I thought to myself.

Provoo looked immaculate and well fed. He was clean shaven, with barbered hair, and dressed in clean, pressed khakis.

The men sneered and jeered as he passed among them, but no one made a move toward him. The Japs wouldn't like it.

He stopped in front of Johnny. "Is there anything that I can do for you Johnny?"

Johnny's answer was polite, but the tone of his voice was guarded. "How about some medicine for those of us who need it. And, maybe a little food. Even some of the coffee and sugar that the officers are getting."

"I'll see if I can find some quinine and maybe some aspirin. The food problem is something else. The Japs are funny about feeding prisoners.

They don't have any respect for prisoner's, and they tell me they never signed the Geneva Convention. That I think is a lie, but you can't tell them that."

After he left Johnny started to talk.

Provoo, he said, had lived in Japan for some years. A couple at least. In the late thirties. He had learned to speak the language fluently, and had aspirations of becoming a Shinto priest.

"Provoo tried to tell the authorities that the Japs were planning to go to war against the United States. No one would believe him. It seems that Provoo, while living in Japan, had befriended some of the Shintoists who were high ranking military men. They had bragged about some of the advances that they had made in landing techniques, the establishment of beachheads. When Provoo had mentioned this to some of MacArthur's people in the Advocate's office, they had merely laughed at him. They had even called him a religious crackpot.

"Didn't anyone listen to him?"

"Not that I know of. And no one bothered with him. He and I were in the Advocate's office. He didn't act or think like a crackpot. And I don't think he made up the stories that he told. He never came across as a bullshit artist to me." Johnny stopped as though he thought back over the past. "Matter of fact, it seems as though all that he told us has come true."

"Well," I countered, "you never know what goes on in the Orient. Maybe those friends of his had some reason for telling him what they did."

"Maybe." Johnny looked thoughtful, and it seemed as though he was hopeful of something good from Provoo.

Johnny's hopes came through a few days later. Provoo came by two days later with some quinine and bandages. There wasn't much medicine, but it seemed to help Johnny for the next few days.

The problems that we all had worsened. Day after day men died from dysentery, malaria, gangrene and other infections that had developed from their wounds. The gangrene was the worst. The wounds blew up to be horrible infected messes. The blue flies seemed to congregate on the wounds, drawn by the putrid smell. There was no medicine and no help from the frigging Japs.

My own wounds weren't healed, but at least I was holding my own. The wounds wouldn't close, but at least they hadn't become infected, yet. I was paranoid about keeping them covered to protect them from the millions of blue assed flies. There were millions of them buzzing around constantly.

The days dragged on miserably. I tried to improve my Japanese at every opportunity. I asked the Jap guards questions. Asked them about the simple things and was laughed at by them, they thought it was funny that one of the round eyed Americans wanted to learn their language. They helped, and I planned. I had the idea that an understanding of their language was going to be very helpful in the future.

Rainy season was about to start. We had hopes that the rains would make the area more bearable. We hoped that the rain would at least wash down the concrete and cool it off. It might even remove some of the stench.

The area was a fly infested mess. The latrines, the cooking areas and the living quarters were all one. Everything being crammed together contributed to the worsening of our conditions. The camp had rightly been named "Fly Camp". There were millions of the big fat blue flies. Someone said that they were rightly called blue tails, not blue ass.

Somehow rumors were started. No one knew how or who. They were just there. There was even the story that Germany had surrendered.

Clouds started to form over the China Sea and move in over the island. It was mid-May. Rain started one afternoon. It was a heavy warm downpour. It came fast. Within minutes we were soaked.

There was no shelter for the hundreds of men. The shelter halves and the salvaged pieces of sheet metal that had been set up as sunshades didn't stop the downpour from wetting everything. Floods of rainwater washed over the hot concrete. Some of the men who had acquired boxes sat on them to stay out of the flood. Everybody held their belongings, keeping them off of the wet concrete to keep them from being washed away.

The rains were sporadic, and although it was cooler, the water just added to our misery. The nights were cold. Fires, used mainly for cooking and now for warmth burned continuously. The night darkness was dotted with the light of small fires. There was also the continuous odor of food of some kind cooking, which didn't help the hunger pangs.

The meager ration of rice issued by the Japs was not only inadequate as a food supply, but it was also infested with larvae and maggots. At first we picked out the maggots and threw them away. Then we were told by one of the Army doctors that the maggots contained protein. So, we cooked the rice again after we received from the Japs to cook the maggots. They tasted funny and a little salty, but they were food.

It became evident to me that the only way to obtain food was to go out on the daily work details. I volunteered for them every day. Some days the work details paid off. One day I managed a work detail that was ordered to the South Mine Dock to load food.

There were bags of sugar, canned fruit and various other canned goods that were being brought by truck from the storage dumps near Cold Storage in the middle of the island. We unloaded the trucks and carried the food to the small boats at the dock. We were told that the food was being shipped to the Jap officers quartered in Manila. Just before the end of the work shift I was handed a box that was open. It contained large bottles of mustard. When I reached the end of the line at the boat, I took two of the bottles and shoved them into my coveralls, one under each arm. The fullness of the coveralls and the tightness of the web belt held the bottles effectively. After I handed down the box I returned to the line at the truck. It took two more trips to empty the truck.

We were lined up by the small Jap guard and told to "Bongo". We bongoed, counted off, and waited. The Jap pointed to two men at the head of the group and told them to pass out two cans to each of the men. Everyone in the group was delighted with the payoff. Two cans of Dole pineapple. I stuffed the cans into my coveralls along with the jars of mustard. When we arrived at the entrance of the camp we were told to bongo again. The small Jap guard saluted the corporal at the gate and left. We were told to wait.

"What the hell do the bastards want now?" someone asked.

"Who the hell knows what these slimy slant eyed shitheads want."

The Jap corporal strutted down one side of the group and then up the other side. He asked questions that were generally unintelligible except for a few of the more common Japanese words.

He stopped beside me and looked up at me from his five foot. Unfortunately I was the tallest man in the group. He scowled.

"Nanda?"

"Beats me. I don't know what you want. Nanda wakaran. I don't know. Nanda?" I asked back.

"Nanda?" He pointed to the bulges in my coveralls.

"Food. Mesi mesi." I opened the front of my coveralls and showed him the jars and cans.

"Doko?"

"Doko? I don't know what you want. I was on a work detail. Everybody has cans."

He scowled again. He stepped back and drew his issue sword. "Nanda?" He repeated.

I opened my hands and spread them palms up in the standard gesture of submission. "I don't know."

"NANDA?" He screamed.

"What the hell do the screwballs want anyway?" I heard someone ask.

"Who the hell knows what the cockknocker wants." Another voice from the group mouthed off.

The little corporal had worked himself up into a sweat. A half a dozen Jap guards stood around the group watching the action.

Suddenly the Jap swung the sword through the air. The blade whistled past the heads of the three of us that were the closest to the little runt. He walked up to face me and jabbed my stomach with the point of the sword. Blood trickled down from the puncture as I backed away. He pointed that he wanted my arms above my head. Both arms went up as high as the coveralls and the jars and cans would allow. A big gold toothed smile spread across the corporal's face.

"Yoi." He said.

Without warning he swung the flat of the blade against my coveralls. The sound of breaking glass surprised him.

"Damn you you shithead." I moved gingerly. I had attempted to duck as he swung the weapon and with the force of the blow I fell to my knees. I looked down at the right side of the coveralls under my arm. I felt the sharpness of the glass from the broken jar and the sticky wetness of the warm mustard, and I thought, something else. Blood. I raised my arm slowly, my face was contorted with surprise and pain. I became angry, but grabbed hold of myself. This wasn't the time.

"Haw haw haw!" The small corporal was doubled over with laughter as were the Jap guards that had been watching. The Japs giggled and jabbered as though they were watching a vaudeville show. Some of the POWs were snickering, while others grimaced.

"You okay?" asked the man on my left as he helped me to my feet.

"Yeah. I guess so." I answered. "I don't know."

Roars of laughter were still coming from the Jap corporal. His face was covered with tears as he stamped his feet in a fit of laughter.

The smell of the mustard spread as did the sticky concoction as it seeped through the cloth. It ran down across my belly and down my leg. I could feel it run down across my hip and across my butt. I though I was burning up when it made contact with my anus. I spit and cursed, careful not to aggravate the Jap.

He finally sheathed his sword and calmed down.

"Yoi. Yoi. Yarushi." He repeated himself a few times. "Kiotski na!" He called us to attention.

I stood as best I could, but the burning mustard kept me jiggling and dancing. I felt as though I was going to piss at any time.

The Jap corporal called something to the guards. He was answered with fits of laughter.

"Oi. You." The corporal stood in front of me, grinning. He reached into his pocket and pulled out a pack of Camels.

"Oi." He handed me two cigarettes.

"Okay?" He asked.

I nodded dumbly, biting my tongue. I thought how much fun it would be to kick out his goddamned gold teeth. But, I also knew what would happen to me if I didn't control myself.

"Okay." I answered as I took the cigarettes.

"Hokay." He answered.

He stepped back, "March." He called out in English.

As soon as we entered the compound the group broke up and gathered around me.

"You okay?"

"Not hurt bad are you?"

"I guess I'm alright. I won't know until a wash off this crappy mustard."

"What the freaking hell do you want with mustard anyway? You gonna have it with some steaks maybe?" One of the men guffawed.

"No asshole. I am going to trade it to the shithead officers for some food."

The man that made the remark shut up fast and stayed shut.

Laughs and guffaws followed me as I made my way to the spot.

"Crap your pants?"

"Your shit stinks like mustard."

The mustard had run down and across my leg. I looked like I had crapped my pants.

"What the hell happened to you?" Johnny greeted me with a frown. Then he laughed heartily.

"You can do without the pineapple if you keep that up." I snorted.

"Ha! You sure look funny." Johnny laughed.

"Thanks." I answered. I handed over the clean can of pineapple and the unbroken jar of mustard. I pulled open the coveralls and examined myself. I could see blood and I knew I was bleeding. There were a couple of mustard covered spots that burned like hell. "May as well leave the can there and wash off everything in the bay. I should be able to fish out the broken glass without cutting the hell out of myself." I pulled on the pants and shorts to ease the burning of my rectum.

The warm water of the bay eased the burning rapidly as I reached into my shorts and washed away the mustard. I swished the water through the brown paste and pulled out the shards of glass. I handed them to Johnny and then washed the other can of pineapple. I finished washing and pulled off the coveralls and scrubbed out the half dozen cuts that had the bleeding stopped by the mustard. I pulled out several shards of glass and washed out the cuts.

Johnny stood in the water near me grinning like a monkey.

Bataan and Corregidor, Philippine Islands

CHAPTER 3 -- BILIBID

Word was passed that we were all to move out of camp. It was Saturday, May 23rd. No one knew where we were moving to.

Johnny, Ed, Schwartz and I fought our way to the gate. We managed to be in the first group of about one hundred men that were being marched to the North Mine Dock. We were loaded onto a small freighter.

The Japs continued to load the prisoners until there were about two thousand men crammed into the holds and on the decks. There had been no food issue, and the only water available was what each of us carried in our canteens. Worse, there were no latrines. The men were crowded into every available inch of space available on the small ship.

Johnny and I fought to stay topside to avoid the suffocating hot cargo hold. We managed to work our way to the deck next the pilot house on the uppermost deck. Soon we had a talking acquaintance with the Jap pilot who remained at his post during the entire time we were on board.

A Jap sailor, who seemed to be a civilian rather than military, brought a tray with steaming hot water, a tea pot, and a couple of very small cups.

We ah'd and oh'd as the odor of the tea spread through the pilot house. The pilot turned out to be a friendly fellow who offered us some tea. Canteen cups were produced with magical speed. Our host doled out green tea with a happy smile on his face. The profuse thanks that he received kept him grinning all the time we were on board. Our expressed gratitude affected him so much that he shared three more pots of tea that were brought to him that day. We tried to question him about the war, but he protested that he knew nothing since he was only a sailor and didn't pay much attention to the war.

We remained at the dock all night, waiting. The men in the holds were miserable. There was a constant stream moving to the water side of the ship as the men relieved themselves over the side. The stink soon permeated the whole ship.

At dawn the ship's lines were freed and the trip started. We headed into the bay toward Manila. The trip was slow, very slow. Around noon the ship stood off of the Pasay end of Dewey Boulevard. Landing barges were brought alongside and we were loaded into them. The barges pulled in to the beach and we went over the side into waist deep water. We made our way to shore and on to Dewey Boulevard. There the Japs that were waiting for us lined us up in a column of fours. We waited in place until the ship was completely empty before they started us marching north through Manila.

I pointed out to Johnny and others that they had changed the name from Dewey Boulevard to Heiwa Boulevard. Some of the men then started to make remarks about the name changes of the streets we passed. The Jap guards didn't strike or punch anyone. This was a surprise. They merely shushed us. "Dekimasen. Shush." Another who spoke English said, "Do not speak. You must all be quiet. Do not talk."

This started us to thinking. What were they up to now? Whispers ran rampant through the column.

We were a bedraggled and sorry mess. Instead of soldiers we looked more like a bunch of starved hoboes. Our uniforms, what was left of them, were rags, dirty and torn. The khaki shirts had the sleeves cut off above the elbows. The trousers had been made into midthigh shorts. Our hair had not been cut in months and our beards were scraggly. We surely must have looked like a bunch of hoboes.

It couldn't be called marching. Not what we did. Men hobbled and walked as best they could. The macadam was hot, burning hot. I could feel the heat through the thin soles of my boots. The sun was hot. The few miles from Pasay up the boulevard to Manila seemed to stretch out to a thousand miles. Men weakened by malaria and dysentery fell along the way. The guards used their bayonets to push us off when we tried to help the less fortunate men. We saw the guards pull and drag the men who had fallen to the side of the street. We were afraid that the Japs were going to bayonet them after we passed so we tried to hold up and drag along the less fortunate ones near us. When a guard spotted our attempt, he motioned with his bayonet and forced the man to be dropped at the side of the road. Our curses and our prayers went unheeded.

Halfway to Manila the Filipinos started to assemble along the route. Word was evidently spreading through the city. Soon there were cigarettes, candy, oranges, bananas, rice balls and money being thrown by the Filipinos.

"Who are you Joe?"

"Where are you from?"

"Corregidor? You come from Corregidor?"

"Bataan!? You are from Bataan?"

"How many are there? Are there more?"

"Do you know John Marshal?"

"Where are you going?"

When the Filipinos finally realized that we were from Bataan and Corregidor they were astounded.

"They said you were all dead!"

"Japs say they slaughter all Americans. Newspaper say so!"

The men in the column were deluged with questions. Names. Any bit of information that could be obtained. The Japs pushed the civilians back, although they could really do little to stop the thousands that had gathered along the line of march. They finally gave up and let the questioning and the donations and gifts of food and cigarettes go on unhampered.

Filipinos laughed, cried and cheered as we passed.

"Victory Joe!"

"We help Joe."

I found it rather strange because Joe was the common term used by the natives when talking to a stranger, particularly Americans.

Words of encouragement that we hadn't heard and never expected to hear came from all. Fallen men were helped and tended to by the people. The Japanese marched along the column and didn't interfere.

An elderly soldier, a Colonel, by the insignia on his overseas cap, collapsed in front of us. Johnny and I helped him to the curb and laid him down. He was very sick. He lost control of his bowels and the mess he made affected even our own callused feelings. We moved him away from the smelly mess and handed him over to a couple of Filipinos who came out of the crowd to offer assistance. A Jap guard came running up to us. I flinched, expecting the bayonet or at least the butt of the rifle.

"You back! March! You." He pointed to the civilians, "You help." he ordered.

I gasped my surprise as we moved back into the column.

We continued on past the Bureau of Posts and then over to the river and on through the business center of Manila.

The end of our march was Bilibid Prison. We were marched in unceremoniously.

"I sure hope that we will be allowed to rest for a couple of days." I said to Johnny. "Let's find one of the cells next to the exit."

There were no orders or instructions issue. The men were marched in and found their own places to squat.

Bilibid was, or had been the civilian prison in Manila. Now it was empty. We never did find out what had happened to the civilian, prisoners, although there was a lot of speculation.

The coolness of the buildings, just due to the shade alone, was welcome after the shadeless heat of Fly Camp, the wait on the ship, and the hike from Pasay.

We had managed to pick up some cigarettes and fruit from the items that the Filipinos had tossed to us. The food disappeared immediately.

We gulped it down without worrying about saving any for later. We were to hungry to worry about tomorrow's hunger. The cigarettes were a welcome luxury. I smoked sparingly.

It was almost sunset when we heard four trucks pulled into the prison compound. Men rushed to the windows of the cells to see what was taking place.

"I'll be damned! Look. Johnny!" I shouted. "They trucked the sick and those who couldn't make the march on their own."

Amazed at the scene, the men found the sight encouraging, something to raise their spirits, even if only for a moment.

The next day more men came in from Corregidor.

The opportunity to rest, to wash with fresh water made everyone feel better. Scissors and razors were obtained by various mysterious means, and even some soap was brought in.

Johnny rented a razor for a couple of cigarettes along with a piece of mirror. Ed, Schwartz and I shaved. We bathed, taking turns in washing each others backs. The clothing, such as it was, was washed and dried in the hot sun. The change in routine took our minds off of our long term problems.

Rice was supplied three times a day. It was brought in in wooden buckets from some kitchen somewhere nearby.

"The freaking cooks must be auto mechanics because they sure as hell can't cook. We could use this stuff as wall paper paste." I complained. "Yeah! I know it is food so I eat it. But they didn't have to ruin it." Everybody agreed that the pasty mess, which the Filipinos called lugao, needed something to make it palatable.

Johnny was quiet and uncomplaining.

We all knew that this was only a stopover point to someplace. May be a hell of a lot worse than Corregidor. Destination? Unknown. There was a lot of speculation and a lot of rumors, but no plans for tomorrow.

The officers were separated from the enlisted men. We wondered why, but couldn't come up with any answers.

I engaged the Jap guards in conversation whenever I could. I asked for specific translations of words and wrote them down on scraps of paper that I found in some of the cells.

"What are you up to?" Johnny asked.

"Studying Jap. Nipongo. I might as well learn their language."

"What for?" he asked in a puzzled tone.

"Hell, it's going to make it easier to get what we need. And, maybe I could put it to some use."

"To get away you mean!" Johnny shot back.

"Maybe." I answered slowly.

"You just won't give up, will you?" Johnny snapped sharply, annoyed at my stupid insistence to escape.

"Guess not. But don't worry, I won't get anyone in trouble."

"Yeah," he snarled, "I'll bet."

Word spread that we were going to Cabanatuan!

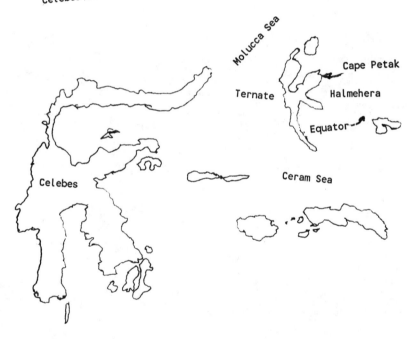

Halmahera, Indonesia

CHAPTER 4 -- CABANATUAN

Cabanatuan lies in the middle of the island of Luzon. To the east, separating Cabanatuan from Philippine Sea, are the Quezon Mountains. Fifty kilometers of almost impassable mountain and jungle terrain. There is only one road leading to the east, to Baler, near the coast. To the west, thirty some kilometers to Tarlac across cane fields, and then sixty more kilometers to the China Sea through the rugged Zambales Mountains. To the north, the inner plain of Luzon is occupied by Japs who are constantly traveling and patrolling the roads leading to the Lingayen Gulf. To the south, the area is again occupied by the Japs. There is no easy way out to the sea and relative safety. They planned to keep us isolated in the center of the island. It would have been easy to have imprisoned us at Fort McKinley only a few kilometers southeast of Manila. There we could be quartered in the barracks. But then we would be too close to the Filipinos. I guessed that they wanted us isolated.

When I mentioned this to Johnny and Ed and Schwartz, they to began to wonder about what the Japs had planned for us.

"How do you know all of this Joe?" Ed asked.

"I've been up there and up further north looking at some of the gold mining potential in the mountains. We were going to mine gold up around Mount Solu. That is only about twenty kilometers south of Pamplona. That is the north side of Luzon."

"Who's we?" Schwartz asked.

"Some friends of Dow Cobb's. Johnny met Dow in New York."

"Yeah. He's the guy that owns the largest pearl in the world. It was found here in the Philippines about eight years ago. That is why we came here in the first place. To meet Dow. Only he never showed." He sounded bitter, and, I didn't blame him.

I had met Dow in New York City at the Explorer's Club. We had become friends due to the fact that we were both interested in exploring the white parts of the maps of Borneo, Luzon and the islands of the South Pacific. I had pointed out to him that there was a Cape Petak on the northeast side of Halmahera, an island northeast of Sulawesi and very close to New Guinea. He had been amazed that a Slavic name had been given to a primary in a predominantly Moslem region. As I explained this to Ed and Schwartz they sat open mouthed and silent. Then they opened up with a myriad of questions. We talked for hours about the southern islands and the riches that were available to anyone

37

with the guts to go after them.

On Wednesday, the 27th, the word was that we were going to be moved out during the night to avoid being seen by the Filipinos.

I decided to scrounge around the cells to see if there was anything useful or worthwhile taking. I passed an empty cell that was littered with papers. I stared at the mess and started to go on when I spotted a newspaper headline, "Corregidor". I walked over and picked up the paper from under the litter. The full headline read "CORREGIDOR FALLS". It was the Tribune, dated May eighth, Friday, 1942. I walked out to the yard reading the story. I realized that the paper was more than likely a historical memento. I folded it and slipped it into my coveralls. I thought the Japs would take it away. I didn't say anything to anyone when I arrived back at the area where we were quartered. I figured I could tell the guys about it later.

It was three in the morning when the Japs rousted us and marched us out of Bilibid along Azcarraga up Antonio Rivera and into the railroad yard. It wasn't a long march, but it did seem long in the dark of the night.

Groups of one hundred and twenty-five men were counted off and jammed into each freight car.

The cars were much smaller than the stateside freight cars that I was familiar with, having ridden the rails one summer while bumming around the country.

The only way that one hundred and twenty-five men could fit into the car was by standing, packed like sardines. The Japs pushed and shoved, cramming us into the cars. The doors were slammed shut and locked.

Men became panicky and frightened as the cars became stuffy and hot. We shifted, shoved and settled as best we could.

"How about some air?"

"I've got to take a leak."

"Open the goddamned doors and let us have some air."

Shouts, moans, threats and pleading brought no relief. We jostled around as the air became stale. The heat and the stink started to take toll of the men. The older and weaker, the sick men suffered first and the most. It was impossible for a man to fall when he passed out or just fainted. There just wasn't room to fall. Hours passed in misery. About the time that the cracks around the doors started to show that the sun was rising the engine whistle gave a feeble toot and the train lurched and chugged to a slow start.

It wasn't long before the sun started to add to the heat in the cars. Johnny and I were on the west side of the car and we were heading north. I told Johnny that we were lucky that we were away from the hot side.

"You sure?"

"Of course I am." I answered. "The sun comes up in the east. The sunlight is coming in around the crack of the door that is on the other side of the car. We are moving north."

One of the men standing nearby agreed. That seemed to settle it. We were moving north to Cabanatuan.

"I gotta go and I can't hold it. Damn you."

"You better hold it or you're going to piss on me."

"I can't!" he moaned.

"You better. Tie a knot in it or I'll tie it for you."

"Got to."

"You bastard! You pissed on me!"

The struggle that started wasn't a fight since there wasn't room to swing. It stopped with a verbal exchange that was a low rumble that continued endlessly.

The car became a stink hole. Soon the vomit added to the incredible stench that filled the stifling air.

Another fight erupted.

"Johnny?" I called in the murky gloom.

"Yeah."

"I thought you moved away. Let's move up against the wall."

The fighting spread. Men slugged, kicked and clawed. One half of the car became a crawling mass of fighting men. In the dim light it looked like a mass of crawling maggots. The train came to a sudden unexpected stop with the brakes squealing loudly.

Unexpectedly the door on the east side of the car opened. Some men fell out on the ground. Shouts in Japanese came over the racket the POWs were making. Bayonets came into action and those that had fallen out were shoved back in. The fighting had stopped of its own accord. The Jap guards prodded the men with their bayonets. Curses and moans of pain answered them. A blessing of fresh air came in through the open door. It was a momentary Godsend.

"What do you want to do with the dead ones?" somebody asked.

"Throw them out and make some room in here," came the callous answer. It was an example of how war changed men.

"What is going on in there?" asked a Jap in English. "Answer me!"

"Come on in and find out you yellow prick," was sneered back at him.

"Somebody started a fight."

"You must stop it! Behave or we will shoot you,"

"Frig you!"

"How about the dead men?"

There was a short conference among the Japs. The English speaking one spoke up. "Pass them out here. We will take care of them."

The bodies of two men were passed out. One body, that of an older man, didn't have a mark on it. He could have died of a heart attack, or he may have suffocated. The body of the other man was bruised and bloody. He had died violently. Another causality of the brutality of war.

"How did this happen?" asked the English speaking Jap.

"He fell from the damned roof you frigging asshole."

"Your insolence will cause you nothing but trouble. There will be no more of this. If another man is injured or killed, ten of you will be shot." His voice was as threatening as his words. "Ten men for one will be the punishment. It is the way of the Imperial Japanese soldier. We will have obedience." The sternness of his attitude seemed somehow ludicrous under the circumstances. The door was slammed shut again and we heard the lock snap shut.

"Johnny, are you all right?" I asked. We had both moved as close to the door as we could.

"Yes. I'm all right. Wasn't that rotten?" he asked in a subdued tone.

"Yeah." I responded in what must have sounded like a indifferent answer. "But what the hell do we do about it?" I didn't feel as thick skinned as I may have sounded.

I thought about how men are driven to the point at which something violent could happen with only the slightest push. The smallest, otherwise insignificant incident, that certain word, could be a trigger. I knew that almost anything could happen. Months of near death, fear, privation and starvation, had brought us to the edge of furious unreasoning fury, if for no other reason than to find emotional relief.

The train traveled on for a few more hours. The stench was bearable only because there was nothing that any of us could do anything about it. The men that had passed out with the heat, or maybe died, were held up in a standing position only because there wasn't any room to fall. Their supporting neighbors relieved them of any loose and accessible possessions without qualm.

There was no warning when the train came to a stop. The doors were opened after what seemed like an hour. Men pushed, crawled and some were virtually carried from the freight car by the rush of bodies. I saw that the other cars were being emptied in the same way.

Word spread about what had happened in the cars. It had been the same in all of them. There was scarcely any reaction and the discussions stopped within minutes after the realization that the violence and death were not at all unusual. There was some talk about the dead that remained in the cars. It seemed as though about twenty or more men in each of the cars didn't come out. Whether they were dead or just unconscious we could only guess.

The Japs lined us up and marched us from the railroad siding to the Cabanatuan schoolyard only a short distance away. It was the only place large enough in the town where they could keep us confined. There was a barbed wire fence around the school which we soon found out had been put up just for us. We were told that we were going to spend the night. In the morning we were going to march to the POW camp. The camp was supposedly some twenty-five kilometers away.

Boiled rice was brought in and distributed. The portion was very small. The Filipinos soon found a frantic market, with skyrocketing prices for anything that was edible.

I wandered around the schoolyard talking to some of my old friends. I noticed that the guards didn't seem to mind the wheeling and dealing that was going on between the Filipinos and the prisoners.

The main item that found a ready market was the brown sugar cake that the Filipinos brought in by the gunnysack. These cakes were about four to five inches in diameter and an inch and a half thick. The going price escalated from five centavos to fifty centavos within minutes as the sugar starved soldiers bought them up by the dozen. The demand soon exceeded the supply and the price jumped to a peso.

I had been one of the first to buy the cakes and had bought twenty of them for a peso. Johnny, Ed and Schwartz had also bought theirs at the same price. Sugar, in any form, had not been available since the first month of the war. It was a luxury that was completely unexpected.

"Don't eat the stuff raw." I warned my group. "You'll get sicker than hell. You will be lucky if the only thing you wind up with is the shits."

"You're nuts man. It's sugar man! SUGAR! You remember what that is don't you?" Schwartz remarked. "Christ! It's been a long time. You should remember. You know the sweet stuff." He jibed at me.

"Yes I know. Look, just look at it. Believe me, don't eat the stuff raw." I countered.

"Why? What the hell is wrong with it? It's only brown sugar."

They all jumped me for an explanation.

"Go and ask the Filipinos what these cakes are. These cakes are made from the sweepings from the floors of the sugar mills. They feed them to the ponies."

"Bullshit!" Ed spit back at me. "Next you'll tell us that the crap that is in them makes them sweeter. Huh?"

"OK OK." I answered. "But I'm going to boil mine first and then let the syrup cool before I eat it. See, you could use the syrup over the rice. That would make a tasty dish. Let's boil ours Johnny. I have had enough of the shits."

"Sure. We'll boil ours." Johnny agreed.

"The stuff is sugar all right. But the rest of the stuff is anybody's guess. There is cane and crap. Dead flies, dried spit, lizard shit, cane and God knows what else. They handle the stuff like coal in sacks. Really the Filipinos just use the cakes to feed the calesa ponies and the donkeys. Animal food." I explained. "I've seen it in the barrios."

"You're nuts."

"How the shit do you know?" asked a fellow POW who had been listening to us.

"Who the hell asked you in?" Schwartz shot at him vehemently.

"Ah! Knock it off. I ain't talking to you anyway." The outsider raised an arm as though to strike Schwartz.

"Hold it man. You just go and ask the Filipinos." I told him.

The man took off in a hurry.

"You aren't kidding are you Joe?" Johnny asked He looked at me in bewilderment.

"No, I'm not kidding." I replied. "The sugar is good. The only thing is that I am afraid of getting some other disease which I don't need. My malaria and dengue is already bad enough. I don't need another case of the runs."

"So what do we do? We hold off until the other guys try it. And we see what happens to them." Schwartz submitted.

"That would take too long." observed Ed.

"Sure, we can pasteurize it. Boil it." Johnny spoke up unexpectedly.

"Hey! That sounds good." I added. "We can break it up into little pieces and let it dissolve in the water as it heats up. The junk will settle in the bottom, the cane should float. Then we can pour off the syrup and leave the crap in the bottom. OK?"

They stared at me.

"Well?" I looked around at the frowning faces. "OK. Then you guys come up with a smart assed idea." I looked around at the group in disgust.

"Ah, come on Joe." Schwartz grinned. "We're only needling you. You are sure it won't ruin the sugar though?"

"When we boil the stuff the heat will kill the germs. The stuff that is left is sugar syrup."

"I'll be damned. A professor we got yet!" Schwartz exclaimed. "How the hell do you know it'll really work?"

"Ah, he's a chemist." Johnny commented. "I guess you have a good point though, I would rather be safe as possible. More dysentery I don't want."

"Sure, it won't take long to boil the stuff. I'll get a fire going if someone will bring water."

Ed took off to find something with which to build a fire.

Robinson, one of the men that I knew had been listening to us for some time. He was a small man with a dark heavy beard and a hook nose that made him look mean for all of his smallness. He had taken off on some errand about the same time that Ed had gone off. He returned after we had built a fire from coconut husks and bamboo that Ed had scrounged. We had four canteen cups of the brown colored concoction that had resulted from dissolving the sugar cakes.

"Hey!" Robinson burst out excitedly, "the Filipino told me that they do feed the cakes to the donkeys because they are dirt cheap donkey food. Does that mean that we can't eat them?"

"No! It don't mean that we can't eat them! It just means that if you don't want to crap your brains out you'll boil them first."

"Won't that ruin the sugar?" he asked skeptically.

"Hell no!" Ed shot back with a know it all attitude. "Won't hurt it at all." He winked broadly at our small group.

"OK! Thanks! I'll do the same for you someday."

Word spread around the schoolyard about the fact that the sugar cakes should be pasteurized. We saw fires burning all through the evening as the pasteurizing continued. Many men didn't heed the warning and ate the cakes anyway.

Johnny sat back after we had finished our rice ball and syrup topping. He looked a little bit odd in a way that I didn't quite understand, then he sprung it on us.

"Did you guys notice some of the dalagas?" He glanced out toward the street.

Ed seemed to come unglued. "Women!? You looking at women!? Jesus Christ! All I see when I look at a woman is their tits. Know why?"

We all stared at him with open mouths. Schwartz had dropped the cigarette he had been smoking and gawked. "Their tits? How come?"

"Milk! You shitty dope! Milk! FOOD! Man! FOOD!"

We all sat stupefied. I though about that I hadn't had an erection in I didn't remember how long. I didn't know if it was because I had been running scared, away from bombs and shells, or because I also had only been thinking about filling my belly. I thought about it for a moment, while the other guys sat as quietly as I did. I was sure that it was because my belly was always empty, and just because I had had the shit scared out of me so many times in the past five months.

"You are out of your stupid feeble mind."

Schwartz swung at Ed with his canteen cup and spilled the hot tea that he had left. The tea splattered on my legs. I jumped up howling as the hot liquid ran down under the bandage on my right leg.

"Holy shit!" I rubbed my swollen leg. "Hey! That felt pretty good." I smiled. "Maybe I should soak the thing in hot tea. Huh?"

"Cripes! I'm sorry Joe. This asshole just made me do that! Tits! Milk! Hungry I can understand, but sucking a pregnant woman's tit for food. I oughta knock your damned head off!" Schwartz was pissed much more than I thought he should be.

"Aw, come on. Hell, can't you take a joke?" Ed bantered.

"Some shitty joke!" Schwartz growled.

"Hell, that would be something. Milk." Johnny responded. "You know I haven't had a glass of milk since the day the war broke out. I don't think I can remember what it tastes like anymore."

"I had some caribou milk on Bataan back in January. Then they killed the caribou so we could eat it." Schwartz reminisced. "Too bad we can't get the Filipinos to bring some in."

"Yeah." I agreed.

"Anyway," Johnny continued, "there sure were some nice looking dalagas out there."

"I'd have to eat it because I couldn't get it up." Ed nodded his head as he thought about it.

"Makes two of us." I concurred. "I didn't even think about sex on the Rock, and there were some nice looking women there that I met."

"Think of what the Japs would do if they caught one of us screwing one of the broads. They'd shit rice I bet." Johnny laughed.

"Bet they would at that." Ed laughed at the thought. "Well, I don't think we'll get the chance for a long time. Right?"

We all agreed. The subject of sex and women died without anymore comment.

Night came fast, as it does in the tropics. We were exhausted and glad that we could rest out in the open. The train trip had been a horrible experience that none of us would ever forget. Sleep came, but it wasn't restful, merely an exhausted unconsciousness. The night was filled with hellish nightmares. I woke up many times and dropped off to sleep uttering prayers of thanks that I had made it through another day. The hard adobe of the schoolyard made for a rough mattress, but there was room to stretch out, and there was cool breathable air.

The standard Jap alarm clock woke us at dawn, a kick with a cloven toed sneaker was the softest version. The point of a bayonet and the rifle but were the other versions.

Boiled rice, wrapped in a banana leaf, a ball about the size of a man's fist, was doled out to each man. We were formed up in a long column, four abreast.

"You must march to Laur. There you will be placed in the camps that have been made ready for you by the kindness of the Japanese Emperor. There you will have shelter and you will be protected from the renegade Filipinos who have not surrendered." He ushed his subordinates and indicated that we were to move out. The four of us, Johnny, Ed, Schwartz and I were up near the head of the column.

The march to the east and north of Cabanatuan started immediately.

"If we are going to Laur we have to march about twenty some kilometers." I told my group.

"How many miles is that?" Somebody behind us asked.

"Over twelve miles." I answered.

"Cripes! How the hell do they think we can make it? Twelve miles! That's going to take us all day. And it's starting to get hot already."

"Take it easy," Ed shot back at the man, "We're all in the same fix."

Word spread as we started to march that anyone who couldn't make the march, anyone who fell out, would be bayoneted. Spirits changed immediately. The up spirits that we had earlier were displaced with a sense of doom. Looking forward to something decent in a camp was replaced by a sense of foreboding. These stinking Japs weren't about to make things any easier for us, not by a long shot. This could very well be a death camp. The grim tragedy of the Death March faced us as we trudged through the dust that was stirred up by the trucks that lead the column.

"If we have to march twenty kilometers I can't understand why the hell they say the camp is in Cabanatuan." I puzzled over the conundrum.

"Maybe because it is the biggest city around here. Laur could be just a barrio." Johnny offered.

"Makes sense." I said and then lapsed into silence as we moved on.

The people we passed on the road, friendly Filipinos, gathered along the path of our march and threw fruit, cigarettes, hard boiled eggs and candy to us. Luckily I caught a pack of cigarettes, Filipino Kings. They were about six inches long, with brown paper instead of white, the way Americans make cigarettes. I grinned happily as I stored away my treasure.

The sun started to take its toll after the first few kilometers. Marching in the tropics is hard work. The tropical sun burns out men in a very short time. The road was bumpy, hard, but dusty. The dust got into everything. It dried out the mouth, caked around the eyes, and blocked the nose. Then the flies came in and made the going even tougher. After about three hours of marching men began to drop back in the column so that it stretched out to twice its original length despite the bayonet jabs. Men dropped out along the road. Sick men, the older ones. Sneaking looks back didn't provide the information as to what happened to them. The guards used their bayonets or sometimes a gesture from a kinder Jap to keep looking ahead was the result of a sideward or backward glance. "No look back. No look."

"How are you doing Johnny?"

He looked weaker than he had at the beginning of the day. I was afraid that he wouldn't be able to finish the march.

"I'm okay. Tired. My gut aches. I'll make it. Don't worry about me. How's your leg holding up?" He looked down at the bandaged leg. His determination was evident.

"Burns like hell. But it's my back that is really raising hell." I arched my back as I answered.

"Do you think that they are killing them?" asked the man directly ahead of me.

"NO! Hell, I don't know." I was angry at him for making me voice my own fears. "What the hell do you think I am? A Jap? Shutup! Save your breath and walk." I kicked dust at him.

"How the hell do I know if they are killing them. I haven't heard anybody scream yet." I snarled.

I was just as afraid as anyone else, I guess. The tongue lashing had been a way of getting rid of some of my fears. It was an unkind way of hiding my fear. I felt a slight release of some of the crawling feeling in my lower gut.

No sooner had I shut up than a shot rang out from somewhere behind us.

"See! See, I told you. I told you. They are shooting them." The soldier I had ranted at broke out in a panicky voice that bordered on hysteria. "They'll kill us if we fall. They'll kill us." He lunged to run out of the column. I made a grab for his arm and one of the other men grabbed his shirt. A Jap came running at us with his bayonet held out in front of him.

"Shut up!" I ordered. "I'll knock your head off if you don't shut up and march." I threatened.

"Nanda," asked the Jap. "Nanda."

"Byoki! Byoki! Yaroshi. Kono stowa byoki des." I answered in Japanese. "Sick. Sick."

The Jap looked at me in surprise. I had screwed up. I didn't want them to know that I understood or spoke some Japanese. I had it figured that if they didn't know that I understood that I could find out things that could be useful.

"Nipongo dekimaska." The Jap asked.

"Skosh." I corrected myself, "Sukoshi."

He gave me a big toothed grin. He forgot about the incident that had brought him running. He kept pace with us for some time. His presence, for some reason seemed to calm the frightened man that we held in line forcibly. After marching about a kilometer the man turned to me, there were tears streaming down his face. I felt so sorry for him that I patted him on the shoulder. "Thanks. I'm okay now, thanks. I'm just scared of getting killed" he strained to keep from looking back. "Do you think they killed someone back there?" His voice was pleading for reassurance. I released my hold and the other soldier nodded to him and moved up ahead as I fell back and rejoined Johnny and the others.

"It's okay. I'm just as scared as you are." I told him.

The man was in his forties. He must have had some bad times during the fighting. He was skin and bone. There were white scars that showed through the deep tan on his thighs and the arm that I had held.

"Maybe. Maybe not." The answer came from the redhead that had helped him on the other side. I became aware of the fact that the redhead was the Marine that had been with me when we had found the tomatoes. "It don't do no good to worry. Maybe the guy is better off dead." His voice was flat and hard. He shrugged. "Who knows?"

"Look. Don't worry about it now. We'll find out later." I soothed him. "Just take it easy now and we'll help you all we can."

I made my way to the outside of the column.

"Where you going?" Johnny asked in a voice that was edged with concern.

"Got to go."

He smirked and shook his head.

I unbuttoned my coveralls and started to take a leak. The Jap who had been pacing us stopped and grinned at me. He set his rifle on the ground and unwound the pant string. He leaned forward as I peed. "OHH! Yaroshi." He grinned again. He let go of his penis and used both hands holding them about six inches apart. "Ookii" He then laughed as he tied up and motioned me back into line.

We saw shacks not far ahead of us. It looked like some kind of a settlement or camp. We passed word back along the column. No one was familiar with the area, and no one knew of any military camps in this part of the island. When we approached the camp we saw Americans and Filipinos behind the double barbed wire fences. Questions, answers and greeting were shouted back and forth. The Japs found it impossible to keep the men quiet and just gave up. The information we gathered as we marched by the camp was meager but enlightening.

The camp was Cabanatuan One. The men were POWS from Manila. Some were from Baguio, others from Clark Field. Some had been captured before the fall of Bataan and Corregidor. They were being fed rice and some eggplant. There was no medicine, no clothing and no doctors. Many men were dying from malaria and dysentery. Some from gangrene and infected wounds.

We kept on marching. Two, three kilometers beyond Camp One we passed another camp. This one was empty. A sign at the entrance gave us the explanation we were looking for. These camps had been the 91st Filipino Army Camps.

CHAPTER 5 -- CAMP THREE

It was well after noon, and about five kilometers beyond the second camp we had passed when we approached another, much larger camp than the other two. We turned in through the barbed wire gate that was standing open to receive us. There were a few men standing around the gate as we entered. "I wonder where they came from?" I commented to no one in particular.

We were divided into groups and counted as we marched in. I noticed that there was some confusion as the Japs were counting us. The Japs were evidently missing their count. A captain was berating a corporal.

"Nanda bongo warui des."

"The captain is asking him why the count off is bad?" Then I heard him say that we would have to be counted again after we were installed in the barracks.

I looked at the barracks that were made of split bamboo walls woven together with rattan. The walls were tied to support and corner posts along the length of the wall. The roof was made of thick nipa thatch. There was nothing in the building, the floor was bare adobe.

Forty to fifty men were assigned to each of these buildings,depending on its size. We arranged ourselves along the sides of the shacks, each man taking a section of the floor.

We went out to take a look at our new surroundings. I noticed that there were much larger buildings, made in the same way as ours, further on in the camp. The camp looked huge.

Soon after we settled in men from the kitchen brought buckets of food. There was pasty rice and a thin eggplant soup. It was flat, without seasoning of any kind, not even any salt, but it was something to eat.

The long march in the hot sun had exhausted us. No one really was that interested in what was going on. The starvation, due to the poor planning, disease, wounds and the mistreatment by the Japs had left their mark on us. Bataan, Corregidor, now Cabanatuan. Most of us were in such poor condition after only six months that I wondered what another six months, or a year or more, would do to us. We didn't know what tomorrow would bring.

My right leg started to swell after the grueling hike. The ragged bandages were dirty from the dust and the sweat, mixed with the oozing goo that was seeping from the open wound. The "Guam" blisters, an
49

ulceration caused by some infectious bacteria, that had developed from the wounds were a dirty red when I took off the bandage. There was a granular green puss that stuck to the angry flesh. I was worried that I was developing moist gangrene which was what one of the doctors had said was what the men had that smelled so bad. The doctor on Corregidor had prescribed sulfathiozole, which wasn't available. At least I hoped it wasn't gangrenous. "How about watching our stuff while I hunt up some water and wash out these things and rinse out the bandages. I don't think we are going to get any medical attention here either."

"Sure," Johnny replied, "and if you find any clean water fill up my canteen."

"Right. Will do." I picked up his canteen and started out to find where our water supply was. I asked around as I hobbled from one hut to the other. The water supply turned out to be a piece of pipe sticking out of the ground about two feet. It was attached to a wood post, and it had a brass faucet. I filled my canteen, then I filled Johnny's. I filled my canteen cup and moved off to an open space about thirty feet away and proceeded to wash the oozing sores, then I washed out the bandages. Then I washed everything, the canteens, the cups and myself. I sat down and rested.

A POW who had been sitting under a tree watching me smiled at me, "Hurt like hell don't they?"

"Sure do."

"I had them on my arm. They used some sulfa on me on Corregidor. Healed them up in no time. Too bad you can't find some. Japs don't have any that I know of."

"I should be so lucky." I replied. "See you." I moved slowly as I returned to our shack.

The sun was low in the sky and the coolness of the evening was replacing the heat of the day. It was a pleasant relief after the trying day. I sat down with Johnny in the shade of our barrack where we were joined by some of the other men.

"I didn't think I could ever be so skinny. " I remarked to no one in particular as we smoked the cigarettes that the Filipinos had been kind enough to throw to us. "I'm turning into a skeleton. Nothing but skin and bone. I'm bruising the skin on my ass because there is no meat to cushion it."

"Your trouble," one of the men remarked, "is that you aren't skinny, you are just stretched out too long for your weight." The group all joined in laughing with us. It was a relief for all of us after the long day.

"How tall are you?" He asked.

"Six foot three. I weighed myself at Bilibid on that platform scale in the old storehouse. Sixty-three kilos. That's about..." I paused to convert it to pounds, "...one hundred and fifty pounds."

"What did you weight before?" Johnny asked.

"A hundred and eighty-five or so, for the past few years." I looked at Johnny. He returned my look. I guessed that he had thought about our problems when we had been living in San Francisco in early nineteen forty. Jobless, and broke, we had had a problem getting enough to eat until we had found jobs.

"You sure lost the weight." Our friend observed. "Were you on Bataan at all?" His question struck me as being particularly harsh for some unknown reason.

"Yes. I was there when the Japs ran all over us. They picked me up on the ninth. I got away from the Death March the tenth and made it to Corregidor." I thought about the trips back and forth on the nightly packet boat. "I used to go to Bataan on photo assignments. I was a Combat Photographer." I explained.

"Hmm, I was lucky. I never was on Bataan at all. I sat on the Rock all through the stinking mess. I'm from the 60th Coast Artillery. I was lucky." He finished pensively.

"Maybe you were."

"You got Indian blood in you?" asked one of the really dark skinned men sitting nearby. "You look like you have. Your skin is kind of bronze just like some of the Indians on the reservations in New Mexico. And you got no beard on your cheeks."

"I don't think so. My mothers people come from Minnesota. Been there for years. But I don't think they married any Indians."

"There are Sioux up there. You could be."

There was a lot of tired small talk as one after another the men turned in to sleep on the hard adobe floor. By a little after sunset everyone had turned in.

The next few days were spent in becoming friends with the men quartered with us and exploring the camp. Also the routine settled in. Up with the sun. Eat. Wash mess gear. Talk, eat, wash mess gear, and to bed at sunset.

On Sunday afternoon, May 31st, there was an order to assemble at the parade ground. It was the area that the Filipino Army had used for drill. No one knew the purpose of the assembly.

A trench-like ditch had been dug along the west side of the open area. It was about four foot deep and about twenty foot long. At four o'clock, a squad of Japanese soldiers marched four Americans in from the Jap side of the camp which was across the road. We parted to let them pass. Questions were thrown at the unfortunates. There were no replies. The Japs marched the Americans to the trench and forced them into it. They were made to stand facing us. All of the POWs had been assembled. It seemed to me that there must have been three or four thousand Americans and Filipinos.

"These men will be executed. They attempted to escape from this camp! We, the Imperial Japanese soldiers recaptured them. Now they will be shot!" The Japanese interpreter shouted to be heard.

There was a roar from the POWs that caused the Japs to place their rifles at port. The mumbling buzz continued as the men realized what they were going to witness.

"They were hungry!"

"They went for food!" Someone shouted.

"QUIET! Quiet! Do not talk!" The interpreter ordered. The Jap soldiers butted some of the men in front to enforce silence. They pointed their bayonets at the throats of others. The POWs moved back, angry.

"There will be no escape! Escape or any attempt to escape is punishable by death. You cannot escape the Imperial Japanese Army!"

The firing squad was ordered to aim and the command to fire was given.

Not a sound broke the silence after the echoes of the rifle fire died. There was a subdued groan from the crowd that seemed to roll out to the borders of the camp. Then there was silence as the stunned Americans watched the execution.

A Jap officer walked to the edge of the ditch. He looked down. He then addressed the interpreter.

No one moved as we wondered at what was going on. Then the officer stepped along the grave and administered mercy shots. From somewhere in the back of us a shout that sounded like "You murdering bastards!" It was muffled by the hands of those nearby.

The Jap firing squad stacked their rifles and proceeded to fill in the grave.

"That is all. Go back. Remember that you cannot escape us!"

When the trench was covered the Japs formed a tight column and marched out of the camp to their compound across the road.

No one moved to disband the assembled men. Anger, surprise and shock filled the men. There was much more emotion that was concealed simply because no one knew what the outcome would be if we let go. Slowly we drifted back to our barracks. No one spoke. The silence was more expressive than anything that any of us could say.

It was later that night that word was passed around about the men who had been executed. The story was that they had all been from Fort drum. William R. Benson, 19048556, Hugh E. Welman, 15065609, Fred

L. Lee, 18014480, and then there was a question about who the other man was. They weren't sure if the fellow named Jordan had been Charles B., 17014320, or Wesley E., 18014490. I noted the informaion.

The effect of the unnecessary execution manifested itself in the caution with which the men used in planning their moves. No one wanted to try an escape without having some outside contact and assistance. The plans of escape became a secretive thing, even from from each other. Only the men involved in an escape were known to each other. We managed to confuse the Japs whenever they lined us up for a countoff. They never had an accurate count from then on in the barracks around ours.

Rumors came in about the fall of Berlin, the fall of Italy, of the African Campaign, ran rampant through the camp. There were also rumors of a bakery that was to be built by the Japs. Rumors of Red Cross food, of medicine coming in, of prisoner exchange. Nothing materialized.

The American officers fared much better than the enlisted men. They had money. Whether by purchase, or due to better treatment, they had much better food. They had yams, papaya, eggs and coffee. Items that were unavailable to the enlisted men.

I had a very difficult time in understanding why an officer rated any better treatment than an enlisted man. They were only men. They were no different than the enlisted man. They didn't die any harder than an enlisted man. Why should an officer be any different than an enlisted man? Officers didn't vote any different than an enlisted man. They didn't fight any different than an enlisted man. As a matter of fact I had seen many of the officers stay back while the enlisted man took the bullet and the shrapnel. What is so democratic about the army? I had had to take command in some pretty hairy situations when there had been an officer around. It was a question that bothered the shit out of me. I could well understand the need of non-fraternization in the services to keep the separation of command, but in a prison camp? They didn't make any kind of a different POW than any of the enlisted men. It was a thorn in my side and it was the same with many of the men to whom I had talked.

My leg hadn't improved. Neither had my left hand. The wounds would close and then I would move too much and they would open up again. I tried a tobacco poultice on one of the blisters. It was an expensive treatment since the price of one cigarette was one peso or one dollar and I had to use five cigarettes to make enough tobacco mush to cover the sore. The tobacco was wrapped in a cloth and then dipped into a canteen cup full of water to make a doughy mass and applied to the sore. The juice from the tobacco burned like hell when it made contact with the open sore. I left the poultice on for three days, wetting it whenever it dried out. At the end of that time the tobacco was a light tan instead of the almost tar black color it had been when I had out it on. The red rawness around the ulcerated wound had faded, but the wound didn't heal. I removed the poultice and hoped for the best.

Johnny wasn't feeling at all well. He looked worn out and worst than he had when we had first come into the camp.

I ran into Ted Brodsky one day when I was exploring the camp.

Ted was from Philadelphia. He was a dark complexioned Jew with a heart as big as a melon. His face was coarse with a heavy growth of beard. He also had a large, typically Jewish nose. We had become friends in peacetime at Fort McKinley, just outside of Manila. He had been in the Finance Office. He was ready to share anything that he had with me. Ted had a buddy, Searcy, that had also been in his outfit. Searcy was a tall rangy Texan. He carried himself as though he had just gotten off of a horse.

I told them about Johnny. We, Ted, Searcy, Ed, Schwartz and I scrounged around to see if we could find some medicine for him. Ted heard that there was some sulfanilamide available, but we couldn't manage to locate any.

One late afternoon we were sitting around in the shade of Ted's hut. Ted had managed to swap for some coffee. We were enjoying a real treat, cigarettes and coffee.

"You know I am surprised about how I find out something new about myself. I never thought that I could forget so easy how something tastes." I drank some of the coffee with relish. It was black, sweetened with some of the sugar from the pony feed cakes that had been boiled. We had bribed a cook at the kitchen for some of the boiling water.

"I didn't know black coffee could be so delicious." Searcy added.

"Yeah, coffee used to be run of the mill stuff. Coffee for breakfast, coffee break, coffee at noon and at supper. No trouble to get coffee. Now I break my ass for some." Ted had always been a coffee freak. There had always been a pot on the hot plate in their quarters.

"Remember the time you spiked the coffee with some of that cheap San Miguel rum. It smelled up the shack for days. Every time the captain came in he would look around for the jug." Searcy laughed at the remembrance. It was good to remember life before the war. And then it was bad too. Bad, because it made me feel so much worse when I thought of the situation we were in now.

Searcy spoke with a Texas drawl. He put it on more at some times than at others. He put it on more this time as he addressed Ted. "Too bad we don't have any of that stinkin rum now, might have some medicinal value, or maybe it would just cheer us up. Does that stuff have any vitamins in it?"

Ted ignored him and asked, "How is Johnny?"

"Not good at all." I answered. Ted noticed the concern in my voice and shook his head. "I wish you could locate some of that medicine. I can't get a line on any at all."

"I'll keep trying." Ted promised.

"So will I." Searcy pledged. "What is that he has? Malaria?"

"I don't know. He had a bad case of dysentery." I stopped as chill caught me. "He has bad bouts of chills. No fever. He suffers with constant cramps. He keeps on loosing weight. I gave him my hot soup last night." I felt pretty good about that. I had gone hungry, claiming I just didn't feel like eating the slop. It wasn't slop, but it seemed an adequate enough reason to refuse eating it.

"I wish I could get some sulfa Ted." I somehow felt ashamed to ask, "If you get any money. I wonder..."

"Hey, you don't have to ask. I know I owe you a bundle. As soon as I get my hands on some you'll have it." Ted was sincere.

I felt that I had somehow ruined the whole mood of the moment. We had been feeling pretty good because of our enjoyment of the treats, the coffee and cigarettes.

"We're going to have to find some medicine soon. "Searcy put in. "If this guy Bakulli is telling the truth we may have some soon. But I don't trust him somehow." He shook his head. "Too goddamned much conniving going around here these days."

"Yeah. That's for sure. Well, I'll see you guys tomorrow." I left with a canteen cup of coffee for Johnny.

The days of the rainy season passed slowly, most of them marked by either feast or famine. At times some pork was brought in. A thick gravy was made with it that was served over the lugao. Sometimes some pineapples and cherries were available which we traded for with whatever we had. The scarcity of these luxuries made us realize more and more that there were harder times ahead.

My hand finally healed but my leg got worse. The doctor didn't have anything with which to treat our wounds. The festering sores that had developed around the shrapnel wounds I had gotten on the fifth were diagnosed as Guam blisters. They were ulcers that were so bad that my leg had swollen to about twice its normal size. The ulcers had eaten into the bone of the leg. I had a hell of a time walking. The trip of about one hundred and fifty yards to the latrine seemed more like a million miles. Many of the trips were made with the help of men that were on their way to the same place.

There were suggestions that I try the camphor from the trees. This burned like hell and didn't do anything to heal the infection. Someone wanted to try cauterizing them with hot coal. I had another session with the doctor. He prescribed scrubbing the sores with some of the yellow soap they had in the kitchen and then sprinkling sulfa on them. Which was great, except he didn't have any sulfa.

Some medicine was coming in through the work details. The POWs made deals with Filipinos for some medicines. It was expensive. A tablet of sulfa was five pesos, or five dollars. Two pesos for a quinine tablet. Fifty centavos for an aspirin.

Another couple of friends Don Miller and Gabby Ellis, promised to buy any sulfa that they could find.

Don was from Los Angeles. He was of medium height and wide shouldered, but skinny. His hair was black. His complexion was swarthy, and he had a heavy black beard. He also had a ready smile and a great sense of humor.

Gabby on the other hand had a slight frame. He must have looked bony even in peacetime. He was older than any of the other men that I knew. Older, maybe near forty, whereas the rest of us were mostly in our twenties.

Don came by and told me he had found someone who had two sulfa tablets. He could buy them for five pesos each. He told me he was going to buy them and that I could pay him whenever I had the money. I sold five of my noontime meals for two pesos each and paid Don.

Johnny and I argued about the sulfa. I wanted him to take them and he refused. He said that he had talked with the doctor and the doctor had told him that two tablets would not do any good. He had prescribed a treatment that required about forty tablets. He insisted that I use them for my leg. He said the same doctor told him that I could lose my leg if the infection wasn't stopped soon. We went back to the doctor.

"Scrub the ulcers and then apply the sulfa. If you can get something to make a salve out of the tablets it would be better."

Gabby said he thought he could manage some fat from the pigs they brought in for the mess. "Hey! Maybe you should try the maggots like the guy said over in the barracks by the kitchen." He suggested.

"What maggots?" I frowned at him in disbelief.

"The guys told me that one of the guys had a shrapnel wound in his right side. He had it covered with a bandage and it started to itch like hell. He said it stunk like dead meat. He was afraid to look at it and let it go for a few days. Didn't wash or nothin. Then he saw some maggots fall out from under the bandage. When they removed the bandage the whole thing was crawling with maggots. He damned near shit a pickle. Got sicker than hell and threw up all over the place. After some of the guys helped him wash it off they found out that the infection was all gone. He's great now."

"That's a bunch of shit," Johnny spit out. "Never heard of anything like that."

"Me neither." I added.

"Well, I just thought I'd tell you about it."

Gabby managed to scrounge up some pork fat from someone he knew in the kitchen. We melted it over one of the cook fires in the kitchen to pasteurize it. I crushed the sulfa and mixed it in with the fat. It was a messy looking salve.

I asked the doctor to scrub the sores, he refused saying that he didn't have the right facilities. I wrote him off as a total loss and made plans of my own.

We collected five men later on in the afternoon after we made the salve. Gabby had also managed to get some yellow soap and a GI scrub brush that had been brought in on one of the work details. The operation was carried out near our hut, on a blanket. Two men held my legs, one guy sat on my chest and two men went to work on the leg. We were surrounded by a about fifty or more men who wanted to see what was going on.

The ulcers were on the upper part of my right leg, just below the knee. One on the inside and the other on the right, outside, near the tendon. The two scrubbers went to work. Hot water, soap and scrubbing brush. As soon as the hot water and the soap hit the ulcer I cringed and tried to keep from jerking the leg away.

"Cripes! Shit, piss and corruption! What the hell are you trying to do? Ease up. Please."

I got my left leg free and kicked, not seeing what I was kicking at. I hit something with my heel and yelled some more.

"Hey. You son-of a-bitch! I'm trying to help you. You kicked me in the face." Fred, the man who was trying to hold my left leg screamed at me.

The spectators yelled at me to hold still. They milled around to get a better look at what was going on.

The team regrouped and started again. I struggled against the pain, but they held me down.

"I got the puss all out and it's bleeding good." Harry the scrubber looked over the man on my chest. "How you holding out? Only a couple of more spots. Hold on."

The tears were streaming down my face. as I groaned. The pain was so intense that I lost control of my bladder and wet myself.

"Hey! Somebody get a diaper." Harry yelled out.

The watchers laughed because they couldn't do anything else. I noticed that some men that I could see winced and turned away.

The burning wasn't letting up as Harry continued to brutalize my leg. He stopped and I went limp.

"Hey! That's the way to go man."

"You got more guts than I have."

"God! Look at how its bleeding now. Wow!"

"All done Joe. Good job." Harry, on his knees, sat back as the man on my chest moved away.

I lay there, relieved that the intensity of the pain had subsided. I brought my right arm over my eyes and cried.

"Hey. It's okay." I heard Johnny say. "You did good."

"Sure. I kick somebody in the face, I cry like a kid and wet my pants and I did okay."

"Sure you did." I heard Ted say through the ruckus of the crowd.

"KIOTSKI! NANDA!" Everybody froze as the little Jap pushed through the crowd and stopped , looking down at me. "Nanda. Doste. What are you doing?" He finished in English. He looked around at the gathering. He looked at the men around the blanket. He saw the blood running onto the blanket. "AHA! You." He pointed his bayonet at me. "You bleed." A grin broke over his face.

"Infection. They are cleaning it for me." I responded.

"So! You are hurting? Yes?" He bent over and looked closely at the wounds. "You hurt?"

"Sure as hell do."

"A so. Okay." He looked around at the circle of men as I sat up. "You shooyoo o suru." He pointed to my wet coveralls.

"If you mean he pissed his pants you are right." Harry stated.

"So." The Jap nodded his head vigorously. He reached into his pocket and brought out a pack of Luckies. Carefully he took out five cigarettes and passed them out to the operating team and handed the last one to me. "Yarooshi. Yoi. Very good." He jerked his head up and down and strode away through the crowd of men who were surprised at the actions of the Jap.

The men laughed at me and told me they were going to put a diaper on me next time. They helped me to my feet and proceeded to strip the coverall from me. Someone brought a couple of buckets of cold water and I washed down. After I dried in the tropical sun I bathed the ulcers and let the bleeding stop, drying them in the sun also. Then I applied the salve and bandaged it with a piece of khaki colored bed sheet that Harry contributed. I felt exhausted and a little humiliated that I had pissed myself. The sores felt warm, but they felt a lot better than they had in many weeks. I applied the salve sparingly for the next six days. The swelling started to go down and the redness disappeared gradually. The scars looked raw and red, and the area was tender, but the fungus and the infection was gone.

Some of the men who had witnessed the so called operation were amazed at the results, as was I. They also complimented me on having the guts to go through with it after the doctor had declined.

Cabanatuan, O'Donnell, Clark Field, Lingayen Gulf.

CHAPTER 6 -- THE RAT

There were always rumors. Rumors that Russia was in the war. That there was to be a POW exchange. That the Americans had returned to the southern Philippine Islands. There were rumors that the Filipinos had offered to feed the POWs, but that the Japs had refused the offer. That the Filipinos had offered medicine and that the Japs had refused that offer also. Why? To save face.

Johnny was having a bad time. We, Ted, Searcy, Ed and Schwartz and I managed to scrounge up some quinine. The supply wasn't steady. Sometimes we could buy or trade for as many as eight or ten tablets, sometimes only for two, three or four. And sometimes none at all for days at a time. Johnny seemed to do all right when he had the quinine. Then he would have a relapse when the quinine wasn't available. But I thought that there was something else that was sapping his strength.

We had many men dying from diseases. Some of the older men, those that were in their late forties and more, were the ones that suffered the most. They had the higher casualty rate.

However, even with the privation and death, the many tragedies, there were times that humor, came into play. Even though sometimes the humor was grim. One of the most fantastic and still somehow humorous incidents occurred at the latrine. It left me with a vivid memory.

The camp's sanitary facilities were peculiar to the tropics and to a primitive situation in the POW camp due to the way it was managed by the Japs. The toilets for defecating were a portable shack or small hut, built of bamboo and nipa, with a wood floor. The shack had seats that had holes in them. Most of the shacks had a back to back arrangement of benches, with four holes on each side. There were lids over the holes in the seats to help control both the odor, which was overwhelming, flies which we were never without. Not that we brought them with us from Corregidor. The shack was positioned over a pit that had been dug into the hard adobe. The pit, or hole was about ten feet deep. When the pit was full the shack would be lifted by the framing poles, one on each corner, and moved over new hole. There were bags of lime in the shacks. When one finished with a bowel movement it was mandatory to drop a scoop of lime over the excrement. The lime was also used liberally on the floors and on the pathway outside. However, with the thousands of men in the camp there was always a shortage of facilities. This principally due to the fact that it seemed that almost everybody had dysentery most of the time. It was surmised that this was due to the food that was brought in as well as from the infectious amoebic dysentery that was taking its toll of the weakened men. It also caused a problem when one had to urinate. That problem had been solved by digging huge pits, the size of swimming pools, that were used as urinals. The pits were about twelve feet wide, forty feet long and about four foot deep. The sides were vertical and slippery from the urine. One stood at the side and peed into the hole. Lime was spread around the sides and along the paths. The paths themselves were hard, foot pounded clay. There were a half dozen of these urinals throughout the camp.

On this particular day there was a storm brewing, with strong gusts of wind preceding the rain. Opposite me, across the pool, there were two POWs. They were urinating and counting out money at the same time. They had a considerable amount of money from the size of the stacks. A sudden exceptionally strong gust of wind blew some of the bills that were being passed from one to the other and scattered them across the surface of the pool of vile colored lime clouded yellow urine. Without even shoving his penis into his pants, the owner jumped into the pool of urine which was armpit deep. He held on to the one stack of money and proceeded to chase around after the bills floating on the surface of the liquid. Everybody stopped. They stopped urinating. They stopped talking. They stopped leaving. Roars of laughter broke out from the men around the pool. The racket drew additional men from around the area. Jibes and instructions were soon rampant.

"Get it!"

"There goes one."

"Hey! One just sunk over here."

"There's a hundred pesos sinking over here."

Men were doubled over with laughter. Some of the men were disgusted at the thought of wallowing in a pool of piss. I thought about the germs that could be living in the pool. Even though there was quick lime being added to the urine, I couldn't shake the thought of the diseases that must be there.

"Hey! There goes another fifty pesos over there in the corner!"

"Get it man! Get it!"

"Laugh! Go ahead and laugh you lousy bastards." The man in the pool yelled. "Laugh you dumb shits. Its money! And money means living. And its mine!" He finished picking up all the money that hadn't sunk and waded to the far edge of the pit. He reached up on the slimy bank for a handhold and fell back in amid roars of laughter and jibes. He sputtered and spit the urine after he surfaced.

"Hey! Give me a hand Rich." His buddy held back. "Give me a damned hand up. I can't get out of here without some help."

His buddy didn't help. No one offered to help him.

"I'll give a hundred pesos to anybody. Help me out."

One of the men not far from him walked back to the edge of a bamboo grove and picked up a long bamboo pole. He held it out to the man in the pool. Three men had to pull on the bamboo to finally drag the piss sodden man out on to the muddy edge. The man from the pool sat there dripping cloudy lime liquid, shaking his head to get rid of the stuff that permeated his hair. He counted out a hundred and fifty pesos, yelling as he counted, and handed the money over to the three men who had rescued him. He struggled to his feet, slipping on the adobe and started off for a place to wash. Everybody stood back as he made his way to the nearest water spigot a hundred yards away. He dripped the smelly concoction all the way. He stripped and stood there looking like something the cat had dragged in and dropped. I watched from a distance as he made a bargain with one of the men who had a wood bucket that he was filling. Somebody else sold him a piece of soap. The man with the bucket carried ten buckets of water which he splashed over the urine soaked man as he washed and scrubbed. He washed his money and then his clothes. We walked away marveling at the incident.

I returned to my barracks and told the story to the men sitting around.

"You're a screeching liar. No one would jump into the piss hole for money." That and similar comments were made in response to my story. It wasn't until the next day, after the story had spread through the whole camp did my cohorts believe that I hadn't made up the tale.

The rainy season was now well on its way. It rained every day. It was mostly a welcome cool rain, but sometimes the storms came up suddenly with torrential downpours. The shacks were poor shelter against some of the gale force winds that made everyone miserable. Fortunately we weren't hit by any typhoons.

Sanitation was another problem. There were no facilities for either laundering or bathing. The river provided the answer for both. One would join a group of men that were being escorted to the river in what was termed a swimming party. Fifty men at a time formed a column at a point near the rear gate on the road that led to the river. We would bango, count off, for the Japanese guards who would then escort us to the river. The usual thing was to strip, wash the clothes we were wearing and any others that were brought along and wash them, and bathe. Most of the time there wasn't any soap, so we scrubbed with the sand along the edge of the river.

One day when we were returning from the river a Jap guard was struck by lightning.

The sky to the south and west had been a veritable fireworks of lightning. The rain blew in as the storm came over us. The lightning display was fantastic. Bolts that split into a dozen forks struck the trees outside of camp. It was one of those storms that sweep in after a hot sweltering day.

We ran along the road back to the gate. A Jap soldier walking guard between the double barbed wire fence that surrounded the camp had stopped to urinate. He was peeing on one of the strands of barbed wire when a bolt of lightning hit the fence about fifty feet from him. The strands of steel lit up like long glowing neon tubes. It seemed as though he glowed, surrounded by a brilliant envelope of light for just the fraction of a second. His rifle exploded. I stopped dead in my tracks. The man behind me, who was also watching, ran into me almost knocking me over. The guard dropped to the ground. He seemed to twitch in the downpour and then he lay there unmoving.

"Hiya! Kura!" The Japs ran us into camp while two of the guards ran to the fallen man.

We were stopped inside of the gate and made to count off before we were dismissed and told to return to our barracks. Some of us found shelter under the eaves of one of the nearby shacks and watched as the camp ambulance came to pick up the dead man.

Some religious soul nearby said a prayer for the dead man, and then callously added, "And may God strike them dead, every last damned last one of them. Amen." He blessed himself sincerely.

A half a dozen of the men around him said, "Amen."

The next day I took a walk to the spot to see what had happened to the barbed wire. The wire was all new. It had been restrung either right after the storm or early in the morning. I was smoking a pipe, a slim Yellow Bowl. As I turned to leave I was stopped by a Jap private. His command "Tomaru." was shouted in an angry tone. I stopped and came to attention, holding the pipe in my hand by my side. The guard approached slowly. He examined me from head to foot, scowling all the time. He spotted the pipe and ushed me to hold it up. I held the pipe out to him. He grabbed it and examined it. Then he looked back at me in a nasty way. I wondered what the little prick was thinking.

"Kore opipu de uri masu ka"

"Wakarimasen. I don't understand."

He glared at me, stuck the pipe in his tunic pocket, and then swung the butt of his rifle. It caught me below my left ear. I went down stunned. He stood over me with the bayonet inches away from my nose. I stayed down. He stepped back and pulled the pipe out and examined it closely. He frowned and stooped, holding the pipe in front of my face. "J A P. Nanda." He was reading the initials that I had carved into the bottom of the pipe.

"My initials. Joseph A. Petak. JAP. My name."

He frowned again, "Your name has initials JAP?" His English was as good as mine.

I stared at the son of a bitch. "Yes. JAP."

"Hmmph. So you have good initials. It is a nice pipe. Do you want to sell it?"

I was surprised that he didn't just take it. "No. I can't find another like it. They are very scarce."

"Yes. They are. I had one like this when I went to school in Chicago. I would like to buy one. Can you find one for me?"

I stared at the sleazy bastard for a minute. He spoke good English and he had pulled that shit on me. "I can try. But you might have to pay twenty or thirty pesos for one."

I had made a deal with an older POW for my pipe for two pesos. I had promised to pay him when I had the money. After I had the money I went looking for the older man and had never found him.

"Good. How long will it take?"

"Maybe three or four days. I have to scrounge around through the camp."

"Okay." He stood up and held the pipe out to me. I got on my hands and knees, and then painfully to my feet. I reached out for the pipe and then stepped back. He smiled at me and reached into his tunic and pulled out a pack of Filipino cigarettes. He handed over the pack, "Keep them. I am on guard duty on days. You can come anytime. Okay?"

"Sure."

"I like the Yellow Bowl. They are a good pipe."

"Okay. I'll see what I can do. No promises because I don't know if I will find one. Okay."

"Sure, I know."

He turned and walked away without giving me his name or saying anything else.

I saw him twice in the next few days and reported that I had made no progress. It was a week later before I found a well smoked Yellow Bowl for thirty pesos. The owner gave me five as a commission.

The incident was another example of the strangeness of the Japanese mind.

I returned from one of the work parties that were a daily occurrence to hear that we were going to be reorganized according to work skills.

The story was that men that were going to go out on road building projects were going to be laborers that were without other skills. The reorganization took place the next day. Every prisoner was classified according to his occupation. The American officers issued instructions that each one of us had to provide information about our past work experience, on penalty of a court martial whenever we were returned to our own command, if we refused. The men were then quartered by occupational groups.

I had reported being an engineer, a draftsman, a radio repairman, and a carpenter. The Japs placed me with the carpenter group.

During the reorganization there had been a general conspiracy among the various groups of men to screw up the count. Men went uncounted by slipping into groups that had already been counted. By the time the Japs had finished the countoff we found that there was an undercount of over two hundred men in the camp that held approximately ten thousand of us. We learned that the Japs never did have an accurate count.

It was only a couple of days after the reorganization that Ted and Searcy brought the man named Arthur Bakulli.

"This fellow is the one that says he can get the sulfa." Ted informed us.

"Yeah. Says he can buy fifty tablets for two hundred pesos. Two hundred pesos. Pretty good huh?" Searcy put in.

"Can you?" I asked skeptically.

"Sure I can get it," answered Bakulli snottily. "It isn't easy, but I can get it. I've got the right connections." He bragged.

"Where I asked?"

"Never mind where," Bakulli answered conceitedly. "I can get it. It'll take maybe two or three days, but I'll get it for sure." He displayed a lot of self confidence for a little guy.

"Only one trouble Joe." Ted muttered.

"What?" I asked suspecting the worst.

"I got to have the money first." Bakulli put in. "I don't have that kind of money. I have to have the cash to buy the drug. Cash only. They won't deal any other way."

"Damn it Ted, I don't have that kind of money. I have only about twenty pesos." I pulled out the money from my pocket.

"I have money Joe. That's not the problem." Ted pulled out a roll of bills. "The real problem is," he paused and looked over the scroungy looking dark complexioned man, "Do we trust this guy?"

It was evident that there was some question about how much we could believe Bakulli.

Bakulli was small and dark. He had lost weight the same as everyone else had. But, there was something else besides that that accounted for the look of the man. His face had a thinness about it, and something that made it look weasely. Maybe it was the cut of the jaw and the eyes.

"Well," drawled Searcy, "if he pulls anything funny, we can take care of him. The Japs won't really mind." Searcy mad a stabbing motion at Bakulli's thin gut.

"I'm not going to pull anything funny." Bakulli spit back. "I get a kickback from the gook."

"Gook huh?" Searcy snarled. "You mean Filipino, don't you?" Searcy sneered his dislike of the term gook.

"Okay?" Ted queried. He looked at me for approval. "We take the chance? You think that the sulfa is what Johnny needs?"

"I think so." I replied. "The doctor says that he has dysentery. He seems to be quite sure that the sulfa will help him."

Ted counted out some of the bills from his bankroll. "Here's two hundred pesos." He handed the money over to Bakulli.

"How about something for me? I'm getting it for you."

"Gawan!" Searcy raised his arm at Bakulli. "You haven't delivered anything yet."

"How about your serial number? And your home address?" I asked.

"What for?" Bakulli asked in surprise. He backed away as he took the money.

"Just so I can find you if the two hundred pesos go and we don't get the sulfa. Then I can find you. Someday if I have to. I don't forget easy."

"Hell, I'm not going anywhere." His voice sounded nasty.

"Yeah, we know." Searcy's voice also had a nasty edge to it. "So if you are not going anywhere, and you bring back the stuff, you got nothing to worry about. Right? So then how about the information?" he insisted.

"Okay. 19052---."

"Hold it!"

"That isn't a east coast number. That's from California I'll bet." Ted was puzzled, and so were Searcy and I.

"I been kicking around the country. So I joined up regular in California. I'm from Albany. New York."

I wrote down the number when he gave it in full the second time.

"Okay. Two three days. No more. A man's life is depending on this stuff. You know we'll be looking for you. If you don't bring it back and he dies--- Too bad for you." Ted's dark brows knitted together as he warned Bakulli.

"I'll be looking for you." Searcy's tone was menacing.

"Couple of days. No more. I'll bring it. You know my barracks. We are the road crew." He pocketed the pesos and walked away without another word.

Searcy watched him as he disappeared among the barracks. "I don't trust the bastard."

Ted spit on the ground after him. "What the hell else can we do?"

"Here Ted." I held out the twenty pesos, all the money I had. My voice broke from emotion. It was Ted that had supplied the money. "Take it. It's all I've got."

"Ah--- Go on and keep it." He shoved my hand away. "It's what I owed you anyway. And besides, you'll need what you got. I won it gambling. I'd only lose it anyway. This was it may do some good." His grin was broad. He was happy with himself.

"It's still a piss poor gamble." Searcy had a quizzical expression on his face. "I can't figure the odds on this one. We have to take the chance, but I don't like it."

I grunted my agreement. Ted shook his head. We knew how serious it was for Johnny. Ted and Searcy left and I hurried off to Johnny's shack to inform him of the situation.

"How is the gut?" I asked Johnny as I lit a cigarette and handed it to him. "Any better?"

He took out his holder and carefully positioned the long brown cigarette in it before he took a drag. "Still about the same. The cramps come and go." He grimaced at his situation.

I told him about the deal we made for the sulfa, omitting our concerns about the trustworthiness of the supplier. "So, it looks like we will have some medicine soon." I ended on a cheerful note. "Of course the damned stuff isn't here yet, but we can pray."

I hoped that his knowing that we were in there pitching for him would be a help. I hoped it would keep his spirits up. One of the worst things that was happening to us was that some of the men were losing spirit, the will to live. In our hopeless situation it was hard to keep on fighting knowing that MacArthur had deserted us. Orders or no orders, he had deserted his men. Me, I was so mad at the Japs that I felt I wouldn't let them lick me no matter what. And then, I did have some plans. But Johnny, he seemed to be losing out on that end of it. He was sick, very sick.

"I sure hope that it comes in." He grimaced painfully. "This gut sure hurts."

"Yeah. I know." I was puzzled, but thankful to someone up there. "I can't figure out how I beat it. Just got rid of it. Just lucky I guess."

"No. You're just mean enough to have burned it out. How long did

you live around the crapper? You were pretty bad off there for a while."
He inhaled on the cigarette appreciative of the effect of the nicotine.
Those black tobacco cigarettes sure had a lot of it.

"About a week." I answered. "And please don't remind me of it." I
shuddered as I thought about the bout that I had had with the runs. It
was so bad that I couldn't wipe my ass. "The damned blood and burning
made me sicker then hell." I shook in disgust. The memory brought back
all the pain and hurt. It made me realize just how bad Johnny was. I had
been there myself. "I still can't figure out how I beat it."

Some men were lucky. They recovered from the dysentery and the
dengue and even malaria, without medicine. Others didn't.

"Did you eat everything today?" I wanted to change the subject.

"Well," he hesitated, "I couldn't get everything down."

I looked at him disapprovingly. "You need all the nourishment you
can get. You finished the milk? I hope." I had made a deal for some
caribou milk with one of the men on the road crew.

"Sure as hell did. It was good. Reminds me of home. Dhobie looked
like he needed the stuff I didn't eat. I gave it to him." He seemed almost
apologetic. "Maybe my stomach shrank and I can't hold as much as I did
before."

"I suppose. But you won't get strong if you don't eat."

We chatted on for a while about anything and everything.

Johnny told us that he had heard that a caribou had found it's way
into camp and had fallen into the piss pit near the road. Forty or more
POWs had struggled for over an hour to pull it out. He said that the
caribou was going to be butchered and stewed for tomorrow's dinner.

I visited the Filipino section of the camp the next day in hope of
finding an old friend, and maybe getting some help from that quarter.
The Filipinos, the Philippine Scouts, attached to the U.S. Army. and
some of the Philippine Artillery units were being held prisoner just as we
were. Their section of the camp was set apart from the Americans by a
shallow ravine that was a natural dividing line. We, Ted, Schwartz,
Johnny, Ed and I visited the Filipinos frequently. Some of the Scouts we
had known in Bataan and some from the Rock were there.

Even though there had been rumors that some Filipinos had been
released, we did not know of any that had been released from Camp 3.
In many ways, even though this was their home, their country, they were
having a worse time of the imprisonment than we Americans. Where the
Americans fought back, spit back, and cursed out the Japs, the Filipinos
cowered, retreated and took the beatings without murmuring. They were
in a worse predicament than we. Anything that a Filipino did to
aggravate the Japs meant that the local civilians would suffer. It made it

rough on the Filipinos.

And, there was something else that happened to the Filipinos that was very surprising and hard to understand. A Filipino would sit down, or lay down somewhere, and give up. Virtually give up. He wouldn't eat, drink, talk or walk. He would urinate and defecate without moving. His face lacked any kind of expression. A complete blank. He wouldn't respond to any attempt at conversation, to prodding, or to any physical means to arouse him. No one would bother him or move to help him. It seemed as though there was some code, or some innate understanding, that the man wasn't to be bothered. The others told us that he had given up his will to live. Usually the man would be dead in about five days. There was no physical evidence of the cause of death. I had asked our doctors about it and they had only shrugged it off. I had never seen anything like it. It was something that none of us understood. The idea of that kind of surrender was completely foreign and sounded impossible. It was one thing to surrender when faced against overwhelming physical odds, but this was something else.

I had been searching for a long time for a friend of mine, a Filipino who had been attached to the Signal Corps after we were bivouacked at Mud Hole on Bataan. I knew that if I could find him he might be able to help. He would have contacts on the outside. I also knew that some of the Filipinos in the camp knew him. Somehow, there was a peculiar lack of information about Vero and his whereabouts. Vero was not to be found. I had been quite sure that I had seen him brought into camp just days after we had been marched in. I repeated my visits, and my questioning for about three days. It was at the end of the third day that I was visited by a tough looking Filipino, a Scout, that I had not seen before. He had been asking for me during the afternoon, according to one of the other guys. We walked off to sit under one of the nearby trees to be away from all ears while we talked.

"You were looking for Vero." he stated flatly after we had settled down and had lit cigarettes that he supplied.

"Yes." I waited for his lead.

"It is not good to look for Vero, Joe." The Joe was the Joe used by the Filipinos for all Americans.

"Should I ask why?"

"No Joe, you should not ask. If you ask, and you know, then maybe Japanese come for you and you do not come back." He answered in a low whispering voice as he looked around. "They would not like what you would know. It would be very bad for Vero. It would be very bad for you Joe. Very bad maybe."

"Okay." I parried with, "But can you help me. I need some medicine for my cousin. Sulfa. He has dysentery. Maybe you could help me buy some."

"I don't know Joe." The Filipino was evasive. "I don't think so. It is not easy to bring in medicine. It is also very expensive."

"I know."

"But I cannot help you Joe." He stood up and started to walk away.

"Okay." I raised my voice so that it would carry to him. "Then I will just have to keep on looking for Vero." I clinched my cigarette and stashed the butt for salvage.

He stopped and spun around quickly. His face was slightly distorted with anger. "No! No." His voice was vicious. He hurried back to stand in front of me. Looking down at me, he continued, "You goddamn fool Joe. You look for Vero--- you get killed Joe. Very quick. Very bad. Vero, maybe he will die too." I couldn't make up my mind if it really was a threat or a warning. The Filipinos acted strangely at times and their messages and meanings had a typical Oriental flavor.

"You going to kill me?" I asked, fishing for an opening to dig out maybe something a little more.

"No Joe. No." His voice quavered. "I mean that you--- Vero--- It would be bad Joe. The Japs, they would kill you."

"Why?" I asked. "They could kill me anytime anyway."

"Because you fight them now, here. We know." He answered. He stopped talking, his face had a frightened look in the evening light. Sharp, and lean, with his high cheekbones, it had a death's head look. He turned without another word and took off. He walked. One did not run in Camp Three.

I sat there until long after dark thinking about the incident. It was evident the that route to help was closed. There was danger there evidently. I didn't know the why or the how. The danger existed for my friends not just myself. I concluded that I had stumbled onto something that must be tied in with the guerrillas, or maybe just the camp underground. Perhaps for the present it was better to leave it alone.

Bakulli hadn't shown up for days. He was making himself scarce. It was the afternoon of the sixth day when Ted and Searcy brought Bakulli to my shack. They walked behind him as though herding him.

"Look what we caught Joe." The sarcasm in Ted's voice carried a message that caused the men sitting around the shack to look up.

"Well, Mr., or is it Doctor Bakulli." I stood up and advanced too meet them. "You brought the medicine?"

"No." Bakulli shrank in on himself. "No, I couldn't get it. A Jap took the money from me and I didn't know how to tell you about it. So I couldn't come to see any of you." The words spilled out so fast that they seemed to be running over one another. "I've been trying to make a deal for the medicine. I'll get it. I promise. I need a little time. I'll make it up." His words rushed out as though they offered some physical defense.

I advanced on him until I was breathing down into his face from my six foot plus. I stood inches taller than the skunk. "You lying bastard." I grabbed the front of his ragged shirt and lifted him. "You're nothing but a goddamn thief. A ghoul. A stinking pronip robber. I ought to beat the shit out of you you bastard." I snarled my hatred at him. I raised my hand to slap him in the mouth. Searcy grabbed my arm fast.

"That wouldn't do any good now." He soothed me as he pulled my arm down to my side. "Let's hold off. Let's find out about the money or the medicine first." Searcy had a way of grimacing where he pulled his lip out of shape by shifting his cheek. It was ugly. Sometimes Searcy could be an ugly Texan. "I can cut his guts out later if I have to."

"Honest. I'll get it for you. You gotta give me a chance." Bakulli pleaded.

"He's so scared he'll crap his pants Joe." Ted motioned gently at me to let him down. "Let go of his shirt before you choke him to death." He laughed. "Not that anyone would really care a hell of a shit."

I released the rat. He backed off and licked his lips. I could see that he wasn't sure what was going to happen next.

"I'll get it somehow. It's not my fault that the Jap took the dough. I was about to make the deal when this bucktoothed shithead got me. Honest it ain't. You know how they are." He was scared. I thought that he could also be yellow.

"If Johnny dies because he didn't get the medicine, I'll rip your throat out with my bare hands, you little shit. Even if it has to be after the war. I'll find you. I promise. Remember that you yellow Jap loving thief."

There was no greater insult than to equate anyone to a Jap. I was working up a sweat due to the frustration of not being able to do anything about recovering the money or getting a supply of sulfa.

Ted and Searcy calmed me down with words of admonishment.

"I'll get the sulfa. " Bakulli repeated. Just a couple of days. Give me a couple of days. When I get money I'll get it out of my own money."

"We'll be looking for you. Tomorrow, the day after that and the day after that." Ted told him. "What barracks you in now?"

"Eighteen." Bakulli answered.

We let him go. We then sat and talked about our plight and then on a happier note, of things in the past, until tenko.

CHAPTER 7 -- ENIGMA

Since the unsuccessful escape of the four men that had been executed I had been leery of mentioning anything about escape around Johnny. One morning, after I had completed my plan, being pretty sure that the Japs would not find out that I had escaped, I figured I would give it a try. I mentioned rather casually one morning that if someone didn't show up for roll call one morning that it could easily be covered up. There were enough discrepancies in the count at the barracks to prevent the Japs from determining that a particular man had disappeared. One of the ploys was to claim that the man was living at the latrine because of dysentery. When the guard was sent to the latrine, another POW was there to claim he was from the barracks in question. It had always worked so far. After the conversation Johnny retorted, "Don't get any more screwy ideas. There just isn't any place to go. You'd never make it to the ocean. It must be over fifty kilometers and its all mountain."

"Yeah, I guess you are right." I answered and let it drop. I made a half a dozen trips to the latrines that afternoon. Johnny asked if I was having any more problems than usual. "No. Not anything special. I have a lot of cramping. Maybe those mangoes weren't ripe enough. It has happened to me before. The mangoes do a job on me. If it keeps up I'll spend the night down there."

Johnny looked at me suspiciously, but he didn't say anything.

At nightfall I made my way across the draw to the latrine nearest to the river. It was one of the least frequented heads, and closest to the barbed wire fence. The lights along the fence were few and far between. I sat inside and waited, pretending I had the runs. I thought about what I had with me. I hadn't taken anything from the shack so as not to arouse suspicion. I had my canteen and canteen cup, my pipe and my sack of tobacco. I also had my little prayer book, which I was using as my diary, some matches and a pencil. I had left behind my messkit and musette bag. It was around midnight, as close as I could tell when a shadowy figure joined me. I couldn't tell much about him in the dark of the shack.

"Going through?" he asked.

I was shocked. I couldn't imagine how anyone could know that I was thinking of going through the fence. "Naw! This is the best place to stay when you have the runs. Not as much stink as the other ones."

"Horseshit! I been watching you. What are you waiting for?"

I stared hard through the gloom of the shithouse. I couldn't identify him, and he seemed to know me. The light wasn't that good.

"Where in the hell would I go?" I countered. And in the middle of the night at that." I hoped to avoid any long discussion or argument.

"Nuts!" He spat the word. "Who are you kidding?" He shifted closer on the bench and lowered his voice. "Look, I don't know who you are and you ain't going to know me. If we make it to the hills okay, then we use names. For now, if you're caught you can't tell them who I am. Same here. Now where we going through and when?" He stopped speaking abruptly and waited.

I decided that lies or argument would be more of a problem than the truth. "Couple more hours. We go to the river. Then north. We stay with the river."

"Okay. But if we are followed we break up. You go one way and I go another. Okay?"

There was no conversation for a long time. Somewhere in between I dozed off and was startled awake by some sound.

"What's up?" I asked in a low voice.

"Nothing. I didn't hear anything. You been sleeping a while."

The night was dark and had cooled considerably, I shivered. I was cramped and my butt hurt from sitting on the wood bench over the hole. I stood up and pulled up my shorts. I walked out and noticed that my unwanted companion followed. I walked around, loosening up and taking in the surroundings. There was no one in sight, not even the guard who should have been patrolling the area between the perimeter fences.

"What say we go now?"

"Yeah. Let's go."

There was no more conversation. We both looked around to make sure that there was no in the area watching. There hadn't been anyone in the crapper for hours. We started to skulk to the double barbed wire fence. We looked for the patrolling guard. He wasn't in sight.

"Go!" I commanded.

"Check."

He rolled under the barbed wire, careful not to rattle the tin cans that were hanging on the wire. The cans were the Jap's idea of an alarm arrangement. He inched along carefully until he was clear of the strands. He stopped, rolled over in his side and watched me after he made it to the path between the fences.

"Okay!"

"Okay. I'm coming." I took one last look left and right. The guard still wasn't in sight. "Go!" I urged.

"Okay." He rolled across the few feet between the two fences as I watched. He inched under the barbed wire and stopped suddenly. One of the cans jiggled but didn't make any noise. "I'm caught!" His voice was shrill and low.

"Christ! Don't rattle the cans.!" I had broken out in a sweat. My heart pounded in my chest. "Wait! I'll help you."

"NO! Christ! Stay there!" He moved back slowly. He inched back until he was back under the strands of wire and grabbed hold of it between the barbs. The can bounced around a bit but it didn't rattle or clang. Cloth tore as he pulled free. "WHOOO! Damned barbed wire." He rolled away from the fence. "I'll wait over there in the grass." He started to crawl away. "Hurry up!"

My heart hadn't stopped pounding. I crept to the fence and rolled on my back. I started to creep under the wire. After my head passed under the wire I could see the lighted area between the fence off to my right.

The Jap guard stood there!

I froze. My upper body was exposed on the bare ground between the fences. I was afraid to move. The guard didn't see me. He was unaware of anything unusual. He was strolling, bored with the duty. He didn't expect any of the POWs to try anything. I remained rigid with fear. I scrunched my shoulders and pushed myself back out from under the wire. I lost sight of the guard. I straightened my legs and twisted around, then I rolled away into the stubble of grass. I stopped when I was about thirty feet inside of the compound. The Jap started in my direction. I rolled over and hid my face in the dirt. Even though my face was tanned I was afraid that it would be a beacon for the Jap. He moved slowly as he looked around, seemingly without purpose. I waited, breathing shallowly through my open mouth. Minutes piled upon minutes as he meandered down the path to the next bulb and then out of sight. I couldn't decide if I wanted to continue or if I wanted to abort and stay in camp to try again some other time. I couldn't see my unwanted companion. I was sure that he had kept on going. If I chickened out now I might not have the nerve to try again very soon. Somehow I decided to go. I moved without hesitation once the idea had firmed up. I started for the fence again. When I reached the fence the second time I didn't wait. I moved under the first strands by wiggling on my back. The guard wasn't in sight. I rolled across the open space to the other wire. As I passed under it I jiggled a can. I sat up fast and grabbed for it. A dull thud sounded as the can next to it swung against the back of my hand. The sound must have been loud, I thought. I searched for the other can and held it. I released it slowly, preventing it from swinging. The cans swayed silently as I said a prayer of thanks. I stretched out on the ground and rolled quietly over the bumpy grass stubble until I was about sixty feet away from the guard path and the fences. I stopped and looked back at the camp. Nothing. Nothing was to be seen, nothing moved. "Nothing." I spoke aloud to myself. I rose to a crouch and scuttled toward the river bank.

"Hey!"

"Quiet!" I shrilled. "Want the prick to catch us now." I was riled at the stupidity of the man. I moved down next to him and squatted as I recovered my breath.

"Hell no!" he answered. "That was close for you. I thought you went back in and weren't going to try it. Wouldn't have blamed you either." he concluded.

"Let's move." I hissed the words. I continued on to the river.

"This way. Up to the hills."

"Yeah. I know. Trouble is we have damned little time to dawn. We better move fast!"

"Right!" he agreed.

"Wait!" I stopped in shocked fright. "Hear that? What the hell goes on?"

"In the Jap compound. They are starting a search party! At least I have never heard of Japs using hounds."

"What do we do now?"

"I don't know." I gritted the words. "How in the living hell could they know? HOW? How? How?" I was frustrated and mad.

"What are we going to do?"

"Across the river. NO!" I changed my mind. "Into the river! Up river."

"Let's separate Joe." My companion sounded panicky.

"What?! What's that?" I was stupefied. "How in the hell do you know my name?" I grabbed for him in the dark."How do you know?" I had his left arm gripped tightly. My right hand was ball up in a fist.

"What the hell do you mean?" He gritted back at me as he struggled to free his arm and face me. "Joe. Just Joe. It slipped like the Filipino Joe. Everybody's Joe to them. You know that." He sounded panicky.

"You better be right." I returned threateningly. My mind was racing. A white rat! He was an American. I was quite sure of that. He couldn't be a plant. It couldn't be true that the Japs had brought Germans into the camps to spy on us! I was the one that was panicking. Then, also he couldn't have let anyone know because he had been here all the time. All except when the guard had passed and I had scrambled back inside for a while. A long while when I didn't see anything because I had my face buried in the dirt. My suspicion was based on fear, not on any real knowledge.

"The can! I hit the can." I thought furiously. "But nobody could have heard it! It didn't clatter. It didn't clatter! And why did they wait until now?" I exerted hysterical pressure on his arm. "They didn't I tell you."

"I know." He answered almost soothingly. "I never heard a thing. And I watched all the time."

The sounds of men came closer. They were moving along the river to the north of us.

"Where? Which way?" He asked.

"What's your name?" I countered.

"None of your business now!" he jerked loose. "If we make it to the hills I'll tell you,. Not till then. Otherwise nuts. Fuckoff."

"Afraid to tell me?"

"Nuts! What's the use of names now? If I get caught you're just another Joe. If you get caught then I'm another Joe."

The sounds moved closer, coming down along the river.

"Let's separate." he suggested.

"Alright" I answered. "Where? Where do we meet?"

"We don't. On your own!" he threw back at me almost viciously.

"Okay. Fucking okay. Good luck."

He moved into the river and disappeared into darkness. I heard him splashing in the river and then up the far bank.

I waited for what seemed like minutes, then I turned south, back along the river. I ran as fast as I could in the darkness, stumbling, recovering and running some more. Then there were noises ahead of me. I stopped. The river wasn't deep. I could cross the river, since it wasn't swift, there might be some deep water, but I could swim that. Across the river I could head north to the boondocks. At the river bank I stopped. Perhaps it would be better to go back to camp. I couldn't make up my mind. The noise and the lights decided me as the source moved closer. I made up my mind fast. I turned and headed for the fence. I stopped and knelt beside the wire. I was glad that the moon had set early. There were no guards to be seen. The gate, well illuminated was far to my left. There were a lot of guards there. Something was going on. I had moved a few hundred yards north. I rose and ran along the wire until I found the latrine in which I had waited for most of the night. I slithered under the wire, snakelike. Then I scuttled to the second fence and rolled under and kept on rolling until I was well clear of the area. Everytime I rolled I rolled over my canteen which made be bump up painfully. I rose and walked to the latrine. Fortunately there was no one around. I entered and lowering my shorts, I sat on one of the thrones. I was panting and soaked with sweat. I sat and waited. Every so often I peeked through the slats of the wall and then sat back again. I heard the Japs as they searched the fence area. They had found footprints outside of the fence but couldn't find any inside. I thanked God that I had rolled and slithered through. There were no footprints inside either because I had rolled away for some yards before I had started to walk. They finally decided that there was no way to trace anyone around the area and took off for the gate.

The sun had risen in the east when I finally decided to return to the barracks. When I arrived I heard that someone had evidently tried to escape. There was a lot of confusion and concern.

The roll call, bongo, was early. After we had lined up and counted off we were kept in ranks waiting for a long time.

"Wonder how many tried it?" asked the man next to me.

"Don't know. I haven't heard anything. I've been at the crapper all night."

"Yeah, sure." Ed, in the row in front of me acknowledged. "How's the gut? Anything left?"

"Better now. But I am tired." I answered honestly. I wasn't just tired, I was pooped.

"Okay. Fall out." the barracks leader called out. The twenty of us from our small shack disassembled.

"Let's get chow." Ed started off to form up the chow line.

The talk in the chow line was all about the search during the night. As soon as we had finished eating there was word that there was no one missing. The consternation of the Japs was enjoyed by all of us.

I wondered about the information. If no one was missing, either the guy had escaped and the miscount the Japs had, which we had caused, was the answer. Or, he had returned to camp just as I had. I was puzzled, confused as badly as the Japs.

"No difference. We'll get it in the end. Wait and see." Ed prophesied.

"Sure. I'll bet we will." I agreed. "Here they come now."

We watched as the squad of Japs approached. The rule was that all POWs had to stand when the Japs came through the camp. Psychic premonition? I broke out in a sweat. Not cold, but a hot flushed sweat. My legs were dead. I sat on the ground, my back against the shack, I couldn't make it to my feet. It wasn't just the back pain. Ed stood at attention as did everyone else except me.

The sergeant and the squad stopped in front of the barracks. "Yasme." The sergeant shouted the order to stand at ease. An American officer reached the barrack at about the same time that the Jap officer approached me. I thought I recognized the officer from Corregidor. Captain Wheat.

"Sergeant, what is wrong?" asked the gawky American.

"Nanda." The sergeant looked at the captain as though he were some offensive child. "This is none of your affair. You know that we, the Imperial Army, will take care of the running this camp and the enforcement of order, and we will police this camp. We also designate work details." The sergeant turned away from the American officer as though he no longer existed. It was an unnecessary speech. He directed his eyes at me as I sat, frozen.

Work detail. What was going on? My Adams apple jumped as I dry swallowed. My mouth was dry, my gut was up in a tight knot. Something behind my eyes and the back of my throat pushed at making tears of fear and frustration.

"You." The small Jap drew his issue officer's sword. "You. Come here." He pointed at me.

I pushed down with both hands against the hard adobe and slipped against the side of the shack's wall to stand against it. My legs quaked. The muscles from my knees, on the inside of my thighs quivered uncontrollably.

"Yes." My voice was hard and sharp, which surprised me. I was surprised that I could even answer.

"Come." he ordered. I swallowed again and moved to the squad of silent soldiers. Nothing else was said as I was marched off in between the squad. My brain was in turmoil. What was going on? The POWs we passed were silent. Captain Wheat stood and watched without doing anything. Everyone stopped and watched as we marched across the camp to the gate. No one followed or moved. No one said anything. They knew what the story was, another interrogation, or worse.

Somehow the Japs had found out that I had been involved in something. It didn't matter that the count was correct. The Japs had information. No one knew how. I thought about the other POW. The cocksucker had known me. He must have identified me. How? I didn't know. I doubted if I would ever find out. We knew we had White Rats. The guys who cooperated with the Japs for favors. There had been some that had been found dead in the latrines, suffocated. I doubted also that the other guy had been caught. Could someone else have seen me? No. Then how? How? The questioned racked my brain as I was marched out of the gate and into the Jap compound.

Tears slipped from my eyes, uncontrolled. I was afraid. I didn't know what I was afraid of just then. Being killed. Torture? I knew that dying would end a lot of grief, but I didn't want to die just yet. I would no doubt get the treatment, then they would march me back into camp, dig a hole and shoot me. I stumbled because of the weakness in my legs. We marched into camp headquarters, the guards remained outside. The sergeant directed me into the big office in the front of the building. There was the Jap interpreter and two other officers seated at a table. The Jap lieutenant issued an order to the interpreter who moved swiftly to approach me.

"Yush." he responded to the officer and then braced, puppetlike, to attention. The officer spoke rapidly for a minute, too rapidly for me to understand any of the words. He pointed at me.

"What have you to say?" the interpreter asked.

"About what?" I countered, confused.

"Escape!" he shouted. "You tried to escape."

I swallowed hard. I was confused about the procedure. It didn't add up to anything that had ever happened before. They weren't sure. They didn't know. But why this approach? Did it mean that the Japs were going to begin treating us as the Geneva Convention prescribed? No! Trick. They were playing with me.

"ESCAPE!" The word seemed to be awfully loud. "Me? No!" I didn't have to feign panic or fear, it was real. "Not me! I was at the latrine all night. I had a bad case of the runs. I had diarrhea and cramps. I stayed there all night. Five or six men saw me while I was there."

The interpreter didn't say a word. He parted his lips and sucked in his breath. I knew it. He swung his fist, his right, at full arm's length. It connected with my cheekbone and my ear. I tried to ride with it. My head bounced. I knew that I was going to fall. I hit the bamboo floor and stayed there. My ear was ringing. The room was quiet I shook my head. The side of my head throbbed. I looked up at the little prick with an expression I couldn't wipe off. He glared at me in return.

"Get up! Stand up!" he ordered.

I rose to my knees with my head hanging. It was then that he kicked me with his cloven toed sneaker. I rolled over and lay there stunned. I crawled to my feet and backed away out of arm's length. I felt the pain in my back shoot down my legs.

"You will answer my questions. You will not lie again. You understand?" He paused as though searching for the right words. "All American dogs are liars!" He stepped in close and swung at me open handed. He connected with my cheek as the heel of his hand smeared across my nose. Blood shot from my nose and my head swung with the force of the blow. I reached for my nose as the blood flowed.

"Kiotski na." the Jap ordered.

My nose continued to bleed as I stood at attention. The warm blood tasted bittersweet and salty at the same time. I heard it drip to the floor from my chin. It still felt warm and sticky as it flowed down my throat and along my chest. I gagged as blood ran into my throat. I remained at attention. He slapped me again. He continued to slap at me as I stood as though glued to the spot. The thought that came to mind was that the little prick couldn't and wouldn't knock me down again. Screw you, I thought. I can take it. Stupid little bastard. I was groggy, dizzy. I didn't remember answering any of the questions. I wondered why they were only slapping me around. I expected more than I was getting. It didn't make sense. Why only slap me around? My head hurt and my ears rang more than what they usually did. This ringing was different than the ringing I had had since the bombing and shelling. I couldn't think clearly. Finally two soldiers grabbed my arms and dragged me away to a cell in the guardhouse at the back of the compound.

I heard the door close behind me as I slumped in a comfortable heap on the floor. The blood in my mouth and the blood I had swallowed was mixed with sour, bitter bile. I choked and puked. I gagged as the raw mess filled my nostrils and mouth. Finally there wasn't anything else to come up and it stopped. I blanked out. When I awoke it was dark. I didn't know I had fallen asleep. I ached. My head throbbed and pounded. My mouth and face were swollen. My left eye wouldn't open all the way. My nose was also swollen. It felt like a big sausage. There was the smell of blood and of the sourness of the puke along with the smell of piss. I struggled to a sitting position and found that I was sitting in my own mess. I was thankful that I hadn't crapped in my shorts even though I had pissed all over myself. I moved away from the mess. The urinal can was in the far corner of the cell. The dim light that came from the small unshielded bulb in the corridor seemed to be painfully bright. I got to my feet and made for the urinal. I dropped my shorts and stepped out of them. I made for the urinal and emptied my bladder of what was left. I wrung out my shorts and hung them on a projection of wood on the wall of the cell. I wiped my hands on the floor.

The night was cool, I left my shirt on to provide some warmth. I sat in the corner of the cell and prayed.

I woke to the sharp pain of a bayonet prodding my ribs.

"Ush. Hi yi." The Jap guard motioned me to move.

I reached for my shorts and slipped into them as the Jap watched me. I moved out into the corridor through the door the guard had opened before he woke me. He prodded me out into the open with his bayonet to where the interpreter and the sergeant were waiting. The sun was just clearing the horizon in the east.

"March!" the interpreter ordered. I marched in the direction he indicated. They led me to the rear of the compound behind the buildings onto a small parade ground.

I sweated. Why would they march me to the back of the camp to execute me. Why didn't they march me back across to the camp and shoot me the way the others had been shot? Maybe they were going to cut my head off with one of their two handed swords. My throat was tight with fear. I attempted to swallow and found that my muscles wouldn't respond. My stomach was a tight knot.

When we reached the center of the open area the Jap called a halt. "Tomaru." I stopped. The Jap soldiers in the area came to attention as they watched.

"Take off your shirt."

I removed my shirt and stood holding it while the Jap sergeant issued instructions to two of the soldiers. They double timed to a pile of long bamboo poles at the edge of the clearing. I watched as they chose a piece about twenty foot long and about six to eight inches in diameter. They hefted it and brought it back to where we waited. The Jap sergeant looked around the area, and at the sun. He strutted off in one direction and then another like a dog looking for some place to pee. He finally found a spot that was to his liking.

"Hayaku. Chikayoru." He paddled his hand at me in the typical oriental style.

As I moved over to the sergeant the interpreter grabbed the shirt from me and threw it on the side.

"Koko." the sergeant pointed to a spot beside him.

The soldiers placed the pole at his feet and moved back, standing at attention. He smirked as he looked at me and then at the sun, then at the pole. He pushed one end of the pole around until it was lined up to his satisfaction. He looked to the east again and nodded. He grimaced a smile and pointed for me to move to the pole. I looked at it and realized that it was pointing north and south like a huge compass needle.

"Kneel." the interpreter directed.

"Where?" I blurted. I wasn't sure of what was going on, but I didn't like it.

"Kneel with the pole between your legs."

I knelt, straddling the pole, facing south. My mind was racing. Was I going to be tied to the pole and beaten with the split bamboo rods? It seemed that a kind of calmness took hold of me. I said a silent prayer. I was resigned to the worst. I knew that I couldn't run away. There was no way out. Maybe, if I ran, I would be shot dead. Maybe being shot to death wouldn't be so bad, it would be a fast death. I didn't make up my mind fast enough. One of the soldiers had a some rope that I hadn't noticed. He lashed my ankles to the bamboo. The Jap sergeant smiled at me. Then he moved in front of me and placed his split toed sneaker on my chest and shoved. I fell back on the pole. I groaned as a shot of pain hit me in the back. My arms and elbows absorbed most of the shock, but my head bounced off of the bamboo. My toes dug into the dirt and my thighs and back burned with pain. I gasped and almost blacked out. My legs were stretched back and I could feel the pulling on the tendons. My ankles felt as though they had been broken. I tried to twist my legs to relieve the breaking pressure on my ankles. The dirt gave way enough to remove most of the strain on the ankles and calves. The private pulled my arms over my head and tied my wrists to the pole. The Jap sergeant said something to him and he checked the rope. He made a reply to the sergeant and showed him that the ropes were loose enough not to cut off the circulation. The sergeant ushed him and grunted. They all walked off and left me to the sun. I blacked out sometime later. When I became conscious I was aware of the hot sun. It was almost overhead. The sun burned into my eyes. I kept my eyes closed and my head turned away from the sun. I was numb except for my head and torso. I didn't seem to have anything but painful stubs for arms and legs. The sky was an orange red light that glared at me. Sometime during the day something stood, somebody stood, between me and the sky. There weren't any features, nothing but an outline of a soldier and a rifle. It seemed a huge black silhouette against an orange red backdrop.

"Mezo."

The word for water was painful to hear. A black arm moved away from the black body and something fell on my lower face. It struck my lips. There was a blistering of pain and the feeling of an infinitesimal amount of wetness that never reached my tongue. The hot wetness was repeated three or four times. Then a cascade of wetness hit my face. Dimly I realized that the Jap had poured some water on my face. The cool wetness was unimaginable relief. I watched the black silhouette move away into the hot sky.

I realized that I was cold. I didn't know why. I was in the hot sun. I shivered with blood pain when I moved. Everything was black. I couldn't think properly. I was very cold and shivering. I made the motions to open my eyes, but there wasn't anything to see. It was all black. I tried to move my arms but nothing happened. I went through the shivering and the pain many times. Once there was water in my mouth. I felt a warm breeze and I moved. My eyes were open but there wasn't anything but a red haze with lighter and darker areas. Someone had removed the ropes from my wrists, that was why I could move. I moved my arms and the pain shot down from my shoulders to the wrists. I was rolled over, groaning. I didn't feel the ropes being loosened from my feet. A foot pushed at me and I struggled to sit up unsuccessfully. Somebody grabbed me at my arms and I groaned again. I was sitting up on the ground. My thighs and my chest felt hot. Dazedly I wondered how badly I had burned from the tropical sun. My underarms felt scorched. Worst then my chest and thighs and face. I couldn't walk. They dragged me back across the parade ground and into the guardhouse. I thought I was back in the cell.

"Koko." It was meaningless. Here, I knew I was here, where ever it was.

A dish was placed in my hand. It slipped out because I couldn't control my fingers. It was handed back and held there until I could hold it on my own. Everything was black. I knew the sun had caused my blindness, but I was too numb to worry about the permanence of the condition. I had kept my eyelids closed. I shoved the tasteless food into my mouth. My throat ached when I forcefully swallowed. I ate everything I could feel was in the dish. Water came later. Someone held a cup of water to my lips and told me to drink. Later I crawled to the urinal and used it as a thundermug. I squeezed hard and strained to force out whatever it was that wanted to come out.

My skin felt hot but didn't seem to be burned as I ran my hands over my body. I wondered if the deep tan I had acquired had made the difference. The real bad spots I felt were under my arms. And, I couldn't see. My body ached. My legs were pulled out of shape. I rolled over on the bamboo floor and passed out.

Time didn't seem to exist. I had violent spasms of chills and then intense burning fever. Food came many times in-between. There were some pills that were forced on me along with some water. It seemed as though a long time had passed, I thought it might have been days. I knew, somewhere in my mind that days had passed because of the cycles of warmth and cold. The days were warm. The nights were cold. A blanket had been thrown over me sometime during the period. Everything was blurred and ran together.

I woke, I was seeing something. A guard was standing outside of the same cell that I had been in when they had first brought me in.

"So. So." he intoned and left. He returned after some time with the interpreter.

"You can speak to me?" he asked.

"Yes." My mouth was thicker than I had expected it to be.

"Can you walk?"

"Yes." I answered not really knowing if I could. I would have to force myself if it meant getting out of the hellhole.

"Then get up and come with me," he ordered.

The Jap guard opened the cell door and let me out. I followed the interpreter and the guard followed me. I walked stiffly and slowly. Neither of the Japs rushed me. I had enough sense to wonder about this. We walked to the Jap soldier's quarters and into the bathhouse. The interpreter instructed me to take a bath. I took off my shoes and stepped into the shower. I dropped my shorts and let them lay there so that they would be laundered as I bathed. I was all muck and encrusted dirt. I stunk. I scrubbed myself with my hands while the two Japs smoked and watched. After some minutes the interpreter spoke to the guard. The guard handed his rifle to the interpreter and disappeared. I watched curiously as the interpreter sat smoking and looking off into some unknown space. The guard returned in a few minutes with a small piece of yellow soap which he handed to the interpreter. The interpreter handed the rifle back to the guard as though it some kind of a ritual.

"Here. Wash." He said nothing after that. He held his nose to indicate how bad it was.

They sat and watched. The guard pointed to my penis and made some remark at which they both laughed. I thought that they were talking about its size, which was small. It had shrunk to the size of a small pork sausage.

I was grateful for the soap which smelled like the yellow GI soap. I scrubbed from head to foot. My beard was scraggly and my hair was long. I laundered my shorts and then put them back on wet.

"Come."

We returned to the guardhouse and I was placed in a different cell. Both of the Japs left.

I sat there and finally had a look at what my body was like under the dirt that I had washed off. I had burned and blistered under my arms and around the armpits. The skin had healed a kind of white. My throat had also been burned. My eyelids still felt thick and gritty. The insides of my thighs were still somewhat raw and red. I also felt kind of stretched out, with a permanent feeling of having a permanent break somewhere in my lower back. The rest of my body hadn't suffered too much from the sun. The bronze tan that I had acquired had provided protection. I hated to think of what shape I would be in if the Jap sergeant had stripped off my shorts.

Four days passed. They fed me Jap soldier rations three times a day. And surprise of surprises, I even had tea.

On the fifth day the interpreter and a guard escorted me to the office where the sergeant sat at a desk in an almost at attention position. He spoke at some length to the interpreter as I stood at attention. The interpreter turned and left.

"You will be returned to the camp." I looked at him, stared at him. "You will say nothing, because no one will believe you. You have been on a work detail that is now over. Any lies you tell, we will hear. It will not be good for you."

The interpreter returned and stood beside me. He handed me a pack of Filipino cigarettes. I started to extract one. "No. Keep them." My mouth dropped open in surprise. I looked at the pack and then at the Jap. "You will go now." As I turned to leave the interpreter produced my shirt and handed it to me. He ordered me to follow the soldier who stood outside of the shack to the camp across the road.

As we entered the camp the POWs looked at me with the same disinterest that any skinny and ragged POW receives. The guard stopped inside the gate and motioned me on. I made my way back to barracks fourteen.

I was greeted by Ed who was sitting on the shady side of the building. "Where in the name of God have you been for the last ten days?" He blurted the words as he rushed to meet me.

"Ten days?" I stopped suddenly with the realization that I hadn't had the slightest idea of how long I had been in the Jap compound. "Ten days?"

"Man you look rough!" He shook his head as he looked me over. "Seen anybody else yet?"

"No."

"Well we all thought you were a goner. The barracks leader will be asking a lot of questions. Johnny has all of your stuff. We sure thought you were a gonner." Ed looked at me and frowned.

"Yeah huh? Well," I started, "the story is that I was on a work detail. Now its finished."

"Yeah! Huh?" Ed snorted.

We sat down and lit a couple of cigarettes just as Ted, Johnny and the barrack leader arrived. The telling of the story took up most of the afternoon. We came to the conclusion that I must have had either dengue fever or malaria. We couldn't figure out what the medicine that they gave me could have been.

The arguments lasted for days. Captain Wheat, who was the acting adjutant, wasn't told the real story by the barracks leader. "If I tell the officers that story they'll swear that you are in cahoots with the Japs. I'll bet. We know that you aren't, and I believe you. But what the hell do you think Colonel Paquet would say?" he stated. "So, what the hell, you were on some work detail."

Johnny was pissed at me and remained pissed off for days. As the days passed I found it harder and harder to believe that the weird experience had actually had happened to me. It made no sense, I couldn't understand the Oriental way of thinking.

CHAPTER 8 -- GUERRILLAS

The Japanese contingent that had been with us since we had entered the camp had been replaced early in July. The new group seemed to be different in some way. We couldn't figure out why the difference, or just what it was. They didn't pay much attention to the comings and goings of the POWs. They took us out on work details and watched us, but not too closely. But it wouldn't be wise to escape while on a work detail because the others on the detail would no doubt suffer.

I decided that maybe, if no one in the group objected, I mean really objected, I would give escape another try. It was the middle of August. There was a POW in another barrack who wanted to be transferred to the carpenter group. I convinced the leader that it was a good thing. I knew that he suspected my motive, but he finally agreed.

"Don't forget, they may have a good count over there."

"Right."

The night of the transfer I told Ed that I would not be around for a while and not to fuss about not being able to locate me. I expected to go out on one of the road or wood cutting details and might be gone for some time. I knew he didn't believe me, especially when I asked him to take care of my belongings for a few days until I got settled in. I asked him not to tell Johnny. I told him that the reason I didn't tell Johnny was because I was worried about how he would take it. I thought I might be able to send in some medicine if at all possible. I started on my way to the new barrack after we had night chow and the new man bunked down in my old place. I turned off on the path to the latrines and scouted out the area. The guards were not patrolling the perimeter fence as frequently as they had before. I made my way to the new barrack and found an empty bay. Then I relaxed for a while just batting the breeze with some of the occupants of the new place. It was well after midnight when I walked back to the latrines. The place was quiet and the whole area was quite dark. When the guy who was using the throne with me left, I walked out toward the fence and dropped to the ground waiting. No one moved around the nearest latrine, the one I had come from. I crawled on all fours to within thirty or so feet of the fence and waited. It was a long time before the guard walked through and headed for the lighted area around the back gate. I said a silent prayer. My heart was pounding and I was sweating. Everything was quiet. The almost new moon had set early and there was only the light from the brilliant stars that was eclipsed at times by heavy clouds. I slipped under the first strands of wire, rolled across no man's land and slid under the other set of wire strands. I stopped and waited, rolling over on my back to watch for the guard. Satisfied that there was no cause for alarm, I started the hundred or so yard crawl to the river. I crossed and walked as fast as I could in the dark heading for what I hoped was Luna, north of Cabanatuan. The brilliant stars were as good as a compass when I could see them in between the clouds that were moving in from the southwest. I suddenly found myself on the road which was empty of any traffic as far as I could see.

I had no real plan. My idea had been to first get out of the camp. I didn't think it was wise to try for the Pacific by following the road through the mountains to Port Aurora. I had heard that the road there was heavily patrolled. Heading west to the Zambales was a better bet. There would be some food from either the banana trees or the mango trees that grew in all sorts of places. There was also rice and sugar cane. Maybe, just maybe I could find some of the guerrilla bands we had heard of that were operating in the area and harassing the Japs.

I was out! I realized that I had made it. It was so simple that it was anticlimactic as they say. I sat down a distance away from the dirt road and lit a cigarette. I held it in my cupped hand and inhaled holding my head down between my knees to hide the glow as the cigarette burned bright. I broke up the butt and stowed the unburned tobacco in my pouch.

I was suddenly shaky. Suppose that the Japs started to track me. I rose and started out. I figured that I could get off of the road and into the brush if any headlights appeared. I moved as fast as I could. After a while I was puffing. I slowed down, realizing that getting winded wasn't the right way to travel. I stopped to rest and smoked another cigarette, then moved on. I realized that I was seeing lights up ahead of me on the road. I stopped. The lights didn't move. It was some small barrio. I wasn't sure which it was. Luna. Or maybe Balangkare that I had heard about. The sky behind me was suddenly glowing. I decided to find a place to hide for a couple of hours and rest. Maybe sleep. There was a thick growth of jungle about a mile to my right. By the time the sun was peeking over the horizon I was at the edge of the thick growth of trees. I noticed that the night had been quiet, or I just hadn't noticed the sounds, but now there were all kinds of noises coming from ahead of me. The mountains in the background looked black with the sun behind them. I had a long way to go if I was going to head for the Zambales Mountains. It was a good hundred kilometers, I converted to miles and came up with about sixty miles, straight line. Maybe ninety miles the way

I would have to travel with the detours and precautions I would have to take. It was a guess. I didn't know how accurate it was since no one had any maps. I didn't know the names of the many small barrios that were along the way, not that it mattered.

The jungle wasn't as bad as it looked from a distance. I found a thicket at the roots of a huge tree, and saying a prayer that there weren't any snakes around I settled down to rest. I didn't think I could sleep, but at least I could rest my legs and my back. I became aware of the stiffness and aching of my back. I put my head back and rested a few minutes before I took a measured drink of water. I expected to have to ration my water until I was sure I could refill my canteen. It had been full when I left camp. I put my head down on my knees to rest.

I jumped and hit the ground at a sudden sound that had jerked me awake. I rolled over and looked around. My heart was pounding in my chest. A huge lizard. over two feet long was only a couple of feet above me on the trunk of the tree against which I had been resting. I released my breath and grinned. The big thing which the Filipinos called an iguana, opened its mouth and stared at me. I looked around for a stick or a rock. He was going to be my meal if I could get him. The heavy branch I spotted lay about four feet from my right hand. I moved it slowly until I had a good grasp and then examined it carefully. It looked like it could do the job. I sat up and the iguana moved. It turned around to head up the tree. I swung the branch and caught it just behind the head. It fell at my feet and twitched. I hit it again and it lay still. I had matches. I would risk a fire if I moved further into the depths of the growth. But, I had no knife. Great! I picked dinner up by the tail and walked deeper into the jungle toward the hills. When I sat down I stared at the carcass and thought. A piece of wood. I left the lizard in a small opening and searched for a branch that I could break and use to butcher the animal. I found a dead branch at the side of a tree that looked like it was some kind of a hardwood tree. When I broke the branch it splintered in such a way that it had some long slivers. I managed to work loose a thick sliver with a sharp edge that I could use as a primitive knife. The whole job was horrible. The skin was tough. The guts were a mess, and the blood stunk. It seemed as though it took hours to butcher the carcass. I found as much dry wood as I could and built a fire that sent up a column of thin blue smoke. I constructed a makeshift spit and skewered the meat and roasted it. The fire burned hot and it seared the white meat. I let it roast until I was sure that it was all thoroughly cooked. I bit into a hot piece of the meat and was amazed at how delicious it was. I hadn't had any iguana since Bataan, back in February. I stomped the fire and threw dirt over the embers. I had eaten only a small part of the meat from the lizard. I wrapped the rest of the meat in some big leaves and started off again. I was full. I decided to rest some more since there was evidently no immediate need to go on. I retraced my steps back to near the place where I had entered the heavy greenery. It didn't seem that anyone was searching for me yet. I was tired. It didn't seem to me that I should be tired, but I was.

I fell asleep again, this time with a full stomach. When I woke the sun was nearly over head. My gut felt full and I felt rectal pressure. I found a place to relieve my bowels. Now I had the same problem, toilet paper. I didn't have any. I reached for some leaves that didn't look to coarse and cleaned myself. I thought about the problem again, toilet paper. It was always the same. You had to scrounge around for paper. The Japs didn't provide enough. It was the same with other toilet articles. It wasn't that they didn't have them, it was that they never planned to take care of the needs of the prisoners, they didn't give a shit!

I made my way out of the undergrowth and west, keeping south of the barrio. I stayed away from the shacks and the haciendas. I saw Filipinos in the distance and turned away from them. I didn't trust anybody. I couldn't. I still didn't see any signs of being followed.

During the first afternoon I crossed three rivers before I came up on a road. The area was a huge flat plain that was planted with rice. I found a bamboo growth and settled down to eat again. I figured that I had traveled about, maybe, nine or ten miles. I was happy that my leg had healed so well. The sun was near the western horizon. I decided to keep on walking until I got tired again.

During the next two days I crossed a half a dozen roads and a railroad. There were a few rivers and creeks that I wondered about. I thought I might follow one of them south, but decided against it and kept on moving west. It rained twice in that time. I found shelter under some trees, but I was afraid of the lightning and moved out fast when it struck in some of the trees in one of the groves. I just kept on moving. I found bananas twice, and a huge mango tree where I found some ripe fruit that had fallen to the ground. I was careful of the mangoes because I had had a problem with some of the unripe fruit before. I couldn't do anything about the water except use the river water. Once I collected some rain water from the fronds of a palm tree.

The mountains to the west were getting nearer. It was day three, and I hadn't talked to anyone, and I was quite sure that I hadn't been seen by anyone that counted. The sound of a train came in suddenly from the north. I crouched and waited. The tracks were only about two hundred yards away. I settled down in the tall grass and watched. It was traveling slowly, a dozen or so cars, freight cars and flat cars loaded with logs.

The Jap soldiers rode on top of the cars as well as in the engine and the caboose. I watched as it disappeared to the south. It was, I figured the railroad that went up to Lingayen Gulf. The road beyond must be the main road to Baguio. There would be a lot of Japs traveling that road. The mountains were just beyond.

I thought about the mountains and the gold mine that we had blasted so that the Japs wouldn't have access to the gold. It had been a stupid order, I thought. It had caused the lives of many Filipinos in one of the little barrios just north of Bataan. I sat looking at the mountains.

"Get up there and blast the tunnel. You are supposed to know where it is, so you lead them. Sergeant Wilcox is in charge of the squad, you show them where it is. Blow it up and get back here. And I mean blow it up." The Colonel was gung ho, but he wasn't going with us.

That had been in February. Six men. I wondered if any of the others had survived. Phil and I had become separated from the others after we blew up the mine.

It had started off as an adventure. Real adventure. I wasn't wise enough to realize how viciously deadly the trip was. I guess none of us really knew what war was like even though we had been on the line and had been bombed and shelled and strafed. It was still gung ho. Making our way through the line east of Olangapo had been no problem. The Japs weren't expecting anyone to try to go north. The mine was east of Castillejos, somewhere near a small river, in the Zambales. Of course there were Igorots there, but I didn't expect them to give any trouble. Hell, they had been selling Japs ears to the Americans at five pesos a pair. We were approaching a small Filipino settlement when Jap patrol picked us up. We fired on them and turned up into one of the ravines. They started after us firing round after round that was ineffective in the heavy undergrowth.

"Stupid shitheads are using the twenty five calibers. They don't penetrate the bush. Gimme a thirty o six anytime." Wilcox was from the Thirty First Infantry. He had been in the service for more than ten years. An old timer by our standards.

We evaded them finally and made it to the settlement that was too small to be called a barrio early the next morning. We had to detour around a small mountain which caused us a couple of hours.

"We have to find the river and head east." I told Wilcox.

"You sure there is dynamite and caps there?" Wilcox didn't believe that I knew what I was talking about.

"Yes. I don't think the Filipinos would tell the Japs about the mine. And nobody else would be there. The place hasn't been operating since about October."

"Okay. Let's check with the natives and then get on with it."

There had been no Japs in the village and the Filipinos assured us that the mine had been inactive since before the war because the owner had left fearing that the Japs would come in. They fed us, a quick meal of rice and pork. We moved out into the hills. We had traveled for about fifteen minutes when we heard shots coming from the settlement. Wilcox ordered us to turn back saying we had to check out what was happening.

"They'll probably put the yellow slant eyes on our asses."

We found a ridge a hundred yards from the small settlement and watched. A Jap lieutenant had the thirty or forty people in the center of the village berating them. The village elder, the leader was on his knees in front of him. We watched as a couple of soldiers dragged a young woman and tied her to a tree on the edge of the clearing. It was about fifty or sixty feet away from the gathering. The old man seemed to be pleading with the Jap officer. The rest of the people were grumbling. One of the women, I figured it must have been the girl's mother, was being held back by a couple of Filipino men. The lieutenant talked to the leader. He ordered one of the soldiers to do something. He was pointing at the girl. We soon saw what it was. The soldier approached the girl, tore her dress off, and then took a grenade from his belt and stuck the handle between her legs.

"Friggin sucker!" One of the men sat up.

"Get the hell down." hissed Wilcox. "We'll take care of the yellow slobs. I got the friggin officer. Pick out a man and shoot the bastard when I shoot. And don't miss. Hear me?"

"He pulled the damned pin!" I heard the small private that was evidently the youngest of our squad.

"Goddamn!"

Wilcox fired as did some of the other men. I saw the girl sag. We all opened fire. It had been a nightmare. The Japs were slammed around by our fire just as the grenade exploded. We continued shooting until the whole squad was wiped out.

"She was dead?"

I didn't know who asked the question. It hadn't mattered. We didn't go back to the village, we went on to the mine. No one spoke, but everyone grumbled under their breath.

The dynamite had been there. We filled the tunnel with about thirty boxes of explosive. Someone spotted the squad of Japs coming up the side of the river just as we were about to set off the charge.

"now where the hell did they come from?"

"Blow the goddamned thing and head down river. If we get separated you all head back. Get me. No deserting into the mountains. We got to go back." Wilcox roared at us as the Japs opened fire from the bottom of the slope near the river. They were coming up along the narrow gage rail that was used to carry ore to the edge of the river and the processing plant down there. Phil and I were behind one of the small ore carts, firing down at the approaching Japs.

"Get a move on! It's going to blow!"

The fuse was lit and we headed for the river.

The mine opening was only thirty or forty feet behind us and the Japs were coming at us.

"Phil! Into the car!"

"Huh?"

"Into the car."

He jumped in as bullets clanged off of the steel. I released the brake and pushed. The car hit the down grade and started rolling. I heard the explosion and saw the whole side of the hill lift and then settle back as we whizzed down through the Japs. Another concussion hit us. A Jap had thrown a grenade which had exploded against the side of the car. Strangely enough nothing penetrated the sides of the car. We hit the end of the rails and were flipped out as the car turned over. I found my rifle before I looked for Phil

"Okay?"

"Yeah!" he answered. "Let's haul ass!"

The Japs were still up on the hill. The fight was still going on. I turned and looked up the hill. I reloaded the Enfield and got behind the overturned car. I rested the rifle on the edge of the ore cart and emptied the clip at a couple of Japs on the track. I wished we had had a BAR. That would have taken care of the Japs in a hurry.

"Let's get the hell out of here! Come on!"

I followed him into the river and across. There hadn't been any shooting at us. It had taken us two days to make it back to our lines. When we returned to the command post from which we had left, we were told that there had been a battle royal there two days before. No one knew about the group that had been there before, they had moved on somewhere else. Phil stayed with them and I was told to return to Mudhole and report to my command by the captain in charge of the unit.

It had been stupid.

I sat wondering what had happened to those guys. Forget it I rationalized, I had my own problems right now.

I could cross the tracks and the road at night.

I was moving along the foot of a small mountain south of a town I could see not far away. The road was north of me. I had expected to see truck traffic along the road and was surprised that it was so quiet. The sun had just risen and I figured that I could travel while it was still cool. I saw something move in the brush along the road. I dropped and waited. I searched the road and the surrounding area. There was a river a hundred yards ahead, in the direction in which I was heading. I took my time and studied the area. There were fifteen, maybe twenty men spread out along the road. All on the southwest side, between me and the river. Guerrillas!?

They didn't look like Japs. Why would Japs be skulking along the road anyway? None of them wore helmets. They had to be guerrillas.

I crawled closer. They were Filipinos! I waited. If I revealed myself now I could be screwing up the ambush. Time inched along. My legs were stiff and cramped. I heard the truck before I saw it. It was coming from the northwest. When it passed over the bridge the gunfire erupted. The burst that hit the cab was from a BAR. The BAR man was using tracers which was a crazy thing to do. He gave away his position by doing using tracers. The three soldiers in the cab didn't know what hit them. The truck bounced off of the road into the ditch. I was surprised that it hadn't exploded. Men rushed out of the ditch and scrambled over the wreck. I watched as they stripped everything usable and searched the truck itself. There evidently wasn't any kind of cargo that could be salvaged.

I heard an order shouted by the man who was evidently the leader of the group, a heavier set man who seemed a little older than the rest. Older. He was probably about thirty, the others under his command were about my age and younger. He was big for a Filipino. Heavyset. They gathered at the side of the road carrying the rifles and ammunition they had taken from the dead soldiers. I counted five bodies. There must have been two men in the back.

I followed at a distance of maybe two hundred yards after they passed over the river and headed west on the south side of the road. They turned south and skirted the mountain, continuing on until they came to another road. They crossed it and continued on down into the valley. It had been maybe two hours since the ambush. I was judging the time by the position of the sun. I decided to close in and approach them when they stopped.

I decided to walk in out in the open. "Hello Joe." I stopped.

The whole group jumped to their feet and pointed their weapons at me. I raised my arms above my head and stood rooted to the spot. The expressions on their faces were something that surprised me. They had amazement spread all over them.

The older man, whom I had taken to be their leader, looked around at them and started to berate them in Tagalog and waving his hands at me.

"I am an American." It sounded like a stupid thing to say, but I couldn't think of anything else at the moment.

The leader moved toward me so fast that I thought that he was going to attack me. I took a step back and stopped. The Filipino wrapped his arms around me and hugged me.

"Man! Am I glad to see you! Where did you come from?" He released me and stood back looking at me while holding my arms.

"I've been in Cabanatuan."

"The prison camp! You escaped?!" he stepped back with his mouth open. "HAH! You see! The Japanese aren't invincible! Come sit. Are you hungry? You don't have a weapon, not even a knife."

"I'm hungry. I haven't eaten anything today except some bananas. Early this morning."

"Come." They gathered around me. "Call me Major Ramos. I am, or was, in the Philippine Army."

"I am private first class Joseph Petak. I was a Combat Photographer with the Signal Corp. We were part of the Seventh."

I wondered about what he had said when he introduced himself. Call me Major Ramos. It slipped away as unimportant.

Someone broke out a can of Spam. It was opened for me and I wolfed it down in a few gulps. I hadn't liked Spam when we first had it on Bataan, but things sure do change.

We talked for some time before Major Ramos said that we should be on our way. It was after eleven by his watch. Ramos said that he had been, was in the Philippine Army. After Bataan, he had made his way north by the roads to the west of San Fernando because the Japs had the Americans and the Filipinos there. Some of his men had made the trip with him. They had found food and ammunition and had been harassing the Japs ever since. They had lost about twenty men, but there were always more that were ready to join them.

"Do you want a Springfield or one of the Jap guns? No. Maybe you should take the BAR. Yes."

I looked at the man who had been introduced as Miguel, the man who had used the BAR so effectively. "No. I think that Miguel should keep the BAR. He knows how to use it well. But you shouldn't be using tracers, they give away your position."

I received a big grin of appreciation from the khaki clad man. "I am using the ammunition which we captured. It is the way it is loaded."

"We should reload the clips. You only want to use tracers to blow up a truck or a car. Or to track your fire when you are shooting at a plane." I smiled at him and then turned back to Ramos. "I would like a thirty aught six." One of the men handed over the rifle and a pouch of clips. "No sling?" I asked.

"We haven't found any slings." Ramos answered.

I checked the rifle to make sure it was loaded and slung the pouch over my shoulder after checking the ammo in the clips. "Where did you find the Springfields? I had and Enfield on Bataan." The bayonet mounted on the rifle looked to be sharp.

"There are a lot of weapons all over the island."

I nodded, "You have a camp somewhere close by?" I asked.

"We have many camps. All around." The answer was given in a nonchalant manner. "We will stop at one tonight. It is not far. It is our main camp."

"Are there any Japs around here?"

"No. Not close by. But they patrol the roads and they are always going back and forth to Lingayen." The Major answered. "We ambush them regularly. But not always in the same places."

We crossed a road and a small river in the afternoon.

"We will stop near Pitombayog tonight. We must pick up some dynamite. We are going to ambush a convoy in the morning. We can rest a while and then start back for the road we just crossed. Then we go back toward Gerona. I will show you how we deal with the Japs."

"How far is it to Cabanatuan from here?"

"Maybe fifty-five kilometers. No more than sixty, depending on the way you came." I figured I had covered about twenty kilometers a day.

The group of shacks was in the foothills surrounded by small patches of garden and pig pens. The children that greeted us stared at me wide eyed as did the rest of the native Filipinos. My height always seemed to amaze the Filipinos.

The evening meal consisted of rice and chicken, followed by some bananas and mangoes. I declined the vicious fermented palm wine. I had found out that I couldn't handle the vile stuff.

"We share with them. They share with us. We bring tobacco and other things that we steal from the Japs."

We talked for hours about my escape and about the plight of the men in the camps. We talked about the war and the guerrillas. Ramos and his men were in contact with two other bands. They had had a radio but the batteries had used up and they couldn't find any replacements. He hadn't seen any Americans, although he had heard that there were some down south.

The Filipinos were interested and surprised at the information that I passed on to them.

It was just before sunset when a man came into the settlement and approached the Major. They retreated to the far end of the porch of the little hut where we had eaten and talked for a long time. I was introduced to the new man whose name was Isidro. He grinned at me and nodded. He spoke no English.

I took the time to look over the group of men. In particular I was amused by one who carried a cesta over his shoulder. I wondered why he was carrying the jai lai equipment with him. When I asked Ramos he told me that the man, Jose, wanted to be a jai lai player. He had picked up the cesta in Manila and had been carrying it with him everywhere. Ramos came over after his talk with the messenger.

"Doesn't he speak English?"

"He has never been to school. He is from the mountains to the north. It is a little place called Tucuccan. It is north of Baguio. He tells me that the other group is already in the hills with some of the stuff we need. All we have to bring is the dynamite. We will leave in a few minutes."

"Isn't it hard to travel at night?"

"No. You will get used to it. We do it all the time. It is safer that way." Major Ramos smiled as he spoke. "We will march along the road during the night. We can rest when we reach the place where we are meeting the others. They are waiting."

"You say that you have dynamite. Do you have blasting caps or electric primers?"

"Blasting caps." He gave me an odd look. "Do you know how to handle dynamite?"

"Yes. What kind of fuse do you have?"

"The fuse from the mines."

"Good."

We stopped only once on the march. The going was rough because of the darkness of the night. The moon was somewhere in its last quarter and it was hidden by big puffy clouds most of the night. We marched along the road, keeping an eye out for any Japanese trucks that just might be traveling during the night. It was near dawn when we arrived at the rendezvous. I was introduced to the leader of the other group, another Filipino from the Philippine army, a lieutenant. We settled down to rest and wait for sunrise.

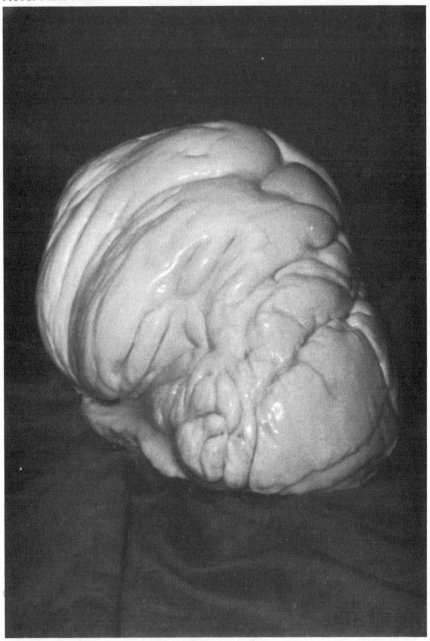

The Pearl of Allah, owned by Wilburn Dowell Cobb. Found by Dyak pearl divers in 1934 in the Sulu Sea. It is 9 1/2 inches long and 5 1/2 inches in diameter and weights 14 pounds and one ounce. The diver who found it was trapped by the giant clam when he reached in for the pearl. He drowned.

CHAPTER 9 -- AMBUSH

The conversation with the leaders was a rehash of what I had already told the Major.

"You are an enlisted man?" The lieutenant was puzzled. "You talk and act like an officer."

"Bullshit! No way. Not me. I was supposed to be shipped out last December to go to OCS, Officers Candidate School, along with Chambers. The war broke out before I was shipped out. So, here I am."

"You were going to be in training for as an officer?" Major Ramos seemed pleasantly surprised.

"No big deal. That was what I had been told. I was supposed to go to Camp Dix, in New Jersey."

"Good! Then you will have the rank of Colonel with us. I am a major. You are an American and you should be in charge. Colonel."

I laughed so loud that the men around us shushed me. "Me? Hell, they didn't even make me a sergeant, and I think I was a top notch combat photographer."

"No matter. Right Pedro?" He asked the lieutenant.

"Yes. A field commission. You Americans gave out many field commissions on Bataan."

"Not me. I don't get along with the officers. Forget it. Let's just get on with what we are doing."

"No." Ramos persisted. "You will have to be an officer. The men expect it. Yes, colonel. Yes."

One of the men came up to the lieutenant and spoke to him in Tagalog. "We should prepare now." He led the way to the road.

A cart that was drawn by a calesa pony was parked on the road. There were four fifty gallon steel drums in the back. One was unloaded by the guerrillas. The men carried the empty drum up the bank to a spot where it would not be seen from the road. When released it would roll down to the road by itself. A group of men rushed in to clear the path which the drum would follow to the road. I watched as the band that held the top was removed, the men started to load it with small stones and clods of dirt that they were collecting from the area. When it was half full, Lorenzo, the man who had carried the dynamite took over. He cut a length of fuse, which he had also carried, and started to set a blasting cap. I squatted beside him and watched. He grinned at me in the pre-dawn light. He inserted the fuse into the cap and clinched the end with

99

his teeth. I flinched at the action.

"You are going to blow a hole in your mouth one of these days." I predicted.

Ramos and the lieutenant frowned.

"Why do you say that colonel?" the lieutenant asked. "I have seen him do that many times."

"That's great if there isn't any loose fulminate in the cap. But, if there is just one grain loose--- POOF. A hole in the cheek."

Lorenzo frowned. "What would you do sir? This is what the engineer at the mine did."

"Sure. I've seen the old timers do it. I use a pair of pliers or just bend it."

"So, the next one you do. Yes?"

"Sure." He placed the blasting cap into one stick of dynamite. I counted as he took out ten sticks of dynamite and tied them together with some cord. I shook my head in disbelief as he tied them together. He placed the bundle in the barrel and held it while the men packed the rocks around it. He coiled the excess fuse on top of the rocks and then guided the fuse cord through the bunghole. The barrel was set on the side of the road with three men assigned to it.

We followed the cart further up the hill and proceeded to set up the second drum a selected spot in the same way. This time I did the preparation. I bent the open end of the blasting cap tube by pressing it against the side of the drum and pulled on the fuse to show Lorenzo that the fuse was well set and wouldn't pull out easily. He nodded and smiled. The same procedure was followed with the other two drums. Now all four were now ready. The drums would roll into the trucks from the upper slope.

We retreated to the up side of the road to wait. Lorenzo, the lieutenant, the major and I were together. I continued on up the hill into the undergrowth.

"Here. This is far enough." The lieutenant stopped.

"Uh uh," I shook my head. "Not for me it isn't."

"Wait! Why?" Ramos asked.

"Hell! You're going to bring down half of the friggin mountain major. Forty sticks of forty percent dynamite! Do you know what is going to happen?"

"We are just going to blow up the convoy."

"And every damned thing in it, and the whole friggin road, and half of the mountain."

"Is it really going to do this?" Lorenzo was wide eyed.

"I wasn't sure I knew what you were going to do. And it is your show, but you are going to blast that convoy to shit with all that dynamite. I'm not going to get killed along with the Japs. I'm going up there where it is going to be safe." I turned after going up a few feet, "You should warn the men to get way the hell back. You have about three feet of fuse in each barrel, that is about a minute after it is lit that it is going to blow the side of the mountain down." I turned and kept on climbing. I heard orders being given as I continued on for another hundred yards.

The major joined me behind the rock I had chosen. Lorenzo and the lieutenant followed.

"You think that the charge is to great?" Ramos asked.

"I think that if you want to stop a truck that at the most three sticks would do the job. Matter of fact, one stick will stop a truck. That stuff is forty per cent. It will blow the truck apart and down into the ravine. How many trucks do you expect anyway?"

"Maybe about ten. They come from Lingayen."

A high pitched whistle sounded from below. "Cover!" Ramos ordered.

The sound of the trucks came from below.

"They are early." Ramos seemed puzzled.

We waited as the first vehicle approached the spot where the first barrel was set up. The signal came again. The lead vehicle was approaching the last barrel, the one furthest up the hill, when one of the men lit the fuse, kicked away the rocks that held it in place. The barrel rumbled down the slope and flew into the air. It ripped through the canvas cover on the back of the truck. The screams of the soldier that were riding in the back of the truck reached us just seconds before it exploded. The three other explosions seemed to occur as one. The blast from below threw debris high into the sky. Pieces of everything shrieked through the air. The shock wave slammed my ears and made the branches of the trees around us quiver. Among the noise was the screaming of the Japs in the convoy. Gunfire broke out immediately. The small crack of the Japanese ammo was mixed in with the heavy bark of the thirty calibers. I heard the burst of the BAR and the spitting of the Jap machine gun. We rushed down the side of the slope and opened fire. Grenades exploded on the side of the road. Men screamed.

Ramos was yelling in Tagalog. I heard the slat of bullets as they passed. I stooped to the ground, kneeling and keeping low. I looked at the scene.

The road was covered with wreckage and debris. Japanese soldiers lay among the ruins of the trucks. It seemed as though there had been ten trucks. There were four large craters where the road had been. The truck in which the last barrel had landed just didn't exist, neither did the three other trucks that had been hit by the explosive laden drums. Two trucks were on there sides. Three others were on fire. One of the trucks, the one in the middle had remained intact, but it was riddled with shrapnel. It didn't seem that many of the Japs had survived the blasts.

A soldier with a grenade had singled us out as a target. I fired at him and ducked as the grenade landed only yards away. A bullet hit the Filipino ten feet away from me. He went down holding his leg, grimacing in pain, but not uttering a sound. I heard the BAR spit a couple of times and then there was a silence so sudden that it was shocking. I didn't know how long the fight had taken. I heard some sporadic shooting from below us.

Ramos stood up about fifteen yards away and shouted some orders. "There will be no prisoners. We cannot take care of any." He directed the statement at me.

I nodded dumbly.

It took only a short time to take care of our wounded and then the salvaging took place. Unfortunately a great deal of the cargo had been destroyed because of the huge amount of dynamite that had been used. The supplies, food, arms and ammunition were carried around the craters to the carts that appeared on the road from the jungle. Men made packs and shouldered them as we prepared to evacuate the area. There was no talk, only the issuance of orders. I helped to bandage some of the wounded. I noticed that both Ramos and the lieutenant, as well as the leader of the other group, watched me at times. They said nothing. I wondered what the reason could be.

We moved out fast into the jungle, following a path that led northwest. We turned after a few miles and turned southwest, skirting the high ground, and heading deeper into the mountains.

Ramos caught up with me as we moved swiftly through the jungle. "We will take the wounded back to one of the camps in the mountains. They will be taken care of there." I nodded. I didn't feel like talking. "You did well. That grenade would have hit us." I nodded again. "Are you alright?" he asked.

"Yes. I'm alright. I don't like us to lose men."

"We will bury ours back here in a little while. We cannot stop until we are sure there are no Japs following."

"Why are they buried just anywhere in the jungle? They should be buried in a cemetery."

"We can't afford to do that. The Japs dig up new graves and look to see if the body has any wounds. They question the villagers and they torture them if they find guerrillas buried in a cemetery. It is the price we pay."

I growled at my own stupidity.

Rain hit us around noon and soaked everything.

"The Japs won't be able to follow us now. The rain will wipe out any sign of our tracks." Ramos was delighted with the rain.

We buried our dead off to the side of a little jungle opening, in shallow graves, smoothing the dirt and spreading leaves and grass over the area. While we rested the rear guard reported that there was no one following. It continued to shower on and off as we followed the dirt road, erasing all traces of our passage. I felt safer as we penetrated deeper into the mountains. The terrain was rough and covered with heavy growth.

The wounded were taken away to be cared for when we reached the small collection of huts hidden under the heavy jungle growth. There was an open area that served as the village square that was not covered. We settled down to rest. Food and beer was brought for us.

"I haven't had any beer since Bataan. It sure tastes great. It would bring a hundred pesos a bottle in camp."

Ramos smiled, a melancholy look on his face. "It will be a long time before we will able to sit in a bar and get drunk." He was frowning as he studied me. "You seem to know the Philippines. Not many American soldiers know much about the islands."

"I was here before. My friend Dowell Cobb is from here, Manila. Wealthy people. He is the reason I am here now. He owns the biggest pearl in the world. It was found off of Palawan, not far from Brooke's Point in thirty-four. It is a long story."

Ramos was distracted. One of the young women passed by as we sat smoking and enjoying the rest.

"Magunda dalaga." Ramos commented in Tagalog. "Yeah." Ramos looked at me and frowned. He didn't seem to be interested in Cobb or the story of the pearl.

"She sure is built. She isn't just Filipino. Is she?" The woman seemed to be in her early twenties, but it was hard to tell. She was about five foot seven, which was tall for a native. Her black hair was long and wavy. The cotton dress she had on hid nothing.

"Could be maybe English or French. You don't seem interested. She likes you you know. This is the fourth time she has passed here."

"Looks great." I nodded and took another swig from the bottle.

"There is something wrong with you colonel. She is beautiful, and, she is a good lover." He studied my face in the fading light.

"I know." I looked in the direction of the woman.

"Her name is Rosa." Ramos grinned, "I bet you haven't had a woman in months. She likes the guerrillas. She thinks they are brave to fight the Japs now that the Americans have been overcome. You should have no trouble. Shall I call her?"

"No." I watched Rosa as she busied herself around the hut.

"But why not? Tomorrow, who knows, you might be dead."

"Could be."

"There is something wrong."

"I don't think I could get a hard on. Look at me. What do you think I weigh?"

"You are very skinny." Ramos nodded.

"I weighed a hundred and eighty-five pounds before the war. That is about eighty kilos. Now I might weigh about a hundred and forty, maybe forty-five pounds. Maybe sixty-five kilos or sixty-six kilos." I smirked as I thought about what I was going to say. "Do you know what I dream about?" I looked at him and he shook his head, frowning.

"The war, surely. Women? Yes?" He grinned knowingly.

"Yes. But I don't dream about women. I dream about food."

Ramos shook his head in amazement. "Food!? You dream about eating?"

"Yes. Steaks. Hamburgers. Bacon and eggs. Not women. Chocalate ice cream."

"Maybe you would not dream about food now. You have food. We have food. So, maybe in a day or two, next week, you will be ready for Rosa." He smiled broadly.

"Could be."

We turned in for the night, finding room in the shacks.

I dreamt of the war that night, not women or food. It was always the same when dreaming about the war, waking up in a cold sweat, heart pounding.

Ramos offered me a safety razor after breakfast. "You haven't shaved in a long time. Yes?"

"Right." I looked a bit more civilized after I had shaved the beard, which was more like a Van Dyke since I didn't have any hair growth between my jaw and sideburns.

Ramos nodded in approval when he returned. "You look more like an officer now," he smiled. "Now Rosa will like you even more. You should have her. Would you like to have your hair trimmed?"

"No thanks."

Ramos frowned at me.

"Suppose she has gonorrhea or syphilis." I continued. " We don't have any medicine. No thanks."

Ramos shook his head, "You could be right. We have a lot of disease now since we do not have any medication. Perhaps you are right." He looked out at some of the women. "I think that she might not like that."

He nodded at me as though anticipating her reaction if there was to be a rejection. "She is the prettiest of the women, and I think she might wonder why you do want to have her. She might think that you would rather have a benii boy. You call them fags. Yes?"

I nodded, "No thanks. Yes, we call them fags. But they don't dress like women and strap up their balls to fool a man into thinking that they are women. When a soldier is drunk and hardup he has anal sex and doesn't even know it. "

Ramos grinned. "But you have them. I met some when I was in San Francisco."

"Yeah. I know." I grinned at him, "There was a young lieutenant from McKinley who was dating one down in Pasay. He wound up being blackmailed by some of his men that found out." I laughed. "He sure was one miserable bastard. I bet he was the only one that was glad that the war broke out. I wouldn't want to be one those men out on a battlefield with him."

The next two days we rested while waiting for information from a group that was operating to the south of us.

I was puzzled by Ramos. I asked about him and was told that he had showed up months ago and had taken over the small group after the Japs had attacked the village looking for guerrillas. He had taken over after telling them that he was an officer. He said it was their duty to continue to fight the Japs. I thought about it for a while and then let it go. It was his business, and right now I was safe enough from the Japs. I was eating and there wasn't any immediate need to do anything else. I was free. And, if he wasn't an officer it didn't make any difference. He was a good guerrilla leader.

Ramos found me near the creek, he smiled as he handed me a colonel's bird insignia. "One of the men had this. Only one, but it should do." I thanked him and pinned it on my shirt.

A runner came in late in the evening of the second day after the raid. Ramos told us that there was some activity on the road south of Gerona. Japanese officers had been traveling back and forth from either Baguio or Lingayen. We were going to attempt an ambush the next morning. Since the targeted area was only about twelve miles distant, we would not leave until just before dawn.

There was a threat of rain as we hiked through the pre-dawn darkness. The moon, somewhere near full, played hide and seek in the clouds.

The road was empty of any traffic and the march was fast, but hot, and the sun wasn't up yet. We deployed on the west side of the road, away from the railroad. We didn't want to get trapped between the road and the railroad if anything happened to interfere with our ambush.

The car that came racing from the north was a nineteen-thirty eight Cadillac convertible with three men in the back and two in the front. As soon as the first shot was fired the rest of our twenty men opened fire. I saw the tracers from the BAR hit the back of the car and then a sudden eruption of flame as the gas tank exploded. The burning car continued on for thirty or forty yards and careened into the ditch on the east side of the road. I heard the cheers as the men ran to the wreck and watched it burn.

Ramos stood with me, "It is the way we have to fight this war."

"I know." I stayed back from the wreck and watched it. "Shouldn't we move on now. There is no sense in trying to hide it." I looked up and down the road. Suppose another car or a truck comes along to investigate? We should move out."

Major Ramos nodded. "Yes." He shouted and order. The men assembled around us. "There is no way to tell who they were and what their rank. It doesn't matter. There are five less now. We shall go."

We heard the train coming from the north. Then one of the men shouted that there were trucks heading in our direction. I could see the soldiers on the tops of the freight cars as the train came into sight. We moved out across the field, heading west into the hills, keeping under cover in the tall grass and brush.

A Zero came in from the south, flying above the road at about a hundred feet. "Cover! Take cover!" I yelled at the men. Everyone hit dirt as the Zero banked and came back over us. "Don't shoot!" I shouted. Ramos repeated the order in Tagalog.

The plane zoomed over us and banked again, going out over the road and the burned out wreck. It turned again and dropped to fifty feet and opened fire. The pilot must have thought he had seen something just off of the road. The bullets strafed the ditch hundreds of yards away from us. The Zero turned again and continued strafing until all of the ammo was gone. The plane flew along the road at about thirty feet then turned and headed south.

"Let's go!" I yelled. We ran on and off for more than an hour before we rested. The sun and the running had made us sweat. We sat and rested for a half hour and then continued our march back to camp.

"Do you just go out and ambush cars and convoys?"

"Yes. But we also have blown up the rails. I don't think that it hurts them as much as when we wipe out their trucks and kill their officers."

I sat thinking about the strategy that the guerrillas were using. There had to be a way to hit them in such a way that they would pay a higher price. I realized that we were limited because of the few men that we had, and that we had only a small supply of arms and ammunition. We could only hit and run. I had no ready answer.

Rosa made her way to our shack that evening. She drank with us and teased the men, but didn't pay much attention to me. I talked and joked with the men, keeping my distance from her. Ramos watched us both.

Just before we turned in for the night he sat down beside me on my mattress and offered me a cigarette. "I think that Rosa is annoyed with you. She has been asking many questions about you. Maybe you should be nice to her."

I frowned. "I don't think she is anyone I would want to play around with. I don't trust her."

Ramos looked at me in the light of the lantern, "You don't trust her? Why?"

I shrugged. "Don't know. There is something I'm not sure of. And, I don't want to wind up with gonorrhea. How do you tell a woman that?"

Ramos shook his head in the manner which seemed to be a habit, "I don't know."

"I have a question for you Ramos. Where does she go when she is gone every couple of days?"

"To see her mother in Tarlac. How do you know that? You have only been with us for only four or five days."

"Lorenzo told me when we talked about her yesterday. She has better clothes than the other women. And she has make-up. I asked Lorenzo."

"It is nothing. Her people in Tarlac own a plantation. They have many friends. She has been with us for many months." He looked puzzled.

"I was just curious."

He laughed. "You are only looking to stay away from her because maybe you could not satisfy her." He laughed again. "You should just tell her that you are sick. No?"

"Maybe you are right. I will."

A runner came in two days after we had hit the Jap officer's car telling us that the Japs were searching to the west of the road below Gerona. They had been seen searching the hills and had a Photo Joe, a spotter plane, around the river and seemed to be heading toward Pitombayog. One of the guerrilla bands had moved into the mountains west of Tarlac.

"I think that we had better move out tomorrow. We should go into the mountains to the west of Burgos until the Japs move out of the area. I'll be back in a while."

We said goodnight and Ramos went out as I turned in.

The gunfire woke me with a shock. It was not yet full daylight. The Jap that stood beside my bed grinned as he placed the bayonet on my Adam's apple. Another held a gas lantern high over his head. I felt blood, warm blood, my blood, trickle along my throat and on my shoulder. I raised my hands over my head as I lay on the mattress. He moved the bayonet away and made a sweeping motion with his rifle. I rose clumsily with my hands over my head. He moved back and motioned me out the door. Ramos wasn't in the hut. I wondered what had happened to him. I hadn't heard him during the night.

There were about fifty Jap soldiers that had crowded all of the men and the civilians into the square in the center of the settlement. Ramos wasn't there. The Japs separated the guerrillas from the civilians after questioning some of the women. I didn't blame them for pointing out the guerrillas. They were trying to save their men from execution. It was a sure bet that we were going to be shot. I was singled out, because I was the only American, and taken in front of the captain who was the highest ranking officer in the Japanese contingent.

The captain walked around me as I stood alone in front of the rest of our band. He looked me up and down as he muttered under his breath. The fact that I didn't have a uniform, or anything that resembled a uniform had him puzzled. He came close and fingered the material of my cotton shirt and then scrutinized my shorts. I was thankful that I had taken the colonel's insignia and had it in my pocket. I hoped he wouldn't search me. He pointed to my issue shoes and addressed one of the lieutenants of his command.

The lieutenant turned to me and asked, in perfect English, "Where did you steal those shoes?"

I looked down at my shoes and then at the captain, "I got them in Manila before I left."

The captain spoke at some length again. I caught some of the words and was prepared.

"You are an American soldier? Yes?"

"Yes."

"Where did you escape from?"

I looked at the captain and then at the lieutenant before I answered. "From Manila." I was taking a chance in lying, but what the hell, it wasn't going to make any difference anyway.

The junior officer translated for the captain. The captain walked over and stood in front of me, looking up at me with a dirty gleam in his eye. Then he swung. I went with the blow and fell to the ground. I figured it would be easier if I didn't show too much resistance. He motioned for me to stand up and then addressed the lieutenant again.

"When did you escape from Manila? Where have you been all of this time?"

"I left Manila on Christmas Day." That was true. I had left Manila on

Christmas Day to return to Fort McKinley. "I have been in the Zambales Mountains ever since." Not true but screw you.

The captain considered the answers for a few minutes. He asked some more questions to be translated.

"Have you ever been to McDonnell? Have you been in Cabanatuan?"

"Nope. Not ever."

The captain glared at me as he chewed over the answers. Then some more questions to be translated.

"Why aren't you with the other soldiers? Are you a deserter? Why do you not have a uniform?"

"My outfit left me behind and I couldn't get into Bataan because the Japanese soldiers cut me off. I am not a deserter. My uniform wore out and this is the only clothing that I could find." I looked at the captain without flinching.

"Ush," was all that came as an answer. He waved his hand at me to join the rest of the guerrillas. I stepped back and stood beside Lorenzo.

"I do not think he believes you." Lorenzo intoned the words.

"Who gives a shit? They are going to shoot us anyway."

The captain spoke to his junior officer again. The interpreter marched over and stood in front of us. "You will all sit and wait. You will all be questioned today."

"What happens to us?"

The lieutenant clenched his fist and slammed it into the left side of my face. I staggered and shook my head. "You will not have the effrontery to question a soldier, an officer of the Imperial Army. But, tomorrow you will be shot." He smiled showing a mouthful of gold inlaid that must have cost him a fortune. "So now you know." He grinned. "Enjoy the rest of your life. Today." He gurgled some laughter as he walked away.

We sat in the hot sun all day. One after another the men were taken away to the captain for questioning. Some came back with cut and bleeding faces. Others had bayonet cuts, and one of the men who had been wearing a Philippine Army shirt with a corporal's stripe came back with a broken left arm. He was in silent tears as he cradled his left arm with his right hand. I moved over to him. The Jap soldiers watched me.

"Lorenzo, get me a couple of pieces of bamboo from the fence. Don't get up. Just pass it on to the men. Let the man by the fence there pass over a couple of pieces about two inches wide and a foot long." I made motions with my hands to indicate the approximate size. The guards watched, they didn't interfere. When the makeshift splints arrived I tore off a couple of strips from my shirttail and prepared to splint the man's arm.

"This isn't going to be easy. I have to match up the bone and then put the splint on it. Okay?" He smiled through his tears as I moved beside him. Two of the guards moved to within a couple of feet of us and leaned on their bayoneted rifles to watch.

"Hold him." I ordered a couple of men. I tried to move the arm as easily as possible. He groaned and sobbed as I felt for the bone to make sure I had it lined up properly set it. I watched as the injured man pissed his pants, "It's okay. Don't worry about it." I smiled at him. The Japs ushed and muttered, but they didn't interfere. When I finished I patted the Filipino on the shoulder gently and offered him one of my cigarettes.

The guard closest to me patted me on the head, "Yaroshi," he nodded.

I ushed him and sat back. I wondered why the hell I had bothered. They were going to shoot us in the morning. Well, he would suffer less anyway.

We had to toilet on one side of the opening in between the huts. The water we received was from the women, but we weren't allowed any food.

It started to rain around what I thought was noontime. The downpour made the open area a mudpool. Whenever we stood up the guards made us sit again. The rain wasn't cold, but it made for a lot of misery.

It was the middle of the afternoon before they took me in for questioning. It was short and sweet, for the Japs. Whenever I didn't come up with an answer that the captain didn't like I was whacked with a bamboo rod across the back, or the arms and shoulders. I was in misery when they took me back out into the open. So much the worse because my back gave me enough trouble without a beating.

At nightfall the guards prodded us into huts and tied us up. They placed kerosene lamps in each of the huts and stood guard outside. There was a lot of speculation about our coming execution which didn't make for a bedtime story.

I wondered, and asked questions about Ramos. No one seemed to know what had happened to him.

It was only because I was thoroughly exhausted that I fell asleep after a while. I jumped awake at the sound of gunfire and shouting. The screams of the women were shrill as they rose above the rifle fire. Grenades exploded somewhere, lighting up the settlement in glaring sheets of red white flame. I rolled over to the door as the gunfire exploded outside of the hut. Our guard jumped inside and directed his fire out through the door. A Filipino with a Springfield leaned in through the open window in the back wall of the shack and shot him. He climbed in, laughing and proceeded to cut us loose. Lorenzo picked up the Jap rifle and ran out into the melee.

"Come. We will go out this way." The guerrilla climbed back out of the window and we followed.

We ducked as bullets whizzed around us and ran into the field and contiued on into the heavy undergrowth.

"Stay with me!"

We ran through the dark until we were panting. Our guide stopped when we reached an opening some hundreds of yards from the shacks.

"We will wait here for the others. There are too many Japs. They will follow us. We must move fast."

Minutes later the other guerrillas came crashing down the path that I didn't know existed.

"Petak. Colonel? Are you here?"

"Ramos!? Ramos! You son of a bitch! How the hell did you manage it?"

"Hey Joe! You are all right?"

"Hell yes! Man you don't know how glad we are to see you."

"No talk!" someone growled, "We must go. Now!"

We started to move out along the path. I noticed that there were some wounded that were being helped by others. The man with the broken arm was there.

"Stop!"

We all stopped and listened. There were no sounds from behind us.

"We rest for a few minutes," the same voice that had given the orders earlier said. "No smoking!"

We sat to rest. Ramos sat next to me. "I went to see one of the women. I heard them coming in this morning but it was too late to sound the alarm. I went out the back window into the jungle. I was going west when I ran into Phillipe and his bunch. We thought it would be best to wait until dark. There must have been fifty or more Japs. Did they execute anyone?"

"No. They questioned us all day. Some of the men were beaten badly. They were going to shoot us in the morning." I grunted, "The pricks are going to massacre the people back there."

"No. Most of them were warned. They ran off. They slipped out before we got there. That was why we didn't go in until three. The only women that were left were with the officers. And they deserve what they get."

"I want to say thanks to everyone. You saved our lives. Did Lorenzo make it? He took off after somebody shot the guard."

"I saw him back there. He's all right."

We kept on hiking through the rest of the night and rested again at dawn. The terrain was rough and there were only a few paths and trails along the way. We continued on into the mountains until mid-morning when Ramos pointed out a mountain, "That is High Peak way over there. We are almost at the camp."

It was near noon when we reached a large encampment nestled in a valley. The cover was excellent. There were no shacks out in the open, everything was hidden under the huge trees. There weren't even footpaths in the open. All were under heavy cover. I had no doubt that Photo Joe would not be able to spot the camp.

We were assigned quarters and told to rest. Two women came to the shack with food and beer. I realized that I was starved and wolfed down the food to the amusement of the ladies. They returned with more beer and passed it around.

"Cold beer? How?"

"We have some in the stream that comes from the mountains. It is cold enough, yes?"

"Great! Just great. Thanks. How did they ever get beer?"

"They raided a Japanese convoy that was going to Baguio. The men like to have their beer. Yes?" the Filipina who spoke English answered.

I finished the beer and relaxed. When I awoke it was dark. There were shaded lamps in some of the huts, shaded in such a way that one could see them from ground level, but not from the air.

I made my way to the edge of the clearing to a slit trench and felt a lot better after I had finished. They even had lime to throw into the trench after one completed voiding. I nodded in approval at the sanitation, it was not the usual Filipino facility that was common throughout the islands.

I roamed around the camp asking for Ramos. He was with a group of men in the biggest of the huts. When I stood in the doorway he greeted me and motioned me in. After the introduction, as Colonel, I thanked them again for saving my life and the lives of the others that were with me.

I was filled in on the activities of the group that was headed by Phillipe. I was also told that there some guerrillas operating in the southern part of Luzon. There were some Americans among them, but only a few. There were none nearby that they knew of. We talked well into the night about the war and the many possibilities that were open to the guerrillas. I listened most of the time, offering only cursory comment when a subject that I knew about came up. I was invited to join the larger group, but deferred in favor of staying with Ramos.

CHAPTER 10 -- CAPTURED AGAIN

Ramos wanted me to come up with a plan to harass the Japs. I confessed that I couldn't come up with anything because I didn't know where they were and what they were up to. The surrender of the Philippines by the Americans had evidently given the Japs control of practically all of the South Pacific. We had no communication with anyone outside of the other local guerrillas.

"We need a radio. We should see if we could capture one from the Japs. They must be using the same frequencies as we do."

Ramos nodded agreement. "I know where we can get one, that is if you want to raid a Jap installation. There is a plantation outside of Tarlac that is used by the local commander. They must certainly have a radio that we could use."

"I think that is the best bet. There is no way of knowing if a convoy has a radio. Do you have any idea of how many soldiers are stationed there?"

"No. But we will find out. I will have information in a day."

He did obtain the information in one day. There was a guard detail of about twenty-eight men. Whoever had provided the information also had found out that there was to be a party of some sort the next day.

"I think that we could possibly sneak in during the party and see if we could steal a radio. If we wait until the party is in full swing the guards could maybe be lax. Is there anybody that knows what the layout of the hacienda is like? Where are the guards? Where is the communications center located? It would make it a lot easier to get in and out without having to fight if we could sneak in, take care of maybe only one or two guards, and get out."

"That is a good idea. I like it." Ramos nodded his approval. "I think that one of our men worked there. I will find him. I think it was Alfredo." He left the shack to find the man. He returned in less than an hour with an older Filipino whom I had seen in the group many times. "Alfredo, this is the American colonel."

Alfredo and I shook hands. He had a deferential attitude. I assumed it was due to the fact that he had been a servant for many years rather than because Ramos introduced me as a colonel.

"Do you know how the compound is laid out Alfredo? Can you draw a plan of it?"

Alfredo nodded, "Yes colonel. I worked there many years. And I was

113

there when the Japanese took it over. I saw the office that they set up in the library. The radio equipment is in the next room. I know how to draw. I was taught that in school many years ago." He grinned amiably. "I know the compound well, and I am sure I know where the soldiers stay."

"Great! Terrific." It was a lot more than I had ever expected. It was almost unbelievable.

I took a child's school tablet and a pencil that had been left in the shack by the owner and handed it to the man. "Make a sketch of what you remember."

Alfredo sat at the entrance of the shack and went to work. I watched as he drew the plan. I was pleasantly surprised to find that he had a great sense of proportion and was meticulous with detail. It was almost an hour later that he looked up proudly and handed me the finished sketch.

"This looks great."

Ramos congratulated Alfredo and asked, "Well, what do think?"

"I think its terrific. Now let's see what we will have to do." We sat and studied the drawing and asked one question after another. The guards were no doubt quartered in one of the buildings that had been used to house the workers. We formulated a plan that we hoped would mean the least exposure to the guards. We would go in to the side of the house and into the office and the room next to it. It had previously been a library and study. I was a little surprised at the library because I couldn't imagine one out in the boondocks in the middle of Luzon. Alfredo assured me that there was one.

"Is there anyone who is good with a knife or a garrote? If there is anyone on guard, or on duty, in the radio room we should take care of him quietly. No noise. No gunfire or we will have the whole stinking bunch of yellow bastards down on us."

"Pedro, the big one, the one who is almost as tall as you. He is good with a knife. He can cut a throat without as much as a gurgle coming out." Ramos smiled grimly.

"Good. Then he should go in ahead of us. Now who is going to go in? I am one. Pedro is two. We should have no more than three more. While three men get the radio one will watch and the other can search the desk for any maps and other information. And if there is money we can use that too."

"There is a safe in the wall behind the desk." Alfredo smiled a peculiar smile. "Would you like to open the safe? It is where they keep the maps and the money. I have seen that."

I stared at him. Ramos slapped him on the back and roared with laughter. "You know how to open it?"

""Yes." he smiled, "I saw the combination one day. It was written on a piece of paper on the desk. I know that maybe I should not have looked at it but I did."

"What is it?" Ramos asked.

"It is three, eighty-three, thirty-three. I remembered it because of all of the threes." He looked at us wide eyed. "All the threes. It was very funny to see all of the threes. It was so easy to remember."

"It sure as hell is. Three, eighty-three, thirty-three. I don't think I could forget it now." I laughed wholeheartedly.

"Yes. The first number, three is to the left. You must turn the dial to the left three times before you turn to the right. And, yes, you must turn to the zero after the thirty-three. Yes?" He bobbed his head up and down a few times.

I thought of how weird the Fates played their games. It was like some movie. Even though it seemed to be a break that really couldn't happen, I hoped that it was true and not some freak dream that this man had made up.

"Good. We will travel during the day." Ramos sat back and looked at me. "But why must you go in? I can go just as well as you. You can stand guard and cover us."

"No. You stand guard and Pedro and three others will go in. It shouldn't take us more than fifteen minutes. Even if we take our time going in it will not take long. Okay?"

"Why must you go in?" he countered.

"Colonel." Alfredo held up his right hand as though asking permission to speak. "I could go in with you and show you. It might be a lot easier. Yes?"

I looked at him dumbly, I hadn't expected him to volunteer for the riskiest part of the mission. I looked at Ramos.

"You don't have to go Alfredo. You have already done enough." Ramos was looking at me as he spoke.

"I agree Alfredo. You have given more than we could have ever expected. No, you don't even have to go on the raid if you choose not to." I placed my hand on his shoulder and gave him a squeeze to show my appreciation.

"I choose to go colonel."

We left it at that and continued our planning.

"I think we should start after lunch. Then we could find a place where we could all get a good night's sleep and be fresh in the morning. If we do four hours today, we can easily do the other two hours tomorrow night. It will take us at least six hours to hike the distance from here. We can a place to hide and rest a few kilometers from the hacienda." I looked to Ramos for agreement.

"Good. We should have a radio and who knows what else by tomorrow night."

The hike through the mountains was without incident. We found a place to settle in for the night on the side of the mountain from which we could see the target. It was only about eight kilometers away. It would be an easy hike even in the dark. The moon would make the trek an easy one since it was near full moon.

At dusk we started out on the last leg of the trip. The grounds were all lit up and the party was in full swing when we arrived.

"They are having a big party." Ramos searched the area with his binoculars. "I don't see any patrol." He turned to me, "Are you sure you want to go in? I could go. You could stay here and cover."

"No, I go. We had it out already. Let it stay the way it is. Okay?"

"Okay." Ramos seemed a little put out. "You should go now before the moon is up."

"Right. Let's go."

Pedro, Alfredo, Hernando and Rudolpho fell in behind me as I moved out, crouching in the brushy grass. We approached the perimeter within a few minutes and didn't see anyone at the gate that led to the garden around the house. We watched for some minutes at the gate before I opened it and ran to the door that Alfredo said was the library entrance. Pedro and I studied the library, which was fully lit. It was unoccupied. The door was wide open. I motioned the men in. Pedro and Alfredo and Hernando made for the door to the study off to the right where Alfredo had said the radio was installed. Everyone moved quietly. There was only the slightest sound of the music coming from the big court in the front of the house. As the men assigned to the radio room disappeared, Rudolpho and I moved to the desk and pulled aside the tapestry that masked the safe. I heard some sounds from the radio room and a thwacking sound that I couldn't place, and a thud. I immediately started on the combination. The safe didn't open. I swore and tried again. Rudolpho stood behind me and watched. I sweated as I started again. I heard the men in the radio room smashing something.

"Rudolpho, search the desk and see if there is anything there." I was trying the combination for the third time when Rudolpho called.

"Colonel. Here. Look! Money in the desk and maps. In this case. Many maps. The two big drawers have American dollars and many pesos."

I joined him and looked at the find as the men came out of the radio room carrying a small radio and a generator. Pedro had a big grin on his face. "We have a field radio. I smashed the big transmitter. How about the safe?"

"No luck."

"Here is a lot of money and there are all kinds of maps in this case." Rudolpho was pulling out the money from the two drawers.

"Screw the safe." I turned away. "Let's take the money and the case and get the hell out of here." I looked around the room for something to carry the money. There wasn't anything like a bag or a box. The rectangular wicker wastebasket caught my eye. I dumped it upside down and started to stack the money in it. Rudolpho helped me. In minutes we had most of the bundles of money packed and ready to go. "Grab the rest and stash it in your pockets." When they had finished there wasn't any left on the desk. "Let's go."

We made it out of the building and through the garden in no time flat. The run out to the others took only what seemed to be an instant. We all moved out and headed west just as the moon rose.

"What is in the basket?" Ramos asked as I shifted the heavy load from one arm to the other.

"Money. Lots of money. Dollars and pesos." I grinned in the moonlight. "The money was in the desk. Rudolpho found it. We took it all and the map case too. Whatever was in the safe doesn't much matter. We also have a field radio that was in the radio room. Pedro smashed the other transmitter."

It was an easy trip to the mountains in the moonlight. After the moon was well up I spoke to Ramos. "Let's take a rest. It's been almost two hours I would guess since we left the hacienda. I could use a rest."

"Fine. No one is following us, I'm pretty sure of that."

"Me too."

He called a halt. "No smoking." He sat beside me and Pedro. "Did you get into the safe?"

"No. Dammit. The combo was either wrong or they changed it. I think that it was changed. But there was plenty in the desk. We took it all." I was happy with the results. "Pedro and Alfredo took care of the men on duty."

"I got one and Alfredo used his machete on the other."

I thought about the thwack and the thud I had heard.

"So, we will be able to contact the Army and we will have plenty of money for supplies." Ramos sounded pleased and happy. "We should continue on to Vigla Aglipay. We could rest there tomorrow and then follow the river most of the way back to camp."

The trip through the hills was easy because of the moon. Ramos called a halt. "We are only maybe a kilometer from the barrio. We should approach cautiously. There have been Jap patrols there many times. I think we should send a scout ahead." He dispatched a man and told him to make sure there were no Japs in the area. "Be back by dawn."

I nodded in agreement as I lit my pipe and settled down. "Somebody else is going to have to help carry this money. The damned thing is heavier than I expected it to be."

Ramos nodded. "We can make small bundles, tie them with vines and make it easy to carry." He called a couple of the men and told them what to do. "We can rest until it gets light." We settled down and rested. Sometime later asked Ramos if he didn't think it was strange that it was taking a long time for the scout to come back.

"Hernando knows the barrio. That is why I sent him. Yes, he should have been back by now. Perhaps we should get going. There is plenty of light now."

Alfredo gave me a strange look. "He will not come back."

I frowned at him. "Why not?"

Ramos looked at him also, "Why not Alfredo?" He sat down next to him.

"Hernando had a lot of the money in his pockets and in his shirt. I do not think he will be back. He will go to Manila. He is rich. He always talked of Manila." He nodded his head knowingly.

Ramos swore in Tagalog, words that I didn't understand.

"You think that he took off?" I asked.

"Yes. He will not come back."

"Why did you not tell me Alfredo?" Ramos was annoyed.

"How could I really know major? I only thought of it because he is not back. He should have been no more than maybe an hour." Alfredo made a wry face as he responded.

"The son of a pig couldn't do that. He has been with us for many months." Ramos stood and looked in the direction of the barrio. "I think we should go. Okay Joe?"

"Sure. Why not. We can scout the place before we go in, and besides that I'm getting hungry. I could use something to eat." I rose and started along the path, following Ramos.

The trail was well defined and looked as though it was in constant use. Everything was very quiet. I wondered at the lack of any noise from the settlement. There should have been something. Gunfire broke out. It was too late. The lack of noise had been realized too late. I saw the two men ahead of us go down as I flopped to the ground and rolled to the side under some growth. A Jap machine gun opened up on us as the men returned the fire. Ramos crawled back to me.

"They are on both sides of us. We have to go back."

"Grenades. We have to get the machine gun. Maybe we can go

through and skirt the barrio."

"Grenades!" Ramos shouted. "Get the machine gun. Use the grenades."

I watched as Lorenzo rose and tossed a grenade. It fell short by about twenty yards. Another man threw another grenade that fell far short.

"Somebody has to get that machine gun." Ramos was crawling toward the gun position as he spoke.

Another guerrilla ran forward and threw a grenade. He took a bullet and went down holding his right leg as he rolled into some underbrush.

"Colonel. Do you have a grenade?" Ramos was nose to nose with me.

"No. I haven't had any grenades at all."

"I know. We never did have many. Lorenzo!" he shouted

"Yes major."

"Do you have any grenades?"

"Four."

"Come back here. Colonel. You play baseball. You should be able to throw it that far."

"I'll give it a try." I took the grenade that Lorenzo held out and moved in behind one of the big trees. Gunfire whistled around our position. I waited until it stopped. I pulled the pin and held the spoon, then I stepped out and threw with as much force as I could muster. The grenade fell short.

"They are coming up behind us." I heard some one say.

"Jose! JOSE!" I shouted.

"SI!"

"Do you have your cesta?" I yelled again over the gunfire that was coming in from behind us.

"Si."

"Come over here."

Ramos rolled over on his side and looked at me. "The cesta? No! Will it work? Maybe." He laughed. "You are crazy!"

"Could be. Look at where I am when I could be sitting in a prison camp quietly starving. Anyway, the pelota is thrown about a hundred and sixty feet, sometimes more depending on the length of the cancha, the court. If I use the cesta I could probably reach the gun."

Ramos stared at me without saying a word. The gunfire started up again behind us.

"Are you sure that this barrio is Vigla Aglipay? May be we missed it in the dark." I looked in the direction in which the settlement lay.

"I don't think that we made a mistake. I am pretty sure it is."

Jose crept up close. "Si colonel. I have the cesta here. I always have it. You want it?"

"Here, strap it on my arm. I'll take a grenade and toss it with the cesta. I will bet it will reach the gun." I took the two foot long woven trough like scooped paddle and started to strap it on.

"Colonel. Do you know how to throw with a cesta? It is not easy you know." Jose stopped working the lacing. I removed the cesta and handed it to Jose.

"I played a few times at the fronton. It's worth a try."

"Me." Jose looked at me. "I can throw a pelota from one end of the fronton to the far wall."

"Yes but a pelota isn't anywhere near as heavy as a grenade. And, the pin has to be pulled before you throw."

"I know. Let me try. Please."

I looked at Ramos and then back to Jose. Maybe he was right. It would be tricky to toss a live grenade just right. "Okay. We'll work together. I pull the pin and place the grenade in the cesta and you be ready to toss. Okay?" The bullets continued to whistle around us.

The machine gun opened up again and swept the jungle on the other side of the path. Jose nodded as he flexed his arm with the cesta strapped to it. He rose to his knees as Lorenzo passed me a grenade.

"Have you checked the grenades?" I asked him. I remembered the grenades that had been sabotaged in Bataan. They had been emptied of their charge and had been filled with sand and sawdust.

"I check all the grenades to make sure." Lorenzo grinned. "We have had too many that have had sand in them."

"Good. Let's try Jose."

Jose got up into a crouch, "Now when you see me place the grenade in the cesta, throw it. Don't wait. Got it?"

He said nothing as I pulled the pin and placed the grenade in the trough. The spoon sprung loose and he stepped out and tossed. The grenade flew out in a flat arc and exploded in the air to the left of the gun position. I thought that I had seen it hit a branch as it descended.

"Got the range Jose. I think it hit something as it went down. Again."

He threw the second one way over the gun. "You got a damned good throw Jose. A little too far. Here we go again. How many we got left?"

"Four." Lorenzo replied. "I took all that we have."

"GO!" I set the grenade just as the gun fired again. The grenade arced through the air and burst as it hit the ground beside the machine gun and the three Japs. The gun stopped. "You got it JOSE!"

Ramos grinned at the youngster. I patted him on the back. More rifle fire came at us from behind and from the side. "They are coming in." Ramos snarled. "Let's go!"

I ran forward holding my Springfield ready. I tripped on something and went down and rolled. Ramos went down from a bullet. He sat up and put his hand to his right shoulder as I reached him and pulled him to his feet.

"Shoulder."

"Keep going!" I yelled and pulled at him as the Japs came up the path from behind.

Lorenzo went down and so did Alfredo. I pushed Ramos ahead of me into the jungle and ran behind him. We reached an open area on the edge of the thick growth. It was a long slope that ended at the river below us. Ramos continued to run. I slipped and rolled down the slope. My rifle was ripped from my hands as I rolled down the gravel slope. I flew over the bank and splashed into the water. The water was about two feet deep. I got to my feet and searched the far bank. I hit the greenery and kept on moving. I stopped and searched for Ramos. I didn't see him. Three soldiers broke out of the jungle and ran in the direction in which Ramos had disappeared. Another group of pursuers appeared. One of them spotted me and opened fire. I ducked into the jungle and ran. Now I had no weapon. The rope sling I had on the Springfield had not been strong enough. I heard them coming down the slope. I kept on running with the branches whipping across my face and arms. Out of breath I stopped to listen. There were no sounds of pursuit. I sat under the fronds of a low growing palm and rested. Still there were no sounds. I waited. My arms were bruised and my face was bleeding. I pulled up my shirt and examined my ribs. I had some bad bruises. My legs were also chopped up from the slide down the slope. I stayed quiet and waited. There was nothing. I wondered how Ramos made out. After the sun had shifted far enough to my satisfaction that maybe two hours had passed, I rose cautiously and looked around. There was nothing. We had run south away from the barrio. The river or creek or whatever it was ran east and west from what I could determine because of the sun and the mountains which had been to our west. I had to go northwest if I wanted to reach our camp. The terrain to the west and the northwest looked rugged. I had to find a route that wouldn't be impassable. I decided that going north would be best, skirting the mountains to find my way to the area around Pintombayog. Then I could make it through the canyons to camp. The jungle was thick and the rain that started made me and everything else sloppy. I broke out of the greenery onto a dirt road that ran off to the north. It was almost dark. I decided to chance the road to make time. I wondered what had happened back there. Ramos had a shoulder wound. I had seen some of the men go down. There was no sense in going back, the place was crawling with Japs. If any of them got away they would head for the camp. After trudging for a long time I saw lights ahead of me. I was hungry, starved. I couldn't make up my mind. Should I go on to camp, or should I stop and find something to eat at the settlement. I decided to stop and find some food.

At the edge of the barrio I stopped and reconnoitered. It wasn't Pitombayog, it might be Burgos. I didn't know of anyone in Burgos whom I could trust. I continued on to Bigbiga. The area looked clean. I remembered the name of the our collaborator. Julio. I approached the house cautiously. Julio was surprised to see me alone. I explained. He was distraught at the news of the Jap ambush. No one else had come through all day. I ate and left, afraid that the Japs might come in during the night. Julio didn't have any spare guns so I was still without a weapon. I continued on a few kilometers until I came to the river. I left the road and found place along the river bank where I could rest for the night. It would be easier following the river west to the camp during the day.

"KURA."

I opened my eyes and looked at the bayonet. Not again!?

The Jap smiled. He stepped back, "Get up on your feet and turn around. Move."

My mouth dropped open, "What the hell is with this Kura shit if you speak English so well?" I climbed to my feet.

"What do you expect from a Japanese soldier?" He looked up at me from his five foot maybe two.

"Where you from?"

"L.A."

"Shit. What the hell are you doing in the Jap Army?"

"Japanese, not Jap. I could stick you for that."

"Don't be so damn touchy. Aren't you an American?"
I stood, arms at my side, studying this phenomenon.

"Yeah. I was born in L.A.. My parents went back to Japan in thirty-eight and I went with them."

We took measure of each other.

"Empty your pockets. Don't you have a rifle?" He looked around the area suspiciously.

I started to empty my pockets, I left the bird insignia in my pants pocket.

He looked at the pipe, tobacco and matches. "Undress and give me your clothes."

I took off my shirt and shorts. "Shoes too?" I asked as I handed the clothes over to him.

"No. That's okay." He found the insignia and growled. "You a stinkin officer?"

"No. I had that with me as a souvenir." I sure as hell didn't want to tell him that story. "What the hell? I'm only twenty-two. I sure as hell couldn't be a shithead colonel at twenty-two."

"I don't believe you. What are you doing here?"

"I was heading up to Lingayen. I have been in the mountains. I came out of Manila. Your army took it over right after Christmas."

"You lie like shit. One big lump. You are telling me that you haven't been in Bataan? That's crap!" He threw the clothes and pipe back at me and kept the insignia.

"You know I can't believe you. You're an American, not a Japanese. What the hell are you doing as a private? You shouldn't even be in the army. Anyway, you should have a job as an interpreter." I pulled up my pants and put on the shirt.

"This isn't the American army I'm in. We don't do things they way you Americans do."

"What's your name?"

"Never mind."

"How come? Afraid I might report you so that you can't go back after the war if you survive? I don't believe this. How can you be like this?"

"What makes you think I would go back after the war? After we win it won't matter."

I studied him for a long minute, "How the hell did you find me here anyway?" I looked around the river bank.

"We stopped up the road a bit. I went to the river to get some water and saw you. You were sound asleep. Why aren't you off in the jungle instead of out in the open?"

I had looked around. In the dark, I hadn't seen that I had come to a bend in the river that was just below a road. I had really screwed myself. The spot I had chosen to sleep didn't provide any concealment. I had been too tired after yesterday's disaster to take a good look around.

"So what now?"

"I take you back with me. I may even get an advance for this."

A shout from the road above in Japanese broke in on us.

The private smirked at me as he shouted an answer. Two Japs appeared on the hill above us. My captor motioned me into the water and up the bank as the two above watched us. When we reached the roadway he evidently explained the situation in Japanese. It seemed the his companions were congratulating him on his accomplishment. They marched me a few hundred yards up the dirt road to where a two trucks were parked. A Jap colonel was standing at the front of the lead truck smoking and examining a map. He looked up at me as the Jap who had captured me stood me at attention, saluted and started a long dissertation. The officer nodded and looked from my captor to me. He walked around me and examined me thoroughly. He addressed the smiling Japanese American.

"He wants to know your name, rank and serial number."

"Joseph A. Pribula. 11052612. Private first class."

My captor translated. The colonel nodded. He asked something again.

"Where have you been since the beginning of the war?" We continued the process of Japanese question, answer and translation.

"Out in the boondocks evading the Japanese Army."

"Why are you not in a prison camp?"

"I was never captured."

"Where were you when the Americans retreated to Bataan?"

"Manila."

"Why do you not have any weapon?"

"I lost it. You know I don't have to give anything but my name, rank and serial number, according to the Geneva Convention."

My captor balled a fist and slammed me in the side of the head. My head rolled and I shook my head to clear it.

"Nanda." The colonel frowned at the private. He spoke for a while and snarled in my direction. The colonel seemed to dislike the fact that he had hit me. He motioned to me and harangued the private, much to my pleasure. I waited at attention.

"You will be taken to a prisoner of war camp after we return to our base in Gerona." My captor gave me a hostile look. "Now get in the back of the truck and don't try to escape or we will be forced to shoot you." He was very unhappy with me.

Everything happened so fast after that that I couldn't believe what was happening. The trucks passed through Pitombayog and then on to Gerona. I was placed in the custody of a corporal who glared and snarled at me through the whole of the trip to Cabanatuan. It seemed as though he was pissed that he had the assignment to deliver me to the prison camp. He sat opposite me in the back of the truck with his sword drawn, the point resting on the floor, ready to take a swipe at me if I so much as sneezed. The Japs at Camp 1 sent the truck on to Camp 3. I was puzzled. It was well on into the afternoon when I was delivered to the Japanese officer at Camp Three. After I repeated the information that I had given earlier I was taken into the Camp Headquarters Office for interrogation which was cursory and straight forward. I watched as the lieutenant had one of the privates check the roster. I sweated as he searched the roster. They didn't find the name or the serial number. I hadn't ever seen the officer or the private before. I waited at attention as they discussed me and my situation. A couple of guards were called in and I was told to follow them. They escorted me to one of the buildings close by and a Jap issued me a blanket. I was led to the gate and escorted to the prison compound and turned over to one of the American officers. I didn't see Paquet or any other officer that I knew. I wondered about what was going on. I was assigned to one of the shacks at the far side of the camp.

"Where the hell did you come from? How come they bring you here?"

The barrack's leader was a sergeant that I had never seen. I decided to stay with the lie I had created earlier on. "I have been running from the Japs since Christmas. I was left behind at McKinley when they pulled out. I had to make it on my own ever since. I couldn't get into Bataan because the Japs had it sealed off. Same with Corregidor. I couldn't risk a boat because I was pretty sure they'd get me." I lied. I fabricated a wild story just to keep up the fabrication. I thought it would be safer to stick with the story because if the truth came out I figured I would be shot for escaping. I waited three days before I looked up Johnny.

Johnny stared at me with his mouth wide open. "Where the hell have you been, Cripes! We all thought you had escaped!" He jumped up and hugged me. "Man! What happened? Ed and Schwartz and all of the rest of us have been going crazy!? What barracks are you in? How long have you been back?"

I explained what had happened. It took me three days to tell the story to the guys. It had been an unbelievable couple of weeks. A lifetime!

Johnny hadn't improved any. Bakulli had never shown up with the medicine.

As the days went by I retold the story a dozen times to our group of friends.

Nothing had happened in the camp. I had not been missed and there had been no reprisal since the Japs had never discovered a prisoner missing. Now I was faced with the problem of regaining my true identity. Why I thought I had to was because I couldn't keep up the fabrication for an unknown time as a prisoner. We all agreed that it would be best if I could return to my own identity. It was the middle of September before we managed to identify a corpse as Pribula. I then returned to the old barracks with the cooperation of the leader and the men who were assigned to that barracks.

I kept sweating every time there was a roll call, or when a Jap came through checking the men. I hoped and prayed that something would happen to change the situation.

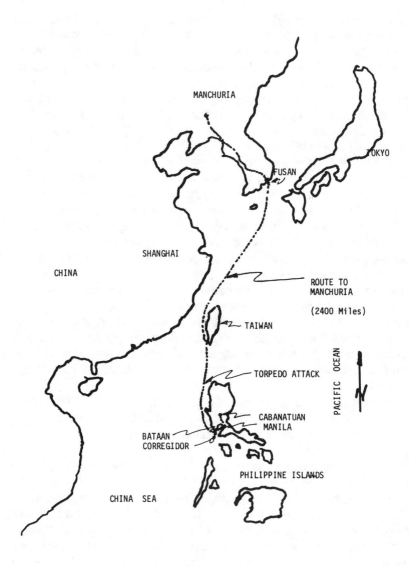

Route of the Totori (Hokka) Maru, October/November 1942

Chapter 11 -- HOKKA (TOTORI) MARU

On the third of October, a group of us were ordered out and issued a blanket each. A total of twelve hundred of us had been selected. After the blanket issue we were returned to our barracks.

There were all sorts of rumors and stories as to the destination and the mode of travel.

Johnny had not been one of those selected in the original group. Neither were Ted or Searcy. Don Miller and I were in the select group as we were termed. No one knew how many would go or why they were selected.

Ted, Searcy and I made a bet. A quart of King's Ransom. I bet that the group would not go to Japan. Ted and Searcy were hard over that we would end up in Japan. We waited for the rest of the day as the tension built up. Everyone was anxious for a change. The lack of news and the monotony of our life was making us all miserable. We couldn't understand the reason for the wait. We were finally called out at midnight. We started to march almost immediately after we were assembled. Word was soon spread that we were going to march to Cabanatuan. We did not look forward to the long hike in the middle of the night. The road was dark. Men stumbled constantly, but the Japanese guards seemed to be unconcerned. We were neither prodded nor abused as we marched. We wondered about this treatment and pondered it as we hiked to our unknown destination. It took us all night to complete the trip since there was no pushing, no pressure to move on fast. We were loaded into freight cars. There was no cramming of the men. There was plenty of room to sit, not like the trip that brought us to Cabanatuan in the first place. We were unloaded in the dark at the railroad yard in Manila and marched to Pier 7 in the port district.

It seemed as though our luck had changed. There had been no incident, or any mistreatment on the trip.

At Pier 7, or rather the remains of the pier, the Japs had pots of cooked rice which were distributed in limited quantity. The rice issue took precedence over any other consideration.

Food! It was always it the forefront of our thoughts.

After the meager meal we were told to find a place to sleep until daylight. We were told that there would be more men joining us in the morning, then we would all be put aboard a ship.

We soon found out that there would be no ship until the next day.

We were joined by another thousand men from Camp Three in the morning. Among them was Johnny. He had had a rough time on the march and was knocked out. I took care of his food and found him a place to rest.

"Why did you come? You knew it was going to be a rough march."

"I couldn't stay behind. Who knows where we are going? We should be better off no matter where we go. That hellhole back there is about as bad as it can get. Besides, I didn't want to stay there alone."

"We are supposed to board ship tomorrow. No one knows where we are going."

"Well at least we will see something different." Johnny seemed heartened by the prospect of the voyage, no matter where it would take us. He was very happy to have left the camp and the "existence" we had had at Cabanatuan.

I left him resting and decided to scrounge around the bombed out rubble of the building. I found an office and some sheets of paper. The papers were registration forms that carried the First Deputy Commissioner's name, Enrico Fabre. I cut the paper into small sheets and made a small notebook. Up until now we had not had any access to any paper. All of my notes had been made in the margin, next to the binding, of the small bible I had found on Corregidor on the sixth of May. I wanted to keep notes, a diary of what was happening to us.

We were marched aboard the Totori (Hokka) Maru, a freighter that was out of Dairen. Two thousand men were crammed into the aft hold. The rest stayed on the deck. The holds were jammed. There was only room enough for the men to lay next to each other. When one man moved or turned over, he had to push apart the men on either side of him. There was no light except that which came in from the open hatch above. Johnny and I managed to find space in the center, directly below the open hatch on the bottom deck. There was a little more light and air at our spot. The areas near the ship's steel sides were hot, humid and stuffy. The air was stale since there was no forced ventilation. In no time at all the hole was filled with the stink of sweating men. Soon everyone was coughing and complaining about the stink.

We stayed in port all day and through the night. No one knew why we were waiting.

It became a hell hole. We couldn't get to the deck to void. The stench of urine and shit filled the ship.

Near dawn Japanese soldiers were loaded. They were quartered in the upper center section of the vessel. They completed their boarding by six thirty. Minutes later the ship's engines started. Somebody yelled, "Seven o'clock and all's well." There were cat calls and boos. Suddenly we felt the motion of the ship as it pulled away from the dock. We were finally under way. It was only a matter of hours before we were out of the bay and into the China Sea. Word spread that the ship had turned and headed north.

The stinkhole got worse as time went on. There still was no plan for the men to relieve themselves and there were no facilities in the cargo holds. Some started to urinate in the far corners of the holds because no one could stay there in the unventilated sections. Others relieved themselves by defecating in the center open area. There soon developed a zonal positioning of the men. The center was a morass of feces, and the regions next to the steel hull and the corners were awash with pools of urine. The area in between was occupied by the prisoners. The men in the hold immediately under the top deck and above us used the lower deck for their latrine. Johnny and I had moved away from the horrible mess in the center of the hold.

We had not been issued any food since we had been loaded on board. The water problem was worse because there wasn't any. The hold was steaming hot with the tropical sun beating on the hull of the ship.

The men's voices rose from all over. "How about water?

"How about food?"

"Water!"

"How about a shithouse? We are suffocating down here."

It wasn't long before the Jap soldiers in the forward hold started to complain to their officers about the stench that was now spreading through the whole ship.

The two hundred or so men on the top deck were lucky. They had fresh air and they were relieving themselves over the side of the ship.

"Johnny!" I shook him. "Johnny. Wake up!"

"I guess I dozed off. I'm so damned tired. I'm having a hard time breathing." His voice was weak.

"Look." I moved closer to him so that only he could hear me. "I think we should make our way up on deck. There's air and sunlight up there."

From somewhere some one shouted, "Hey! This guy is dead! Get him out of here!"

That triggered riotous shouting about the filth and lack of water and food. We had been under way only a day and all hell was starting to break loose.

I wondered at the way that the Japs planned things. They had screwed up the handling of the men on Bataan. They hadn't done any better on Corregidor. The transport of the men to Cabanatuan had been a horrible affair. Now we were in another horrid situation. It was no wonder that the Japs had not succeeded in taking the Philippines in less time. The poor bastards couldn't plan properly. I thought that it was something that they lacked as a people. They still had a barbaric mentality that couldn't deal proper planning and management. They could only work in groups and not as an independent individual.

"Come on Johnny," I prompted, "we're going to get up on deck. The hell with staying down here in this cesspool." I helped him to his feet. We pushed and shoved our way over to the ladder.

"Give me a hand up there." I yelled to the men on the deck above.

"Stay the hell down there, there isn't any more room up here."

"You guys can't come up. No room."

"Goddamn! Give me a hand. He's sick and he needs air." I shouted back. I wasn't going to let them keep us down below deck no matter what.

Someone gave Johnny a hand and helped him up the ladder. I followed as he made his way to the next deck and then up to the top deck. We pushed our way to the port side, stepping over and on the men on the deck. We rested a minute as I held him up and breathed the beautifully fresh air.

"Better now?" I asked.

"Okay." he smiled, then laughed. "Okay. This sure is different. I didn't think we could make it."

We pushed our way to the rail. He slid down to the deck propping his back against the metal side rail. The men grumbled as they made room for us.

"What is the matter with you?" Johnny looked puzzled. "You look like you're burning up." He reached out and placed his hand on my forehead. The sweat was pouring off of me.

"It started below decks. That was why I figured we had better move out of there. I thought I wasn't going to last the night." I felt hot, but the air made me feel a lot better.

We rested a while and recovered a bit of strength from the clean sea air. Talk was at a premium. Everyone was hungry and exhausted, much too concerned with the new problems to talk. It was late afternoon when some men were put to work building a latrine of sorts. A wood deck was built hanging over the starboard side of the ship, on the aft section. The wood deck had holes cut in it. The idea was to climb out on the deck, squat over the hole and let go. Hoses with salt water were laid so that the deck and the side of the ship could be washed down. It didn't take too long to finish the makeshift latrine which started to immediately do a standing room only business.

Near sunset a food ration was passed out to each man. This

consisted of a small cloth bag that contained a hardtack biscuit that reminded me of oysterettes. There were also some small colored candies that really were tiny sugar balls. This we were told were the Jap soldier's emergency ration. Fresh water, one canteen cup per man was also distributed.

The American officers had a meeting with the Japs that were in charge of the prisoner contingent. The officers pointed out to the Japs that if the men weren't fed and issued water rations they would become ill and the death rate would be enormous. The Japs agreed to set up a kitchen to cook rice and issue water. When the word was spread it eased the situation somewhat. The men calmed down.

The hot deck cooled off rapidly after the sun went down and the blankets we had proved to be very necessary. We slept on the deck where we had settled. The steel was hard, but it was much more desirable than the stinking hold.

The officers had laid claim to a portion of the deck near the fan tail, allowing themselves more than enough room for each of them to stretch out. They also had their belongings. It was evident that they were much better off than the enlisted men. They had brought food and they even had dog robbers serving them.

The men in the hold were having problems. The heat from the men and the stink from the urine, feces and puke, made the Black Hole of Calcutta a Paradise compared to the hold we had now on board the Tottori (Hokka) Maru. There was a constant bellowing from below. Shouting, moaning seemed never ending. Fighting broke out around the middle of the night and the Japs threatened to open fire at the men below if it didn't stop. The fighting died down as the threat was circulated.

A story was passed around that a Marine by the name of Dougherty, an old guy by comparison to the rest of us, near forty, tried to commit suicide by cutting his wrists. All he did was bleed a lot. He didn't die. He would have been the twenty-fourth dead man if he had succeeded. Men were dieing off fast. Most them were men in the hold. All were being buried at sea.

I slept in fits and starts. I felt hot and cold. I thought that what had brought on the fever and the chills was another attack of Malaria. I didn't think I had Dengue again. From what I had been told Dengue was caused by reinfection, Malaria could come back at any time. The night dragged on for me. The water rushing against the sides of the ship and the steady throbbing of the engines were the only meaningful sounds after the racket from below stopped. I was awake before sunrise. The sunrise looked beautiful after the time spent down in the hold.

We had to go to the latrine in relays to protect our territory. Everyone on the upper deck had established territorial rights to a portion of it. When Johnny returned he seemed refreshed.

"It feels good to wash even if it is salt water." The water came from the hoses that ran along one side of the ship, in the scupper. The hoses were provided to aid in sanitation. The hoses were used to wash after using the latrine as well as to wash down the latrine board and the side of the ship.

A man approached us and asked, "Do you want to swap places for a while? My buddy and I are over there on the hatch." He pointed to the center hatch. "We sit here for a while, then we come back. Okay?"

"Sure." Johnny answered. We changed places like a relay team, one man remaining at a spot until replaced by the other.

"How about pancakes and some hot coffee?" I asked jokingly.

Johnny smirked in answer.

"You nuts? Wise guy, huh?" The man on my right looked at me. His sense of humor had been shot away somewhere in the war, or lost in the prison camp. "You're cracking up fast mac. Real bad." He turned away to talk the skinny man next to him.

"Have some." I offered Johnny some of the hardtack.

"Yeah." Johnny picked up the mood, "Pour some syrup on please." He took some of the sugar balls and chewed and then took a swig of water from his canteen to wash it all down.

"You know," I talked while I was chewing the hard biscuit, "you know I haven't heard anyone talk about women or sex in the camp. The guerrillas have women around, maybe that is why they talk about it and have it with the women.

"Didn't you get any when you were with them? I never understood that part of it." He frowned at me.

"No I didn't. I didn't trust the women. What the hell kind of a fix would I be in if I came down with the clap, or worse? I heard that some of the men in camp died of syphilis." I remembered my conversation with Ramos, "I guess it is because we are so damned hungry and fighting for food. I wonder if that happens to all of the people when they are starving? Not thinking about sex, I mean."

"Yeah---" Johnny paused, "I don't know. I used to think it was something I couldn't so without for very long." He chewed some more hardtack and washed it down. "I haven't thought about women in months. Know what I dream about?"

"Yeah! Like I told Ramos once. Food! Meat, butter bread eggs and milk---"

"And how! Me too!" Johnny interrupted me. "Me too."

"TORPEDOES!! TORPEDOES!!" The shout caused panic. Everyone jumped to their feet. No one could tell where the torpedoes were coming from.

I looked around the deck wildly. There were no life jackets!

"Over there! Over there!"

"Starboard! Torpedoes!"

I looked out to the starboard, to the east. There was no sign of a periscope. There were two frothy trails just under the surface of the almost calm sea. There was nothing else in sight. Not a sign of a another ship anywhere. The torpedoes were still some distance out from the ship, but coming fast! The hatch we stood on was about two feet above the main deck. This permitted us to watch the trails as they closed in, closer and closer to the ship.

The torpedoes were about a hundred yards apart and two hundred or more yards from the side.

I was scared. I knew what a torpedo could do! I had seen the PT boats attack the Japs.

Men on the starboard side of the ship started a mad scramble for the port side, the side away from the torpedoes, jumping, pushing and shoving each other to reach the safer side of the vessel. Men in the hold had heard the screams above and clawed and fought for the ladders. It was every man for himself.

I grabbed Johnny's arm and pulled him to port. I yelled, "The rail! Let's get to the rail!

There was a sudden clanging of a bell from somewhere forward. The ship's horn blasted away with an ear piercing shriek.

I heard the Jap soldiers from the center hold shouting as they fought to get above deck.

The ship started a hard turn to port. It heeled, the deck tilted. It seemed that the ship turned almost immediately.

Johnny and I moved with the panicked mob and struggled to reach the rail before the torpedoes hit.

The ship's horn shrilled and blasted us with sound repeatedly.

The Japs on the superstructure raced for the port side just as madly as we did.

It seemed that everything was registering as though it were in slow motion. The torpedoes sped toward the ship. The ship turned. The men clawed and fought to escape the impending blast. I expected to have the deck blasted out from under me at any instant. I somehow took time to wonder why no one jumped overboard! The same slow motion permitted seeing the unbelievable escape.

"Thank God!" I mouthed

The ship heeled and turned just enough for the torpedoes to miss us, one in front and the other in behind. They continued on past us as the ship wallowed in the water.

I was watching the wake of the two terrible weapons as they suddenly disappeared. One instant they were there, the next instant their wake was gone. They had disappeared only about a hundred yards from the ship.

A whooping and a hollering went up from the men. The hold below was roaring. Japs and Americans cheered and shouted. Whoever had been at the wheel, Jap or not, had been guided by the hand of God. I thought about it. Believe in Fate if you wish, but somebody up there sure had something to do with it.

The ship was brought around, straightened on course, turned about ninety degrees to the starboard and put under full steam. We were heading north again.

We kept watching the sea to the east nervously for more torpedoes. There were none. There was no sign of a periscope or of the sub that had fired at us.

"Those bastards must have fired at extreme range or they wouldn't have sunk so close. They just ran out of steam."

It took some time to settle back down. Men in the hold had been injured. Doctor Kaufman, Captain, U.S. Army, went down to help.

There was a lot of fighting about the spaces lost on deck. It took quite a while for the problems of territory to be resolved.

Some of the men said a prayer of thanks as I did.

Maybe the sub commander couldn't mark up the ship as a sinking, but I thought he would be just as happy as we were if he knew what his failure meant to us. Our lives, such as they were. I think that he would have thanked God that he had missed if he only knew.

"What time was it when the torps came?" I asked around.

"Time! He wants to know what the hell time it was yet!" The man that said it made a circular motion with his right forefinger close to his temple.

"It was eight twenty."

"Eight fifteen!"

"Eight thirty! It was eight thirty!?" another insisted.

"Okay okay! I just want to write it down in my book. If I ever find any guy that was on that sub I'll buy him a drink." I responded. "Even twenty years from now." I wrote the time in my book. "10/9/42-torpedo attack at about 8:15-8:30 China Sea, North of Philippines."

Two days later we anchored off of Taiwan. It was Saturday, the eleventh of October. We remained at anchor and waited for we didn't know what. Again, we didn't know what tomorrow would bring.

I had managed to visit the Japanese soldiers in the center hold frequently. There I put the Japanese that I was learning to use while I was in the process of learning more. Some of the soldiers were getting a charge out of teaching an American POW to read and speak their language. Learning the language could give us a big advantage. I could find out what was going on. Maybe I could do other things also. What other things? I didn't know, but I wanted to learn and be prepared.

We were having a bull session and bumming cigarettes from the Japs in the center hold when a shot rang out. It echoed hollowly within the metal shell. Japs and Americans sprang to their feet in shocked surprise.

"Where did it come from?" Someone asked what seemed to be a foolish question.

"It is in the prisoner section!" answered one of the Japanese soldiers.

"What prisoner section?" I asked.

"We have prisoners. The Japanese prisoners are being returned to Japan," answered Suzuki, one of the Jap soldiers with whom we had been talking.

"You're kidding! We thought that you shot all soldiers that disobeyed," I threw at Suzuki.

"No. We do not shoot all of them."

Word came to the soldiers in minutes. A prisoner had wrested a guard's pistol from him and had used it to shoot himself. Evidently, the prisoner, to save face, Oriental face, found it much more honorable to commit suicide rather than face prison and disgrace. He had succeeded, he was dead. There were no words of condolences or consolation. Everyone returned to the activity that had preceded the interruption to the day's course of events.

The ship pulled up anchor and entered a bay in Taiwan, the port of Tiekow. The harbor was a well protected one. Entry to the harbor was gained through a very narrow channel bordered by high cliffs. We anchored in the bay and waited for three days.

Johnny hadn't improved at all during the time we had been on board. His trips to the latrine were innumerable. He didn't have any appetite. I argued with him constantly about his not eating. I tried to convince him that he had to eat to survive.

The kitchen that had been set up had been providing us with a watery soup. It was in the least hot if not appetizing. I appreciated the hot food for some reason. It seemed that the heated liquid was more palatable even if not very nutritious. I thought that in a way it was no better than the slops that we had fed the pigs on the farm in Jersey. It was just something to fill the belly.

Don Miller asked me how Johnny was doing day after day. The answer was that he was going from bad to worse. He needs medicine, I don't know what kind, but he sure needs something." I was so helpless that it was frustrating and maddening. "Do you have any sulfa left?"

"Yes," Don hesitated, "I have a few." He was reluctant and seemed embarrassed to discuss the medicine situation. This was quite common and understood by all of us. Medicine was a personal thing, like life itself, your life. If you were sick, and you were lucky enough to have medicine, you might live. If you didn't have any, your chances of pulling through were pretty slim. Piss poor.

"I'll buy whatever you have if you will sell it to me." I begged. Or, I'll trade you anything I own. I have a good pipe here." I pulled out the Yellow Bowl. "Or I will swap you my food ration."

"No." Don refused, "I don't want anything. I'll give them to you," he offered. "You do me a favor sometime." He dug into the watch pocket of his ragged khaki shorts and pulled out a small box that looked like an aspirin box. It had a dispenser opening. He pushed out two tablets into the palm of my hand.

"Thanks Don." I was so grateful that I choked up. I was even afraid that the tears were going to show. It was hard to keep control. "Thanks a lot." I looked at the pills and left.

"Something for you Johnny. Sulfa! Two tablets." I held them out to him. He smiled weakly. I never saw a skeleton smile before, but his one smiled. "Don Miller. And for nothing too!" I was exuberant. He took the pills with some water. They stayed down.

It was sometime later that I saw the Jap interpreter walking around our part of the deck. Suddenly an idea was born. It hit me! If the officers couldn't do anything, maybe I could.

"I'll be back." I smiled at him and took off after the interpreter. I knew him to be Major Kito. He looked more like a Chinaman than a Jap to me. I was about to do something that could cause me a lot of grief. By the time I caught up with him he was talking with Major Hankins and Captain Kaufman on the starboard deck just aft of the superstructure.

"Major. Captain. Major Kito. I'm Petak." I stepped in when the conversation had evidently concluded. They looked at my skinny frame as though they thought "So what?" That didn't stop me. "That man over there, Corporal John Urban, is very sick. He needs medicine. Isn't there anything that you can get for him?" I was in dead earnest and I had a firm determination to be heard. "Major, he is nothing but skin and bone. Isn't there anything that you can get for him?" I pleaded. I was addressing the Jap officer and not the Americans. Hell, our officers were little better off than the enlisted men. I knew that they couldn't do anything, but I knew the Jap could if I could convince him.

The men around us stared at me as though I had flipped my cookie. No one ever addressed a Jap the way I had. I knew that they expected me to get knocked on my ass.

"What is wrong with him?" Major Kito asked politely as he looked at Johnny.

"Dysentery and Malaria," answered Captain Kaufman to my surprise.

"We haven't anything for him and there isn't anything we can do." Major Hankins added.

I was grateful to them for the help. I hadn't expected any support from the officers, particularly since I was doing this all on my own.

Johnny Urban was only one man, and the only one that was looking after him was me. Yeah, he was my cousin, so what? The help I was receiving, even though only words were more than I had expected.

"Let us take a look at him." The Japanese motioned for us to follow him. We walked to the stairs where Johnny was stretched out near the latrine.

Kito looked at him for a long time. He made wry face and shook his head as though in disbelief.

"He is in really bad shape. Very bad. He has been this was ever since June." I offered.

"Yes, he is very sick." The Japanese officer spoke in very precise, clipped English. He turned and looked at me. "I will see if we can do something for your friend." He bobbed his head and walked off leaving us standing beside Johnny.

"You sure as hell have one hell of a lot of nerve! If I hadn't been here and seen it for myself I wouldn't believe it. The Jap was more considerate than I expected," Hankins frowned at me.

"I am not sure that anything will be done." Kaufman offered disdainfully. "How is your fever?"

"Comes and goes. Mixed with chills." I answered. "I sure hope he will do something for Johnny." I looked in the direction in which the Major had disappeared.

"Let us hope so." Kaufman said rather hopelessly.

I watched them as they retreated to officer territory.

"What the hell was that all about?" One of the bystanders asked. I told them what I had done. A few shook their heads in disbelief. "Nervy bastard, ain't you?" commented another.

The next morning Don came by and gave me three more pills for Johnny. I hadn't asked for them. I didn't know what I could do to repay him for his generous offer. I did say a prayer for him.

The ship remained at anchor in the bay and the rumors started all over again. The latest one was that we were waiting for a convoy from the South Pacific that was heading for Japan. We were to join the convoy for protection.

The next day Kito arrived with two men in white hospital orderly uniforms. We were told that they were going to take Johnny to the military hospital on the island. I couldn't believe it! It was something that was totally unexpected. I had thought that Kito might have some medicine brought aboard, but to have him taken to a hospital was amazing. A stretcher was brought aboard and we were told to load Johnny on it.

"We will take your friend." Kito had a big smile on his face. The POWs on the deck crowded around to watch the unprecedented event. They craned and gawked at the orderlies. "Do you want to go along with him?" asked Major Kito. "We will bring you back after we take him to the hospital. There are three other men who are going also. Two of them are also very ill."

"Sure. You bet. Gee, thanks. Thanks very much." I couldn't believe this either.

Hankins and Kaufman pushed their way through the crowd. "Where is he going?" asked the major, "Are these hospital orderlies?"

"Yes they are." answered Kito. "We are taking this man to the hospital. His friend will help." He made the statement sound as though it were an order.

"I'll be damned!" I heard someone say.

"A kind Jap! Oh boy!"

"What's going on Joe? Where are they taking me. I'm not dead yet." Johnny looked apprehensive.

"We are going to take you to a military hospital ." I told him. "You'll be okay. You'll see. It's like I told you. I talked to Major Kito the other day."

"Really!?" He couldn't believe it any more than I did.

I picked up Johnny's belongings and followed as the orderlies moved off to the hanging stairway on the starboard side of the ship. The two small orderlies carrying the stretcher were having a tough time. I took one end of the stretcher and another big American offered to take the other end. Kito looked on in approval, a thin smile on his narrow face. We carried Johnny down into the small boat that was standing by without too much trouble. I could see that the shifting and jarring was causing Johnny a lot of pain. Three other POWs joined us in the boat. I looked at them but said nothing. The water of the bay was calm and the trip to the dock was short. We picked up the stretcher and carried a short distance down the dock to an ambulance that was waiting for us.

The dock workers watched the procedure with intense curiosity. We climbed into the back while the Japs climbed into the front.

I examined the three other POWs. I didn't recall ever having seen any of them before. "I'm Joe Petak. That is my cousin on the stretcher. His name is Johnny Urban."

The others introduced themselves as Sol Fromer, Sigh and Jim. The last names weren't important to the two others. I guessed that was why they didn't give them.

"Man, you are one lucky guy Johnny," Jim, the man who had helped me carry Johnny on the stretcher started, "if you get more treatment like this you're bound to pull through." He nodded in approval.

Johnny smiled grimly, the ambulance ride wasn't a limo ride. The jarring was causing him a great deal of pain.

"Thanks fellows, thanks for helping."

"Nothing. Nothing at all. Glad I could help," he responded.

"I didn't think that they would do anything, I really didn't." Johnny's voice was evidence of his disbelief.

"Thank God they did Johnny. Just say a prayer of thanks." I meant every word of what I said.

Sol (Abe) Fromer sat through the ride without saying a single word. He had a bad eye. I wanted to ask him what was wrong with it but figured that the guy was having enough problems without talking about it. Sigh just seemed to be worn out. He wasn't a young man like the rest of us.

"Looks like we're here." Jim observed as we turned into a driveway that led to a series of one story buildings. We pulled up near one of them and then backed up to the entrance of one of them. The Jap hopped out from the front and opened up the back door. Jim and I carried Johnny to the entrance of the building and into a clean septic smelling room. Sigh and Sol were led away to the interior. Nurses popped in, all in white, short, stocky and definitely not Japanese. A small Oriental, not Japanese came in.

"Take those filthy rags off of him," he directed us in English.

Jim and I removed the bloody shorts and the shirt.

"Lift him onto the bed. The nurses will clean him." He issued orders to the nurses in what sounded like a Chinese dialect.

Jim and I wrapped the shirt and the shorts in the blanket on which Johnny had been laying. A nurse took the bundle from me and walked out with it.

"That will be burned." The oriental said softly. "I am a doctor. I am not Japanese, I am a Korean." He said it as though proud, and also as if he wanted us to know it. "The nurses are also Korean." He answered my unasked question.

"What is his name? What do you think is wrong with him? He is an American? Yes?" He asked the questions in quick succession.

"Corporal John S. Urban. The doctor on board the ship diagnosed him as having malaria and dysentery. And yes, he is an American as we are. We are from the Philippines."

While we spoke two nurses started to sponge and clean Johnny from head to toe. Another nurse had started an intravenous injection. Johnny flinched as she inserted the needle.

"Ah," said the Korean doctor, "we will take good care of him. You say your goodbye now." He started his examination of Johnny. "He is my first American patient. I will take good care of him." He smiled almost benevolently.

"So long Johnny. Get well. I'll see you sometime soon. God bless and goodbye." Tears came to my eyes as I headed out the door to the ambulance. The last I saw of Johnny was through the window, there were four very busy people around him. Jim joined me in our silent walk to the vehicle.

"Friend of yours?" he asked me as we rode back to the dock.

"My cousin."

"Tough. Pretty sick guy." He looked at me sympathetically. "At least he is in the hospital. I never saw anyone go to work so fast. All nice and clean. And man, that bed. I think I could be sick just to be able to lay in a bed like that. Remember what it is to sleep in a bed? With sheets yet!" He shook his head in wonderment. He kept on talking all the way back to the harbor.

After we were back on board the ship I shook hands with Jim and thanked him for his help. "Thanks Jim. It was great of you to help. Thanks again."

"Nothing. Glad I am still strong enough to help somebody yet." He took off in the direction of his squat and I got back to where Johnny and I had been staying.

Chapter 12 -- HOKKA (TOTORI) MARU 2

We remained in the bay, at anchor, for another couple of days. It was early one morning when the anchor was hoisted and the ship, smokestack belching, passed through the channel and made its way to the open sea. We headed north under moderate steam. There wasn't another ship in sight. So much for all of the rumors that we were to join a convoy that was waiting for us off of Taiwan. We were under way for only half a day when the course was changed. We turned and headed due south. There was a general consensus that the Japs were confused. All of us on board had a sense of unease, of pending doom. This included the Jap soldiers that were on board. Sometime during the night the ship turned east. I watched as we changed our heading as the stars swung around. The ship's speed was cut back drastically. I dozed off near dawn and woke to find that we were back in the bay. I had slept so hard that I hadn't even heard the anchor go down. Word spread soon, evidently from the Jap crew, that there were American submarines patrolling the seas around Taiwan. Another rumor was that the convoy from the south had been torpedoed.

We had now been in and out of the harbor three times.

We were given orders to pack up our stuff and be ready to disembark. After we pulled up anchor the ship was docked at a pier that was enclosed with barbed wire and patrolled by soldiers. The Japs disembarked first and marched off. We never saw them again. There were a group of non-coms that were led to a separate area on the dock. It took a long time for us to vacate the ship.

A crew of laborers, Koreans, cleaned the holds and the decks. The whole ship was scrubbed down and fumigated. They made comments about a benjo ship. A shithole ship. They couldn't understand how men could be kept in such dirty, unsanitary conditions.

We were provided with soap and told to wash and scrub everything. It was a blessing since we had lice of sizes, kinds and shapes. I didn't have any head lice because I had shaved my head to get rid of them. Everybody had body lice. They had been impossible to get rid of because they were in the clothes and the bedding, and the blankets as well. Crabs were another problem that we didn't have any way of treating. We scrubbed everything we owned. I kept a couple of bars of soap for future use.

We were loaded on board again along with the Jap soldiers, mostly non-coms, that were to accompany us as guards. The Japs had learned that we had a plan to mutiny, take over the ship, and head east to escape. The guards were all armed and more alert than ever before.

There was a little more room and we now had a lot cleaner ship. All of us were now below decks. I was told by one of the Jap non-coms, one Yukinoro Suzuki, that we were going to a very cold country to work in the factories. It was assumed that we were going to Manchuria.

I studied the language with Suzuki's help. I also managed to be assigned to the chow detail. Among my chores were trips to the forward cargo hold where rice and other food had been loaded. Among the cargo were hundreds of wicker-like crates of onions that reminded me of the Bermuda onion. I managed to open one of the crates on one of my trips and stashed a half dozen onions in my shirt. When I returned to the hold I hid them in the musette bag that I had borrowed. At supper time I broke out one of the onions. After peeling and cutting it I bit into it with relish. It tasted better than an apple. The odor spread throughout the hold.

"HEY! Where the hell did you steal that? It's an onion, isn't it? An honest to goodness onion." The guy next to me was having conniptions.

"Shush. You'll have the whole stinkin hold over here." I tried to quiet him down. "You'll have the crazy Japs on us."

"How about some. Come on. Just a little tiny slice," he pleaded.

I gave him a slice, and then another to another POW and then another until the whole onion was gone.

"I'll give you a cigarette for a slice," offered a man from across the hold. I hesitated. "Two slices," he upped the offer.

"Okay. Two will do." I traded the second onion off in slices for cigarettes.

"Where the hell did you steal the those beautiful things?" asked one POW after another as they traded for generous slices of my booty. I also had forty cigarettes. I was left with only one onion of the six I had started with. I peeled it and bit into it as though it was an apple. It was delicious.

"Here, have some salt." The POW that I had given the first slice of onion to offered with a smile.

"Thanks." I sprinkled some of the coarse salt on the onion and bit into it again. If the grains had been any bigger it would have been rock salt. I finished off the onion in between mouthfuls of the soup that we had been served.

"You going to get any more onions?" asked the salt giver.

"Maybe. I hope so." I answered, "That is if some loud mouth doesn't leak word to the Japs and I get clobbered."

"Jap stuff huh?" he asked. "You stole it from the Japs! Holy hell! Sure.

Where the hell else would it come from. Hah hah hah." He laughed in appreciation of my accomplishment.

A couple of days later I managed to steal another half dozen onions. I approached Don just before the evening meal.

"How about having an onion with your soup walyo?" I thought I remembered that Italians liked onions as well as garlic.

"Huh? An onion? You're kidding." He waved me away, "You're nuts."

I held out a big onion to him, sheltered from view of the others around. His eyes popped and his mouth dropped open.

"Sabis." I said as I handed it to him.

We had all started to pick up and use Japanese words that lent some emphasis to our actions and conversation. Sabis in Japanese means present.

"Holy cow. A real onion! A real onion!" he repeated. He looked at me in disbelief and grabbed for the onion. He shoved it out of sight under his mess kit. Then, after looking around he placed it under his nose and inhaled. "It even smells like a real onion!" There was a tone of amazement in his voice.

"Shhh! Not so loud. They'll hear you. Don't spread it around. I'll bring you some more when I can."

"How come?" he frowned as he looked at me.

"Favor you did me Remember?"

"Aw go on. You mean the sulfa for Johnny?" He asked. He was awed that anyone would remember a favor in our predicament.

"Yep. Thanks."

"How about that? How about that now?" He held the onion and just looked at it. He looked up, "I wonder how he is doing now?" His concern was genuine.

"He's dead." I let it drop coldly. I didn't want the emotion to show. Especially since tears welled up whenever the subject came up. "Johnny died in the hospital on the sixteenth or the seventeenth. Sol told me after the brought him back to the ship when we were in Tiekow." I took a deep breath. "I asked Kito to check if it were true. He checked. He also said that he was given a military funeral. I'll see you later."

The onions were a gold mine. I traded them for cigarettes and other food. I also bought the borrowed musette bag for two onions. Now it was mine. I found a piece of canvas and borrowed a needle and some thread, paying for its use with some onion, and sewed a false bottom into the inside. I hid the newspaper and the notes in the secret pocket.

The language lessons continued with Suzuki and his cohorts. We held bull sessions with them in the evenings as the ship continued on its way north. The sessions helped us to understand just what kind of people we were dealing with, and how to deal with them. When we were swapping stories in the Jap quarters the Japs were always asking questions. The typical questions they asked were: "Are you married? Do you have a sweetheart? Do you have children? Do you have any pictures?" Pictures were a prized possession of the Japanese. They were always ready to pull out pictures of their family, wife and home. Few of us had anything left. Pictures were a rarity. Our method of communication was to tell a story to one or two of the Japs that understood English. They in turn would translate it for the others. On the other hand a Jap would tell his story to the translators who would in turn repeat them to us. I practiced as much as I could. One of the other POWs, Jim Hinds, Heinzey was also an active participant.

"Immersion. Language immersion is the way to learn to speak Japanese." Heinzey repeated many times.

On one occasion the subject of food came up. We were asked about our food rations on Bataan and Corregidor.

"We were always starving," I started. "I ate monkey, snake and iguana. See these spots on my hand?" I held up my right hand for all to examine, indicating some white spots that had been tender for months. "Well," the translation went on, "in April, just before the fall of Bataan, I had been on an assignment in Bataan. I had been all the way from Limay to Bagac and around again. The food situation was so bad in the places that I had been that there wasn't even any iguana left." The Japanese were surprised to hear that Americans would ever eat the big lizard. In fact, they didn't even know that the iguana was edible. That statement surprised me because I had heard that they had been taught to live off of the land. I explained that the meat of the lizard was very much like chicken, white and tasty, but a bit oily. I had been on assignment for about a week. I had finished all the film that I had with me. I had to return to Corregidor to have the film processed and to pick up some more film. I took the midnight packet put of out of Cabcabin. I arrived at Middleside barracks, where we had set up our darkroom, at about one thirty in the morning. the only soldiers that were living in the barracks were the kitchen detail and the Photo Lab men. The rest of the huge buildings on Middleside were empty."

Whenever we talked about Corregidor the Japanese always had a thousand questions. They wanted to know what had happened during the bombings and the shelling. They had a strange fascination, an obsession, about Corregidor. So, when relating a story, the general trend of the story was there but it went slowly because of the many interruptions. This particular session was peculiar because the only questions that were being asked were those pertinent to the story.

"The Coast Artillery kitchen was right next to the Photo Lab. I stopped at the kitchen before going on to the lab. The mess sergeant was the typical fat cook." I made motions to help the description of the sergeant. There was unanimous agreement by both the Americans and the Japanese that all mess personnel were fat from the food that they stole from the other men's rations. There was much genuine laughter which led to a greater than usual interest in my story.

"I asked him for something to eat. He told me I would have to wait until breakfast the next morning. I explained that I had just come from Bataan and that I had not eaten since early morning. I pleaded and cajoled, he relented. He opened the oven door of the huge range. I saw a large pan of beef ribs that were being baked. There was gravy and potatoes and carrots. The sergeant took a a knife and sliced a very thin slab. He placed it between two slices of field bread. He held it and said that was all I was getting, no more." We became involved in describing what field bread was since their bread, or pan, was a small bun about the size of a hot cross bun. "Just as he was handing it to me the air raid siren blasted. Everybody stopped what they were doing and headed for the doors and up to the air raid shelters. The shelters at Middleside were two tunnels dug deep into the side of the hill. It was about a hundred yards from the kitchen to the shelter. All uphill."

I was asked why I didn't go with the men from the kitchen. Wasn't I afraid of the bombs?

"Mati mati. Wait and I will tell you." I made motions for them to be patient, I would explain everything. "Yes, I was afraid of the bombs. I had been in many air raids and had been injured. I had had two concussions and had a back injury that was due to a bomb." I explained. "But I was so hungry that I didn't give a shit. I was going to get something to eat."

The Japs made many remarks, "Bakaro, fool." laughing at the same time. They had known what it was to be starving they said. On the other hand, some of them thought that I was being pretty clever. As a matter of fact I remember thinking at the time that I was being very clever.

"After they had all left I grabbed a loaf of field bread and cut off a section of it and scooped out the soft inside to make a big bowl of the crust. I opened the oven and with a big ladle," I elaborate with pantomine, "and filled the hollow loaf with gravy and potatoes and carrots."

"Niku nie." Suzuki asked.

"Sure. I took a big whole rib of the beef, by the bone, and ran out of the barracks."

They made various comments. Some roared with laughter and others shook their heads as the translation was made.

"I had the hot bone in my hand." I showed them the tender spots, "But as hot as it was I wasn't going to give it up. That is how hungry I was, starved. I could hear the bombers almost overhead as I left the barracks. I knew that the bombs would be exploding within seconds but I couldn't go to the air raid shelter with the food I had stolen."

There were many questions, pats on the back and shaking of heads on the part of the Japanese. Some of the POWs had many varied comments, such as, "you slick bastard; you must have been nuts; Cripes! you stayed out during the air raid, you must have cracked up."

"So," I continued, " I ran up the side of the hill, about a hundred yards to the east of the tunnels, to a big wide staircase that led from the road to the shelter.

"Sure. They built the stairs so that the soldiers could get from the barracks to the shelter. They must have been about fifty or more foot wide." Explained one of our men.

"Yeah, I know, I was quartered there," offered another.

"I found a place under some bushes and settled down to my feast. " I smiled at the people gathered around me. "The bombs had started to fall just as I started to eat. They landed on Morrison Hill and a lot of them dropped west of Middleside. I ate the meat first, then the vegetables and some of the bread. That meat was delicious. My hand was singed, but it didn't matter. I flinched and ducked as the bombs came down. I could hear them screech as they came through the air. I ate as fast as I could, but not so fast that I would be sick. I was scared as hell, but I kept on eating." I laughed at the thought of the experience. A cold shiver hit me also as I thought of the bombs.

There were various comments. One of the Japs felt my stomach and made motions and comments about the size of the loaf of bread and the capacity of my stomach.

"Did you eat it all?" Suzuki asked.

"No," I laughed," I couldn't. There was too much. I ate until I was busting and then wrapped the rest in a pliofilm bag that I used to protect my film. I stuffed it into my musette bag along with my film and photo equipment. The fires that the bombs had started were far enough away from me that they didn't bother me. I curled up and went to sleep."

All were laughing at my story. One of the men remarked that I was just like a hog.

"I stuffed myself and went to sleep. I was wakened in the morning by the flies buzzing around my face and my clothes. They were after the meat gravy that had spilled on my clothes and smeared on my face. I finished the cold meat and the rest of the bread. I made my way down to the barracks and waited until there was no one around and made a fast dash to the Photo Lab. I picked up a clean pair of coveralls and went to the shower room. I showered and washed my gravy stained clothes."

"You were very clever. Very smart." Suzuki commented. "But you could have been killed just for a stomach full of food." He shook his head in reprimand.

"Well, I think I would have done the same thing, only I would have had my pants full, not just my stomach," drawled one of the other POWs.

There was a lot of laughter and good natured bantering.

"You sure you ain't lying? Maybe you had to wash your pants because they was dirty on the inside and not on the outside like you say."

There was a lot of ribbing after that. No one would have thought that that group was made up of enemies.

"Maybe you are stealing food even now." Suzuki remarked.

"From where?" I asked. All eyes turned to me. Many were surprised and questioning, others were not surprised at all.

"Only a few men have onions. Where do onions come from Petaku?" asked Suzuki.

"I don't know Yuki." I lied, with a blank look of innocence. "But, if I find out I will let you know. Okay?" I countered.

"Okay okay." Suzuki smiled, not believing a word. His face was broken into a huge jesting smile. He changed the subject. "Maybe someday you have family visit. After war."

"Oh!" I looked at him.

"Yes. Japan will win. We must win. We are small and China is full. No place to go. Korea. Nie. Samui des. Cold. Only place to go is United States. Big country. No place else to go. Japan is very old. More than three thousand years. We know what to do to survive. United States young. Not very smart. We will make a colony there. We have plans for the next hundred years. We will go there." He nodded his head meaningfully.

The group dispersed quietly, morosely, immediately after that.

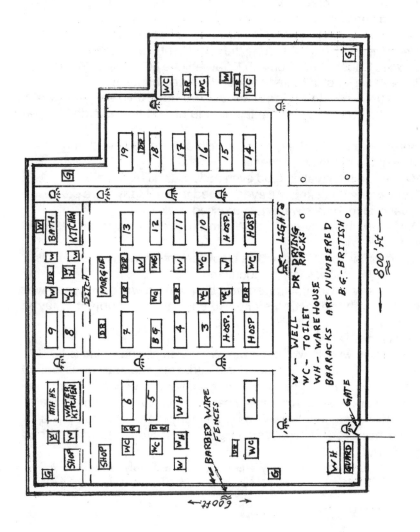

Splinter Camp, Hoten. Old Chinese Army Camp. 1942/1943.

CHAPTER 13 -- MANCHURIA

We docked at Fusan, Korea, on the ninth of November. We knew for sure that we were on our way to Manchuria, or Manchoukuo as the Japanese knew it. We also now knew that we had been selected because we had some kind of a trade that the Japanese thought could be useful in the factories they had built.

We were lined up on the dock as we disembarked and counted. There were huge piles of clothing already stacked on the dock. We were each issued a Japanese uniform without any markings or insignia. A jacket or tunic that buttoned up all the way to the throat, tight fittings pants, a light grey colored shirt, flannel-like underwear that looked like pajamas and cotton socks. This was topped off with a knit cap and a heavily padded quilted overcoat. The inside of the overcoat was a paper-like material that was sewn in between the inner and outer layers of fabric. We had to strip and put on the clothing that had been issued. The guards wandered around as we changed, searching, poking, and examining anything that caught their fancy. They were looking for contraband. Small articles such as knives, watches, rings, razors and money were secreted or passed along into safekeeping while stripping and changing.

A small skinny individual a few feet away from me was acting very nervous. He was asking for help without receiving any from the men around him. I was sitting near Don, I turned to him, "Watch my stuff." He nodded in response. I walked over to skinny guy and sat down.

"What's up?" I asked him as I watched a guard who was coming in our direction.

"How about holding this bundle until after I change?" he pleaded.

"Sure. What's wrong?" I noticed the sidelong cautious looks from the men around us.

"Got something that smells?" I joked.

"Naw," He tried to be nonchalant, "just something I been hanging on to. Honest."

"Okay, let's have it."

He handed over the bundle. When I had it firmly in my hand my eyes widened and my mouth dropped open in surprise. I snapped it shut fast.

"No! No. Don't say it!" he warned in near panic. He looked around for the nearest Jap. "Don't say the word. Cripes, if anybody hears you there'll be all hell to pay."

149

"Damn! Holy damn!" I gasped. The gun, a revolver, was wrapped in the cloth. It couldn't be mistaken for anything else.

"Quick! Gimme it!" he grabbed for the bundle and quickly sat on it after shoving it into the pile of clothes heaped on the ground. "JAP! JAP!" he warned. His head bobbed in the direction of the guard closeby.

Somehow, it seemed that the Japs sensed something out of the ordinary. They wandered around among the men without purpose or direction, never taking their eyes off of us.

"We have to hide it somewhere," he was panicky, "where the hell can we put it?" He looked around while I watched the guard that was heading in our direction. Someone close by whispered hoarsely, "Over here. There is a hole in the curb." Skinny looked around nervously. There was a hole about five inches in diameter, it looked to be a drain hole. Skinny held the bundle close to his left thigh and slid on his butt until he reached the hole. I saw him reach behind and push the bundle into the hole. The Jap stopped. He looked at me and then at Skinny. Then his attention was attracted by something that a POW near him did. Skinny slid back to his pile of clothes.

"Better start dressing," I warned him. "I'll keep an eye on it for you."

"Right."

While he changed into the new clothes I watched. The Jap came over to me and made a circle around me. He examined me suspiciously but said nothing. He stopped a few feet away and glanced around. His attention was not on anyone in particular. Then he turned toward me and examined me from head to toe. Rather than cause myself any headaches I moved back to my pile of clothes. Don nodded, no one had touched anything but only because he had been dog watching. I stripped and stood naked for a minute or so while figuring out the underwear situation. The pants were a good bit short for my height. They had a tie string to hold them in place. No belt. The air was cold and I shivered as I put them on and then slipped on the undershirt. The Jap watched me almost nonchalantly. No one was rushing us. It was about a half hour later that the order to form in fours was given. Everybody scrambled, collecting their belongings and started to line up. Skinny moved toward the hole. He was nervous and clummsy. He was hidden from the Japs by the line-up that was taking place. He reached into the hole while keeping an eye out for any Jap who might move around to the rear of the line-up. I saw him freeze and then grope frantically. He laid down on the ground and reached in with his arm. I couldn't see his face. He pulled his arm out and shucked the heavy overcoat and the tunic. He thrust his arm back into the hole. Seconds later he withdrew his arm and sat disconsolately on the ground looking at the hole. His at the hole. His face was downcast. He looked up and caught my eye. He shook his head and scowled. He stood up and picked up his coats and threw them over his shoulder. He picked up his burlap bag and came to me slowly.

"The small hole," he stopped as he searched for the words, "there is a big pipe about two feet back. I pushed the goddamn thing into it. It's gone. Maybe it's better that it's gone." He turned and walked away.

"Yeah," I said to his back. "Maybe it was better, it could have led to tragedy."

I turned and joined Don in the column. It was a sunny day, but cold. You could see the vapor of your breath. The clothing was warm. We marched to a railroad siding nearby and were loaded into passenger cars, not freight cars. Each man settled into a seat. We were amazed that we were traveling in such luxury after the month we had spent on the prison ship.

One of the guards strolled through the car soon after we started our journey to the north. "Why are we in passenger cars and not in freight cars?" I asked one in English.

He responded in English, "You are of value to the Emperor. You will be good workers in the factories." His English was pretty good.

"Where are we going?" I asked, not really expecting an answer. The men around me were quiet and expectant.

"You all go to Hoten. You will work in the factories there."

"Hoten?" I was puzzled, "I don't remember a city called Hoten in Manchuria." Having been in and around Asia before the war I had become somewhat familiar with China and some of the other countries. "Not Darien?"

"No, no, Hoten." He frowned and then stopped as though searching his memory, or maybe trying to make up his mind about continuing the conversation, "Chinese, Manchu, call it Mukdem. Japanese now. Call it Hoten." He smiled as though proud of the fact that the Japs had wrested Manchuria from the Chinese.

"Arigato." I thanked him in his own language.

The men spread the word through the train in minutes.

Sometime later food was issued. The ration consisted of a ball of cooked rice wrapped in paper. There was also a small paper funnel package that contained some kind of a sauce, not suey. Food was food, as little as there was of it, it was certainly welcome.

It was soon after we ate that an amusing incident occurred. One of the men had found the toilet. He came out bitching like hell and berating the Oriental mind and the way they designed the john.

"You know that these stupid assholes didn't even put a seat on the toilet? No kidding, you have to sit your prat on the freezing toilet. And man it is cold?"

I laughed to myself. I had seen the toilets when I had been in Shanghai and had traveled by train.

"Aw, go on!"

"Let's see."

The men crowded around the door to the toilet at the end of the car.

"Yeah! How about that?"

"Ha! Look at that. They built it without a seat! How about that?".

The compartment was fair sized. The bowl, stool, had very wide flat lips on each side. They were close to eight inches wide. The top of the stool was about fifteen inches high. There was no seat or lid. There was a bar about an inch in diameter, like a towel bar, attached to the wall about eighteen inches above the stool. Closer examination of the lips of the bowl showed that they had depressions about an inch deep and six inches wide and about twelve inches long.

A Guard came through the car and stopped at the crowd gathered around the door of the john. "Nanda. Doste. Benjo. Kura." He started to push his way through using the butt of his rifle as he moved. The men separated for him. "Nane," he asked as he looked into the little room, puzzled by the crowd.

"Benjo samui," one of the men pointed to his backside and then to the toilet. "Cold on the ass when you sit," he said.

"BAKA, baka." He laughed at the men as he looked around. He pushed through into the room, holding his rifle in his left hand he stepped up on the stool, facing the wall. He stooped and grasped the "towel bar" in his right hand as he squatted facing the wall. He grunted as though straining with a bowel movement. He looked around at the POWs grinning a gold-toothed grin. "So. So." He grunted again as though straining a gut. He continued to grin at the men in the doorway. "Baka des." He thought that they were all a bunch of dummies for not knowing how to use the john.

Looks of understanding and surprise spread over the faces of the men.

"Hey, how about that? They ain't so stupid after all."

There was general agreement that the design was not only efficient, but effective. The fact that one did not sit on the seat meant that there was no contact with a dirty seat. Lice, crabs and disease were, therefore not transmitted by way of the toilet seat.

We had boarded the train on Monday. It was the ninth of November. The train moved north at a steady rate. We had little to do except to bat the breeze and wonder what the future was going to be like. We slept in our seats. Food was provided in the same way that we had had our original meal.

The country changed gradually. There were black rolling hills and the mountains. It was a barren God forsaken land. There were many small towns and villages through which we passed without stopping.

On Wednesday morning, the eleventh of November, Armistice Day, one of the guards told us that we were almost at our destination. The countryside leveled off and there were more signs of civilization. More and more towns and signs of industry.

"This is Hoten." The Jap guard pointed out of the window at the city that we were entering. You are here now. This will be your home for many years." His toothy grin was glittering with gold. "This is where your factory is."

I looked at him wishing I could spit in his face.

"Your home for many many years. Maybe, sometime you have visits from your family." He grinned again.

We stopped at a siding, not a depot or station. We were told to disembark in an orderly manner and wait for the trucks to be loaded. We were counted off as we boarded the trucks. We passed through the outskirts of the city and along a highway that led back out into the country. After a few mile drive we arrived at a camp.

It was bleak and desolate. There was a double barbed wire fence, actually two fences that were about ten feet apart. Each was about six foot high and consisted of eight strands of barbed wire strung with tin cans. The area between the fences, No Man's Land, was constantly patrolled by guards. Looking at it from the bed of the military trucks, it was about six hundred by eight hundred feet. There were a series of rolling hills that started about five hundred yards behind. Barracks for the Japanese guards were on the west side of the camp, to the left of the main gate, which was the only entrance to the camp. North of the Jap quarters were a series of warehouses and what looked to be a bathhouse. The prisoner barracks were to the right, the east side of the road that split the camp in two. Before the hills started to the north was an open field with a scraggly row of low brush and a few barren trees. Open fields bordered the east and west sides of the camp. The south side of the camp was bordered by a narrow field and a lightly wooded area. We had approached from the south, the only road to the camp. The guards told us that we were about eight kilometers from Hoten. This had been a Chinese Army Camp. The guards at the camp were not the same as the ones that had been with us on the train. The contingent of camp guards were assigned to POW guard duty only. We were told by the guards that were escorting us into camp that the guards were from the Kwan Tung Army, and that they were mean.

Men were counted off into groups and marched off to the barracks. There was no selection or separation. We were counted off as we stood as we had formed up after getting off of the trucks. No one had a chance to find a buddy or a friend so that they would be assigned to the same barracks. If one was lucky enough to be with a friend, then they went to the same barrack.

The barracks were not like anything I had ever seen before. They were built almost half underground. Each building was about one hundred and thirty feet long and about twenty feet wide. The roof pitched in two directions. The peak was about twelve foot above ground. It was about a quarter of the distance from the front of the structure. The front wall was about eight foot high and the rear was only five foot high. There were two main rooms as we entered from the center, each about fifty foot long. The center, between the two rooms was an anteroom that served as a foyer. There were two similar rooms, ten foot long at each end. The roof was covered with eight and more inches of sod. The floor of the barrack was more than three foot below the surface of the surrounding ground. Each main room had raised decks or platforms along each wall, running the full length of the room. These were a foot above the floor. They were seven foot wide. The aisle that ran between was about five foot wide. There were shelves that were eighteen inches above the platform that were about a foot wide.

In the center of the aisle, halfway down the length of the room was a massive piece of brick masonry. This we were told, was the stove. It was two foot wide, six foot long and five foot high. The front end, facing toward the center of the structure, had a step that was two foot lower than the high end. A metal lid was set in the top of the step and two metal doors in the front, one above the other. One door was for the firebox, the other was for the ash box. At the end opposite the step was the flue that passed up through the sod roof.

The barrack was cold. Ice cold. There was an odor of cold, if cold has an odor, that permeated the whole place. There hadn't been a fire for a very long time.

A guard came through even before we had settled down and ordered two men to come along with him. They returned in short order with newspaper, wood and one bucket of coal. Some men went to work starting a fire immediately.

I grabbed at the papers and scanned through them to see if there was anything that we might be able to read. They were in Chinese and were evidently quite old. I had to surrender them to the fire. There weren't enough of them to keep, the fire had to come first.

Four more men were called out to go to the kitchen. They brought back sour dough buns and buckets of hot soup. Each man was then issued two of the buns and a canteen cup of the soup. Soup. It was a watery broth that had been made by boiling pork bones in it to make the broth. There was no meat, but the soup was hot and it did have some flavor. It was flat and tasteless because it had no salt. There was enough of the soup to go around for seconds. It helped to warm us and fill our empty and shrunken stomachs. We didn't have any water for either drinking or washing. I stored my canteen cup on the shelf and started to look around for a source of water when a guard came in and ordered us outside. We formed a line and were marched to one of the warehouses where we were each issued five army blankets and a mattress cover.

"Hey, what the hell we gonna do with five blankets?" asked one of the men.

"Yeah, who wants to buy a blanket? Five cigarettes I'll take for a blanket," he offered.

One of the Japs who understood and spoke English came by and stopped when he heard the offer. "You will not sell the blankets. You are each responsible for them. You will find that you will need them here. Very cold. Samui. Very, very, very cold here in Hoten. You will find out," he nodded his head in a knowing manner, the way I had seen many Orientals nod.

"Aw, five blankets. How cold does it get anyway?" asked one of the men of the same Jap.

"Very very cold," repeated the guard. "If you go outside to pee, by the time the pee hit the ground you have ice," he answered seriously.

The laughter that rang out was low and ghostly in the chill of the darkness of the night that was being stirred by a wind from the northwest. The story struck the men as funny in a world that had no fun.

"You will not laugh when you see for yourself." The Jap was honestly put out at the way the men accepted his tale. "The temperature is maybe forty and fifty degrees below zero at night. In the winter, January and February it has been seventy below zero Centigrade." He was deadly serious.

"How much is forty below zero centigrade in Fahrenheit?" asked someone.

"Forty below centigrade is forty below in fahrenheit. And fifty below is fifty-eight below in fahrenheit," Fleming converted the corresponding values in moments.

"Yea! He's right," put in Driver, another of the men from our room.

"I don't care how right he is, that is damn bitchin cold, too cold for me. I ain't gonna survive," chirped another man.

"Boy! From one extreme to the other. First we roast our asses in Cabanatuan, now they freeze them off of us in Manchuria. What the hell did we do to deserve this?" This was voiced by one man, but it certainly must have been in the minds of many.

We returned to our barrack and started to fix our sleeping area, our bunks. This involved folding of the blankets in half, the long way, and laying them on top of the empty mattress cover. I sat on the top of the pile of blankets and listened to the various conversations that were going on around me.

The fire had been roaring merrily and the room had warmed up some, but the place was cold. You could feel the cold from the floor, the walls and the ceiling.

"Why is it that they build that Rock of Gibraltar in the middle of the floor like that?" The question came from Kane, one of the sailors. Kane was short, but even starved, he looked ruddy and chubby. His short cropped hair and walrus type mustache were set off by blue eyes.

"Well,--- I'll tell you what I think, in case you are interested," offered one of the men cautiously. Driver, Fleming and Kane sat down, waiting for him to continue.

"Well?" said Kane. "Why? Come on, let's have it."

"Well," started the man who had volunteered the information. "The fire is built in the fire box, now if it were a potbellied stove, the fire would heat the metal and the heat would be radiated out from the sides. This warms you up because it throws out the heat. Besides that, the air is heated as it passes around the hot metal."

I listened to the discourse. He had the right ideas.

"Yeah sure," put in Fleming, "we use a lot of pot belly stoves in New Mexico. It can sure get cold there."

"Only they don't have pot belly stoves here," said Driver.

"'Right. Iron must cost too much or they don't know how to make them. So they got a lot of clay and they make bricks. So they build the stoves out of bricks. The reason the thing is so long is because the hot gasses flow through the passages they build in. They must go back an forth maybe two or three times before they go out the back and up the flue at the end and then out the chimney. This gives the hot gas more of a chance to heat the brick."

"Okay, so we got hot bricks. So what?" someone asked him.

"Well, the bricks don't cool off fast, see?"

"No, I don't see," said Kane.

"Well stupid, since the brick is hot and it keeps the heat in it takes a long time to cool off. All the time its throwing out heat to the room. Get it?" He had a smug look on his face.

"Sure. Just like a radiator," Fleming added. He nodded in agreement. "Must be so. Pretty good thinking, huh Pete?"

"Sure sounds good," I agreed. I relapsed into silence, listening.

"Thanks," he said.

"Sounds right to me," agreed Driver.

"Maybe so," said Kane, "but it looks like a lot of wasted brick to me."

The others laughed. Everyone started to head for their bunks to turn in. It was warmer in between the blankets. Two and a half underneath and two and a half on top. I draped my overcoat over the top of the blankets for additional warmth. The day had been long and eventful. Sleep came fast and easy.

I jumped from under the blankets still only half awake. "What the hell was that?" Fleming, in the bunk next to mine, stared at me blankly in the dim light of the small bulb in the middle of the room.

"What?" Fleming asked back.

"That racket. It woke me up. Scared the hell out of me." I listened intently. I couldn't remember what it was that had jarred me awake. It was as though I had dreamt something and couldn't remember it after I had wakened.

A horrendous howling came from outside of the window in the back wall. It was followed by the barking of a half dozen animals.

"Coyotes!" Fleming sat upright.

"Dogs!" I corrected him. "No coyotes here. Wolves maybe, but no coyotes."

The howling started again. The whole barrack was awake now. "How the hell are you supposed to sleep with that racket going on?" some one asked.

The window next to Kane's bunk seemed to be the source of the howling. I scooted around Kane and scraped the frost off of the window. I capped my hands around my eyes and moved up close to the pane. The howling came again. I knocked Kane over as I scuttled back from the window. Two large red eyes had glared at me only inches away. "Cripes!" I yelled.

"What is it? What's the matter?"

"Hell!" I laughed sitting down. "It must be a dog."

"Well I wish it would shut the hell up."exclaimed Fleming. "I want to sleep."

"Pipe the hell down you guys."

"Get to sleep!"

"Let the friggin dogs alone and get to sleep!"

""Nuts to you to." I responded. I crawled into my bunk and pulled the blankets around me to shut out the dogs as well as the penetrating cold.

The dogs kept me awake for a long time. I would doze of and they would start the racket again. It kept up for most of the night.

Morning started off with a bowl of corn meal mush and a couple of the sour dough buns. Shortly after our breakfast we were ordered out to another building similar to our own except that there were no bunk platforms. We were told that this was the hospital. We were all lined up for a medical. Stethoscope to chest, open mouth, bend over and spread cheeks and cough. Those with dingleberries, small balls of shit collected on the hair around the anus, were listed and ordered to the bathhouse immediately. They were given priority. The rest of us were told that we could bathe later.

We were returned to our barrack and issued numbered red fiber tags, one and three quarter inch by three and three quarter inch. The number was stenciled in white paint. There were two small holes in each corner, We were ordered to sew these tags on our tunics. We were to wear these at all times under penalty of severe punishment. This meant that we had to have our number id no matter where, hospital, benjo or outside. We were to answer by number, not by name. I figured the Japs couldn't remember our names and found it easier to give us numbers. It was also easier for them to keep track of us.

My number was six nine four.

Fleming wanted to move next to one of the men further on down the line. His number was six nine five. We decided to move up when Fleming took six nine two. The Japs wanted us to stay in proper sequential order. The shift made me six nine five.

Fleming, six nine two, was a tall lanky individual. He was as skinny as the rest of us but it seemed to show more on him than on the rest of the men. His hair, what there was of it was a sandy color, kept in a crew cut like most of the men. We hadn't licked the lice yet. His face was long, cheekbones high and a narrow jaw with a long thin nose sticking out from the sallow face. He was friendly and considerate. He moved slowly, but could move fast when it was required. He said that he was from North Solano, New Mexico.

Six nine four, the man that moved up next to me was Driver. He was a little shorter than Fleming, but broader in the shoulders. He presented an image that was bulky, but not fat. No one was fat. He had shaved his head and the fuzz was starting to show. His face was round and he frowned a lot. He was always sniffling from some allergy and one would have thought that the had a cold all the time. He had a shuffling gait, not slow, but his feet seemed to follow him instead of carrying him.

Friday, the first Friday in the camp was Friday the thirteenth. It snowed. It was a fine snow that was driven hard by the wind as it howled and whistled through the eaves of the buildings. The sounds were eerie, like the howling of the damned crying for mercy. The damned were the POWs. It was a wind that came in from the west, from the Mongolian Plateau. It was the coldest wind that I had felt in a long long time. Not since Alaska.

The Japanese commander of the camp, Colonel Matsiumo made an inspection of the camp the same day.

He told the officers that the men would be put to work in a machine tool factory. We were given a form to fill out detailing our skills and work experience. We balked at the order. We had been told that according to the Geneva Convention we were to give only name rank and serial number. Then we argued with the officers who ordered us to comply with the Jap order. If we did not obey we were told we would face a court martial for disobeying an order. The reason they gave for cooperating was to not endanger other men. Reluctantly we filled out the forms. Many of the men supplied all kinds of false information and work backgrounds knowing that the Japs had no way of verifying any of the information.

I indicated that I was a design engineer who had had considerable experience with machinery. Sure, I was good with mechanical things, my father had had me working with him repairing automobiles since I had been only eight years old. I had learned a lot from him. But, I wasn't a design engineer. I was a good draftsman.

Nothing happened immediately as a result of the forms. We waited for any word of what the factory was like but there was no information and not even any rumors.

The food rations that were provided were meager. Mornings the meal was corn meal mush, watery. Noon and night there was about pint of hot soup, which was the broth in which maize had been boiled. There was about five tablespoons of maize in a noonday ration and one quarter to sometimes one half a cup of solids at night. There was also an issue of a sour dough saltless bun with each meal. Doctor Herbst estimated that each man was receiving just about seven, and with luck on some days, eight hundred calories a day.

Our medical situation was even worse. There wasn't a man that didn't have some disease. The month that we had spent on board the Hokka Maru had wreaked havoc with us physically. Our feet were swollen and our mouths were sore. Our scrotums were swollen, red, scaly and puffy. The skin peeled off of the scrotum like large flakes of dandruff. All of this was caused by the lack of any vitamins according to Herbst. We had pellegra, scurvy, beri beri plus malaria and dengue fever. The standard treatment, for the lack of any other medication was two aspirin. Men with scurvy and pellegra received half a tangerine. Since there never were enough tangerines the rest of us would receive a quarter section of the peel of an orange or of a lemon.

The beri beri was worse than the scurvy. Legs, feet and arms, and the hands also, swelled to almost twice normal size. The skin became red and tender. It was impossible to put on a pair of shoes. Some of the men cut their shoes open from the tongue to the toe, then crosswise just in front of where the ball of the foot fit into the shoe. The shoe was then folded over the foot and laced to hold it on. It was also difficult to walk because each movement of the legs caused scraping of the scrotum which brought hot searing pain.

Those of us who had pellegra and scurvy had sore mouths. Our lips were swollen and scaling. The hot broth brought tears to my eyes. A lot of the men simply let the food go cold before they would eat it.

It was a common sight to see men shuffling slowly like old men with arthritis. Anyone who didn't hobble, shuffle or show some signs of starvation and vitamin deficiency was suspect of anything up to and including cooperating with the Japs.

There were no restrictions that prevented us from visiting the other barracks or walking around the camp. I wandered around, shuffling, because there wasn't anything else to do in Splinter Camp. Since everything was built of wood we had tagged it Splinter Camp. South of the camp, some few hundred yards was a large tower. It was about twenty foot square at the base and at least eighty feet high. When I asked one of the guards about it he told me it was a battle monument from the Russian Japanese War of nineteen aught five.

On one of my walks I found the garbage dump behind the Jap cook house. I watched as a Jap emptied a slop bucket across the ditch from the building. I waited until he had returned to his chores before I investigated. The stuff he had dumped was a mass of steaming peechi (Chinese cabbage) leaves, meat bones, and other scraps. I moved the mess around with my toe as I watched for the Jap to return. I saw orange peels, scallion tops and turnip peelings. This was sprinkled with masses of large tea leaves. I kept watch on the kitchen door afraid that the Jap would come out and chase me away before I could salvage anything. I saw a piece of newspaper to one side. I stooped and pulled the paper free being thankful that it had not frozen into the ground as was some of the other garbage. I picked out the orange peels first. They were the real treasure. I kept on digging for all that I could find. After that I picked out the chunks of rotten turnip and the scallion tips. I worked frantically. I picked at the tea leaves and made a small ball. I wrapped the whole treasure trove under my overcoat and shuffled back to the as fast as I could. All the way back to the barrack my heart was pounding with pleasant excitement.

I called Fleming out into the foyer, out of earshot of the other men. "Bring two canteen cups of hot water and our mess kits," I instructed him.

"What for?" he frowned in puzzlement at the strange request.

"I got some stuff that we have to wash. Hurry up."

He took off and came back in short order. We sat down out side the barrack's door, away from most of the traffic. The snow made a cold seat even through the overcoat material. "Here! Look at this!" I showed him my treasure trove of food.

"Holy cripes! Where did you find that?"

"Never mind that now. Let's scald the stuff." I wiped off the tea leaves and dumped them along with the orange peels into one of the mess kits. We scraped and washed them leaving the tea leaves.

"GARBAGE!?"

"Uh uh," I answered around a mouthful of orange peel. I flinched as the juice hit. I chewed the peel until it was mush and swallowed it.

We shared the rest of the orange peels, seven each. I shoved mine into my pocket and picked up the mess kit and canteen cup, "Let's make soup out of this," I looked at him for approval. We entered the building from the end foyer and pushed through to the stove. There was a large pot of water that was used to provide humidity.

"What you got there?"

"Where the hell did you steal that?"

"Is there any more where that came from?"

"No," I lied. I placed my mess kit with the vegetables in it on the stove and poured some water in from the pot. Fleming did the same.

"Hey! Don't forget to replace the water!" some one reminded us.

"Sure sure. How about watching this stuff until it cooks?"

"Will do." Fleming sat on the edge of the deck close to the stove to keep watch.

I moved down to my bunk and sat on it. "Hey Driver." He turned over and looked up at me sleepily. "How about some of this?" I held out one of the orange peels.

He bolted upright and grabbed for the peel. "I'll be damned! Were the hell did you get this?" He shoved the whole thing into his mouth and started to chew. He winced the same as Fleming and I had done when the juice hit the tender inflamed tissue of his mouth. "Well? Where?"

"Never mind," I evaded giving an answer. "Think a couple of those will get rid of the scurvy?"

"Sure as hell will," he answered hopefully.

I smiled at him and returned to Fleming by the stove. The greens were boiling merrily and the odor from the broth filled the room. There were jealous comments as the other men watched us down our soup greedily.

It was always difficult to be selfish. Invariably I still felt rotten when it was necessary to refuse to share something like the soup. We were, however, developing the hard core philosophy of me first. It was understood that the me first, I take care of me was the way it had to be to survive. The "Semper Fi" of the Marines was that kind of a philosophy. After Bataan and Corregidor, the 92nd Garage and Cabanatuan, the Totori (Hokka) Maru, it was assumed without disagreement that it was every man for himself. If some one shared with a friend or friends it was accepted gratefully, and never forgotten. No one asked what the motive was for sharing. If it was given it was taken, with thanks.

There was an unspoken code that had developed. There was always the search for an opportunity to get food, medicine or whatever could be useful. There was also the code of not asking. There was little enough available. Sometimes a man would break the code and beg. Men watched enviously the good fortune of another, hoping that their turn would come next. For many the chance never came. Others made it their turn, but they sometimes took extraordinary chances for even as small a thing, such as the core of an apple. It was probably because of this that some were surviving and others weren't. There was no way of identifying the survivor. There was no way of predicting who would survive. We had many deaths. The average now was one a day.

The Japanese started to cremate the bodies. The dead were sent to the crematorium in Hoten. However, as the word spread that there were many POWs dying, the Japs stopped shipping the bodies to Hoten. They didn't like the stories that were being circulated in the city. They decided to bury the men instead.

That was how the grave digging detail started.

The hill to the north of the camp was selected as the site for the cemetery. It was a treeless terrain. The hill was exposed to the winds that whistled in from the cold miles of the tundra of Siberia and the Gobi. It howled around the top of the hill, cold and biting. The ground was frozen solid for some unknown depth. Digging a grave was like trying to dig a hole in a glacier. Shovels were useless. Picks made small golf ball size chips that stung like a bitch when they hit the face and the legs. We dug for a week. The twenty-five of us had only six graves that were only a foot and a half deep. The second week the Japs brought in cartloads of firewood. Fires were built in the graves to thaw the ground. The fires thawed the ground about three inches after about two hours. The ashes, embers and burning wood was shoveled from one grave to another, more wood being added after the maneuver to build up the fire. The mud that resulted was then shoveled out into a pile that froze in minutes. After another week the project was abandoned. It was decided that burial would take place in the late spring after the ground had thawed.

The only good thing about the detail was that we were kept warm by the fires as they burned. But even then we all had some degree of frostbite.

The bodies were stacked in coffins, pine boxes that were brought in, in one of the storage sheds in the middle of the camp. It became the morgue, a natural ice box that was a grim reminder of the fate we were all trying to avoid.

Our food situation was worsening. The maize and the cabbage was cut out as a daily ration and the soupy corn meal was cold when it was brought to the barracks. We banded together and went to the officers who were faring a lot better than the enlisted men.

Lieutenant McCarthy was sent to our barracks to talk to us. The session broke up on a sour note in a bedlam of noise, accusations, recriminations and name calling. All of the men felt and believed that the officers, both American and British, were skimming the best of the food for themselves.

The officers had separate quarters and orderlies to serve them. They had first choice of the food in the kitchen. Some of our men had seen how the food was being separated and rationed. The officers were taking care of themselves first. This caused a great deal of discontent among us.

A few days after the bitching session an inspection of the camp was conducted by a two star general and the new commandant of the camp. The new commandant, Colonel Matsuda, had a directive distributed after the inspection.

One of the junior officers read it to us.

*   *   *

Men will be put to work as soon as positions are found for them. Men will be employee according to knowledge, ability and skill. Pay will vary according to position held. No complaints of any sort will be entertained.

Men who are ill should strive to gain health, and they will be put to work.

Disciplines should not be lax. If the civilians find a lack of discipline it will be a disgrace to the wearer of the khaki and blue as guardians of soldiers of this country.

*   *   *

"Sounds like some of the officers helped Matsuda write that!?" Someone in the rear of the room shouted.

"What kind of work we gonna do?" I heard Kane shout.

"Nobody knows yet." The lieutenant answered. "The work will be in the factories. We'll let you know as they find places for you."

"What do you mean for us? Ain't you officers gonna work? You special or something?"

"Well, no we don't work. We don't have to according to the way the Japanese look at it." The young lieutenant answered awkwardly, embarrassed.

"Oh! La di da!" came another retort. "You sit on your fat ass and we work. Real democracy in our American army. Ain't it?"

There was a great deal of hissing and jeering. Others booed the officer out of the room. The atmosphere and the dissension he left behind showed the rift that was growing in the camp. Our officers were supposed to be looking out for the men, standing up for them. Our officers weren't standing up for us. The contempt for the officers was growing every day.

A small group of men were selected to start work at a factory that was about four miles away in early December. I was sent out on the first detail.

CHAPTER 14 -- CHRISTMAS IN MANCHURIA

Christmas. It was the second Christmas of the war. The first in prison camp, but the second of privation and hardship.

There were rumors.

Rumors that there was going to be a good meal for all on Christmas day.

A rumor that there was a food shipment on the way to the warehouse.

We waited anxiously. The food shipment did come in. It was on the twenty-third of December. Everyone that could walk wanted to be on the unloading detail. Our barrack and barrack eleven were assigned to the detail.

It was a cold and snowy night. The floodlights around the warehouse illuminated the fine fuzzy snow that drifted down in a fine haze. The whole camp was masked with the white veil that cloaked the death and privation that lived there.

We found that the food shipment consisted of potatoes, carrots, turnips, flour and pork. PORK! MEAT! A magic word that was mostly a vague memory as was a woman and candy and beer.

There were four trucks loaded with the vegetables and flour. The fifth was loaded with the meat. The meat wasn't wrapped or boxed. The slabs of pork, side and ribs, were piled high, filling the back of the truck and covered with a tarpaulin. There were two Jap guards with each of the vehicles. There were also guards about twenty feet apart all around the area. In the warehouse itself there were Jap guards, Jap officers and the Manchu drivers.

The slabs of meat were handed down by a POW, loaded onto the shoulder of another POW and carried into the warehouse to be stacked. Each of the slabs of meat weighed maybe about twenty to twenty-five pounds each.

On my third trip to the warehouse I had figured out a way to steal a slab of pork. It had to be a small slab, unfortunately. I unbuttoned my overcoat and tunic. Next I unbuttoned my shirt and tightened my pants cord. I left the shirt tails firmly tied in place.

"Give me three slabs," I told the man on the truck. "I can handle them."

"Okay okay. But take it easy," he warned.

He loaded three slabs on to my left shoulder. As I passed between the truck and the side of the building I shifted the weight and my hold on balanced the one on top with my right. When I reached the cab of the vehicle I looked around quickly. There was no one on the truck and no one behind me at the moment. Just for an instant there wasn't a Jap in sight. I slid the top slab of meat down onto my chest and shoved it under my shirt. The shirt tore somewhere under my arm. The sound of the tearing was loud in the hush of the falling snow. I placed my right arm across my chest and held the coat closed as I passed the next truck. I was in an instant sweat. I quickened my pace as I approached the warehouse door. I moved in close behind a man carrying a sack of flour and stayed almost on his heels. I cautiously reached under my shirt and centered the hunk of meat to prevent it from bulging out under my arm. My hand was cold and stiff. My fingers wouldn't work well. I buttoned two of the buttons and then my fingers wouldn't work any more. The line stopped at the entrance of the warehouse. There were so many men unloading that the line had backed up because the stackers couldn't handle everything fast enough. I moved over to the section where the meat was being stored. I unloaded the two slabs of meat. My heart was pounding and my mouth was dry. I expected to be stopped at any moment. I rejoined the line as it formed at the trucks again. A little Jap guard grabbed my arm as I started to pass him. I thought I was going to shit.

"You," the small Jap smiled as he hissed, "you work hard. I see you carry two, not one. Yes?"

"Yes." I smiled a sickly smile of relief. I exhaled the breath I was holding. The Jap took it as though I was exerting myself and grinned.

"Good. Yaroshii. When you finish I give you tobacco. I not forget." He pushed me back into line.

I almost sagged with relief as I left the warehouse.

The man that fell in behind me was Driver. "I give you tobacco," he mimicked. "You work hard."

"Nutsu to you too," I sneered.

"I like you. You worku hard," he grinned as he joked.

"Shut up," I growled, "I have to leave here fast." I threw the words over my shoulder.

Instantly on the alert Driver sensed the urgency and knew that something was afoot. "Got something?" We had all developed a sense of awareness, a special sense that identified the "not normal."

"My stomach is cold and damn near frozen." The chunk of meat was a block of ice plastered against my stomach and chest.

"Go benjo," Driver suggested.

When I reached the truck I walked over to the guard and danced from one foot to the other as I addressed him, "Benjo. Haiyai benjo."

"Ush. Baka," the Jap growled. "Haiyai. Hayaku."

I ushed him back and moved off in the direction of the toilet shack, the benjo. When I reached the path between the barracks I made a quick turn in the direction of our building. I walked around the near end. I stopped and looked around in the snowy darkness. There was no one in sight. I dashed to the snowbank at the west side of the building. The snow half buried our barracks and new snow was piling up on it. I shoved the meat deep into the snow and then smoothed it over with my hat. I swept the snow over my footsteps and headed for the john. I went in and emptied my bladder. I thought I had to go more from being afraid than from having a full bladder. I picked up a handful of snow and washed my hands and then fell back into line at the trucks. I searched for Driver but couldn't spot his shuffling gait among the men in the line. Men were grabbing for potatoes, carrots and turnips that were crammed hastily into pockets and under coats whenever the guards weren't watching. I managed to squirrel away some of the vegetables on the four trips that I made. Amazingly, no one was caught. I wondered if they were permitting us to get away with it. We finished unloading and were told to return to our quarters. The Jap sergeant who had promised me the cigarette wasn't to be seen in the area. I really hadn't expected him to keep his word, but then I had hoped he would.

Driver was sitting on the end of the bunk when I returned to the barrack. He was grinning. "How did you make out?"

"Not bad. Not bad at all," I grinned back as I started to unload my pockets. "They let us get away with it. They didn't search us." I showed him my four large carrots and two large potatoes. He held up a bag that held maybe two to three pounds of flour and a few turnips.

"Flour. Real flour," I exclaimed.

"And turnips. What else did you get your sneaky bastard?"

I looked around and moved closer to him. " A slab of pork," I whispered. "About ten pounds." I indicated with my hands, "About so big."

"Kidding?" His eyes were rounded with surprise.

"No. Honest. I hid it outside. I glanced around at the men that were watching us. That sense of the unusual was shared by others, not just Driver and myself. They knew that there was something up. "How about a big pot of stew? Tomorrow is Christmas Eve," I warmed up as the idea germinated. "Let's cook up a meal. We can use the meat, the potatoes and carrots. You throw in the turnips. We can use the flour to thicken it and we can even make some dumplings. How about it?"

"What a Christmas present! Man!" he roared.

Eyes turned toward us immediately. Something was up. The men knew it.

I worried about the dogs all night. They howled as they roamed around the compound. I made two trips during the night to check the stash.

Christmas Day just didn't work out for our feast. First there was an inspection by the Japanese Commandant. Then our officers came through for their inspection, Lord knows why, except maybe they wanted to show their presence. Then there were some work details called out. We sweated through the morning and into the late afternoon. At four o'clock we gave up any plans for the day. I was afraid the dogs would find the meat. That worried me more than being caught. My only consolation was that it was frigid cold and that the deep snow made for good cover. We spent the evening caroling and swapping stories of better days.

Christmas Day Driver and I pre-empted the water pot. It was the biggest thing we could find. Going to the kitchen for a pot would be stupid. The kitchen crew would immediately know that there was something stewing and would demand a cut. The pot held about three gallons. I dug up the pork and brought it in without being spotted. We peeled the potatoes, carrots and turnips. This extravagance, peeling the vegetables, we felt we could afford today. We were food rich today. But even so we traded off the peels for cigarettes. Driver delegated the cooking to me saying he thought I was a better cook. I wasn't in the least bit reluctant to do the cooking.

Neither of us had any salt so we traded off a three cups of broth for a quarter canteen cup of salt. Payoff was to be made after the stew was cooked. Before we started cooking we hired lookouts. We were in possession of contraband food. If we were caught with meat and potatoes and flour, plus the fact that we had turnips, we would wind up in the guardhouse for weeks. And, no food!

The guardhouse sentence was a bad deal. Seventy-one and fifty-six had been caught with stolen food from the kitchen some time ago. They spent a week in the guardhouse. The guardhouse was unheated. No blankets were permitted, only overcoats. A man had to stand all day. Sitting or lying down brought a Jap with bayonet. The food ration consisted of one day of food every third day. Neither of us wanted any of that.

The lookouts were stationed in the anterooms and also outside. They were to relay a warning in the event of the approach of any Jap and also of any of our own officers. The price for each of the lookouts was a cup of broth. We left it up to the lookouts to arrange their own shifts, who was inside and for how long and who was outside. It was colder than a witch's tit out there.

The cooking started just after noon. We first thawed out the frozen slab of meat in the boiling water and then cut it up into small chunks. We allowed it to stew for about an hour before the carrots, turnips and potatoes were added. I added the salt sparingly until it had the right amount. We let it cook for about three hours. Neither of us left the vicinity of the stove during that time. I took some of the broth and mixed it with some flour and made a pasty ball of dough. I used half of the flour to make the dumplings. I browned the other half in my messkit on the top of the stove. I mixed it into the stew making the whole thing more like a thin gravy than just a watery stew.

I wondered what would happen if a Jap came in. We could hide the pot but we could never mask the odor that permeated the room. When I mentioned it to Driver he suggested that we smell up the place with a burning rag. The men howled their dissension. We decided to let things take their course. Fortunately no one bothered us the whole afternoon.

When our evening food ration was brought in we found that we had two hot buns instead of the regular one cold bun. So much for Christmas. The watery soup was no different than at any other time. We had expected to see some of the food that had been brought in just before the holiday. There was however a ration of coleslaw, made of the blue cabbage that was common to the area. There was no special meal as had been rumored.

We traded off our issue meal as we had our noon ration. We were saving our appetites for our special stew. We paid off the salt first, then we paid off the lookouts. Then we dove into our treasure of food. We set the pot between us and started with the meat. Most of the pork had just boiled apart leaving only the larger chunks along with the bones. I filled each of our messkits with as much meat as they would hold. I filled the canteen cups with broth. We sat and ate slowly, relishing every mouthful amid the snarls and envious remarks that were made. I ate the meat and the vegetables and washed them down with large drafts of the broth. I felt bloated and I was. I couldn't hold any more. The meat had been delicious. I couldn't remember a meal that I had ever relished as much.

"Pigs. Stinking pigs."

"Hope you heave your guts out gluttons."

"Slob."

"Hog. Stingy damn hogs."

It was no more than was expected. It hadn't blunted my appetite at all.

"How about we share with some of our guys? I can add some more water and let it boil, then we can give it out."

"Sure. Why not?"

I added about a gallon of water and let the pot come to a boil again. We doled out half canteen cups of broth magnanimously. Kane, Fleming, Storey and many of the others shared in our good fortune. The mercenary spirit existed even on Christmas. We traded off the remaining broth for cigarettes. After washing up and cleaning the pots and things, we sat around with our glorious bloated feeling and enjoyed our cigarettes while telling tall tales from the past and singing Christmas carols.

A paper was brought in by one of the men that had been issued by the officers. It was a double folded sheet that had been mimeographed. The story was that the Commandant had generously donated the paper and the stencil out of his own money. Not by the glorious Japanese Army, but out of his own pocket.

CHAPTER 15 -- MANCHU KOSAKI KAI KIBOSHA KI KAISHA

The dogs had been a constant annoyance ever since we had arrived at the camp. They howled as they roamed around the camp every night. No one had thought of them as a potential source of food. The dogs were wild. They traveled in packs. They were the scavengers and many times, we had been told by the guards, they killed livestock that was not sheltered or protected. Somehow the subject came up that the dogs might be good to eat. I mentioned that I had been at Baguio and had seen the Filipinos eating roasted dog. Others agreed that they had seen the same thing. They were meat. Food. We decided to trap and kill them.

Buns, and bones that had been filched from the kitchen, were laid on the ground in the middle of a noose. We waited inside of the anteroom of the barrack for the pack to come in. A big black and brown mongrel who was either hungrier, or bolder, than the rest sniffed around the noose. He stopped, head low to the ground and looked around with mean looking eyes. He snarled and looked around again as though he heard something. I shushed the men. The dog growled as he moved in closer and then made for the bait. I yanked on the end of the rope and yelled for the guys to get him. While I dragged the dog off of its feet they rushed in and started to beat the dog to death. The other dogs of the pack barked and snarled and then took off. Normally I would have expected that a man could swing a thirty inch long piece of two by four and kill a dog with one blow. This wasn't so. We were so weak that they couldn't hit the dog hard enough. It must have taken twenty or more blows to kill the animal. None of us were bitten. I would have bet that some of the dogs could have been rabid. The carcass was dragged behind the latrine and butchered. It was a very tedious and messy job. We fried the meat, making dogburgers, on the stoves, the petchukas, in the barracks. No one ever got sick from eating the dogburgers. We never thought about getting rabbies from the meat. I didn't particularly like the taste of the meat, it had a very odd flavor. I had had bear meat and wild pig and python, even some monkey meat. None of them tasted like the dog meat.

The country was cold and dreary. The temperature according to the thermometer outside of the Jap barracks showed temperatures of fifty-five and sixty below zero. Our main problem was trying to keep warm. Frostbite was a common affliction. The coal ration was one scuttle of coal per day. This was apportioned for morning and late afternoon. This made the barracks livable during the day. It was the time when we could move around. The barracks were nearly comfortable in the evening when most of the socializing went on. At night we just huddled in our blankets. With the fuel for the petchukas in short supply it didn't surprise anyone when it was discovered that there were sixteen coffins from the morgue had disappeared. We had stolen some ourselves.

Fleming and I had left the barracks just after the supper chow had been brought in. Driver was going to get our soup and watch it for us. There was a light snow drifting down that made everything eerie quiet. No one was out except the two of us. It was what we wanted. Nobody would want to miss their supper. We made our way to the morgue and slid inside. It was pitch black. There were no lights on the path that ran between the morgue and Barracks 8 and the kitchen.

"I better leave the door open so we get some light in here." Fleming whispered.

"What are you whispering about. They aren't going to hear us." I retorted, amused.

"Yeah. You're right." Fleming answered.

I could discern the note in his voice that implied that he knew it was stupid to worry about making any noise. We knew that the Japs never came around the morgue at night. I always figured that they were very superstitious about the dead.

"Let's do it and get out of here."

I pried the lid off of one of the coffin that was stacked on the top of two others with the coal shovel that we had borrowed and set it aside. "Know him?" I asked.

"Shit! I can't see my own hand in the front of my face and you want me to identify the guy!"

"Yeah. It is black as hell in here." I proceeded to remove the lid from a coffin that was against the south wall. I figured that the next coffin was going to be stacked on top of this one. "Okay. Let's move it."

We lifted the frozen body and laid it on top of the body in the coffin on the floor. Fleming moved back and let me fiddle with the nails in dark.

"DAMN!"

"What happened?"

"I hit my hand with the stinking shovel. The hell with it. Nobody is going to count how many nails there are anyway. Let's take that thing apart."

It took a short time to kick the wood sides apart and break the boards into pieces that were about twelve to fifteen inches long.

"I'll take the first load. You stay here."

"Right."

I heard Fleming shut the door as I left. I scrambled across the ditch on the other side of the path and into the center foyer of the barracks. Since it was the last one in the compound, up against the north fence, there was no one walking around.

"Hey?! What the hell?" Kane shouted as I entered our room.

"Give me a hand you guys. We got more coming. How about stacking it under your mattresses? We can have heat for three or four days."

Everybody pitched in and stashed the wood as we brought it in. Some of the pieces had to be broken into two because they were too long.

Fleming smiled as he sat down to eat. Driver had kept our soup warm on the petchuka. "Well? Who did you move anyway?"

"I don't know. Not that it makes any difference. Maybe they liked each other."

"That is damned nasty." Fleming observed as he filled his mouth with beans.

"Yeah. I know. I'm just getting to be a real callous bastard."

"Hey! Did you hear about Boushey? In barracks nine." Driver asked after we had settled down.

"What?" I asked.

"He and a couple of other guys stole half of the dog that and his guys had hanging in their foyer. There was holy hell to pay for a while."

"Anybody get bruised?" Kane asked from his bunk.

"Nah! Just a lot of pushing and yelling. Some deal huh? Stealing dog meat." Driver laughed. "I bet nobody ever heard of dogburgers stateside."

"Maybe not in the states, but they eat them in the Philippines. Specially up in Baguio." Kane put in.

"I can't see eating dog if you don't have to. I mean in the states." Fleming shook his head in disgust. "They make great company."

"Yeah. I had a great pet before I enlisted." Driver added.

The conversation turned to other things as the room heated up with the wood from the coffin.

The Japs raised a ruckus about the coffins. There had been thirty-five coffins, each with a body. First they wanted the coffins back because we they said it was indecent to place two bodies in one coffin. They searched the camp twice and didn't find a trace of them. Then they raised hell again because one of the Jap officers suggested that the wood was being used to shore up the roof of an escape tunnel. I laughed at that because it was impossible to dig through the frozen earth. Another Jap warned us that if they found the ladders that were probably being built they would shoot the perpetrators. We smirked while they searched. The only thing they could possibly find would be the ashes, wood ashes, and nails. We burned the coffins to keep warm. Our officers warned us to stop stealing the coffins or the Japs would take some drastic measures.

It was always cold. I felt the cold even more in the bath house. The floor was covered with slatted duck boards over heavy planks. There were deep troughs under the duckboards to drain off the washwater. The damned thing was unheated and that made bathing an ordeal. Hot water was supplied in two square tanks that were out in the middle of the room. One wasn't allowed to dunk in the tubs. The method of bathing was to use one of the wooden tankards that held about six pints of water and splash it on oneself. Once you started you had to keep on using more water to keep warm. After each splashing there was about a twenty second period in which to scrub down before you started to freeze. The room was so heavily masked with water vapor that it was impossible to see more than four or five feet. The windows, the duckboards and the troughs near the windows and along the walls were coated with heavy layers of ice. We had argued about the temperature in the bathhouse. No one believed that the temperature could be over thirty-two degrees Fahrenheit. Some of the men argued that the temperature was closer to zero. A bath took only about three minutes, at the longest.

The drying process after a bath was also unique. We didn't have any bath towels. Only a small face towel had been issued to each of us. That and a wash cloth that was maybe eight inches square. After bathing the wash cloth was used to wipe off most of the water and then the small towel was used to finish off drying.

There were times when there were surprise dingleberry inspections. An officer would be stationed at the door of the bath room. One had to bend over, spread cheeks and show clean. If there was a dingleberry it meant a return trip to the freezing cold room for another scrub down. There were few men that were returned for a second bath.

When we had started work in the machine tool factory I was assigned a job as a design draftsman. The leader, hancho, wanted me to do design work. I told him that I wasn't prepared because I didn't understand enough about what had to be done. He explained that that would come in due time, first we had to layout the factory. The job wound up to be an Industrial Engineering job. The factory was new. The shell of the building had been completed and the interior was empty. Our task was to layout the machine shop. This meant that we had to define the flow of parts to be machined and arrange the machines in an orderly manner to provide an efficient flow of parts to be processed.

Yamaguchi, the design leader, was a mechanical engineer. He managed to speak some English, but my Japanese was much better than his English. Yami said that he was fortunate that I could speak Japanese, Nipongo, because it made his job easier.

Yamaguchi San was one of the big Japanese. He reminded me of the wrestlers, the biggest hunks of men that they had in Japan. Big was meant big for a Jap. He was about five foot nine. One hundred and eighty centimeters, metric, as he said. He weighed a three hundred pounds plus. One hundred and thirty eight or more kilos. He insisted on using the metric system since we would have to do all of our design work using the metric system. He had his hair cut short, but not crew cut. His face was round and usually covered with jovial, but slant-eyed expression. He neither had or needed gold teeth. His age, according to our best guess, was thirty-three to maybe thirty-eight. Whenever we asked him how old he was he gave us a bland smile and mumbled, "Wakari massen." Translated it meant, "I don't know." We didn't have any idea why he should be sensitive about his age. But then, Orientals are peculiar. Maybe he was concerned about his Oriental face. I wondered if in fact maybe he didn't know how old he was. Even with the the wartime rationing Yamaguchi managed to keep his weight up there. Somehow he managed more food and other rations than any of the other Japs we encountered.

He was very much surprised at how thin and starved we all were. His response to my six foot three frame was a sad shaking of his large head.

He proved to be easy to work with. He had somehow had an implanted idea that Americans were born mechanical geniuses. He believed that we all knew everything about machines and factories and could fix anything mechanical. He never pushed or pressured us and was a willing source of information.

My assignment was to lay out the machine shop. Yamaguchi explained that MKK, the company, had built the factory in conjunction with, and under the command of, the Army. It was built to employ the POWs. The buildings were huge. The main building was Building Number Three. It was three hundred foot wide and eight hundred foot long. I was built into four bays by the main support columns. There were overhead cranes thirty-five foot above the floor and they were already in place. There were two other buildings of near the same size. One to the north and one to the south. There was an alley about twenty-five foot wide in between them. We were to provide a layout for the lathes, turret lathes, drill presses, radial drills, broachers, milling machines - both horizontal and vertical, surface grinders and planers. Some of the equipment had come from Japan. Most of the machines had been shipped in from the Philippines, Singapore and China. The machines had been manufactured in the United States, Germany and England. It was the booty that the Japs had taken after they had captured other countries during the war.

We were to plan the layout to emulate the factories in the states for mass production of machine tools.

The soil on which the buildings stood was very sandy. It could not readily support the heavy machines on just a concrete floor. It was necessary to design bases or foundations for some of the huge planers that were going to be installed.

Kozakevitch, 660, Kozy for short was added to the design staff. He was a Polack from Brooklyn. He and I started the design of the footing for one of the biggest pieces of equipment in the shop, a Gray planer. It was a monster of a machine. It was eight foot wide and eighty foot long. We asked Yami if he knew how much the thing weighed. He said he didn't and that there was no way to find out since there were no papers with it. It had come in from one of the countries that the Japs had overrun. We estimated the weight to be about a hundred and twenty tons. When Yami asked how we had arrived at the figure, we explained that we had measured it. Then we had computed its weight by determining the number of cubic feet of iron it contained. We had then looked up the weight of a cubic foot of iron and came out with its weight. It was determined that the base had to be twelve foot wide, ninety foot long and seven foot deep. The trouble was that there wasn't any reinforcing steel available for the foundation. The pit for the base was dug and POWs started to pour the concrete.

The factory floor was crammed full of lathes, drill presses, gears for the lathes, tools, grinding wheels, vises and milling machines. The overhead crane was in operation. A POW was manning it and was busy hauling concrete to the pit where the huge planer was to be installed. There was about six foot of mushy concrete in the hole.

I watched as the pouring went on. I had been measuring the building, checking on the dimensions against my set of prints. I stopped by the POW crew and struck up a conversation with the group leader, Savoie.

"How's it going?"

"Pretty rough. He's working our asses off," complained Savioe wiping his brow. Even as cold as the building was he was sweating. "He wants all of the concrete poured by six tonight or we don't go home."

"He sounds like a prick," I agreed. "Any other Japs around?" I asked as I eyed the mounds of steel machinery.

"Nope, not another shitty Nip out in this cold."

"No guard?" I was puzzled. "There is supposed to be at least one guard."

I had not been out with any of the factory crew and I didn't know that they weren't guarded at all times.

"None. They figure we can't get over the fence, so no guards no more." Savoie looked at me, "Hey! What you got in mind?"

The Jap civilian who was their hancho, lead foreman, came over to find out what was going on. "Nanda," he asked. "You. Something is wrong?" He pointed to the blueprint I was holding.

"I don't know yet," I responded in Japanese. "We are trying to find out if there is anything wrong."

"You, you speak English. I practice," he stated proudly, "You can speak Nipongo to the others. To me you speak English." It was an order.

"Okay, okay," I complied hastily.

"You call me if there is anything wrong. Yes?" He walked away leaving Savoie, 905, and me alone.

I spit mockingly at his back. Savoie laughed.

"How about reinforcing the concrete?" I asked.

"With what?" he sneered. "These Nips don't want to use any reinforcing. The think that the concrete will hold together all by itself. If it don't freeze." He made a disgusting sound of contempt. "Besides, they need all the steel for the war."

"Hell, I see plenty of reinforcing around," I observed innocently. "Steel gears, shovels, grinders and wrenches."

Savoie looked at me with a blank stare that looked stupidly silly. "Hot damn, why not? That stinking hancho can be kept busy and we can reinforce the concrete for them," he laughed. "How about that now? But if we get caught?"

I shrugged my answer. Beatings and the guardhouse were common occurrences. "Always make it look like an accident, you know, slip and fall. But be careful." I followed the Jap hancho with my eyes as he moved around through the men on the far end of the factory. "Post lookouts," I cautioned.

"We will. What's the most important stuff that'll kabosh the works?"

"Gears. They use them to change the speed of the lathes. Grinding wheels are hard to come by. Cutting tools." I pointed out the most difficult things to replace. "I have a doozer for you," I urged in a conspiratorial tone.

"What?" asked Savoie with a puzzled frown.

"I'll get the Jap to check the floor plan with me, the factory layout. I'll get him over to the far end of the building. You get the crane operator to hook on to one of those lathes over there. The turret lathe," I pointed out the one that I had in mind. "Then have him dump it, quietly, in the pit. Looks like there is enough concrete to cover it." I finished discussing the details and what some of the men had to do.

Savoie looked at me as though I had proposed a plan to blow up the Imperial Palace. "You give us five minutes. Five minutes and it's done."

"There are about ninety lathes. When they start counting them they'll go nuts. Cuckoo," I laughed in eager anticipation of the frustration of the Japs sometime soon.

"Okay. Let's go," Savoie went off to carry out the plan. He turned back, "Hey, you think it's deep enough?" his voice was anxious.

"I'll measure it." I found the measuring stick the hancho had been using and probed the pit. Then I walked over and stood beside the lathe. I had found the depth of the concrete to be shoulder high by standing beside the concrete covered stick. The lathe was about six inches shorter. I looked at Savoie in the midst of a group of men. I nodded at him with a smile. I joined them, "Give me the high sign when you are ready. I'll get the Nip."

I spent about ten minutes checking the floor plan while Savoie made the arrangements. He had set up the crane operator and instructed the men. I approached him wondering if the whole thing would work or whether we could wind up with our asses in a sling. He gave me the sign that he was ready. The crane operator positioned the crane over the lathe and gave me the middle finger indicating the Jap. He smiled broadly and waited.

"Hancho! Mongai arimas!" I yelled at the Jap.

"Ha. Nanda. Hay nanda," the foreman came trotting over to us. "I tell you to speak English!" he was angry.

"Gomenasai. I'm sorry. But I think there is a problem," I pointed to the dimension on the floor plan that represented the width of the building anxiously.

"What trouble? No trouble. Everything fine." The Jap couldn't conceive of a problem or a mistake that could be made by any of the Japs.

"I think one meter is missing in the width of the factory. Not one hundred meters wide. Only ninety-nine."

"Nah! Nie. Nani," he reverted to his own language in his excitement. "No, cannot be," he assured me. "Hayaku des. Hayaku metoru."

"We measure. Okay?" I asked. "you see." I took the tape measure off of my belt and shoved the blueprint under my arm.

"Okay okay. Where?"

Savoie walked away toward the pit.

I walked toward the north side of the building threading my way through the stacks of material. I heard the crane start as we neared the end of the factory. I handed him one end of the tape and moved toward the opposite wall.

"Two minutes!" someone shouted.

"What? What they say?" the foreman looked toward the crane from behind the pile of machinery that was stacked between us and the pit.

"Nothing that I can make out," I answered. I wet my dry lips with my tongue, "Here, here it is." I pointed to the blueprint trying to keep his attention away from the operation that was going on at the other end of the building. "See! The plan shows that the building is one hundred meters wide inside the wall. See," I pointed out that the dimension arrow was to the inside wall, "it is an error. It should be to the outside!"

He peered closely at the dimension line. He stuck his nose almost against the paper and mumbled in Japanese. "Ah so," he smiled a buck toothed smile. "You are right. So. The draftsmen make the mistake. Ah so," he grinned happily as he looked at the wall of the building. "You very good man. Good worker. I remember," he bobbed up and down with his torso. "What your number?" He reached for my tag.

"Rocco ku go, six nine five," I answered.

"Very very good. Here you have tobacco," he fished for a pack of cigarettes and handed me one. He was happy and smiling.

"Hancho! Concrete Hancho. All clear." Someone shouted. My heart pounded in sudden excitement.

"What is it?" the Jap asked.

"Concrete. They are ready to pour more concrete," I answered.

"Okay okay. You come," He ordered.

We threaded our way back through the maze of machinery to the pit. A huge bucket was being emptied just as we reached the side of the foundation. Savoie was standing near one end of the excavation. We stopped beside him and watched as the bucket was emptied. His signal, thumb and forefinger forming a circle, a nod and a smirk, caused an uncontrollable sigh of relief to escape. I felt a bit deflated, but elated.

"Everything okay?" asked the foreman.

"Fine, fine," answered Savoie. "Finish in a hurry. " He smiled at the Jap.

"Good. We see." He picked up the long measuring rod and shoved it into the concrete. We held our breaths. He shoved hard on the rod and then stood back and examined it. Savoie's face had gone white. He stood frozen.

"Ah, good." The Jap withdrew the rod and tossed it to the side. He strutted to the far end of the pit as he looked at the surface of the wet concrete.

"Man! I almost pissed," Savoie gasped.

"What's wrong? Something there?"

"Wrong! Cripes sake! Another foot and he would have hit the lathe. It slipped the sling and it's just about where he probed." Savoie's voice was hoarse.

"Thank God he missed. Everything else okay?"

"Yep! Real good reinforced concrete we gonna have here. Tons of it. Gears and tools. The guys wouldn't stop once they got the idea. Boy I hope they don't find out."

"Hell. If they ask you you can tell them that there is no way that we could use the stuff. You can't sell it. You can't steal it. Hell, they search you when you leave the factory." I tried to pacify him.

"Yeah. So?"

"So. Who are the only people who could steal the stuff? The Japs or the Manchus. Right?" I spread my hands and shrugged. I had a shitty smile on my face.

"Sure. Somebody is trying to sabotage our factory and it can't be us. Right?" He strutted around in mock concern.

"Right," I smirked. "Look, I'm due back at the drafting room. Be careful," I cautioned. "Don't say anything to anyone."

"Okay Pete. I'll see you." Savoie waved as I left. Some of the men gave knowing smiles.

The hike to and from the factory was about four or more miles each way. The weather wasn't letting up at all. There was some snow, but it was mostly cold and overcast. The shoes I had when we were captured on Corregidor were just about worn out. We asked about having shoes repaired and were told that it couldn't be done. I am one of the unfortunates that have big feet. I fit into an Army size twelve. The largest that the Japs had was a ten, or maybe an eleven. A size twelve didn't seem to exist in Manchuria. The soles had worn through so badly that the cardboard no longer worked when I stuffed it into the bottom. I couldn't make it to the factory with the cardboard. It wore through about three quarters of the way to the factory.

One morning when the temperature was thirty-five below zero, I fell out of the line-up that was to march to the factory. I told the American officer that my feet were freezing and showed him my shoes. When he informed the Jap lieutenant about my problem. It befuddled him completely. It was something so unanticipated that he didn't know what to do. After a few minutes of baffled consideration they decided that I should remain in camp. I returned to my barrack and spent the time resting at my bunk. Mid-morning a Jap sergeant came through on an inspection tour. He stopped and looked at me as I stood at attention.

"Why do you not work at the factory today?" he asked in schoolroom English.

Unthinkingly I answered, "Shoes shot."

"Shot? Shotsie?" he asked, cocking his head. He didn't understand the vernacularized answer I had given him. He bugged his eyes at me and then frowned in consternation. I picked up my shoes from the floor and showed him the worn out soles. He examined them with some interest and a lot of bewilderment. "I take," he stated.

"Hey! That leaves me without anything at all," I objected weakly. I knew better than to show any strong objection.

"Bango. Nani bango." He pulled a small notepad from his tunic pocket.

"Rocco ku go," I told him.

He entered the number in his book and then after pocketing the book he picked up the shoes and strutted out through the end door. There was nothing for me to do, I let him take the shoes. The other men laughed at my predicament. Some understood the seriousness of my situation. Going outside, even to the latrine now presented a problem. I sat confused and frustrated. I had, I thought, a temporary solution. I dug through my musette bag for some pieces of canvas that I had stolen from the ships stores.

I had sewn a false bottom in the inside of the bag. It was where I hid the papers that I had brought along. Whenever there was an inspection, a guard would pick up the bag and turn it upside down, dumping its contents for inspection. They had never reached into the bag and felt around in it. I had my diary and some old newspapers stashed there. I sat and looked at the canvas.

Kane came over and asked me what I was going to do.

"Make some booties." Someone offered.

"Nah. Make clackers. Like in the Philippines," he suggested.

"That is a damned good idea," I agreed. "Now all I have to do is managed to get my hands on some wood."

"Rip out a thick piece from the bath house partition."

"Sure. Great! All I have to do is fly there. My feet will be a couple of chunks of ice by the time I get there."

"I'll get it for you," Kane offered.

"Great, but don't get caught or you'll wind up in the guardhouse and freeze your damned ass off."

He was gone only about fifteen minutes. He returned with a piece of two by six that was about three foot long.

"I owe you Kane." I turned to Driver who was sleeping on his bunk, "Hey, how abut borrowing your knife?"

"Sure." He looked at the board, "Don't break it." He retrieved the knife from its hiding place and handed it over.

I started to carve the clackers. I roughed out the soles to the shape of my foot, but a half an inch larger all the way around. I managed to pry enough nails from the barrack wall with the knife and my spoon. I was careful not to take all of the nails from any one board. I took only one nail from any one board. I made a wide strap from the canvas. I nailed it to the sides of the sole piece at the instep. Then I carved out two pieces that were an inch by an inch and the width of the sole. One piece for the ball of the foot and another a little back from the heel. I then nailed the one by ones to the bottom. It was late afternoon when I had finished the clackers.

The men congratulated me on my project. The following day I borrowed a needle and sewed up a pair of oversized booties. I had picked the thread from the canvas that I had left. I also traded for some string with which to tie the booties around my ankles. The clackers were my salvation. They made it possible for me to get around camp without shoes. This lasted for two weeks.

While sitting around doing nothing, bored, we discussed the affliction we were having with farting. Soy beans had been added to our diet when we had started to work at the factory. The beans caused huge farts to be emitted almost constantly. A fart that would have been an embarrassment Stateside was a common occurrence that was practically unnoticed unless some asshole blasted the roof off of the place. Otherwise a fart was as commonplace as a sneeze or a cough. It was also noticeable that some men were greater gas generators than others.

The subject had been farts. "I bet the stuff burns." Bill stated emphatically.

"Like hell it does," was the heated reply from a named Jim.

"Betcha that we can prove it easy enough," countered the Bill.

"How?"

"Let's put a match to it," was the nonchalant answer from Bill.

"You're friggin nuts." Jim shot back at him

"You're just chicken shit," retorted Bill.

The rest of the men in the barrack quieted down. Here could be some diversion and entertainment.

"Like hell I am," snorted Jim. "You got the guts to face it when I fart then I'll let you light it."

The barracks became and uproarious shambles. Betting started. It would burn it wouldn't burn. It was an even money bet.

"Okay," Bill retorted.

"Okay, I'll drop my pants and bend over on the bunk and you light it. And don't get any ideas jarhead. I heard about you swabbies at sea," Jim snarled. That brought a lot of laughs and snide remarks. Tim got up on the bunk by the petchuka and dropped his pants he knelt and turned his head, looking over his shoulder, "I'll let you know when I'm ready, then you light it. And don't burn my damn ass."

"Okay." Bill got ready. He had a long splinter of wood that he lit in the petchuka. The bantering started.

"Come on, let's go."

"Let her blast."

"What the hell you waiting for? Can't you build up any pressure?"

"Sure sure," Jim answered. "Just take it easy. Okaaaay, here it is."

He let go a blast of gas just as the flaming splint was placed inches from his butt. The gas blew out the match.

"There, it doesn't burn," shouted Jim as he prepared to rise.

"Horseshit. You blew out the match. Ya have to try again." Bill insisted.

The arguments broke out hot and heavy. Some argued that the match was blown out by the force of the gas while others insisted that it wouldn't burn.

"The shitty stuff is too putrid too burn," someone insisted.

"You need a small torch."

"Like hell you do," disagreed Jim. "You ain't going to give me no singe job."

"Hell, we ain't going to burn you. We just want to make sure it is and honest test." Bill insisted.

A larger splinter was wrapped with a small piece of paper. "Don't blast yet. We ain't ready."

"Yeah, hold on a while. Don't blow the experiment now," someone in the background advised.

The splinter was lit, "Okaaaay! Let'er go!"

Jim let go an unbelievable volume of gas. The torch ignited it and a long blue jet shot out. Tim let out a tremendous yelp that could be heard at the front gate. The flame seared his butt. He shot forward on hands and knees. "HOLY CROW!" he screeched as he sat on the bunk. "You burned my ass!"

Man oh man! Did you see that?"

"That's some blowtorch!"

Roars and shouts and laughter rocked the crowd of men surrounding the experimenters. Jim sat holding his butt. The men continued to laugh and harangue Jim. Some were rolling around on the bunks. Others had tears streaming down their faces.

"You shithead you! You did that on purpose. You burned my ass!" Jim shouted. "I'll fix you for that. Wait and see."

"Aw! I did not." Bill replied. "The flame just caught up with you. Besides, you ain't got no dingleberries now."

Everyone roared.

The story spread all over camp the next say. By the time it made the rounds and came back to us it was unrecognizable. We heard in the days that followed that the guys had tried the experiment in some of the other barracks.

Kane came by a few days after the experiment with some other bad news. Johnson, 698, had died in the hospital on January the 20th.

It was soon after that that a notice came out that a shoe repair shop and a tailor shop was going to be set up and that it would be staffed by POWS.

It was now the second week of January, the week that the sergeant brought back my shoes. Repaired! As he handed them to me he smiled a self satisfied grin. " Sabis. Presento, me to you." He was well pleased with himself as he should well have been. He had accomplished something.

I thanked him profusely and sincerely. I took off my canvas booties and before I could put on the shoes the sergeant indicated that he wanted to see my foot. I took off my socks and waved my foot at him and wiggled my toes. The men gathered around to see what was going on. He looked at the swollen joint of the big toe. "Nane." He asked.

"Rifle butt," was all I said.

He frowned. I knew that he knew damn well what had happened.

"Big. Taksan, big. Ooki. You got big foots." He was grinning like a happy little monkey.

"I sure have. Size twelve. Maybe thirteen." I pulled my socks on and then put the on shoes on. Whoever had done the job had done a very good one.

The sergeant made remarks to the men. It was evident that he was enjoying himself immensely. In light of his good humor he became very generous. Laughing and joking he passed out two packs of cigarettes. The object of his amusement, me, managed to be presented with a half a pack of cigarettes. I was extremely thankful for the shoes and the tobacco.

I returned to work the next day to the great pleasure of Yamaguchi who told me that not much had been done while I was gone. He showed his pleasure by presenting me with a pack of cigarettes. Cigarettes were like money. Like gold. They were the medium of exchange with which you could buy anything in the camp, or from the Manchus at the factory.

A few days later the camp Commandant issued and address with regard to the purchase of canteen items.

ADDRESS

With regard to the canteen promised, by the former commander, we have, after negotiating with the various parties, been able to give it a start and will begin selling today and from the coming Monday. Canteen commodities will be, due to strenuous efforts on the part of the staff, far cheaper than in civilian circles, and I wish to give you a few instructions as regards the canteen and its operation.

1. With consideration to the low price of the canteen commodities resale of same is forbidden.

2. In spite of the best efforts of the staff, shortages will occur from time to time and you must bear with us in this difficulty.

3. Making purchases outside of camp is prohibited. Exception for this ruling will be made on articles of special necessity upon applying to the Superintendent Officer.

4. To prevent overcrowding and jamming in selling in the canteen, the Superintendent Officer will give further instructions as to date, time and methods used in making sales.

5. Greater individual precaution must be taken against loss of money and valuables in this camp.

6. Cigarettes will be sold, and smoking allowed at places designated according to Camp Regulations.

Full care must be paid as to fire prevention.

It is particularly desirable that members of the camp adhere more strictly to religious teachings and strive towards a higher standard of conduct. Among the men on the factory are those who are negotiating through the employees of the factory and others for outside purchases and the change of money in violation of previous instructions. Should the need arise for the above application should be made to the Superintendent Officer. I wish to again reiterate my personal feeling to work in your behalf.

January 21, 1943   Colonel M. Matsuda
          Commandant Mukden War Prisoners Camp

There were many comments about the reference to the religious note in the speech. Some of the men felt that the officers were at it again. Enough said, except for the religious hypocrisy.

Kane always seemed to be the bearer of the bad news about the men in the section. I was sitting on my bunk after having finished eating on a cold night, the tenth of February, two days after my birthday when he sat down beside me. "Did you hear that Witter died today?"

I looked at him sorrowfully, "Another one?" I looked to the new empty spot, 701, and shook my head in discouragement. "He was from Long Beach California, right?"

"Yeah. Navy. Like me."

I watched him sadly as he walked away.

There was a government prison about midway between camp and the factory. One morning in late February we saw a body laying by the prison wall as we were on our way to work. The body was fully clothed with a heavy padded overcoat and even a pair of shoes, not sneakers. Sneakers were the common footwear of the Manchus. They were cheap by comparison to leather shoes. It was about seven-fifteen which was the usual time that we passed that point. Our path was across a field that bordered the prison. At five thirty, on our way back to camp, the body was still there. No one had bothered to move it.

I questioned the guard about the body. His answer was simple and straight forward, "Just another dead Chinaman." There was absolutely no emotion. He thought of it as garbage.

The next morning I saw that the body had been stripped of all clothing. All during the next week I observed what happened to the corpse. First the dogs gnawed at it. On the third day the head had been separated from it. I started to throw pieces of ice at the crows that were picking away at the head the next morning. Others joined me in chasing the crows. Not that it did any good, it was just an exercise in frustration. The guards laughed at us. The gradual dismemberment of the dead man didn't bother the Japs or the Manchus. It didn't bother us much either, to be perfectly honest about it. There was a great deal of discussion about the incident of the body and the psychological and philosophical meaning of the culture that didn't react to the death of a man, and the insignificance of death. Nine days after the corpse had first been observed it was gone.

Everytime I saw another body being carried into the morgue I thought of how different we were in the way we treated our dead. We were having many deaths throughout the winter and into early spring. The count rose to almost two hundred Americans, Australians and British.

CHAPTER 16 -- ESCAPE AND SABOTAGE

Spring passed toward summer without any noteworthy incident other than the number of deaths that we suffered. Disease and starvation combined to kill off a number of the older men who had suffered the most during the month spent on the Hokka Maru.

The advent of summer brought on a change in our attitude. Just the fact that it was warmer made us feel better. We didn't know what was going on in the outside world. We were isolated, and we had to survive. Survival was the only thing that mattered. There was talk of escape, but escape brought seemingly insurmountable problems because we, as Caucasians, stood out in the world of yellow men.

The escape attempt of three men ended in disaster.

Meringolo, 1125, Pallaita, 444, and Chastine, 516, had been together ever since Corregidor. They had escaped from the Rock and had been recaptured on Bataan. Since the Japs didn't have any record of the POWs, they didn't know that these three had been previously captured. The Japs merely took them captive again and let it go at that. They had been lucky that time.

They had been planning to escape ever since we had arrived in Manchuria. They decided that it was too difficult to escape during the winter since the frigid cold was as much an enemy as the Japs themselves. The discussions, and the planning, the secret discussions, were held at the factory. Their decision to try for the Russian border had been prompted by the fact that it was only about four hundred to five hundred miles to Russian territory, but it was over fourteen hundred miles to Chunking. The final decision was made in May. Maps were purchased at the factory at exorbitant prices from the Manchurians. There were few other items that they could obtain for the trip. There was no way to acquire the food that would make it an easier, but in no way less dangerous trip. They would have to find food on the way. There were two main concerns, forgetting about the Japs, water and speed. If they could make twenty miles a day, or if only ten miles if they had to travel at night, it would take more than a month to reach Russia. The route would be east northeast, to the closest Russian border.

They stayed in camp on the twenty-second of June. At the time that the guards were at the gate, checking out the men to the factory, the group made their way through the fence and headed north, away from Mukden.

187

The escape was discovered at tenko that night. The Japs became vindictive. More guards were brought in to supplement the detail that had been with us through the winter. They then cut the food ration. The men who were in the same barracks as the escapees were taken in for questioning. The Japs method of questioning was always accompanied by physical violence. The men who were interrogated didn't go to work for two or three days. The men told us that the favorite method of interrogation was the water treatment. A hose was shoved down a man's throat and water was poured in until it overflowed. It was an easy was to drown a man. There were some men who were so badly beaten that they had to stay in camp for two weeks.

The interrogations went on for a week. On the twenty-ninth of June they came to an end. The Japs told the officers that the three men had been captured. There were no other details available. The escapees were in the camp guardhouse under constant guard.

On the fourth of July the Japanese Propaganda Corps came into camp. We were told that there would be still and movie shots taken of the POWs to show how well we were being treated. Extra food was issued. Fresh vegetables were provided. Cigarettes were passed out in profusion by the members of the Corps to butter us up.

One of the men was given a prepared statement to read while the movie cameras rolled. After he read the statement he refused to cooperate. The Jap sergeant with the Corps pulled out his sword and beat him across the back and shoulders with the flat of the blade. He collapsed into unconsciousness. The episode, we were told later had been photographed. We became sullen, angry and completely uncooperative. Another group of men was brought in to replace us. This group was warned not to cause any trouble or the whole camp would suffer.

The statement that the Corps wanted us to attest to was:

"The English are a warmongering nation. They have been responsible for starting most of the major wars in the past two hundred years."

We found out that the statement had been written by a member of the Corps who had been educated at Oxford. I remembered that the Japs hadn't had any Western World contact, except for the Portuguese, until Dewey went to Japan in the middle of the nineteenth century. So the Propaganda Corp had dreamed up their own version of world events as they saw them.

During the three days that the Propaganda Corps was in camp there had been no mention of Meringolo, Pallaiti and Chastine. On the morning of the seventh of July, the morning after the Propaganda Corps left, the escapees were taken to the cemetery on the hill north of camp and executed by firing squad.

One of the Jap guards told someone, we never found out who, that the Americans had killed a Chinese policeman and that that was why they were executed, not because they had escaped. I wondered about the truth of the story, but then, they had not shot me when I had been returned to Cabanatuan, so maybe there was some truth in the story.

The effect of the execution left a mark on us. We became vindictive, vengeful and surly. We became uncooperative at the factory and slowed down the work tremendously. Sabotage increased tenfold. Sabotage went on a rampage. No one could accept the punishment as being justified. The Geneva Convention was not being observed by the barbaric medieval Japs.

The machinists were the cause of the greatest sabotage. They overloaded the machines. A typical depth of cut on a piece of stock being machined was ten to fifteen thousands of an inch, depending on the metal being machined. The men increased the depth of cut to eighty and one hundred thousands of an inch. The tool would overheat, the metal would gouge and the tool would break. Most of the time the gouging would cause the workpiece to rip our of the chuck and cause damage to the lathe bed and the chuck. The production in the machine shop dropped more than sixty percent in less than a week. The draftsman also caused a lot of problems. There were dimensions missing from the blueprints, incorrect dimension lines, improper views of the components of a design. Bills of lading were bollixed. Gears, screws, shafts, cotter pins and other pieces used to assemble the machines that were being manufactured were called out incorrectly. Quantities of items were wrong. Either too many or to few. The planning group and the production control group helped to add confusion to the effort. Pieces were missing and machines could not be assembled. The production line bogged down. Excess quantities of some components were spelled out, and again shortages were found in other components. The bills of materials were always correct.

The Japs were furious. They threatened the men and informed us that our food rations would be cut down and our privileges curtailed.

Chang, one of the Chinese engineers, warned me that the Japs were at the end of their rope. He suggested that we should stop or in the least relent for a while. "You will have trouble Pete," Chang warned me. His English was better than even that of the stateside educated Japs. "The interpreter suspects you of being involved. He doesn't know what or how, but he knows that a lot of the paperwork originates here." He was endangering himself by warning us.

"You should warn Pinson, and Leon and Felix."

"Thanks Chang, I'll pass the word," I assured him.

Fleming, 692, who was assigned to the blueprint room, was the man who produced the bills of material had been the key to most of the paper work sabotage. He printed up the bogus bills and then made sure that they were replaced by the correct bills. There were only two of us that were involved in that conspiracy. We felt that it was safer that way. If we were caught, then there would be only the two of us punished.

The gang that worked in the drafting room was known officially as the Planning group. The men in the group worked well together. It consisted of Pinson, 438; Kozakevitch, 660; Ravin, 517; Elliot, 453; Balcer, 568; and myself, 695.

The next day Chang warned us that Mr. Ki, the interpreter, suspected the nature of our scheme but that he couldn't prove it.

Ki was the Japanese interpreter in the employ of MKK. Ki said that he had attended the University of Chicago and had lived in the United States for ten years before the war. He acted as the liaison between the Jap Army, the factory and the POWs.

During the noon meal Ki joined us in the drafting room. He was being very friendly, talkative and very generous with the cigarettes that he passed out. "Everything all right?" he started in a nonchalant manner.

"Everything is okay," was the general tone of the answers he received.

"It seems rather odd that there are so many problems with production. Is it possible that there are mistakes being made in here? Could it?" He attempted to be naive. He eyed us one after the other, looking for any sign of weakness or fear.

"Nah, not here. Couldn't be," Pinson answered.

"Just standard SNAFUs," threw in Kozie.

"Maybe the Chinks just can't read the blueprints."

"Humph," he snorted. "Maybe, but I will tell you this. There is sabotage going on. How it is accomplished we don't know, but I will find out." His manner changed, "We suspect that it comes from here. When I find out it will be too bad. Just too bad. It may be that there will be a few less Bastards from Bataan." He had become angry during the course of his interrogation. "There is too much that goes wrong. It cannot be accounted for by run of the mill problems. The Japanese are not as stupid as you Americans think. You will see." His voice had changed. "Now go back to work," he ordered.

Chang gave me a broad wink as the session broke up and we returned to our drafting boards.

We had heard threats before and they didn't phase us. The fact that

Ki had admitted defeat in finding the source of the sabotage bolstered our spirits considerably.

Two days later I was informed that I was being transferred to the construction gang. Yamaguchi didn't like the idea but there was nothing that he could do about it.

"I can imagine just how much work they will get from you," commented Kozie. "With that bad back and gimpy leg you won't be worth much too them. They're making a mistake. You are doing more for them in here."

"I guess that Yamata figured you in on it somehow," offered Johnson in consolation. "But they haven't proved a thing." He smiled encouragement.

"Don't forget," Kozie spoke up, "they really don't have to prove anything. They could just up and shoot you."

"Great! Thanks for the thought." I replied. "Guess tomorrow it is." I felt as though I had failed somewhere along the line. The construction gang didn't offer much of an opportunity for sabotage.

The following day I reported to the construction gang. This was usually composed of sixty to eighty men who were the labor gang for the factory. Whenever there was a job that was just menial labor, it was the construction gang that was assigned the detail.

My previous notions of the lack of opportunity for sabotage were changed drastically. An example of my education was the ditch digging detail. They had been assigned to dig a ditch for a water main. The ditch was staked out. It ran through the sandy soil that was worked easily. There was no shoring so the sides kept caving in continuously. It looked kind of queer to me that twenty men had dug only sixty foot of trench, four foot deep in three days. The trench had been two foot deep when we were assigned the job and the Manchus pulled off of the job. Eight working days later the trench was "V" shaped, two foot wide at the bottom and six at the top, and only ninety foot long. The Jap hancho agreed wholeheartedly, with much ushing and yushing, that it was extremely difficult to make progress in the sandy soil without using any shoring. There was no wood available to shore up the sides he told us.

There was also the unexplainable loss of tools. Picks and shovels were always being lost or stolen. We knew that the civilians valued the tools highly. And, they did bring excellent prices. The tools were picked up for sharpening or repair by a special group of POWs.. The men carrying the tools detoured as they made their way to the blacksmith shop. When they passed the fence of the adjoining factory the tools went over the fence to the waiting shohis, the Manchu kids. Sometimes half of the tools were consigned to trade and never made it to the shop for repair. The next day aspirin, cigarettes, canned goods, usually fish of some kind, and sometimes socks and even a sweater, or two, were made in payment on the next day. It was all conducted on the honor system and never violated.

I arranged for some other items such as gears, diamond dressing tools, grinding wheels, drills, wrenches and all kinds of other small tools that were in great demand. The construction gang operated as the go-between and collected their share of the take. I estimated that a thousand items a month were making their way to the black market. The Japs, even though they patrolled the area, never caught up with any of the men involved.

Then some of the men in the tool room informed us that they had been told that some tools, marked with the MKK stamp, had turned up in Dairen. I was enthralled with the thoughts of how those tools had ended up so far away.

One of the men came in with a story about how the guys were really screwing the Japs. He said that Joe Gozzo had told him that the Japs had put them to work straightening out nails. Boxes of bent, rusty and otherwise used, nails had been brought in. A crew of men were told to straighten them out and sort them according to size. Soon one of the men proposed that they form the assembly line. They formed an assembly line and went to work. One man was to straighten the nail. The next one was to bend it, then the next guy was to straighten it out again and pass it along to the man at the end of the line who was to sort the nails into boxes by size. The majority of nails didn't survive the two or three straightening cycles and were broken. The Japs never caught on as to what was going on.

CHAPTER 17 -- NEW CAMP

We were informed that the new barracks into which we were to move were almost complete. The new camp had been built to house us as had the factory to employ us. The camp was a half mile east of the factory, across an empty field. Empty, except for a lonely old tree that stood, alone - the only one for hundreds of yards, alongside the road that had been built for us. This, we were told was going to be our home for the next twenty years. And, we were told, to show how generous and kind the Japanese people were, they would even allow our relatives to visit us after the U.S. became a Japanese colony. Naturally, the Japs were going to win the war and we would work for them for the rest of our lives.

Moving day was the twenty-ninth of July. We evacuated Splinter Camp early in the morning and were pretty well established in the new camp by late afternoon.

The new barracks were in a compound that was six hundred foot east to west and twelve hundred foot north to south. The wall around it was a foot thick and twelve foot high. On the top of the wall were strung three strands of high tension wire. In the prisoner side of the compound there was also a barbed wire fence that created a no man's land that was fifty foot wide.

Access to the prisoner side, after entering the main gate in the west wall, in the northwest corner of the compound was through a reception and search building. There was a hospital building, a kitchen, a warehouse, a bath house, a kitchen, the barracks and a boiler room. the prisoner side was set apart from the Jap side which was in the northern sector. That held an office building, the jap barracks, a Jap kitchen and a bathhouse as well as two warehouses and a guardhouse and garage.

The prisoner's barracks were two story buildings one hundred and sixty foot long and fifty four foot wide. At each end was a foyer and a staircase. Each floor of the building was divided into five rooms or bays. A center aisle ran the full length of the building from foyer to foyer. Each bay had a six foot aisle that ran across from one side of the building to the other. A large round petchuka stood at each wall, two to a bay. There were two platforms. One a foot above the floor and another five foot above it. These were seven foot wide. At the wall of each of the platforms was a shelf, two foot above the platform and a foot wide, to hold personal belongings. Six bunks were laid out in each of the eight platforms for a total of forty-eight to a bay, which became known as a Section. The three barracks were connected at the east end by a single story building that housed the washing sinks and the latrines. Each of the barracks was eighty feet from the other. They formed a huge "E".

The parade ground occupied a section that was three hundred foot by two hundred foot in the southwest corner of the prisoner compound.

Watch towers, thirty foot high had been built in each corner to provide an unobstructed view of the no man's land and the barracks.

The Japs were becoming more fanatic. They had been infuriated by the sabotage that had followed the executions, and were not making any allowances for any infraction of the rules. The guards strutted and pranced as they made their rounds. The Jap officers became even more vicious.

The "Bull", a short fat slob, was the worst of the lot that we had at that time. He was a captain. Taii Miki, in Japanese. Another was a lieutenant, chui, in Japanese, Murata. Enlisted men and non-coms were no better. Most of the Americans were most happy to use the title Taii when addressing the Jap captains. Taii in Filipino means shit. So we were only to happy to comply.

The Bull was a sword rattler. He liked to walk through the barracks or the factory grounds eyeing everyone of us. He had the habit of drawing his saber and charging at a man as he stood at attention. A man would back off as the saber whizzed around him. Bull would back a man up against a wall and would order the man to say "America lose war." At first we would comply, repeating the words to pacify the asshole. He would order the men to repeat the phrase three times. Then the Bull would whack the man with the flat of the blade and then told to go about his business.

One of the men refused to comply with Taii Miki's order. This sent the Bull into a rage. He backed off, pointed his sword at the man and charged at him. The man stood his ground. The point of the saber was driven into the wall and inch from the POW's arm. The Bull then placed the point of his weapon at the man's throat, drawing blood. The American refused to comply. The Bull beat him unmercifully with the flat of his blade. The American took it all and didn't wince. This infuriated the Bull even more.

Word was passed around about how easily the Bull was frustrated. We became more defiant of the man. The next time he pulled his stunt the POW laughed in his face. The Bull went livid and left the man without touching him. The Bull came across a Jap guard, a private, who did not salute fast enough to suit the Bull as he went racing past him. The Jap private was beaten by the Bull.

Everytime the Japs were short on temper was an indication that they were not faring well in the war. It was an excellent barometer as to the progress of the war. Sometimes it was a painful way to find out because they were prone to use rifle butts and cuts from swords and bayonets.

It was shortly after we were settled in the new camp that we found a way to hold religious services. Previously it had been impossible to assemble any number of men to hold a service since all of the buildings had not had enough room. In the new barracks we held services in the upper foyer at the east end of the building. The second floor had an open area by the stairs that was twenty-five by thirty feet. Here it was possible to assemble fifty and more men. Since the Japs did not allow a gathering of more than ten men at any one time, it was necessary to post lookouts to warn us of the approach of a Jap. We used lookouts for many of our other activities also and had developed a system. When a guard made an inspection tour, he had to enter by one of the only two doors to the building. To enter the east door he had to walk the length of the building out in the open and could be spotted through the windows. Then we would exit through the upper floor of the barracks. If he entered the west door and started upstairs, the lookout would alert us and the men would disperse through the upper floor and down the east stairway.

The first services were only gatherings on Sunday morning, the only day of rest. One Sunday a month we had readings from the bible and prayers. The frequency of the inspections kept the services to only short sessions.

The main past time was gambling. Blackjack, craps and poker were the usual games. A lookout was required because the Japs would try to sneak into the barracks. When they caught the men gambling they confiscated whatever booty they found. This meant that cigarettes, buns and money, and whatever else was being gambled, was taken. Cards were permitted only for social games, not for gambling.

The favorite game was blackjack or twenty-one. It was fast. The stakes were as varied as one could imagine for a prison camp. Money and food as well as cigarettes, and personal services were the typical stakes. The personal services were peculiar to our life in the prison camp. Washing a man's dishes, bowl, canteen cup and spoon after each meal for a month was worth three to five yen depending on how badly the man that was gambling wanted the money. The yen and the dollar were equal in value. Doing laundry for a week was going at two yen. Chow detail, carrying the chow buckets and washing them for each meal was a rotating chore shared by all men in the section. Chow detail went for a yen a turn or a day's duty.

Money, the yen, was obtained from various sources. The pay of the factory workers and the proceeds from the sale of contraband to the Manchus were the primary sources. The men working in the factories were paid fifteen to twenty-two sen (cents) a day by the Jap Army. The factory actually paid the Army between fifteen and twenty-two yen (dollars) a day. The other ninety percent we were told bought the food, clothing and medicine for us. If it cost ninety percent of a man's pay for the food, since we never received any additional clothing and there was no medicine, then the Japs were paying through their flat nostrils for the food. We did find out that the camp commandant was pocketing hundreds of thousands of yen a month through some of the disgruntled Jap soldiers.

Our food consisted of meager portions of blue maize (Indian corn), soybeans and corn meal. Eight hundred calories a day.

Food bought at the factory, from the Manchus was quite inexpensive. A stack of ten paper thin pancakes, pan as the Manchus called it, about twelve inches in diameter, cost only a yen. A can of fish, Lord only knows what kind, was only two yen and fifty sen. Those of us who could deal for the food at the factory, that is those who could manage, could supplement our meager rations.

There were a lot of health problems among the men. One of the these was the damnedest that we had ever encountered. We had worms. Intestinal worms. It was anybody's guess as to where the infection had started. Abe (Sol) Fromer had told me that he had worms. But one incident that almost made us puke our food occurred one night when everything seemed to be going along quite well.

We were eating the supper meal, batting the breeze at the same time when Fleming started to cough.

"Getting a cold?"

"No. I feel alright."

He continued to cough and then started to choke.

"You okay?"

At that time Fleming put down his bowl and started in a real fit of coughing. Suddenly a worm about ten inches long came out of his nose. He jumped in amazement.

"Jeez!" He looked at the worm he held in the palm of his right hand. "What the hell is that?"

"Ah, nothing but a worm." Pinson answered. "I seen a lot of them in the Philippines. Nothing to worry about. Too bad we haven't any of the worm medicine they had in the Navy. Clear them up in no time."

"Hey, maybe we could go fishing?" some wiseass across the section called out.

"Shit! You mean I got those in my gut. The Goddamn thing nearly choked me to death. I'm going on sick call in the morning. I got to get rid of the damn things."

"Don't worry about it. It won't kill you." Pinson smirked.

The doctors told us that they didn't have any medicine for the worms and that we would have to live with them until the Japs brought in some worm medicine.

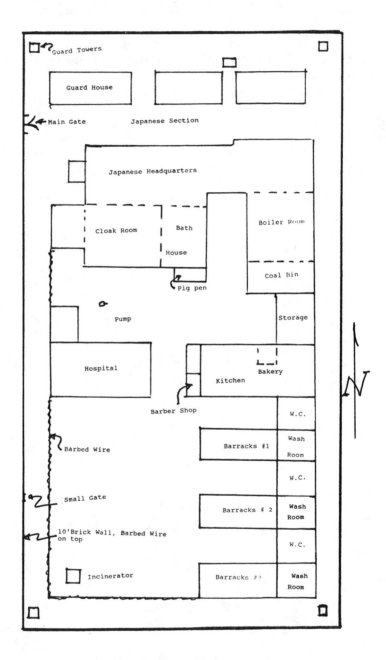

Mukden (Hoten) POW Camp, Manchuria.

CHAPTER 18 -- THE SMUGGLERS

The officers and men that remained in camp were an excellent market for the contraband that was available at the factory. Some of the men remained in camp to run the camp. The officers remained in camp because they were the so called "elite". The Japs didn't require them to perform any duties. Some of the officers, to keep from being bored to death before they starved to death, volunteered for some functions such as the go-betweens in the factory, and one of the English, who spoke Nipongo well enough, acted as an interpreter. The other officers sat around playing cards, or they bitched and moaned, feeling sorry for themselves. Usually moaning about the lack of advancement in grade. Some men worked as cooks and janitors. Others worked in the hospital. Then there were some men who were sick or otherwise too incapacitated to work. All of these were a ready market that supported the smugglers.

Smuggling was a high risk business, so the prices for the contraband were equally high.

There were inspections when leaving the factory and when entering the compound. Personal body inspection was not carried out as we left the camp. The normal procedure we went through was to fall out and line up in formation at seven. We counted off and sick call was carried out. If a man was too ill to work because of malaria, dysentery or some other problem, he would step out in front of the line-up. We would then be questioned as to the nature of the illness by either a Jap officer or a non-com. After describing the symptoms we would wait for a judgment. If accepted as valid, we would go back to the barracks and then report on Sick Call at ten to the hospital. If the symptoms were not convincing enough, or if the "judge", the Officer of the Day, acting as the instant doctor, didn't feel like accepting the symptoms, he would send us to work. Byoki was the term used for sick.

The easiest going Jap on the byoki call was Yamogushi, a non-com and the principal interpreter. The worst was the fat prick Taii Miki, the Bull. The next in line to the Bull was Murata Chuii.

After the byokis (sick men) fell out, we marched out through the reception hall, through the inspection stalls without any inspection, out through the main gate and across the field to the factory. At the factory we passed through the inspection hall at the gate and into a compound where we were counted off again. Sometimes there was a cursory inspection as we entered the factory grounds.

Leaving the factory was quite another matter. We would line up in the compound and count off. Then we entered the building through six doors, single file. Inside the building were six corridors formed by waist high fence of two by fours to keep the lines separate. We would then be searched on entering by a factory guard. This was done holding hat and all legal possessions in our hands and with arms raised. The searchers would feel under the arms, pat all pockets, and feel the arms and legs. When wearing an overcoat, the coat had to be unbuttoned and held open. If anyone of us was caught with contraband the search intensified. Shoes would have to be removed and shaken out. Pants would also have to be dropped and the crotch searched. Occasionally a strip search was carried out. We would then walk through the building to the gate end and go through another search by the camp guards. After counting off again we would march off to the camp. We lined up again and counted off before we entered the reception hall through six lanes separated by rails for another inspection carried out by the camp guards.

The possibility of smuggling an item of any size through the series of inspections was negligible and presented formidable obstacles. It taxed our ingenuity. There was, of course, high personal risk. The risk was not just the confiscation of the contraband which was usually quite valuable, but also personal punishment. A beating with the flat of a sword or saber, a kick or a rifle butt in the crotch, a rifle butt in the face or ribs, or a knee in the gut. Then came the questioning session. One would have to stand at attention until fatigue would cause one to drop to the ground. There was also the water cure, and the sneaker beating during the questioning. The Japs wanted to know about conspirators, partners and sources. The guardhouse sentence usually followed. Confinement could be three to sixty days depending on the kind of contraband. While in the guardhouse the food ration was the same as when we had first been confined to the first camp. One day's ration every three days. Standing all day in a crouched position because the cell was not high enough to stand up straight. The guardhouse was unheated.

Due to the risks involved, the price of the contraband items was relatively high in camp. A can of fish was fifteen to twenty yen. Aspirin, a box of twelve, was ten yen. A one pound, half a kilo, of salt was five yen. A kilo of sugar was twenty-five yen. Candy, three to five yen depending on the type. There three kinds available, Russian, Manchu and Japanese. A hard boiled egg was five yen while a fresh egg cost eight to ten yen depending on the size. At the factory the price was usually about one tenth of the camp price.

The techniques that we developed to smuggle were ingenious and as varied as the smugglers themselves. The easiest method was to observe the guard and watch what kind of a search he was conducting. If a guard was a crotch feeler he would not be searching under the arms or in the pockets. One would change lines and place the smuggle items where the guard wasn't searching. The same technique applied to the other kind of searches that were being conducted. For some unknown reason the belly was the least likely to be searched even though the small of the back, the armpits and the shoes were searched. Another method involved a member of the construction crew. The accomplice on the construction crew would pick up the contraband and secrete it in a hole in the sandy soil beyond the inspection building at the factory. The item would be retrieved just before leaving the factory grounds. This involved only a slight risk at the factory end. It still left the inspection at the camp entrance which many times could be only a cursory inspection.

One of the safest ways of secreting the contraband was in something that would not be inspected. I had made a new pair of clackers because the repair job on my shoes hadn't lasted long because of the cheap Jap leather. The Japs permitted us to wear them to the factory simply because they were an accepted piece of attire among the Japs themselves. We made the single strap style across the ball of the foot whereas the Japs used the cross strap version or the between the toe type. My new pair was contoured to fit the bottom of my feet at the toe, ball arch and heel I had carved the wood and the sanded it smooth with sandpaper that I had obtained at the factory. This pair had no cleats. They were almost three inches thick The result was a clacker that resembled a Dutch wooden shoe except that the feet were placed on the top of the shoe instead of inside. The strap was a good piece of high grade leather that had come from a machine drive belt that had come from the factory.

There had been a rash of apprehensions at the factory gate and the contraband was scarce in the camp. The intensity of the searches increased daily. Prices of aspirin and cigarettes went up to the highest they had ever been.

I listened to a group of men that included some Aussies and English as they discussed the smuggling problem.

Jack Hodgen, eleven ninety-one, had been ogling my clackers. "How come the Dutch shoe?"

"It's not really a Dutch shoe. It's my version of a clacker. Easy to walk in and it keeps my feet out of the muck and mud," I explained.

"Still looks like a Dutch shoe," he smiled, "only it's not hollow."

"Yeah, I guess it does," I agreed. "Too damn much work too hollow it out."

"You're not kidding," sneered someone in the group. "especially with the size of that hoof you've got. You would wind up with canoes."

This remark brought a roar of laughter and some more kidding. I wasn't paying much attention because of the unintended brilliant suggestion. Now to carry out the idea that had been sparked by the remarks. I had to hollow out the clackers. The job needed a little planning to execute. I headed for the carpenter shop at noon and made a deal with a couple of the guys that worked there. One was to act as a lookout for the Jap foreman who always took long lunch hours. He went home to eat and sometimes didn't return for more than an hour and a half. I used the band saw to slice the clackers into two pieces. One was about two inches thick leaving the other piece at about one inch. I used a router to gouge out a cavity an one and a quarter inches deep and a little over four by three inches in the other dimensions. I worked fast and was sweating all the time. I acquired some wood screws in a deal with another carpenter shop worker. After drilling guide holes for the screws with recesses for the heads, I assembled the shoe with the secret compartment. No one in the shop had paid any attention to me during the whole operation which had taken about a half hour. I thanked the men as I left, telling them that I would take care of them for the favor.

I bartered for three packs of cigarettes. I found a safe spot in the yard and stowed the cigarettes in the secret compartment of my clacker. That night I was in business. The price of cigarettes had increased a hundred and fifty percent. The next day I performed the same operation on the other clacker. Now I had a capacity of sixty cigarettes. I felt super safe in smuggling with my new method. The men were puzzled as to how I managed to bring in the cigarettes. Some were peeod because they couldn't figure it out. I was afraid to share my secret with just anyone. A sloppy craftsman could undo the whole business by making a poor clacker. Or at worse, constructing a clacker that would come apart at the wrong time. That would be a major disaster.

Finally I decided to cash in on my invention. I made a deal with one of the men at the carpenter shop. The contract was fifty fifty. I sold twenty pair of custom made clackers at one hundred yen a pair, plus a pack of cigarettes. Payment had to be made in camp, not at the factory.

All through the summer, the warm weather period it was the only foolproof method of smuggling that was never uncovered by the Japs. Neither was the secret revealed by any of the smugglers. Each felt it was protection of their source of income. I turned to other items after the price of cigarettes dropped to an unprofitable level. Candy and fish always brought high prices and had a ready market. The size of my foot was a thing for which I was thankful. A can of fish, a sardine can, was one by three and a quarter by four a half inches. After careful measurement I discovered that I had clackers that were large enough to secrete one of the cans plus fifteen cigarettes that would act as cushion material. I enlarged the cavities in both of the clackers.

The winds that came in from Mongolia and Siberia in September caused a drastic change in the weather in a short time. I had to abandon the clackers because of the cold weather. There was little smuggling activity during the fall.

The construction gang enjoyed some of the contraband, but only at the factory.

My bad back and gimpy leg usually kept me off of the hard labor details and I wound up doing most of the paper work for the Jap hancho. I had to check a lot of the stores in the warehouse. This turned out to be a fortunate turn of events.

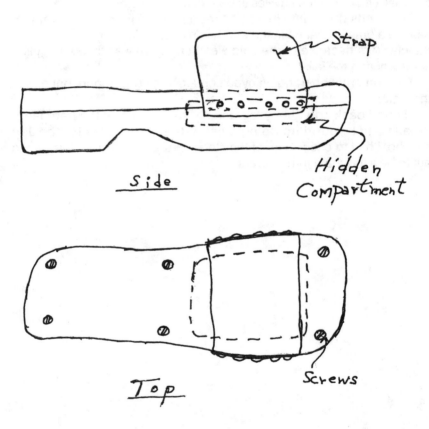

Go-aheads (clackers) with secret compartment.

CHAPTER 19 -- PINK LADY

It was just the weirdest of accidents that we discovered that one of the warehouses contained a huge supply of alcohol. The alcohol was in the anti-freeze stored in fifty-five gallon drums. The winter temperatures dropped to forty and fifty degrees below zero. Alcohol alone didn't keep the water in the engines from freezing, so it was mixed with glycerin. A pink coloring agent had been added. From what the Japs had told us we assumed that the alcohol was methyl, wood alcohol. That made it poison. We wouldn't touch it. It tasted sweet because of the glycerin. No one wanted to take a chance and drink the stuff. No one that is, except Hank.

I found Hank drunk a dew days after we had discovered the cache. He had stupidly disregarded all of our warnings. He was out cold, dead drunk. Fortunately it was midmorning. I told a couple of the men about Hank's condition and asked them for help. We dragged him back to the construction gang's shack nearby. The story I told was a doozer. "A Manchu came in on a cart, he had a bottle of some kind of brandy. Hank stole it and drank the whole frigging thing," I lied.

"What kind of brandy?"

"Any more around?"

"No," I continued my story. "I think the name of it was Dragon Lady."

"Hell, let's get the chinks to bring some in for us."

"Let's check with them this afternoon when they make the deliveries."

Hank woke up in the middle of the afternoon. "Don't say a damned word about the stuff. There'll be all kinds of hell to pay and you could be in big trouble. So will the rest of us. I don't know if you are going to be sick or not. We'll have to check with Herbst and find out what happens when you drink wood alcohol."

"Pete, I won't say a thing, not a thing. Promise," he promised groggily.

"Don't you know that you could die from the stuff? It could ruin your damned kidneys. You could maybe go blind." I was concerned and also mad at him for taking such a stupid chance. "How much did you drink anyway?"

"About a half of a canteen cup. I feel fine. Just got one hell of a headache. I've had worse hangovers before," he responded.

I figured that a half a canteen cup was maybe as much as eight ounces. "You sure smell sweet though," I wrinkled my nose, "like some of the ladies at the barrio bar. Or maybe a two bit whore. That's it! I've got a name for it! Pink Lady! I think you're going to shit pink too. Pink Lady."

"I'm all right, " he continued to grumble. "But what the hell are you talking about?"

"Okay. But don't say anything. I told them that you stole a bottle of brandy from one of the Manchu carts." I warned him. "I'll see you in camp tonight. Maybe we had better talk to Doc Herbst tonight." I was worried since I didn't know how wood alcohol affected the system. "What drum did you open?"

"Only one by the column, not with the rest of them. All by itself. I had to break the seal."

"Okay. I'll go and take a look when I'm checking the stock. See you later."

The Manchus couldn't get any brandy I was told that evening. They didn't know what Dragon Lady was, and had never heard of it, which didn't surprise me since I had dreamed up the name on the spur of the moment. They told the men that brandy was rationed as was all alcohol and it brought very high prices when available on the black market. And, no Manchu would risk bringing it into the factory compound.

I went to check on Hank after chow. "Seen Hank?" I asked one of his buddies from his section.

"Yeah. He's in the crapper. He didn't even eat."

I went to the latrine at the back of the building on the first floor. "I walked along the row of stalls. "Hank. Hank."

"Yeah. Over here at the end," came the strained answer. "That you Pete?"

"Yep." I opened the door to the cubby, "Sick?"

"Man! I got them! The runs," he accentuated this with a rectal blast that reverberated through the room.

"The alky. Damn. I told you. How bad is it?"

"Just like a dose of castor oil."

"I'll go and see Doc and ask him. Maybe he can tell us something. I'll come back."

Doc Herbst was quartered with the rest of the officers in Building One. He asked many questions which I avoided answering because of the situation. The outcome of the session was that if Hank had drunk about eight ounces of methyl alcohol he would probably be heaving his guts all over the place instead of just having the runs. Hank had told me that it was sweet. Herbst explained that it was probably the glycerin that made it sweet. He couldn't say what internal damage would result. The runs was due to the amount of glycerin that Hank had consumed and would stop in a matter of hours. I said I would get back to him and left to reassure Hank that he would be alright in short order if the stuff was grain alcohol.

"Hank? How are you doing?" I asked from outside of the stall.

"You mean now that I shit my brains out. I'm cleaned out." He pushed open the door and smiled dejectedly.

"Doc says you will be okay if it is grain alcohol. You are in deep shit if it's wood alcohol."

"When will I know?" He sounded worried and anxious.

"By tomorrow," I told him. "Better see if you can go byoki in the morning. Then take it easy."

"Okay."

"Need any help?"

"No. I'll squat here a while. I'll wash my pants later and then sack out. Thanks."

"I'll see you tomorrow after work."

I didn't see Hank until the evening because he made sick call and stayed in camp. I found him in his section after the evening meal. "How's it going?"

"Okay. I'm fine." He sounded relieved. "I went over and talked to the doctor this afternoon. He said that if it had been wood alcohol I would be in deep shit right now, and not with the shits. The glycerin was what gave me the shits. Man that was rough."

"Did you tell him what you drank and where you found it?"

"Nope," he smiled. "You know if there was a way to get rid of the glycerin that stuff would make good drinking whiskey." He looked at me slyly. "Do you think that you know how we could get rid of the glycerin?"

"Yes. I think I know a way." I smiled at him in my own self-satisfaction.

"And I suppose that you are going to keep it a secret."

"Yep. But, you and I, fifty fifty?"

"You nuts or something Pete? You think that you can really keep that kind of stuff from the other guys for long?"

"I know that we can't keep the guys from the antifreeze. But what happens when they all have the runs?"

"It's rough," Hank agreed. "But there are a hundred drums of the stuff. Five thousand gallons!"

"Yep," I sat back complacently and started to fill my pipe. "First, a final test. Just to prove that it is ethyl alcohol." I mulled some ideas.

"Suppose we drink it just the way it is?" Hank asked, playing it coy.

"We won't have much of a market." I predicted. "And the shit dippers will be busy." I laughed.

"Rat! You think you are pretty smart. Don't you?" Hank sneered, but jokingly. "Once the word gets out they'll drink it no matter what." Hank predicted.

It was a possibility that I had already considered. "I know, but probably not for long. I wonder what the stuff would sell for?"

"I'm going to find out, I'll get some tomorrow. No matter what." Hank decided. "And I won't keep it a secret either."

"Okay. I have plenty of benjo kame for sale. You know how much good toilet paper goes for these days." I wasn't going to be bluffed.

I paid a visit to the drafting room about midmorning of the next day. There was an issue of the nineteen thirty-six issue of the Handbook of Chemistry and Physics that gave me the information I needed. Ethyl alcohol boiled at seventy-eight degrees centigrade, methyl alcohol at sixty-four degrees and glycerin at two hundred and ninety-one.

I had found a small still in one of the warehouses some time previous. I could never figure out why they would need a still. It was a puzzle that I never solved. I moved it to a new site and checked it out. It had a temperature controlled heater that checked out pretty accurate with a thermometer. I built a hidden cubby with the drums by moving them around with the portable crane. It was only large enough to hold me and the still. I had to crawl under the drums along the was of the warehouse to enter the distillery. A short extension was all that was necessary to connect up to one of the wall outlets. It was three days before it was in full operating condition.

Since we were allowed to carry our canteens to the factory it made it easy to smuggle the alcohol into camp. The canteens had never been opened or sampled by the guards. The guards would shake a canteen to see if it would rattle or gurgle. If it gurgled then all was well.

The first batch of alcohol proofed out at one hundred and ninety proof. I had lucked out, there had also been a hydrometer with the still. It looked like water. I filled my canteen and brazenly carried it through the shakedown and inspection lines. It wasn't for sale. I gathered some of the gang together, Kozie, Pinto, Johnson and a few others. The whiskey I made was mixed by adding an equal amount of water to the alcohol. It was a little sweet, but otherwise flavorless. It reminded me of the vodka that the Slavs made from potatoes.

I established a price of fifty yen for a canteen which was about thirty ounces. I made three canteens of drinking whiskey from each canteen of the alky. It was a profitable enterprise as long as it lasted.

Hank brought in the straight stuff which had acquired the name I had originally given the antifreeze, Pink Lady. Hank goofed and let some of the other members of the construction gang find out where he was getting the stuff. A flood of Pink Lady flooded the camp. For two weeks the latrines were doing a standing room only business. Toilet paper was in great demand. The drinking spree came to a sudden end when one of the gang got stoned at the factory. We had all agreed that there was to be no drinking on the factory grounds. But as always, there is one guy that will screw something up. The man refused to be searched as he passed through the inspection line. The guard slapped the shit out of him and then moved up close enough to smell his breath. The guard immediately let out a squalor and alerted the other guards. Everything went haywire at once. The guards started to smell the breaths of the men and one of them decided to check a canteen. I watched as the guards picked up six canteens of Pink Lady. I slid my canteen into the crotch of my pants, leaving only the canteen cup in the carrier on my belt. Searching now consisted of checking for alcoholic halitosis and opening the canteens and checking for alcohol. There was no searching of the crotch, pockets or jackets. I breathed a heavy breath at the guard as I passed. Most of them knew of my gimp and paid no attention to the way I walked. The canteen made it look like I had a full load in my pants. I made it through without any trouble. The men who were caught got the guardhouse for a week. It was also the last of the Pink Lady coming in by canteen. The Japs ran a search through the camp for alcohol. I sold off all of my stock. I was going to leave well enough alone. I was eating quite well from the proceeds and didn't want to risk any time in the guardhouse.

I was buying food from the men who sold it for various reasons. If a man wanted to sell his food, meager as the rations were, no one stopped him. It didn't do any good to try.

Some of the guys said that I was going to get my ass in a sling the way I took chances. Kozie was always on my back about the stupid escapades in which I was involved. It wasn't just the fact that money was needed for food that I was maybe challenging the Fates. I liked the taste and the feel of the excitement, the danger and the conniving. It was an interest, a preoccupation that made the imprisonment bearable. The monotony, lack of direction, the lack of knowledge that we had served any good purpose was a spirit killer. The not knowing when the war would end was in its own way terrifying. Two years had been like two hundred. So it wasn't just for the food. There was an attitude, a camouflage that was just for the Japs. This camouflage was our apparent condescension to imprisonment. The humility of taking orders from the yellow barbarians was a mask. The kowtowing to the megalomaniacs was also a mask. Underneath there was a feeling of purpose. The purpose was sabotage. There was still a war going on even though it was not a battle of the kind we fought on Bataan and Corregidor. We were fighting our own war even though we were prisoners. There were many men who could not, and some who would not, chance sabotage. It was their business. Our officers warned us constantly not to cause any trouble. That was, I suppose, their business too. They were considered chicken shit by the enlisted men. But there was a group that didn't give a damn. The Japs were still the enemy. We planned our own secret war.

The electricians that worked in the factory, POWs, had access to the room that housed the jig borer. The precision machine was the only one that MKK possessed. The room had a thermostat for controlling the room temperature to make sure that precision could be accomplished when machining the jigs and fixtures. Heat was supplied by electricity. The machine had a peace time value of maybe sixty thousand dollars. In these critical times we figured that it was worth a great deal more to the war production of the Japs.

There had been numerous discussions about a means of sabotaging the jig borer. We concluded that the best way was to use fire. The heat would either melt or warp the machine so that it would be useless. We devised a methods that we thought would be almost foolproof. A test was run to make sure the technique would work. A steel bar was placed across a power cable and across a hot plate. The steel was heated and it short circuited the cable causing a fire. It was thought that if the bar was found after the fire it would be considered an accident.

The night that the building burned was a cold one. The water froze as the firefighters poured it on the building. There was also the lack of any good fire fighting equipment. The building and the jig borer were in complete ruin and totally useless.

The Japs suspected sabotage, but not by the POWs. They though that some of the Chinese had used incendiaries. It was also concluded that they had fired the wrong building. It was evident, said the Japanese that if the warehouse they had intended to burn there would have been much more damage and it would have been much harder to have brought the fire under control.

Now that MKK did not have a jig borer it was necessary to have the jigs and fixtures machined by another company. This caused a delay in production. So we had achieved our goal. Total success!

Winter came in in a hurry. Along with the cold weather came the demand for alcohol again. Since it was no longer permissible to carry canteens, a new method would have to be found to bring in the alcohol. I settled on finding some kind of a flexible bottle as the means of bringing it in. I tried to inveigle Chang and a couple of the Manchus to bring in a hot water bottle or an enema bag. They said that such items just didn't exist. I tried the camp hospital without success. It looked as though my plan would not work. I searched the warehouse for an inner tube without success. I tried the garage and still didn't succeed in finding anything. I was frustrated. I sat by the stove in the construction shack one afternoon and decided I had to do some research, some logical thinking. What could I use? Did it have to be rubber? Even if it was rubber, how could I conceal it? I doodled and made list. I concluded that it would have to be rubber, flexible. I would have to conceal it on my body. I thought of the falsies I had seen. The kind that the women blew up and inserted in their bras.

I chuckled to myself as I remembered a dance I had been to years before. An escort went to pin a corsage on his date's dress. He stuck the pin through the falsie and it blew up. I snickered to myself. The crew around the stove eyed me suspiciously.

I made a list of rubber items. Hot water bottle, enema bag, blowup falsies, balloon, tire tube, hose, swimming wings, life preserver, life jacket, basket ball bladder, football bladder and rubber gloves. I locked on to the tire tube because the other items were not of this culture. China was not like America. They didn't have the things that we had. Then it hit me. I was being stupid. Not an auto tire tube! A bicycle tire tube. Everybody used a bicycle for transportation. They were all over the place. I had hit on it. A bicycle tire tube.

The tube, stolen by a couple of the men on the gang, cost me five packs of cigarettes. It was one of the fat ones. It was magnificent. It was also new.

I set the still into operation. Then came another obstacle. How the hell could I fill the tube? The small hole in the stem seemed to a formidable problem. It took some experimentation to find a way to fill the tube. I solved it by using a piece of rubber hose that slipped over the valve stem. I had a can made with a small spout at the bottom to which I attached the hose. After flattening the tube I held the can with the alcohol above it. It didn't fill easily. I had to hold the can six feet above the tube to create enough pressure to fill the inner tube. I replaced the air valve and had a leak proof assembly that held almost two quarts of alcohol. I was in business again. The tube went around my skinny belly twice. I had to become a gymnast to fit it around my waist. A bellyband, standard with many Japs, was wrapped over it. Then my underwear, shirt and jacket. The jacket was a tight fit. By the time I had finished I was sweating. When we lined up to go through the inspection line I had my eyes, fingers and toes crossed for good luck.

The Manchu I caught for inspection merely patted me. I swallowed hard and walked through to the Jap search team at the other end of the inspection building. I came up against the Yasme Kid. He was a real prick if there ever was one. He eyed me and started to poke at me.

"Open coat." His English was not extensive, but he knew enough to be obnoxious with the way he used it.

"Okay." I opened my coat and sweated.

"Nanda." He drawled the word. "What? Taksan niku." He Poked at my flabby waist. He sneered. "You fat slob," he said in clear English. "Okay, go." It must be true that the first words that one learns are slang and swear words because he had the right ones down pat.

I fell in behind Kozie. "You carrying?"

"Hi Koz. Yeah, five pounds of fat." I chuckled

"Meat or lard?" He turned to look at me with a frown.

"Lard." I laughed.

"How come that Yasme called you a fat slob? How the hell did you get fat? Huh?" asked Hinds from my left. "What kind of food you eating that you fattened up?"

Hinds, 400, was short and thin. He had a peculiar way of walking, almost as if he were prancing. His feet were always shuffling when he stood and talked. His face always had a wry expression and almost always showed some degree of belligerence. The lines around his mouth always made him look drawn and tense. They also made him look a lot older than he was. He had learned to speak Japanese very well.

The camp inspection was a snap and I sailed right through without a hitch. I sighed with relief when I left the reception building.

Kozie came up behind me as I wiped the cold sweat from my face. "What are you up to now conniver? More trouble huh? One of these days---" He laughed.

"Just like I said, no trouble. No conniving." I lowered my voice," Who'll pay a hundred for a quart of whiskey?"

"Alky? You kidding?" He was amazed. He looked at me as though he were trying to fathom my secret. "Anybody will pay a hundred for a quart. But who has any?" He bugged his eyes at me and stopped dead in his tracks. "You!? You no good louse!" He laughed, shaking his head. "You are almost rotten enough to make a good Polock." He made a motion as if to slap me on the back and caught himself in time and stopped. "You never quit."

"Come on over later and I'll buy you a drink."

"Okay. After chow. Never drink on an empty stomach. How much do you have to sell?"

"A gallon." I told him in a low voice.

"Alky or Pink Lady?"

Whiskey. Pure alky, three hundred a quart."

Kozie said nothing as he walked off shaking his head in disbelief.

I asked one of my bunk mates to draw my chow. I headed for the latrine and the cubby at the end. The place was empty because it was chow time. I had to practically undress to remove the tube. I hid the tube under my overcoat and returned to my bunk. I hid the thing under my blankets and headed for the chow. Willy, who had drawn my chow, had saved a place at the table for me. As I sat down He eyed me oddly.

"What's up?"

"Nuthin." I answered between mouthfuls of beans and bun.

"You got seconds coming," he informed me.

"Want them?" I offered.

"Yeah? Sure. Thanks." He finished his food, stepped over the bench and formed up in the seconds line.

The food, soup, mush or beans, that was served from the buckets usually went around, with some left over after each man received his regular portion. The remainder was doled out as far as it would go as seconds. A record was kept and the next round of seconds started with the man after the last one to receive seconds. Willy collected my seconds and sat down beside me.

"Need help?"

"Later. Stick around the bunk and keep an eye on it."

"Okay." It was all that was necessary.

After cleaning up the eating dishes I turned to Willie, "I need four canteens for a while tonight. How about borrowing yours? I'll let you have dregs."

"Sure. Just leave a mouthful."

"Don't worry, there'll be more than that," I promised. "The best stuff available."

"Fine. I'll scrounge up a couple more." Willie went to borrow the canteens. He returned within minutes.

I secreted the tube in my overcoat and headed for the latrine with Willie following with the canteens. We squeezed into a cubby and started the transfer operation. The canteens rattled as we went through the operation. I draped the tube around my neck and unscrewed the valve stem with the back of the cap, inserted the stem into a canteen and squeezed gently.

"Holy cow! What next?" Willie asked.

"Easy. Quiet! Someone will hear you," I cautioned. Almost all of the alcohol drained out of the tube. As we left the cubby someone whistled insinuatingly.

"Shithead." Willie threw back over his shoulder as we left.

"Not a word about the gimmick," I warned Willie. He nodded agreement.

I stashed the tube under the loose board under my bunk without anyone seeing it. "We need water, then we're in business."

"I'll hunt up the bucket," offered Willie.

Water was a problem. Many men drank it from the tap, but they were taking chances of coming down with some disease. Water was boiled before drinking. It was one of the duties of the kitchen. It was then brought to the barracks in large wooden buckets. Canteens were filled from the bucket. The last man who emptied the water bucket had to refill it. It was one of the rules that was seldom violated.

Shouts went up for water when Willie brought it in. We borrowed canteen cups and started the dilution. I intermixed the resulting whiskey by mixing from one canteen cup to another until I was satisfied that the whiskey was well mixed and all of about the same strength. The word had spread that there was alky by the time I had finished.

"How much a canteen?"

"One hundred yen," I answered.

"Cripes! You want to die rich?" the potential customer complained.

"Only six quarts available," I replied emphatically.

"Okay okay." He counted out a hundred yen and handed over his canteen. I filled it from one of ours.

Kozie joined us as the whiskey was being transferred. "Got any left?" He looked at the customer as he left. "How much?"

"One hundred."

"I have one sold." He counted out the money. "I'll be back in a few minutes."

Within a half hour all six canteens of the whiskey had been sold. It looked as if there was a potential market of two to three gallons a day.

Willie brought out the pill bottle that held about an ounce and a half. We passed the whiskey around to the men in the section and to our friends until the two quarts were gone.

"How did you get this into camp?" Kozie asked after his third drink.

"Secret," I answered slyly. "It's here. And there will be more."

"Know anything?" asked Willie. He was in great spirits as were the rest of us after consuming a few shots each. "Nobody ever talks about women." He looked around the group gathered around the table wisely. "Why I ask you?"

"I dunno," answered Kozie.

"Me either," Johnson stared at him dumbly.

"Seems to me," I started voicing my thoughts, "that I am too busy thinking about food. I'm too hungry to think about women. And I don't think that I have the strength to do a damned thing to a woman except to chew the hell out of her." I smirked as I made the observation.

"Maybe that's it," Willy made a funny face, "you don't think about women on an empty stomach. I guess if I had one now I could grab a feel and look."

We all laughed.

"You don't think about women on an empty stomach," I parroted. "Come to think of it I think you are right. Hell I remember that I used to dream about women when I was in the Philippines. You know, white women. Not the tan ones down there."

I was greeted by whooping laughter from the group. The alcohol had had its effect on all of us. For the moment we forgot about the prison camp.

"I dunno," put in Kozie, "they got whiter all the time. Hell, I remember one was so white you couldn't find her on the sheet." We all laughed at the exaggeration.

"Hell, that wasn't a bed sheet, it was the bamboo she was laying on, and that was why you see her. Hell, they didn't have no bed sheets anyway. Especially the 803rd Engineers." He meant the remark for Kozie.

"Aw, come on. There were some white ones down there," Kozie insisted.

"Yeah sure, just like these Manchus, huh?" Johnson smirked. "By the way, I haven't seen any good looking Manchu women. Come to think of it, I haven't seen any women. Have they got any women here?"

"Hell no!" Willie yelled.

"Oh yes they have," insisted Kozie. "I saw one. Young and juicy too."

This generated a lot of laughter since it seemed funny to us in our alcoholic induced mood.

"Now just a minute. I mean it, really. I haven't dreamt about a woman at all since the damned war started." I was emphatic and insistent. "Bet you can't tell me what I have been dreaming about. I don't mean the screeching nightmares either."

"Sure I can," Kozie grinned. "A great big juicy steak." He held up his right hand with the thumb and forefinger held about three inches apart. "That thick."

"Yeah," agreed Willie, "with gravy and mashed potatoes and bread and butter."

"And a piece of pie ala mode, with a real cup of coffee," concluded Johnson.

"Right," I admitted. "But no women. We must be psycho." I screwed up my face in alcoholic wonderment. "We just can't be normal if we don't think about women," I concluded.

"Oh I'm all right," squeaked Willie in a high falsetto, "I like boys." He raised his eyebrows and flicked his eyelids.

We jumped him enmass and pounded him in fun.

"Nut!"

We all laughed as we let him up and relaxed again. The rumpus had caused the other men to throw envious glances and jibes at us.

"I guess I better scram. Only ten minutes to tenko." Kozie rose to leave.

"What!? Twenty after already?" We were all surprised at how swiftly the time had passed.

"Thanks Pete. See you." Kozie slapped Willie on the back as he walked away.

"Yeah, thanks." Johnson grinned happily as he left for his section.

"I'm going to have a smoke before I turn in. What some?" I offered Willie some of my pipe tobacco.

"Uh uh. Not tonight. I feel a nice glow right now. I'm just gonna wash and turn in. I'll probably sleep like a dead man tonight. Thanks for everything."

"Hey Pete. Any whiskey left?" asked Stanko as he stopped on his way to his section for tenko.

"All gone."

"I'll buy a quart tomorrow if you have it."

"Might have some. But don't count on it. You know how it is."

Tenko, the night countoff, that was a check on the men, was held at eight thirty and lights out was at nine.

I slept well that night. The alcohol business went well from then on. It was also very profitable.

CHAPTER 20 -- RIOT

One of the most sought after items of contraband was the local newspaper. Even more so was the Nippon Sun or the Nippon News. Those items brought a high price. The Japs forbade the Manchus and the Japs at the factory from passing copies of these to the POWs. The officers always paid well for any copies that were available. We had a couple of people who could interpret them. I myself, was still not too good at deciphering the hieroglyphics.

There was also a great demand for writing materials of all kinds. Paper, pencils and pen and ink were in demand from men who wanted to keep permanent records, brought high prices.

My own supply of pencils, which I had acquired when I had worked in the drafting room had been depleted, so I was on the lookout for a resupply. Johnson and Kozie had provided some pencil and some paper which were available in the drafting room.

I walked outside of the shack one afternoon and saw a Jap guard exercising Hank. Then the guard searched under the cart and came up with the bottle of ink. He held it up in front of Hank and started to berate him. They marched him off. Hank spent three days in the guardhouse. He was beaten and starved for those three days just for a bottle of ink.

In late November, a cold day that had been brought in by the winds from the north and the northwest, Sigh, one of the construction gang had a run in with the Weasel. The guard ordered Sigh back to the shack. He pushed Sigh to speed him up. Sigh lost his footing on the icy ground and fell. I heard the thump forty feet away. Sigh got to his feet mad as hell at the small Jap. He turned on the Weasel and said something to him, then he picked up a long pole from a stack nearby and went for the Weasel. It was a pole that was used as a fence post. It was three inches in diameter and almost seven foot long. Sigh swung it like a baseball bat. The Weasel jumped out of the way and started to yell at the top of his lungs for help. Sigh advanced on him, swinging the pole back and forth. I yelled at Sigh to drop the pole and leave the Weasel alone. He paid no attention to me. As the Weasel turned and ran to the guardhouse I grabbed Sigh by the arm just another man appeared from the shack.

"Let's get the hell inside."

We grabbed Sigh by the arms and rushed him to the shack. He was mad as hell and yelling at the Jap. "I'll kill the stinking skinny yellow
217

bastard. I'll brain him," he shouted as he struggled in our grasp.

Everyone in the shack was on their feet. The sirens blasted loose at the guardhouse. "Riot signal! Now there's hell to pay."

"Everybody pipe down!" someone yelled.

Men were trying to evacuate the shack as we tried to enter. We were pushed out by the gang of men that were rushing out. Jap guards came running toward us with bayonets fixed. The machine guns on the garage roof were uncovered and pointed toward us. I heard the camp siren join the one at the factory as we milled around in front of the shack surrounded by the guards. Trucks roared out of the camp gate as I watched. They sped to the factory across the field. The factory guards and the army guards formed a ragged semi-circle about fifty feet away and stood their ground. A Jap sergeant appeared from somewhere and took charge. The trucks stopped at the gate as the soldiers from camp came running to reinforce the guards. Takeuchi, the fat Jap army interpreter waddled to the line of guards.

"Line up! No more rioting! Line up!" he screamed at the top of his lungs.

The Jap sergeant issued orders. We were formed into a double line and ordered to stand at attention. The company guards stood by the machine guns while the rest of the guards ran around the yard. They rounded up the members of the construction crew from all over the factory grounds.

"Who started the riot?" Takeuchi screamed.

No one answered.

"You will tell. We have orders to shoot! Who started this?" He walked up and down along the line. I looked around to see if all of the gang had been rounded up. I did a quick count and estimated that there were about eighty of us, just about all of the construction gang. Takeuchi turned toward the sergeant and spoke to him. They were joined by the Weasel. They jabbered for about three minutes, then Takeuchi turned to address us. "You will return to camp," he fumed. "You will not be allowed in the barracks until we find the man who threatened to kill the guard." The response was a lot of snickering and odd razzing sounds.

We were marched out without being searched. Outside of the gate we were double timed to the camp gate. Once inside we were lined up in the Jap compound outside of the inspection hall and stood at attention. I started to feel the cold immediately. The temperature had been ten below zero Centigrade by the thermometer outside of the construction shack just before all of this had started.

At five-forty the rest of the men from the factory entered through the gate. They were marched by us and directly into camp.

The wind started to blow from the north. The camp lights had been on for some time and the dark that surrounded the lighted area was like a cold black curtain. My nose was freezing and my fingers were numb. I felt my cheeks tingling from the cold. I rubbed my face with my right hand and was sent sprawling as a rifle butt hit me in the back.

"Nane."

"Samui des." I answered.

"Kiotski na."

I rose and stood at attention as ordered. My feet were freezing. I thought that it must have gotten twenty degrees colder since we had been standing there.

The man in front of me started to march in place. One of the guards walked up to him and stamped his rifle butt on the toes of his shoes. The man screamed in pain and doubled over. The guard shoved him with his rifle and laughed when he fell. "Samui" The Jap smirked at him. The man next to me slumped to the ground and lay there. I moved to see what I could do for him. The rifle butt caught me in the shoulder and I sprawled over him. I rolled and lay on the ground for a moment looking up at the guard who held his bayonet inches from my nose. He motioned for me to stand up.

"Kiotski na." I stood at attention as best I could. It was cold. Frigid cold.

I saw that there were six men laying on the ground. No one made a move toward them. They just lay there freezing.

I moved my toes inside my shoes and started to exercise my fingers. My face was numb and tingling.

The guards changed some time later. I had no real idea of how much time had passed. I estimated that we may have been standing there for more than two hours before Takeuchi appeared.

"Undress! Everyone undress!"

I stared at the fat bastard. Then I thought that the men who had passed out were lucky. They were going to keep their clothes on.

"Take off your clothes and pile them up in front of you. Take off your shoes too. Then stand at attention," he ordered. "Move!"

He walked along the line of incredulous men. No one started to undress. I would have bet that the temperature must have been at least thirty degrees below zero. They must be nuts I thought. We were going to freeze our balls off and die.

The guards started on the men. Rifle butts and bayonets came into play. We started to undress. Slowly. The wind bit through us as we removed our clothes. There were mutterings and swearing as the bitter wind bit at us. Numb fingers, they must have been as numb as mine, couldn't unbutton the jackets or untie the strings on the Jap issue clothes fast enough for the Japs. They came through with rifle butts and bayonets again.

I stood shivering and freezing as I watched the Japs search through the piles of clothing. I never thought that I would have to experience the cold that I had once experienced when I had been in northern Canada. I had almost frozen to death that one winter. I knew that soon it would start to feel warm. That was the danger sign. The false warmth that signaled the freezing process. The worst had been when I had started to thaw. That had been miserable. I thought for some reason about that I must be a real jerk. I had not had the sense to stay home, in the states. No, smart assed me, I had to see the world. All just because of a freeking huge pearl, the Pearl of Allah.

I noticed that the Japs searched through the coats and pants. They threw them where ever they pleased. They did not return them to the original pile from which they had taken them.

I started to shiver uncontrollably with my teeth chattering. Every breath was like inhaling ice water. My chest started to hurt as I breathed. I took shallow breaths to see f it would be less painful.

I saw more men fall. three, then four. I danced in place without regard for the friggin guards. I saw the others doing the same. I rubbed my hands over my belly and my thighs as the cold got worse. The Japs couldn't keep us at attention any more and I noticed that they didn't try.

"Put on your underwear." Takeuchi ordered.

I fumbled with my clothes to find the long sleeved undershirt first. It was hell trying to control my fingers. The tips were numb. My feet felt like chunks of ice half way up my calves. Parts of my face felt frozen. Tears streamed from my eyes and froze. My chest and nose were numb. I was sobbing. I didn't know why. I stepped into my long drawers and couldn't tie the string to hold them in place. I sat on the icy ground without feeling the cold and fumbled with my socks.

A Jap guard stopped in front of me. "Nanda socki, no socks," he glowered at me and threatened me with his bayonet. He prodded me as I ignored him and pulled on the socks with numb hands. I felt only a dull pressure from the point of the sharp bayonet. He jabbed at my butt again and then just walked away.

There was no accounting for the way a Jap acted I thought.

"Okay. Put on your clothes," Takeuchi ordered.

Another guard watched me as I dressed. "I know you," he muttered and then stalked off. I wondered what the hell that had been about. I shivered. I couldn't stop shivering. The man next to me, an older man, still hadn't put his pants on. He stood quivering with cold as the wind picked up. I helped him into his overcoat first. I rubbed his hands and found that I warmed my own hands as I did. He was slim and skinny, about maybe forty years old, but, who could really tell how old he was. We, none of looked young in the condition we were in due to disease and malnutrition. It was harder on him than on me. He mumbled something like thanks, as I helped him with his pants and shoes. He sat on the frozen ground and tried to tie them and then just gave up.

I counted twelve men lying on the ground. Some of the others were dressing them.

"Stand up! Every one line up! The colonel is very angry. Line up and listen," shouted Takeuchi.

Lieutenant Murata came out of Jap headquarters and stalked, pranced, up and sown the ragged line of frozen men. He turned to Takeuchi and spoke to him. I knew that Murata could speak English very well, but it was beneath him to address the POWs directly. It lowered his social status, or something. It was a matter of face for the uncivilized Japs. As he spoke Takeuchi translated.

"You have broken faith with the Imperial Japanese Army," he paused and looked at us. "You have rioted and attacked a Japanese. This is a serious crime. You will be punished. You will no longer work at the factory. You will no longer earn any more money." Another pause. "If there is work, you will work in the camp. We will have no more riots! The MKK people will be afraid to work with you Americans. You will apologize to them. Now you will register your numbers as you go in."

Orders were given to right face and march. The men who couldn't manage on their own were helped by the rest of us. Our POW numbers were listed as we went through the inspection gates.

As we left the inspection building we were met by small groups of men who had come on the run when they heard that we were being released. They helped the men who had collapsed. They carried them back to their sections. I made my own way. When I got to the barracks I was surrounded by a crowd who wanted to know what had happened. There was a lot of swearing at Japs as I was helped out of my overcoat. Willy and somebody else lifted my almost paralyzed arms as they removed it and sat me down on my bunk. My shoes came off. Four men worked on me. They rubbed my hands and feet. The pain of returning warmth hit me.

"Here. Have some of this. It's hot."

I wasn't sure of who it was that offered the cup. My vision was blurred and I was shivering uncontrollably. My face felt hot and the inside of my nose and throat felt raw. I tingled and burned all over.

The hot liquid was tea. Some one had shared some of their treasured stash of tea with me. I was grateful to whoever it was. I felt the hot liquid sear as it went down and hit my stomach.

Tears started to flow unmanageably.

"Willy," I managed between my rattling teeth. He placed his head close to me, "Aspirin. In my mussette bag. Wrapped in tissue paper. Reach in under the false bottom in the bag." I whispered so as not to be overheard by anyone else.

Willy felt around the bottom of the bag and dug out the tissue with the aspirin.

"So that's how it is. No wonder the Japs don't find the stuff."

"Yeah." I answered as I swallowed the aspirin with a mouthful of tea. "Don't tell."

"What the hell happened?" Johnson asked. He had joined the group of men around me.

"There are all kinds of stories about you guys out there," started Willy. "They say that somebody tried to kill a Nip."

"Nuts. I was there when it started. I saw it happen. Sigh got mad at the Weasel after the Weasel pushed him. Sigh fell. He grabbed a pole, a fence post, and started after the Jap." I stopped for a breath of warm air. "We stopped Sigh, but the Weasel blew the whistle. The yellow bastard."

"Did Sigh hit him?" someone asked.

"Shit no! But he scared the shit out of him." I laughed as I remembered how fast the Weasel had run away.

"You should have let Sigh kill the prick. He's one slimy snake." Willy sneered.

"Sure. Kill a Jap and they'd shoot ten of us if not more. Don't be a nut!" Johnson came back. "That's all the more that we have to have happen to us."

"Ah, they wouldn't do it," replied Willy.

"Don't kid yourself," Johnson responded. "Remember Cabanatuan. And at Splinter Camp. They shot those three."

"But that was months ago. They wouldn't do it now," countered Willy.

"The hell they wouldn't." I commented wryly. "I wouldn't trust the stinking slant eyed liars as far as I could push this stove. There wasn't any riot. The stinkin Weasel lied about that, and look at how they reacted. They had the machine guns all ready." I vented some of my anger and frustration. I had warmed up quite well. "I'd bet that they would have used the machine guns if everybody hadn't quieted down as fast as we did."

"No. We are too valuable in the factories," disagreed Willy.

"Man I hope you are right. But I don't believe it," I finished. "Let me up. I got to piss something awful." I slipped into my clackers and wrapped the blanket around me as I headed for the latrine. Things had quieted down by the time I returned. I sat down on my bunk and pulled the blanket around me again as I started to shiver again.

"What happened to chow? I bet we got screwed out of the food!" I looked around for any sign of our night soup.

"No," Willy informed me, "your chow is in the kitchen. The kitchen crew passed the word around after you guys didn't get in. They saved extra and it will be brought over soon. They got a list of numbers." He picked up my canteen cup and soup bowl and left.

"Why did they keep you out so long?" Johnson asked.

"I don't know. Maybe punishment. No one would own up to who went after the Weasel. Man my hands and feet burn. So does my face." I rubbed my cheeks and my feet.

"That stripping business is something new. Cripes it's cold. And that stinking wind." Johnson shook his head.

"I froze my bones." I shivered again at the thought of it.

"There's going to be a lot of sick guys I'll bet," Johnson shook his head at the thought of the ordeal.

"I'll bet. There are eighty-four men on the construction gang. The ones that keeled over had it bad. I don't doubt that some us are going to come down with pneumonia."

"Now what? No work at the factory for you guys anymore. Isn't that what Murata said?" Johnson asked.

"Yeah. The Japs at the factory don't trust us anymore."

Willy came back with the bowl and the canteen cup both filled with hot bean soup.

"More beans than what we had tonight. And plenty of hot soup." He sniffed the cup as he handed me the bowl. "Somebody must have trapped a rat. Smells like there is meat in this stuff." The group of men laughed.

I watched as other men passed by carrying the soup they had picked up for their buddies.

I ate the beans and drank the soup. When I had finished the banquet of hot food, the double ration that had been provided, I rose to clean up the dishes.

"You stay wrapped up. I'll wash this," Willy offered.

"Thanks," I appreciate the help. I felt wiped out. The rest of the evening was a constant go around of repeating the story and answering questions. There was a great deal of concern expressed about sickness as an aftermath to the freezing treatment we had received. I laid back and fell asleep to be wakened for tenko. I woke up shivering.

Morning came after a few trips to the latrine to empty my bladder. I shivered constantly and woke up a number of times during the night from some unremembered nightmares. Word came in the middle of the morning that some of the men were down sick. There was a lot of anxiety by the crew in camp that we would be called out into the cold and lectured again, but nothing happened.

The next day there were twelve men who had been in the freezer treatment in the hospital. The next day there were another sixteen men for a total of twenty-eight out of the eighty-four of us in the hospital. Eleven came down with pneumonia, the others had the flu. I only had a bad cold and frostbite. We were fortunate. There had been no deaths as a result of the so-called riot freeze treatment.

Our death rate was high enough as it was. We never had any funerals anymore, and the number of dead was known only to the officers.

CHAPTER 21 -- CHRISTMAS NUMBER TWO

Christmas was not far off. The third Christmas of the war, the second in Manchuria. It was December 25th, 1943.

The kitchen crew had arranged to cut back slightly on the rations for over a month. They saved some beans, maize and corn meal which they had to keep hidden from the Japs. The Christmas Day meal was supplemented by this hoard of food.

The corn meal was used to make corn bread. Some sugar had been obtained by devious means and it was used to sweeten the corn bread. It was a delicacy that we had not had before. The beans had been boiled and then baked. The maize had been added to the soup to thicken it. There was actually a half a bowl of solids instead of the three or four tablespoons that was the normal daily ration. It turned out to be a real meal, a feast compared to our standard rations. This was supplemented by special hoards of private delicacies that had been smuggled in by the factory workers. Some men were more fortunate than others, but there was a lot of sharing.

The camp commandant gave the factory crew the day off in his magnanimous generosity.

It was a day of friendly visits, bull sessions and caroling.

We had hoped that there would be letters from home, but the Japs didn't acknowledge that there were any. We had hoped against hope that there would be some Red Cross packages. But there were none. The Japs were not cooperating with anyone that we knew of about the welfare of the POWs. I wondered how the civilians that had been left in the Philippines were making out. They were the hostages that should have been exchanged a long time ago. They had been the unfortunates that really suffered at the hands of the barbaric and backward Japs. We were soldiers. We had been sacrificed and were POWs, but the civilians were the sorry unfortunates.

The camp commandant even permitted a newspaper to be mimeographed and distributed in limited quantity. It was written by some of the men, and it included some artwork.

CHAPTER 22 -- POW POETRY

The weeks that followed became monotonous. There was nothing one could do to occupy the time in the camp. There was no recreation. The past times were like the past times of the living dead. There just wasn't anything in the form of sports or any other things that the Japs allowed. There was no equipment supplied by the Japs.

Most of the men slept, attended bull sessions or gambled. Some wrote poetry. Most of the poetry had to do with the war. There were some poems, ballads, call them what you will that weren't too raunchy. I had collected some, hoping to take them back with me whenever the war ended.

One of these was the Bastards of Bataan. I had seen the original copy on Corregidor when it had been written and had copied it and had even added to it. I had met the author, Frank Hewlett, the United Press correspondent, in February when I had been on the Rock on one of my resupply trips. I reflected on the photo printed page I had written as Tunnelitis Joe. I had come up with the tag for MacArthur of Dugout Doug. I had tagged him that because he made only one trip to Bataan and had never even made it to the front. I never admitted to be the originator of the term because I was afraid of official reprisals from the officers.

"What's the reading stuff?" Pinson asked as he sat down beside me.

"Poems. I have a collection. This one is the Bastards of Bataan, and the Army That Was Betrayed." I held up the ragged copies.

"Let's see it."

I passed it to him. He started to read it silently. Then he started to read it aloud from the beginning. As his voice echoed through the section a few men gathered to listen to the poem that was written soon after MacArthur left the Philippines and Wainwright, Skinny, took command of the sacrificed troops.

"THE BASTARDS OF BATAAN.
We have no father and do not care
We have no mother anywhere
We have no Uncle Sam at all
Just the same we'll never fall
The Bastards of Bataan.

We are the men of an Army lost
Given up, the hell with the cost
Young and old, we have been told
That we are cast in a heroe's mold
The Bastards of Bataan.

We fight, in spite of promises broken
We have no food, arms in token
A bunch of kids, far from home
Burying many in a foreign loam
The Bastards of Bataan.

Miracle men, our fame did spread
Miracle men, whom the Japs did dread
A brave little band, both near and far
But to the Japs, we always are
The Bastards of Bataan

We drink and fight to drink again
A toast to those whose life did end.
When the Japs did choose to fight,
They did not turn their back in flight,
The Bastards of Bataan.

We live and carry on the show,
We fight and fight and God knows how.
Mid tropical fevers running high,
Causing many brave men to die,
Among the Bastards of Bataan.

Protectors of an orphaned land
upon which the Japs did stand
On what was to them a promised land,
Until the Bastards made their stand
The Bastards of Bataan.

We live on fame and hope to fly
We pray, too brave to cry
But our shuddering pain and graying hair
Have gained us naught but despair
The Bastards of Bataan.

We must live to fight another day
For our convoy is on the way
And it will be in Manila Bay
To help us save the fight today
For the Bastards of Bataan.

Wainwright's Warriors - when MacArthur fled
Wainwright's Warriors - of whom half are dead,
Fighting on without a grumble
Until the last defense did crumble
So did the Bastards of Bataan.

Throw down your arms
Return to your stores, your markets, your farms
We go back to our occupation
Which we know have been taken,
But not by the Bastards of Bataan.

Peace at last to a troubled world
Homeward bound to our best girl
To a draft dodger she did wed
While on Bataan her brave soldier bled
And will remain, the Bastard of Bataan.

Stocks, taxes, tariffs and tolls
Will disgust the weak, destroy the bold
Communism, Socialism, Nazism too
With life, living I am through
As are, the Bastards of Bataan.

The crowd that had gathered was very very quiet. Men lit their
smokes quietly and said nothing.
I handed him another sheaf of papers. "This one is about us here. I
don't know who wrote it. I kind of think that it was some Limey."
Pinson looked at the handwritten pages for a moment and then
started to read.

A War Prisoner's Dilemma
There's not much to do
In this land of Manchu
Especially for "guests" of Nippon;

We get up in the morning,
Just before dawning
And start the day off with a yawn.
Our breakfast is bad,
But it is all to be had.
So about its shortcomings we'll hush,
Suffice to say
It's the same every day:
God awful sugarless mush!
So after our meal,
Not eaten with zeal
We sweep up and straighten our gear;
Then, we might mention,
We stand at attention,
While they count us to see if we're here.
Most of us go
Thru the sleet and the snow,
To a factory that's not far away;
Few of us talk,
While making the walk
'Cause there's nothing of interest to say.
Tho we've been through a battle
Thru the gates while they search as we enter;
With our coats open wide, You've nothing to hide,
It's the same thing both summer and winter.
But work there we must,
It's not too unjust.
There's not any reason to doubt it,
But as Prisoners of War,
Such as we are,
We can't do a damn thing about it.
We eat at twelve-thirty,
In a mess hall quite dirty,
Mush, beans and maize cooked together;
We get it each day,
Fixed the same way,
So the less said about it the better.
When five o'clock comes,
We're hungry as bums,
And our supper we anticipate;
So we put on our coats,
Line up like goats,

And get searched as we go out the gate.
Back at the camp,
Wet, dry or damp,
We line up and count off once more,
It's routine you see,
But "t'ain't funny McGee,"
Oh, what a hell of a bore.
Our supper at night
Is quite a delight
In contrast to breakfast and dinner;
But good, bad or just,
We'll eat it or bust,
We can't afford to get thinner
At home in the States,
We'd be out on dates,
Back where there's fun and there's laughter;
But here all the time,
At half-hour past nine,
We're in bed, and asleep quite soon after.
But we live in Hoten,
Try to smile and grin,
And look to the future that's hazy;
Since we're not back in Kansas,
We write silly stanzas,
It's do that or go crazy.

"How about that? That's good," I praised his rendition of the oddly written poem.

There were some twenty men sitting around the room listening. All that smoked had an ash tray near at hand. If a Jap walked in and a man was smoking without an ash tray within reach it meant a jolt from a rifle butt. The Japs feared fire maniacilly.

Other comments ranged from snide to praiseworthy.

"How about it, any more?"

"Here's one that I have some guy's name on the bottom, A.P. Herbert. I am not sure who he is."

"The portion of a woman that appeals to man's depravity
    Is constructed with considerable care,
And what at first appears to be a simple little cavity
    Is really an elaborate affair
Now doctors of distinction have examined these phenomena,

In various experimental dames,
And made a list of all the things in feminine abdomina
    And given them delightful Latin names.

There's the vulva, the vagina, and the jolly perineum,
    The hymen, which is sometimes found in brides
And lots of little other things you'd love if you could
see 'em
    The clitoris, and God knows what besides

Now what a pity 'tis when we common people chatter
    About these things to which we have just referred,
To give such a delicate and complicated matter
    Such a short and very unattractive word.

The erudite authorities who study the geography
    Of that obscure and interesting land
Are able to indulge a taste in intimate topography
    And view the scenic details close at hand

But ordinary mortals though aware of its existence
    Of secrets underneath the pubic knoll
And normally contented to survey them from a distance
    And view the apparatus as a whole

So when we laymen try to probe the secrets of virginity
    We exercise the simple sense of touch
We do not cloud the issue with meticulous lativity
    But call the whole affair a such and such

For men have made this useful but unpicturous commodity
    The subject of innumerable jibes
And though the name they call it is not without its oddity
    It seems to suit the object it describes."

There were roars of laughter and a lot of dirty jokes.
"What is the name of it?"
"I don't know. The top of the page has been torn off, or maybe just
worn away. It looks like the title I have is, 'Ode, After Reading a Medical
Textbook'. I don't know where I got it."
"I think it's great," commented one of the guys in the back of the
room.

"This one was also written by some Englishman. I don't have a name for it. It has the typical Limey flavor."

"So what?" Rogers commented, "Let's hear it."

I handed the unfolded sheets of lined paper to Pinson. The penciled words were hard to decipher in some cases, but he read on.

"Oh how I hate this tragic land
    Its watery sun, its yellow sand
Its heavy humid sticky heat
    With odour of decay complete
I hate the feathery coconut trees
    Languidly swaying in the breeze
The fragijam's cloying smell
    And all the other smells as well."

"What the hell is a fragijam?" Rogers asked.

"Who knows? Don't make any difference. It's a poem."

"I hate the morning's blinding light
    I hate the suffocating night
I hate the listless afternoon
    I hate the dark that comes too soon
The amorous chickak's plaintive trill
    The crickets serenading shrill
And mossies whining round my net
    Have failed to fascinate me yet.

The tropic moonlight leaves me cold
    And all myriad stars untold
The black Sumatra's sudden rain
    The tom tom's maddening refrain
The rubber trees - unlovely whores
    With obscene scars and running sores
And none of these (for me at least)
    Appears the glamour of the East.

I hate the food, I hate the drink
    I hate the all pervading stink
Of squalid crowded Chinatown
    Of bodies yellow, black and brown
Of clamorous murky, native shops
    Of ancient fish and sundry slops

The blend of odors unsurpassed
    Where East and West have merged at last.

Cancerous diseases of foot and ear
    Encountered nowhere else but here
Yellow bodies soft and slim
    Incubating horrors grim
Malaria nurtured in a lamprey's skin
    A TB incidence which is a crime
Drink through boredom makes one a sot
    Do ya wonder I hate the flaming lot

The Tian Benars, a motley crew
    The Tonkays, Datos, Tenglas too
The petty spite, the stupid brag
    The social trips in the local rag
The empty chatter, vapid bleat
    From girls of the local Fishing Fleet
The lovelies of the Bomber Ball
    By Geary, I hate them all.

The careless quest for quick romance
    The shuffling mob at the Raffles dance
The curries satin evening jackets
    The blaring bands, the shaded lights
The futile fleck from flick to hop
    The floor thrums at the Cathay top
The little men, their squalid wives
    The snug intrigue, the double lives

I hate the tunic drab
    The stupid spurs, the scarlet tab
The portly blokes in naval rig
    Who execute a stately jig
The Army subs with weak mustache
    The RAFs so short of cash
But those for whom I save my tears
    Are the conscripts known as volunteers

Heathen Chinese with indecent hoards
    The numerous piffling local Boards
Officials jailed for ethics lax

Objections to the income tax
The local beer, the enervation
   The dearth of modern sanitation
The shriveled dames so quick to please
   From all of these to have release

I loathe each yellow muddy stream
   I hate the lack of milk and cream
The jungles lecherous tenuous claw
   The dredges open, gaping maw
Which swallows the earth in its hungry quest
   For tin which makes war twixt East and West
So back to hills and cold and snow
   Dear Lord above please let me go

Yes, how I hate this futile clime
   The unmarked flight of value time
The heedless passing of precious days
   Faces that vanish in the haze
Of half forgotten memories dim
   Of apathetic boredom grim
And things being such, this is my stand
   I hate and loathe this cock-eyed land."

"Man! That friggin Limey sure as hell didn't like being down there, that's for sure."
"Must have been in Singapore."
There were some other remarks about how disgusted the author must have been.
I passed some more pages to Pinson. He read through Dangerous Dan McGrew, The Convict Rose, Ivan Skavinsky Skavar, Down the Sewer and The Pit.
I handed him the last one of my collection. "This is it. The last one I have. It's about the Limeys."
"The Army That Was Betrayed? I never heard of this one before." Pinson remarked.

The Army That Was Betrayed.

They smashed us back to Singapore,
From Kedah to Collyer's Quay,
And I would that my tongue could utter

The thoughts that arise in me,
So I could tell the story
Of the gallant stand that was made
By the Army that was never beaten,
The Army that was betrayed.

You'll hear of our lack of numbers,
You'll be told we were short of planes
But you'll never hear tell, that in Malaya's grim hell,
What we really lacked was brains.
It was in brains that the Nips had us euchred,
And not in the troops arrayed
Against the Army that was never beaten,
The Army that was betrayed.

The enemy came in the dead of night,
And attacked in yellow swarms.
Jap H.Q. wanted quick results
Whilst ours wanted Army forms:
For it was Army forms we were given
When for air support we prayed,
In the Army that was never beaten,
The Army that was betrayed.

And for the alibi, "unprepared"
Just save your loudest jeers,
For the time we had to prepare defense
Was well over two long years.
But laughs won't help the dead and maimed,
The unfortunates who paid.
From the Army that was never beaten,
The Army that was betrayed.

We won at Waterloo and Eton,
At least so I've heard tell
Well, Singapore was lost in the rooms
Of a famous old hotel
Here gathered the cream of our General Staff
All scarlet tabs and braid,
Leading the Army that was never beaten
The Army that was betrayed.
Deported from Simlu and Poon

"Deadbeats", from Mysore
Got together in a motley mob
For the defense of Singapore
No wonder the Nips who "knew their stuff,"
Pressed onwards, unafraid
Of the Army that was never beaten
The Army that was betrayed.

And in our sorry Saga
Of this unsavory mess
A special place must be reserved
For brilliant M.C.S.
Obstruction successful, and graft "mon sut"
Not many, it is noticed, stayed
With the army that was never beaten
The Army that was betrayed.

And now we sit in durance vile,
Held thrall in an alien land,
We know not whether to curse or smile
At Malaya High Command,
Still strutting around in armbands red,
Unshamed and undismayed
Blaming the Army that was never beaten
The Army that was betrayed.

There was a sprinkling of applause when he finished. The crowd
broke up while a few of us remained to talk.
"We should find something to do besides just reading poetry. That is
not really entertaining for a lot of guys."
I leaned back on my bunk after stashing the poems in the secret hole
under the platform.
"How about we put on a play?"
"Sounds good to me." Pinson agreed.
"Who wants to follow it up?" I asked.
We talked about the props problem, the kind of play and the real
hurdle, permission from the Japs.
"We have to get the officers to go along with it first." Pinson observed.
"Yeah, what about it?"
There was general agreement that it would be an interesting project.
We worked on it for days. There was no way that we could get a play
we found out. The officers said that the Japs couldn't come up with

anything. They would agree to let us put on a play, although no one knew just when they would give their permission.

In anticipation of obtaining permission we started planning. First we had to have a script. Pinson. Rogers, Hewgley, 223, sat with me, beating on the kind of a play we should consider. First we had to have dames. Without dames we would be lost. No one would want to sit through a play with only men. That was all there were in camp, men. We had to have a plot, a theme. A comedy. Costumes.

The idea was fine except that I was elected to write the damn play. It had to be a comedy. There should be only four characters. Three acts. Scenery? That was a problem in the camp. Costumes had to be made. The play had to fit the restrictions that we had. All of these seemingly insurmountable hurdles were a challenge. And it was something to do! Ideas were hard to come by under our situation. For every story, every plot, every character that was presented there were a hundred reasons why the thing wouldn't work. Finally the idea came from some discussion that dealt with a story that someone had read.

"There was this dame, a witch, with supernatural powers. She could read minds. She meets this guy and really charms him. Hypnotizes him. The guy's loaded with dough."

We argued, discussed and modified, but followed the general theme.

"How about calling it the Passionate Witch?" asked Hugely.

"Sounds good to me," I agreed. "I seem to remember a book by that name."

"Not that I heard of before," Pinson frowned.

"Well I don't know. But it sounds familiar." I scratched my memory trying to recall whatever it was that was bothering me about it.

"Ah, forget it. Who's gonna know. So, now go to work Pete." Rogers coaxed.

"You get it written and we'll get the stuff together. How long do you think it will take?"

"Hell, I don't know," I puzzled over the question. "Might be a week or a month."

"Okay. Holler when you need things."

CHAPTER 23 -- TAKAI

The Japs had made arrangements with another factory to employ POWs. The overhead crane factory, Takai Kabushiki Kaisha was across the road east of the camp. The contract was for twenty men. Two draftsmen and eighteen men with various other skills, mostly structural steel and machine shop. The cranes would be shipped to factories and machine shops in Manchuria.

I wondered about what had happened to the men, Manchus, who had worked there before.

The list was posted on Sunday, the rest day for February.

The work days had been increased. We had had two days off every month for some time, then the Japs wanted to increase the output at MKK and had cut back to only one day off a month. The work hours had been adjusted to eight to six, and there was a lot of overtime ordered.

We all crowded around the bulletin board to find out who was assigned to Takai. I found my name on the list. The first name. Number one. My job assignment was as design draftsman. Tommy, 917, Francis Thompson, was to be the drafting detailer. Among the names on the list were, Morris, Dhobie, Crowley, Art Rice and Leon C. Adams. Some Aussies and Englishmen, Mitchell and a few others.

We were to start work the next day. Excitement and anxiety hit the group that had been selected. Here was something new. New opportunities in new surroundings.

By nightfall the "Takai" crew had checked around and had become acquainted with each other.

The group formed up separate from the MKK workers on Monday morning. Since we were a very small group we bangoed, counted off, and marched off amid wishes of good luck, good hunting and watch out for the women, ha ha.

It was a short ten minute walk from the main gate in the west wall. We went north along the compound and then east along the north wall of the camp. Then we turned south along the camp's east wall to the second road heading east, no more than half a kilometer in all.

The factory compound consisted of the office building There was a small apartment house on the east side. A small warehouse, and the factory on the north side of the grounds. These were all enclosed by a fence and a ten foot brick wall. There was only one entrance, a gate, on the south side next to the office building.

After we were marched in we were lined up inside of the gate and counted. The Jap sergeant, Hono, reported to the owner, Takai San.

Takai was a squat, heavy built Jap. Heavy by comparison to the Japs we had come to know. He reminded me of a bulldog. Flat faced. A large flat nose. Close cropped hair, salt and pepper, and a multitude of wrinkles lining his forehead. He also had a couple of deep furrows on his cheeks. He gave the appearance of having flabby jowls that reminded me of some kind of a dog that I had seen somewhere. I couldn't recall the breed.

Takeuchi, the interpreter, came through the gate and joined the two Japs. After a few minutes of conferring among themselves, Takai turned to us and spoke. We waited as Takeuchi listened and then translated. "You are all welcome by Mr. Takai. He will treat you fair. He expects obedience to all orders and instructions that the Japanese foremen will issue. I will take you to the factory and the foremen will take over and instruct you in your jobs." He paused and turned to Takai. After some lengthy discussion he turned and addressed us again. "Six nine five and nine one seven. You two will remain here. You will be working in the office. Mr. Takai will supervise you directly. You, six nine five, since you understand Japanese, you will be the leader." He turned and conferred with the Jap sergeant and Takai at some length. "You," he addressed me, "You will also help as interpreter in the factory. That is whenever Takai and the foremen need you."

Takai motioned to us to follow him into the office building. The first floor was an office with two drafting tables and a large desk. Takai indicated that we were to work here. We sat at the drafting tables and checked out the equipment. I wondered how we could do the job Takai wanted us to do when he spoke no English and my Japanese was mediocre. He spent some time with us showing us the drawings and details of the overhead cranes that he was building. I tried to find out who had done the work before but Takai ignored the question. When I pressed the point, hoping that someone was around who could initiate us into the mysteries of his operation he became annoyed. I let it go and just listened and watched as he showed us what was needed. During the following weeks the frustration due to the language barrier made it very difficult to do the job. I learned more and more of the technical language because I had to to do the job. Tommy just let me handle all of the communications. It was a major achievement when we turned out the first set of blueprints for an overhead crane.

I was accused by Takeuchi of making things difficult just to slow down the operation. He didn't come out with it and accuse me of sabotage, but he had the opinion that I was obstructing the manufacturing progress. Tommy warned me that Takeuchi was going to get me in real trouble if I continued to "frig up the works." We decided it was best for the whole crew to go along with Takai and not drag our asses on the job. Somehow the officers found out about what was going on and told us that we should not ask for trouble, that it would be better if we did the job that the Japs wanted us to do.

We, Tommy and I, found out that the locked room on the first floor was the Japanese workers commissary. The stores were rice, potatoes and beans. Takai always kept the room locked. Besides the regular door latch there was a heavy padlock. We pondered the problem on a daily basis after we found out what it contained. Another hurdle was the fact that the upper floor of the building was the living quarters of Takai and his family.

We observed that there had been a ditch dug from the house out to the garden area between the office building and the factory. The ditch was three foot wide and five foot deep. It was for a sewer pipe that was to connect up to a septic tank. The project had come to a halt because the ground had frozen. There was a hole in the foundation directly under the store room of the office building.

Tommy and I decided that it was worth investigating. It could be a way to get at the stores. After considerable planning we decided that we would explore the hole and the foundation at noon one day. Since we ate our noon meal in the yard on nice days, it would be relatively easy to duck into the ditch and find out if there was a way into the room from underneath. Our food was cooked at the camp kitchen and brought over by a couple of men just before noon. The buckets of food were usually set up near the pile of structural steel where it was served. The steel pile was right on the edge of the ditch. There was rarely a guard around at noon time. They usually patrolled the perimeter of the compound and toured the factory about once an hour to make sure that we were there and working.

We had planned that if the area under the store room allowed access to the room it would be easy to lay the blame on the workers. Since the ditch allowed just about anyone to crawl under the building, we couldn't be blamed unless we were caught in the act. Tommy was to go in and see if he could knock the floorboards loose. He would then remove the nails and allow the boards to rest on the joists just by their own weight.

Tommy finished his meal fast. I took his cup to wash it as he slipped down into the trench. He crawled the twenty yards to the building without incident. We had arranged that three sharp whistles was the danger signal.

The men sat around talking and smoking as we watched Tommy

creep in under the building. Mitch, Clancy and Jack sat with me and helped as lookouts.

It took about ten minutes. Tommy called, "Is it okay to come out?"

"Yeah, pop out in a hurry," intoned Clancy.

Tommy climbed out and sat beside us. He let out a sigh of relief. "Man that floor is nailed down tight. I couldn't budge the freaking thing. There was a large piece of masonry under there. I thought I heard someone walking around in the office. Maybe Takai was checking on us. I must have made too much noise." He was in a sweat. "It's black as hell down there and I couldn't see worth a damn. Maybe there is some other way."

"You're taking an awful chance," Warned Mitch.

Mitch, Mitchell, R.G. was an Australian. He was a thin wiry individual with a leather tanned skin and dark wavy hair and sharp features. I estimated him to be about thirty. He was not afraid of the Japs. Nor was he afraid of any of the punishment they imposed. He was a cautious man. He didn't ask for trouble, but if trouble came, he was there to be counted on.

"You'll probably get a couple of potatoes or a cup of rice," he cautioned. "But it could put us all in a bad way. The others are sure to suffer. It is not worth it under the circumstance."

"You are probably right Mitch," I agreed. "We better not try anything that is so risky."

The problem was that I couldn't forget it. I had spent all the money from my smuggling activities and was broke. I was hungry. Now I had trouble sitting because I didn't have any meat on my ass. I weighed in at sixty kilos, or just around one hundred and thirty-two pounds. I was skinny. I always seemed to be loosing weight. I had been under one hundred pounds back at the old Chinese camp. And I was having sieges of beri-beri and scurvy, along with the continuous migraines. I looked fatter when I had beri-beri because of the way the disease caused me to bloat. The only answer was to get some food. I always scrounged through the Takai garbage for lemon peels and used tea leaves.

In between planning on how to break into the storeroom, I spent a lot of time working on the play.

CHAPTER 24 -- PROPS

I finished the play. I made arrangements with Fleming for a typed copy. I had also made up a list of the props that would be required. The gang that was going to put on the play was enthusiastic about the project. The list of props was duplicated and passed out to the men who volunteered to cooperate in finding and making the props.

There were four main characters, Sonja, Wanda, J.P. and Doc. We made a list of the props that we needed.

<u>Sonja</u>
high heel shoes
low heel shoes
flowered skirt
wig
sweater
turban, same material skirt
silk panties
bracelet and earrings
wedding ring
bra and breasts

<u>JP</u>
robe (smoking jacket)
tie
silk shirt
trousers

<u>Other</u>
bottle and glasses(label)
desk and nameplate
steno book/pencils
pictures magazines
papers
knife
picture frame (battle axe)
telephone
radio
tag for Rogers
lipstick

<u>Wanda</u>
high heel shoes
wig
black silk ? skirt
necklace
pink ribbon garters
panties
bra and breasts

<u>Doc</u>
shirt and tie
trousers
coat

<u>Other</u>
desk call button
small benches
single seat bench
curtain (blankets/asbestos)
clock
cork
top hats
mustache
pipe
makeup

We enlisted anyone and everyone that could possibly help. It was a beg, borrow steal operation. Mostly steal. The mere fact that it was a challenge helped to enlist more men than we ever expected to become involved.

There was one thing that brought the men together, screw the Japs. Outwitting the Japs was a game. It didn't matter what the consequences were as long as you could screw them. Naturally all of the men weren't like this, but the group that we had formed were dedicated to the cause.

Anything in the warehouses, the factories, as well as the factory workers personal belongings, were subject to acquisition. Everyone involved went to work with gusto. I had never experienced the kind of cooperation that I was seeing. The two items that aroused the most enthusiasm were the panties and bras. As we accumulated the props we had to hide them from the Japs. The floorboards under the mattresses were loosened. The nails pulled and the shank cut off leaving only the head. These were reinserted in the nail holes to make it look like they were still nailed down. Wood boxes were built under the floor with the assistance of the camp carpenters. In some cases the nails were replaced by wood screws to make the hiding place safer.

The wigs became one of the most interesting and fascinating props that we had to make. One had to be blonde and the other brunette. The solution was a magnificent example of ingenuity. The blonde wig was made of yellow silk that came from a Japanese kimono. Some Jap lost it at the factory. Don't ask me how, all I know is that we had a yellow silk kimono. The kimono was cut into pieces and the fabric taken apart thread by thread. These threads were stitched in small bunches onto a cotton skull cap. Bunches of twenty to thirty threads were sewn in close rows and then combed out. The silk was curly and formed waves that made the effect more realistic. When viewed from a distance of fifteen feet the wig looked great. The brunette wig was made in the same way and then dyed in tea. The task occupied a few men for many hours.

There was a general air of hazing and razzing going on about the props and their acquisition.

The bracelets and earrings were made in the MKK machine shop.

Clothing was stolen from the Japanese in the factory.

There was a near riot on the lower floor of Building Three when the silk panties surfaced. No one claimed the honor of having supplied the panties. They were the real thing. I found the panties under my mattress bunk after the evening meal. I sat on the bunk and wondered what it was that didn't seem right. I swung off of the bunk and lifted the mattress for looksee. The small bundle of silk, pink silk, surprised me. I couldn't imagine what the thing was. One of the panties dropped as I picked them up between thumb and forefinger. Someone let out a howl.

Willy, in the next bunk, let out a howl. "Well kick my ass! Where is the dame that goes with those? YEAH MAN!!" He made a grab for the pair that had fallen to the floor. I scrambled for them myself but he beat me to them.

"Hey! Let go! Don't mess them up!" I shouted. "They're for the play!"

"Sure mister! I'll play," yowled Jimmy. "Gimme a feel. Cripes! I haven't seen anything like that in a hundred years!"

Men around the section jumped off of the upper bunks and ran over. The men across the aisle crawled over to get a look.

"Panties---"

"WOMEN!"

"Silk---"

"Lemme feel."

"Gimme a look."

The section was a shambles. The noise and the shouting brought men from the other sections on the run. There was a great deal of pushing, shoving, grabbing, yelling and laughing. Willy and I were trying to defend our panties. I was afraid that the grabbing and pulling would tear the panties to pieces.

"Hey gimme a smell."

"Knock it off goddamn it! Don't ruin them." I yelled.

We had been pushed back on our bunks by the mob.

"Okay okay! Here. Feel them." I passed the panties around. "Don't grab!"

"Won't take a big ass to fill these. Must be a skinny one."

"You particular or something?"

"Picky. Who cares?"

"Hey! I haven't had a turn."

The men were in a mood that I hadn't been seen in what seemed ages.

"Who's gonna wear them?"

"A sailor. Who else?" answered one of the marines.

"Like hell!" answered a sailor.

"JAP! Jap coming."

Bingo! The crowd broke. Men disappeared to their bunks, across the hallway, around the tables in the sections. Thirty seconds was all that it took to clear out the fifty or sixty men that had crowded into the section.

The Jap entered the far end of the building without sensing that anything unusual had been going on. He passed through the section and on to the stairs at the other end of the barrack.

"Who has the other pair of panties?" I shouted. I had only the one pair that I had shoved under my mattress when the guard came through. The other pair was missing.

"Come on guys, come on." I looked around the room. "Let's get the damn things back here." I turned to Willy," Who had the other pair?"

"Hell I don't know. There were maybe a hundred guys here. I didn't see."

"Why the hell didn't you watch?" I asked annoyed. "Nuts! Now we have only one pair."

"You gonna wear more than one pair at a time honey?" someone from across the room asked nastily. There was an uproar of laughter in response to the quip.

"Aw! Hell!" I remarked. "What a bunch of stinkers you turned out to be. I hope you wind up with the clap." I sat on the bunk, "Gimme a hand Willy. Let's stash these in the box under you."

"Under me! WHEE! Will I dream from now on." Then in a more serious vein, " Hell! I'm sorry Pete, I couldn't help it." He moved his mattress and started to unscrew the board to the box.

"It's okay, we'll manage. We'll have the typed copy from Fleming soon. The whole thing is just about finished. We have to get the rest of the stuff together. We should be ready in about a week."

CHAPTER 25 -- FIGHT

Takai had me acting as an interpreter on many occasions. This caused some resentment among a couple of the men in our group. The two men made nasty remarks many times. It was something I ignored because I knew that we were not working under the best of circumstances.

One of the men was Blackie. He was a dark haired, heavy bearded man of twenty-six or twenty-seven. He was almost as tall as I was and heavier. He worked the steel gang at the plant. Blackie Brennan resented taking interpreted orders from me. He complained that, he wouldn't take orders from a private. I was told that he went to see the officers. He supposedly received little sympathy from the officers when he asked them to do something about the situation. He was told that it wasn't a matter of rank. The fact that the interpreter was only a private was immaterial. We were in a peculiar situation and he had to go along with it or learn to speak Japanese himself, which he was not about to do. He had a lot of resentment toward me. On innumerable occasions he ribbed me about the story that I had been busted from sergeant three times. Which was not true.

The other man was Polack. He was of Polish descent and had been tagged with the nickname because of that. He disliked me because he thought I was too cooperative with the Japs.

Assembling the cranes, hauling around the heavy steel kept those men in tough condition, as tough as any in camp. Both Blackie and Polack were among the two men that were in good shape.

Takai demanded that the crew put in more time, and overtime, to complete the construction of one particular job that was needed as soon as possible. After I had translated Takai's demands the men grumbled and complained. Takai was annoyed and threatened to take it up with the Jap Commandant. After pacifying Takai, and coming to an understanding with him, Takai said he would not file a complaint with the camp officials. We all agreed to see if we could speed up the scheduled delivery.

Blackie made a nasty remark. "What was that?" I asked him, annoyed at his attitude.

"You heard me you pro Nip bastard!" he spit back at me.

I made for him and started to swing when Mitch and Tommy grabbed me and backed me off. "Knock it off Pete!" ordered Mitch," you'll get us all into trouble."

"I'll knock his rotten head off," I retorted. "Who the hell does he think he is anyway? You're one son-of-a-bitch!" I snarled at him.

Jack, one of the other Englishmen, had stepped in front of Blackie. "Knock it off! Here comes the guard!"

The Jap guard walked in through the factory door and looked around with a questioning look. We broke up and returned to work.

At ten o'clock I returned to the factory to check some measurements on one of the cranes.

"Well? You looking for something to tell the Nips?" asked Blackie.

"No you creep," I turned away. "Mitch, how much steel are you short on the struts?"

"Not more than a dozen pieces. We're all out of stock." Mitch looked at the structure.

"Takai says..." I was interrupted by Blackie.

"Takai says. Takai says," mimicked Blackie. "That all you can say?"

"Look knuckle head, you want your face pushed in? Say so. I'll do it for you." I threatened.

"Hell, if you two want to mix it up why don't you have a go at it at noon time? Out behind the warehouse. Nobody'll be around," suggested Jack as he listened to us harangue each other.

"Fine with me," I agreed.

"Okay," Blackie smirked. "Before or after we eat?"

"After," I answered.

"Alright. Then settle it, and no more after that." Mitch walked off.

I returned to the office to steam over the incident.

We finished eating just after noon and washed up our cups and the buckets in which the food had been brought. It was a sunny and warm day. The rain during the night had left the ground muddy in spots. All of the crew moved to the end of the pile of steel and settled down to watch the fight. The word about the fight had spread like wildfire. Fights were rare, and, they were also forbidden by the Japs. There was to be no interference from the men. Everything was to be settled between the two of us.

We walked up behind the warehouse out of sight of the Takai's house. The Jap foremen had gone home, to the worker's apartments, for lunch and the guard had made his round just after the food had been delivered.

""Well, Jap lover, come on," Blackie egged me on.

"Just yell when you have had enough," I said between gritted teeth. Then I rushed him. Both fists pounded at his ribs. I had decided that body blows were the best way to attack him If I avoided the face then I

wouldn't cut my hands on his teeth. He threw punches at my face. I felt
a couple of solid blows on my shoulders, chest and cheeks. I continued
to pound on his ribs, short jabs, with all of my weight behind them, not
that I was that heavy. The breath shooshed from Blackie as I forced him
back. His arms flailed at me ineffectively. He started to double over as I
followed him.

"Knock it off!"someone yelled.

"He's had enough Pete!"

No one interfered as I continued to pound away at his ribs and chest.
I was in a blind rage.

"Okay okay Pete okay!" Blackie wheezed.

I backed off, heart pounding. I was panting. I was all worked up and
killing mad. All of the frustration and hatred of the Japs had been
channeled into the punches, I didn't want to stop. I wanted to go after
him and knock his teeth in and smash his face.

"Pro-nip huh?" I panted. "You ever gonna say I'm for the stinking Japs
again? Huh?" I gulped air between the words. I was shaking with anger,
emotion. "Well! Are you?" I started toward him again,

"NO! No!" Blackie backed away. He was holding his chest. "No. I'm
sorry, honest. I don't mean it Pete. Honest I don't." He sobbed and
swallowed hard. "I know you're not. Honest.Just jealous maybe," he
panted.

"Okay." I dropped my hands to my sides and relaxed my fists. "Okay.
You want to shake and forget it?" I reached out.

Blackie reached out and shook. "You're pretty damn tough you
know." He gasped.

"No. Just mad. I'm not for the frigging Japs and never will be." I wiped
my hands on my trousers and then wiped the sweat off of my face. I
noticed that some of the men had stood up in their excitement during
the fight.

"Hey you two! Come on over and sit down," yelled Mitch. "You both
better rest up."

We walked over and sat at the foot of the pile of steel. We both lit up
cigarettes and smoked as we cooled off.

"That didn't take long." Jack looked at me with a funny look.

"What do you mean?" I asked in a shaky voice.

"You blokes fought for only about two minutes you know." Jack
exploded."Not even a full round!" he joked.

"That's all?" Blackie's face had an astonished look.

"Yes," agreed Mitch. The others around him nodded.

Blackie was having a hard time recovering.

"When you are fighting you never know how long a fight lasts." Jack watched Blackie. "You okay?"

"Yeah, I'm okay." I glanced at Blackie.

"How about you?" Jack asked Blackie.

"I don't know." Blackie looked down, "I'm not so good."

I looked at him closely. His face was alright because I hadn't hit him in the face. I felt as though I had a couple of bruises on mine.

The factory whistle blew ending the lunch hour. We returned to work slowly. I missed the talk among the men as I headed for the office with Tommy.

"That was a rough beating you gave him," Tommy spoke up as we walked alone.

"I was just mad," Was the only explanation I made, which was more of an excuse than anything else.

"He looks beat," Tommy looked back over his shoulder at the group heading for the factory. "Think he's okay?"

"Sure. I only gave him body punches."

"Yeah, I saw." Tommy looked at me strangely. "You okay?"

"Yeah. Just a headache."

It was late in the afternoon when I had to make another trip to the factory to check on some of the work. I had to measure a gusset on one of the cranes. Blackie came to meet me as I entered the big doors. "Can I talk to you over here? The Japs won't see us."

"Sure." I was puzzled.

"I think I have a couple of busted ribs." Blackie kept his voice low.

I looked at him in surprise. I didn't believe him. "You're kidding," I said half laughing. "I couldn't have!"

"Honest. I hurt like hell."

Mitch came over and joined us. He carried a blueprint. He pointed to it as a cover for our conversation. "Shohi's watching." The little Jap foreman was looking in our direction. He wasn't a bad Jap. We knew that he wouldn't turn us in to the guard. "Pete, he's really hurting." Mitch was very serious.

"But I couldn't have hit that hard," I disagreed.

"Maybe you don't think so, but I feel it."

"Better go on sick call." I was still unbelieving.

"What can we say happened?" Mitch pondered and excuse.

A reason had to be provided to the Jap guard if Blackie was to return to the camp sick.

"I could say that I slipped on the wet steel when I was carrying a bucket of rivets. The steel plate at the front door is all wet from the rain last night." Blackie pointed to the entrance of the factory.

"Okay. I'll back you up. I'll say I saw you fall." I agreed.

"So will I," offered Mitch.

"We can get the Jap to take me back. Okay?" Blackie pointed to the Jap guard nosing around the far end of the building.

"Right." I walked over to the guard and brought him back, explaining the situation.

"Oh so! Byoki. Sick?" he asked Blackie. "Doko." He looked at him to see what was hurting.

"Here," Blackie pointed to his ribs.

"Dame dame," muttered the guard.

"Bad is right," I said. "He'll take you back," I told Blackie. We'll take care of the count. Bango okay?" I asked the guard.

"Yosh. Bango okay," the guard smirked. Then he smiled for a reason known only to himself.

Blackie and the guard left. "I still don't see how he could have broken ribs. Are you sure he didn't fall?"

"He didn't fall," Mitch replied coolly.

"I hope he's wrong," I shook my head. "It'll be rough if he has broken ribs." I turned and continued my checking of the steel structure of the overhead crane.

That evening, after chow I looked up Blackie. "How you doing?" I asked as I sat sown on the foot of his bunk.

He looked up at me. He winced as he moved to sit up. "Rough Pete. Real rough. Look." He lifted his shirt to let me see that he was all taped up.

I looked at him in surprise.

"Doc says that he feels four broken ribs," Blackie shook his head and frowned.

"Damn, I'm sorry, real sorry." I felt awful. "I didn't mean to do that. A fight is a fight, but I sure didn't want to bust you up that way." I tried to convey my feelings.

"I know," Blackie answered. "You sure pack a wallop for a guy that is starving."

"Can I do anything for you? Anything I can get for you?" I really wanted to help. I regretted the painful injury that I had inflicted on him because of my anger. It should have happened to a Jap.

"Nope," he answered. " I won't be working for about two weeks. And," he smiled, "I'll be paid. Hurt on the job. They bought the fall story. So everything is okay."

"Well let me know if there is anything that I can do for you." I left, not wanting to stick around because I felt pretty bad about having caused the pain and suffering to one of our own.

Francis Thompson, 917 and Joseph A. Petak, 695. Photograph was taken by Takai junior.

Chapter 26 -- SUKI SAN

Takai sprung a surprise on us, Tommy and me, one morning. He told us that the office was going to be moved to the factory. The small store room that stuck out of the north side of the factory was going to be remodeled and we would move as soon as it was finished, maybe a week or two. Tommy and I weren't surprised. We had heard that the camp commandant didn't like our working in the main building with the Takai family quarters.

"Well Pete," mused Tommy, "looks as though we'll never get in there?" He looked very unhappy at the thought of loosing out on the food that was stored there.

"Yep, I guess so," I agreed, half lost in a wild scheme. "I wonder if we couldn't work on the door somehow? Take the hinge pins out?" I studied the double locked door.

"Nah. Too much in the open," Tommy disagreed. He was also studying the door. "Someone coming."

We both heard the footsteps on the stairs. The outer door was unlatched and by the time the Japs came in we were both busy at our boards. I looked up to see the elder Takai followed by a rather pretty Japanese girl. She stood about five foot tall, and without the bulky kimono, probably about one hundred and fifteen pounds. Not fat, zoftsig would more be the term.

"Ohio," Takai greeted us.

"Ohio gozaimasu," I returned his good morning greeting.

"Rocu ku go, Petaku, konostowa Suki San desu." He introduced the girl.

"Omaeni kaheete yaroshie gozai masu." I acknowledged the introduction, telling her I was glad to meet her. Her eyes widened perceptibly. Takai grinned. He was tickled that he had a POW, an American, that could speak Japanese, working for him.

Suki San bowed low and stared as she straightened. Her eyes were lowered the way that the Jap women showed that they were observing the protocol of polite society.

Takai turned to Tommy and introduced him. "Ku ju sichi, Toemmie, Suki San."

Tommy muttered, "Ohio," and stared.

This was the first pretty Japanese girl that either of us had seen, much more that we should be introduced.

253

Takai told us that Suki San had just come from Osaka and had been placed with the Takai family by the government to help in the war effort. Tommy and I looked at each other. We had never heard of any of this type of placement of civilians. She was going to work in the house and she would also take care of the bookkeeping and other office work. He also told us that we were not to molest her or we would be shot. We were to tell that to the other men. Suki stood there silently as we received our instructions. Takai then led her out to the factory for a tour.

"Well how do you like that?" I asked. "A mistress."

"Aw go on. She's not his mistress, is she?" asked Tommy incredulously.

"That is the way I heard that they work it," I watched them as they walked through the compound.

"You mean a geisha?" Tommy was gawking at Suki.

"No, not a geisha. She works here. Right? And he's the boss. The women don't have the kind of rights they have in the States." I smirked.

"Sure looks nice and clean, doesn't she?" he smiled, a silly look on his face. He shook his head as though to clear it. "Even smells like a woman."

"Yep. Maybe you can get her to scrub your back for you in the bath." I smiled at that thought.

"Huh? How do you mean that?" Tommy frowned.

"Just like I said it," I stated flatly. "don't you know that the men and women bathe together?"

"That's only a story. Isn't it?" he asked. His face was screwed up, eyebrows up, and mouth half open.

"Aw come on Tommy. Don't you know anything about the Japs?"

"Well," he turned and cocked his head a little. "I can't see how come the men and women get together in the bathhouses."

"They do. Used to be that in the big hotels they used to fix your bath and then come in and wash you down." I looked at Tommy and wondered if he had had any interest in the customs of the Oriental culture.

"You ever had your back scrubbed by a cookie like that?" he asked with intense interest that surprised me.

"Sure. In the Jap bathhouse in Manila. Didn't you ever go there? I thought all of the guys knew about the places."

"No," Tommy said bluntly. "Was there one there?"

"Sure. Down from Escolta, over near Rizal. Somewhere around there from what I remember." I didn't remember the exact location.

"In the Biando District?"

"Yeah. I guess it was. Used to cost only two pesos."

"Umm. That's for me." He grinned.

"Yeah, well, how about those gusset plates?" I changed the subject abruptly. "We have to have the details up there if the guys are going to meet their schedule."

"All done, "Tommy moved back to his board. "You know," he paused, "I don't care much for this setup here. I think I'll ask for a transfer." He looked around the room.

I was kind of surprised because it was a fairly easy job, and it was also a warm place to work by comparison to the factory. "Think that they will transfer you?"

"Sure. I wasn't on the construction gang you know." He turned back to his board.

The noon meal brought the men together and the conversation was centered around Suki San, girls and women in general. It had been the longest and most interesting conversation about women in months.

"I wonder if these blokes will ever allow us to have women, that is if we behave ourselves," wondered Jack.

"You nutty or something?" asked Mitch.

"Naw. I mean it," answered Jack seriously. There are a lot of places where they allow women to visit prisoners. Spain, Mexico. Right in their cells. Conjugal visits."

"Yeah, sure," Tommy agreed sarcastically.

"It's the truth. So help me," retorted Jack.

"I've heard of it," I nodded my head in emphasis. "But not for POWs. Don't forget, we're POWs. They are civilian criminals who have been allowed visits by their wives. Maybe sweethearts too. Only I don't know what countries allow it."

"Sure. And, they allow them regular too." Jack was hot on the subject.

"Who the hell wants a Jap or a Chink?" Mitch frowned.

"Who's gonna be here that long?" I asked.

"What is the difference how long you been here? A woman is a woman." Jack looked around the group. "I could use a woman."

"They keep on getting whiter and whiter," Tommy laughed.

"Yeah, if you go dhobie like the guys in the islands." I smiled at the thought of the guys and their offspring. Guys that had been in the Philippines for ten and fifteen years.

"Hell! I had a dalaga," Scotty said unashamed. "And when I get back I'll get me another."

"Not for me," Mitch shot back. "I'll take me a big buxom Australian woman." He held his hands out in front of his chest indicating the size of the bosom that interested him.

Everyone laughed. Mitch was tall and skinny as a rail. Imagining him with a huge buxom gal was funny.

"Aw, what the hell is the sense of talking about women," Scotty put in, "it'll be another cold winter before we see any dames."

"I'll say. Anybody hear any new rumors?"

"Same old stuff. Landing in France. You know, second front stuff. Pushing in. Rome taken back. That's all." Jack repeated the stuff we had been hearing for some time now.

"I heard that the Americans are in the Philippines. Island hopping."

"Yeah,but they aren't in the Philippines yet." Scotty tried to sound pessimistic.

"Can't be too long low," I said smiling. "Heck, they are supposed to be mopping up Europe. When the Russkies get the Nazis back to Germany they'll turn on the Japs."

"I don't understand why the damned Russkies aren't fighting the Nips right now," Scotty complained.

"They probably have their hands full on the Nazi front," Jack said thoughtfully. "I was at Dunkirk. I bet the Nazis have been giving the Russians all kinds of hell. They won't be easy to clean up."

I nodded in agreement and started to rise. "I hope that it won't be long now. See you later." Tommy and I started back to the office.

Suki San soon picked up the name Peachi. No one was quite sure just how it came about. Peachi is Chinese cabbage.. Maybe it was because she was something to eat. Or, maybe it was because she was a peach of a woman. No matter, Suki was stuck with the tag.

One afternoon she came into the office, muttered her "Ohio Gozaimus" and started to unlock the door to the storeroom. She was having difficulty with the locks so I offered to help her. I took the keys and unlocked the sticky lock. The padlock opened with a little jiggling. The regular latch wouldn't open unless the door was pulled as the lock was turned. I had seen Takai do that.

"Warui des. Very bad," I explained to Peachi.

"Arigato," she bobbed her head and went into the store room.

I watched her for a moment to make sure she was going to be busy for a few minutes and scooted back to Tommy's board. I grabbed a piece of paper and a pencil.

"Hey, take it easy," Tommy complained.

"Shhh!" I admonished him. I slapped the padlock key on the paper and started to trace the outline with the sharp pencil. I looked over my shoulder quickly. I marked the grooves on the outline. Peachi was still busy picking out some vegetables. I traced the other key and quickly folded the paper and hid it under Tommy's board. I stepped back to the door and held the keys out in front of me. I heard Tommy's snicker behind me. I turned to him with a self satisfied smirk on my face. Peachi came out carrying the basket of potatoes and carrots and a small container of rice. She smiled at me when she reached the door.

"Kagi," I said as I handed her the keys.

"Doet tasti mashita. Tank you," she mouthed the English words with some difficulty.

"Okay." I smiled at her.

She set the basket and container on the floor and relocked the door. Then she quickly picked up the containers and left.

I stood by Tommy's board until she closed the door behind her. We heard the latch click. We both looked at one another smiling like two Cheshire cats.

"You are rotten. Clear through rotten." Tommy put on an act of being disgusted with my sleezy act. "Not only are you rotten to the core, but the core is rotten too." He shook his head in mock disgust. "Taking advantage of a poor little innocent like that." His face broke into a smile he couldn't hold back. Then he broke into laughter. I joined him.

"I'll apologize at the end of the war." I crossed my heart with my right forefinger. "Honest Injun, or honest Jap." I laughed again, a happy laugh.

"How much luck can a guy have?" Tommy shook his head.

I pulled the paper out from under his board and studied it. Neither key would be difficult to make. "Shouldn't take much to duplicate?" I asked, "should it?"

"Nope. I guess not. Who's going to make them?" Tommy asked as he studied the outlines.

"Let's trace this. Make two copies," I looked out of the window, unseeing, as I planned. "MKK machine shop can knock them out in a day. I know just the guy for the job." I nodded with self approval. "Sailor. Know him?"

"No," answered Tommy. " Is he good at it?"

"Sure. Probably cost a pack of butts each. In camp," I mused about the price.

"Cheap," commented Tommy. "Want me to trace them?"

"Sure. And take off about a thirty-second all around. That will make them just about the same size." I estimated the enlargement of the pattern due to the displacement of the pencil line from the exact size of the key. "Then mark the grooves and we're all set." After he finished the tracings I cut them out and folded them. I slipped them into the slit in my belt. I patted it with satisfaction. "Won't be found there, I hope."

"Looks okay. Hope we're lucky," Tommy sounded a bit pessimistic.

"They'll work," I promised.

I looked up Sailor that evening after supper and arranged for a set of keys to be made. The price was as I had estimated, one pack of cigarettes for each of the keys. The keys were delivered three days later. There had been a delay at MKK. I took the keys with me the next morning.

"Tommy," I started, "I want to try the keys. After the guard makes his round at ten, you keep an eye on him to make sure he doesn't double back. I'll find out what kind of a job Sailor did on them."

"Okay." Tommy didn't pursue the matter beyond that.

The guard came early. As soon as he left I crossed the room to the stairway and tried it. It was locked. I hurried back to the store room. The padlock key was the one that worried me since it was the most complicated. I was pleasantly surprised when the key turned easily and the hasp popped open.

"That one is perfect," I turned to Tommy with a smile.

"Great! Now how about the other one?" he asked anxiously. He kept glancing back and forth between the window and the door.

I tried the second key, pulling the door toward me as I turned it in the lock. The lock turned smoothly and the door opened. "Anyone around?" I was excited and exhilarated at the good luck we had with the keys.

"No."

"Okay." I popped into the store room and looked around. The first thing that I saw that would give us no trouble in preparing was the basket of potatoes. I grabbed two in each hand and rushed back to the door. I glanced around the room to fix the other items in my memory. I moved out and dropped the potatoes in Tommy's hands. Then I rushed back to the door and pulled it shut, slipped the hasp of the padlock through the hasp and snapped it shut. I locked the bottom lock and pocketed the keys. I turned back to Tommy and took a deep breath and held it. "Where did you put them?"

"Here." He pulled open his unbuttoned coat and showed me the stolen food.

"Raw or cooked?" I asked.

"Cooked. Roasted." He had a thoughtful look on his face. "I'll even settle for margarine instead of butter. Salted."

I swung at him playfully, happy about the food. "Butter yet. How?"

"The foundry at lunchtime," Tommy smiled in anticipation of the treat. "We could do it on the rivet stove. Good hot charcoal fire."

"Only it will take a while," I said thoughtfully. "How about getting Mitch to cook them for us? He can bring them out to us at lunch."

"We'd have to split with him," He answered reluctantly.

"So we give him one spud. We still have three to split." I was ready to agree to the payment. Food was food.

"Okay. I'll take them up now. That should give him plenty of time," Tommy agreed.

"Do we have any salt left?"

"Some in the back of the drawer." Tommy picked up a stack of prints and started for the door.

The potatoes were delicious, a real treat. We had our soup first, then we squatted behind the steel pile and split the potatoes.

"Where is the stash?" asked Polack as he watched us from his vantage point on top of the pile.

"In the office. Locked up," I responded. "Jap commissary."

"Okay, so you got it. How many butts for a spud?" he asked as he watched us wolf down the potatoes.

"I haven't even thought about a price."

"Well how about thinking about it?" he asked.

"Alright, I will." We finished eating. The signal to go back to work sounded and we started back to the office.

"What do you think a potato is worth" Tommy asked speculatively as we walked slowly.

"I don't know. I guess it depends on how big it is."

"When are we going to try again?" Tommy asked as we sat at our boards.

"I've been wondering about the best time," I screwed up my face as I gave it some thought. "I think morning is best. After Takai comes down here he goes to the factory for his checkup. Then Peachi comes down for the day's rations. Takai keeps busy up there for an hour or two. In the afternoon he is usually upstairs or he goes to town." I watched Tommy doodling with his pencil on the edge of the drawing on his board while I was talking. "If he is upstairs we never know just when he'll come down. I think Takai is the problem," I mused. "Once the daily ration is drawn they never come down for more. So, if the guard has been here and Takai is in the factory, we stock up. Can't do it every day though. And we can't take too much. We don't know how they keep track of the stuff."

"What else is in there besides the potatoes? Rice? Any meat?" He asked hopefully.

"No meat that I could see. Maize, beans rice, onions and flour." I scratched at my memory for the details I had of locked room and its boodle.

"How about beans? And maybe an onion. I haven't tasted an onion in years." Tommy looked at me and expected me to make the decision.

"Onions may smell up our breath too much. I guess they have some vitamins. Beans take too long to cook. Potatoes seem to be the best bet." I decided.

"Okay. Spuds it is," he agreed.

"I have to take a look and see if there is any bean cake. No. That still would take too long to cook. Rice might work though," I wondered which of the foods were the best for us.

"Let's just stick to the spuds. Okay?"

"Right. Let's see what tomorrow brings."

During the next week we robbed the store room four times. Then came bad luck. Takai came in after lunch. "We move to the factory this afternoon," he told me in Japanese. "You get some men to help. Bring the cart. The office is ready."

I translated for Tommy. "Nuts," he muttered.

"Nanda." asked Takai.

"He said fine," I told Takai. I frowned at Tommy to be careful.

"You start packing the stuff so we can move it. I'll go up and get a couple of guys and the cart."

We moved everything, drafting boards, files, prints, supplies and the desk along with the stools and the chair. It took the whole afternoon to re-establish the operation in the room that had been renovated. It was separate from the factory proper. It was about ten feet wide and twenty feet long. It stuck out on the north side of the factory. The door that gave access to the room from the factory was in the southeast corner along with a big window. There were other windows in the other walls. Two in the north wall and one in each of the other walls. The windows were double casements, swinging out on large hinges. There was a grill of half inch thick bars on the inside that were fastened solidly to the brick wall. The desk, Takai's, was at the east end, near the door. One drafting board, Tommy's was under the west window. My board was under the window in the north wall, close to the west wall. Against the factory wall were the blueprint files and the supply cabinet. There was a pot bellied stove in the northeast corner. The brick walls had been whitewashed and a new concrete floor had been poured. New light fixtures had been hung over the boards and the desk. There was also a light near the stove. This was our new bailiwick.

"Well this won't be so bad," I said optimistically. "No store room, but maybe something else will break. How about it Tommy?"

"Couldn't last forever," Tommy sighed. "Maybe just as well. They might have started counting spuds. Then we would have been in trouble," Tommy smiled as he looked around our new surroundings.

CHAPTER 27 -- THE PASSIONATE BITCH

The play was finished. Fleming had managed to type one copy of the script. It was our master copy. I sat on my bunk to proof read it.

ACT I

(8 minutes)

2 minutes ad lib

Curtain rises on office scene: as it does ??? makes his way through the audience and takes a seat, left stage front, and commences to read newspaper, remains in this seat throughout whole performance, paying no attention to proceedings, just smoking and reading. (Three Little Words - Orch.)

Through the main entrance enters J.P. Dobie, a leading citizen, lodge member, leader of the Men's Bible Class and President of Dobie Enterprises. A widower and more a vegetarian than a war prisoner. A clean liver who cares nothing for his blonde secretary who is hot for him, nor does he care for any other woman.

Takes seat at his desk, rattles through his papers, calls secretary:

J.P.- "Sonja!"

(Music _ Take A Letter Miss Brown) (Papers on desk)

SONJA - (Enters from off stage, with a steno pad and pencil, and with a sensuous hip movement walks very close to J.P., throwing her breasts practically into his face and in a love filled voice asks)

"What is it Mr. Dobie?"

J.P. - (Ad lib) - Letter. MKK 100 butt shooters, Pinklady, etc. (Backing away).

J.P. - (Clears throat an number of times) "Ahem, ahem, - There was a large fire last night at the Hoten Arms Hotel. I appeared and rescued one of the guests who lost everything. (Pause) Check through our files and see if the Hotel's policy gave full coverage, the woman I rescued and none whatsoever."

SONJA - "Why Mr. Dobie!!!"

J.P. - "Oh yes, I am expecting a call from Dr. Sherbst on the condition of this guest.

SONJA - "The Dr. is waiting outside now."

J.P. - "Send him in."

Exit Sonja - Enter Dr. Sherbst with Sonja. She sits down, resumes work going through papers, etc. Dr. shakes hands, sits down. J.P. sits down.

261

DR. S - "Good morning J.P. How are you after your gallant deed?"
J.P. - "None the worst, except for a few singed hairs."

DR. S - "Well you sure screwed up. I told you to breath steam, not flames (pause for laugh), a little cure I picked up in Manchuria."
    (Sonja looks shocked at Dr. Sherbst's language).
J.P. - "All joking aside, how is that woman I carried out of the fire?"
DR. S - "Extraordinary. Her condition is wonderful, but why did you take her clothes off?"
J.P. - "I didn't take her clothes off!!! They were burned off!!! She came through a sea of flame."
DR. S - "That woman came through no sea of flame, only a witch or some supernatural being could come through such a furnace unscathed."
J.P. - "Well then, she is a witch, but I never pictured a witch so beautiful."
DR. S - "For heaven's sake, don't talk so loud, I brought her down - and she is waiting in the outer office." _ (Continuing, and trying to be sly so as to catch J.P. in his story) - "How long did you say you knew this woman?"
J.P. - "I tell you I just met her yesterday. I was passing the fire, and being the honorary Fire Chief, and the apparatus not there, it was my duty to enter the building. Once inside I saw this woman enveloped in nothing but flames. When she collapsed, it was my duty as Fire Chief to carry her to safety."
DR. S - "Hah, I take it then that she is a new flame rather than an old one." (slaps his knee, laughs at his own joke and gives a knowing wink).
J.P. - (Getting hot under the collar and a little pissed off at the way Sherbst is acting) "Wait a minute Handlebars, don't go forgetting that I had you put on as the insurance company medic, and I can have you taken off just as easily."
DR. S - (In an extremely friendly tone) "Take it easy J.P. old boy, you know I was only joking."
J.P. - (In an exasperated tone) " O.K., O.K." (changing to interest) "Did you say she is in the waiting room now?"
DR. S - "Yes, I brought her a few new dresses then charged them to your account."
J.P. (Dirty look) "I'll go out and invite her in." (Rushes out, upsetting chair in his anxiety.)
DR. S (Walking over to Sonja and sizing her up with X-ray eyes - at the same time resting a fatherly hand on her shoulder and neck)
"Say now, you have a gorgeous line to the covering over your medula oblongata."

SONJA - (Tearing her shoulder free from his caress and in a hurt and insulted tone.) "Fresh! Take your hands off me. I'll have you know I am loyal to my employer, he is a gentleman."
DR. S - (Trying to quiet her down)
"Easy no, watch your hypertension."
(Striking a listening pose)
"I hear them coming - we should see some hot stuff when these flames get together." (He laughs heartily at his own joke.) (Resumes previous position sitting)

The witch, ravishing beauty with cat - like eyes and a shape that would buy any man, walks on stage looking back over her shoulder at J.P. as he follows her on. (Snake Charmer - Orchestra)
WANDA - (In an adoring voice)
"Oh, you were so brave, risking your life for poor worthless me. I owe you my life, my soul, my body. Take it, it belongs to you alone." (with this she sensuously moves her hips towards J.P.)
J.P. (Taking a step backward and warding her off with his outstretched arm)
"Easy now, easy. I merely saw my duty and did it, you owe your body just as much to the fire department, give it to them. (very flustered) er ah, I mean, I don't want it, I mean they do, damn it all. They do their duty, I do my duty. We all do our duty, the Doc did his. Just stay over there where you at."
Off stage - Glass of water
DR. S (Interrupting) "Yes, and my duty now is to give you something for your nerves. Sonja, get me a glass of water please."
(Sonja off stage for water)
J.P. - (Continuing his oration, only a little calmer)
"I am a respectable widower and I lead an honorable life. I have been true to the memory of my late wife. I loved Mrs. Dobie, and I can never love another."
WANDA (In a deep, dramatic frenzy)
"What? You cast me aside? Well if you won't have me, no one shall. You saved my life and it is yours. Whole or not at all."
(Music - Walk of Skeleton)
J.P. (Resignedly) "I want no part of you."
(At this statement the witch moves fast, grabs paper knife off desk and swings arm wide to take a plunge at her breast) (J.P. makes a step closer to act and her arm swings him into an embrace, as she holds him, he is succumbed by her femininity and then he clutches her and holds her to him passionately and pulsatingly. It is then that he realizes that he wants her as he kisses her, he keeps repeating) "I love you, I love you, I

must have you."
WANDA (Slyly and cleverly, turning her head to evade his kissing her)
"And will you marry me? Soon dear?"
J.P. - "Yes, yes of course, of course, but I can hardly wait."
CURTAIN

ACT II
(7 minutes)

(Music - Temptation)
Scene 1 - One month later. Wanda and J.P. enter bedroom that is well
furnished, walking arm in arm.
WANDA - "This is a gorgeous home you have Percival dear (Pause) and
just think (sighs) tomorrow we are to be married. Then it will be mine
too."
J.P. - (Dryly) "That's what I'm afraid of."
WANDA - "Now don't my itty joyty peaty be a meany (changing and in all
seriousness points to a wall picture) whose picture?"
J.P. -(With some pride) "That is the first Mrs. Dobie. A fine woman too."
WANDA - (Cat-like, in a pout) "I don't like her."
(Turns picture and walks by, as J.P. passes picture he turns it back)
J.P. - (Looks at watch) "Well dear, it is time I took you home. You have a
busy day tomorrow."
WANDA - (Clutches at her head and gasps as she starts to crumble)
"Percy... I feel faint..."
(J.P. catches her and starts to help her away from the bed as she looks
at it with a longing look)
WANDA - (Frightened voice) "Where are you taking me?"
J.P. - "To your home, (calling) Rochester!"
WANDA - (Coyly) "Put me to bed dear and you won't need Rochester."
(She strokes his cheek as she talks) (More because he can't carry her
any further, he sits her down on the bed) (She stretches and writhes on
the bed like she feels good inside and out)
WANDA - "My shoes dear."
(He doesn't know what to do at first, then realizes that she wants them
removed. As he removes the shoe he lifts her foot slightly and causes
her skirt to slide down - to get a better look he kisses her foot)
WANDA - (She continues) "Oh you are so romantic." (Barefooted she
jumps up on the bed and frolics around, happy as a chipmunk, while he
sits on the edge of bed and watches)
WANDA - "What a bed, what a bed. We shall live, eat, sleep and take our
exercise in it. A Madison Square Garden of a bed, built for wrestling
matches. Hand in hand we shall pace up and down in it. We shall hang

a white sheet at one end and give motion pictures for our friends, we shall have twelve children, my little husband, and they shall all sleep down there in the far corner, while we curl up in this one. You, you poseur, you and your righteousness, you vegetarian, you slave to a vitamin and calorie chart. Look at me Percival, (shaking her torso in her same sensuous manner) does flesh still revolt you?"
J.P. (He studies her up and down and as she starts to squirm he covers his face with his hands and slowly spreads his fingers to peek, but seeing how he likes if, he takes down his hand and she continues)
WANDA - "Don't fret your little head my darling, it is late, it is time for bed, you in your corner and me in mine, How do we communicate? By telephone or yodel? You might come over to see me some time." (Mae West)
(Where he is sitting he starts to rub earnestly the upper inside of his thigh, she notices it, smiles smugly and then in a bedroom voice)
WANDA - "Your love for me rising isn't it dear?"
J.P. - (Flustered and standing up) "No, but (still rubbing) No. NO. Just scratching a flea!!"
WANDA - (Exasperated) "You're impossible." (Seeing radio beside bed - in a voice filled with glee)
"I'll see if I can get some good music."
(She starts on push button while J.P. sits on edge bed and starts untying shoes. From backstage the following radio programs snap in: (Music) Little Orphan Annie's theme song; Fred Waring's theme song; Lights Out introduction; Barabosol's theme song. Piece - "All of Me.")
(As last piece is reached, Wanda seems satisfied and lays back on pillow)
(J.P. having taken off shoes, walks to wife's picture and turns it face backward. The piece ends as the curtain closes and the piece played is "Under a Blanket of Blue". All the while there is a commotion and shaking of the curtain, then a hand and arm comes out through the curtain holding his pants and drops them. More motion behind the curtain, then her hand comes out holding silk panties and daintily drops them. Music "Under a Blanket of Blue" continues.
                    CURTAIN

                    ACT III
                  (8 minutes)
Dobie's office - Same as Act I. One month later.(J.P. is seated at his desk chewing on the end of a pencil and rustling through papers, very fidgety and nervous. He gets up, walks up and down stage and runs hand through hair, rubs his face and shows nervousness on every hand.

He snaps on desk phone.) (Three Little Words) (She Got Me This Way)
J.P. - "Hello, Sonja?"
SONJA - (Voice coming from inner office phone) - "Yes J.P."
J.P. - "I've sent for Dr. Sherbst. When he comes, send him right in."
(Turns off phone and talks to himself)
"Cursed witch, with the power to read everybody's mind. Some people would give a fortune to know what others are thinking about them, now I hear, and hear that no one thinks much of me. Dr. Sherbst is a good medic, he might know a cure."
SONJA - (Voice comes from off stage)
"Go right in Dr., Mr. Dobie is expecting you."
(Enter Dr. Sherbst)
J.P. - (Jumps up anxiously, runs over and shakes Dr. Sherbst's hand violently)
"I sure am glad you came Doc. I really need you."
DR. S._ (Calming him, taking his wrist and holding his pulse)
"Easy partner, you are under a great nervous strain. Look like a man with a nicotine fit."
J.P. - "You're telling me, I'm going around in circles."
DR. S - "All kidding aside Doc, it's my new wife. You said once that she must be a witch. Well, she's a bitch of a witch. We have been married only a month and she goes through all sorts of antics. She gets up in the middle of the night, entirely nude and climbs down the vine outside of the window and rides a goat bareback through the orchard. Last night at midnight I caught her killing a rooster and mixing a concoction with the blood."
DR. S - "What does she have to say about this?"
J.P. - "That's the worst part. When I told her about this, she cursed me with the power to hear the thoughts of others."
DR. S (Turning his head and cupping his hand over his mouth so as to give the idea of his thoughts) ("This old Dobie bastard has really stripped his gears. He has gone around for years telling people to live a clean life, stay away from meat and drink. He had so much meat in the last month that he is under the delusion he can read minds and...)
J.P. - (Interrupting)
"Delusion my ass, it is downright fact. I hate soliloquies. Even Shakespeare, and now I have to listen to your lousy babble."
DR. S - (Embarrassed)
"I didn't say anything J.P. Honest I didn't. I have been sitting here thinking."
J.P. - "I know you have and I have to listen to it."
DR. S - "You imagine it."

J.P. - "I wish I did."

DR. S - (His thoughts talking as he has his hand over his mouth)"It must have been coincidence that he guessed what I was thinking. Poor Dobie, he's really slipped his cookie. I wonder where he got that Dobie, it must have been in China when..."

J.P. - (Interrupting)

"No, it was Manchuria."

DR. S - (Amazed) "Say! You must be able to read minds."

J.P. - "I am and it is no fun, you would be surprised to know the opinion that people have of you. Everyone is a hypocrite."

DR. S - (Thoughts talking out of the side of his mouth)

"And you J.P. are the biggest hypocrite of all. If it weren't that I received such good money for these calls, I wouldn't spend so much time here. Damn it, from the expression on his face, he can hear my thoughts."

J.P. - "Yes, every one of them, you have a most evil mind."

DR. S - (In a professional attitude)

"The best way to cure this ailment is to get at the cause. I shall go to see your wife and see if I can have the curse lifted."

(Thought voice)

"If I hurry I might catch her still in her negligee."

J.P. - "Watch what you think about my wife."

DR. S - "I can't keep my thoughts straight." (Thought voice) "The old bastard is too slick for me."

J.P. - I am no bastard, only an orphan."

DR. S - " I give up."

Enter Sonja

SONJA - "You rang for me J.P.?"

J.P. - "Yes, phone my wife and tell her to be ready to receive Dr. Sherbst in a short while."

DR. S - (Eyeing up Sonja and his thought voice goes on) "This Dobie gets the dolls. Look at that pair of mammaries on this one, and the curve to her gluteus maximus. I wonder what her..."

J.P. - "You better hurry Doc."

DR. S - "I'll be back soon.

Exit Dr. Sherbst

SONJA - (Talking in a thought voice) "Dear old J.P. worrying about that useless wife of his. She doesn't love him, while I am wild over him."

J.P. - "What did you say?"

SONJA - "Nothing , I was just thinking." (Thought talking) "If that heavy hung darling only knew that I was thinking of him and being with him, of how I have always loved him, and he goes and marries another."J.P. - "Don't let me interrupt your thoughts."

SONJA - (Thought talking and tapping pencil against hand) "Someday I might tell him that I love him, but while he is married to this other I can say nothing, can I J.P. honey?"

J.P. - (Forgetting) "Yes you can... Er, ah, ahem, I mean, I have something to tell you Sonja,"

SONJA - (Anticipatingly) "Yes, yes, what is it?" (Thought talking) "Here is where I lose my job and my boyfriend too."

J.P. - "Since the day when you were a girl out of training class and first stepped into my office, I have been mad for you. If I hadn't been bewitched by that sorceress I would have asked you to marry me."

(He stands and steps toward her, she stands and they clutch hands)

J.P. -(Continuing) "Now I am married to another, but even if she were out of the way I couldn't marry you., as I am afflicted with a strange malady."

SONJA (Thought talking) "I wonder if it would prevent us from having children."

J.P. - "Even now I can read your sweet thoughts."

SONJA - "Then you know how I feel towards you?" (She starts to sob, and he takes her into his arms and she sobs on his shoulders)

(Music - Get Out Of Town in background - low)

Enter Dr. Sherbst followed by Wanda

WANDA - (Rushes in and separates Sonja and J.P. emitting a wild scream) "Kura??!!"

WANDA SONJA - ad lib - seconds

DR. S - "Easy now Wanda. Remember we have something to tell these two schemers."

WANDA - "It was your idea, you spill it."

DR. S - "Here it is J.P. Wanda and I were talking it over and we find that we were made for each other. She will give you a divorce and remove the curse forever. You can have Sonja and I'll take Wanda."

J.P. - "Doc, you really cure without medicine." (Grabs Sonja in his arms, kisses her, he comes up breathless and gasps) "Sonja."

DR. S - (Tries to get a kiss from Wanda and she gives him a sharp slap. He curses Wanda)

CURTAIN

Pinson sat beside me reading the copy that I had proof read.

"Well, what do you think?" I asked when he had finished.

"Sounds good to me," Pinson answered as he lit a cigarette.

"I think that we should have Rogers and Hewgley read it. If everybody agrees it's okay then we'll start rehearsals, if not we'll fix it and then start." I collected the pages of the script and leafed through them slowly.

I examined them with interest again.

Fleming had filched some paper and had typed the script at MKK. He had to smuggle the script through the inspection lines. I wondered what the Japs would have thought if they had caught him. There was no telling what would or could have happened to Fleming. Unless the Jap officers would have understood that it was just a play, he would have wound up in the guard house for a few days.

"How about if we have them read them now? We have about another hour." Pinson suggested.

"Okay." I agreed.

" I'll find them. You just take it easy."

"Nuts," I answered, but I did appreciate that he was trying to save me from walking too much.

"Can I read it Pete?" asked Willy. He had been sitting quietly taking it all in. He had not interfered in our conversation before.

"Sure," I handed him the sheaf of papers. "I'd like to know what you think of it. It's plenty corny, but I think it will get some laughs."

Willy started to read as Hewgley and Rogers came in and sat down on the bench by the bunk.

"Here, let's see what you think of it," I picked up the pages that Willy had read and passed them over to them. They chuckled and laughed as they read the corny script. Rogers pointed out some specific phrases to Hewgley. When they finished I asked, "Well? How about it?"

Pinson came in just as Rogers started his comments. "Pretty good. I guess it should break out some laughs. I think the way it's put over, you know, the costumes and the get up will make it a real show."

"It sure as hell will. I think it is great." Hewgley was enthusiastic. "You have women here. You have some of the things spoofed that the men know about so it makes them feel close to it. Associated with it. They'll like it. Ya got pazaz. Especially the dames," he smiled. "That Sonja, Sonjama!" He finished by pinching Pinson's leg. "Hey Sonja!"

"I'm gonna be Wanda," Pinson swacked at Hewgley's hand, femininely.

"The hell you are, you're blonde. That means Sonja. I'll be Wanda!" Hewgley was emphatic.

"I think Hewg's right. You would do much better as Sonja. You're naturally blonde. You would look more natural," I agreed with Hewgley. Pinson was a natural for the blonde part.

"I think so too," interrupted Willy. "He'd look better as a blonde."

"Okay, so I'm Sonja." Pinson conceded.

"Anybody else have any suggestions? Anything that will help to put it over? Anything that will get the guys to laugh?"

it." Pinson urged.

"Right," agreed Hewgley. Rogers nodded agreement.

"Okay. Then we'll have to make copies of this. I'll go see about it. Maybe Johnson can print three more copies in a hurry." I picked up the script, "See you guys later."

Johnson thought he could have the copies in about a week. We had the props, so we planned to start soon.

CHAPTER 28 -- RALPH

We wound up our rehearsals with bull sessions that lasted until tenko. It was during one of these that the discussion centered around sabotage. It was due to the rumors that were floating around about the war effort and whether or not we could hinder the manufacture of war supplies in any way. Sabotage. Someone suggested that we could possibly sabotage the cranes we were building at Takai. The idea came about when Pinson told us about the overhead crane that had broken down at MKK and caused a lot of delay in the production line. The larger castings and machinings were backed up and most of the heavy machine production had stopped. I mentioned the story to Mitch and Jack at lunch in the yard, cautious about being overheard by any of the Japs. They both agreed to do some serious thinking about it.

"Foolproof or it's no go. Don't forget, if they can trace it to us we're dead." I cautioned them. "If the Nips can prove anything it will mean our necks, so it has to be good. It has to be better than good, it has to be great. It has to be one terrific idea to work at all."

"Well it won't be bloody easy that is for sure," Jack agreed.

"Humph! I can't figure anything right off hand. But we will give it a go." Mitch looked pensive. "I'd like to screw the slant-eyed snakes but good. You know that Art Rice is puttying in the extra holes in the gusset plates mate."

"I know. They don't really weaken the plates, it's more cosmetic than anything else. But Takai doesn't want the extra holes showing."

We left it at that for the time being, hoping that someone could come up with and idea.

Tommy transferred out of Takai early in the fall. He was replaced by Ralph Sharp, number eleven forty-two. Ralph was an Englishman who had been captured at Singapore. He had been at Dunkirk. When he came in he admitted that he didn't know a thing about drafting. Much more that he would know about structural design. He hoped to learn something that he would find useful and therefore have something good come from being a prisoner. I felt the same way. Whatever experience I could gain would, or could be useful in the future.

"Whatever experience is gained here, even if it is for the rotten Japs, forced labor, is still experience. If one takes advantage of this period to learn then one has gained something. It's not the same as though you were working in industry at home, but it might be something that you can use in the future. Maybe even profit by it." I was verbally offering justification for the job that was being done for the Japs.

"I agree old boy. And I certainly intend to learn anything that you can teach me," Ralph answered sincerely.

"I'm not sure that I can teach you much. But anything that you learn will probably be helpful." I felt rather foolish, Ralph was at least ten years older. He had been in the service for some years. But, it did help to bolster my ego.

"You know, I think there is one really good way to learn. If you can design a mechanism or a machine and make it work, then you have learned something. Now suppose that you would want to sabotage the machine, the one that you designed. It would be easy to have some part of it fail. Analyze the machine and find its weakest point. Then make that part weak. It could look like a natural failure. An unpredictable failure. Then I think that you really know how to design something." I felt like some professor lecturing a class instead of having Ralph as a captive audience.

"Sounds rather fascinating Pete." Ralph said thoughtfully. "But it is a rather difficult project. Isn't it?"

"Sure. But I think that it can be done."

Days passed into weeks. Ralph learned rapidly. I found him to be a ready partner in crime. He was ready to help with any connivance at any time. It was more than a month before we concocted a scheme that we were sure was worth trying. One midmorning, after looking around the factory and seeing that there were no guards, and that all of the foremen were busy, I called Ralph over to my board. "I have been working on a project." I started a cross sectional view of a structural part of a crane. I drew a rivet holding three pieces of steel together. "See this. The diameter of the rivet is such that it fits and fills the holes that are drilled through the plates. A heated rivet is inserted and then the head is formed by bucking it and hammering it with the rivet gun. This pounds the metal into the holes, filling the cavities. The metal is hot so that it flows and deforms. When you are finished there isn't any void, the metal fills up everything. No clearance is left. The head is shaped by the riveting gun. Pounded round. Okay so far?" I didn't know if Ralph understood my point.

"Yes, quite clear," Ralph nodded. "If the original hole is bigger that the rivet, and it is, so that you can insert the rivet easily, then pounding the metal from the outside pushes the metal into the holes and fills them. Right?"

"Right," I smiled approvingly. He picked up ideas fast. "Now suppose that the rivet is much smaller than it should be, and not long enough to provide enough material to fill the hole. You will have to see how they use a bucking tool and the rivet gun to pound the heads. If you shape the heads fast, you don't fill up the holes in the plates."

"Okay." He looked at me to finish the explanation.

"Now if you use a bucking tool and a riveting tool for a larger diameter rivet on a smaller rivet than the tool was intended for, the material of the rivet is formed by the head and it looks like a large rivet. The hole isn't filled by the metal. The only thing that holds the plates together it the tension of the two heads." I paused to let him absorb the idea.

"Logical. And you cool the center by holding it with the rivet tongs."

"When the plates vibrate there isn't any metal in the hole to keep the plates from shifting. After a few months of use the plates tend to shift because of the load. The heads finally loosen and the plates start to shear the rivet."

Ralph looked as though he were mulling over the action over a period of time to see what the results would be. "After enough of this motion," Ralph placed a pencil between the first and second finger of his hands, palms together, pencil sticking out of both sides, and then he moved his hands in a circular motion. "Then suddenly, one day, POP goes the rivet." He smiled. It crinkled his whole face.

"I hope," I said with a somewhat perturbed tone.

"What do you mean, you hope?" Ralph looked reproachful. "It certainly sounds logical."

"I guess it could be, but I just don't know. And we don't have anyone in camp that can prove or disprove the theory," I informed him.

"Have you checked with any of the officers?" he asked as he looked out of the factory window.

"Yes. But there isn't any mechanical engineer around. The officers don't know anything. The draftsman and designers at MKK, Kozie for one, says it sounds right, but no one knows for sure." I looked around and then tore the sketch into little pieces and dumped them, half into one basket and the rest into the other.

"You are taking a lot of extra precautions, aren't you Pete?"

Ralph hadn't been at Takai long enough to know about the kind of surveillance that went on. "I saw Takai checking the waste baskets a couple of times. It doesn't pay to take chances." I told Ralph as I looked out of the window into the factory.

"He checks on us that way?" Ralph asked in surprise.

"Sure does. So do the guards. They'll come in and check while you sit here."

"Well," he puffed the word, "So we have to be careful of what we write and sketch."

"It always pays to be careful." I assured him. "Takai just came in through the door. Look busy. Here, let me explain about the design of the drum."

Ralph glanced out of the window and then pointed to the drawing. "How does one determine the radius of the groove?"

"You use the handbook. All worked out." I picked up the reference book, an American edition, and started to thumb through it.

Takai came in and slammed the door. "Ohio." He walked over to the board and studied the drawing. "Nanda."

"Ralph will do the drum detailing," I informed him in Japanese. "I think that he can do the job very well."

"Good, good," Takai bobbed his head a couple of times in approval. He had been unhappy about Tommy being transferred. He looked around and then walked out. He stopped just outside the door and studied the factory, and then headed to the left to the foundry.

"Well Ralph, guess you may just as well start on the detail of the drum." I picked up a sheet of paper. "Here is the information and here is a similar drum. We need the drawing this afternoon."

"Righto old boy. I'll be right on it," Ralph returned to his own board.

"We're going to try the rivet trick on the crane that has to be shipped in November."

"Good show. Good show Pete. I hope that the bloody thing takes a half a dozen Nips along with it."

"We'll see," I said hopefully as I turned to my board.

There were only five of us in on the actual conspiracy. Six, if Ralph was to be counted, only he did not have to do anything as far as working at it. The riveters, the hot man - who heated the rivets, the warehouse man and myself. The fewer who knew about what was going on the safer we all were. The other men knew that there was something on, but they weren't told the details. The way it figured was that if they didn't know about the plot they couldn't break under questioning. A drowning man can only hold back for so long before breaking down. Or, the sneaker beating could break a man down readily.

The crane that we chose to try our scheme was to be delivered to a machine shop in Dairen. The men involved went about their business as usual and the Japs weren't aware of what we were doing.

We returned to camp one evening to be greeted with sad news. "The Japs have issued an order that there are to be no gatherings of any kind. I guess everything goes to pot." He was disgusted. "No special privileges and no entertainment."

"Why not? What goes on now?" no one had said anything during chow.

"The Nips figure that the Americans are robbing the commissary at MKK. So, since nobody says who, we all get cooked for it. Just like that." Pinson snapped his fingers in my face.

"What happened?"

"No one seems to know just how it was done. But for two or three months now food has been disappearing. It's the storeroom by building one. How? Who? And last week the outside gang was sent in to unload a boxcar of food, sweet potatoes and such. Half of the stuff disappeared. Now the rest of it disappearing from the warehouse." He shrugged and smiled.

"So they take it out on all of us even though it could be the Manchus. It figures." It was the way the Japs did things. "No privileges. How does that solve their problem? It's not logical. Not to me anyway. Nuts! That means the play is off. All of the work we all put in too."

"Guess so. Well, that's that," Pinson stated flatly. "Guess we leave the stuff where it is. What do you say?"

"Oh, I guess so." I was disheartened and not interested in the props if we couldn't use them. "Guess anything that could be put to use should be taken out. The rest we might as well leave." I thought it for a moment, "Maybe we should just leave it all."

"Want to dig through it now?" Pinson didn't seem to be that interested anymore either.

"No, let's leave it for now. Maybe the stinkers will change their minds in a month or so. We could put the show on then." I hated to see all of that work go to waste.

"Okay, well we'll leave it and see." Pinson left in a down mood.

"Didn't you hear that the order was posted this afternoon Pete?" Willy asked as I lay back on my bunk.

"Nope. I guess they'll bring it up at tenko to make sure that everybody knows about it." I lay there thinking about the way that the Japs did things. No way near like the Westerners. Their logic, their philosophy was different. That was probably the reason that we got away with so many things. It worked both ways. They couldn't figure us out. But we had the edge, we were pretty good at figuring them out. A Jap wouldn't steal food in the same manner as an American. We knew the penalty and we still went ahead and tried. We weren't fatalists. We were gamblers. The Japs would fight on to the end, to the death, suicidal, just to save face. We, Americans, would fight to the death too, but not uselessly, not to save face. We were too realistic. We were sleazy, but with a purpose. We used life because being alive was a weapon in itself.

"Guess we are just different. What do you think Willy?" I turned my head, my chin resting in the palms of my hands. "Think we can ever really be beaten by the Nips?"

"Well, I don't know. We're prisoners, but we still keep on giving them a hard time," Willy voiced some of my own thoughts, "but they won't win the war, that's for damn sure."

"Yep, that's for sure."

Maybe the Japs couldn't see that they wouldn't lose the war any more than we couldn't see that they would win.

"What say Willy, who's in on the commissary deal?"

"Well," he rolled over on his side to face me, "if you were at MKK I probably wouldn't tell you without breaking a promise. I promised not to tell anyone at MKK."

"There's a gimmick, huh?"

"Yup. You know the head at building two. The crapper sticks out between two and three. On the north side." He waited for my nod of acknowledgment. It had been a year since I had worked at MKK. "Well the Japs turned the extension on the south side of three, just opposite the crapper on two into a storehouse. The commissary storeroom. They put a couple of locks on the big door. The windows all have bars now. It's like a big safe. And," he paused dramatically, "the floor is about a foot thick. Poured concrete."

I waited, puzzled at the buildup.

"Anyway some of the guys thought up this beaut of an idea." Willy rolled over to look around the area. The card game was at the other end of the bay. No one was paying any attention to us. "The hole at the east end of the crapper has been blocked off. Not really blocked off, just a sign posted that it isn't safe to use. It's so dark there that no one uses it anyway. That is where one end of the tunnel is. The other end is under a corner of the commissary."

"You kidding?" I asked unbelievingly. "In the crapper?" I shook my head. "Somebody's going to get crapped on for sure."

"Naw! Nobody ever uses that end. Besides, there is always a lookout when there is a lift going on."

"But how about the other end? How the hell that the Japs haven't found it?" I frowned at the story. It sounded like a bunch of bullshit.

"It's a beaut!" Willy enthused. "The hole is in a corner. It's plugged. A tapered plug! Comes up from the bottom! You can't even see it. Looks like some cracks in the floor. I've been there, believe me."

He practically convinced me that I wouldn't be able to find it. I backed off in disbelief. I couldn't believe that somebody couldn't find the thing.

"Can't see it. The dirt is always filled into the cracks when the guys go in to stack the supplies. The thing rests on a big stump. Piece of a telephone pole. There's boards, planks, on the tunnel floor. The stump is on the planks. The plug is held up tight. Then there's the wedges. You have to knock out the wedges to drop the plug. Then you use the wedges to lock the plug into place."

I kept looking at him in disbelief. It just didn't seem possible. "And you can't see it or knock it loose from the commissary?"

"Hell no! I've been in there loading and unloading stuff. I was even on the repair crew. We fixed the plug when we were putting in the concrete floor."

"Well how about the tunnel? Why doesn't it all cave in? Somebody's going to get killed if the sand caves in. The whole area is nothing but sand."

"Yeah. True. But the whole tunnel is lined with planks. Two inches thick. Right from the crapper to the storeroom. And," he glance around the bay again, "the tunnel runs right out from the crapper to the foundation across from it. So, one of the walls of the tunnel is the footing of the building itself. The planks are right up against it and it's all stable as hell." He looked at me with a bland look of self assurance.

I studied his face for minutes.

"Well?"

"Bullshit! I don't believe it!" I lied. I could believe that they could do it, but it was so far fetched that it seemed like a pipe dream.

"Hell! Why not? Think I'm lying?"

"Well," I stopped to think up the words I wanted. "Well, how the hell do you crawl into the tunnel without wallowing in crap?"

"Easy," Will answered with a smirk, "the crapper floor slopes downhill, away from the crapper to the urinal. It's the highest point of the whole frigging thing, and there's a block under the crapper floor to prevent the stuff from going back up toward the tunnel. Right?"

"Yeah, I guess so." I was trying to draw a mental picture of the setup.

"Don't forget," Willy pressed on, "the floor slit where you squat to take a crap is narrow, you have the floor hanging over the thing. It's like a roof, an overhang on each side. The hole under is about four, maybe five feet across. You can hide under the overhang and not be seen from above. That's how come no one sees the end of the tunnel."

"Sounds real crazy to me. If they ever find anyone crawling out of there..." I didn't finish the statement.

"It works. We can't bring in any food from the factory, but we sure eat good at the shack whenever there's a lift."

"How big is the tunnel?" I asked, still not believing the tale.

"About eighty feet long. I guess maybe three foot high and about three or more foot wide. No trouble getting in and out. You need a candle. And man, sometimes the place stinks!"

"I guess it would," I frowned at the thought that struck me. "It's a wonder that the smell doesn't come up in the storeroom."

"Yeah, I suppose."

"Tenko, tenko. Come on line up and get counted off before you all roll in and grab your cocks."

We lined up for the nightly roll call that was conducted by the Japs to make sure that no one was missing.

"Now don't forget," Willy nudged me, "not a word to anyone. Okay?"

"Sure, okay Willy. So that is why the Japs stopped everything. Too much has disappeared."

"Yup." He smiled and formed up as we started to count off.

CHAPTER 29 -- TOBACCO

The problem of supplying the men in camp with cigarettes and tobacco taxed the ingenuity of all of us. The Jap commissary allowed only two packs per man whenever there were any cigarettes available. Two packs per week was a short supply. When you didn't have anything to eat you wanted a smoke. And smokes were hard to come by. Sometimes there were no sales for three weeks. And, as long as six weeks. So, the demand was always high. It didn't matter what kind of tobacco it was, as long as it was smokeable. The price was always way up. Since some of the cigarettes and tobacco came in from MKK, they had the corner on the market. Tobacco that came in was usually rolled into cigarettes with any kind of paper that was available. Pipe tobacco, when available, also was very high in price.

The only pipe tobacco that was in abundant supply was a Russian import. The package was blue with the name Janko spelled out in large white letters. "Janko" translated into John in English. What puzzled me was that the name was not printed in the Russian alphabet. Maybe it was packaged for the export trade. The tobacco was a licorice black. It was so strong that only the hardiest smoker could finish a pipeful at a time. It reminded me of the black cheroots that the old Italians smoked in lower New York City, the place I had known as Little Italy

Since none of us knew anything about tobacco, how it was processed, dried or blended, we couldn't figure out what could be done to the stuff to improve it. We tried to blend it with some of the other tobaccos that came in but never succeeded in making it any more smokeable.

There was also another kind that was available, Manchu Dust. This was a flake tobacco. We had seen the Manchus smoking the stuff in their little bowl pipes. The pipe looked like a shallow thimble sitting on a little stem, like a piece of pipe, about the size of a pencil. The bowl held about three pinches of the dust. It was about all one could smoke regardless how much of a hankering one had for nicotine.

A lucky accident led me to the discovery of a method of treating the Russian tobacco so that it rivaled the "Toasted Blend of Lucky Strike".

One rainy morning after we had entered the factory compound I saw one of the Manchu workers drop a package of Janko. It fell into a puddle of rain water. "Wamba tusa. Malakapi!" he cursed. "Ding bu how." He looked at me in disgust and gave a sharp shake of his head. Then with

the odd Oriental humor with which he was endowed, he pointed to the
sodden package soaking in the puddle, "Ding bu how." He laughed and
pointed to me. I picked up the the tobacco and gave the old man a smile
and thanked him. I squeezed the package and made a wry face as a
black liquid ran out from between my fingers. The Manchu laughed
aloud and took off for the factory. I looked at the mess I was holding and
curled my upper lip in disgust. I squeezed it until there was no more
water coming from it. I carried it back to the drafting room.

"What the blimey hell do you have there?" Ralph stared at the mess in
my hand. "Don't tell me that you have been chasing horses old boy."

I had removed the paper and held a brown moist ball that looked
exactly like a wet horse turd. I looked at it and had to agree with Ralph, it
did look just like a ball of horseshit. "Nuts," I retorted as I discarded the
paper wrapping. "Don't be funny." I kept looking at the ball of tobacco.
Ralph watched as I squeezed it again. A few drops of juice dripped to
the floor.

"Yahh!" he responded in distaste. "You gone balmy or something
mate?" He made a face that seamed into folds like loose old leather. He
had that kind of a face. Old in some ways before its years. "Pete?" he
looked at me with honest concern.

"No, I'm not balmy, and I am as nuts as I can be already," I answered
with some degree of sarcasm. "From years of incarceration with a bunch
of Limeys." I added with a smirky grin. I had moved my hand over the
trash basket and waited until the dripping had stopped. I reached for a
rag under my drafting board. I spread the tobacco as well as I could on
a piece of paper and placed it under my board to dry.

"What the bloody hell are you up to anyway?" Ralph shook his head,
peering at me with wonder.

"I don't know right now. We'll see after it dries."

"What is it anyway?" Ralph asked in exasperation.

"Tobacco."

"That! Tobacco! You are joking!" He laughed. "It's nothing but a horse
turd. You are going balmy. Like a bat." He waved at me and turned to his
board.

"Okay, okay. So I am balmy. And I am going to smoke dried
horseshit." I turned to my board and got busy.

There had been no one in the office all morning. Peachi hadn't been
in, and neither had Takai. It was late afternoon before the tobacco had
dried out completely. Ralph had been gone for some time gathering
information out in the factory. Making sure that there were no Japs in the
vicinity of the office, I picked at the strands of dried tobacco. They were
light and fluffy, light yellow in color. I was surprised at the change in the

color. I remembered the tobacco poultice that i had tried on my leg in Cabanatuan. There were dirty brown stains on the paper on which I had spread the stuff to dry. I filled my pipe and lit it. I puffed away enjoying the best smoke that I had had in ages. Horse turd! Well, he could call it whatever he wanted to call it. It was real honest to goodness tobacco. I stored the light yellow strands in a little cloth sack that I carried to collect cigarette butts. Ralph opened the door to the office and sniffed the air. He opened his mouth and stopped. He sniffed the air again. He closed the door carefully and looked around. I watched the expression on his face. I was enjoying myself immensely. I watched as he approached me and sniffed at the smoke I exhaled as I puffed on my pipe.

"Pete," he said, sniffing at the pipe, "where did you get that tobacco?!"

"Horse shit!" I puffed away and blew smoke at him.

"Don't be nasty," he retorted. "Where?" he shouted.

"Easy now. Not so loud." I put him off. "Just you never mind."

"Well now," Ralph walked over to his board, placed his papers and the scale on the board with great deliberation and sat down facing me. "Now I say that that is not at all cooperative you know. Aren't I entitled to know where you got the tobacco?" He sounded querulous.

"Well, maybe you are entitled and maybe you aren't. You really might be upset if I tell you." There was so little about our existence that wasn't boring, the same routine day in and day out that I was milking the occasion for all it was worth. "It might be just some horseshit that I picked up and rinsed out. You wouldn't want to smoke horseshit, would you?"

"Well at least let me try some," he begged. "I have some excellent paper here, rice paper, and the making of a fag would be in order."

"Sure, sure," I laughed. I couldn't string him any longer. "Here," I handed him the small sack, "Make yourself a smoke."

He rolled a cigarette and lit up. He inhaled as I watched. His face lit up as he exhaled the light blue smoke in appreciation of the fine tobacco flavor. He held the cigarette up close to examine it and then sniffed at it again. "Now that is a real good smoke. Thank you."

"Horseshit," I said, "you wouldn't really smoke it would you?"

"Okay I give up. Break it off Pete. Just what is this stuff?" He was bewildered.

I told him about the incident. I stopped at the point in the story that he was familiar with and waited for his response.

"You mean this is the Black Death?" he sat with his mouth open as he stared at the smoke curling up from the cigarette. "The Russian stuff?"

"Yep!" I was tickled pink at his reaction.

"Well I'll be!" Ralph intoned. He shook his head in disbelief.

"Now you have to promise not to breath a word to anyone. Not one word. You can't show anyone how it is done. Our trade secret. Promise?" I pressed him.

"I swear. I promise. Not one word." He looked at me with a peculiar expression. "Are you sure that it will work?"

"Yes. I am sure. We'll fix some tomorrow. Now, let's see if I can get Shohi to bring in about five packs of the stuff tomorrow. I have the buckets tomorrow night. That means that I can smuggle the batch we process tomorrow."

The carpenters in camp had worked over the wood chow buckets that were used to bring our lunch from the camp kitchen. The bottoms had been modified so that there was a second, false, bottom. Since the buckets were almost a foot in diameter, the cavity under the bucket bottom, was about ten inches in diameter and about an inch and a quarter deep. The contraband was stored there and carried into camp under the noses of the Japs. I figured that I could carry at least eight packs of tobacco at one time.

"That's a bit of all right. How much does the little bastard hang us up for a pack of the stuff?"

Ralph seemed to have some kind of distrust about the little Manchu kid that worked in the factory. It seemed that he and the other Englishmen didn't trust natives.

"He charges a yen. I think he pays about fifty sen. So he makes a hundred percent profit. It is still damn cheap."

I found the little Manchu boy out in the foundry and arranged for him to bring in five or more packs of what was called the Black Death.

Shohi was a real gem, he brought in eight packs of tobacco. I also ordered ten for the next day. I warned him not to tell anyone and not to take any chances. He assured me that he would not have any trouble. I returned to the office just as Takai came in. He checked our work and then left. Ralph acted as lookout as I opened the packages and dumped the black tobacco into a large can of hot water that I had had heating on the stove. I let it steep for a while and picked out the soggy strands with a small wood paddle that I had found in the factory. I let the water drain out and then gingerly squeezed the strands dry. I spread it all out on some paper under my elevated drafting board. By mid-afternoon the tobacco had dried to a golden brown color that gave off an aromatic odor of rich mellow tobacco. I didn't know if nicotine was water soluble, I wondered if some of it was removed in the process.

"Well, what do you think of that? Real fine smoking stuff." I was elated at the prospect of having a tobacco supply that was known only to the two of us. "Mild."

"Absolutely marvelous," intoned Ralph as he sniffed the tobacco.

"I figure that it should bring in about fifteen yen a pack."

"Fifteen yen!" He shouted. "Fifteen yen?"

"Why not? It's the best stuff ever."

"A good price. A real good price," he agreed enthusiastically.

"Suppose that we pack it in the little brown bags. That way nobody will ever suspect." I proposed.

"Jolly idea. That will camouflage it perfectly."

The little brown bags reminded me of the bags used in the candy stores. They were used to hold small rations of tea or beans or other items that were distributed by Takai in small rationed quantities. We had a plentiful supply in the warehouse. I measured the tobacco by filling the original package and then transferring it to the brown bags. We had ten bags when we had finished. That was a bonus that we hadn't expected. The tobacco had fluffed up.

"You're cheating old boy. The Chinese measure you are using might put you in trouble and not make us rich." He warbled happily.

"So we make a little profit," I answered, undamped by the accusation. "Who takes the chance of winding up in the guardhouse?"

Ralph shrugged. "Are you going to load the buckets now?"

"I guess I had better. I'll do it now." I stuffed the packages under my jacket, checked that they didn't bulge too much and headed for the warehouse where the buckets were stacked until they were to be picked up and carried back to camp. I secreted them in the hidden compartment and set the buckets for pickup.

"Any problems?" Ralph asked as I closed the office door.

"None. Nobody around."

There was no problem in the trip back to camp. I dropped the buckets off at the kitchen. Ralph acted as lookout as I unloaded the stash. Charlie, one of the KPs came around after I had unloaded the stuff and took the bucket to the special rack. He came back to talk to us.

"How'd it go?" he asked as he wiped his hands on his apron.

"No strain Charley." Ralph nodded in agreement. "Here," I handed him a bag of tobacco, "if you don't use it yourself it sells for fifteen yen the bag. Right?"

He opened the bag and sniffed. He peered inside with a puzzled look. "Hey! Real tobacco! Pipe tobacco!"

"Real good makings too," Ralph added. "But not a word now, hear?" he cautioned.

"Heck no! I won't breath it around. How's it for chewing?" He shook some of the tobacco into the palm of his hand. "Looks good. Smells good." He popped the tobacco into his mouth and started to form a cud.

Ralph made a sick face and turned away. I smiled at Charlie. "Well?" I asked.

"Good. Great! Best I've ever had here." Charlie moved the cud around his mouth.

"Do all Texans chew tobacco Charlie?" Ralph asked.

"Naw. We don't all chew." He laughed, "But I do. Thanks. You gonna sell?"

"At fifteen yen a bag. Ralph or me."

"Okay. Let me know whenever the special." Charlie spit some juice into the drain gutter.

"Right. I need them tomorrow and from now on until I tell you."

I handed over five bags to Ralph as we headed toward our barracks. "You take five now. I'll make up mine tomorrow."

"I'll take four now. It was your money." He handed back one of the bags.

"Okay." I took the bag and shoved it into my pocket. "See you in the morning." All five bags moved in no time at all. There were requests for more after the goods had been sampled. No one complained about the price.

We proceeded to supply the tobacco regularly. Either Ralph or I carried the bucket, or we paid the bucket carrier for smuggling in the tobacco when it wasn't our turn to carry the buckets. Sometimes we paid the carrier for the privilege when it wasn't our turn.

Kozie and Mac were steady customers. Our customers, we found out, were reselling at a profit. The only customers that were sold three and four bags were Kozie, Mac and Gene Scarcelli, 1271, after that since they were special friends.

I bought a Navy blanket from a swabie for a hundred yen. It was a holdup price, but I wanted the blanket for a special reason. I wanted a wool coat. I had Shohi bring in some needles and thread. It took me six weeks of night work to sew a heavy coat using a sailor's pea coat as a guide. It was the only one in camp. It was also one of the warmest coats anyone had.

In late October, nineteen-forty-four, we had a pleasant surprise. We arrived in camp to hear that the Japs had lifted the non-assembly order. They had lifted the restrictions and restored privileges.

"Wow! Wow!" I yelled as I danced around to the amazement of the guys around me. "We can put on the play."

"Hey! That's right," roared Ralph, "that means that you blokes can put on the play."

"Man! I have to collect the guys and see about starting rehearsals."

"We'll spread the word." Ralph stopped short. "Hey! When do you think you blokes can be ready to put it on?"

"I don't know. We'll figure it out tonight."

My bay was in an uproar. Pinson, Hewgley and Rogers and the cast had started to check out the props and costumes.

"Hey Pete!" Pinson spotted me in the crowd as I tried to push through to my bunk. "How about it? We can be ready and put the play on the first time on Saturday night. Sunday's yasme. It'll be great."

"How about a rehearsal after chow?" Rogers was enthused.

"Great!" Hewgley agreed. "Let's have a couple of readings and then a full dress rehearsal." He grinned happily. "Okay?"

"Sure." I agreed readily. I had been waiting to present my play and find out how the guys, my public in this case, would respond to the presentation.

Chow took forever. After the bowls were cleaned up a crowd started to gather. The word had been spread through the whole camp. Someone asked if we were thinking of putting on a show just for the hospital patients. I said that I thought we could do it sometime in the future if the play went over. The bay was jammed. Men were sitting in rows on the lower and the upper decks. Cigarette and pipe smoke turned the place blue. The readings caused an uproar. There were jibes and jokes. Everyone was relaxed and enjoying themselves. Tenko broke up the gathering with the cast happy at the way they had remembered their lines and cues. We rehearsed three times before the presentation on Saturday night.

The orchestra was located in the lower bay behind what was the main stage area. The bays, upper and lower, that weren't used for the stage were crammed. Men were sitting in three rows on the bunk area. The bunks had been stowed and the tables had been removed to make room for more benches. I was afraid that the upper bunks were going to collapse from the number of men that were jammed in to see the first performance. Men were sitting side by side and knees to backs in the aisles as well. All of the floor space was covered. Hewgley told us that someone had counted three hundred and forty men.

The orchestra, a harmonica and a guitar, opened with Three Little Words and then went into Please Take a Letter Miss Brown as the background music for the first scene of Act 1. When Wanda the Witch entered the music picked up with the Snake Charmer. The closing scene was backgrounded with The Walk of the Skeletons.

The audience laughed, roared and joked. They were enjoying themselves as they never had for the last three years. The cast was so overwhelmed by the response of the spectators that they went overboard in their portrayals. The cast and crew, including me, were bursting with joy at the reception of the play. What had started out as just entertainment turned into a fiesta of fun. The congeniality of the moment was so overpowering that the actors were almost flubbing their lines because of the laughter and distracting jibes. No one made any obvious mistakes. Ad libs covered so well that no one knew the difference when a line was flubbed. The applause at the end of Act 1 just about brought down the barrack. Act 2 opened with Temptation and blended into Little Orphan Annie's theme song, followed by Fred Waring's theme song, the Barbosal theme, and All of Me. It closed with Under a Blanket of Blue.

The uproar during the bedroom scene was uncontrollable. The actors had to stop until the men quieted down before they could continue. It took minutes before they quieted down enough for the third act could go on. The music began with Three Little Words and the mood setting She Got Me This Way. The audience sang and hummed. There was a continuous hushing so that the actors could be heard. The act concluded with Get Out of Town and It's All Over Now. There was a tremendous crash of applause along with whistling and cheering. Men from Barracks Two came over to find out what was going on. There hadn't been any guards coming through the area since early evening. The play had started at eight and had run until almost nine. I wondered if the Japs knew that the play was going on and had kept the guards out of the way.

Everybody, officers and enlisted men were crushing with their praise. There were hundreds of questions about the props and the costumes. The women's getups were the ones that generated the most interest.

We promised to repeat the play for the other barracks and the hospital.

There were no repercussions from the Japs about the play.

CHAPTER 30 -- AIR RAID

The Japs reorganized the camp in November. We didn't know why they did. We supposed that it was to prevent any long time associations progress of the war played some part in the move. Men were shifted around and the old sections disbanded. I had been in Barracks Three. After the reorganization I was located in Barracks One.

The change was made during one of the rest, Yasme, days.

A few days after the move the air raid sirens blasted the area with the fact that there was no place that the war didn't touch. We were returned to camp on the double. After being counted we were ordered to report to our sections and wait there. We sat in our bays wondering what was going on outside. Rumors that were absolutely fantastic were circulated.

Paratroopers were landing outside of Mukden.

American forces had landed in Dairen and there were air attacks into Manchuria.

The American fleet was in the bay off of Dairen.

The Russians had entered the war and were going to bomb the Japs out of Manchuria.

Japan was surrounded.

Peking had been retaken by Chinese forces, Chang Kai Chek's people. And a guy by the name Moa Tse Tung was organizing the Chinese Communists.

Anything that you wanted to hear was there for the listening.

An hour after we had first heard the sirens the All Clear sounded. We were counted again and marched off to the factories again.

Two day later near the end of November, the same thing happened. The alert sounded and we returned to camp. This time we were told to spread out on the camp parade ground. We lay face down on the frozen ground until the Air Raid Alarm sounded. The eerie sound evoked memories of Bataan and Corregidor, and the hundreds of air raids that we had gone through. Jap air raids. This time it was American air raids.

I decided to head for the southwest corner of the compound, near the incinerator. It was the farthest from any of the buildings. I was only fifty feet from the south and the west walls. We waited. Nothing happened. The All Clear sounded and again we returned to the factories. We did not see any aircraft.

Rumor had it that the port cities had been heavily bombed by planes from the south.

287

Our plans for repeat performances of the play were canceled.

On the seventh of December, nineteen-forty-four, the Air Raid alarm sounded. The alert came first, evidently triggered by telephone alerts from the south. It blasted again a second time only minutes after the first alert. The day was very cold and the sky was brilliantly clear. A clear, freezing blue. There was none of the usual winter temperature inversion that fogged the sky so that visibility was only a few thousand yards.

We had been in the barracks since the first alert. We had just settled down, wondering if there was really going to be a raid when the sirens blasted again. Every siren in and around Mukden shrieked into the frigid air. We piled out of the barracks on the double. There was something different in the air this time. My mind worked furiously as I pelted out of the building. I ran, for some unknown reason, to the middle of the compound, not to the southwest corner where I had gone before. I ran west, almost to the barbed wire fence that was some feet away from the wall. I hit the ground and looked up. There in the sky was something I had never seen before in my lifetime. There were tremendously long cloudlike white streamers. There were nine of them arching across the brilliant blue frigid sky. They were the whitest white contrasting against the azure blue. They were high, very high. I couldn't imagine what they were.

Men were still pounding out of the barracks and spreading themselves over the solidly frozen ground. It was bitterly cold.

I hit the ground about thirty feet from the barbed wire fence, only about twenty feet from the hospital. I was at the foot of the rise, much like a plateau, on which the hospital was built. It was about three foot higher than the parade ground, the yard inside the compound. I rolled over and watched the cloud trails. At the head of each was a shiny point. The airplane! The American bomber! There were a bunch of gnats skittering around the nine bombers. Tiny, nasty gnats. Japanese fighters.

There were shouts from the men as they lay on the ground waiting. Waiting helplessly as the battle in the sky, thousands of feet above, raged on. There were cheers. There were cries of terror and fear. We had been through this before. We lay there waiting for bombs to fall.

The hospital patients that could not walk had been brought out by the corpsmen and the able patients. They lay there like the rest of us and waited through the eternity that always preceded a bomb fall. In the seconds that followed we heard the sounds of gunfire, faint, far off gunfire.

A small plane, one of the gnats, one of the Jap fighters, started a long fiery trail to the ground thousands of feet below it. One of the heads of the trails also blew up. There was a series of orange flares that blossomed suddenly. Huge fireballs that were born explosively in the air and died there. Men, Americans, died there too. I saw great chunks of metal, parts of the bomber, spin wildly as they screamed to the earth. The whistling of the falling metal reached us seconds after the gigantic flares had mushroomed in the freezing sky. Tiny specks fell from the region where the bomber had blown up. A few parachutes snapped open only seconds later.

One of the men close by jumped to his feet and ran around in blind terror. He ran in a crouched position, first in one way and then another. Suddenly he turned toward the barbed wire fence. "Tell them to let us out! Let us out into the field! We'll all be killed here!" He screamed his panic as he ran.

"Hit the dirt! Hit the dirt!" I raised up on one elbow cautiously and I yelled at him as he came close.

"LET US OUT!! LET US OUT!! We'll all be killed here." He continued to run around in circles, blind with terror. I knew what it was like for him. Bataan and Corregidor came back. The bombs, the tearing and rendering that followed as they hit.

I looked at the trails again. The gnats were darting in and out of them. The sound of high powered engines and gunfire, muffled by the distance, came again. The trails were almost over us, but to the south and west, not directly over the camp. "Get down!" I yelled at the man screaming to be let out. "It's too damned late to go anywhere! Here they Come!" I yelled as I hid my head under my arms. The shrieking shrill high pitched scream that only comes with bombs that are hurling down only yards away pierced the cold air. Corregidor flared in my mind. There were two violent ripping explosions. Rocks, dirt and brick, mixed in with shrapnel flew around us and thudded onto the ground and the building. I heard screams of wounded and dying men, the sounds of breaking glass and the sounds of things as they continued to whistle through the frigid air. I dug my nose into the ground, cold and frozen. The whistling sounds stopped. My ears hurt as they continued to ring from the explosions. The chunking of metal and brick into men and dirt stopped. The screams didn't stop. I raised my head. I was in a cold sweat. I looked around. The man I had yelled at had hit the ground a short distance away. Something had hit the man only feet away from him.

I looked up at the white trails in the sky. They were moving fast as they passed beyond us. They had changed course and were now moving to the north and east.

The incinerator in the far corner of the compound didn't exist anymore. Neither did part of the west wall. I rose to my hands and knees and scooted to the man who had been hit. Thank God I didn't know him I thought as I looked down at him. I didn't know what had compelled me to go to him. He was holding his hand over a hole in his pants. He lay curled partly on his right side. There was blood oozing between his fingers as he covered the hole. He was deathly white. His eyes were almost fantastic in size as he stared at the place he held with his hand.

"Okay! Okay. Get the hand out of there!" I knelt beside him I reached for his waist and started to undo his pants. A corpsman appeared beside me. We ripped his pants down to his knees together. We ripped down the long john underwear also. There was a hole in the back of his left thigh. Through the bloody smear it seemed to be about the size of a half dollar. The corpsman took the belt out of the pants and tied it around the man's thigh. He pulled tight. The wounded man mouthed some moaned words.

"Okay, you'll be okay!" The corpsman kept on repeating. "Let up on the tourniquet every couple of minutes." His instruction was directed at me.

The blood was congealing around the wound. The blood on the ground was already frozen.

"It hurts like hell! It's burning!" The wounded man groaned.

"Sure. It sure as hell does!" I agreed as I tried to soothe him. I knew what it was like. I had had it too.

"He'll be alright until we can move him. He won't bleed much now," the corpsman assured me. I worried anyway. I didn't know who he was, nor did I know the corpsman.

The wild man. The berserker, the one who had been running around in terror, was sitting and watching us without saying anything. He just sat there and watched. He began to rock back and forth, slowly, just back and forth, moaning, as he watched.

There were screams and cries of pain from the area around the incinerator. Men from the hospital corps were running to help.

There was all hell spread around the southwest corner of the compound.

I stood up to take a look and sat down promptly, jarring my tailbone on the frozen ground. One body had no head.

The smell from the explosive had blown toward us. There was also the smell of blood and death.

The munitions factory southwest of us, about a mile away, was burning. There were explosions going on and the smoke was lifting into the sky. I looked around the sky. The Jap planes were not to be seen anywhere. There was a single parachute north of us, thousands of feet in the air, drifting away to the north of Mukden. I didn't see the other chutes that had come from the bomber. I wondered about how cold it was twenty thirty thousand feet up.

Men with stretchers were running from the hospital. There was nothing but confusion and general milling around where the bombs had burst. There were a few men on the ground, some stretched out, some sitting and moaning with pain. The majority of men were sitting all over the compound waiting for the All Clear to sound.

The Japs were racing around in near panic. A cordon had been thrown up outside of the break in the wall. The wall had been blasted away for perhaps thirty feet. A machine gun had been set up commanding the break, pointing in at us.

The Jap interpreters were not anywhere around.

Shouts of gangway cleared a path from the bombed area to the east end of the hospital. Men were being rushed in on stretchers. Others were being helped by the uninjured.

"Hey! Somebody give me a hand here." One of the men from nearby came over and helped me. We made a crossed hand seat for the man with the hole in his thigh and had him hold on to us as we carried him into the hospital. I sweated and grunted as we carried him weaving our way through the men still sitting on the ground. A corpsman stumbled along with us as we made our way inside to pandemonium. Stretchers were laid out in the corridors. There were corpsman tending to the wounded who were moaning with pain. We pushed out way into a large room that had served as a clinic. We put our patient on a table, face down. I straightened up and winced as the strain came off of my back.

The Japanese doctor came in with Herbst. A quick survey was made as I watched. The most critical were being move into the operating room for immediate attention. Herbst and Yomata, the Jap doctor, were going to operate on the men.

I walked out into the corridor. The smell of blood was almost suffocating. I made my way through the hall wanting to get out as soon as I could. I looked down at a man on a stretcher. His chest and belly were ripped apart, a real mess. He was in horrible pain. "Please Mother, don't let me die." He sobbed painfully. After grimacing he continued, "I don't want to die. It hurts. Oh how it hurts." His moans of pain were heartbreaking. He was young, twenty-two, twenty-four. My age. A good looking, if starved, young man, but a dead one. His sobs and groans grew weaker. I stood there wishing that there was something that I could do for him. I prayed for him silently.

"Take it easy man. They'll help you soon." I lied to him. "They'll work on you."

A corpsman, Brownie, rushing by, stopped. He looked at him in pity. "Help him. Talk to him. Hold his hand."

I stooped and took a bloody hand.

"God what a mess." The corpsman mumbled softly. I heard him but I didn't think that the dying man did.

"Any morphine?" someone shouted. "Give the poor guy a shot."

I hoped that there was something that would ease the man's agony.

"Yeah! The Japs, God Bless them, they just brought in some. Thank God for that!" The corpsman continued on to the surgery. Another corpsman came out with a kit.

"Here! Gimme one of those!" The corpsman who had been talking to me demanded. He snatched one of the hypos. The man on the stretcher squeezed my hand and moaned. The corpsman pulled down the shirt at the neck and thrust the needle into his arm, squeezing the the syringe. I watched. I held on to his hand, hoping that I was providing some comfort.

"Please help me," He moaned.

I prayed for him. The tears in my eyes were tears of frustration and pity. He died in a few short minutes, with less pain because of the drug. After all he had gone through to get here, he died. Life sure is a bitch I thought, a real bitch.

I realized that I was outside. I heard the order being passed around. Everyone who was not wounded had to return to his section for roll call. Tenko.

I mad my way back too my bunk and sat quietly. I wasn't in the mood for any of the talk that was going on, the speculation about the bombers and where they came from. I rested. My back ached from the strain and the activity. The All Clear sounded as I sat there.

Someone placed a hand on my shoulder. "Why don't you go and wash your hands Pete? There's blood all over them. And on your jacket too." I looked up. It was Joe Stanko, 1397, talking to me. I stared at his number tag blankly. "Pete."

My hands were covered with blood and I should have known it but I didn't until Joe said it. I didn't really remember when. I hadn't felt it. My coat sleeve was sticky with blood.

"Yeah. I had better." My nose wrinkled, the smell of the blood penetrated. I got up and walked out to the wash basins and stripped off my coat, removed my number tag and shoved it into my pocket. Men that were passing looked at me curiously. Some serious and some just curious.

"You hit?" One asked as he looked me over for a sign of a wound.

"Man you are a mess. You hit?"

"You hurt?"

"No." I answered repeatedly to their questions. They were concerned. That made me feel better down inside. I felt that there was still some humanity left in some of us. Some concern for the other fellow.

I filled one of the sinks with the cold water and dunked the coat. My shirt had some blood on the sleeves so I stripped it off and dunked it with the coat.

Johnson, 277, came by. "You okay Pete?" he asked. "you didn't get hit did you?" He looked at my still bloody hands.

I washed my hands of the rest of the blood. "No, I'm okay Johnny," I smiled weakly, "I just messed up a bit and have to wash up." I continued to scrub the spots of blood off of my hands and arms.

"You sure you are alright?" he asked again.

"Yeah. I'm alright. Really." I drained the water and refilled the sink with the shirt and coat still in it.

"TENKO! Tenko everyone! Everybody inside."

I turned the water off and started back to the section. I took the number tag out of my pocket and pinned it to my undershirt. We lined up in the center if the section and waited for the count. When the non-com tenkoed our section he strutted around. He stopped in front of me, glowering. "Roku Ku Go, nanda."

"Where is your coat?" asked the interpreter that accompanied him. It was standard practice to have an interpreter with a non-com whenever they conducted the count.

"In the sink having the blood soaked off of it." I answered.

"Were you wounded? Why are you not in the hospital?" He looked at me, cocking his head from one side to the other.

"No, I wasn't wounded. The blood is from somebody else."

The interpreter turned to the non-com and translated. The non-com, a little shrimp with accentuated slant of his eyes came up close to me. He reached for my left hand, took it, and held it up for close inspection. He looked at the back and then at the palm. I still had some clotted blood between the fingers and in the creases of the skin of the hand. He looked at Takashi, the interpreter and instructed him to obtain an explanation. Takashi ushed him and then turned to me again.

"Why do you have blood on your hands and on your clothes? You are wounded."

"I helped some of the men that were wounded. I carried one to the hospital. He had a wound in his thigh."

There was a general mumbling from the men in the section. The interrogation struck them the wrong way. They were in no mood for Jap horseshit.

"Yasme," the non-com commanded. The men stood at ease. He looked around at the group. "KIOTSKI NA!" he ordered. We all snapped to attention.

Takashi relayed the information to the non-com.

"Yush." The non-com accepted the explanation. He turned, with Takashi following, and went on to the next section.

The at ease command, Yasme was given to our section. The mumbling dissension continued.

"Stinking prick. Slant eyed cunt." Cy, the man on my left spit out. "Aw, they are just trying to make things tough. Don't worry about it."

Now the reaction was starting to take hold. It was sinking in. These had been American planes. American bombs. The Japs were being clobbered at last. Sure, our own bombs had killed our own men. WAR! That was why. It had been an accident! We were in the right place at the wrong time. The fortunes of war. We, "The Bastards of Bataan", had that kind of frigging rotten luck. We must have been born to that weird quirk of fate. We had already gone through one kind of hell. Bataan, Corregidor, Cabanatuan. The prison ship. Splinter Camp in the winter. Three years of war. That was it! Three years of war! The 7th of December! Three years after Pearl Harbor! That was why Mukden had been hit! That was why the sneaky Japs had been hit! The poor bastards out there had died because the sneaky yellow Japs had declared war. The men had died because of the fortunes of war! God help them and rest their souls in peace forever.

I hadn't realized that it was just the third year. It seemed as though it had been three hundred years! Three whole centuries. Not just three years. Three thousand years! But here for the first time in three years the Americans had struck back at the treacherous yellow bastards! Our Americans! Fighting men. American bombers! I smiled at my thoughts. This meant that the war was moving close to us. I wondered about the men who had parachuted from the downed bomber.

"Tenko oware." The roll call was over. I went back out to the sink to finish my chore. The cold water had done a pretty good job of loosening the blood stains. I scrubbed some more and washed out the rest of it. I wrung out the shirt and jacket and carried them back to my bunk. It was cool without the outer clothing since the fires in the stoves never raised the temperature above sixty in the sections. I hung the coat on a line around the stove and the shirt at the head of my bunk.

"Got it all cleaned up?" Cy asked.

"Much as I could." I examined the sleeve of the coat closely, "Can't see much if any at all. It hadn't dried, so maybe it's all out."

"Yeah, maybe. I don't guess we go back to work today," Cy said hopefully.

"No, I don't think we will," I agreed. "Me. I'm going to try and rest. Sack out." I laid down on my straw mattress. The bunk was an upper, not a lower as I had had in barracks Three, and it was near the window. My mind was in a muddle. I watched the men moving around outside. Somewhere along the line of thought about the war I fell asleep. I awoke when Cy tugged at my foot.

"Chow Pete."

"Check," I answered. I picked up my bowl and climbed down the ladder to join the chow line.

"Hear the latest." Pappy Rose, 1466, asked.

"No. What is the latest?"

"The planes came from Okinawa. They say that most of the islands are retaken, and, Russia is going to come into the war against the Japs."

"As fine a bunch of bullshit as I've ever heard Pappy. All this came from the bombs no doubt. And as for the Russians, they sure as hell waited long enough no matter what they had to do in Europe against the stinking Nazis. How many men got killed? Anybody know?" I asked as I held out my bowl for the bean water ration.

"Twenty they say." Snuffy answered. "And about thirty are wounded. And Bill Darnold, 778, they say he lost his arm, the right one, below the elbow."

"Man that is rough," Santak, 641, put in. "I heard your buddy Fleming got it." He looked at me sorrowfully.

I stared at him rigid, frozen. "Fleming. Shit! Damn it all anyway." I climbed up to my bunk and sat there without moving. I dug out one of my buns and ate morosely in silence. I washed my bowl after eating and put it away. My mind was numb. I checked my shirt roboticly, then my jacket. I sat on the bunk and closed my eyes. I said a silent prayer.

Word was passed around to the barracks that no one was to approach the hole in the fence or they would be shot. Everyone was to remain in their barracks until told otherwise.

Card games started. It was one way to pass the time.

The following day, the eighth, we went to work as usual. The Japs at the factory wanted all the news about the camp. We told them that twenty had been killed by the bombs. They were surprised and shocked. The war had never touched them before. It was all very new to them. It was fate that our men died at the hands of their own countrymen.

They told us that the center of town had been hit. Many more Chinese had been killed than Japanese. The railroad terminal had not been hit. The bombs had landed in a residential section east of the railroad yards. The only military target that had been hit had been th munitions factory. They also told us that there had been three of the bombers shot down. The Americans had all been captured and were being questioned at military headquarters in Mukden. We spent the rest of the day in anxiety waiting to get back to camp to compare notes with the men from MKK.

We hadn't even finished our evening meal before the rumors and the news were under comparison.

The bombers were definitely American. New and huge, something we had never seen before.

Four bombers had been shot down.

The center of Mukden had been bombed and many civilians had been killed.

A Jap pilot, unwounded, who had bailed out at high altitude had frozen to death before he had hit the ground.

Whatever the truth was about the bombers, the bombing and the war, we knew that finally the war was moving against the Japs. The morale of everyone in camp had changed. We had seen our own bombers in action. Yes, we had lost men, by some weird accident, some quirk of fate. We also knew now that it couldn't be very long to the end.

Our officers convinced the Japs that there had to be foxholes dug. These were to be dug out in the parade ground. There was only one problem, the ground was frozen so hard that the picks couldn't dent the frozen stuff. It was finally decided that the foxholes would have to wait until the ground thawed. We would have to take our chances on the open ground if there was another air raid on Mukden.

The death toll rose to nineteen.

1	Carr, Ulyssis	370
2	Buck, William,	624
3	Fleming, J.W.,	692
4	Gooby, L/Sgt.,(English)	1235
5	Grizzaro, Herbert	1088
6	Jette, Leon,	730
7	Lane Arthur,	741
8	Long, Roy,	317
9	Mabry, Lonnie,	119
10	Mitchell, Robert E.	327
11	Privatsky, E.,	984
12	Ravin, Fredrick S.	517
13	Roetshke, Ralph,	575
14	Sabo, Alex J.	1260

15 Scholl, J.A.   1184
16 Skabicki, Leo   103
17 Sutton, Bill   764
18 Wall, Thomas   366
19 Wood, Kenneth C.   1060

I wondered who the poor soul was that had died while I held his hand. I had been brought up as a Roman Catholic and I felt that a silent prayer was always a help, even if it only helped my state of mind and gave me some peace.

Southwest corner of Mukden POW compund. Boarded section is where bombs hit. Gutted building, munitions factory, in background was destroyed by B-29s from the 58th Group out of Chegtu, China on December 7, 1944.

CHAPTER 31 -- CHRISTMAS NUMBER THREE

Christmas was coming. The bombing had been accepted as an early Christmas present. When the Japs passed out the word that a carload of Red Cross packages had been received we didn't believe them. We had heard the story before. Then one day a work crew was called out to unload Red Cross packages. It was the middle of December. It was amazing news. Good news. Red Cross packages! Three years! Three years for the Red Cross packages to come. A second Christmas present. The packages were stored in the warehouse on the Jap side of the compound. The news was terrific! Coffee, sugar, cigarettes and meat! Each man was going to receive a package. The distribution would be in time for Christmas. I said many prayers, silent and thankful for the Godsend.

We noted that the Jap soldiers, our guards, were smoking American cigarettes and eating candy bars. It was for sure that they had been in the packages in the warehouse.

We started to plan for Christmas. We would have a Christmas tree! When I presented the idea it was greeted with great enthusiasm. The cooperation of a few men was required. Paper! Dyes and a stick! It took a few days to smuggle in the paper and the Prussian blue dye from MKK. Everything went off smoothly. We would have a tree for Christmas.

The packages were distributed just before Christmas. There was margarine, Spam, candy and cigarettes. Also canned crackers. All of the cans of meat and beans had been punctured. If the food wasn't eaten within two days it would spoil. I knew that the idea was to circumvent any attempts at escape. A cache of food was required if anyone tried to escape since there was no food easily available on the outside. The other items, cigarettes, margarine or butter, whatever you preferred to call it, the sugar, coffee and candy offered a brand new trading fest. The Jap cigarette market fell flat on its slant eyes. The American cigarettes were mild and tasteful. Mild! It was the first that we knew that the Lucky package was white instead of the trademark green. I figured it out after we talked about it. The aniline dye had been coming in from Germany.

Christmas Eve was cold, but our spirits were warm.

The Japs gave us Christmas Day off.

Our tree. It was an ersatz tree. The trunk was a broomstick stuck into a bucket of sand. The branches, graduated cones of paper dyed to a deep green with the dye from the machine shop at MKK. The largest

299

cone was on the bottom and succeeding smaller cones were arranged above it to make a perfect tree. The decorations were colored balls cut from paper and colored with stolen chalk and crayon. There were metal curlicues from the machine shop that looked like tinsel. And, there was a star on top made from a piece of sheet metal and polished bright.

We sang Christmas carols. And believe it or not there were even some Christmas presents exchanged between friends. A pack of tobacco, a bar of candy, a pack of cigarettes. Little as it was, it meant something to each of us. On Christmas Day we had many laughing, joking visitors. Everyone wanted to see our tree. It was Christmas!

The holidays had given us a break, a change in the monotony that was our existence. We returned to the same miserable routine. There was however, a change in our attitude. We knew that the war was going against the Japs. The news we received was always late.

One cold morning it seemed that everyone was in a more onery mood than usual. One of the Jap guards volunteered the information that it was go ju san, fifty-three degrees below zero! Fahrenheit!

"Cold enough to freeze a Jap to death," commented Ralph.

I laughed a nasty agreeing laugh.

Mitch and Jack snickered behind us as we marched to TKK. The short march to the factory usually didn't warm us up. This particular morning it didn't warm us either. We froze our noses in the arctic wind. We had knitted caps that had been issued by the Japs. These were pulled down over our ears, our chins were tucked into our overcoats. Some men had been fortunate enough to have held on to the knitted Navy caps. One of these men was Polack. He had the type of cap that had an opening for the eyes and nose. The chin and neck were covered by the lower part of the cap.

"Hey Polack!" I called after we had entered the factory grounds and had started for the factory. "I'll trade you for the cap. What'll you take?"

"Nuts! I'm not trading," Polack answered through the knit cap. He hulked his broad shoulders under the heavy coat. "In particular with you." He sneered.

"How come? What did I ever do to you?" I asked, surprised at his attitude.

Polack and I had never seen eye to eye. He was Polish, and me, a Czeckoslovak. For some reason or other the Poles, some Poles, not all, didn't get along with the Czeckoslovaks. We had never had a run in about anything in particular, we just tolerated each other.

"How come?" I asked again.

"Aw forget it." Polack slowed his walk and I caught up with him. "You always want to trade somebody out of something."

"So? What's wrong with that? Gotta have something to do."

"Well, since you ask," Polack turned on me, "how come you always have trading material?" His voice carried his belligerence. "Maybe you're with the Japs?"

"Knock it off you!" Ralph interrupted. "That's a lot of crap Polack! Wise up!"

"It's okay Ralph," I admonished. "Let's hear it. I don't think I like what he means." Polack had triggered me. The one thing that made me go blind with rage was ever to imply that I cooperated with the Japs. I was fuming. The fact that I spoke enough Jap to do a job that made it easy for me physically, but it also made me look bad.

"You know what I mean. You always have trading goods. Tobacco. Fish. Who had Pink Lady? Huh?"

"You're a lot of crap. I wouldn't help a Jap unless it was to help push a knife into his guts," I retorted. "What's the matter? You jealous I manage to finagle stuff that you can't? You're just jealous! That's what it is, you're jealous! Envious!" I smirked. I had figured out what the reason was and I was ready to drop it.

"Come on Pete," Ralph took hold of my arm as we started through the big doors to the factory. "He'll cool of fast enough."

"You're a lousy Jap loving bastard!" Polack spit the words at me.

I saw red. I pulled loose of Ralph's hold and swung on Polack. I pounded him with lefts and rights. He struck back hard. His fist caught me in the mouth. The freezing cold had my face tender. The blow pained so much that I exploded. Somehow I knew that the body blows weren't taking effect. The heavy padded clothes absorbed the force of the blows. I struck for Polack's face. I smashed blow after blow into his face. The knit cap slid around and blinded him as I hit him.

"STOP IT! Hold it!"

Men jumped at us and pulled us apart.

"ENOUGH!" Ralph commanded.

"I'll kill the Polack bastard! I'll kill him if he ever calls me a Jap lover again," I panted. "I'll smash his face to a pulp if you ever say anything like that to me again." I heard my voice strain in anger.

Polack didn't answer. The men that held us apart let go.

"Get inside before a Jap comes along!" ordered Mitch in his sergeant's voice. "Come on! Move or we'll all be in for it!"

We all moved inside through the big doors. A couple of the men guided Polack while Ralph and Mitch dragged me to the office.

"Damn him. The son of a bitch! Jap lover huh?" I cursed out my anger.

"Cool it Pete," Ralph advised. "It's not going to do you any good to stay worked up old chap. Calm down."

"Yes. Take it easy! You bashed the hell out of him. Now calm down." Mitch continued in the same vein as Ralph.

"Okay." I exhaled a long breath. "I'm okay now." Tears of frustration and rage had streamed down my cheeks. Maybe some of them were because of the cold, there wasn't any pain to be crying about.

"Come on. Let's go in." Ralph opened the office door. Mitch and I followed him in.

"I'll start the fire." Ralph busied himself with the stove.

"You sure you are all right now Pete?" asked Mitch.

"Yeah." I pulled the cap off of my head and opened my overcoat. "Yeah, I'll settle down in a minute. Thanks Mitch." I slipped out of my coat and sat on the stool by my drafting board.

Mitch reached for my coat and hung it on the wall hook. He stood looking at me with a sad expression. "I'll see you two later. Okay?"

"Sure." I answered.

"Right Mitch. Later old chum." Ralph crinkled his face at him.

"See how Polack is, will you Mitch?" I asked him as he walked toward the door.

"Sure. Later."

"You alright Pete?" asked Ralph. "You sure laced into him."

"Yes. I think I'm alright. My mouth feels puffy." I felt my lips. "My lips feel numb." I looked at my fingers. "No blood though."

"No." Ralph peered at my lips. "There is no blood, but they seem to be swollen. How about the ribs?"

"Nothing. Not a thing. Here comes Takai." I warned Ralph as I saw the Jap enter the factory door.

"Righto. To work we go." He turned and sat at his board. He busied himself as I turned to my board and stared to fill in some details of the crane truck drawing that was tacked to the board.

Takai didn't include the office on his round of the factory. Both Ralph and I kept busy for the next few hours, not talking at all. It was hours before anyone bothered us.

"Hey!" Mitch stuck his head in the door, "Polack's got a black eye and nasty bruises on his face. What have you got?"

I turned from the board. "I got a fat mouth."

"HAH! That's all?"

"Yes." I smirked.

"Well chappy you got off easy again old man. Just like the last time. You sure are a nasty one you know." Mitch's leathery face crinkled into an amused and appreciative smile. "You for my side. Come visit me in Australia." He winked and shut the door.

"How's Polack going to explain to the bloody Nips?" Ralph wondered out loud.

"I don't know," I answered thoughtfully. "I don't think that they will bother him."

Nothing happened as far as the Japs were concerned.

Polack's eye was a nasty purple blue green and puffy. My mouth was sore for a couple of days. No one asked any questions, but I was sure that the men back in the section knew just what had happened. Neither Polack or I bothered to talk to each other. One day after a rough session with Takai, Shohi, the Jap foreman, and the riveting crew, over the work schedule, I was approached by Polack. When he came close I turned to face him cautiously.

"Pete," he started, "I'm sorry," he held out his right hand.

I was so surprised that I just stood there and looked at him.

"Well? What say? Want to forget it?" he continued, "I don't know what got into me. You know how we all get sometime, don't you? We just been here too long. It gets rough."

"Sure." I agreed. I shook his hand. "I'm sorry I blew up. I guess I exploded. Know what I mean. Let's forget it."

"Okay." Polack smiled at me. He turned and went back to join his crew.

I stood and watched him for some minutes, thinking about the incident. I didn't like myself for the way I had acted. There were all kinds of excuses I could offer myself. None were any good. I couldn't really forget the incident. This was the second time I had injured some one because of an insult. I wondered about myself. I walked back to the office slowly, morose.

We had attempted to pump Peachi for news about the war many times. She was afraid, deathly afraid of the Japanese soldiers. She warned us that the Army would deal harshly with any civilian that passed information on to any POW. The Jap workers at TKK would never pass on any war news. The news we did get came from the Manchus that worked with us.

On one of the blustery wintry days that were common to the country brought Peachi running into the office. She ran up to the stove and turned her back to warm her fannie. She rubbed her hands together and hugged herself to get rid of the chill. It was about seventy-five yards from the factory to the living quarters. Even though she had run all the way she had been chilled by the twenty below zero air.

"Samui des." She exclaimed. "Petaku San. Anata wa samui nie." She wondered if I was cold.

"It is cold," I told her. Then I went on to question her about why she hadn't worn anything more than the kimono that she had on. Her answer was that she didn't think it was really that cold. We joked, between Ralph, Peachi and myself while we kept watch for either Takai or a Jap soldier.

Peachi invariably asked questions about American women, English women and the movies, movie stars clothes, feminine makeup, and other everyday things. She was fascinated when I told her I had worked for a while in Hollywood as a photographer. She was amazed at the stories we told her about our world. We also joked about her figure. She questioned us constantly about how we liked living without women.

Once she became very angry when Ralph told her that we were kept so hungry by the Japanese Army that we never thought about women, only food. She did not believe that they would treat us as badly as what we told her. This had been when she had first come in contact with us. She had gradually changed her opinion. Not drastically, but enough for her to believe what we told her. She had seen how we had scrounged for anything edible. I thought it made her ashamed.

There were many times when Peachi brought Ralph and myself little gifts of food that she had no doubt filched from Takai's kitchen. We often found little packets of cooked rice in the back of the drawers of our drafting tables. At times there were even little pieces of some kind of coconut candy. We were always grateful for these gifts. Many times we warned her to stop bringing these things because if she was caught she would be punished. She was too nice a person to have to suffer on our account. She never listened to us.

She came in one morning soon after that looking behind her as she entered the office. She had on a warm coat to ward off the freezing cold of the January weather. She seemed to be glowing.

"Peachi, what are you so happy about?" I asked her in Japanese after we had completed our greetings.

"I have something special for each of you today." She responded with a great smile. "But you must be very careful, very very careful. Here." She handed me a nice little rice paper package wrapped around something. She quickly handed one to Ralph also. Then she looked around quickly, to make sure that no one had seen us. She was bubbling, excited and happy.

"What is it?" I asked eagerly. I opened the paper and nearly dropped everything. "HOLY COW! An EGG! An honest to goodness egg!" I practically shouted.

"SHHH!" Peachi admonished in Japanese. "Someone will hear you. "She kept glancing out of the window into the factory nervously, but smiling.

"A hard boiled egg! Heaven help us!" Ralph said almost reverently.

"You will like this egg. No?" she asked in Japanese.

"Yes!. Yes, Thank you Peachi San. Thank you a thousand times." I responded in Japanese.

"Thank you Peachi. You are a veritable angel with beautiful slanted eyes." Ralph smiled at her as he stared at the egg.

The eggs had been peeled. I looked at the egg in wonderment.

"Eat it! Eat it." Peachi moaned. "You do not look at it. You must not be caught with it. Eat it please." She sounded desperate.

"Thanks Peachi. Many thanks." I turned to my board and dug out some salt I had stashed in the drawer. I sprinkled a bit on the egg and took a small bite to make the prize last longer. It was the most delicious food I had tasted in a long time. There was no way to describe the taste. It was better than the Spam, or even the candy from the packages. I chewed the mouthful of egg until I had drained out all of the taste. Each succeeding mouthful was dealt with in the same way. Peachi stood and watched us through the whole procedure grinning from ear to ear. She had as much pleasure from the eggs as we did, if not more because she was watching the both of us. Her face was wreathed in a great smile that really surprised the both of us.

"It gives me great pleasure to have been able to make you both so happy." She bobbed her head and smiled again.

"What did she say?" Ralph asked. I translated for him. "Well you just tell her chappie, I haven't been so delighted about anything since I was in Singapore. You tell her that chappie." Ralph's voice was as sincere as I had ever heard it. The sincerity of his tone penetrated the language barrier better than my translation. "Arigato. Domo arigato." He thanked her himself.

"Peachi, did you steal those eggs? You are going to get into trouble if you are not careful. And we will feel very very bad if you get hurt because you are helping us." The lengthy spiel in her own language left her smiling and happier than before.

"No, no trouble. Now I must go." She avoided answering any of my questions about how she had obtained the eggs and the trouble it get her into. "I must go now. If sometime again I have eggs I will bring them." She smiled broadly, bobbed her head and responded with a further greeting, "Konitchiwa Petaku San." She left the office very happy about her good deed.

"Now how do you like that ?" Ralph sat, astounded. "I would never have believed it. Never." He shook his head in amazement.

I was so overcome with gratitude that my eyes teared. Ralph noticed but he was gentleman enough not to remark on it.

Peachi continued to provide us with delicacies that were always a surprise. On another occasion she managed enough pork so that both of us had a sandwich. We sliced our buns and toasted them in the stove on sticks. The pork was in small chunks. We sliced them carefully, salted the pieces and made delicious hot pork sandwiches. We also had a bad case of runs since we were not used to the rich meat.

February was a cold month. February also brought my birthday. The fourth of the war. Nineteen forty-five. This was the last one during the war I hoped. I thought back on the birthdays as I sat at chow that evening.

The first had been on Bataan, or was it Corregidor? One or the other.

The second had been in the original camp, Splinter Camp. The Old Chinese Camp here in Manchuria.

The third had been here And now the fourth.

Kozy showed up with Mac after chow.

"Hi! Happy birthday. I have something for you from Chan." He smiled. The dimples in his cheeks made him look younger than he was.

"Yeah. Happy birthday." Mac was in a happy mood. "You must be an old bastard now, huh? About twenty-five?"

"Yeah." I quipped. "More like two hundred and fifty after these years up here."

Kozy handed me a small paper wrapped package and a folded note of tan rice paper. The note crinkled as I unfolded it.

"You took a chance smuggling this in. Thanks." I smiled my appreciation. "Who was on?"

"That son of a bitch Murata. Who else?" He laughed. "I get a kick out of smuggling the stuff though when he's OD. You know how your old buddy is? Don't you?" He joked.

"Well how about that?" I passed the note to him. "I didn't know that Chan was a poet. He's a pretty good egg. Read it."

The folded paper was really a birthday card.

A Birthday Wish
I wish you Health and Wealth
and all the things
A man wish a dear friend
but besides this
I wish you Keen enjoyment
of the common things of life.
The fresh smell of clean
earth after rain,

The warm touch
of a beloved 's hand
The joyous laughter
of a little child,
I wish you this, and I can
wish you no more.
For this is happiness.
          Chan

"That's pretty good," Kozy handed back the poem. "Yeah, he's a pretty slick Chinaman. Better look at the package." He smiled again.
I opened the package. "Tangerine!" I was amazed. "In February. A tangerine? Where the hell did he ever manage a tangerine?"
Kozy smiled again. "I told you he was a pretty slick Chinaman."
"Here." I broke the tangerine by pressing in both thumbs and pulling. I handed Kozy and Mac a few segments each.
They both thanked me.
"Hey! That's pretty good."
We ate our portions one segment at a time, savoring each of them to the extreme.
"I haven't tasted anything this good in years. Thanks for bringing it in."
"No sweat," Kozy answered.
"Hey! What do you want for the peel?" asked one of the men sitting at the table below. "Give you two cigarettes." He held up two Jap fags.
Kozy quickly picked up half of the tangerine peel. "It's a deal." He reached for the cigarettes and tossed the peel to the man.
"How about you Pete?" asked another man.
"Okay."
"Well, another birthday. How many more in this place Pete?" Kozy asked.
"I don't know really. Maybe this will be the last in Manchuria." I paused. " I sure as hell hope so. I don't think we can last too many more. Too many sick men."
"It better be the last," Mac commented sourly.
"Yeah," Kozy agreed, "just like Brody," he shook his head sorrowfully. "Seen him lately?"
"No. Last time I saw him he was shuffling along like --- like a moron. An idiot who just wasn't with it. He's better off in the hospital instead of roaming around. The goddam Japs are going to shoot him and then claim it was his fault." I felt very sorry for the sick man.
"Think he'll be alright after he has an operation? Or maybe just some

medicine." Kozy mused.

"I don't really know. I feel sorry for the big guy. He hulks around as though he has lost his wits. I can't understand how a sinus infection can affect a man that way. It must be putting pressure on his brain. You'd almost think that he has become a moron."

"He's not really that bad. He recognized me." Mac stated. He sounded hopeful.

"Maybe, but he can't even speak properly anymore. It's as though he can't control his thoughts or his speech." The surrounding group of men were listening intently. "At least Doc Herbst is holding out hope for him from what I heard."

"Yeah," Kozy lit up one of the fags that he had traded for, "but he can't even take care of himself in the benjo department. Sure is a shame to see a big guy like that suffer that way. Hope the hell he comes out of it all right."

"I guess he will be, that is if it isn't too long before he has help. Otherwise I suppose that the brain could be permanently damaged." I shifted back on my bunk as Kozy and Mac puffed smoke all over.

"Yeah," Kozy agreed. "Hey, what do you hear at TKK?"

"Nothing. The Japs are quiet. The Manchus are leery of passing on any info. The Japs have been pistols. They come over and listen as soon as we start to talk to the Manchus."

"Well, so much for that. Happy birthday again Pete." Kozy slid off of the bay, "I'll see you soon."

"Take care of yourself Pete." Mac slid down to join Kozy.

"Yeah, great. Thanks again"

CHAPTER 32 -- HOSPITAL

I had a cold that I hadn't been able to shake for more than a week. I felt particularly weak and whoozy a few days after my birthday. I would have liked to sack out and rest but I knew that I couldn't. It didn't matter to the Japs that a man was sick, he still had to go to work. My head felt hot and my cheeks were flushed.

"You don't look so hot chappie," Ralph commented as he stood next to me as we waited for the count off before we marched off to the factory.

"I feel like shit that has been stepped on." I responded.

"Fall out for sick call." Ralph prodded me.

"Not with Murata on." I watched as the Jap officer inspected the men that were lined up on th parade ground.

"I couldn't even eat the mush this morning. I traded it off. I don't feel so hot."

The count started off with the Jap OD following it section by section. I counted off when it came my turn. Then I saw the ground coming up at me. When I awoke, my head was buzzing. I searched my memory. I looked around I didn't remember hitting the ground, now I was in some kind of a steam bath. I was all fuzzy and confused. I was lying in a bed, not my bunk. I looked to my right and saw another bed with someone in it. "This the hospital?"

"Oh! Awake huh?" The man turned away and yelled, "Hey Fred! He's awake." Then he turned to me, "They wanted to know when you came to. Fred is the corpsman. He'll be here in a minute." He smiled broadly.

"What time is it anyway?" My voice was thick in my throat. My mouth was dry and I couldn't raise any spit.

"Eight o'clock." He smiled again. "The third day after." He watched me closely.

"What-do-you mean?" everything ran together on me. "The third day after what?"

"The third day since they brought you in," he laughed. "You been here three days already. This morning." He was gleeful. It was something that tickled him. Some kind of a private joke.

"Okay okay! Just don't shake him up now. Everything is going to be alright now. Okay. Just relax." The corpsman stepped in between the bunks.

"I've been here three days?!" I couldn't digest the statement. I didn't remember anything about those three days. "You must be kidding. I just keeled over early this morning."

"No way. Three long miserable days. You've been ranting and raving and sweating for over three days. More or less." The corpsman stood looking down at me pathetically.

"What the hell is wrong with me?" My head was clearing a bit. I felt hot and felt soaked. I was thirsty.

"Doc Herbst says malaria and flu. Great combination." Fred, the corpsman, informed me. "But since you are awake it looks like you are going to make it this time. Here, here are a couple of pills and some water." He held out two white pills and a cup of water.

I propped myself up on one elbow and accepted the medicine. My head spun as I moved it back to swallow the pills and the water. I handed the cup back and dropped back onto the bed. "Whew! Everything is going around and around." I closed my eyes and put my hand to my forehead. It felt hot and moist.

"You'll be okay. Just rest a while." Fred advised.

"Thanks. I feel cold now." I shivered.

"You should be okay now. Sleep if you can. If you need anything just holler." he fixed the blanket around my neck.

I closed my eyes as everything spun around.

"Hey! How about some breakfast? How about breakfast?" The voice was close to my head.

My eyes didn't want to open. I waited a while and forced them open. I looked up to see a blonde headed man standing by the bed.

"Okay. Sure. Fine. Mamondi." I moved to a sitting position and propped myself against the wall behind me.

The blonde man handed me a bowl of thick mush and a spoon. "Buns coming right up."

I held on to the bowl and spoon and blinked, shook my head and stared at the food.

"Good morning. How are you this morning?" The man in the bunk on my right was watching me hawkishly.

"Better, I think. I must have slept kind of hard. I remember the pills and the water, and that's it. I passed out huh?"

"You sure did." The man on my left quipped. "You snored up a storm. More like a typhoon." He yukked at me.

"Sorry. I guess I kept you guys awake. Sorry."

"Nothing. Nothing at all." The right hand bunk poohed the apology.

"I'm Petak. Joe Petak. Everybody calls me Pete."

"I'm Lew," said the man in the bunk on the right. "And that over there on the other side is Jamie."

"Hi."

"We know you pretty well even though you don't know us. Great stories. Great entertainment.

"How's that?" I frowned.

"Never mind now." Lew advised. "Better eat that mush before it gets cold. We'll tell you later."

I started spooning the hot corn meal into my mouth. "Hey! This has salt in it!" I was surprised. "Makes it taste good." Our regular mush was always flat and tasteless. You had to add your own. If one was fortunate enough to have acquired some salt by trading for it.

"Yeah. Even once in a while we get sugar. Hospital chow you know," laughed Jamie.

The meal, including the bun which was delivered by the corpsman, was finished in short order. The bowls were then picked up for washing. I had never had such service before.

"I must have been pretty bad. Must have been out of my head." I looked at the men on either side of me.

"Say that again. You fought the battle of Bataan all over again. Miss any part of it?" Lew asked.

"I was a Combat Photographer. Always sent into the places where there was something going on. MacArthur always wanted blood and guts pictures. He was nuts."

"Sure sounds like you were there. What happened at Quinan Point? You got chewed out for that." Jamie was watching me.

"Quinan? What about it?" I was wary about the incident and the question.

"Why didn't you go down with the troops?"

"Well," I swallowed, a bit relieved that that was the only question. I was scared. I couldn't get up the guts to go down with the men. I had only my camera and no weapon. The fire was heavy and a lot of men had been wounded. I held back. I had seen some jocko from the 31st carrying thirty caliber machine gun, advancing and firing. I had taken pictures and pulled out. When I had returned to Mudhole, base camp, the lieutenant heard about it and chewed me out. I asked for a weapon and was told that there weren't any available." I felt relieved that that was all I had mouthed off about. I wasn't afraid to admit that I had been afraid. I wondered again how I would have reacted if I had had a rifle. "It wasn't until after that that rifles were issued to the photographers. Got them from the front."

"Hell! Who wasn't scared?" Commented Jamie. "Anybody that says they were never scared is a damned liar!" he sounded off.

"That's for shit sure." agreed Lew from the other side.

"Didn't say anything else did I?" I looked from one to the other.
"Like what?" Lew perked up.
"Something that might still interest the Japs?" asked Jamie eagerly.
"Well might be." My answer was evasive. I didn't want talk too much.
"Like maybe silver? Hah?" asked Lew. "Silver dollars?" he pressed me.
"Hell a lot of people knew about the silver." I countered.
"Yeah, I guess so." Lew lost interest in pursuing the matter.

I was glad that there wasn't more. I lay back and closed my eyes. I had hoped that the Japs would never find out about the code book. I prayed that maybe it had done some good when it got back to the States. I thought about the book and about Sherman. Poor Sherman. He had walked into an ambush not long after that. Machine gunned. Somebody had said he had been peppered with eighty bullets. Maybe so much bull shit, but possible.

Sherman and I had been assigned to the mop up operation on Quinan. We had come across the Command Post that the Japs had been using. The image came back vividly. I had seen the small hump that stuck up above the rest of the ground in the macerated jungle floor. I approached it cautiously as Sherman stood back and watched. It was a dugout, more like a short tunnel under the dirt that had been piled up over it. A trench that was about twelve feet long had been dug and tree trunks had been laid over the middle of it so that they formed the short tunnel. A flat area had been excavated to form a table or bench. I had moved in slowly and heard a warning from Sherman about a booby trap. There was a body in the dugout, sitting on a low bench of bamboo tied together with vines. It was sprawled over the dirt table. I had watched for a time and then moved in. I took a picture and hoped that there was enough light to expose the film and form an image. We didn't have any flash equipment. The body had been that of a Major. I prodded the body cautiously expecting a booby trap. The body rolled to the ground exposing a black book that had been hidden by the body. I looked at it closely to make sure it was safe before I picked it up. I heard Sherman call. I shoved the book into my musette bag and crawled out. I still had the book, which I had not examined, when I returned to Corregidor a few days later. There was a Nisei in the Signal lateral that I had look at the book. He had become very excited. He had determined that the book was a code book! The Japanese Secret Code! The title page had the name of the unit, the 515th Corps. What had followed was worthy of a super spy story. I smiled at the thought of my special secret. We had photographed the book and sent it and copies of it to Australia. I lay back and relaxed.

Three days later a corpsman brought me a note.

"From some Limey," he said disdainfully. "No visitors in this ward."

The note was written on YMCA crested paper, a red triangle over the Australian insignia, in the upper left hand corner.

24 Feb /1945

Pete

Please accept my apologies for neglecting to visit you, owing to the late hour I now get home from work and pressure of rehearsals, my spare time is pretty well used up.

However, through the medium of this note I wish to express my thoughts, which are that you will soon be in running order again and ready for some more "Strenuous" toilings "on the board."

Your partner-in-Crime,
Ralph E. Sharpe

"Well now, how about that, the Limeys are rehearsing for a play."

"What'd you say?" asked Lew from the next bed.

"Nothing." I answered.

Four days later, the 28th of February, I was on my feet. Doc Herbst, old "Handlebars", had been around a few times. He had told me that the malaria had knocked me for a loop. That in combination of the flu had done a knockout job on me. He also told me that I was lucky to have made it through the attack. "If you had had dysentery along with it you wouldn't be here now." Thanks a lot.

"Only the good die young. You bastard." Jamie had commented.

It was two more days before I was discharged and returned to my section. The next day it was off to work even though I felt shitty and weak. The Japs wouldn't let anyone take it easy, no matter how bad off we were.

Rumors were rampant. We had heard late in the winter of landings in Europe, Italy and France. We had no way of knowing how valid the information was. It was logical and we accepted most of them as fact.

The happiest news was when we heard about the fighting in the Pacific. Europe was remote to us.

March was cold, but not the bitter cold that we had had in January and February. March also brought news of fighting in the Philippines. We felt that it couldn't be long to the end of the long frigging war.

April came in warm. Unusually warm for Manchuria. The Manchus brought in scallions. These were usually not harvested until May.

Now the news that was coming indicated that the war was snowballing to a fast finish. The Manchus told us that Okinawa had been invaded. They also told us that MacArthur had landed in the Philippines.

The POWs held in the Air Corp Compound. USAF Photo taken after liberation. September 1, 1945

CHAPTER 33 -- PEACHI, TOMADACHI

Peachi came in one day wearing a light outfit that was very becoming to her. She greeted us and then asked us about the clothes that our women wore. Ralph made a remark about women's figures and shaped a woman in the air with his hands, indicating a buxom shape.

"Petaku San, Ralph San is saying that English women have big breasts, yes?" she asked in all innocence, speaking in Japanese.

"Yes. But I think that American women have bigger breasts than the English women." I answered her in Japanese.

Ralph looked at me. He figured that I was up to something. "You kidding old boy? We have a lot of big bosomed women in merry old Australia too you know chappie," he stated fiercely. "I'll bet bigger than American women and a hell of bloody lot bigger than the Japanese or the Manchu women."

"Oh hell yes," I acknowledged. "Ralph San insists that Aussie women have breasts bigger than American, Japanese and Manchu women." I translated for her.

"Tsk!. Not so," Peachi said in English. She had learned a lot of English words in the months that she had worked with us. "American women," she continued in Japanese, "have the biggest bosoms." She made the statement as though she had the final determination.

I translated for Ralph.

"Oh no they don't!" he disagreed heatedly. "No bigger than our English gals." He concluded emphatically.

"Well, Peachi, he still insists that the English women have the biggest tits. Bosoms I mean." I smiled at her. I found the exchange very amusing.

"How do they get so big?" she asked seriously.

Peachi's breasts were small. I would have bet that they were more like a couple of baseballs encased in skin.

Ralph broke up when I translated. "How do they get so big? Now why don't you just tell her Pete." He howled at the thought.

"Take it easy," I warned him as I looked out of the window into the factory. "Somebody will hear you for sure," I cautioned him.

"Why does he laugh?" asked Peachi. She looked at him with a hurt serious expression.

"Nuts," I said to Ralph. I turned to Peachi, "Well," I smiled at my own thoughts, "well, American women usually exercise their breasts to make them grow." I explained in Japanese.

315

Peachi's eyes rounded and her mouth ow'ed in astonishment. Ralph sat watching me, not interrupting. He had a rapt snicker on his face.

"How do they do this?" Peachi asked. "I would like to know this." She had a very serious look on her face. "Kudasie Petaku San."

"Well, I heard that they undress and stand in front of a mirror. Then they take their breast," I made the motions as I described the method, "right breast in the right hand and toss it up to the shoulder. Then the left breast in the left hand and toss it up." I kept a straight face, no sign of a smile.

Peachi looked at me. She didn't know whether I was serious or not. Ralph sat with his mouth open. He had interpreted my actions, but still he said nothing.

"How many times?" asked Peachi.

I shrugged, "Oh, fifteen or twenty with each one. You know Peachi, after a time some of them toss them over their shoulder and kick them back up with their heel." I struggled to keep a straight face. The actions I had made had been followed by Ralph. He had turned back to his board, his head was buried in his arms and with laughter.

"OH! Only a very few could do that! No?" she asked. "Mae West? Yes?"

"Yes. Yes. That is right." I agreed.

"Oh so. Thank you." Peachi bobbed her head. "Domo arigato." She thanked me for the information and then turned and ran from the office.

Ralph broke out in a howls of laughter. I put my head down on my arms on my board and roared. I heard a crash and jumped up. Ralph had fallen from his stool. He sat on the floor and laughed.

"Boy," he spoke in between fits of laughter, tears streaming down his leathery cheeks, "I can't understand Japanese, but I didn't have to." He dragged himself up and grabbed for the stool. He set it up and sat on it, doubled over. "My stomach hurts," he moaned. "Wait until she finds out what a line of shit that was. Man oh man oh man! How could you do that to her chappie? How could you?" He was holding his stomach and laughing.

We were brought back to the real world by the appearance of a Jap guard making his rounds. We quieted and returned to work.

Later in the afternoon I was leaning over my board, spread out making notes on the drawing on which I was working. The layout was of a railroad crane that I had worked on for weeks. I heard the office door slam, but I didn't turn to look immediately because I wanted to finish the note.

"Petaku San," Peachi was standing beside my board. I turned my head without changing my position. I looked at her over my left shoulder. I could see that Ralph had stopped working and was listening. "Petaku San," Peachi repeated. Then in clear, enunciated English, she continued, "You goddamn liar."

My eyes popped round and my chin dropped. I was flabbergasted. I just stayed there on the board and looked at her. She stood for only a moment, mad looking, then she turned on her heel and ran from the office, slamming the door behind her.

I turned and looked at Ralph. He stared at me with open mouth. Then we laughed. Tears came and I was gasping for breath, almost choking. The muscles across my stomach ached. I wiped tears from my eyes and looked at Ralph, a little bit more settled. "I'll be damned. Cut me open and spit me."

"You sure as hell will be you bloody coot," Ralph laughed. "Boy, she sure told you. Didn't she?" He broke out into more laughter.

"Who the hell taught her that? Not me for sure. Damned sure." I was amazed at her choice of words.

"I don't know who did, but it sure is true Pete."

"I'm going to have to apologize to her. I know that I shouldn't have done it, but I got carried away. I just couldn't help it. It sounded so damn good.

"You damn well better apologize." He laughed. "She sure told you you bloody bloke."

"Man I sure did do that up brown."

It was two days later before Peachi was back in the office alone. She had been in the following day but Takai had been there all the time. She was polite and made no attempt to speak to us. On the second day Peachi was in the office with Takai, and then Takai left.

"Peachi," I started, "I am sorry about the story I told you. It wasn't true. I was pulling your leg."

She looked at me with the bland Asiatic look, "You lie to me," she answered in Japanese."It is not nice to lie stories to someone who believes you. To someone who wishes to learn." She was abject in her response. "It is not nice to lie to friend Petaku San." She was being very formal.

"Yes I am sorry, truly sorry,"

Ralph looked at me and frowned. "You are a liar," he mocked me. He shook a finger at me school teacher fashion. "Bad, warui, dame dame." He spit the Japanese words in a staccato manner imitating Takai.

Peachi looked at him and then at me. She opened her eyes wide in a manner that was Peachi. "You are not nice when you tell friend lie." She softened and continued, "But you tell good stories," her mouth formed a smile that she erased almost immediately. It came back immediately in full flow. Then she couldn't control it any more. "You pull my leg." She put her hand over her face and laughed. She bent almost double and then straightened. She laughed hard and it started us off.

"Nanda. Nanda." Takai hollered as he opened the office door. We had not seen him come back.

"Gomenasie," Peachi lowered her head, snapping out of her laughing fit. She bowed low to Takai.

"You. Petaku. Nanda." Takai turned on me.

"Just a joke. We were laughing at a joke Takai San."

"Joku. Nanda joku. Jokuu nie. Dame das." He was stern in his denouncement of our actions. "Suki San. Yuke." He commanded her. Peachi, Suki San, ran from the office.

"No more of this," ordered Takai in Japanese.

Ralph made a face at him as he turned and left the office. "Old freeking bloody bat!" he spit out.

I smiled, relieved that there had been no more than a reprimand. "It could have been worse."

There had been a rumor going around for some time that the survivors of the crews of the American bombers that had been shot down on December the 7th were in the compound across from the Takai factory. We couldn't verify it for months. It wasn't until we learned that there was food being sent over from our camp kitchen that we knew for sure that we knew that there were Americans there.

CHAPTER 34 -- RAPE

We heard rumors that the war effort had been stepped up since the weather had been so good. It was the end of April when the news that Roosevelt was dead reached us. None of us believed it. We thought that it was a story fabricated by the Japs.

There were also rumors about Mussolini and his death. More about the fall of Italy.

Then there were the rumors that were of great interest to us. The Pacific. There were stories about the Philippines and Burma. All of these helped to keep our spirits up.

Ralph was looking out of the back window, watching the road that ran past the factory. We were waiting for the Shohi, the young Manchu kid with whom we were doing business. "Pete. Look. The guard is patrolling out back again. Do you think he suspects something is up?"

"No. I think that he gets around there once in a while for a look see." I tried to calm him down. "There is no reason for him to suspect anything. Nor anybody else. The kid has been pretty smart."

"I sure hope not. The bloody bastard could foul things up for us. We will have to keep an eye out for him. Never do to have him catch the poor Chink kid slipping anything in through the window to us. Be in a bloody pickle, both of us, if he catches him doing anything like that." Ralph got up and inspected the road from all three windows.

We had made contact with a Manchu boy. He bought whatever was available in the local market place. He passed it in through the bars of the windows to us. We were always careful in timing our transactions so that neither a Jap guard or worker, or Takai, were ever around. A red cloth that we tied to the bar of the window signaled a dangerous condition.

We watched, heads down over our boards as though we were working. The Jap walked past the window, about twenty-five feet away from the building. He watched us through the window as he strolled along. We pretended that we didn't know that he was there.

"It's that bastard. The Yasme Kid." Ralph muttered as we watched.

A Manchu woman, young and not bad looking, came from the opposite direction. The Kid stopped her and told her to go to the factory wall. The woman, about twenty, was dressed quite well. Clean and neat looking. She obeyed and walked to the building. I could see that she was apprehensive, not scared, but worried. The Yasme Kid looked
319

around to make sure that he wasn't seen and then forced the woman into the corner of the building formed by the office and the factory.

"Hey!" Ralph went to the window to follow what was going on. "What the bloody hell is he up to?"

"I don't know. I don't think that he's up to anything good." I joined him at the window near the corner into which the Jap and the woman had disappeared.

"Should we watch?" Ralph frowned as he stretched to find out what was going on.

"Sure as hell we should. I can't see him. He has her right up in the corner. RAPE!" I gritted. "He's going to rape her."

"NO! He bloody hell wouldn't!" Ralph threw back at me. "He bloody wouldn't dare! They shoot them in the Jap army just like in ours for rape!"

"Yeah! So who's going to stop him. She sure can't fight him off!"

Ralph tried to push his head against the wall by the window to get a look at what was happening. "I can't see the bastard. I don't think that he would try that right there in the open. Would he?" I though that Ralph sounded as though he hoped that I was wrong.

"Look Ralph old man, as you say, these stinking Japs don't have any use for these Manchus. If this drip thinks he can get away with it he'll try it." I pounded the facts home to Ralph.

"Damn it I don't see him." Ralph spit it out.

"Hey! The roof. Let's get up on the roof. No. We can't go. We have to send somebody up there and fast. Sandy! Go get Sandy. He can make it up there. He works on the crane. He can climb out there easy."

Ralph moved fast. He was gone about maybe three minutes and then he rushed in, out of breath. "I got Sandy. He's on his way. Can you see them yet? Hear anything?" He pushed up against the window, "Sandy has the crane over us now. He should be out there any sec."

"The latrine!" We can see into the corner from the latrine window!"

We rushed out into the factory and into the latrine. The windows in the back wall of the latrine were small squares with bars on them. The window casement swung in. Both were open. I looked around and then headed back out into the factory for a large sand box from the foundry. I placed it under one window and climbed up, pushing my head up against the top of the window and between the bars. I saw the Yasme Kid and the neat looking Manchu woman. More like a girl. He was talking to her in Manchu. I listened. First he was talking about money. She shook her head back and forth and tried to push past Yasme. He pushed her back into the corner roughly. She was crying quietly and holding the Jap off. Yasme reached for her long skirt and pulled it up as she fought to pull it down. I noticed that the rifle was in the corner against the building. I made room for Ralph on the box.

"Hey you two chummies having a go at something up there?" Farmer quipped at us as he stood in the doorway of the latrine.

"Quiet! The bastard out there is trying to rape a Manchu woman." Ralph explained.

"You're damned well kidding!" Farmer yelled.

"QUIET! For Jesus sake." Ralph turned to Nobby.

"Well what do we do to stop him?"

"We have Sandy up on the roof."

"What the hell is he going to do?" Farmer asked.

"He's going to drop something on his head."

Yasme slapped the girl. Then he backhanded her. She had both of her hands up to protect her face. She cowered against the wall, cringing in fear. Yasme pulled up her skirt and told her to hold it up. He used both hands to untie her underwear which was like a pair of longjohns. He pulled the underpants down around her ankles and passed his hands over her thighs and her crotch as he straightened. He was so involved in the woman that he never looked at the window.

"OI!" he muttered as he looked appreciatively at the smooth young body.

He started to undo his pants and pulled out his small erect penis. He maneuvered to get into her.

"What the hell is Sandy doing? Does he think this is some kind of a show?" I was alarmed that Sandy wouldn't do anything in time to prevent the cockknocker from succeeding.

"NIE! NIE." I yelled in Japanese.

Yasme looked around. Ralph and I ducked. I saw a brick come down outside the window. It thunked into the ground. I looked out again. The brick had missed the Jap by inches.

"KURA." Yasme screamed as he looked up on the roof. Then he turned back to the Manchu woman.

Another brick came down a foot away. Yasme wasn't going to be stopped so easily. The poor girl was crying and cringing against the wall.

"KURA." I yelled as he positioned himself again, pushing against the girl who had crossed her legs and tried to push the Jap away. "Tomeru. Tomeru," I shouted.

A brick whumped into Yasme's shoulder. He jumped back as three more bricks landed around him. He started to shout, "Kura nanda bakero." He tried to button his pants as another five bricks thumped around him making him dance and duck to avoid being hit. Ralph and I both shouted "Kura." Farmer had disappeared I noted as I balanced on the box.

"Run! Run!" Ralph was yelling at the Manchu girl. He wasn't thinking whether or not she understood him as he shouted. He just wanted her out of harm's way. She looked up at the window and then up to the roof above us. Her eyes went wide as she must have realized that there were people helping her.

"Hai yai!" I yelled at her waving for her to run.

The Yasme Kid disappeared from view as he ducked another couple of bricks and went for his rifle. He pointed it at the roof making threatening gestures. He backed off into the road to get a better look at the roof. The Manchu girl bent over and pulled up her underpants and held them as she started to run down the road toward the houses farther on.

"TOMERU. TOMERU." The Yasme Kid shouted for her to stop. The girl kept on running until she disappeared down a side street some hundred and fifty yards away. The Yasme Kid shouted something in Japanese and then headed west to the road that led to the factory.

"Cóme on Ralph," I jumped down, followed by Ralph, I picked up the box, "back to the office before he makes it around to the gate and up here." We checked on Sandy to make sure that he was back in the crane cab before we made our way back to the office. As I closed the door I heard the crane move to the west end of the factory. I sat down and waited for Ralph looking out of the west window for the fat Jap. He came in with the biggest grin I had ever seen on that leathery mug.

"See him anywhere?"

"Hell no! He's probably running his ass off to get in the front gate. He'll be here in about a minute. Wait and see." I turned to the board and picked up a pencil.

"Maybe we should be outside in the shop?" Ralph looked nervous. I didn't blame him. There was no telling what the crazy Yasme Kid would do.

The Kid was a fat, dumpy Jap, a prick. He enjoyed beating up on POWs. He didn't need reason. If somebody looked at him and he didn't like it he would use the butt of his rifle on the guys back or shins, or smashed his face. I had been on the receiving end of his rifle more than once. He also liked to bring a man to attention with a "Kiotski na." then have him go to parade rest, "Yasme." He would repeat the procedure twenty to thirty times while grinning like a gold toothed monkey.

"No. We'll be alright right here. We have been working all the time. He won't be able to prove any different. All we heard was some shouting from outside. Right?"

"Sure. Okay." Ralph bent over his board and pretended to work. I smiled at his attempt. He turned and looked over his right shoulder. His eyes crinkled in a smile. A second later we were both laughing uproariously. We were happy at what we had done. Including Sandy. The bastard had been run off and hadn't gotten to the girl. We both felt great about having foiled the rape of the unknown Manchu girl.

Sandy opened the door with a big grin plastered across his freckled homely face. "Well? How about that? How about that bloody stinking bastard?" He growled. He stood just inside the door. "Farmer warned the guys to watch out for any Japs while I was up there."

"So that's what happened to him." Ralph grinned.

"You sure clobbered him a couple of times. Great! Just great!" I congratulated him. The cockknocker didn't know what the hell was happening. I hope you broke the son of a bitch's shoulder."

"Good bombing old sock." Ralph spewed the words happily. "You did a fantastic job."

"We better be careful," I warned, "he's going to be heading right for us any minute now." Just as I spoke the Jap rushed in through the big front door and came for us, headed right for the office. "Quick! Let's get around this drawing." Sandy and Ralph both leaned over my board with me. "Now when you lift this side you have to be careful in aligning the sections." I was pointing to the structure as the Yasme Kid threw open the door. We all turned in surprise. He had the bayonet pointed at us, more like at my stomach.

"KURA." He shouted. His face was flaming red with anger. His mouth was working uncontrollably. "You. Six nine five." He pushed the bayonet against my stomach. "Kiotski na." I stood at attention as he ordered.

"Nane. Doeste kiotski." I questioned him as I thought an innocent man would. I hoped that putting up a front would dissuade him from violence for which he was noted. He could easily beat the three of us and make up a story for the camp commandant.

"You, you kiotski," he motioned to Ralph and Sandy. Both came to attention. "Dore." he questioned, "Who?'

"Who what?" I countered, "What is wrong?" I asked in Japanese.

"Who throws bricks at me from the roof?" he asked in Japanese.

"I don't know," I looked at Ralph and Sandy. "We were working here and we did hear some shouting outside, over there," I pointed to the east end of the office. "Then we saw a Manchu girl, woman, running over to the houses." I explained in Japanese.

"Hunto des." he turned on the others.

"What does he want?" Sandy asked. Neither he nor Ralph understood enough Jap to have been able to follow the explanation.

"Hunto. True. I told him that we were here working and heard some shouting and a girl running. He wants to know if that is true?"

Yasme watched us closely as I talked. I knew that he understood one hell of a lot more English than he let on.

"Sure! Oi. Sure it's true." Ralph and Sandy nodded their heads in unison like a couple of puppets.

Yasme pushed the bayonet threateningly into Ralph's midsection. Ralph backed off and Yasme snarled at him.

Takai walked in and stopped at the door in shocked surprise. "NANDA. NANDA DES KA. DOESTE." his voice was the loudest that I had ever heard it.

Yasme went into a spiel that I had difficulty in following because of the rapidity of his speech. I picked up that someone had thrown bricks at him from the roof and that he had a sore shoulder, but he didn't mention the Manchu girl at all. Someone of us was responsible.

Takai turned to me. He knew that I had followed enough of the conversation. "Hunto des." He asked me directly. "Hunto."

"Nie. No. It is not true. We have been working here. We heard some shouting a few minutes ago and we saw a Manchu woman running down the road. That is all. I, we don't know anything about any bricks. What happened to your shoulder?" I indicated his shoulder and lied blithely. They both understood my Japanese.

"Girl. What girl?" Takai asked in Japanese. "What girl? He said nothing about a girl." Takai looked at Yasme. "Where is the girl?"

Yasme pulled back his rifle from Ralph's gut and slammed the butt on the floor. He looked at Takai and then at me. "No girl. Maybe the bricks were loose and fell from the roof. I saw no one." Yasme lied.

"Ah so." Takai looked at each of us and then turned to Yasme. "Come." He led Yasme out into the factory. We watched, making nasty comments to one another for about ten minutes while Takai harangued Yasme heatedly. Yasme looked in at us a number of times and made gestures. Then he ushed Takai and did a fast exit from the factory. Takai watched him leave and then came back to the office. He pulled out a pack of cigarettes and passed one to each of us. He looked into the pack to see how many cigarettes were left and then handed me the pack.

"Nane. What happened?" His voice was low and friendly. Was he trying to rape a Manchu?" He looked at each of us in turn. No one uttered a word. He looked out of the window and then turned on us, "Alright. Nothing is to be said. There are too many of these things going on with the soldiers. Shigoto. Work." His face broke out into a big smile as he turned and left the office.

"Well, how about them apples?" Sandy watched Takai as he walked out of the factory door.

"He bloody well knew that we had done it! He knew and he wouldn't let the bastard do anything!" Ralph sat on his stool. "He isn't going to do a damn thing about it. And what's more, the bloody Kid can't say a word about it to anyone. If he does he gets burned for attempted rape." Ralph started to laugh. We joined him.

"Hey, that Chink girl looked pretty good you know. She was slim and trim." He winked at us. "I wouldn't mind shacking up with her myself."

"Nutso! You know we could never get anything around here. And besides, you would have to eat it because you couldn't even get it up old chappie." He snuffed out the cigarette that Takai had given him. He peeled the paper off of the butt and stowed the tobacco from the butt in a little bag that he carried around for loose tobacco. "How many fags did Takai give you?" Ralph craned his neck to watch as I pulled out the pack and counted the cigarettes. I figured that Ralph was changing the subject, women talk was an endless road.

"Five. One and a half each. I hog the other two. Possession."

"Sure. Better than nothing. Even if I did do all the work and took all the chances. The shithead could have shot me you know." He smirked as he left the office.

"We could have been in a bit of a mess old boy." Ralph was looking out of the window toward the houses where the Manchu girl had disappeared. "It was a bit close," he mused with a quirky smile.

"True. The Yasme Kid won't forget," I pointed out. "We are going to have to keep an eye out for him. Real sharp. I think that he was hurt. We haven't heard the last of this yet."

That night the story spread through the camp. The following day everyone in camp and at MKK had heard about the Yasme Kid. We heard that there were a couple of guys who had bruised shins because they jeered the Kid about "Skivie nie." Yasme's rifle butt was busy for a long time after. Unfortunately it was determined that the Kid didn't have a broken collar bone as we had hoped.

Yasme informed the other guards about us and we had to be extremely cautious of everything that we did. The guards now made extra trips around the back of the factory which they had patrolled only rarely. It also caused our Manchu boy to be very careful.

Ralph and I were extremely cautious whenever the Yasme Kid had duty at Takai. We were extremely wary when the Manchu boy was to deliver anything. We had acquired a particular liking for the thing we called a pancake. It was made of maize flour and evidently had some soy bean meal in it. It was paper thin and about twelve inches in diameter. I guess it was cooked on a hot plate. It was something like a large tortilla, plain, no filling. They were brushed with some lard and sometimes soy bean oil. A stack of five cost a yen, delivered. We didn't know what the Manchu paid and we didn't care. We ate ten each whenever we could get them. We shared with the men in the factory at the same price at which we paid the Manchu.

It was late April when we were watching for our Manchu when we saw, to our surprise, a bunch of Americans marching down the road heading for the camp. I counted about two hundred and fifty Americans. Sixty odd rows of four.

"Where do you think that they came from?" Ralph asked in surprise that was equal to mine. "I never heard anything about any new men. Did you?"

"No. They have to be from Japan. They must have pulled them out of the Philippines into Japan. Now they move them here. It means that things are really getting rough for them. I wonder why here?"

"Do you think they are all Americans?

"I think I saw some Aussies. The hat you know. And maybe some English officers. They had the shorts that you blokes wear, you know." I accented the last words for Ralph's benefit.

He looked at me with a frown, "I guess that things will be lively for a while in camp now." He rubbed his hands in anticipation.

"Yeah. And I bet we'll get the shitty end of the stick old boy." I sat looking at the road. "Those guys aren't going to work. Especially if they are officers. They looked like officers and not enlisted men. The uniforms." I explained.

"Oh I don't think that you can be too sure of that yet." Ralph said optimistically. Maybe some news to chew on though."

Ralph passed the word to the men in the factory.

Camp was a bedlam when we marched in that night. They were, as I had guessed, almost all officers. And, they had come from Japan. The stories that they told us, who had been isolated for two and a half years, were unbelievable.

One of the enlisted men was a Corporal Weiner of the 4th Chemical Company. He was in a sorry state.

The trouble started immediately. The men that had come in were voracious, immoral. We had thought that some of us were bad, we had some moral values we found out.

The price of everything in camp went up. Buns sold for two yen instead of one. Cigarettes doubled in price. Ten yen a pack from five. Soup and maize jumped from two yen to five yen.

Everyone had new problems. We had not had to watch our

belongings. Now thievery was rampant. All personal belongings had to be stashed away. Guard duty was assigned to the men who did not go to work in the factories. Clothing and other personal belongings that had been considered inviolate were open season to these new men.

There was a Catholic Chaplain in the group. Plans were made to hold Mass instead of just the prayer meetings that we had had before. The first Sunday in May, the fifth, was the first time a Mass was said in Camp Mukden. The altar was set up on the second floor of the barracks. Guards were posted at the first floor doors. Only thirty men were allowed to attend since it was thought that that many men could disperse readily if the Japs came through. The altar was a box placed on a table. The vestments were the field vestments that the Chaplain had been allowed to keep. The Chaplain did have a crucifix. The factory workers, MKK, managed to smuggle in some candles. There was wine and bread. The wine was some raisin jack that had been made from the raisins in the Red Cross packages. The altar was covered with a blanket and some towels. The scene had a sense of sacredness for all of the primitive accessories. The room was very very quiet. The sun was just rising and shining through the windows casting a haloed light over the room. The Mass was short without any interruptions or alarms. The Japs would no doubt find some reason to stop the service when they found out. We knew that they would find out. We still had white rats amongst us.

I left the makeshift chapel feeling much better than I had imagined.

The second group of men came in on May twenty-first. Officers, and all from Japan. This group was composed of all senior officers, mostly colonels and above.

The rumor was that General Wainwright was coming proved to be false. It was word from MKK, from our Manchu friend Chan, that gave us the answer. Wainwright had been taken to a special camp to the north and east of us, Sian.

The officers decided that it would be a magnanimous gesture to distribute the remaining Red Cross packages to the new POWs. There was a small amount of disagreement and dissension from the old timers in the camp. After the boxes were distributed the camp was in an uproar. The new men were selling everything from the packages on the open market. We had given them the packages intended for all of us and now they turned around and were profiteering.

A committee of enlisted men took the matter up with Major Hankins and the other senior officers. As a result an order was issued that anyone caught selling Red Cross material would have it confiscated and turned over to the hospital for distribution to the patients.

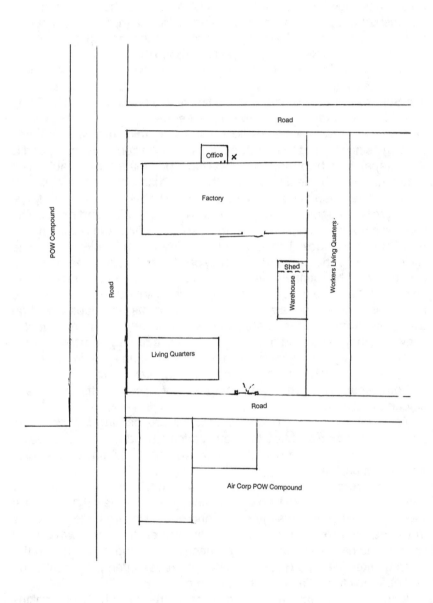

The Takai factory where we were building overhead cranes. The X is the place where the Manchurian girl was attacked.

CHAPTER 35 -- THE CHICKEN

The chicken appeared from under the wall of the Jap workers compound, next to the factory, clucking happily as it searched for whatever was the natural food in the area. I was looking for some cast iron drum and gear castings. The green castings were stacked on the south side of the factory, against the wall, to age. The wall was almost eight feet high, built of red brick. There were arches that were about ten inches high and three foot long built on the bottom of the wall. They were evidently intended as drainage sections, to permit rain water to pass out from the yard. The chicken had found its way through the arch. I was amazed. I moved behind a stack of iron and stepped out on my clackers to watch the big beautiful bird. I was engrossed in planning a delicious chicken dinner, completely oblivious to anything else. I felt something smash against the middle of my back and I hit the drum casting over which I had been standing and fell, sprawling to the ground on top of some smaller castings. I rolled over on my back. Pain shot down my legs to my toes. I propped myself on one elbow and looked up at the stinking Shohi. I hadn't heard him come up behind me at all. He stood spread legged, left hand on his hip, holding the barrel of his rifle in the other hand. His head was back as he laughed gleefully at me. His flat moon face was split open in laughter, his mouthful of gold gleaming in the early morning sun. He laughed for minutes as I recovered from the shock of the blow from the stock of his rifle. I quirked my lips and then sneered, "Go ahead and laugh you sawed off son of a bitch. Very very funny," I winced. "Now I won't be able to straighten up for a week. You stinking prick."

Shohi stopped laughing and looked down at me, "You rest. You should be working! Getup! Hiyah! Hyaku. Shigoto." His Japanese came out in a torrent as he motioned for me to get to my feet or get another hit. "What you say?"

"Nothing. Nothing at all." I answered in English. I struggled to my feet painfully and arched my back, wincing with pain.

"You go. Must work. No stand and do nothing. Wakaru. What you do here?" I understood him well enough.

"I was counting the drums and looking for a set for a crane," I spat back.

"Nanda counting. Drums. Nanda this counting."

"Hitotsu, futatsu, mittsu, yottsu. Bengo." I indicated with my fingers. I had learned that the Japs were so utterly stupid that they had four systems for counting, depending on what was being counted. There was one for counting in general, the way we counted off at tenko or bengo. Another for counting things, another for counting people, and another specifically for counting buildings. The attention span of the stupids was such that they had to be told what they were counting. So they had four systems. So much for the Jap mentality. Nuts. I smiled at him sarcastically. "You stupid stunted jackass." I kept on smiling as I berated him to relieve myself of my anger. I would have loved to have shoved the bayonet up his ass. He searched my face, suspicious, but not sure.

I moved by him and stepped into my clackers and then ignoring him, I started back to the factory. I saw him watching me out of the corner of my eye. He searched among the stacks of iron, through the barrels of rivets and then the shed attached to the warehouse. I heard him muttering as he searched. I made the rounds of the factory and listened to the latest rumors before I returned to the office. By the time I sat down at my board my mood had changed from morose to vengeful. I knew I couldn't wreak vengeance on the Shohi, but I could against the Japs, all Japs. Ralph watched me as I sat down. He raised his eyebrows, then frowned. This was typical of the signal language that had been developed. He had asked "What's up" and "is something wrong?" I nodded and jerked my head in Takai's direction at his desk. Ralph understood that I meant "Later".

A half hour later Shohi came into the office and saluted Takai and then stated to spurt off a tirade of Japanese that I had difficulty in following. I heard Takai's response which was in my defense. I was surprised. He answered that I had evidently been doing my job since it was my responsibility to determine what was available in the stockpile.

I turned from my board and leaned back on my board with my elbows. I had a satisfied smirk on my face as I watched the Jap guard. Takai motioned for me with his hand, Japanese style, hand out, palm down, fingers flapping up and down. I rose and approached them.

"Yes," I spoke softly in Japanese.

"You were in the yard earlier?" asked Takai.

"Yes I was."

"What were you doing?"

"I was counting the drum casting. Counting them and looking for a set for the twenty meter crane we are building. We need a drum about a meter in diameter." Takai knew that we were working up a design for a new crane.

"You lie!" Shohi shouted. Takai frowned at him because of the shout.

"You were resting, sleeping." Shohi ended his tirade with a threatening motion of his rifle.

I stood without flinching, which was something that aggravated the pip squeak even more.

"I was not sleeping." I directed my answer at Takai. "How could anybody sleep standing over a drum that is over a meter and a half high? Impossible!" I finished with a Japanese expletive of disgust which made the guard even angrier. He didn't like it at all that Takai was defending me.

Takai eyed me speculatively. He knew that he had a bunch of POWs that were clever. He had seen some of our activities in the past. He turned to Shohi, "You must be mistaken. I will have no more of this." He motioned for me to return to my work. "If you insist on reporting falsely and causing trouble in my factory I will have to report it to Lieutenant Suzuki." He flipped his hand toward the door as a sign of dismissal and turned his attention to the papers on the desk in front of him.

Shohi glanced at me and then ushed Takai and departed unhappily.

I turned, tongue in cheek, a happy smile on my face. Ralph, his face broken open in silent laughter gave me the thumb circle sign. Even though he didn't understand Japanese he had understood quite well what had happened. He knew that I had scored one over the guard.

The penetrating blast of the horn in the factory signaled the end of the morning and time for lunch. Ralph picked up the canteen cups and took off for the chow line. As I joined the other men for chow the conversation died.

Charlie looked up from his unfinished soup, "What have you done now?"

"Nothing. Oh! You mean Shohi. The little prick. Why? What's up?" I looked around at the men.

"The Shohi had been snooping around and raising all kinds of hell out in the factory." Ralph finished up a mouthful of food before he continued. "He is in a nasty mood ever since he and Takai talked."

"I guess that he didn't like what Takai told him."

"What the hell happened?" Randy burst out. "What did you do?"

"Nothing. Shohi caught me out in the stockpile and thought I was goofing off. I was watching something that was going on, and the shithead came up behind me and swacked me in the back with his rifle butt. Takai told him to quit interfering with me when I was doing my job or he would tell Suzuki. Shohi didn't like it. Of course I didn't tell Takai about the chicken." I had held back on that tidbit.

"WHAT?"

"Where?"

I related the story to the men and then started to outline a plan to make us a dinner.

The subject changed to rumors. Germany was supposed to be about wiped out. Italy was supposed to be mopped up and the Americans were in the Philippines and moving up to invade Japan proper. The Manchus were deathly afraid of air raids. Most of this was supposed to have come from Chan at MKK.

I kept an eye out for the chicken, planning on how to make a pot of soup. A large pot was filched from the warehouse and stashed in the factory, under the sand in the foundry. We decided that the best place to cook the chicken would be in the well of the planer not far from the office. The planer foundation was about twenty foot long and about three foot wide, and two foot high. In the center was a bridge that held the tool post. Under the bridge was a cavity over which the table that held the piece that was being machined. By setting the stops properly the center of the foundation was never fully exposed, hiding the cavity between the walls of the foundation. One of the men acquired a hot plate that was of no earthly use where it was. Since there was no outlet in the well of the planer one would have to installed. A convenient accident was arranged that required some electrical repairs to the planer. One of the trucks used to carry castings was rammed into the power conduit on the side of the planer. The power line was sheared. This required digging up the floor near the machine to replace the conduit and restore power. At the same time an outlet was installed inside of the planer. Charlie, the Aussie did a terrific job on the installation.

I found the chicken in the factory yard only a few days later. It had a brood of fluffy chicks running around with it. When I relayed the information to the men we decided to grant the mother hen a reprieve until the chicks were big enough to fend for themselves. The chicks sprouted fast to the feather stage. It was decided it was time for dinner, chicken dinner!

We were trying to anticipate any problems that could develop and decided that if we had to, we could hide the pot with the chicken in it in the cab of the overhead crane. Sandy operated the eighteen meter crane that rode on rails twenty five foot above floor level. We figured that no one would inspect the cab and that the pot would be safe there.

I made a half a dozen trips to the yard watching for the chicken. It was the first trip after lunch that the chicken, clucking merrily, stuck its head under the wall. It looked around inquisitively and after looking around, slid under the wall to mosey around the yard. I tensed, heart pounding and prayed violently that there was no one around. I glanced around the factory yard and saw no one. I dropped my pad and scale and shuffled out of my clackers. I found a gear casting about the size of a baseball and hefted it. It was heavy. I watched and poised for a fast throw. The chicken moved along the wall. It must have sensed me because it froze suddenly and stretched its neck to look around. I uttered a silent prayer and threw the piece of iron. It caught the chicken in the neck, just below the head. The chicken was only inches away from the wall. The chunk of iron crushed the neck against the wall almost decapitating the chicken. It hadn't even had a chance to croak a sound. I only heard the thunk of the iron against the brick wall and the chicken was ready for the picking. The wings started to flop and the legs paddled as the bird struggled in its death throes. I grabbed it and finished the job by wringing its neck. I wiped my hands clean in the dirt and stated for the shed, first picking up my pad and scale.

"Greg."

Greg came out of the warehouse. "What's up?"

I held the chicken up for him to inspect. "I need your knife and some newspaper. I have tomorrow's dinner here. It needs cleaning."

"WOW! The chicken! Where the hell---" He disappeared and returned in no time flat with the knife he kept hidden in the warehouse.

I worked with the speed born of three years and more of hunger. I saved the liver, heart and gizzard. I wrapped the trash in one sheet of paper and the chicken in another. "I need a bucket for a while, and some rivets. Dump this stuff in the garbage pit and then set the thing on fire."

"Where do I come in on this?" He stood stubbornly waiting.

"You come in with the rest of the crew. Chicken soup for lunch tomorrow. Help me with this now. You carry the bucket. Shove some rivets on the top of it. Tomorrow the buckets are to be brought inside. One will be emptied and the chicken soup will be dished out at lunch. We will have to stash the regular soup. Okay?"

"Sure. Okay. Well, you know how it is. A guy has to take care of himself too." He looked abashed, on the verge of embarrassment.

"I know. Hell, you don't I'd take a chance on sixty days in the guard house if there wasn't a good reason. Let's go. Not a word to anyone. This is going to be a surprise except for the guys who are doing the cooking."

"And how!! Chicken soup. You know the last time I had chicken soup was from a can. Lemme see. It was on the strip on Corregidor. I went to Malinta Tunnel on a detail and swiped a couple of cans of soup. No labels. When we got out to the strip I opened one and ate, drank the stuff cold. Must have been Campbell's. It sure was good even cold."

Greg deposited the bucket by the planer and had Randy sign the sheet for the rivets. I stood at the planer and examined the casting that was being machined. He signed and then came over to me as Greg tore off the paper and crumpled it into a ball. He waved as he went back to the warehouse, no doubt tasting the chicken soup already.

"The chicken?" Randy asked with surprise. "When do we cook?"

"Set it up now. The pot holds about five gallons. Set it on low and let it cook till we leave. Then we cook it tomorrow morning so it will be ready by lunch."

"It'll cook out and burn."

"No. Not five gallons."

"Okay, but how do I fill the pot and set it up? Suppose a Nip shows up? He'll want to know if I'm going to take a bath or something."

"Nobody'll show. I'll watch. You got about ten minutes. Now get going."

"What do you mean?" He looked at me suspiciously.

"Don't worry. Just fill the damned thing up. And, don't go outside if there is a rumpus."

"What's going to happen?" He was apprehensive.

"Never mind. I'll tell you later."

"Okay. I have some rice and Charlie stole spuds. We were going to roast them. Also I got some pichi, cabbage. It'll make a beautiful stew." He offered.

"Fantastic!. Go ahead."

Just as I turned there was shouting outside and everyone except Randy ran to the door. Randy looked at me. I stood with one foot on the planer bed with my pad resting on my thigh. I watched, not budging. Randy realized that something had been planned. He snorted, pulled the stop dog on the planer and ran the bed back exposing the pot and the hot plate. He threw the rivets on the ground and placed the chicken in the pot. He picked it up and ran to the water spigot and turned it on full force. It filled in no time. He ran it back and set it on the hot plate, turned on the hot plate on low and clamped the lid on. He then ran the bed back and reset the stop dog. Everything had worked perfectly.

"I'll get the spuds and stuff." He ran to the sandpile at the foundry end of the factory and retrieved the stash. "The spuds are washed but not peeled." He was breathless.

"Who the hell cares. Dump them." I responded.

"I got salt too." He dumped everything into the pot after exposing it again. "Hey! What if it boils away?"

"It won't." I assured him.

"Hey! What if a Nip smells cooking? Holy Jap! There'll be hell to pay. Me for it."

"Set the tool for a deep bite. Slosh it with cutting oil so that it sizzles. The oil stinks to high heaven when it sizzles."

The men came trickling back to the factory.

Ralph stopped to tell us what had happened. "See what happened old boy?"

"No." Randy and I answered together.

"The garbage pit caught fire. It stinks all over the place." He laughed. "All okay now?"

"Sure. It only took a minutes to clear it off you know. Coming in?" He started back to the office.

I gave Randy an offhand salute and followed.

"Chicken is cooking." I offered, with a satisfied smirk.

Ralph looked at me in shocked surprise. "IT IS!?" Ralph's eyes lit up. "How the hell did you manage that?" His eyes lit up. "The fire! You---"

"Greg. Chicken dinner tomorrow at noon. Don't spread it around."

"Good show old man. Good show."

The old cliche, "The best laid plans of mice and men." It had its place in Manchuria too!

The afternoon wore on endlessly for me. Riveting guns clattered. The overhead crane ground on its tracks. The foundry furnace spit and sputtered, and, the Jap guard stuck his small yellow nose into things.

Shohi. It was Shohi.

Shohi was making his rounds. He grinned happily as he observed the sweat on the backs and the brows of the POWs. He scowled a the lathe hands who were sitting and watching their lathes whittle away at the steel. He walked by the planer and wrinkled his nose.

I watched him. I decided to take a walk through the factory so I could watch him more closely. I approached Randy and was stopped by Shohi.

"Oi. You. Roku ku go. Oi." He motioned for me to come to him. He walked around the foundation of the planer and asked, "You smell?"

I cocked an eyebrow at the Jap, "Sure I do. I've been sweating and I haven't had my bubble bath today darling." I smirked at him.

"Oi. Nan da. Bath?" He shouted and everyone in the factory that heard him looked at us. His eyes glittered behind thick lenses. "You no joku. Business! Business!." He motioned toward the machine. "Niku. I smell meat cooking. You smell meat?"

"MEAT!?" My surprised tones surprised even me. " Meat? I haven't smelled meat in so long that I won't recognize it if I did smell some. I don't know what meat smells like anymore." I retorted. I turned to the planer, sniffed around, frowned for Shohi's benefit, and sniffed again as Randy sloshed cutting oil on the red hot tool. I burst out laughing. Shohi became infuriated.

"NAN DA. Bakaro." he screeched. "You laugh at the Imperial Japanese Army. You insult the Emperor. You will be punished. Why you laugh?"

I walked over to Randy's side and picked up the pail of cutting fluid. I turned to the little bastard and pulled the dipping brush out of the pail. It was still hot since Randy had held it against the hot tool only seconds before. I held it close under the Jap's nose. "Here's your meat Shohi." I said thoughtlessly. Too late. I had slipped and called him by the POW nickname. More than one POW had bruised and bleeding shins when they had referred to him as Shohi. He was allergic to his nickname which meant little boy. Shohi was bent on the trail of something much more important than his abusive nickname. He darted his head forward in a quick birdlike motion. He misjudged the distance to the brush, which I helped along, and pushed his nose right onto the brush. The oil smeared his nose.

"Nan da. Oihi." he reached for the brush and grabbed it from my hand. He leaned over to smell it again. The brush was still smoking vapor. He grunted and tossed the brush back into the pail in disgust.

Randy offered him a clean rag. Shohi took it and wiped his nose and hand and handed it back.

"Yarushi," he hissed.

"There is bean oil and fish oil in the cutting fluid. When the steel is machined it heats up and has to be cooled. The oil smells like somebody is cooking fish." I managed a smirk and a wink at Randy.

"Ah. So." Shohi was extremely disappointed. He grunted and sneered. He started another round of the factory, looking back at us every few minutes as though he was still suspicious of something but couldn't figure out what it was that we were doing.

Randy sat down on his stool and exhaled in relief. I continued to watch the Jap until he disconsolately meandered outside. I turned to Randy and was surprised at the look on his face.

"Hey man! What's the problem? He's gone. What's wrong?"

"Nothing."

"You got a mean look in your eye. Murder. Glad it's not for me."

The afternoon was a drag. The clock had stopped as far as I was concerned. Finally the horn blasted the end of the work day. I checked with Randy to make sure he turned the hot plate off and joined the men for bengo and the march to the camp. We alerted the camp to send half rations the next day.

The march to the factory was unusually quiet. No one went near the planer all morning. The office was empty of Japs. Takai was in Mukden and Suki San had not showed. I checked with Randy at ten.

"Lunch ready?"

"Yep. Looks damned good too. Can't you smell it? I'm glad there aren't any Japs around today. You'd think I had the plague or something. Nobody's been around."

I laughed, "You don't have plague. We're just damn lucky today. Maybe the Gods are on our side at last." I puffed at my pipe and looked around the area. "Have you been using the oil?"

"Yep. But I don't think it does the job. I can smell chicken cookin."

"No problem. When the buckets come we'll dump the soup into one and then fill the empty with the chicken soup. We'll take the chicken in the small pot and stash it in the crane cab with Sandy. Give me a call when the buckets come."

At eleven Randy came into the office and dropped a print on my board. "Everything's set."

"Ralph, how about a hand? Pretend to be checking a part on the lathe. Have Ed come over and keep you eyes open. Whistle God Save the King if anyone starts in our direction. Randy, slide the table back while I empty one bucket into the other. Then you give me a hand with the chicken soup. I'll put the chicken in the small pot. Ralph, you come when I call and we'll get the buckets outside. Serve the chicken first, then everybody can do what they want for seconds with the soybeans."

"What happens if somebody comes at the wrong time?" Randy was figidty.

"We'll just have to play it by ear and pray for the best. Let's go."

I watched as Randy left the office and then a few minutes later Ralph. When I saw that they were all set I joined Randy. Randy was nervous as he fixed the stop dog and moved the table to clear the pot. I poured the camp chow together and was gratified to find that the one bucket was filled to within an inch of the top. I stole a quick glance around the factory. Only Ralph and Ed were watching us. Randy jumped up on the planer bed and down into the pit. He switched the hot plate off and handed me the bucket. Randy removed the lid and I almost dropped the bucket in apprehension when the strong odor of the chicken hit me. Randy inhaled deeply and grinned. I poured the surprisingly thick stew into the camp bucket while Randy got the small pot out of the tool locker. He caught the chicken as I shook it out of the cooking pot. The rest of the broth went into the small pot leaving the cooking pot empty. There wasn't anyone around to give us a problem during the minute it took to complete the operation.

"Go."

Randy covered the small pot and ran over to the ladder that led to the crane. I waved at Sandy in the crane cab. and hid the cooking pot in the tool locker. As Randy climbed the ladder Sandy drove the crane to meet him. I smiled as I watched the transfer and got the high sign from Sandy. Randy joined me and we carried the buckets out to the chow area.

"That went off as smooth as anyone could hope for." Ralph was sitting at his board when I returned to the office. "I guess we can have a delicious meal even if we starve again tomorrow. Good show, eh?"

The chicken soup was served first. There were looks of amazement as the soup was doled out. I saw everyone of the men smell the soup, which was more like a stew, thanks to Charlie's stolen spuds and Randy's rice and pichi. The salt he had contributed had been the finishing touch to the gourmet meal. I watched as the stew was wolfed down. There was enough for a second half dipper for everyone.

"Who do we have to thank for the feast?" asked Blackie. "God! I didn't know that chicken soup was that tremendous."

"Randy, I saw you doing the cooking," Jack looked at him and then at me. "Who supplied the chicken and where the hell did it come from mate?"

"I don't know from nothing." It had been Jack's day to dish out the chow. "And I don't think anybody else does either. That way no one gets blamed if there is a chicken found missing." He made a smirky face at the group. "Wakarimasu."

Ralph and Sandy gave me knowing and appreciative looks.

"Hey we can say thanks anyway. Right?"

There was a surprising long spell of silence, then somebody behind me said thanks first. It was like a roll call as each of the men muttered a verbal thanks, some loud and clear and others just a mumbled phrase.

I said thanks with the rest of them, only my thanks was directed to God for having been so generous to us for the delicious meal.

"Hey guys, there's a lot of camp chow. Save it for later."

Everyone lined up for a cup of bean soup that would be a mid-afternoon snack. I took my share too.

It was well after three before Sandy, Ralph, Charlie, Randy and I finished off the meat of the chicken. I belched for the rest of the afternoon and all evening. I traded off my camp chow back at the barrack because I was too full to eat anything more.

CHAPTER 36 -- TECHNIQUES

The stinking Japs had discovered the false bottoms of the chow buckets which Charlie, the kitchen hand, had been sending over to TKK. This meant that we couldn't supply the camp with the contraband. Charlie swore that somebody had squealed. It was very probable that that was true. We had White Rats in our midst. Anderson was one of them, and he was a pariah that was ostracized. These characters were so anti-social and selfish that they informed on their fellow inmates to curry favor from the Japs.

The White Rats had been ferreted out by the Japs and used by them. They were pitiful men who couldn't stand up to pain when the Japs questioned them and beat on them. Perhaps it was just the lack of physical courage. Or maybe it was the lack of mental courage and they may not have believed in their country, their fellow Americans, or maybe just in themselves. The Japs paid them off in food and cigarettes for spilling their guts and informing on the rest of us. They were a constant threat since we didn't know who all of them were.

Charlie found out the hard way. But the White Rat could also be a useful tool. We used them as Red Herrings. Information was leaked to the suspected Whiter Rats either through an unguarded conversation or by bragging about a plan to smuggle in some contraband. It was very effective.

A discussion would be held concerning a plan to use hats to smuggle something on Tuesday. The Japs would concentrate on headgear and totally ignore belts, armpits, crotches and pockets. Only cursory examinations would be made of everything else except hats. The Japs would display silly-assed grins as they searched our hats and caps. The fact that they found nothing on that particular day was never disconcerting to them. They would concentrate for three or four days afterward on hats.

Usually a hat could be used to conceal contraband either in a special pocket that had been devised or by simply holding the item being smuggled in the hat, bunching the material around it, and shaking the hat in front of the Jap. If nothing fell out the Jap would pass the man through without examining the hat himself.

We always hoped that the Japs would become disgusted with the false information and give up using the White Rats. That wish was never fulfilled.

339

Charlie told us, after he did three days in the guard house, that a Jap sergeant and two soldiers had walked into the kitchen and headed directly for the bucket rack. They picked them up one by one and separated the false bottom buckets from the others in a matter of minutes. They knew exactly what to look for. They had questioned him for hours. He wound up in the guard house alone since he didn't squeal on any of us.

He was pissed and swore he would find out who had ratted. The rest of us that had used the buckets tried to find out who had ratted without any success.

We decided that we had to find another means of secreting the contraband. The buckets were still the most likely candidates. Since the Japs were looking for false bottoms we decided to use the lids of the buckets. All the food buckets and the lids were made of thick wood. The buckets had been manufactured from staves, the same as a barrel, that were about three quarters of an inch thick. The lids were also about three quarters of an inch in thickness. The pieces were tongue and groove, with two crosspieces to hold the assembly together and to reinforce the lid and keep it from warping. The crosspieces were about an inch wide and stuck up about an inch and three quarters above the lid. The tongue and grooved pieces were dadoed at right angles after the lid was assembled to a depth of three eighths of an inch. The dado was wider at the bottom and than at the section that sat on the top of the lid. These crosspieces slid out after some loosening was done with a knife. The inside of the crosspiece was hollowed out and slid back to form the lid. A couple of pegs were added to hold the crosspiece in place. The only problem was that the pegs dried out and fell out. We kept soaking the pegs constantly to keep them from drying out. Each cavity of a crosspiece held two packs of cigarettes. Four packs of cigarettes could be smuggled in in one lid. Since these crosspieces were also used as handles to lift the lid we passed through the inspection lines lifting the lid and turning the bucket over to show that there was nothing concealed in the bucket. There were only a couple of the kitchen crew who were privy to this information. They kept the smuggling lids separate and they received special handling.

In May a new group of officers, all of senior rank, were brought into camp. And with them many more problems with the food rations. None of the procedures that had been accepted as satisfactory for almost two and a half years suited the senior officers. They proved to be cheap, dirty and selfish.

These same men offered a new market for some of the handicrafts that had developed in the factories.

The officers were said to have bought and traded for the pipes that were being manufactured at MKK. The basic material for the pipes were the hardwood knots, usually oak, that were selected from the wood piles used as fuel to run the cars and trucks at MKK. Since gasoline was not available to civilians, only to the army and high rank government officials, all other vehicles used wood gas. Each of the vehicles had been converted by adding a closed circuit wood burning attachment that produce gas that was filtered and piped to the modified carburetor. The burner used small chunks of hardwood under controlled conditions to generate the gas, mostly carbon monoxide. The fumes were the fuel. Most of the engines ran poorly, but they ran. The wood chunks provided beautiful grained wood. I had designed one of the first pipes. It was a squat bowl, with the diameter of the bowl about twice the height. The top had a flattened curve that was met at its circumference by a large curve that formed the bottom of the bowl. The stem was round, a half inch in diameter. The stem blended into the bottom curve to give the pipe a distinctive design that was both pleasing and functional. The mouth piece was a piece of black hard rubber that had been stolen from an electrical switchboard at MKK. The metal piece that connected the stem which was the mouth piece to the bowl was a hollow screw that came from a melted down aluminum messkit. I traded the design for the pipe. Pipes sold for anywhere from twenty-five dollars to one hundred dollars depending on the grain and the finish.

Besides the pipes that were manufactured at MKK were the officer's insignia we made at TKK. Colonel's eagles, major's leaves, and bars for the captains and lieutenants.

Since we had a small foundry and not many Japs, we cast the insignia from pure tin. The tin was used to pour bearings for the crane mechanisms. A peculiar property of a piece of pure tin is that a thin piece that you could bend would creak when it was flexed. The mold was made from a white, easily carvable, fire brick that was used in the foundry. The insignia was carved as an intaglio and that was used as the mold to pour the finished insignia. I prided myself on some of the work that I did. Eagles sold for ten dollars American, pilot's wings for seven, maple leaves for five and general's stars and sets of bars for two dollars each. One day as I was smuggling in a set of eagles I bought trouble. Murata Chui, the lieutenant, half Portuguese and half Jap, was on duty. I started through the camp inspection line and Murata stopped me. He asked me for my web belt, the standard issue gun belt. I unbuckled it and handed it to him along with the canteen still attached. He removed the canteen and felt around in the carrier. I sweated. I knew that there was something wrong. I watched him curiously and apprehensively. I instinctively knew that I had been ratted on. I knew that he would not search so diligently himself if he didn't have some information. He spread the overlapping portions of the belt. I wet my lips and swallowed. He had me. I gritted my teeth and waited. I looked at him poker faced. He pried out a set of colonel's eagles and held them in his palm. He looked at me with a mean and dirty look. I took in a deep breath and held it. I knew what was coming next.

"Kiotski na."

I snapped to attention as he walked behind me. I was set for a blow and intended to roll with it and fall to make it look good. The gun belt caught me across the shoulders. I let out all the air from my lungs and fell forward. I grabbed the wood rails of the inspection line and held myself erect. I hadn't fully recovered when he kneed me in the small of my back. I heard noises and saw lights. That was it.

I woke up and winced with pain. My left leg was numb, paralyzed. My back felt like I had been horsewhipped. I looked around and found I was in my bunk, stripped from the waist down, with my blanket over me. My head ached, my back ached and my leg ached. My right leg felt numb.

I propped myself up on my left elbow, "Who brought me in? Who helped me?"

"Couple of the guys," Cy answered. "You okay? Herbst was here and took a look at you. He wants you to see him at the hospital when you come to. He says."

"Thanks. What happened? Why was I stripped?" I was foggy.

"You pissed your pants. We stripped and washed you. John and me. I washed your pants. They're drying outside. I saved your chow for you."

I started to eat and gave up. My stomach felt queasy from the pain. "Here, Cy, you take it. My stomach isn't in the right place.

"Thanks." He wolfed down the rest of my food ration.

"I guess I'll go and see Herbst. How about some help? Dig out my coveralls for me." He helped me into the remnants of the coveralls I had treasured ever since Corregidor. "Man that yellow bastard clobbered me." I complained. I straightened up to some degree and winced myself into a slight forward crouch that relieved some of the pulling down the leg. Cy helped me limp over to the hospital. Herbst told me that I probably had a some additional injury to the spine. The previous injuries were compounded by the latest trauma. Herbst's words.

"You could have a ruptured disk."

"Disc? What disc?" I winced with pain.

"Spinal disc. Have you had any trouble with your bladder?" he asked.

"Well ---" I hesitated. "Not that I can't control it, but," I paused, trying to choose the right words to describe the problems, "whenever I have had back problems. Mostly after I had been knocked out. I lose control."

"Hmmm. Well maybe there is some kind of nerve pressure. The disc may be protruding and pressing on the nerves. No way we can really tell. I'm only guessing."

We talked for some time about backs and back troubles. The end result was that there wasn't anything that could be done. "Don't worry about the bladder. If you loose control when you are unconscious just don't worry."

"Don't worry he says," I smirked.

Herbst suggested that I make a girdle from a couple of web belts and a piece of canvas to help support my back.

I spent a miserable night. When we lined up for work the next morning I fell out for sick call. Murata, the bastard, was still OD. He pushed me back into line and sent me off to work.

I traded for some cloth and a couple of belts and sewed up a passable back brace that helped one hell of a lot.

I never found out how Murata knew about the insignia. None of the guys could find out either.

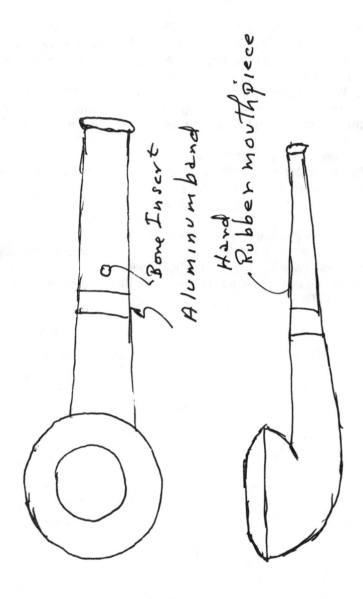

Pipe that was designed by J. Petak and manufactured at MKK.

CHAPTER 37 -- SALT DEMONS

The new batch of officers, senior rank - major and above, started to raise hell about the food rations. They complained that the enlisted men were receiving more food than they received. It made no difference to them that the Japs had established the rationing. The Japs fed the workers more than the men who either did not work or could not work. They said it made no difference to them that the enlisted men worked and they didn't. They insisted that they be treated equally when it came to the rationing of available food. Officers privilege was their reason. Whatever that was supposed to be. Working men received five buns a day. Non-workers, and officers, received three buns a day. That was not the only complaint that they had. They complained about the way the kitchen was being run and about the rations that the men who worked in the kitchen received.

The senior officers organized a kitchen patrol that was dubbed the Kitchen KPs by the enlisted men. The Kitchen KPs kept watch on everything that went on in the kitchen. They policed all of the cooking and the distribution of all meals, and all of the bakery products. The hospital ration was analyzed and criticized.

The officers were all quartered in Upper Two. The officers barracks. The enlisted men came to despise this group of officers even more that the White Rats. They were supposed to represent role models for the enlisted men. Instead they showed up as petty, mean and selfish. They were referred to as the Silly Bastards of Bataan. They commanded no respect whatsoever from any of us.

They went to extremes such as we, who had been there for over two and a half years, had never dreamed of. They first concentrated on the distribution of soup. They insisted that all of the solids, maize or beans, in the soups be separated from the liquid. The solids were then divided equally, bean for bean and grain for grain, before a bucket was sent out of the kitchen to the men. The liquids had to be doled out the same way. This caused the meals to be late just because of the additional work involved in measuring the food. They stated that it was the only way of assuring that everyone received an equal amount of food. The Jap version of distributing the food was unacceptable to them. They worked so hard at the selfish and asinine task of rationing that they considered themselves workers equal to the men who worked in the factories.

Their pettiness reached its peak when it the story of the bun crumbs circulated through the camp. Even the Japs laughed at the officers because one of them incurred a black eye.

The buns were distributed from the kitchen in large trays. After the trays were emptied of the buns, there were crumbs left in the tray. The officers had established a distribution of the crumbs in an orderly fashion and a record was kept of the last man's turn to have received the crumbs. We had never bothered about the crumbs. They were the reward for the man who carried the tray from the kitchen and then returned the tray to the kitchen. The officers said it wasn't fair, they had to distribute the bun crumbs fairly. Soon after the seconds, the crumb rationing started, two of the officers in Upper Two got into a fight about whose turn it was to receive the seconds. One of the officers got a black eye out of the fight.

General Parker, the ranking officer in camp, then became embroiled in the dispute. It was the last straw for him. He chewed out the officers and ordered the childish practice stopped. Thereafter the crumbs in the tray went to the man who carried the tray, the same as it was before. The officers made it known that they considered the order extremely high handed and that they were very unhappy about the situation, including the way it was handled by the general.

The next item on their agenda of complaints was the kitchen work crew. They complained that the cooks, pot washers and the firemen were not on strict rations as were the rest of us in camp. None of us had complained for all of the time we had been in Manchuria. It was known by everyone that the kitchen crew always ate more than the rest of us but no one bitched about it. The Upper Twos demanded that the kitchen crew go on strict rations. They established a twenty-four hour police force in the kitchen. They watched every man in the kitchen and the amount of food that he received. They formed a committee and petitioned the general demanding that rationing be strictly enforced. Parker lost his cool. "Knock it off! Quit acting like a bunch of silly kids. Start acting like men and officers."

The enlisted men had a good opinion of General Parker, but they though he was very lax in not controlling the officers and letting things get out of hand. Parker was the only man in camp about whom the enlisted men didn't bitch.

We had seen favoritism in the distribution of food, but it had been straightened out without the pettiness to which the officers in Upper Two had succumbed. The men at TKK avoided becoming involved in the bickering. We had at times noted that we were short changed in the rations that were brought over in the buckets to TKK. The noon meal was watery and the maize soupy. There was no use in complaining to the officers or the kitchen crew. If anyone bitched they suffered with shorter rations for a longer period of time. The men at TKK were usually driven to dealing more with the Manchus for food. This food never reached the camp. It was safer to eat it at the factory.

Rumors suddenly became more rampant and unbelievable. Some sounded so astounding that no one believed them.

Germany was supposed to have surrendered in June.

There were some kind of jet propelled airplanes.

There were some huge new bombs.

Rockets were being used to carry explosives for many miles without using airplanes or bombers.

Rumors about continued fighting on Okinawa were being circulated by the Manchus.

In July the Japs changed the factory work hours. On the twelfth MKK started to work from seven to five. On the sixteenth the hours were changed to seven to six. The reason given was that it was necessary to increase production. We suspected that there was another reason.

There was an atmosphere of change. The Japs as well as the men in camp were edgy and nervous. The Manchus were becoming furtive jumpy. There were some undercurrents that no one could put into words. We suspected that something important was going to happen very soon.

Next the Japs rearranged the personnel at the factories. At the end of July, Perry, Casey, Farmer and Arnez were replaced by Morris, Dhobie, Nobby and Crowley. Some of the men in the TKK work crew read a lot into the change.

There rumors that some of the men were being shipped to Dairen where there were some experiments going on with the prisoners. When men were shipped south we never heard of them again.

It was interesting to observe the induction and education of the new men into the mysteries of the operation at TKK. We had, each of us, experienced some unique educating after we had started to work at TKK. Some of the episodes were enlightening and others were quite amusing.

Nobby, one of the new men, was an Aussie. He was a big framed man. He looked bulky, even though he was as starved as the rest of us. His hands were huge, gnarled and knobby. His nickname was derived from his knobby hands. He had a large frame and a large head to match. His face was leathery and dark complexioned. This was all set off by a mass of dark wavy hair and a thick walrus mustache.

Nobby had a gimmick that fascinated the men who worked with him and amazed the Japs and the Manchus. Nobby's fingers had such thick calluses that he could pick up a hot coal from the rivet furnace and light a cigarette without showing any discomfort. At first he would bum a cigarette from a Jap or a Manchu and then light it in his unique way. Soon after he never had to bum a cigarette from them. They would come to him and offer him a cigarettes just to see him light it with a hot coal. Nobby profited by the practice. When anyone asked him to light a cigarette he would put away the offered smoke and take out a butt that he had previously smoked and pinched and light it. Nobby used the cigarettes he collected to trade for food.

Nobby was assigned to the construction crew. He had never seen a rope drum pour. The casting of a rope drum for use in a crane. Some of the drums that were manufactured were as large as thirty inches in diameter and five foot long. The wall thickness was as much as three quarters of an inch. A drum of that size weighed approximately twelve hundred pounds. There was just about three cubic feet of iron used in the pour.

At Takai we poured all of the blanks for the gears, bearing housings and drums. The foundry was located in east end of the factory. The blast furnace was in the southeast corner. Sand molds and frames were stacked all around the walls with the pattern and mold making equipment in the northeast corner.

We needed a drum for a crane that would be constructed in thirty days. The drum had to be cast now so that it could be set to age before machining. The Jap foreman Suzuki, had scheduled the pour for late in the afternoon. Nobby had been listening to us and approached me after Suzuki had left to instruct the men and check on the iron in the furnace.

"What's it alabout mate?" he slurred.

"A drum has to be cast today if they are to meet schedule."

"Meet sched hell. The frigging war is going to be over by the time you have to machine the frigger." He pulled on his mustache as though he was going over some kind of a plan.

"I sure pray and hope that you are right Nobby. I sure do. But we might as well keep busy. If we just sit around we'll get mighty figidty. If we are wrong about the end being close we'll just be disappointed again."

"Sure, sure." He ran his words together. "But even so, what'sat about?"

"What is what about?" I asked in puzzlement.

"All 'at preparin?" he pointed to the blast furnace.

"The blower is just forcing air in to help bring up the heat and melt the iron. It's going to take hours to make a melt. You just watch, you'll see something you've never seen before." I promised.

"Like 'at matey?"

"Well," I smiled as I thought about the way the Japs poured steel, "Ever hear of the demons? Salt Demons?"

"'At? You must be outa your gore! Demons? Yuk! You must be nuts Pete." He glared at me.

"No, not kidding. You never heard of their demons?"

"Sure I heard a demons. The bushmen got 'em all over the Outback. But what's 'at gotta do about pouring a mole?" He screwed up his mustache and eyebrows.

"Demons ruin pours," I responded. "There are all kinds of nasty demons around according to the Japs. And if the atmosphere isn't right, zap, bad pour. No casting, no drum."

"Ya outa your mind man. Don't put me on or'll cuff ya one."

"No. I am not out of my mind, and I am not kidding you. They believe that stuff. You'll see. Suki and Shohi will pour. You watch them. Everybody else will be watching too."

Nobby stepped back and gave me one of those looks that people give when there is someone mentally unbalanced around.

"No kidding Nobby." I continued the buildup. "You know how the Japs are about the Night Air Stomach Demons. Right?"

Nobby nodded his head.

"Well then you know that they think that the windows have to be closed at night so that the cold air doesn't come in and give them stomach problems. They wear those belly bands, particularly at night, to protect their stomachs. Right?"

"Yeah," Nobby drawled. "You puttin me on Pete? I'll nail ya," he threatened.

"I'm not putting you on Nobby. They actually believe in demons. Don't forget they aren't all Christians. They even believe that the stars have to be in the right part of the sky before they start a project. Just like the people who believe in astrology.

"Yeah. Astrologers huh?"

"Yes."

"Well we'll see, won't we?" Nobby turned and joined the rest of the men in the construction crew.

"I'll give you a call when they are ready to pour." I spoke to his broad back.

"Okay."

"Hey Suki," I shouted to the foreman. Suki heard me over the noise of the factory and gestured. "What?"

I motioned to him in pantomine to call me when the pour was ready. He motioned okay and I returned to the office.

Ralph watched me as I sat at my board. "What's up? Something's up!"

"Nobby has never seen a pour. He don't know about the demons."

Ralph's eyes got big and he frowned. "Oh no!" He looked at me suspiciously.

"I think it's a wet mold. I think the crew set it to blow, but I'm not sure."

"Shouldn't we ask?"

"Yeah, at lunch. We have to make sure no one is close enough to get hurt. Hot iron can do a lot of damage in a hurry."

"How about Suki and Shohi?"

"Ah! They should be okay. They are always skittish anyway. They'll run like rabbits when the thing starts to blow. Anyway Shohi has his hot suit."

"Yeah." Ralph turned to his board and his own thoughts about the matter.

It was at noontime that we were informed that the mold had been sabotaged. Everyone was alerted.

When a mold and core were set up to pour, they were packed, tamped and dried thoroughly. They had to be bone dry. If there was the smallest amount of water in the mold the molten iron, at a couple of thousand degrees, would turn the water into superheated steam instantly. The result, an explosion. The steam would form so fast and build up enough pressure, hundreds of pounds to the square inch, that the sprue hole would not vent the steam fast enough. The molten iron would be blasted out of the sprue and the case of the mold could rupture. It was a very dangerous situation.

I was told that some one had poured water into the mold earlier in the morning. I had noticed that there hadn't been any Japs or Manchus when we had arrived early in the morning. Someone had poured water in through the sprue, the hole that was provided to allow the molten metal to flow into the mold itself.

Suki called me at three o'clock. "We are ready to pour Petaku San!" he smiled broadly.

Suki, Suzuki, was on of the good natured civilians. He was always a happy soul. He was easy going and friendly with all of the POWs. He was also very considerate and sympathetic. He said he didn't understand about why the army was so vicious in their treatment of the Americans.

"Okay. This is a big one Suki. Better be careful There is a lot of hot steel." I realized I could say no more.

"So. So. Never know. Sometimes good, sometimes bad. This," he paused as he looked at the huge frame of the mold and jerked his head up and sown, "not good day today. I know. You see," he prophesied.

"No. Everything will be alright." I consoled him.

"Ah so." He didn't sound convinced.

""Let's go Ralph."

We followed Suki to the foundry end of the factory, joining the whole factory crew who had gathered to watch the pour.

The fire wagon, a water pump on a wagon that had a huge tank of water, had been wheeled over close to the mold just in case it was needed.

"Hey Nobby," I called to the Aussie as we found a spot from which to watch. I had selected a place that was far enough away to be reasonably safe. "Watch Shohi." I pointed to the other Jap civilian, a gawky character in his mid-twenties. Shohi was the foundry man. He took care of the blast furnace and the making of the molds. He had on an asbestos long coat and a hooded helmet.

The furnace was spewing white hot metal. The glare and the heat were terrific. Some white hot metal blasted out of the top of the cauldron. Shohi went over to the wall of the factory and picked up a small bucket.

"Hey Nobby. Watch!"

Shohi went into a dance step and pranced around the mold and the furnace as though he was tip toeing on hot coals. He reached onto the bucket he carried and threw handfuls of salt into the air. Nobby watched in astonishment. Ralph nudged me. I turned to see a big grin on his crinkly face. I nodded.

"Demons!" I yelled, "He's chasing away the bad demons!" I was laughing at Nobby, not at the antics of the Jap.

Nobby shook his head in disbelief. "BALLS!" he shouted to me.

Ralph and I doubled over in laughter.

Shohi finished his ceremony. None of his incantations made any sense to us. No more I figured than a Mass had any meaning to a non-Christian oriental. He put the bucket down from where he had picked it up. He moved over to the blast furnace. Suki helped him to ready the pour. The plug was tapped and the dazzling white stream of molten iron gushed into the mold. Almost instantaneously the molten metal caused a reaction.

"HI! HI! DAME DAME!" Suki shouted as he made for cover as the huge sparklers of white hot liquid spewed fifty feet into the air sizzling with heat.

Shohi scrambled for the furnace with a long iron rod with a clay plug on the end. He tried to stop the flow of metal by plugging the pour hole.

A blast of glowing metal and steam was followed by hot sizzling noised. Everyone had ducked for cover. The roar of sound shook the factory. The end of the mold blew out and hot metal and sand sprayed the factory. Small fires and little columns of smoke erupted wherever the molten iron landed.

"FIRE! FIRE!"

The POWs who had scattered started back immediately. Shovels appeared as if by magic as the men started to shovel sand onto the liquid iron that flowed like hot lava out of a volcano.

Ralph and I ran to the sand pile where Suki was on fire. We slapped and brushed at his burning clothes, ripping off his shirt.

"Okay?"

"Hai! Hai." He looked at us gratefully as he brushed at his smoldering clothing. "Doko Shohi." he asked as he looked around.

Shohi was dancing up and down. He was cursing in Japanese as he ran around the furnace and the remains of the mold. His face was contorted with rage.

"He mad." Suki smiled. "He mad at the demons."

"Hai." I watched as Shohi ran around the disaster area.

"So. I tell you. Yes. Bad day. Yes?" Suki asked me.

"So. Anybody hurt? Burned?"

"Doesn't look like anybody is hurt. Everything seems to be under control The guys have all of the fires out." Ralph looked at me with relief showing on his leathery face.

"We better check. Huh Suki?"

"Yes. You check. I talk to Shohi." Suki nodded.

We checked the men. No one had been hurt or burned.

Nobby stopped me, "Demons huh?" His face twitched, "More like American bastards if you ask me." His face split into a big grin.

"How can you say that?" asked Ralph. "Not very sporting you know."

"Balls," responded Nobby. He nodded in the direction of the Shohi, "He just wasted a bucket of good salt. I could 'a used it."

"Guess we'll have another pour as soon as the Shohi has another mold ready. I don't see how we can meet the schedule."

Nobby let out a snorting bellow of amusement and joined the work crew that was being directed by Suki to put things back in order.

"I wonder who will be blamed for this?" Ralph mused as we returned to our office.

"No one."

"Why not?" He sat at his board and looked at me quizzically.

"It's been damp on and off. High humidity. So, Takai will probably figure that the mold didn't dry out enough, too green, too damp. Anyway we'll be a couple of weeks behind on the crane. We don't have a drum that big in the yard. Too bad? Huh?" I smirked.

"Maybe so. Maybe." Ralph was unconvinced. "I'll bet the guards are going to do a lot of looking around. Especially Murata."

"Yep. He'll be around." I agreed.

Word of the blowout spread through the camp after we got back. There were a lot of smirky comments about strange accidents at TKK also.

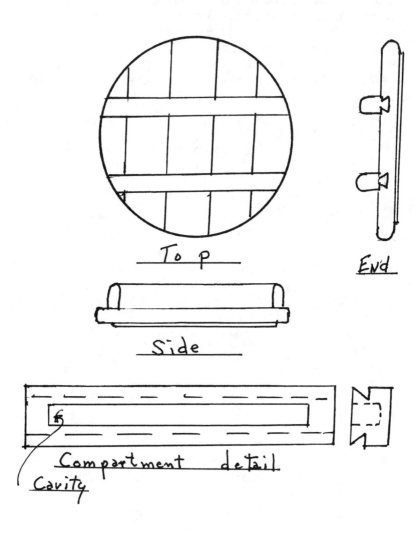

Top

End

Side

Compartment detail

Cavity

Lid of chow bucket with secret compartment
compartment in the crosspieces.

CHAPTER 38 -- THE DAYS OF AUGUST

August came in with a batch of rumors. Some were fantastic and unbelievable. We had been out of touch with the outside world for over three years.

On the eighth of August the people at MKK brought in a story of a Japanese city that had been wiped out by a single huge bomb. The Manchus didn't know any details. They didn't know how many planes had been in the raid.

"What kind of a bomber could carry a bomb big enough to destroy a city?" puzzled Ralph as we discussed the rumor.

"Beats me. I suppose that we have bombers that are maybe bigger than the ones that bombed us last December. But we don't even know how big those were. I'd heard about bombs that weighed two thousand pounds, but I don't think that one ordinary bomb could do it. Maybe somebody had an opium dream."

"I am not too sure of that old boy," Ralph disagreed. "We've been in this asshole of the world for a long long time. A lot of things could have happened outside."

"True." I conceded. "Ever read any science fiction? Atom power? I---"

"Quick. Here comes Malakapy." Ralph warned. "Man they sure are hounding us ever since the blowup."

I frowned at Malakapy as he entered the office. He was a short stocky Jap, and one of the nastiest guards in camp. He always had a swollen look as though he suffered from wet beri-beri. It showed mostly in his face. The skin of his face was also pockmarked as he had had Chicken Pox when he was a kid. Actually his face looked as though there was putty padding concealing the bones with skin stretched over it. His facial features gave Malakapy a deceiving appearance, as though he was bland and innocent, instead of the prick that he really was. He was one of the sleaziest bastards in camp.

He looked first at one drawing and then the other on our boards. He smirked and gawked at the complicated details of the structure of the crane. "Nanda." He pointed to the drawing on Ralph's board.

"Crane." I pointed to the overhead crane in the factory. "Oki. Big. Crane."

"Ah so." He smiled. "Yoi des. Taksan shigoto."

"Yes. Much work." I repeated in English for Ralph's benefit. "Yaroshii. Asita kora wa oware des."

355

Ralph frowned at me.

"Tomorrow these will be finished." Ralph nodded at the interpretation.

"Yaroshii. Very good." Malakapy commented. "Very good."

He nodded as he studied the drawing, then he glanced around the office, out of the barred windows, and left.

"Yaroshii." Ralph spat after him.

In the evening there were many bull sessions about the bombing of the Jap city, Hiroshima. When we turned in that night almost everyone was in high spirits because of the news of the war.

We were blasted out of bed at four twenty in the morning. It was the ninth of August. The sirens were wailing continuously. All of the lights came on in the barracks. Everyone was up and dressed.

"What the hell is going on anyway?"

"Who knows? I don't hear any planes."

"We going outside Pete?" asked Cy.

"Don't know. Haven't heard anyone say so." I looked out of the window and saw nothing.

"Here comes the Yasme Kid," someone spoke up.

The Jap ordered that no one was to leave the barracks.

"All lights out! Lights out!"

No one went out to the fox holes. The fox holes had been dug in early spring after the ground had thawed. They had not been used since they had been dug.

"Might as well see if we can some sleep." Cy climbed into his bunk.

"Might as well," I agreed. "I guess the Japs are pretty goosey. Nobody has heard any planes."

"Yeah. Maybe there is something to that story about one plane wiping out that city, huh?" Cy rolled over.

Tenko was called at six fifteen, early, earlier than usual.

Cy dressed slowly, as he was tying his shoes he looked up at me, "Guess the Japs are pretty well shook up. Huh?"

Word was passed to the MKK workers that only two hundred and twenty-nine men were to report for work detail. That was only about twenty per cent of the regular work force. All of the TKK work force was to report for work.

Rumors were rife.

"All of the guards are being called out for defense duty."

"The Manchus say that the Russians are moving into Manchuria."

"Come on! How the freaking hell can anyone know that all of this is going on?" Cy grunted. "Nobody's been out of camp this morning. How the hell does the scoop get in?"

"Beats me Cy," I grinned, "Yup know how it is. You can never track the stuff. Go with the tide. What the hell, it makes life interesting."

"Yeah. I guess."

"See you after work," I smirked, "I'll bring you a few juicy ones from TKK."

"Yeah sure," he growled. "See you later."

TKK was quiet. There wasn't a word said about the middle of the night alert. There wasn't a rumor. This was unusual. We knew that something big was happening. Something that had never happened before. The Japs and the Manchus were too quiet.

That night, the ninth of August, brought many rumors. Cy was busting to talk even before I sat down to wait for chow.

"Hear about Arkey?"

"No!" I was surprised. "What is he doing in camp? He was at Camp Two. Or was he at Sian with Skinny?"

"Sure, sure. They brought him in from Sian today. He says that they heard that the Russians declared war on the Japs yesterday." He paused dramatically. "Russia invaded Manchuria this morning!"

The men in the section all crowded around to listen. Amazement and disbelief showed on every face.

Eddie grinned at Cy. "You been smoking some poppy maybe Cy?"

"Hell no! Manchuria was invaded by the Russians this morning. Swear to God! No kidding. Wait till Arkey gets back. He's over at the hospital. He'll tell you." Cy's seriousness wasn't lost on the men.

"Okay okay! But it sure as hell is kind of sudden. Right? You gotta agree to that." Eddie shot back.

"Sure does," I agreed, "we didn't hear a whimper of a rumor at TKK today. Something is sure as hell going on. Everybody was just too quiet."

"Yeah, maybe, but Arkey says that that's the reason he was brought back to main camp."

"Hey!" One of the men in the other bay yelled out. "Here come the guys from MKK."

Everyone rushed to the center aisle to question the men as they dispersed to their bays.

"The Russians are coming down from Siberia," were the first words that we heard.

"Japan has been invaded."

There were plausible follow-up stories that placed the landing on the morning of the ninth. This coincided with the alert time.

We turned in at nine-thirty. Everyone was excited and no one could sleep.

The sirens blasted through the warm night at ten-thirty. The lights came on but no one left the barracks. Every man stayed in his bunk, waiting. Calm.

Orders for a strict curfew were issued. No one was to go outside for any reason after nine-thirty at night. Everyone was to stay indoors after curfew, even in an air raid. Anyone caught violating the order would be shot.

It was ten-thirty when we were ordered out and into the foxholes. At the same time blackout orders were issued.

"Anybody hear any planes?"

"Not me. I have that buzzing in my ears all the time and I don't know if I could hear a plane at high altitude." I offered. "Besides, I don't think they have to bomb at night."

"Why not?" Cy asked from his end of the foxhole.

"Yeah. Why not?" chimed in Benny from his part of the foxhole.

"Hell, they didn't have but a couple of fighter or interceptors up there last December. And none of us have seen a Jap plane in months."

"Maybe you are right," agreed Benny. "But," paused as though from some thought that shocked him, "But maybe it's the Russians coming in from the north that they are afraid of."

"Yeah, how about that?" Cy sat up straight and looked over the edge of the foxhole. "Maybe they are going to bring paratroopers at night. That sure would be slick."

"Sure," I acknowledged. "I never thought of that. But I sure wouldn't want to make a night jump. It's bad enough to jump in daylight into a combat zone."

"I think we're lucky that there aren't any bombers tonight. Or bombs." Cy spoke over his shoulder as he watched the parade ground. "Those senior officers sure took a long time getting into those foxholes."

"Yeah. You got to remember that some are still in pretty bad shape." Benny put in defensively. "Don't forget, they aren't as young as some of us."

The camp was completely blacked out. There were no lights or light reflections from the city of Mukden.

There was a low murmur of voices from the parade ground foxholes.

"What do you think will happen to us?" Benny asked suddenly.

I was stumped for an answer. We had talked about the many things that could happen at war's end, but no one had an answer.

Cy was the first to voice his thoughts. "I don't know. I have heard some rotten things about how the Japs treat their prisoners. I heard that in China they just slaughtered the POWs. It was to get rid of them because they couldn't pull them out with them."

"Yeah, that's what I heard too." Benny's voice carried a funny note. "I guess that that is why they put the machine guns in the towers. Maybe they plan on using them on us."

"Could be," Cy mumbled.

"Why worry?" I tried to cheer up the despondents. "Some of us should be able to make it no matter." I warmed up to the need. "We sure as hell will try to fight and make it out no matter what. I think that the Manchus will be there to help us when we need them."

"Yeah. Could be." Cy warmed up to the call of courage. "Hell, after what we have been through they're not going to wipe us all out now. Bet your ass on that. I'll take my chances and fight if I have to."

"Hope you're right," Benny squirmed in his crouched position.

We were ordered back into the barracks at midnight. The all clear sounded an hour later.

August the tenth was relatively quiet.

Rumors of the declaration of war by the Russians were heard in both factories.

New orders were issued that the factory workers were to return to the compound when an air raid was signaled.

Even with the changes that were evidently taking place in the outside world the Japs wanted production. Their plans for evacuating the men from the factories was to get as much production as was possible. Work crews that were not direct production personnel would return to the camp on the first alert. Production workers, such as machinists, lathe, drill operators and the forge crew, would return to camp when the short blasts of the second alert were sounded.

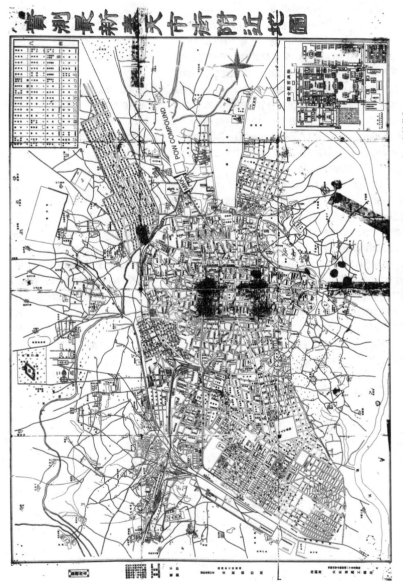

Mukden. The POW compound was built close to the factory by MKK.

CHAPTER 39 -- SIGNS OF PANIC

Saturday, August the eleventh was another work day.

The stories we were hearing and the rumors were starting to form a pattern. The Russian Japanese War was acknowledged by the Japs. There were rumors of the planned evacuation of the Japanese nationals.

There was a more threatening action. An ultimatum was supposed to have been issued by the Russians to the Japs to evacuate Mukden or it would be bombed.

Lending credence to the story was the heavy traffic and truck movement on the nearby roads. People, food and supplies, as well as some equipment was being moved south. Some of the vehicles were antiques that had been converted to run on charred wood gas.

Ralph was unusually quiet. "What do you think Ralph?" I interrupted his reverie. "The end is here now. Everything just depends on the breaks for us now."

"Yes. You could bloody well be right. Looks like we have made it. Bloody well good you know. We, you and I, are in pretty good shape for all of the crap we've taken through the years."

"Yes. Thank God for that."

"Thank God! You? Yes, I suppose so," Ralph looked at me as though he was surprised about something. "Didn't ever think of you, of all people, as religious."

I stared at him, puzzled by the statement. Suddenly I had a new impression of myself. I had never thought about what kind of an image I presented to the men. It had never entered my mind to evaluate myself in that respect. Now Ralph's statement carried an implication of something I had never even considered. Was I supposed to be some kind of a hard, cold bastard? Heartless and independent?

"Come on now," I looked at him and wondered what he really thought of me. "You don't think that I am some kind of an atheist? Do you?"

"Well," Ralph paused as though he were collecting some phrases and thoughts, "you, well- you don't give out being a puff you know."

"A what? A puff? What the hell is a puff?"

"A softy. A cream puff. You know what I mean. You're no bloody softy that's for sure." He rushed the words out as though embarrassed by the explanation I had forced from him.

"Yeah, sure," I grinned, "Hard as bone. Right? No heart?"

He looked embarrassed now. "Well really old man, you know what I
361

mean. We've been pals around here and all that you know. I know you've got a lot of heart. You take care of you and yours. I wouldn't say you have no heart. It's just--- Well I wouldn't cross you. And I bloody hell don't want you for an enemy. You play dirty. Raw and dirty. That's not for me."

"Thanks. I guess I should feel complimented. Somehow it sounds kind of backhanded. But, I guess there is a compliment in there somewhere." I turned to my board and became absorbed in my own thoughts.

The door burst open soon after and Sandy came through in a rush. "Hey men! Hear the latest?" he let go in a rush of words as he slammed the door behind him.

Ralph beat me to the question, "What?"

"The Chinks are forming guerrilla bands. Chang Ki Shek's men are supposed to be coming out of the woodwork. All over the place. All around Mukden. The Japs are finally getting it from the Manchus!" He paused for a breath. "Man! Nobody knows just what the hell is going to happen now."

"Where did you hear that?"

"The Manchus! Then Suki told Mitch that the Chinks are giving the Japs trouble. Wouldn't say what, but man - you know what that means. Huh?"

"I guess it means things are coming apart for the Japs."

"Guess it could be," Ralph agreed. "Bet the Manchus have been waiting for their chance to get back at the Japs since nineteen-thirty-one."

"Wait'll we get back to camp tonight. We should be able to check with MKK." He turned and left the office without waiting for any further comment.

The story was verified when we returned to camp. I kept making notes in my diary. If this was the end I wanted to be sure I had the story on paper.

August the twelfth was Sunday, another work day. The aura of excitement, the sense of nervous anticipation, was evident everywhere and in everyone. Comments were made about the tenseness of the guards.

"Machine guns in the towers," Ralph intoned as we started the trek to the factory.

I glanced at Ralph, then took a quick look at the tower behind and to the left. The machine gun had been set up and sandbagged. The snout of the gun was pointed directly at our backs.

"Guards patrolling." Someone behind me growled.

There were guards patrolling inside the wall, in the "no man's land" between the barbed wire and the wall itself. There had never been a patrol in the area except at night.
"What the hell's up?" asked Jack.
"Looks like they're expecting trouble. That's what palsey." Nobby cooed as though he would welcome some trouble to break things open.
We had four guards and a corporal to escort us to TKK instead of the the normal contingent of two guards.
The only Jap that was in the factory was Suzuki. The women and children were all moving out. After the women left the men followed. The only things that they were taking were their personal belongings, their prized possessions. Nothing of any size or bulk were to be seen on the carts and trucks that were all heading out of Mukden, south.
Rumors cropped out early in the morning. Paratroopers landing on the Quantung Peninsula. Hordes of paratroopers in Korea. The Russians were said to have captured one hundred and fifty-three thousand Jap Army soldiers.
"Pete," Ralph was talking before the door to the office closed as he rushed in. "Pete! They are burning all the records from Takai's office. The Manchus say that everything at MKK, drawings, warehouse slips, everything, is being burned. No matter what it is, if a POW wrote it they're burning it."
I looked at him in amazement. Without saying a word I left the office and crossed the factory to the big door from which I could see the incinerator in the yard.
Takai and Suzuki were burning heaps of paper. I could make out the drawings and the colored slips of the warehouse records. They threw the account books in also. The ones that Takai kept in the house.
Mitch spoke from behind me. "No records of any POWs. Looks like they are out to clean the slate old boy."
"Sure as hell does. I wonder what is really behind it."
"Look over at MKK." Mitch pointed to the west beyond the camp. "Those columns of smoke are the fires at MKK. Everything is being burned over there too."
"They haven't taken the drawings from the office yet Mitch. I think that they will wait a few days before they burn those."
"Why?" Mitch asked.
"Just to keep us quiet and keep us busy," I answered thoughtfully. "They'll keep us working to keep us out of trouble."
"Maybe. I don't know though." Mitch rejoined his crew. The riveting started soon after.
Suzuki showed in the office late in the afternoon. He had a furtive air

about him. He kept glancing around and over his shoulder nervously. "Ohio." he clipped the greeting nervously.

"Ohio Suki. Nane dekimasu." I queried in Japanese.

"Burn papers," Suzuki answered in English. "Every paper is to be burned soon."

"Why?" Ralph sat back and leaned his elbows on his board. His voice was friendly and cajoling.

"War is over. Oware desu. Over. Maybe one, maybe two days." Suzuki nodded his small head. "Blueprint," he pointed to the drawing on Ralph's board. We moved to the board and leaned over the overhead crane drawing. To anyone watching us it would look as if we were discussing the drawing. "Much talk," Suzuki continued, "Manchu is together to fight the Nippon Army. Very bad for Japanese. Good for you. They on your side. Any bad thing then Manchu there. Chang. Chang Ki Shek. They are every place." He produced a pack of cigarettes and passed us each one. After we had lighted them Suzuki continued. "Russia, Nippon, war maybe. War over maybe two days."

"Japanese leaving because of war's end?" Ralph asked.

"So. Yes, yes." He glanced around nervously. Then he smiled in an odd way. "Soon it all over. I go." He knocked the fire from his cigarette and placed the butt in Ralph's ashtray. He bobbed his head in a friendly goodbye and left the office.

Ralph sat on his stool as I leaned over the board in deep thought. The end of the war. It was a numbing thought. It was still an unbelievable thought. Years and years of prison. Starvation. Death. Sickness and pain. Fear and terror. Now a sudden end. I had never thought about how it would really end. Now it was here the end. My brain wasn't capable of absorbing the shock. I looked at Ralph and without a word turned and walked to my board and sat down. I felt numb.

Ralph snapped me out of wherever I was. "It's five-thirty and the guards aren't here yet Pete." He was looking out into the factory. "Think that they forgot about us?"

"Maybe we had better find out."

We walked to the big door of the factory that led out to the compound.

"Here comes Shohi," Ralph pointed to the Jap guard who had just entered the factory compound. "Looks like he's going to talk to Takai. I wonder what's up now?"

We waited as we watched them converse after which they both came up to the factory.

"Shigoto. Sichi jun." Takai informed me as the Shohi stood by and nodded.

"Work until seven he says." I translated for Ralph. "Guess there is something up."

The men stopped working, sensing that there was something in the wind. I passed the order to them amidst their grumbling and cursing the Japs. The speculated on the meaning of the extended work hours as they resumed their tasks.

Seven o'clock came fast. We were escorted back to camp with four guards and a corporal.

We were greeted with more news and more rumors. The Russians were suppose to be moving in from the north in a five point pincher movement that was to include Mukden and make contact at the port city of Dairen. More troops were moving toward Harbin three hundred miles to the north of us, The fastest moving Russians were the ones coming down the valley along the railroad.

Cy was almost busting with news. "They are burying equipment at MKK. And the Japs are moving all of the records out of the camp office." Cy attached a great deal of importance to that. I agreed with him.

"I would guess that they are getting ready for something really big." I frowned with puzzlement at the way things were going. "I can't see what the Japs will gain by destroying the records. Hell, there are enough men to tell the story."

"Yeah" Cy gushed the words, "unless they make sure that we ain't around to tell it."

"Sure. Could be." agreed Ed from the bench by the table.

The bay had filled with men from other parts of the barracks. Men sat on the low bunk platforms, others on the upper platforms. I counted over sixty men in the group. It was a gathering that came from the need to clarify our situation.

"What about the machine guns and extra guards?" someone asked.

"Yeah! And what about the bars on the windows? They just put those on in the past two days."

"Maybe we should get the officers down here and make some plans in case the Japs decide they are going to wipe us out.

"Hey! That's a good idea," someone from one of the upper decks shouted. "We should figure a plan. The officers should help us."

"Hell no!" Ed disagreed loudly.

No." Cy shouted to be heard. "The bastards will just screw up everything. Like usual. They ain't got no guts. We can do it ourselves. It's our neck's we got to worry about. The officers always get special privileges. Hey! Did you know that not one officer died here. It's only the enlisted men. And I don't think that they are going to worry about us getting killed. They only worry about their own asses."

"Sure," Ed followed Cy's lead, "we don't have to be told we'll be court-martialled after we get out because we clobber some stinking Jap. We're going to have to take care of ourselves. Like always. Screw the officers."

"Hey guys! Maybe we don't have to worry about anything." I tried to talk and found that I had to shout to be heard over the racket of agreement with Ed's ideas.

"What do you mean?" Cy asked after things had toned down a bit.

"Maybe we'll have help from outside."

I was quieted by the shouts and jeers and questions.

"Okay, come on spit it out Pete." Cy urged. "What the hell do you know? Give."

"There are plenty of Manchus out there that are just aching to get a chance to get even with the Japs who have been occupying this country for the past fourteen years. Suzuki told us that the Manchus are getting together and there are some stories about Chang Ki Chek's men. You heard about the guerrillas .Well if the Japs start anything around here the Manchus will come in. We'll be okay." I concluded confidently.

"Horseshit. Plain old horseshit." Someone threw back at me. "They will machine gun us before the Chinks have a chance to get here."

"Yeah!"

"Sure!"

"The Chinks won't move that fast." Ed argued. "We'll never have a chance."

"I'll bet we do." I countered.

"You act like you know more than you are telling us. I know you talk Jap and Chink. So what do you know?" Everybody quieted down.

"Come on, speak up Pete."

"Sure, you can tell us." Cy urged.

"I can only tell you what I have been told about the Manchus. You know how that goes."

"Yeah sure. But I don't think that you tell us everything." Ed blurted. "You always have good contacts. We all know that. Some pretty straight stuff. So how about now? Is it straight? Will they help?"

"Suzuki told me that the Japs are having trouble with the Manchus. And I'll bet that they'll be around when we need them. If we need them."

Some newcomers pushed their way to the table. They had come from upstairs and the other sections because of the ruckus that was going on.

"What's up anyway?" They looked around at the group.

"You guys up to something?" Scarcey asked.

"Hell no," Ed answered. "We are just trying to figure out what's going

"How about it Pete?" asked Scarcey. "What's with the Manchus?"

Scarcey was a big man. He was a black bearded Italian with a dark complexion. I looked at his tag, twelve seventy-one. I wondered why I noticed the tag now? It was one of those senseless diversions.

"Nothing more than what has been passed on before. If the Japs try to wipe out the POWs the Manchus might be there to help us. Maybe some of Chang Ki Chek's people. "

"Yeah," Scarcey looked around. "Seems to be a lot more going than just talk. Somebody making plans?"

"Just talk. We'll figure out what we have to do in the next few days." Ed spoke for us. "If we have time that is."

"Well don't forget it's all our asses that are in the sling. Not just a few of you." Scarcey drawled the words. The undercurrent was understood by everyone.

"Officers too?" some smart ass jibed.

"Screw 'em." Ed rapped the words. "Just like they been screwing us for years. Remember Corregidor?"

There were many nasty, profane and vengeful remarks in response to the reminder.

"Well don't forget," Cy interrupted the general harangue, "nobody'll blame us for taking things into our own hands and taking care of our own asses." He grinned broadly at the group.

The gathering disintegrated slowly. Everyone wanted to be gregarious because they didn't want to be alone in the uncertainty of the war.

"Well," Cy mused, "what else can we do? If the Japs try anything we'll be in one hell of a mess.

I pulled out a pack of smokes and offered them to Ed and Cy.

"Man, it must be getting near the end." Ed's voice had a sarcastic tone, "Pete's passing out cigarettes."

"Nuts," I grunted, "if you don't want one just give them back."

"Like hell!" Ed scooted back as I reached for the pack. "This could be the last one you give away," he laughed sarcastically.

"Balls! When did you ever give away a cigarette?" I retrieved the pack and flipped out a cigarette for myself.

"Never," Ed responded. "I can't afford them like you do. I ain't got the contacts."

"Bah." I changed the subject. "I think that the story about the war and the Manchus is pretty straight. If the war is over in two days or so, we should have some idea of what we are going to do."

Ed nodded his head as though he had decided that there was only one course of action. "We will have to rush the Japs. If we work it right we should lose only a few men before we get them."

"Agreed" Cy nodded, "We'll make it. Most of us anyway."

"Yeah. I hope so." I snuffed my cigarette and stashed the butt out of habit. "I'm going to hit the sack. No telling what will happen tomorrow. Don't make any plans for tomorrow! We'll have to take it as it comes."

CHAPTER 40 -- THOSE DIRTY RUSSIANS

We stood in formation on the morning of the August the thirteenth, Monday morning.

"What do you think Pete? Something happened?" Ralph looked around at the men lined up in the MKK formation. "Think the bloody Japs are up to something?"

"I don't know Ralph. We've been here about a half hour. Something is happening." I craned my neck to look toward the Inspection Room through which the Japs entered the compound.

"Think we will go to work?"

"I don't know why not. Nobody has said any different. "Here comes Murata."

Murata issued some orders to the Jap guards who summarily dismissed us. No work at either TKK or MKK.

Men found many things to keep busy. Some did laundry, others got some rest. Card games started early and then the rumors started.

The rumors were brought in from the men who had been summoned to the Jap side to unload food that had been brought in by the Manchus.

Again the persistent rumor that Russia had declared war on the Japs. The Jap guards had made reference to the "Dirty Russians". They had stabbed Japan in the back. The Russians were supposed to be advancing on Harbin which was about three hundred miles to the north and east of us.

I couldn't understand the rumor about Dairen because it was to the south of us, about two hundred miles and there was no way the Russians could get there without tangling with the Jap navy.

War was supposed to have been declared on the eighth of August. Supposedly the Russians had notified the Japs that a state of war would exist after midnight of the eighth.

The Japs were complaining that the Russians have stabbed them in the back. Kitanai Roshiyajin. Dirty Russians. It was supposed to be in retaliation for the Russo Japanese War of nineteen aught four.

On the morning of the fourteenth the same thing happened. We lined up for work and were told there was no work for anyone at TKK. Only half the crew would have to report for work on the next day. Only half of the MKK crew went to work.

The rumors spread in the afternoon were brought in from the Jap

369

side of the compound. Martial law had been declared in Mukden. Most of Manchuria where there were Japanese troops was also under martial law. New rumors about Harbin and now Port Arthur were brought in by the MKK crew in the evening.

Troop activity in the area had increased. We noted that the air activity had surged. Now there was air activity to the east and north of the camp.

Records at MKK had been moved out. No one knew where the Japs had taken them.

Charlie came over from the kitchen in the evening with the latest goings on there.

"We got orders to bake nine hundred white buns and one thousand spuds," Charlie panted the news. "It's all got to be ready early in the morning. Thursday. We have to have everything ready before daylight."

"What's going on? Somebody going to move?" Cy asked him.

"Who knows? The Japs didn't say anything else. But something is up." Charlie continued in his excitement. "General Parker and Major Hankins have been trying to get over to see the Japs but the Japs aren't talking." He paused and looked at the group, "There is another story from the Chinks. They think that the Japs are going to move out small groups of POWs, spread them around the countryside. The Japs aren't saying but the Chinks are." He sat back after dropping his blockbuster on us.

"What the hell are they going to feed us if they move us out of camp?" someone in the back asked.

"Who says they are going to feed us? There are two thousand of us. There are only a thousand buns and spuds. How long do you think that is going to last?" Ed asked. "Maybe when they get through they won't have to feed us! Maybe---"

"Hey!" Cy interrupted, "you don't know what the food is for. The travel bread could be for anything and anybody. Don't start a story that will cause a lot of trouble."

Most of the men had heard Charlie's story and Ed's harangue. It was too late to stop the wild versions that would spread through the barracks in no time flat. Excitement, conjecture and a sense of fearful foreboding spread through the camp in a matter of hours.

General Parker passed word around that there was to be no action of any kind, and no plans to act against the Japs.

No one was sleeping much during the night. There was furtive movement, restless activity in the dark barracks all night. There was a nervous tension that defied definition.

Tenko was early as was the lineup and bango for the work crews.

The work hours were announced as seven thirty to six thirty. Only half crews were sent to the factories.

There was no word from the tannery, the canvas factory or the steel mill. Nor was there any word from the Air Corps compound south of TKK.

Suzuki came into the office only minutes after we had settled at our boards. There was something different about his actions. He acted sneaky, as though he had something to hide. "Ohio," he greeted us. "Petaku San, anatawa tsukuro springu."

"Fix a spring? What kind of a spring?"

"Toki. Watch. Watch spring. Yes?" He switched to English. "Takai San, wife sister, her watch. I think the spring is ---"

"Broken." I supplied the word for him. "Takai's sister in law's?"

"Yes. Broken." Suzuki's smile was sickly. "Maybe it can be fixed?" he smiled as he spoke. It was a rather submissive smile.

"Maybe.

I smiled back at him.

"What kind of a watch?" Ralph asked.

"Wristu." Suzuki blinked his eyes happily and he glanced from one to the other of us.

"Let's see it Suki. Maybe we can do something with it."

Suzuki brought out a small bundle of cloth. The watch was in pieces. It was a small Swiss ladies wrist watch. I spread the handkerchief in which the watch was wrapped. I sorted the pieces. I examined it closely and determined that all of the pieces were evidently there. The main spring had been removed from its case. I reached in the table drawer for the magnifying glass that I had and inspected the spring.

"What does it look like Pete?" Ralph bent over the collection of parts and poked them around with a finger.

"It looks like the retaining hole at the end of the spring broke." I pointed to the end of the spring with the tip of my pencil. Ralph and Suzuki crowded in close to take a look at where I was pointing.

"Can you fix it?" Ralph asked with a surprising show of concerned interest.

"Maybe. I could try annealing the end of the spring and then drilling a new hole. I have to take the temper out of just the smallest section at the end of the spring. After that it only has to be reassembled."

"Okay. You fix it?" Suzuki smiled. He brought out a pack of cigarettes and passed out one to each of us. "Taksan tobacco. Hokay?" Suzuki grinned at us. "Fix watch? Hokay?"

"Sure Suki. I'll try. I'll see about a candle at the warehouse. I should be able to anneal the end and then it shouldn't be too bad. I'll work down at the warehouse. Gregg has some tools. I'll see you later Suki."

"Hokay." Suzuki grinned happily. He left the office in high spirits.

"Why is he so hot to have the watch fixed anyway Pete?" Ralph watched through the factory window as Suzuki headed for the foundry. "Shouldn't be any real problem in having the watch fixed in town."

"Maybe. Maybe not." I placed the watch parts in the table drawer except for the spring. "I'll see about annealing the end of the spring and drilling a hole in it. I shouldn't be too long." I paused before leaving the office, "If Takai comes around send word down to me. Hokay?" I mimicked Suzuki's okay.

"Hokay." Ralph mimicked and grinned.

"Hokay. I'll see you later."

I met Peachi at the main entrance to the factory. She came close and greeted me. "Ohio goziemus," she smiled. "Papeeru." She handed me a roll of blueprints. She intoned, "Tomago." I took the bundle gingerly, quickly transferring it under my arm. Eggs!

"Arigato." I thanked her as I continued on to the warehouse. I was surprised at her generosity. Eggs were hard to come by.

"Hey man! How about boiling a couple of eggs? We'll share."

Gregg stared at me in disbelief. "Where the hell did you get eggs?"

"Well? Yes or no?"

"Sure, sure Pete. No sweat."

I passed the eggs to him. I had a bun in my table drawer. I thought about that. Toast. I would have to get the bun and we could have eggs with toast. "I'll be back." I carried the blueprints back to the office and left them there. Ralph was out somewhere and not in sight. I took the bun from the drawer and hurried back to the warehouse.

Gregg had the eggs boiling as I sat down at the table in the back of the warehouse and started to work on the spring. Gregg produced the candle and the tools. The spring was so small that I had to be very careful in heating it or I would destroy the temper of the whole thing. I clamped it with the small pair of pliers, allowing only an eighth of an inch to stick out in the candle flame. It turned blue and then red and then a straw yellow in the flame. I let it cool and then drilled the tiny hole in the very end of it.

I turned to see Mitch come in on the pretense of getting a light for a cigarette at the grinder. He held a piece of steel against the grinding wheel until it turned red and then lit his smoke. "Air raid coming up." He turned to leave.

"When?" Gregg growled.

"Now. Coming up."

I watched him as he walked swiftly to the door of the factory. I didn't know where he had gotten the information. I didn't question the truth of it. "Later Gregg." I shot out of the warehouse and into the office.

"Air raid buddy. Coming up now."

"I know." Ralph threw back at me.

I looked at him and said nothing, puzzled about the how the news had come in. I put away my drafting tools just as the sirens started to blast the alert. The clock pointed to nine twenty-five.

The guards had been on duty at TKK since they had marched us in. They had been jittery all morning. They were like scared rabbits when the alarm sounded. They made us double back to camp. We were sent to our barracks. No one left the barracks for the foxholes. The MKK crew did not return to camp. This caused a lot of conjecture. Something that we did not understand. There was no all clear, but the Japs spread the word that it was all clear at ten fifteen.

We were ordered back to TKK.

MKK. The factory was supposedly designed by American engineers before the war.

CHAPTER 41 -- SAYONARA

The Japs were pissed for some reason so they made us double time back to TKK. We passed Takai's wife's sister and her two small children as we entered the compound. She was lugging a huge blanket wrapped bundle as she hustled the kids out into the road. Suzuki was standing by the door of the house and waving good-bye. He followed us up to the factory and into the office.

"Petaku, hiyai. Toki." He pointed to his wrist indicating he wanted the wrist watch.

I retrieved the small bundle of parts and then added the spring that I had secreted in one of my pockets.

"Thank you. Thank you very much."

He turned and ran from the office like a rat with a cat on its tail. Ralph and I followed him to the door and watched him as he ran out of the gate.

"That bloke is in a hurry." Ralph commented. "Guess he wants to make sure that she takes the watch with her."

"Yeah," I mused. " Maybe she can find someone to reassemble it for her. I think it is a very expensive watch. Good Swiss works. Twenty-one jewels."

We walked back to the office slowly.

"Hey!" Ralph pointed out of the window to the road behind the factory. "They all have rifles. Manchus! They're heading east."

"Sure looks like it."

We rushed to the window and watched as they disappeared down the road.

"Sure looks like everything is going to pop in a hurry. What do you think Joe?" He sat at his board and lit a cigarette as though to calm himself.

I looked at him for some time before I answered. He seldom called me by my given name. He always called me by my nickname, Pete. He was disturbed. "I think we are over the hill now." A strange thing happened then. I shivered for some unknown reason. "Short timers now." I couldn't shake the apprehension that I felt, or account for the reason for it.

"Yes," Ralph was preoccupied, "I wonder what it is like at home."

Suzuki interrupted our musing. "Doeste."

"Doeste. Nane." I questioned him back.

"Why did everybody go back to camp?" Suzuki asked in English.

"Air raid alert. The guards ran us back to camp. There wasn't a plane in sight. Nothing happened." I glanced in Ralph's direction and warned him to be careful with a frown. "Some say that Russian planes were flying over Hoten."

"Nie, nie. No no." Suzuki shook his head emphatically. "No planes. Hikoki nie."

"Why are your people leaving?" I asked boldly.

"Oi," Suzuki spluttered uncomfortably, "Russia, how you say?" he motioned with his hands, "Semeru, koogeki suru."

"Susmeru. Attack. No advance. The Russians advance to Hoten. Zenshin chu. No Zenchin suru. Advance on Hoten. Yes?" I pushed for information.

"Yes. So. Russians coming. "Suzuki stopped suddenly. "No talk. Dame. Bad. Dame. Warui des. So." His reaction was not what I had expected.

"We will not tell anyone that we heard the news from you," I assured Suzuki in Japanese.

"So. Good." Suzuki looked out of the office window to the factory. "Tabete nieji hon."

"Two thirty for the food from camp you mean. How come?" I asked. "The chow won't be here until two thirty instead of at twelve. I explained to Ralph.

"Wakaran." Suzuki shrugged. "I do not know. Gonso."

"That damned sergeant," I snarled. "Well I guess we had better pass the word to the guys Ralph."

"Yeah. I guess so." Ralph agreed. "We'll starve by the time the food gets here."

"I'll go out and tell them."

Suzuki left with a strange smile on his face as he looked around.

After passing out the word I headed for the warehouse. Gregg had boiled the eggs and had hidden them along with my bun. "How about toasting the bun while I keep an eye out?"

"Check." Gregg stopped as though to say something.

"Something up? I asked.

"No. Just keep an eye out for that frigging gunso. He's the sneakiest sergeant in the whole stinking Jap army."

"Right."

The egg and the toast were a real treat. I saved a portion for Ralph. Gregg watched but said nothing.

"How the hell do you manage this stuff Pete?" His tone was intense and searching.

"Luck. Luck and a little prayer." I smiled.

"Yeah. Sure."

"I'll see you later. Thanks a lot."

"Thanks to you Pete." He waved happily as I left.

Peachi was alone in the office checking some of the records that were kept in the desk. She had sorted the papers into small piles. She was crying quietly. A soft sob broke through every few seconds. She looked at me with the most peculiar look I had ever seen on her face.

"Arigato Peachi San." I looked at her sadly. I felt a sudden wave of compassion for her. "Domo arigato."

She sobbed loudly. She shook her head, tears flying from her cheeks. She said nothing.

I placed the portion of egg and bun that I had saved for Ralph in the drawer of his drafting table.

"Peachi."

She looked at me with a very odd, sad look. Still she said nothing. She then moved quickly and picked up a stack of the papers and turned to look at me. Her face was an amazing array of expressions that I had never seen before. She smiled, sadly. "Sayonara Petaku San." She turned quickly and ran from the office. I sat on the stool, suddenly all alone in a strange world and watched her through the window as she ran out of the big door and down the path to the main building.

Ralph came in, stopped at the door and gave me a weird look. "Something wrong Pete?" There was a note of serious concern in his voice. "You okay?"

"Sure. Yeah, I'm okay." A sigh that I couldn't control escaped me that surprised me more than it did Ralph.

"You sure?" He repeated. His leathery features wrinkled in a frown.

"Yeah sure. Thanks. I'm okay. Something in your drawer for you."

He wolfed down the treat without a word. When he had finished he smiled, "Thanks. That was great." He wiped his lips, "The guards just left the factory compound. Some say that there are paratroopers around. Another story is that there are guerrillas around and that the Chinese are rioting."

"Could be." I nodded. "Remember the Manchus we saw earlier?"

"Sure do."

"I guess we'll be seeing a lot of action in the next few days." I looked up at the clock. "Only eleven forty-five. Sure has been a busy day so far. Wonder what else will happen today? Let's see," I stopped to recall the day, "It's Wednesday today. The fifteenth. According to Suzuki the war will be over tomorrow."

"Man I sure hope so." Ralph had a faraway look. " I sure hope so."

We settled down and lost ourselves in our work to help the antsy feelings I was sure we both had.

It was two o'clock before the sergeant and two guards took two men to camp to bring our food. They brought back two buckets of soup. One of the buckets had rabbit meat in it.

"RABBIT!"

"Rabbit!"

"Meat!"

The word spread through the mess line.

"Oh man! What happened?" Gregg was ecstatic.

Polack, who had been one of the chow carriers, explained. "That bucket should have gone to the hospital at twelve forty-five. Somebody goofed and the buckets got swapped. So we lucked out."

"Great!"

"Too bad for the guys in the hospital." Gregg commented.

"Yeah. Too bad." Polack smirked.

Everybody had their fair share of the windfall. We returned to work much happier.

At four o'clock a sergeant, a Jap medic and two guards ordered us out of the factory and ordered us to line up and count off. Suzuki stood by as we bangoed. He exchanged some words with the sergeant. Suzuki nodded, then backed off and saluted the sergeant. As we left the compound I waved good-bye to Suzuki. His mouth formed a silent "Sayonara". I looked back with some strange feeling. I had a weird premonition that I would never see him again. A chill across my shoulders made me shiver on the very warm day.

The guards started us at double time and kept us running all the way back to the camp gate. When we entered the main gate the MKK crowd was already there. No one knew the reason for the early return to camp. MKK said that they had had a delay because two men were missing. They had been found sleeping behind one of the shacks. Unbelievably the guards hadn't beaten them. We knew something was up for sure.

Cy and Ed were waiting when I arrived at the section. They had collected all of the latest information. "Chow is going to be late." Cy started as I rid myself of my work gear. The clackers remained on the floor, the web belt and canteen I placed on the shelf over my bunk.

"Wonder why?" I tossed the words down at him as I squatted on my thin straw mattress. "What's going on in the kitchen?"

"All kinds of fuss about rations." Cy answered.

"Not the officers again?" I interrupted.

"Nah! The Japs." Ed replied. "Charlie has been in and out a half a dozen times today with the stories. You can't believe half of the stuff he is telling us."

"Hey! I think that some of the stuff is really straight poop." Cy came back excitedly.

"So okay. Don't keep it a secret. Out with it."

Ted, Scarcey, Johnson and Stanko, and a half a dozen other MKK men, plus some of the men from the other section had collected at our end of the section.

"Yeah, come on. Let's hear it. We know a hell of a lot had been going on."

"Okay okay!" Cy settled himself on the edge of the upper bunk. "First, thirty-six men came in from Camp One at about two thirty. They were covered with a canvas in the back of a truck. The trucks they were on were stopped a few times. They don't know who or why. When they were unloaded on the Jap side of the camp Murata was there. Murata told them that it was for their own protection that they were kept covered. The rest of the guys from that camp were supposed to come on a little later but they haven't showed yet." Cy paused.

"What happened to the rest of those guys?" Scarcey asked. "I know a couple of them."

"Nobody knows yet. Maybe they are alright. There's some story that the Manchus put out that doesn't sound to good." Cy paused again as he looked around at the men gathered in the section. "There shouldn't have to be any panic you know. Don't go twisting what I've told you. I'll tell you ..."

"What?" Somebody interrupted.

"Yeah, spill it. You don't expect us to go out and take over from the Japs right now. What the hell do you expect us to do?"

"Aw knock it off!" Scarcey shouted to quiet the rumble that had started. "Let's hear what the hell it is that he has to say."

"Yeah. Come on Cy. What the hell is the rest of the scuttlebutt?"

"Come on!" Cy started. He stopped and shook his head before continuing. "The Manchus are telling the men that we are going to be taken away in groups of four and five. Small groups. And ..."

"What the hell for?" Scarcey shouted.

"Who said that?"

"The Chinks told them. Who knows what for? The Chinks don't like what the Japs might do. The Chinks don't trust the Japs."

"You mean that the bastards are going to take us out and execute us? Right? Is that what you mean?" Ted's voice rose a few notches as he spoke.

"Naw! Damn it! Now quiet down. I knew that was what you were going to do. Go off half cocked! I told you not to panic. But there you go!" Cy threw up his hands in disgust.

"Okay okay. So maybe the Chinks don't know from nothing." Ted conceded.

"Right! Well, anyway the Chinks just said that the word should be passed around that we should be careful. Okay?" Cy looked around the group of excited men.

"Sure," Ted nodded, he looked ashamed of his moment of near panic.

"Now the rest of the stuff sounds real good. The Russkies have cut through from Vladivostok, over in Siberia, by the Sea of Japan, all the way across to Sinuiji in the Yellow Sea. They are headed straight for Dairen. They have Manchuria and Korea separated. The Russkies drove a spearhead right through cutting everything off." He stopped. The racket was so loud that he couldn't shout loud enough to be heard. "Hey! Quiet! Quiet down if you want to hear the rest of it. You can all talk later. Let me give you the dope. Okay? They took Harbin in eighteen hours. And, the Russkies are collecting all of their heavy forces at Pies Pass, about eighty miles north of here for a straight push to the sea."

"WOW! Wowie. It's all going to be over soon!" Ted yelled. "Sayonara Manchu!"

"Hey! Be quiet and let him finish."

"Here is the real clincher." Cy paused dramatically and wet his lips as he looked around the crowd. "The Japs are going to move all of us down south. Someplace down in Korea. There are supposed to be four groups."

There were questions, shouts and curses. The racket drowned out Cy's last words. "Hey! Quiet and let me finish."

It took only moments for quiet to settled in.

"The generals and the senior officers are to be the first group that moves out. Then the rest of the officers. Then ..."

"You mean we are going to get rid of them at last?" Someone shouted the interruption.

"Aw quiet."

"Then there are to be two large groups of enlisted men. But ..." Cy stopped and looked around again as though he never was going to have center stage again. "Something changed their plans. There aren't going to be any moves."

"Hey! What the hell you doing giving us a story like that if it ain't going to happen? Huh?"

"Yeah! What the hell is the idea?"

The assembly broke up in dissension. There were discussions and arguments. Some of the men expressed the opinion that it was all bullshit. The bull sessions went on for hours.

It was seven thirty before the chow buckets were brought in from the kitchen. Seven sections received extra rations. The extra was supposed to have been the rations for the men from Camp One.

"Hey!" Charlie stuck his head over the edge of my bunk. "The nine hundred extra buns and the spuds are going to be used for chow tomorrow. How about that?"

"No kidding? Wonder what the hell that is all about?"

"Don't know. It will be spread pretty thin." Charlie chuckled.

"So what? It's extra right?"

"Hey!" Charlie shucked his clackers and climbed the ladder to climb up to the upper bay. He squatted at the end of my bunk. "You know that Sections Seven through Thirteen each got six men from Camp One? And then seven more got in from Camp One a little later. They were in a truck and surrounded by equipment to hide them. All of the gardens have been stripped of food. How about that?" Charlie bobbed his head in emphasis, a habit that he had when he was excited and talking.

"It sure sounds like a lot of things are happening around here."

We sat and talked until the call for tenko came to end our day.

I thought about the events of the day. I also smiled when I thought about the promise of "taksan tobacco" that Suzuki had made if I fixed the spring for the watch. He had forgotten all about his promise. There were no cigarettes.

Mukden POW Compound, looking to southeast.

CHAPTER 42 -- OPERATION CARDINAL

August the sixteenth, Thursday, was to be the fateful day. Nothing happened, there were no moves. The Japs had had to change their plans.

It was a rainy day.

There was no callout for the factory workers of either of the factories. At nine o'clock there was a call for volunteers for tomato picking and potato digging. A hundred men responded. It was always a detail that was volunteered for happily. There were a lot of tomatoes eaten that would have gone only to the Japs. The same with the potatoes. Raw potatoes were good food. A little starchy tasting, but edible and stomach filling.

Cy, Ted, Ed, Kozie, Johnson and a few others started a Black Jack game. During the play the rumors spilled out.

"Hear that the reason for lights out around the camp was because of the guerrillas." Kozie related the story. "It was about nine twenty-five when the Japs thought that they had spotted a band of them just to the north of camp. They didn't want them to spot the camp so they put the lights out."

"Don't make sense. All the Manchus know that the camp is here."

"Yeah. But the Japs at the warehouse told somebody that the group was too small to attack the camp." Ted took up the story. "The Japs think that they might collect a couple a hundred more and then raid the camp and free us before the Japs do anything stupid."

"That's only talk." Johnson shot back at him. "I sure wish it was true."

"Sure," I agreed, "but you can't tell just what could happen. Maybe it would be best for all of us if we prepared for something like that."

"Yeah. How?" Johnson asked. "We haven't got a thing to fight with."

"Well," I hesitated. "if the Manchus attack the main gate and the towers, we could probably break out."

"Then what?" asked Kozie as he looked up from his cards. "There are more Japs all around Mukden."

"Sure. But they are going to have their hands full." Ted got in his thoughts.

"I guess we'll just have to sit and wait," conceded Ed. "So, let's play cards, huh? Hit me."

The game continued hot and heavy for a long time.

"I'll see you guys later. I'm going to check outside and see what is
383

going on out there." I glanced out of the window. "It looks like the rain let up out there."

The clouds had broken somewhat. There were still patchy rain clouds spread around with a lot of clear blue sky in between.

Planes buzzed somewhere among the puffy clouds. There some small specks over Mukden and off to the north.

"What time is it anyway?" I asked one of the men at the kitchen as I watched what was going on inside.

"Eleven o'clock."

"Check." I turned away and started to walk through the compound, walking around the foxholes to the southwest corner. A half a dozen men were sitting on some of the flat rocks around the foxholes. I wondered if they were playing it safe and staying close to the foxholes just in case something happened.

One of them jumped up and pointed to the north of camp. "Hey man! Look at the size of that sucker will you?"

"Hey!" shouted another as he jumped up. "He sure as hell is low. Can't be more than a thousand feet or so."

"HEY MAN! Look at that!" another shouted.

Men all over the grounds were on their feet staring at the huge plane.

"Man he is close. He can't be more than a couple of miles from here. He's heading for the open field just to the north of camp."

"Hey, that's near the airfield. Bet the Japs are going to get him in a hurry."

"Not if the guerrillas are around."

"They sure as hell ain't going to stop the Japs from shooting the plane down."

The next instant shocked everyone watching. Specs dropped from the belly of the plane and chutes started to open soon after.

"WOW! Paratroopers!"

"One, two, three, four, five, six. Six chutes!"

"Hey! There come some more!"

The startling incident had everyone on their feet. Shouts, hurrahs and then pandemonium broke out in the compound.

Ten chutes floated gently to the ground. They dropped out of sight behind the compound wall. The huge plane made another pass over the area and then turned to the southwest and roared away into the clouds.

"They're down by the granary."

"Hey! How many were there?"

"Did you see if any of them had guns?"

"Who the hell knows? They were too far away to see."

Excitement spread through the camp like wildfire, not only on our side but also on the Jap side. The guard towers became a hive of activity. There were no shots fired but the machine guns were manned.

I returned to the barracks area to witness men pouring out into the parade ground.

"HEY! MAN! Did you see them? What's up Pete? Did you see them?" Cy grabbed my arm as if to force the answers to his questions.

"Yes, I saw them. I counted ten parachutes in all. Looked like maybe six men." I sat down on a bench at the table in the section. Men crowded around to hear the telling.

"Well! Come on tell us. What happened?"

"This huge plane flew in low from the south. When it passed to the north of camp ..." I paused for breath, not realizing that I was excited as everyone else. "Six chutes dropped out of the belly. Then a little later there were four more. Ten in all."

"Where at?"

"What kind of a plane was it?"

"Were they Americans?"

There was a multitude of questions being thrown at me. "Hold it! Hold it!" I shouted at the questioners. "I don't know what they were. I couldn't tell what kind of a plane it was. It ain't Jap." I halted dramatically. "It looked like the American planes that bombed us last December. Big! Four engines. I never saw anything like it in the Air Corps before the war. That's for sure. It must be a new bomber. Bigger than a seventeen or eighteen that we had at Clark Field."

"How high was he?" Cy asked.

"I don't know. I'd guess about a thousand feet, maybe lower." I concluded.

"What makes you think that it was American?" Ed challenged me from the end of the table.

"I'm just guessing. Then maybe it's gut feel. But it didn't look like it was Russian. And, I sure as hell don't think it was a Jap. I'll bet on that!"

"What do you think they want Pete?"

"My guess is that they are Americans. I think that maybe the war is over like Suzuki said it would be. Today is the sixteenth and Suzuki said that the war would be over on the fifteenth. That was yesterday." I was surprised at my own self assurance. Surprised at the confidence in my own voice.

"Yeah sure. You're dreaming."

"Aw, come on now," Cy offered in my defense. "He heard the stuff from a Jap. The dope was pretty straight in the past."

"Sure. But who can trust a Jap?" Ed countered. "Do you really trust them Pete? You Cy?"

"No." We both responded together.

"We'll soon find out I'll bet." I hadn't lost any of my outward display of confidence, but inside I said a silent prayer that I was right.

Arguments, discussions and general sweating continued for hours as we wrestled with what had been seen and what the incident held for us in the near term. Noon chow didn't put a damper on the talk. The talk went around mouthfuls of food.

The rain started again at about one o'clock. A summer downpour lasted for an hour. Soon after the rain stopped the men from Camp Two came in. They had wild rumors that spread through out the camp in a manner of minutes.

"The war in Manchuria is over. The Russians have taken just about everything." Cy repeated the story, "And the Russians are still coming. They are going straight through Manchuria."

"Sure sounds good. But we'll have to wait and see."

Word started on the upper floor of the barracks that there was something going on outside of camp.

"A whole mess of cars and trucks just pulled off of the road. They're heading for the Jap side. Let's go see Pete." Cy started for the exit.

"Okay." I followed close behind him.

We ran down to the fenced area between the hospital and the main entry to the POW side of the compound. The double fenced area permitted a good vantage point from which the main gate and the Jap office entrance could be seen. Strangely enough there were only three other men in the area.

Cy crushed me to the fence. "Here they come!" he shouted.

All of the men in the area rushed to the fence to see what was going on. The compound gates were opened by the guards. Two Jap army trucks and two cars drove in and out of site behind the Jap administration building. Men, four white men, Americans, marched around the corner of the brick building.

"AMERICANS! AMERICANS!" Cy gasped in and attempt to shout.

I stood dumbfounded.

The Americans were dressed in Air Corps coveralls! All except two, who I thought were officers. One was a Jap in an American uniform and the other was plainly a Chinaman. The other four were Caucasians. One of the men in coveralls, a blonde young soldier, smiled and waved at us. They disappeared through the doors of the Jap offices.

"The parachutists!" I mumbled. "Cy, they're the guys who came out of the plane! You see! I told you so!"

I saw one of the men near us take off for the barracks with the news.

We waited.

Within minutes a crowd assembled around us, filling the area near the fence with anxious men.

The Jap guards walking the perimeter didn't make a move toward us or "Kura" us away. No warnings to get the hell back from the barbed wire. They spouted something in Jap that I didn't catch. They laughed and then continued their patrol.

Cy was pressing me to the barbed wire as the other men strained to get a looksee at what was going on.

"What do you think is going on?" someone behind us asked.

"Who knows?" somebody answered.

"Who were the guys that the Japs brought in?"

No one answered.

We waited.

At five o'clock there was a flurry of activity at the Jap office entrance. Jap soldiers marched out, they looked around at us and then continued to march around the building to the Jap side.

Minutes later the camp commandant, Colonel Matsuda, Lieutenant Murata and the six men came out into the compound. One of the men waved at us vigorously, a big smile on his face. None of the six spoke to us. A piercing whistle was let out by one of the team.

There was a gap in time! No one moved. Someone started to say something. Then someone shouted, "THE WAR IS OVER!!"

Shouts, yells and unintelligible words filled the air with a horrendous volume. It was deafening as the shouting continued.

"THE WAR IS OVER! WAR IS OVER!!"

The six Americans stood stock still. Two of them waved to us. One man clasped his hands and waved them over his head. Everybody could interpret the sign.

"THE WAR IS OVER. THE WAR IS OVER."

Hell broke loose in Mukden! It was as happy a hell as one could imagine. Men grabbed each other and danced around the compound. Laughing, action of joy. Everything broke all of a sudden.

The news spread immediately through the camp.

There was no way to hold back the emotions that broke loose. There were hundreds of crying men. It was the end!

Three years! Three years and four months!

The end!

THANK GOD!

There was no discipline. There was no attempt to break out. No one bothered the Japs at the moment. No one attempted to cross over to the Jap side of the compound. There was a continuous outpouring of such emotion that it was just impossible to contain the men and their exuberance.

Tenko, just through sheer habit, was held at eight thirty.

There was no sleeping. Everyone was up and around and talking. It was one continuous round of talk, talk, talk. Men were laughing and crying in sheer relief. Three years, which had been like three hundred years, of suffering and tears and terror were at an end. Actually three years and four to five months. But for us they had been an eternity. Now it was over. The Jap guards continued to patrol the "No Man's Land".

Malakapey came through at nine thirty. He was the last Jap to ever make a patrol through the Mukden Prisoner of War Camp.

I walked out into the night and sat under the stars and said silent prayers of thanks.

The morning of the seventeenth of August was a grand and glorious day of anticipation.

Breakfast was delivered early. Then for some unknown reason there was a bengo at eight thirty.

"Cars coming in from town!" the word was sent down from the second floor and spread through camp. They could see the road outside of the camp from the second story windows. There were lookouts at the windows constantly.

"Let's go Pete!" Cy called.

"What time is it?" I asked anyone who would answer.

"Nine thirty. Put it in your book Pete!" Ed laughed. "put it in your notes."

"I sure as hell plan on it." I retorted.

Cy and Ed joined me outside of the barracks.

"Let's go." Cy urged.

"Think it's the Americans?" Ed asked almost prayerfully.

"I think so." I answered, hoping that I was right.

There were men gathered around the wire fence between the hospital and the entry hall, the cloak room. We heard the cars pull up outside of the wall and stop. A horn tooted. The Jap guards ran to the huge wooden gates and swung them open. The cars drove in and parked behind the building, out of sight. Seconds later a Jap Colonel and five of the six men that we had seen the day before appeared from around the structure. They move rapidly into the offices. A dozen Jap officers of varying rank followed. The Americans, and the Japs with them had broad smiles on their faces as they walked into the building.

"Who do you think the Jap is?" Cy asked me.

"Nisie," I answered smartly. "You've seen the American born Japs haven't you?"

"Yeah sure," Cy nodded. "I've seen them. Think maybe he is an interpreter?"

"Yes!" I spit out. "Sure as hell must be. I wonder what happened to the Chinaman that was with them yesterday."

"Yeah. That's right." Ed spoke up. "There were six of them yesterday. How about that? I wonder what did happen to him.

"We'll find out in a hurry I'll bet." I had a know-it- all tone that didn't sound at all out of place. Let's move around to the cloak room doors." I urged. "If anything happens we can be in on it."

"Check." Cy agreed as we made our move.

The three of us moved away from the fence and toward the doors that led to the cloak room.

"Here comes Murata." Ed pointed out .

Murata and four Jap guards, guns at port, hurried through the cloak room. Murata glance at me and then looked away in a hurry. I wondered what thoughts went through his head as he saw me. I had no love for the bastard even now that the war was over. No one made a move to stand at attention as had been the rule when a Jap officer came by.

They headed for the barracks.

"They must be headed for the officers sections in Two." I remarked as they passed us. "I guess that the war is really over. The guards went with him to protect him. I'll bet. The shithead is due for some retaliation." I promised.

"Yep," Cy agreed. "You sure as hell are right Pete. He'd have a ball otherwise. Now it's our turn."

"Think it's going to be too long before we find out?" Ed sounded very impatient.

"I think that they went for General Parker and Beebe and a couple of others. The staff types." I mused.

"That's no bet. You know a sure thing." Cy countered.

Generals Parker, Beebe and Pierce and three other American officers and the Englishman, Major Beaty, crossed the compound in our direction at double time followed by Murata and the guards. They rushed through the cloak room and into the administration building.

"Bet it won't be long before the Japs are taking orders from us." I offered hopefully.

"Horseshit," Cy spat back.

We waited for over an hour, venturing all kinds of suppositions. Then the American officers, the Englishman, Beaty, and the five new men, the parachutists, entered the cloak room and out into the yard.

"THE WAR IS OVER.!!" General Parker spoke hoarsely.

Pandemonium broke loose.

Shouting, yelling and laughing men went berserk. We all danced and pounded each other on skinny backs as the news was verified.

"Hey," I approached the group of five, "Where did you come from?"

"Hsian. In China. On a B-24."

"What the hell is a B-24?"

Laughter was the happy answer.

Two of the crew that had parachuted in were majors. The others were various grades of sergeants.

"We are here to make sure you fellows get home okay. We're here to take you home. It's all over. WE WON!" The major had to shout to be heard.

The generals had broad happy smiles on their faces, and tears on their cheeks.

"Hey! What's an atom bomb?"

"Who the hell is Harry Truman?"

"Is Skinny okay?"

"Hold it fellows. Hold it! We'll get around to answering the questions. Right now we have to make arrangements to get you people fed and then home." The major's voice was a shout so that he could be heard.

We quieted down slowly, realizing that there was more that we were to be told.

"The Russians are moving in. We'll fill you all in later. We have to find General Wainwright. He's at a place called Sian. Up north in Manchuria."

Shouts drowned out the major. Everything went topsy-turvy. There was no quieting down for hours. The exuberance was unimaginable and seemingly never ending.

"The war is officially over." General Parker issued the statement as an official edict at two thirty.

Everyone in camp was in the compound except for the non-ambulatory patients in the hospital.

The general called order so that he could speak. "The Japanese are still officially in charge of the camp. The Russians will be here in a few days." Parker paused. "The war is officially over." A solemn quietness greeted the general's repetition of the momentous statement.

I thought that he repeated it because he couldn't believe it was so.

"We will all be going home soon. Very soon. Be generous, be kind to the Japanese. Remember, WE WON!"

There was an immeasurable time during which there was singing, shouting and crying as our emotions reached their peak. Finally, after much waving and shouting for order the general started to speak again.

"General Wainwright is in Sian. Major Hennessey is sending Major Lamar and Sergeant Leith to Camp Two in Sian to bring the general back to Mukden. And, then, there be supply planes dropping food an supplies, arms and clothing for the next few days. Good luck to all of you and thank God we made it."

The shock of finding out that the day we had prayed for for such a long time left me in a shocked state that made me feel melancholy. I didn't know exactly what the future would bring, but I thanked God that I was still alive at the end of the horrible time that we had lived through.

AND THEN!!!

CHAPTER 43 -- AIR DROP

When the announcement was made that there was to be an air drop the officers asked for Signal Corps men to assist. They needed a "Drop Control Operator" to talk the planes in and coordinate the drop. The field between the camp and MKK was the perfect drop zone. It was directly west of the camp and clear of any structures. There was nothing in the field, no shrubs, nothing but a single old tree that was right at the side of the road that had been used by the men as they marched to MKK. Also it was easy to keep the Manchus out of the drop zone. The main gate faced the area.

The camp buildings were marked with huge white crosses painted on the roofs. I didn't know where the paint came from. I was given what was called a walkie talkie. It was a new gadget to me. A hand held transceiver. It was an example of the new technology that had been developed during the war.

The Air Corps made good its promise to bring in supplies. After contacting the huge planes, C-89s, I directed them to fly in from the north and start the drop just before they came over the north end of the field. I had been told that the chutes were opened by a static line. The supplies were to be strapped to pallets. My radio contacts explained that the planes would drop the load at between three hundred and five hundred feet. The air speed would be around a hundred and fifty miles an hour.

I took up my position at the fence at MKK, west of the camp, because it offered an unobstructed view of the approach and the field itself. The drops started perfectly. All of the planes that came down to three to five hundred feet and made their drops landed in the field. As the drop continued, problems developed. The pilots that came in too fast, but low enough, smashed the supplies into the ground because the chutes never fully deployed. Some who were leery of coming in too low, missed the drop zone completely.

I had finished evaluating the damage to the cargo of one of the chutes that had come in too fast. The sky was clear, and all planes were supposed to have dropped and left. I started across to the camp, about two hundred yards away, when I heard a plane. I was almost in the middle of the field. I spotted it to the north, coming fast. I triggered the radio switch and shouted into the mike, "Hold! Abort. Why the hell don't you contact before you drop?" I scrambled for the tree. "Abort! Veer off!
393

You're too damned fast and too low. This isn't a damned bombing run!. Abort!"

"Sorry buddy. You're too late."

The radio response came just as the cargo came out of the plane.

"You're nuts!" There was more that I wanted too say but the cargo was heading straight for me. I saw the tree. It was a thick trunked old oak. It was about a foot and a half in diameter. It had twisted and broken branches, sparsely leaved. I ran for the tree watching the cargo coming at me at fantastic speed. I ducked behind the trunk and plastered myself against it. I heard the whistling whooshing sound as the cargo came flashing through the air.

The speed of the plane had been so high that the chutes had ripped loose from the cargo. The pallets and the cargo thundered and smashed into the ground around the tree like bombs. I coughed and choked as a dark brown cloud of powder spread around the tree and all over me. I winced as something stung my face and hands and splattered my body. I was coated with a sticky liquid and the powder. The slight westerly breeze blew the powder away. I became aware of the nature of the stuff. "COCOA!"

"Hey! Hey buddy. Mac" The walkie talkie spouted words at me. "Sorry. You okay?"

"Damn it! I don't know you stupid son of a bitch. I'd like to get my hands on you. I'd knock your head off and kick it around the field. I'll kick your guts out. Don't you know how to drop cargo?"

"Hey," laughter came from the speaker. "You must be okay. You're mad, but you're okay. Great!" The voice from the radio sounded relieved.

"Yeah. I'm okay you shitty jackass. Can't you fly a plane? You should be in the infantry."

"Hey man! That's no language to use to an officer of the Air Corps." The walkie talkie squawked.

"SCREW YOU! In capital letters. Court martial me."

I examined myself. The liquid that had spattered me was ketchup. Large bottles of ketchup. It was splattered all over the tree and the surrounding landscape. Mixed in with the ketchup was cocoa. I was covered with huge splotches of the red liquid. I didn't feel as though I was bleeding, but I couldn't tell. The cocoa was mixed in with the ketchup in a weird looking mess. I didn't hurt anywhere. I was a big mass of ugly red brown goo.

"Hey You okay?" Men were coming from camp and shouting as they ran toward me.

I heard the engines of the plane and looked up to find that it was circling and bearing down on the drop zone again.

"HEY!" I shouted into the W.T.. "Don't make the drop. Hold off! Men in the drop zone." I shouted into the W.T. I released the button and waited.

"Roger buddy. Got you loud and clear." The W.T. twitted the words, "We are just checking to make sure you are okay. We have more cargo."

"I have to clear the men out of the drop zone. Circle around one more time. I'll give you the word."

"Roger," replied the radio voice.

"I started to shout at the men who were approaching in a dead run from camp. "Back! Get back! there is another drop. More stuff coming in! Go back!" I waved fruitlessly. I started to run east, back to the camp wall.

"Holy hell! You okay?" Asked Macarovitch as he reached me. "Pete? Is that you?"

"Yeah. It's me. Ketchup, cocoa and me. Take a lick. "I joked.

"Man you look like the Goo Man himself," Mac laughed.

Six or eight more man caught up with him. They made jokes and funny remarks once they had determined that I wasn't injured.

"Come on! Let's get the hell out of here before they clobber the bunch of us."

We ran toward the compound wall as the W.T. squawked again. "Hey man! We're getting close on gas. How about it? Do we drop or go?"

"Yeah! Drop it! Throttle back this time. What were you doing the last run?"

Moments passed as the plane made a wide turn to the north and came on track again.

"About one fifty."

"Cut it to one thirty if you can. Then drop. Try about four hundred feet. There isn't anything in your way" I advised.

"Roger."

It looked like the plane was at about five hundred as it came in over the houses at the end of the field. The engines were throttled back. Colored cargo chutes blossomed and floated gently to the ground as the plane roared over the south end of the field and made a wide turn. The plane dipped its wings left and right and then headed for home.

"Beautiful! Beautiful!" I complimented them.

""Thanks buddy. We'll be seeing you tomorrow. Roger. Over and out."

"Thanks guys. I'll send you the cleaning bill. You lucky bastards!" I waved at them even though I knew they were far gone and couldn't see me.

"Man! You sure are a mess. You sure you aren't bleeding? Look." Mac reached for my side. "Here's a hunk of glass sticking to you." He threw it into the field.

"I think I'm okay. That's the last drop for today. We had better get the stuff picked up fast before the Chinks run off with it."

I saw the pickup crew on the truck coming out of the main gate.

"Hey! You think maybe you taste sweet?" the truck driver shouted as he slowed to pass us.

"Nuts!" I replied laughing.

I was the butt of many jokes as I made my way through the compound to the bath house. I placed the W.T. in a safe place and took off my shoes. Men watched me curiously, pausing in their bathing, as I made my way to the water tubs in the center of the floor.

"What'cha cooking man?" one of them asked.

"Cocoa," I answered as I picked up one of the wood buckets and dipped water. I washed my shoes and set them aside.

"Hey! Ain't you gonna undress?"

"What for?" I answered as I doused myself, clothes, ketchup, cocoa and all. After repeated dousings the goo came loose from my hair and clothes. I stripped and washed thoroughly. After I finished I walked back to my bunk naked, carrying my clothes, shoes and the WT. I dressed in clean clothes, hung my wet stuff to dry and headed for the Administration Building to report on the drops.

I was introduced to the men gathered in the large room that the Japs had used as an office. The men who had parachuted in were identified as an O.S.S. team. They told me that the mission had been named "Operation Cardinal".

Major Hennessey, in command of the operation.

Major Rob Lamar, Medical Officer.

Sergeant Ed Starz.

Sergeant Harry Leith.

Sergeant Fumico Kido, Nisie, interpreter.

"What happened to the Chinese that was with you?" I asked Major Hennessey.

"Major Cheng-Shi-Wu took off for parts unknown." he answered non-commitally.

"How come Major?"

"Who knows? Looks like he wanted to join his Chinese buddies."

I wondered at the nonchalant answer. It seemed to me that there was too little attention being given to what could have been turned a defection or maybe even desertion. I looked around at the other team members who didn't seem at all concerned with the event. I wondered if maybe there was more to it than that.

"You ask a lot of questions for an enlisted man." Hennessey gave me a look that struck me as being more than just ordinary.

"I was a combat photographer and I worked with G2. Guess maybe I was just interested. Then the people who have worked with us are in contact with Chang Ki Chek's group. I guess there is an underground all through the area."

"Good."

I was baffled by the remark and the fact that there was nothing else said by the team or by our camp officers.

Major Lamar and Sergeant Leith were preparing to leave. Their mission was to head north to Sian to find, free, and return with General Wainwright. They ordered one of the Jap officers to accompany them on the trip. I gathered that they were taking one of the camp staff cars for the journey.

Sergeant Starz and I sat on the side and listened as the discussion concerning the take-over of the camp from the Japs. We asked questions and I supplied answers about the camp and the factories that the Senior Officers couldn't answer.

"How did the air drop go?" Hennessey asked after the discussion turned to other things. "Was there much stuff lost?"

"Not much. Only the stuff that slammed in because the chutes didn't open. Some of the stuff went through the roof of the warehouse and Takai's factory. Everything was recovered. There are a couple of big holes in the roofs of both places. About a dozen holes. The happy fly boys were having a ball. Couple of cowboys I guess. And the truck in the yard got clobbered. No one hurt that I know of." Everyone laughed at the results of the cargo bombing.

"How about the rifles and the ammo?" Hennessey asked.

"No strain. Everything came down okay. Everybody wanted to make sure that we recovered the stuff before the Manchus got to it." I emphasized our anxiety concerning the arms and ammunition. "I don't know if we'll need them, but I am not going into town without a rifle. That is for sure!"

"Can't blame you." Ed agreed. "You could have your throat cut for a pair of shoes out there."

" How do you expect to make it into town?" Hennessey asked, frowning.

"I have already picked up a bike. It's the best way to travel around here."

The officers looked at me. I saw some frowns.

"When are you going to town?" someone asked.

"As soon as we are told that the Russians have cleared up this official release business."

"Seems to me like you haven't waited for that. How the hell did you manage to get a bicycle?"

"Well, I made a deal for one with one of the Manchus that I know. No one stopped me from going out, so I started to explore."

I got some head shakes from a couple of the officers and a smile from General Parker.

I figured that it was alright. I wondered if the fact that I had stepped out and offered to take care of the air drop had set me aside for some reason. Whatever it was, I was taking advantage of it.

CHAPTER 44 -- THE MUKDEN RUSSIANS

The Russians came in on Monday, August the twentieth, nineteen forty-five!

Colonel Kamrakoff of the USSR, and twenty-five of his officers and enlisted men arrived at ten in the morning. The official transfer of the camp to the Americans took all day. There were all kinds of little things that the Russians wanted understood because they were the ones who officially occupied Manchuria. There was very little that really affected us. I was under the impression that the formalities were due to the fact that the Russians wanted to lay claim to whatever they could strip and send back to Russia. It took until eight thirty in the evening before the Russians left and we were in charge of the Mukden POW Camp.

Colonel Kamrakoff wished us good luck and drove away.

General George Parker was now the official camp commander.

I tried to locate some whiskey or beer in the settlements around the camp to celebrate. I was told that the Japs hadn't allowed any alcoholic beverages. I didn't believe that. I decided that I would locate something in Mukden.

On Tuesday, the twenty-first, Kozie, Mac and I, decided to search Mukden for something to drink. We had never been in the city before. We asked directions of the Manchus who were very cooperative and evidently quite happy that the Japs were no longer in charge. We found the Old Walled City, the ancient site of Mukden, Shenyang, that we were told dated back some two thousand years. It was the old palace. It was a fascinating structure that reminded me of the other cities in the interior of China.

It turned out that it was only a few miles from camp to the center of town. We were gawked at, stared at, and questioned as we walked through the city. The Manchus were dumbfounded at the sight of Americans in the city of Mukden. Those that spoke English wanted answers to a thousand questions. We were directed to a colony of White Russians, survivors and refugees of the Russian Revolution. They lived near the center of the city. They were not only friendly but eager to welcome us into their midst. They introduced us to the middle and upper class Manchurians, the business people and the influential group that were evidently going to take over Manchuria now that the Japs had been defeated. Invitations to the homes of both the Russians and the Manchus were numerous. Since the three of us, Mac, Kozie and I were a venturesome trio, we visited with the Russians, partied with them, and celebrated our freedom. We stayed with them for three days and enjoyed ourselves. We decided we had better return to camp and find out what was going on, and to find out when we would be leaving for home. We found out that very few men left camp, happy to stay there and enjoy their freedom, and the food that had been delivered in the air drops. No more air drops had occurred in the three days that we were gone.

"How come that you haven't gone to town?" I asked Cy.

"What the hell for? Who the hell wants to roam around China? Not me! I ain't interested in any of the Chinks. It's white women and American food for me. I'm taking it easy until we get out of here." He eyed me curiously. "Where the hell have you been for the last few days anyway?"

Ed had joined us while Cy was spouting off. He waved and sat down.

"In Mukden. The people still call it Hoten. I guess it is because the Japs have been here for so long that they do it out of habit. Some of the Manchus say that the old name is something like Shenyang. And as for hobnobbing with the Chinks," I teased Cy, "you should see some of the rich ones. We were at a banquet yesterday that was like something out of Hollywood."

"What?"

"Where at?" Cy jumped with the question. "What do you mean," he paused, "a Hollywood production?"

"We were at Chang's place. Man what a spread! You wouldn't believe it! Terrific! We had a ball!"

"You kidding?" Ed asked in utter disbelief.

"No, I guess he isn't kidding," Cy said with a show of envy. "The son of a bitch will fall into a shit trench and comes up with a diamond ring! Where was this at?"

"In town. And we ran into a colony of White Russians that have been living here since the end of World War One."

"What? White women? Where?"Ed was suddenly interested.

"Hey! You mean that there are white people in this country?" Cy's eyes were bugged out in surprise.

"Sure are. And you should see some of the women! Blondes yet!" I was enjoying myself immensely as I related our adventures.

"Go on! You're kidding." Ed looked at me as though I was crazy. "You mean that there are white people who have been living here all these years!And we didn't know about it."

"Yes. Sure as hell are."

"What the hell makes you think that white people are special?" Cy looked annoyed as he questioned Ed. "They live all over you know."

"Yeah .. but... well, I mean," Ed stuttered into silence.

"Well, anyway we got to know some of them. Melichka, Millie for short. Her sister Vera ... oh! They happen to have some family, a sister I think, living in Brooklyn. Name of Murphy. I have the address here somewhere." I searched my pockets for the piece of paper on which I had written the address.

"Brooklyn? Who's from Brooklyn?" Sol Fromer had joined the group during the discussion.

"Somebody that lives here in Mukden had some relations in Brooklyn." I smiled at him.

"Really! White people or Chinks?" He pushed through the group to get close. "Who are they?"

"Some White Russians in Mukden have relatives in Brooklyn, not Coney Island Sol." I laughed. "Brooklyn is pretty big. They couldn't be neighbors of yours." I had found the paper I had been looking for. "Here. Murphy, Olga. Three six six Evergreen. That can't be close to Coney Island. Now can it?"

"Nah! I don't think so," Sol answered. "But hell, it's Brooklyn. That makes us neighbors " Everyone enjoyed a good laugh.

"When are you going back?" Ed asked.

"Later on today." I settled back on my bunk. "We heard that there is a brewery in town, somewhere in the southwestern part of town. Not far from the railroad depot from what we were told." I snickered at the group. "We are going to requisition some beer. Melichka lives at 18 Wu Wei Lao. She says that it isn't far from her place."

"Do you think that the stinking Japs that own the place are going just hand it over to you because you ask?" Cy's curiosity and thirst were both aroused.

"Nope." I reached into my musette bag and brought forth the Luger.

"HEY!"

"What the hell?"

MAN! Let's see that."

I released the magazine and pulled back the slide to eject the cartridge. The men crowded around. More men came in from the other sections as the ruckus spread word of something going on.

"Man! You would be the one. Wouldn't you?" Cy puckered his lips and shook his head in admiration.

The Luger was passed around from hand to hand as I watched it closely. Handling the weapon made the men realize that in truth they weren't prisoners any more.

"Pete! How? That's all I want to know. How?" And where?" Cy sat staring at me in wonder.

"A Russian pilot that I met. Tolek. A-n-a-t-o-l-i U-g-a-r-o-f-f. Tolek. He's a junior lieutenant from what I can gather. A pretty good egg too. I traded." I lorded it over the group, enjoying their praise and amazement.

"It's a beaut. But where did Tol ...Tolek? get a hold of it?" Cy bounced around in his eagerness.

"He picked it up in Berlin a couple of months ago." I informed them. "He's from Moscow." I pulled out my new notebook and flipped through the pages. "Tolek. Really Anatoli S. Ugaroff. Poselok Kostonaevo, No.1 Flat 7, Moskaw."

"Here's some numbers on this Pete, I mean Joe." Cy looked close at the frame of the Luger. "Number 621469 and the slide has a 1257 on it. Where did he pick it up? Berlin you said?"

"That was his story. I repeated as I reached for the Luger. I loaded the cartridge into the clip and slapped the clip into the butt.

"Do you think that that is going to help you requisition some beer?" Cy asked.

"Sure as hell gives him some bartering power. Huh?" Ed smirked. Everyone laughed.

"Hey, how come you got a permanent pass Pete?" Sol asked. "The rest of us got only one day passes. You some thing special?"

"Well." I slipped the Luger under my belt under my shirt. "I managed to get my hands on a camera. I borrowed one from Murata." There was a lot of happy laughter at the information that some one had gotten something of Murata's. "And then I was handed a thirty-five millimeter camera, Army issue. I am supposed to take pictures around here. Officially I am still a Combat Photographer." Snickers and remarks like "horseshit" were heard. I laughed. "Well, anyway, Major Hennessey thinks that we should have pictures for the official record. Parker and Beebe aren't so sure. I don't know why the hell not. I think that they are afraid of some kind of horseshit about war crimes. But, since the generals don't want to cause the Major any problems I am the photographer and I have a permanent pass." I dug out the pass and held it up for all to see. It was grabbed for and passed around and then handed back.

"Hey!" this says from seven in the morning until seven at night. You haven't been around for three days." Sol squinted from his good eye.

"So it ain't safe to roam the streets at night. I stay with friends."

"Man! You are a sneaky conniver!" Sol muttered.

"You sure can snow people." Ed snickered. "Wait when they catch up with you." He warned.

"Yeah. could be. But until they do..." I left it unfinished.

CHAPTER 45 -- SABERS

Kozy came by after lunch and we searched out Mac. We started for town in a happy mood.

"Let's try the other avenue," Kozy suggested after we had left the Walled City. "We might run into something interesting and we can see more of the city."

"Great." Mac agreed.

"Hell! I thought we were going to find ourselves a brewery." I objected. "It's the middle of the afternoon already. After two I guess."

None of us had a watch. We had all been relieved of watches and jewelry in the Philippines.

"Hey! Hey! Over here!" We heard someone shout in English after we had traveled about a mile through the streets of the city, heading in a generally westward direction.

"Where's that coming from?"

We searched the fenced yards along the street. We didn't see anyone right off hand.

"Over here! Over here!"

"Look! Over there." Mac pointed up the street to an iron fenced area.

"HEY! HEY! Over here!"

We double timed to the fence which was about a hundred yards away. There were three people leaning over the fence waving and shouting to attract our attention.

"Hello hello hello!" Smiles and laughter greeted us.

"Who are you people?" Kozy was the first to reach the fence. "How long have you been here?" Kozy stood in the street in the same state of shock as Mac and I.

"Who are you?" They shouted. "Are you Americans? Where are you from?" They asked questions in machine-gun rapidity. We couldn't answer the profusion of questions that they were asking. "Come on in. Around the side here."

We made our way up the street to the gate in the fence. We managed to piece together their story after about an hour of questions, answers and conversation. We told them our story and they told us theirs.

There were some twenty odd people in the compound. English and Americans. It was a Civilian Internee Camp. There were women, men and children. They had been interned in December of nineteen forty-one. Neither the Red Cross or any other agency had ever contacted them. No one but the Japs knew they existed or were interned in Mukden.

Our own story was as incredible to them as theirs was to us.

"We'll pass on your location to our officers at camp. I'll make certain that they will inform the Red Cross and our Embassy. I guess they will be able to find the right people in Japan to inform the British." We promised to visit them again soon.

"Man it's too late too try and find the brewery now. Suppose that we head for Millie's for the night and then tomorrow we can find the brewery and pass on the information about the Civilian Internees."

We partied well on into the night at Millie's along with a bunch of Russians that we rounded up in the streets.

"Let's go." Kozy was anxious to get started after we had breakfasted on a Russian feast of a breakfast. "Millie gave me directions. I can't miss." Kozy assured Mac and me as we started up the street in front of Millie's. "So let's go."

After we walked about a half a mile, Kozy led us into a large circle, a hub with a monument in the center. The streets radiated like spokes from a wheel.

"That is some monument." Kozie stared at the huge stone memorial. "I wonder from which war it's from."

"Who cares. Where the hell is the brewery?" Mac quashed Kozie's curiosity with a note of sarcasm.

"We make a right turn," Kozie ignored Mac's sarcastic tone.

"Better be right or we're lost." Mac snorted.

"Supposing that we get separated?" I asked. "Where do we meet?"

"How about at Tania's? Or should it be Millie's place?" Kozie mused. "Maybe it will be easier to find Millie's since it is on the main drag."

"Suits me. How about it Mac? Think that we could find Millie's place again?"

"Sure, no sweat!" Mac retorted. "Now let's get balls out and find that damned brewery. I'm thirsty."

"Okay okay!" Kozie answered and led us to the northwest around the circle. After about five blocks we approached a bombed out building.

"That must have been where they dropped the bombs last year, in December." I observed.

"Yeah!" Kozie answered. "Too bad they didn't drop one of those atomic gizmos on it." His voice had that nasty tone that most of us found coming through when we spoke about the Japs.

"There! That looks like some kind of a factory. Let's take a look." Kozy decided for us.

"Tovarich! Tovarich!"

"RUSSIANS!" Mac yelled. "I'll be damned."

The Russian soldiers descended on us enmass. There were a half dozen of various grades of ranks that we couldn't decipher.

We introduced ourselves as Americans, ex-POWs.

"Vun Kozakovich," I pointed to Kozie. "Macarovich," I pointed to Mac and then to myself. "Yah Petak."

After much handshaking and bear hugging, back pounding and helloing, we squatted on the street curb. The Russians broke out a batch of thick water glasses, tumblers, and unslung the magnum bottles that they had slung with rope slings over their shoulders. They pulled the corks with their teeth and started to pour the liquor. They poured half glasses of the liquid.

"Vodka! Piit! Truman!" The Russian tilted the glass and drank. His comrades followed suit.

"Holy hell! What kind of drinking is that?" Mac bug-eyed the Russians.

The glasses were refilled, three quarters full this time. They passed them to us and waited.

"Stalin! Hoy!" I had heard from Tolek about Stalin as the hero of the Russians all through the war. I figured it was the best bet. The warm sweetish liquid scalded my mouth and my throat as it seared its way to my belly. My eyes watered, I inhaled and choked. "Whoot! What vodka!"

The Russians roared. They liked the response they got from me. Kozie and Mac had been watching me intently. Their glassed were still three quarters full.

"Tovarich!" Mac downed the liquid dynamite. He gulped and gasped.

"Stalin! Roosevelt!" Kozie drained his glass. He smacked his eyes closed and snorted. "Man! That stuff is worse than Pink Lady!"

Everyone laughed. Mac and Kozie started the conversation. They both could speak Polish and Russian well enough to carry on an easy exchange.

"Yah, I, Sartok. Sergeant!" One of the Russians thumbed his chest. He pointed to the GI issue camera, the olive drab colored Kodak that I had slung over my shoulder. He opened a leather pouch that hung at his waist. He opened it to expose packets of ten yen notes, neatly stacked and cramming the case. I estimate it to be about eight by six by six inches. "Okay?" He pointed to the camera.

"Nyet!" I shook my head. I explained that it was Army issue, "Not for sale" in my brand of Russian. I wasn't getting through. "Kozie. Kozie. Explain to Sergeant Sartok that this is U.S. Army property and that I can't sell it to him. Not for sale at any price. Its my ass if I loose it."

He started a heated discussion with Sartok that left me behind.

Another glass of vodka was thrust into my hand. I gulped the fiery stuff and handed back the glass amidst admiring looks by the Russians.

"Mac," I grabbed his arm to break him loose of the conversation that he was involved in with one of the other sergeants. "Mac."

He turned to me, straining to focus his eyes. "Hey Pete! How's it going?"

I was surprised to note that in the fifteen or twenty minutes that we had been sitting there that the alcohol had taken effect. I wondered, momentarily, if we had been there longer.

"Mac," I shook him, "listen. I'm going to bug out. I don't want to get into any trouble with the Russians over the camera. I'll see you guys at Millie's. Okay?"

Mac straightened his back with an effort, then with a stiff wrist he passed his hand in front of this face, palm out, "Check you Czech." He gave me an idiotic smile, happy and not giving a damn about anything.

"See you later." I rose and left as the group continued some heated discussion. The Russians didn't notice my hasty retreat to the main boulevard some hundreds of feet to the west. I turned the corner and took a fast look back, no one bothered about me. I continued on for six blocks. I heard the rumbling of hundreds of people and wondered just what the hell was going on. I turned a corner and entered a broad street that led to a building that couldn't be anything else except a railroad station. The street and the depot were swarming with Manchus and Japs. People. Women, children, men, were all rushing around in what was near panic. The scene was something that was out of a movie. Both Manchus and Japs kowtowed, bowed, fumed at me and skittered out of my way. I towered over the mass of people and had a good view of what was going on in the huge shed that housed the trains. Occasionally I spotted a tall Manchu. All were rushing to the station. I noticed then that there was a clear space of about ten feet all around me. They all avoided me. The circle, was a No Man's Land for any of them that followed me as I moved to the building and entered the station. An engine was puffing steam as though ready to race away to the south. It was a pandemonium of bodies that were pushing, yelling, pushing and screeching as they fought their way into the cars that were already cram packed. The men started to climb on to the tops of the cars, leaving the cars for women and children. There was all kinds of baggage littering the floor. There wasn't enough room for the people and their personal belongings on the train.

I called to a young Jap that was rushing to climb up on one of the cars. "Oi. Nanda. Doeste." I pointed to the train.

"Oi..." his speech was so fast that I couldn't grasp a single word. The noise mad it additionally difficult.

"Matti matti," I commanded him to wait. "Yukkuri harase. Speak slow."
""Oi, gomenasie," he bowed and apologized. "Dozo. Kore wa. Kiska..."
The train whistle hooted and drowned his answer. The engineer blasted
the whistle again as a warning as the engine started to puff massive
clouds of steam. He ran to the nearest car and started to climb aboard.
He lost a cloth wrapped bundle as he joined the men on the top of the
car. The drive wheels of the engine spun and screamed as the steam
drove the piston back and forth. The train started to move slowly. The
crowd of people all crammed into and onto the train leaving only a few
who made their way, running, to the exits. I wandered around the
station. I found a check room at one end of the building. By the time that
I had reached the door the station was empty. I wondered if it was the
last train south, away from the advancing Russians. I paused
momentarily and wondered about the how and why of the train with the
Russians already in Mukden. I was puzzled by the total evacuation. I
received some strange looks from some unsavory looking Manchus as I
entered the check room. I unbuttoned the flap of the Luger holster
pulled the weapon out. I checked to make sure that I had loaded a
cartridge into the chamber and snapped the safety to show "Gesichart"
and hefted the solid deadly mechanism. I was glad that I had traded a
pair of GI shoes for the gun. Tolek had been insistent on the trade. I had
figured it to be unequal, but Tolek had been happy. There was some
kind of hard assurance of power in the feel of the butt of the gun in my
hand. The eight rounds I had loaded into the magazine washed away
the sense of helplessness that had flooded me momentarily as I realized
that I was all alone. There was no other American, no other Caucasian
around. I knew that I was stupid to be wandering around alone in a war
zone with God knows what kind of characters around. I shoved the
Luger back into the holster and entered the baggage check room.

I stood open mouthed at the sight. There were hundreds, thousands
of bundles of clothing, kimonos and other personal belongings that
overflowed from the immense adjoining back room. The bundles had
been ripped apart and scavenged for anything of value. Expensive silk
embroidered kimonos, obiis and a variety of clothing were scattered
everywhere. I rummaged through the bins that formed the walls of the
room. I was in sudden shock as I moved some clothing and exposed a
hoard of sabers. "WOW! Sabers!" A coveted treasure. Japanese officers
sabers. I counted twenty-two. I selected a tapestry like cloth and spread
it on an area of the floor that I had kicked clear with my feet. I laid the
swords in a neat pile on the cloth except for one that I laid aside. I
bundled, rolled and tied them. I hefted the bundle and staggered under
its surprising weight. They weighed about seventy pounds. I lowered my

booty to the floor. I fastened the saber I had laid aside to my belt and hefted the bundle to my shoulder. I kicked aside bundles and packages as I made my way to the door. One package broke open as I kicked, spilling yen as it skittered away. I dropped the sabers and methodically salvaged the paper money. There were thousands and thousands of yen. "Hell!" I complained aloud to no one, "Probably not worth over twenty dollars American." I realized that the actual value of the money at the rate of exchange made the huge amount practically valueless. "Oh well," I caught myself speaking aloud again. I stuffed the money into various pockets of my coveralls. I picked up my sabers and continued on to the street. I hailed one of the local taxis, a horse drawn open Victoria, and directed him, left here, right there until we reached Millie's. I paid him with some of the money I had found. He grinned happily as he drove off with the Japanese money.

The gathering at Millie's were a terrific audience, they thoroughly enjoyed my story of the acquisition of the sabers.

Kozie and Mac put on a real smash and were in no shape to return to camp. I didn't want to travel alone at night with my treasure trove in a panicky city of Manchus, Japs, and trigger happy Russians. I decided to stay and go back in the morning.

CHAPTER 46 -- BEER

Saturday morning was hung over for most of the crowd. I was more fortunate since I had spent my time eating instead of drinking. I had also done a lot of talking. I was clear headed and hungry. Millie served up a massive breakfast of eggs, fried pork and heavy black bread. I washed mine down with sweet milk that had been obtained by devious means.

It was decided that we were going to find the brewery come hell or high water. I left the sabers, except for the one I carried on my belt, and started off with Kozie and Mac. We had clearer directions this time. We hired a large barouche, a four wheeled horse drawn carriage, with the driver sitting up high in the front. It had two double seats facing each other, and had, at one time had a folding top over the back seat that had long ago disappeared. Millie gave the Manchu explicit directions in Chinese. The trip to the brewery took under twenty minutes at a leisurely pace.

We approached the grounds which were extensive. There was a great open are of lawn that bordered the road. The factory itself sat at the bottom of the "U" shaped driveway. The front of the building was of red brick. There was a porticoed terrace that was the entry to the main building through what was an extensive office area. The terrace was flagstoned and raised three steps above the level of the driveway. Umbrelled tables were scattered about. One of the tables was occupied by a few Japs, fat, prosperous looking Japs.

"Pretty nice looking place, eh?" Mac made a wry face of approval. "Wonder what the beer is like?"

"Jap beer is supposed to be pretty good. Not that you would remember though." I joshed him.

"What do you mean, not that I would remember?" Mac drawled back at me.

""Hell, I don't think that you could tell which the chaser was last night, the vodka or the beer." I laughed.

"Ah!" Mac waved me away.

The barouche stopped at the foot of the stairs that led to the terrace. One of the plump Japs, sweating and worried looking trotted out from the door that was held open for him by a younger Jap.

"Ohio goziemus. O hairi dozo." He bowed and scraped and kowtowed. He ushed us on to the terrace.

"Hotori po Ruskie?" Kozie asked him.

"Wakaran. Gomen kudasie." The rollie pollie Jap bowed to Kozie.

"He doesn't understand," I mouthed the words over the Japs head. "Speak Russian." I pointed to the three of us.

"Nippongo dekimas ka." The Jap turned and addressed me.

"Hai." I spat the word out with a gutteral sound. "Oramae wa non desku ka."

"Honashi."

"So, Honashi San. Watakushi wa Petaku." I placed my fingers on my chest. I indicated Kozie, "Kore wa Kozakevitch." I pointed to Mac, "Kore was Macarovich."

"Ah so. Roshoyajin. Omeni kokette ureshu gozai masu." He bowed as he professed how happy he was to meet us. He had assumed that we were Russians.

""Kore was - biiru kaisha ka." I questioned him, asking if it was a beer company.

"Hai. Kooba" He acknowledged, calling it a factory.

"Kudasie." He indicated that he wanted us to sit down at one of the tables. "Raku ni shite kudasie." After we had seated ourselves he shouted in the direction of the brewery entrance.

I noticed that the Japs that had been sitting at the table had disappeared inside.

A young Jap came out so fast that he must have been waiting there for the order. He carried a massive Japanned tray with four large moisture coated bottles and four mugs. The bottles were ice cold and wet.

"Kudasie." The beer was poured all around.

Mac held up his glass, looked at it momentarily and proceeded to inhale an immense draught. "Yoi!" He exploded after he had downed half of its contents.

The Jap smiled at the appreciation that Mac exhibited. He sat and joined us.

Mac and Kozie started a conversation in Polish. The Jap brewery manager sat and listened in amazed silence.

"How about we ask him to load up the wagon with beer for us?" Kozie asked in Polish.

I nodded in agreement. I informed the manager in Japanese that we wanted the carriage loaded with cases of the one liter bottles of beer. Loaded to the top. He needed little urging as he eyed the saber and the Luger. I had no doubt that he was well aware that it was a Luger. It seemed as though the weapons made him extremely nervous. Within minutes the beer was loaded. The barouche was stacked with cases in the foot well and up to the top of the backs of the seats.

"We had better leave before there any problems," Mac warned us in Polish. "I wouldn't want to loose any of that beer."

"Let's go Pete." Kozie continued to speak in Polish.

"Doomo arigato gozaimus." I rose and bowed to the Jap, expressing our thanks.

"Do itashi mashite."

"Arigato." Both Kozie and Mac bowed politely to the Jap.

We started to walk slowly to the barouche when shouting started at the gate as some commotion broke out.

"VAMOOS!" Kozie shouted. "RUSSIANS."

We made a dash for the Victoria. The Jap manager stood petrified. I took time to wonder if he was going to shit his pants as I joined Mac and Kozie. Our Manchu driver was shaking. The shouts were now being punctuated by shots. A burp of machine-gun fire erupted.

"RUSSIANS! Stinking Russians!" Mac shouted. Russians coming." He pointed to two carriages bouncing and rattling as the Russians riding them urged their drivers with the muzzles of their guns.

Mac and Kozie jumped to the top of the beer cases as I bounded up to join the Manchu driver in the front seat. The driver knew exactly what was expected of him. He didn't want to be caught by the Russians either.

The horse exploded into a run. I urged the driver and the horse to greater speed as the Russians raced down the driveway to the factory entrance.

I really didn't know if the Russians would raise hell with us and confiscate the beer, but we weren't about to wait and find out. The beer was there for the taking and we took.

We broke out into the street shouting at the people, the carts and the skies. We waved the Chinese away from in front of us as we urged our driver to keep going come hell or Russians. Kozie and Mac were pantomining, waving the people in the streets to bunch up behind us and block the Russians.

The Russians had been so excited that they locked the wheels of their carriages as they made the turn near the terrace. I caught sight of them as they separated the carts and resumed the chase.

"Let's go! GO! GO!" Mac was shouting at the driver.

Chinamen cursed and made nasty motions at us as we raced along the crowded street. "Wamba. Wamba tuso." There were other unintelligible remarks that followed us as they scattered in front of us and then closed in behind the carriage as we raced frantically through Mukden.

The peculiar sense of humor that the Chinaman exhibits at times came to our rescue even as bullets whizzed through the air from the Russian burp guns. The Chinese refused to move out of the way when the Russians entered the street. They moved sluggishly as the Russians threatened them and then cajoled them. The Chinese shouted back at the Russians, the drivers and the horses. The Russians dropped behind as we pelted down the road now being urged on by the crowd in the street. Bottles of beer jogged out of the cases and exploded in great blobs of foam and froth as they hit the street. We, Kozie, Mac and I, bounced and rolled around on the top of the cases as we grabbed for bottles and hung on to the cases. Laughter and jibes and shouts of amusement followed us until we turned a corner some eight blocks from the brewery.

"HOI. Hoi. Mati." I ordered the apoplectic driver.

The driver pulled back on the reins and the panting horses slowed to a walk.

"Man oh man!" I laughed as I settled down on the top of the cases. "That was like a Keystone Cops movie scene. Fantastic!" I burst out into uncontrollable laughter, relieving laughter.

"How about that? How about that now?" Kozie shouted between his chortling laughter.

Mac lay doubled over with laughter on top of the cases. The Chinese in the streets smiled at us as we drove through the streets. We directed our driver to Millie's place. There were many helping hands at Millie's. The carriage was unloaded in record time and the well paid driver, happy with the money we paid him, drove off mumbling and waving at us as he drove out of sight.

That evening we returned to camp in another barouche with our booty. We smuggled the beer into camp. We had gotten away with thirty cases. We had left a supply of fifteen cases, less the bounced out losses, at Millie's. The cases of beer were arranged into bunks, with our mattresses on top and blankets draped over the sides and ends. Sunday, after Mass, turned into a beer bash that took its toll of the beer supply.

In the afternoon Sergeants Ed Starz and Harry leith, Fumico Kido and Major Jim Hennessey, the OSS Team, joined us. The bull session brought out the details of their adventure when they parachuted in on the sixteenth of August. Hennessey and Starz did most of the talking.

They had never seen Mukden before. It was a blind mission and they had been told that it was a very high risk mission. It was code named Cardinal.

"Major Lamar was the first to go through the hatch. By the time I jumped everybody had dropped, their chutes were open and everything seemed to be going pretty well. We had been sweating the fuel situation ever since we had left Hsian just after midnight. The crew was sweating the return trip." Hennessey paused, "We dropped in on a vegetable field over there." He pointed to the north of camp and wet his whistle with a large slug of beer. "When we finally got all of the equipment together I ordered Ed and Major Cheng to stay with the gear while the rest of us went off to make contact with the Japs. The Manchus gave us the directions we needed and warned us about the Japs. They said the Japs were ready to shoot any paratroopers on sight. It wasn't more than a matter of minutes when the Japs from the camp surrounded us. We told them that the war was over. They said they didn't know anything about the war being over. That made me sweat. There was no telling what they might do. We couldn't tell what the hell they were thinking. I suppose the worst was that they would shoot us as paratroopers."

"And," Ed Starz filled in, "it started to rain. We got the Manchus to help us carry the equipment to a shack that is just on the edge of the field."

"The Japs started to prod us with the bayonets, damned bayonets." Hennessey snarled. "They moved us out of the rain into one of the Manchu houses. After talking to Kido here, they sent some of the soldiers to bring in Ed and Cheng. We had some time hassling with the Jap officers. They were a couple of pricks. I think that one of them may have been Murata, but I am not sure."

"Yeah, that was okay, but you didn't get stripped like we did. They didn't give us our clothes back until the truck came to pick us up." Ed Starz filled in.

"Yeah, we know only too well. The Japs have this thing, I guess it's a psychological approach, they like to strip the captive. Gives them some kind of an edge over the guy who doesn't have any clothes on. They've done it to us regularly, and it ain't too see how big a dick you've got either." There was a general spattering of laughter as I finished my input.

"They took us to some military installation. Then after some more talk they got in touch with Matsuda and told him our story. They brought us here when you people saw us." Hennessey paused and motioned to me, "You were the first guy I saw, weren't you?"

"Yep. We figured that you would be brought in through the gate and into the Jap area." I smiled in self satisfaction.

"Right. Well, Matsuda said that he would have to have higher authority give him the word. In the meantime, so as not to mess up any more than necessary, we would be put up in the hotel in town. We spent the night at the Yamato in downtown Mukden. You know the rest Pete, except that Cheng took off for reasons of his own."

"Sure scared the hell out of you for a while didn't they?" someone in the back commented.

"Sure did." Hennessey admitted.

"Now you have an idea of what it's been like for three and a half years."

"Amen!" I interjected. "What about Wainwright? Think he's okay?"

"We haven't heard from Lamar. I guess that they should be getting back from Sian either tomorrow or the next day. They are overdue now." The words weren't emphasized with much confidence I noted.

Everyone expected trouble at Sian.

CHAPTER 47 -- GENERAL J. WAINWRIGHT

Sunday, the twenty-sixth of August, word spread through camp that General "Skinny" Wainwright was to arrive in Mukden. He was to be quartered at the Yamato Hotel. Everyone that I talked to was relieved and happy to hear that their General was in fair health and safe.

I decided to pay him a visit on the twenty-seventh, Monday. The rest of the guys told me I was nuts. I left camp at seven thirty in the morning and pedaled my way into town in just about a half hour. I found a safe place for the bike and headed for the lobby. American officers eyed me skeptically. Some of them waved and some smiled in amusement at my outfit.

"What kind of a getup is that?" The lieutenant was one that I did not remember seeing before. He had a broad amused grin on his skinny face. "A Jap saber, and," he looked at the holstered Luger, "and what kind of an automatic is that anyway? Not a real Luger?!" He stared at the weapon in surprise.

"Sure is lieutenant," I answered with a self satisfied smirk.

"How in the hell did you manage that stuff? We've only been free for about a week!" He was genuinely admiring my acquisitions.

"Well..." I hesitated.

"Yeah, I know, better not to ask questions. But what are you doing here?"

"I came to see the General. I was told that he was here. Word is that he is leaving right away and I wanted to see him." I was hoping that the officer wasn't going to be an obstacle.

"But you're an enlisted man!" The lieutenant was surprised at my answer.

"Yes sir. I am." My response was staightforward. "I happen to know the General personally. Fort McKinley and the Rock. Corregidor. I photographed him during the war. I was a combat photographer."

"Yeah! So now you think that he will see you?" He smiled at my temerity.

The other officers that were around the lobby, a couple of majors, some colonels and three generals looked at us occasionally, but they didn't seem overly concerned.

"What makes you think that you can see the general if that brass over there can't?" The lieutenant was amazed.

"Just tell him Combat Photographer Petak is here and wants to say
415

hello." I stated with self assurance that stopped the officer cold.

"He's on the second floor. I think that you should leave your artillery with me. I'll take good care of it."

I looked around the lobby, eyed the officers and then re-examined the lieutenant. One of the colonels broke away from the group of officers and joined us.

"What's going on lieutenant?"

Staid Army protocol had already returned.

"This man says that he is a friend of the General's. He wants to say hello." A smile played around the lieutenant's mouth as he answered the major.

"WHAT?" The colonel was upset by the idea, especially since it came from an enlisted man. He turned and walked away to rejoin the group of officers without a word.

The lieutenant looked at me and shrugged. "I can't let you up there. I have orders."

"Want to sell any of your souvenirs?" he asked.

"I may have a few sabers to sell, but not the Luger."

"Really?" The lieutenant's interest was sparked. "How much?"

"I don't know. I haven't found out what the going rate is yet." I remarked.

I headed for the door and camp.

No one in camp believed me when I told them about the General being at the hotel. I was disgusted at the reception and decided to get out of camp and take a ride. I picked up the camera and a couple of rolls of film and started out with no particular destination in mind.

I started toward town when a thought struck me. I would retrace the route that we had used to the old Chinese Army Camp. I had no trouble finding the path that we had used in the first days that we had trekked to MKK. Only... there wasn't any camp. The Japs had torn it down completely. I could make out traces of the road and the paths that had existed in between the barracks. The barracks pits had been filled in and leveled. There were no fences, no fence posts, and no guard tower. I would not have been able to locate the area if I hadn't been very familiar with it. The old war memorial had been the key to its location.

I stared around at the bare ground. "I'll be damned. They covered their tracks." I wondered, perhaps aloud. "They didn't want any traces of the POWs left."

There was no proof, not a shred of evidence that a camp had ever existed at the spot. There was absolutely nothing to be seen. I rode down the road to the Jap-Russian War Monument and stopped to photograph it. The thought struck me that the graveyard must still be up on the hill north of the camp. I returned to the camp site and turned on to the dirt road that led to the highway and up the hill to the graveyard.

Surprise! There were a lot of people gathered there when I arrived. A mass was being held for our dead. I had not heard of anything about it in camp. I attended the Mass and then photographed the ceremonies. I found that the people were the local population and clergy, Protestant and Catholic, had gathered to pay homage to our dead. After the Mass ended I started back to town.

I had traveled for about ten minutes, moving rapidly toward Mukden along the surprisingly smooth roadway when I overhauled a group of Jap soldiers. I stopped a distance back, not sure of what I should do. They were all armed. I watched the group as they marched ahead of me, a distance of about fifty yards. I was puzzling about passing them or turning into the fields and by passing them when my course of action was decided for me by one of the soldiers who had turned and looked behind. He spotted me and shouted. "HOI. Shosa."

The officer at the head of the column turned and looked back. When he saw me he called the column to a halt. I decided to make a bold move. I started to pedal toward the head of the column. The soldiers waved, saluted and shouted pleasant greetings in Japanese as I passed them. My surprise was even greater when I stopped at the head of the column beside the officer who was a major. I confronted the officer boldly. The major bowed and ushed me politely, he stepped back and saluted smartly.

I looked closely at the men while the major held his salute. They all looked as though they had had a rough time. They looked tired, exhausted and bedraggled. I returned the officer's salute for lack of any thing else that I could think of. I noticed that the major looked at the saber at my belt, but he said nothing.

"Dokokara kimashita ka." I asked.

"Sian," the major answered.

"Sian. Chutai no heiryoku wa doredaka arimasu ka." I continued the interrogation, asking about how many men he had.

"Goju nin," he responded.

"Fifty," I repeated, surprised. "Doko yuki masu ka."

"So," the major spoke in English. "I speak English sir. You are an American soldier."

"Yes." My surprise didn't last long. "Yes," I repeated. "Where are you going with your men?"

"To Mukden sir. To surrender to the Americans that are there. We were told in Sian that the Americans were in Mukden by the soldiers that came for the General."

I stared at the Jap officer. "To surrender to the Americans?! Why?" I was puzzled. "Why not surrender to the Russians?"

"No no," the officer was visibly shaken. "They will send us to Siberia. We have seen the men that they have taken on the trains. They are taking them to Siberia."

I was completely flabbergasted. This was an eventuality that I had never considered. I had already witnessed the Russians stripping the factories of tools, machines, materials and supplies. We had discussed the activities of the Russians and had wondered if we should do something about it. The officers had sent back reports to the headquarters in Hsian, Chunking and Okinawa. But now to hear that the Russians were actually taking prisoners and actually shipping them to Siberia! It struck home. The Russians were not really that friendly! They were going to take care of themselves.

"Are you positive that the Russians are taking prisoners of war?" I questioned the major.

"Yes! Yes!" he assured me. He turned to a lieutenant who was standing a few feet away. "Tell him what we have seen."

The lieutenant saluted me and started in English, "Yes sir, they have loaded many men at Sian and at other places where the railroad is. They are taking the men north."

"So," the major interrupted, "we wish to surrender to you, an American. We do not wish to be taken to Siberia."

"Oh no you don't! You can't surrender to me. Not on your tin Buddha or what ever. I can't take you to our camp as prisoners. No sir!"

The major started to argue.

"Tell you what major. You follow this road, then you turn left, east and then you follow along past the prison..." I gave him explicit directions on how to reach the camp across from MKK east of Mukden.

"No! No sir! We go with you sir. Then if there are Russians around you will tell them that we are your prisoners." The major was insistent.

"Oh no!" I disagreed. "By the way, why are you still armed? If the Russians find you armed there may be a battle."

"We carry arms to protect ourselves from the Communist Manchus. They have formed bands and they are looting, stealing, and killing the Japanese. We have had to fight them several times already."

The situation was taking on a darker side the more he talked.

"Well." I paused. I didn't want any part of the situation that I saw developing. If I was with the Japs and we came across some Russians there could well be a lot of shooting. I looked at the group of soldiers who were squatting or had laid down to rest during the time that we had been talking. I was very sure that I didn't want any part of the deal. I looked at the major, his saber caught my eye. "How about surrendering your saber to me?" I asked cautiously. An experiment in courage on my part.

"No. I cannot." His voice was filled with emotion.

I glare at him. Something happened to me. I remembered Cabanatuan. I remembered the Filipina with the dynamite between her legs. I remembered. I lifted the flap of my holster and withdrew the Luger. I thumbed the safety and pointed the pistol at the major. Somewhere back in my mind I knew I was being very stupid. There was a scurrying of men, a rolling whisper of sound as the Japs rose expectantly.   Before anything else could happen the major acted. He unbuckled the saber and held it out to me. He held it flat on the top of both palms. "I surrender to you. You are an honorable American. I and my men are your prisoners. We place ourselves under your protection." He bowed his head, the saber extended to me.

I gasped. The Japs all stood at attention and bowed. They were frozen in the position waiting for me to act.

The goddamn Japs had the nerve to ask for me to protect them from the Russians. The bloody nervy bastards. After the way they had abused us, killed us, starved and tortured us. They wanted to be protected by an American from the Russians. Screw you. I reached for the saber. "Well, I'll take the saber." I reached out with my left hand and took the saber. "I still can't take you as my prisoners. Orders from headquarters."

The major looked at me. The soldiers were all watching us.   "But you must," insisted the officer. "We have surrendered to you. You cannot leave us to the Russians." His voice carried his plea. "They will ship us to Siberia and we will never see our homes again."

Ludicrous! Absurd! The amazing situation had me petrified. The thoughts I had had minutes ago came back.

These Japs were in the position I had been in for years. Now they were pleading, begging for mercy. "Save us from the Russians." But they were still only trying to save face, save their asses. They were insisting that they were my prisoners, America's prisoners, and that we therefore, the stupid Americans would save them, protect them from the Russians.

The thoughts I had were vengeful and vindictive. After years of prison camps I couldn't just wash away the hatred and bitterness. I couldn't blow away the memories of the sickness, and the suffering as I would blow my nose to clear it.

"Major, all I got to say is it's tough. If you want to follow me back to camp, it's up to you. But if we run into any Russians, or if you can't keep up with me, it's just tough shit."

It looked as though I had slapped the major with his saber. His face went pale, he licked his lips and bowed stiffly.

I holstered the Luger and mounted the bicycle, turned down the road and started to pedal. Fifty Japs started to follow. They ran to keep up with me. I looked back after a few minutes and saw that they were running as fast as they could, but they were falling behind rapidly. I couldn't see the expressions on their faces, but I had a good mental image of what those expressions were like. I didn't slow down, I just pedaled along. About five minutes later I saw that they could never catch up with me. I continued on to Mukden with a great deal of satisfaction. I didn't bother to stop at Millie's. Or at Tania's. I kept right on going to camp. I hoped that the major would not be able to find the camp.

CHAPTER 48 -- RUSSIAN LOOTERS AND HOME

The men who were roaming around town came back with various stories about the Russians in the days that followed. Mostly the stories were about the looting and moving of booty by the Russians. It was the primary occupation of the soldiers. We heard of only a few incidents of skirmishes with the Japs that were holding out outside of town.

The Americans were collecting souvenirs, sabers, kimonos and other paraphenalia that struck their fancy. The Russians had an organized process of collecting industrial equipment and machinery.

Cy, Ed, Kozie, Mac and I sat around swilling some of the beer that remained. "We were lucky to make it to the brewery before the Russians got there." Mac was happy to have beaten out the Russians.

"You're not kidding," I agreed. "A couple of the guys were run off by the Russians yesterday. Johnson said that the Russians now have a patrol around the grounds out there. Armed patrol."

"Not only that," Ed added, "but when some of our officers tried to get some beer they were told that it all belonged to the Russians. Americans - nyet. How about that?"

"And, then there is the story that when Major Hennessey talked to the Russians they told him to see the Russian general in charge of Mukden. Name was something like Malinovski or something." Cy frowned at the idea of the Russians being so high handed.

"Hell, the beer is the least of the things that are going on. What happened to you Pete? Weren't you at MKK and the foundry?" Ed prodded me.

"Yes. I went over to see what was going on. Part of building one is stripped." I informed them. "Looks like they are planning on cleaning out two and the foundry and the forge of all of the machinery. I went through the fence to the Mukden Foundry on the other side, the big place behind MKK. There were a whole bunch of Chinamen working the place over. Looks like the Chinks and the Russians are racing to see who can steal the mostest the fastest."

"What are they doing with the stuff anyway?" Ed asked us.

"Shipping it to Russia is my guess. And I guess the Chinese are shipping the stuff to Peking or Nanking or places like that. I wonder if the Chinks are moving the stuff out so that the Russians don't get it?" I looked around for comment.

"Beats me," Mac retorted. He took another swig of beer from the big

421

bottle. "But I'd like to see the stuff burned before either of them ship it out."

"Sounds like we need a fire bug," Cy agreed.

"Better it should be blown up." Ed snorted the words. " There was a lot of dynamite at MKK. I saw it over in one of the shacks by the office building.

I frowned at that. I couldn't understand why there should have been any explosives at the factory. Unless it was to destroy the plants so that the Russians wouldn't get it. If that was so then the Japs must have expected that something like this could happen.

There was a deadly meaningful silence for a few seconds.

"Is there any problem in fusing the stuff? Is it tricky?" Cy broke the silence.

"It really is no problem, perfectly safe if you know what you are doing." I answered with only half of my mind on the words. "If it's an electric fuse then you need a battery. If it's a combustible fuse you only need a match to light it and run like hell." I smiled.

"Hey! Hey!" Kozie exploded. "The mad bomber from Manhattan knows how to do it." He laughed a dirty laugh.

"Yeah, and just get yourself caught by our officers. Those damned dipheads will court martial you as soon as look at you. They're all army and regulations again. The pricks. They don't understand." Mac spat to emphasize his dislike.

"Well, so you just don't get caught." I started. "And..."

"You sure as hell had better be watching out for the Russians and the Chinks," warned Ed. "They'll shoot you first and then ask questions later."

"You sure as hell are right about that," I agreed.

"How come that the Chinks or the Russians haven't taken the dynamite already?" Cy asked. "Seems to me that the Chinks would just love to get their hands on the stuff."

"Yeah, I wonder why not?" I expressed my puzzlement too.

"They just haven't found it yet. It's not out in the open. It's all the way back out of the way. You have to go down the alley and turn in behind the building."

"Might be a good idea to stash it someplace where it would be hard to find. Maybe bury it." I mused.

Arguments followed and continued for some time. No one wanted to become openly involved in the venture.

"Hey you guys, come on out and see what's going on out here." Ted had come running out of the cloak room.

"What's up?" Mac asked as we scurried to the fence between the cloak room and the hospital.

"A bunch of Japs just came up to the gate and said that they wanted to surrender to the Americans." Ted laughed breathlessly as he gave us the story. "They say they were told to report here by some American a couple of days ago. Now they say that they are our prisoners. POWs. How about that?" Ted was really amused by the goings on at the gate.

I carefully avoided exposing myself as we watched the scene just inside of the front gate. I couldn't recognize anyone at the distance we were at.

We couldn't make out who the American officers were, but we could make out that there was a violent disagreement going on.

"The officers don't want the Japs!" Ted roared.

"The Japs told them that they were told to report here." Ted was coughing in between his explanation. "I was just coming in the gate when they got here a little while ago. The officers told the Jap major that there must a mistake. We don't want any prisoners. The Jap says that we have to take them prisoner since the war is over. Man that is what I call funny."

We watched the comical proceedings for a few minutes and then gradually the guys lost interest and started to drift back to the benches where we had been drinking beer.

"Guess that the Japs don't want any part of the Russians," Mac laughed. "I don't blame them I hear that the Russians are shipping the Japs up to Siberia."

"Tough gashitsky," Kozy spat out. "Real tough."

"Yeah," agreed Ed. "Ain't that just too damn bad."

"Yeah." I swilled some beer to cover a little apprehension that I had about the incident at the gate. "Guess I'll roam around. Anybody want to go?"

No one wanted to do much of anything.

"Don't blow yourself up Pete," Cy yelled after me.

I ignored the remark and made my way to my bunk. I waited until the Japs at the front gate had left. They had been sent off to Jap Military Police Headquarters. Even then I checked to make sure that none of them had remained anywhere around camp. I rode off on my bike and headed toward Mukden, then I doubled back and approached MKK from the southwest. There was no one around at MKK. I searched the Mukden Foundry and found no one there either. I went back to MKK and explored the factory to see just what had been removed. There were still some large pieces of equipment in place. Most of the smaller machines, the lathes, broachers, grinders and drill presses had been removed. The huge Grey planer, with its reinforced concrete foundation, the big radial drill and the large automatic turret lathes were all still in place. At the MKK foundry the drop hammers were still in place. All of the drafting equipment and all of the hand tools had disappeared. I went back to the Mukden Foundry by slipping through a hole in the fence. Vacant spots, clean because they had been protected by the bases of the machines that had been there, told the story. The foundation bolts formed a small forest of steel on the otherwise empty floor. Dozens of pieces of machinery had been moved out. I found the laboratory. Most of the lab equipment was gone. There were a few microscope objectives on one of the benches. These were valuable pieces of optical equipment. I picked them up and stuffed them in my pocket. I turned back to MKK to search for the dynamite. If there had been any in the shack that Ed had told us about, it was gone. I searched the warehouse and the construction gang area too. There just wasn't any dynamite around. I turned back to the Mukden Foundry and searched through all of the shacks and the warehouses. Finally I gave up. I had covered just about every place where there could have been any explosives. I found that the tires of my bike needed air as I started out of the grounds. I walked it to the MKK garage, parked it, and started the air compressor. I filled both tires and shut down the compressor. No one came around as I had expected they would after hearing the compressor running. I decided to look in the office and found the door locked. I smashed the window of the door with a steel bar that I found on the floor. There was nothing of value in the office. It had been stripped by others before me. I sat on the desk and looked around. The ink incident came back to mind. I shrugged it off, thinking about how Hank had paid for that escapade. I had seen the box that was shoved back under the desk and had ignored it. Now it had my attention. The box had some indecipherable hieroglyphics stenciled on its sides. I pulled it out and pried it open. Sawdust packing spilled out. There were sticks of dynamite under the sawdust. I pawed the sticks and piled them on the floor. I searched the garage for a sack or some kind of a bag. As luck would have I couldn't find anything. I didn't want to leave the dynamite, and I didn't want to carry it exposed for anyone to see. I saw some newspaper on the desk . With some wire and twine from the benches I bundled the dynamite into bundles of six. I wrapped them in the newspaper. I had dynamite, but no fuses. I found a place under a small platform in the MKK messhall to store the bundles. Then I started my search for blasting caps or fuses. After an hour I gave up and headed out of the west gate for Millie's. The afternoon had passed more rapidly than I had expected. It was almost six o'clock by the time I reached Millie's place.

I found Kozie and Mac when I arrived. I didn't say anything about the dynamite. In answer to the questions about my activities of the afternoon I displayed the microscope objectives.

The following day, Saturday, we decided to explore some more of Mukden.

We were stopped at one time by a very friendly group of Russian soldiers. They were interested in obtaining some ammunition for what looked like seven millimeter automatics of Jap manufacture. We directed them to the Headquarters of the Japanese Military Police. They thanked us and shared a glass of vodka with us before they left on their search.

We roamed around in various places, just sightseeing. We couldn't find any of the Japanese that had been at TKK or at MKK.

We were anxious to get out of Mukden, restless at the waiting. We had to keep roaming around to pass the time. On the afternoon of the sixth of September we ran into another group of Russians. These guys weren't interested in looting, they were interested in women. Whores was what they wanted. Kurvas. We teamed up with them just to see if anything could be found. We stopped at a Jap restaurant in the Japanese settlement. After a good meal, topped off with generous helpings of sake, the Russians insisted on continuing the search. The Jap told us all of the geishes were gone along with the rest of the Japanese who had fled the Russians.

"Geishes hell," Mac laughed, "just plain old whores is what they mean. They ain't looking for dancing girls to entertain them."

We followed a couple of leads that didn't pan out. Then we found one of the houses that we were told about by some of the Manchus.

"They sure put up a good front," I commented. "Looks like a real light and clean place to me. Look at all that tile."

The Russians unslung their grease guns, Tommy guns which they loved, and pushed on into the huge room. There were a number of small door sized openings that led off of the main room into small cubbies. A curtain provided privacy to some small degree. The cubbies had a knee high shelf across one end that was covered with maize cane to pad the wood.

"HOI! HOI!" the Russians shouted to bring out whoever was supposed to be there.

We had formed a tight group in the center of the big room. We waited as the Russians shouted some more to attract attention.

A big, fat Chinaman, dressed in a conventional Manchu robe entered from a door at the back, the far end of the building. He was very dark. But not completely identifiable as a Negro. His face was fat, his eyes were not slanted.

"Hey guys! You! You're Americans! For Christ's sake! You're

Americans. Hello hello hello. Come on in." He shouted all of the words as he descended on us.

"What the hell?!" Mac exploded.

"I'll be damned!" Kozie stared at the English speaking Manchu.

"How the hell come you speak English so well?" I asked.

The Russians interrupted, wanting to know just what the hell was going on as they expressed themselves in Russian.

"Ze kurvi?" they asked.

"The girls? ho-ho-ho," the Chinaman roared. "Kurvi, ho-ho-ho."

We stared at the amazing character. We looked at each other, Mac, Kozie and I, not understanding.

"My girls! Hoi!" he shouted to the back of the room.

A dozen women, in various kinds of kimonos, and of various ages came in from the back door.

"Hold it!" Kozie yelled. "Just a stinking minute!"

"It's okay okay." The fat Chinaman started to placate Kozie as the Russians backed off and took a hard look around. "I am a friend." He pounded his large chest. "I'm from Brooklyn!"

We stopped stock still.

"From Brooklyn?!" Kozie's voice broke with disbelief.

"Yeah. Sure. I've been here in Manchuria since nineteen thirty-four. How's little old New York? Man I sure as hell miss old Broadway. Bright lights! Times Square! Vaudeville. Man that sure is a town! And Coney! Coney Island! Now there is a place for you. How long since any of you guys have been in New York? Where you guys from? Anybody here from Brooklyn?"

"Hold it!" I laughed. "Hold it. I'm from Manhattan. Kozie here is from Greenpoint. Mac here is from Pennsy. The Russians- who the hell knows. Maybe Moscow." The Russians perked up at the name.

"Great! Just great! You guys want dames? Broads. I got them." He motioned the women forward.

The Russians started to laugh and smirk, joking in Russian. They started to jab at the women.

"Fifty yen. Take your choice." The Chinaman pushed the women forward toward us.

I gagged as one of the younger ones came close to me. She smelled to high heaven from something I couldn't identify. I backed off.

"What is the matter?" Kozie asked, he frowned at me.

"She stinks. They stink." I continued to back away.

"Naw, she don't smell bad at all. She's pretty clean." The Chinaman offered.

"Like hell she is! She stinks!" I spat back at him. "She needs more than a bath. Open up the kimono." I commanded.

"Aw, don't be like that. What the hell do you want in a cathouse anyway? When you're in the sack it don't matter anyway. You won't mind." There was a nasty tone in the Chinaman's voice.

"Tso? Tso?" The Russians unlimbered their greaseguns. They didn't understand the words but they sure as hell knew that there was something that wasn't kosher in Moscow.

Mac took the time to explain to the Russians. They gathered in close to us, the bolts of the machine guns snickered menacingly. They motioned with the snouts of their submachine guns. I pulled the Luger and pointed it at the fat man.

"Hey man! No need to get rough. Don't forget that I am an American too!" he complained.

"Yeah?" I backed away.

"Sure man. I was born in Brooklyn. My old man was from South Carolina. My old lady was Chinese. I was born in Brooklyn, no kidding. I wouldn't screw ya on that !"

We stared at the character. He sure was one for the book, a Chinese Negro. Chinegro. I'd heard the term before.

"Have them open the kimonos." I emphasized the order with a flip of the pistol in my hand.

"Aw come on," the Chinegro started. He stopped suddenly and moistened his fat lips. He ordered the women to open their kimonos in Manchu. The women, from twelve to forty, muttered and mumbled. They opened their kimonos slowly.

I swallowed. They were disgusting. Everyone of the women had open sores on their bodies. There were ugly green puss sore around the breasts, the folds of the abdomen and around their crotches.

The Russians started to curse in Russian. They pushed the women back with the snouts of their guns. They started to mutter angrily in Russian.

"The damned Russians are mad!" Kozie yelled.

I shoved the Luger back in my holster and started backing to the door through which we had entered. Mac and Kozie joined me.

"They are mad as hell that the Chink would let them get diseased." Mac informed us. His understanding of Russian was better than ours.

We kept on backing out to the door.

One of the machine guns spit out a burst of bullets that brought glass showering down from the skylights overhead. Another burst caused whistling ricochets from the tile walls.

Everybody scattered.

The women ran for the back door. The Chinegro beat them through it. The rest of us headed for the street.

The Russians fired a few more bursts and came scrambling out of the door laughing. They jostled each other as they rushed out.

"Let's get the hell out of here!" I shouted and started to run.

"Aw, what for?" Mac laughed. "The fun is just starting."

"Like hell! I'm leaving." I started up the street.

A few more shots came from behind me.

A Russian vehicle, a small truck, turned into the street ahead of me and continued to come toward me.

"Mac! Kozie!. Look!" I yelled and pointed at the racing truck.

The Russians in the doorway spotted the truck. They turned and ran back into the building. The three of us raced into an alley across from the whorehouse. We ran down the alley and out into the street, in through a yard around a house and into another alley that led us out into another street. I stopped for breath. Kozie and Mac stopped. We looked at each other and laughed.

"Those were Russian MPs." Mac laughed. "I heard the Ruskies yell before they beat it through the cathouse."

"Hell, I bet that that Chink won't forget us ever. Right?" I laughed.

"And how!" Kozie agreed. "And from Brooklyn yet. I still don't believe it!" Kozie was shaking his head in disbelief.

"Did you see those stinking women?" Mac asked.

"You kidding? How the hell could you miss? My stomach still hasn't settled down." I spat. "I was ready to throw up just as the Russians opened fire. I need a drink. Vodka, sake or something. Some alcohol to disinfect my mouth."

"Me too." Kozie agreed. " Let's get back to Millie's and get a decent drink."

"Check." I nodded as we started to walk slowly, laughing and smirking as we headed for Millie's.

Our story met with a great deal of laughter at Millie's. She kidded us about the nice clean Russian girls that we knew and warned us not to go searching for any of the locals again.

There was little else to do but wait for the arrangements to be completed to move us out of Manchuria.

The Russians issued warnings to the Americans that drastic action would be taken in the sabotage of the factories continued. The Russians informed the American contingent at the Prison Camp that there were suspects in our camp. There had been fifteen incidents of sabotage in the industrial area that the Russians believed were deliberate cases of sabotage. Heavy machinery had been blown up, dynamited. The American officers denied any knowledge of the incidents or of any parties that might have anything to do with them.

Even so, despite the warnings, the Russians acted hospitably.

On Saturday, the eighth of September, a troupe of Russians, under orders from the Commanding General, put on a show for their American Allies.

On Sunday afternoon Cy came running into the area, panting. "Hey! We're leaving! Word just came in. We're on our way!" Cy couldn't contain himself. "Monday! Monday! We're on our way! Tomorrow, the tenth, we go home."

Joseph A Petak (695) and one of the Russains he met after being liberated by the OSS Team.

AFTER ALL

There is more to tell about the end and the trip home. To keep it short, only the high lights are recorded.

After we were loaded on the train we met some more Russians at a station stop on our way to Dairen. They had their women with them. They took many photographs which they said they wanted to show their families when they arrived home. We were the Americans that they were supposed to have liberated from the Japs.

When we arrived at Dairen we were loaded on the U.S.S. Hope. On our way to Okinawa we were hit by a typhoon that smashed us with eighty foot waves.

Some of the men from Mukden were aboard the U.S.S. Holbart which ran into a mine at Buchner Bay. It went dead in the water and had to be towed. None of the POWs were injured.

Some of us we were loaded into the bomb bays of B-24s and flown to the Philippines. One of the saddest incidents was the loss of nine men from the bomb bay of a B-24. A Black Dutchman, a Dutch and native marriage produced what are called Black Dutchman. He pulled the manual bomb bay door lever and dumped nine men nine thousand feet into the China Sea.

When the bomber I was on reached the island of Luzon it was fogged in. As we were flying into Clark Field we flew through the mountains. We missed a cliff by only a few feet as the plane descended to the field.

I roamed around the South Pacific for weeks before being sent home on a transport. We landed in Seattle and were transported by hospital train to Utica, New York, and admitted as patients at the Rhoads General Hospital. From there I was sent to Halloran General Hospital for two spinal operations to repair the damage I had sustained during the war. I was discharged, due to disability, in August of nineteen forty-five.

This manuscript is the result of psychiatric counseling and treatment. The doctors insisted that I write my experiences to help me overcome the problems I was having with nightmares and other bad memories. It was completed in nineteen forty-seven, handwritten. It wasn't typed until nineteen sixty-five, when my son wanted to read it. It was then stored in the attic, in a box of memorabilia, until nineteen eighty-nine. I found it when my wife wanted something from the attic. I decided to edit it and put it into readable form.

The photographs were taken with an Army Kodak and a Japanese

431

camera that I had requisitioned from Murata. There are over two hundred photographs in the collection.

The entry to the POW compound at Mukden. The area, right foreground, is where the Japanese made the POWs strip in below zero temperatures after the so-called riot.

POW parade ground. The Japanese camp guards, now POWs, are filling in the fox holes. Barrack two in center, barrack three extreme right.

Anatoli Ugaroff, (Tolek), Russian Air Corp, Joe Petak, Millie Plohotenko, Walt Macarovich, Felix Kozakevitch at a party at Millie's in Mukden. August 1945.

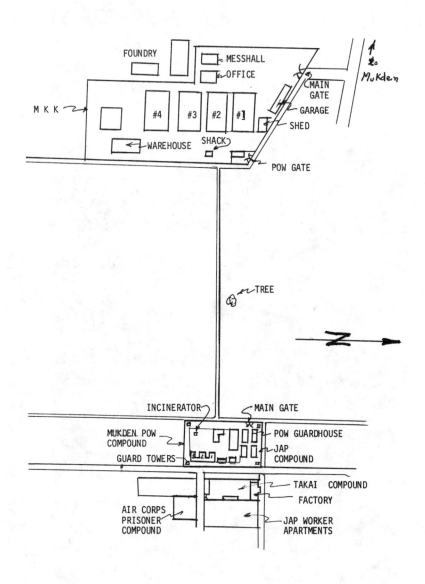

The Mukden POW compound and the factory, MKK.

Mukden Roster - Original Group   1

Name	Unit	Number	Address	No.
Abernathy, Carl W.	USMC	281443	Route 2, Altus, OK	1429
Abraham, Ned L.	515 CA	38011938	Silver City, NM	931
Acam, J.E.	194 Tnk	20900642	15 N. Seabright Ave., Santa Cruz, CA	167
Adair, James	60 CA	19056347	419 Lighthouse St., Erie, PA	545
Adams, John M.	USN	3556691	626 S Palace St., Tyler, TX	650
Adams, Justin J.	60 CA	18042216	905 S State St., Abbeville, LA	842
Adams, Leon C.	USMC	282618	269 2nd St., Yuma, AZ	389
Adams, Raymond C.	USMC	276750	Pomona, KS	1421
Adams, Rufus D.	724 Ord	33050318	1633 N. 29th St., Philadelphia, PA	173
Adams, William E.	194 Tank	3510052	Orleans, IN	684
Adams, William M.	60 CA	18036367	Box 7, Smyer, TX	721
Adamski, Joseph W.	2 Sqdn	6148580	113 Everett St., Easthampton, MA	1449
Adkins, Deward D.	MC	6253231	West Monroe, LA	404
Ahlstedt, James I.	59th CA	17012219	635 S. 19th St., Lincoln, NE	205
Ahlstedt, John D.	60th CA	17012221	635 S. 19th St., Lincoln, NE	206
Aitken, T.L.	124 ORD	19052834	3801 Lincoln Ave., Oakland, CA	1570
Alex, Stephan H.,	200 CA	20843948	513 1/2 Bullard St., Silver City, NM	16
Alexandowicz, Casmir	QMC	6947996	705 Hess Ave., Erie, PA	509
Allen, Albert L.	192 Tnk	35001458	21 Linden Road, Mansfield, OH	1362
Allen, Fred J.	17 ORD	7041074	3630 Greenwood Ave., Louisville, KY	1535
Allen, Oliver C.	7 Mat	18029940	Medill, TX	362
Allred, Harvey A.	60 CA	18038734	204 Paradice St., Ft. Worth, TX	937
Althaus, Rubin M.	200 CA	38030757	Route 1, Fredrickburg, TX	1529
Alves, John F.	194 Tank	20900688	Salinas, CA	1107
Alvis, Wm. B.	24 Grp	6809683	Big Stone Gap, VA	1303
Ammons, N.J.	200 CA	20843790	Artesia, NM	1540
Anderson, Fred A.,	SC	19012256	924 1/2 Euclid Ave., Beloit, WI	36
Anderson, James C.	HDSMB	7021023	2220 Riggs Ave., Baltimore, MD	1515
Anderson, John A.	194 Tank	20900689	407 California St., Salinas, CA	553
Anderson, Leonard V.	60 CA	16003920	1215 5th Ave., Rockford, IL	666
Anderson, Milan E.	194 Tnk	20700194	1713 Oak St., Brainard, MI	1560
Anderson, Robert A.	60 CA	19054316	10 20th St., Great Falls, MT	1324
Anderson, Vincent M.	USMC	17011898	400 N. Main St., Ainsworth, NE	348
Andrews, Leland M.	USMC	230220	15517 Lauder St., Detroit, MI	379
Anger, W.D.	RAMC	Cpl	London, N.I., London, England	1160*
Anstis, R.	SAIF	Pfc	Nicholis Pt., Mildura, Victoria, Aust.	1234*

Mukden Roster - Original Group   2

Name	Unit	Serial	Address	
Antonio Sam J.	200 CA	28012665	Box 1059, Grants, NM	475
Arentzen, Chas.	USN	3684081	226 Ave. B, Billings, MT	957
Armijo, Ernesto J.	200 CA	38012513	Route 1, Box 588, Albuquerque, NM	873
Armijo, James G.	60 CA	18016879	Glorietta, NM	711
Armijo, Manuel R.	60 CA	18016885	Glorieta, NM	1136
Armijo, Salvador J.	200 CA	20842950	Route 3, Box 1215, Alburquerque, NM	178
Armour, LaFaye	515 CA	38012586	2407 Washington St., Parsons, KS	1507
Armstrong, Howard R.	4 CGAC	6489804	720 Washington Ave., Alton, IL	626
Armstrong, Ralph E.	60 CA	6995999	51 Madison Ave., Hagerstown, MD	1078
Arney, Dewey J.,	60 CA	17000637	708 Garfield St., Kansas City, MO	108
Arnott, V.,	RAMC	Sgt	London, England	1168*
Arrington, James R.	60 CA	14043782	Route 1, Waynesville, NC	800
Asher, Preston H.	27 Bomb	39158784	1356 A Indiana Ave., Detroit, MI	210
Atchison,Earnest D.	USMC	275139	Snyder, OK	1524
Atkins, Ralph P.	USN	2684456	Alhambra, Coral Gables, FL	1142
Aulds, James V.	16 Bomb	7602615	301 2nd St., Monroe, LA	1563
Autrey, Francis R.	60 CA	15061694	811 Laurel Ave., Hattiesburg, MS	1270
Baca, Aligio	200 CA	38012017	Chimayo, NM	303
Baca, Ignacio	200 CA	xxx	Socorro, NM	1283
Bacsik, Stephen C.	USN	2283618	434 Berg Ave., Trenton, NJ	1106
Baffo, Victor	USN	2717875	265 Kasarinian St., Snt Ana, Manila, PI	1541
Baggett, Alonzo T.	803 Eng	7085802	3148 NW 57th St., Miami, FL	1422
Baier, Oscar	60 CA	19019936	Route 1, Staples, MN	899
Bailey, Ivon J.	USN	3857999	Malone, WA	877
Baine, Harry M.	60 CA	6568911	529 S Virgil Ave., Los Angeles, CA	608
Balcer, Julian H.	USMC	269109	3122 Chatam St., Philadelphia, PA	568
Baldassare, James	QMC	R598972	4 Baldwin Place, Boston, MA	291
Banach, John	SCAW	13026986	6315 Torresdale Ave., Philadelphia, PA	200
Bangs, Ralph J.	60 CA	18016840	Liberal, KS	996
Barber, Alton L.	60 C A	14043793	Route 1, Temple, GA	1468
Barkowski, J.J.	SC	6881920	12 Greenwitch St., Natrona, PA	201
Barna, Joseph L.	20 Bomb	11020430	Box 95, Martin, PA	1059
Baron, Chas. R.	31 Inf	13027870	31 Ackerman St., Hellertown, PA	431
Barone, Salvatore J.	USAFFE	6976407	64 Caddy St., Rochester, NY	832
Barton, Robert D.,	CA	0408462	205 South Wells, Kosciusko, MS	6
Bates, Robert K.	724 ORD	33035525	464 2nd Ave., Koppel, PA	826

Mukden Roster - Original Group   3

Name	Unit	Number	Address	
Bazewick, Casey T.	USMC	255449	3000 N. Christain Ave., Chicago, IL	439
Beadle, Waldo J.	809 MP	6274076	Nelson Route, Antlers, OK	718
Beard, James E	59 CA	13000768	Route 2, Chambersburg, PA	823
Bearden, Carl R.	803 Eng	38043169	Chico, TX	259
Beauchat, Eugene P.	USMC	268911	625 Allison Ave., Canon City, CO	551
Beaurman, William	USN	xxx	McPherson, KS	915
Becker, Geo.	59 Ca	19002005	Route 4, Box 147, Fresno, CA	674
Beckman, Gail	60 CA	19020671	1943 Orchard St., Klamath Falls, OR	565
Bee, H.G.	L/Mt	Cpl	Nedlands, W. Australia	1195*
Begay, Keats	200 CA	38011850	Many Farms Area, Chin Lee, AZ	476
Begaye, John Y.	200 CA	38012002	Coyote Canyon Store, Tomatchi, NM	712
Begley, Wild Bill	34 Pursuit	19051934	2330 Filmore St., San Francisco, CA	114
Beliveau, C. N.	USN	2044531	84 Mechanics St., Lebanon, NH	410
Bell, R.K.	59 CA	18050427	Oswalt, OK	1531
Bell, W.A.G.	AAOC	Pfc	N. Melbourne, Victoria, Australia	1217*
Bellstrom, Leonard D.	USN	3930471	5333 SE Rhone St., Portland, OR	1128
Bendele, Wesley H.	FEAFC	6260650	Hondo, TX	935
Bender, Jack	USN	2503607	3111 American Ave., Long Beach, CA	722
Bennet, Robert A.	60 CA	17009588	771 S Ave., Springfield, MO	965
Bennett, Owen D.	59 CA	18052388	Lawton, OK	1091
Benson, Ed E.	7 Mat	19050511	Route 3, Hutchinson, KS	409
Berndt, Elmer L.	QMC	6276648	472 E 10th St., Winona, MN	335
Bertram, W.P.	USMC	271548	410 E 12th St., Littke Rock, AR	1579
Beshears, James D.	454 ORD	14049258	5892 Sunnyside Ave., Winston Salem, NC	385
Besserra, Julio T.	200 CA	20842396	1531 52nd St., Albuquerque, NM	447
Bidgood, Clyde E.	724 ORD	14003007	326 N Ave., Los Angeles, CA	1286
Biela, Ralph E	USMC	xxx	1925 S Drake Ave., Chicago, IL	942
Biggs, Carl W.	803 Eng	34044955	726 Elnorst, N Chattanooga, TN	661
Bilbo, Harry A.	USN	3600209	Mauriceville, TX	944
Bird, James	USN	3761145	971 S 7th St., San Jose, CA	1148
Birkinsha, Harry E.	59 CA	17010417	Fayetteville, AR	770
Bishoff, David	60 CA	6581195	Sugar City, ID	1477
Biszaha, Joseph	59 CA	13038251	230 Fairview Ave., Pittsburgh, PA	638
Blalock, Joseph G.	31 Inf	6393256	51 Ash St., Rome, GA	386
Blevins, Geo.	USN	2660363	Big Stone Gap, VA	955
Bo, John	60 CA	6980707	Spencerport, NY	1431

Mukden Roster - Original Group   4

Name	Unit	Serial	Address	No.
Boatwright, L. L.	59 CA	18046440	Colordao Springs, CO	383
Bobulski, Casimir T.	17 Bomb	6489799	unknown	182
Bocksell, Arnold A.,	AMPS	C.W.O.		14
Boehme, Arthur A.	USN	2992291	1743 58th Street, Brooklyn, NY	945
Boeshart, Chas. R.	192 Tank	20500754	628 S Oakland Ave., Villa Park, IL	669
Bogart, J.H.	194 Tnk	20700219	209 E 3rf St., Clinton, OH	163
Boltock, James J.	16 Sqdn	14014589	Pine River, MN	1439
Bond, Duane G.	USN	3163693	Route 1, Box 10, Eunice, LA	1526
Book, Elmer R.	31 Inf	18042319	6920 Malasar St., Huntington Park, CA	420
Bosko, Nicholas	17 Pursuit	11019064	Lake Providence, LA	125
Bostie, Hobart E.,	USN	2874337	9 Cooper St., Norwich, CT	22
Boushey, Hershel	60 CA	6582007	Rt. 1, LaFollette, Tenn.	687
Bowen, James H.	59 CA	19002217	1914 Pacific Ave., Everett, WA	1058
Bowen, Roy D.	60 CA	18015209	Killeen, TX	503
Bowers, Robert T.	60 CA	14040516	Box 923, Wink, TX	1436
Bowman, Geo. R.	USN	2582194	107 Spring St., Charleston, SC	1281
Boyer, Manforo C.	19 Bomb	6569648	Ridgeway, Severn, MD	294
Bozric, Frank C.	60 CA	15017290	Farmington, WA	1124
Bradley, Hardy E.,	3 Pursuit	6296956	2137 Georgetown Road, Canton, OH	123
Brakin, A.C.	60 CA	17001753	Box 34, Branson, CO	134
Branch, Robert K.	HDMSB	19015320	Loman, MN	1007
Branchaud, F.E.	USN	3281511	Salkum, WA	1508
Brandt, Edward A.	59 CA	19006196	610 N 10th St., Brainerd, MN	585
Brannon, Winifred B.	60 CA	14040416	805 E Washington St., West Chicago, IL	689
Brasel, Joseph	60 CA	17010418	Route 1, Greenville, AL	1097
Brennan, D.J., Captain. MC	Austral.	Austral.	Route 1, Altus, AR	25
			Sydney, Australia	
Brennan, Harold R.	28 Mat	6714454	810 Broad St., Pleasantville, NJ	1434
Bressie, Jesse A.	31 Inf	17016231	2929A Michigan Ave., St. Louis, MO	1538
Brevington, Wm. I.	USN	3369173	915 W 18th St., Tulsa, OK	1312
Bridges, Wilson C.	59 CA	6288947	Dime Box, TX	373
Brierly, E.	Loyals	Pfc	Umstron, Manchester, England	1208*
Brignall, Geo.	17 Pursuit	7030722	731 S 5th Ave., Canton, OH	1087
Brill, Arthur	59 CA	12007085	489 Shephard Ave., Brooklyn, NY	1438
Brincefield, Fitzhugh	17 ORD	15047583	Crumpler, WV	450
Brink, Ralph S.	515 CA	20833719	928 Tilden St., Las Vegas, NM	597
Brister, Thomas H.	60 CA	14042483	Route 1, Durant, MI	898

Mukden Roster - Original Group   5

Name	Unit	Serial	Address	
Britt, Ellis T.	34 Pursuit	6823773	860 Bush St., San Francisco, CA	217
Brittain, Jack P.	28 Mat	6562306	1616 E St., Sacramento, CA	435
Britton, Albert E.	803 Eng	32070223	504 Myrtle Ave., Woodbury, NJ	614
Britton, Kay Dee	59 CA	18015216	Wink, TX	749
Broney, Andrew T.	803 Eng	6774369	427 Robinson St., Baltimore, MD	372
Brookens, James O.	FEASC	6718112	1108 A 1st Ave., Hyde Park, L.I., NY	1349
Brookes, S.	Loyals	Pfc	Little Lever, Nr. Bolton, England	1174*
Brookover, Sherrill R.	21 Pursuit	15018748	Hamlin, WV	415
Brosnan, Irvin M.	17 ORD	39152043	Trona, CA	646
Broussard, Albert G.	17 ORD	34018782	1922 Levin St., Alexandria, LA	468
Brown, G.J.	FEASC	R56595	9 Loomis St., Chicago, IL	1562
Brown, James E.	20 Pursuit	6914061	Westphalia, IN	333
Brown, Kenneth D.	91 QMC	6578600	1061 Acacia Ave., Sacramento, CA	395
Brown, Leslie L.	60 CA	18049878	Route 2, Yale, OK	583
Brown, Robert E.	803 Eng	37085742	5 Cross St., Chelsea, MA	635
Brown, R.A.	MC	19000652	617 C St., Marysville, CA	190
Brown, Sharkey	USN	xxx	Timpson, TX	1465
Brownell, Richard C.	809 MP	17001777	Treat Creek, MI	930
Bruce, Geo. D.	USMC	279308	29 Sand St., Denver, CO	1520
Bruce, Paul H.	192 Tank	38053804	Box 86, Conroe, TX	356
Brumley, James R.	USN	xxx	Edinburg, TX	349
Brunner, C.A.	60 CA	19015982	Ontario, OR	148
Bryan, Chas. L.	60 CA	18036283	Box 1882, Panpa, TX	1472
Bryant, Riley J.	17 Pursuit	6970953	726 E Henry St., Savanah, GA	1130
Bryant, Chas. J.	59 CA	xxx	118 Anderson St., San Francisco, CA	828
Buck, William E.	60 CA	17014268	Arkadelphia, AR	624
Buckner, Calvin C.	200 CA	20843737	Hope, NM	760
Buckworth, A.	Loyals	Pfc	xxx	1218*
Bullock, Thomas S.	60 CA	19010858	184 E 5th St., North Provo, UT	513
Bumgarner, Melvin R.	60 CA	1901744	606 Henderson Ave., Williamstown, WV	821
Burgess Joseph A.	60 CA	18033911	Route 1, Roanoke, TX	1074
Burgon, J.	Loyals	Pfc	Fallowfiled, Manchester, England	1230*
Burkett, Albert	803 Eng	6837676	USA Engineers, Washington, DC	604
Burkholder, Arthur W.	USN	2658521	802 Cenadala St., Lynchburg, VA	1023
Burrola, Joseph M.	200 CA	20843294	602 S 7th St., Gallup, NM	1259
Burrola, W.M.	200 CA	20843308	602 S. 7th St., Gallup, NM	300

Mukden Roster - Original Group   6

Name	Unit	Number	Address	
Burroughs, D. S.	454 ORD	14050703	712 Nash Drive, Raleigh, NC	355
Bush, Donald A.	60 CA	14043813	Box 132, Claremont, PA	331
Bush, Ray J.	USN	2581095	Box 1371, Clarksburg, WV	1374
Bushman, Francis S.	60 CA	17024991	Grand Portage, MN	498
Butler, Frank	31 Inf	17031797	718 W Markhan St., Little Rock, AR	920
Butler, John B.	60 CA	17014270	Ethel, AR	1392
Butler, L. R.	21 Pursuit	6262059	New Madrid, MO	130
Butterbaugh, Robt. E.	USN	2503915	615 4th Ave., Lakemont, PA	37
Byrne, Lawrence H.	200 CA	20842452	Deming, NM	892
Cahill, Marvin D.	803 Eng	37037613	Woodstock, MN	499
Cahoon, Celon L.	USMC	277904	Old Trap, NC	397
Cain, Carson	60 CA	15065657	Liberty, KY	633
Calahan, Sameul S.	USN	xxx	Rt. 2, Gladespring, VA	105
Calderon, Arthur J.	59 CA	20843309	Box 3, Gamberco, NM	1024
Caldwell, Carl E.	59 CA	7023361	Route 2, Box 48, Colborn, VA	620
Caldwell, James R.	MC	19052384	Route 1, Portageville, MO	1247
Callen, Bruce C.	60 CA	17016179	Tory, IL	1354
Cameron, John D.	60 CA	6149158	12 Washington St., Caribou, ME	833
Campbell, Andrew M.	USMC	267547	Route 1, Eugene, OR	1085
Campbell, Arthur L.	34 Pursuit	6573980	Box 332, Rigby, ID	350
Campbell, Emil G.	20 Bomb	19018023	2101 Ellis Ave., Missoula, MT	940
Campbell, Leon W.	17 ORD	35153085	Pleasantville, PA	613
Campbell, Oscar	60 CA	19015210	541 Mill St., Salem, OR	256
Campbell, P.	RAMC	Cpl	Liverpool, England	1158*
Campbell, Thomas C.	60 CA	14042461	Shugalack, MI	1371
Campbell, Virgil E.	59 CA	19002216	Weinert, TX	504
Cannella, John D.	USMC	xxx	415 6th St. SW, Mason City, IA	986
Cantwell, Melvin T.	60 CA	18038740	Richland, TX	563
Capell, Henry A.	USN	3420638	1112 Minnesota Ave., Kansas City, KS	1278
Capes, Carl R.	7 Mat	19030463	PO Box 123, Bremerton, Wa	311
Cappelano, Peter J.	803 Eng	32035490	125 Whitney Pl., Buffalo, NY	429
Caravela, Ralph E.	59 CA	20434663	2320 SW 59th Ave., Coral Gables, Fl	470
Cardamon, Frank	USMC	xxx	413 Jackson Ave., Des Moines, IA	755
Carey, Ralph J.	USN	2656141	Rawl, WV	993
Carlos, Felix H.	7 Mat	19050712	1410 Maud St., Los Angeles, CA	925
Caron, Henry L.	USMC	267082	16 Glen St., Adams, MA	1310

Mukden Roster - Original Group   7

Name	Unit	Number	Address	
Carpenter, Harold F.	59 CA	39302688	Mahomet, IL	1090
Carpenter, Morton E.	27 Grp	6972450	Route 3, Booneville, MI	1318
Carr, Ulyssis B.	60 CA	14046208	Star Route, Albertville, AL	370
Carroll, Weston	HDMSB	6146749	Union, ME	599
Carson, Geo. R.	USMC	276733	532 Alabama St., Vallejo, CA	304
Carter, Arthur F.	USMC	xxx	Route 3, Oak Grove, AR	387
Carter, Harold B.	USN	3466963	Route 1, Docahontas, AR	580
Carver, A. J.	60 CA	14037824	Route 1, Guilford College, NC	323
Casey, Geo. R.	34 Sqdn	6293469	317 Sadie St., San Antonio, TX	1517
Cast, Ellie L.	200 CA	38012187	Encino, NM	1322
Castle, James E.	60CA	15017066	330 1/2 N. Broad St., Lancaster, OH	454
Castleberry, Roy C.	200 CA	20843829	Artesia, NM	339
Castriani, Sam J.	60 CA	6003826	813 Grand Ave., Racine. WI	763
Cata, Jose I.	200 CA	38012060	San Juan Puevlo, Chamita, NM	543
Catt, Boyo	59 CA	14043912	Cherokee, NC	1071
Cauthon, Elmer T.	59 CA	17019788	509 Osbon St., Fort Scott, KS	480
Cecil, Waverly J.	60 CA	18048910	Vona, CO	1296
Chacon, Manuel	31 Inf	18048869	Mercedes, TX	1245
Chaffin, Chas. P.	192 Tank	20500756	522 E 5th St., Port Clinton, OH	791
Chaffin, Rex M.	200CA	20842681	510 Kelcher St., Albuquerque, NM	401
Chandler, Paul B.	28 Mat	6372060	Coburn, VA	1552
Chapman, P.	Loyals	Pfc	Barton on Humber, Linconshire, England	1209*
Chase, Chester O.	USN	3811216	1225 S 2nd St., Arcadia, CA	725
Chastain, Jos. B.	USMC	2170992	Waco, TX	516
Childress, Winifred L.	QMC	6582842	Box 351, Laredo, TX	347
Chislom, Ross M.	60 CA	19002116	Route 2, Box 265, Chowchilla, CA	1306
Chorak, Milan M.	60 CA	18029119	325 E Northern, Pueblo, CO	1149
Chosnyka, Joseph	31 Inf	6896944	5005 Forest Blvd., Washington Park, IL	374
Christie, P.	Loyals	Pfc	Hanley, Staffordshire, England	1210*
Christmas, John F.	434 ORD	14049180	426 State St., Rock hill, SC	1132
Christopher, Harold J.	7 Mat	19014977	Elmira, OR	1246
Church, A.E.	Loyals	Pfc	Kensington, S.E., London, England	1236*
Ciboch, Geo. B.	USMC	301037	North Judson, IN	846
Cigoi, Walter F.	192 Tnk	20600398	2235 W Huron St., Chicago, IL	1565
Cinnfrini, Anthony	31 Inf	13004915	3240 N. 20th St.,Philadelphia, PA	299
Cisneros, Luz R.	60 CA	19060862	PO Box 501, Clifton, AZ	603

Mukden Roster - Original Group   8

Name	Unit	Serial	Address	No.
Clancy, J.P.	MJAIF	Cpl	Perth, W. Australia	1199*
Clark, Vonley	60 CA	13017019	St. Paul, VA	255
Clark, Ward S.	16 Bomb	xxx	332 Riverside Blvd., Rockford, IL	170
Clements, Donald R.	59 CA	19017577	807 Wilson Ave., Yakima, WA	893
Clouse, John J.	USMC	270044	2315 SE 32nd Ave., Portland, OR	507
Clymer, Milton I.	803 Eng	33070087	457 Main st., Quakerstown, PA	500
Cochran, Donald F.	USN	2579790	Relay, MO	992
Cochrane, Rochell	200 CA	20843584	111 Sheldon St., Clovis, NM	1297
Cohen, Ray E.	USMC	269014	4106 Berryman Ave., Culver City, CA	677
Coleman, W. R.	200 CA	38011613	Hot Springs, NM	381
Coley, Edward S.	60 CA	14039223	215 S Haywood St., Raleigh, NC	1095
Collins, Alfred D.	24 Pursuit	6998842	815 E. Molar Ave, Martinsburg, WV	287
Collins, Leonard G.	ORD	15067947	PO Box 15, Cincinnati, OH	337
Colvin, Wesley M.	698 Ord	19045992	1600 S. Olive St., Alhambra, CA	297
Compton, Bobboe B.	59 CA	18014487	Route 1, Los Crucas, NM	733
Comstock, Wayne V.	SC	6592678	1822 Holly St., Kansas City, MO	106
Confer, Russell W.	60 CA	18045738	2434 S. Filmore St., Denver, CO	571
Conley, Howard H.	59 CA	19044367	1744 1 st Ave, San Diego, CA	574
Cook, Charles A.	16 Sqdn	6973560	650 Ornwood Ave., Southeast, PA	1454
Cook, Henry H.	SC	6592679	866 Hill St. S.E., Atlanta, GA	587
Cook, Iray	59 CA	19019959	Fort Benton, MT	856
Coorer, James	3 Pursuit	18004746	Route 2, Poteau, OK	307
Cordoxa, Robert R.	59 CA	18000435	Gardener, CO	514
Corley, Richard C.	48 Mat	6881419	106 2nd Ave., Scottdale, PA	1366
Costillo, Herman B.	31 Inf	18049164	117 Austin St., San Antonio, TX	482
Cotton, Harry F.	USN	3930287	3939 NE 67th St., Portland, OR	1536
Couch, Elbert T.	USMC	280846	Piedmont, OK	1417
Covey, Donald L.	USMC	268104	Box 16, St. Maries, ID	784
Cowgill, John D.	31 Pursuit	6569667	5008 Lacey St., Spokane, WA	928
Cox, C.S.	16 Bomb	15067586	Thorpe, WV	169
Cox, Ishmael W.	31 Inf	6882537	Route 1, Leaksville, NC	939
Cox, James C.	60 CA	14043991	Route 2, Conyers, GA	736
Cox, Woodrow T.	192 Tank	38020773	Tishomongo, OK	970
Crabb, Jesse W.	200 CA	20843807	Carlsbad, NM	606
Cramer, Bruce O.	59 CA	17023982	Menville, WY	1040
Cramer, Thomas L.	59 CA	6557283	1001 Hayes St., Emmett, ID	1345

Mukden Roster - Original Group 9

Name	Unit	Number	Address	
Crass, Arthur J.	USMC	268291	Route 1, Monticello, AR	804
Crawford, Walter N.	60 CA	19042018	1827 Norfolk Ave., Dallas,TX	1365
Crea, Joseph	Phil Div	6881561	777 2nd Ave., New Kennsington, PA	278
Creecy, Roy E.	60 CA	19019937	Willow Creek, MT	860
Crenshaw, Harvey L.	60 CA	18038651	Dawson, TX	786
Cress, Harry F.	60 CA	14037700	China Grove, NC	688
Cresswell, Clifford J.	60 CA	18050018	5772 Agnes Ave., Kansas City, MO	732
Crider, Harold L.	45 ORD	14049116	Pomona, MO	1400
Crisp, Carroll	93 Bomb	6259224	Sulphur Springs, TX	742
Crossland, C.R.	21 Pursuit	18013669	Route 3, Lott, TX	132
Crowley, B.	Loyals	Pfc	Liverpool, England	1204*
Crummett, Leland L.	60 CA	19020528	Route 1, Vale, OR	794
Cuchessi, Albert	17 ORD	32059907	299 Sherman Ave., Newark, NJ	645
Cuniffe, V.	RAMC	Pfc	Staffordshire, England	1166*
Cunningham, Sheldon W.	HDMSB	6588986	312 Lewis St., Silverton, OR	1435
Cutler, John W.	DEML	R2021028	184 Nadaturta St., Manila, P.I.	1427
Cydylo, Theodore I.	31 Inf	6978018	2133 Green Point Ave., Schenectady, NY	1263
Dale, Glen E.	59 CA	17010074	Route 2, Bentonville, AR	789
Danehey, Donald E.	USMC	301134	Lawrence, NE	868
Dapron, George I.	USN	3374587	829 Ridge Ave., Festus, MO	1055
Darby, Theodore J.	803 Eng	36032672	6042 S Mozart St., Chicago, IL	1100
Darnold, William T.	60 CA	19006448	Deerpark, WA	778
Davidson, Roy L.	59 CA	18039651	Alexander, IL	792
Davies, D.B.	RAMC	Pfc	Ferndale, Glam, Wales, England	1165*
Davis, Benjamin F.	59 CA	18050020	Fort Lawson, OK	1094
Davis, Earl M.	USMC	xxx	Boone, CO	714
Davis, Elvin D.	34 Pursuit	19015707	Myrtyle Point, OR	227
Davis, John E.	USN	xxx	Navy Dept, Washington, DC	1448
Davis, Wm. W.	60 CA	14376771	2053 Peidmont St., Newberry, SC	1415
Day, Arlin W.	803 Eng	34033399	211 3rd Ave., Cullman, AL	399
De Broise, MD	RAMC	Cpl	Halifax, Yorkshire, England	1155*
De Harrar, Valdemar	515 CA	38012214	Costilla, NM	803
Dean, Ben J.	USMC	xxx	Brownwood, TX	1572
Dean, Mathew W.	59 CA	6583782	Route 1, Dardanelle, AR	600
DeAngeles, Anthony N.	59 CA	6946306	Dysart, PA	1098
Deck, Leonard J.	USN	2484437	2217 N 17th St., Philadelphia, PA	1356

Mukden Roster - Original Group 10

Name	Unit	Service No.	Address	No.
Dees, Carlos A.	60 CA	18043754	Shasta Dam, CA	581
DeKoch, Edward	31 Inf	17016215	4708 Michigan St., St. Louis, MO	1341
Delanty, James E.	DEML	6547508	2605 H St., Bakersfield, CA	451
DeLisle, Wilfred	17 Sqdn	11014634	47-49 Central St., Manchester, NH	1444
Delmuth, W.F.	808 MP	13020847	2706 C St., Philadelphia, PA	1553
Denobile, Wilbur E.	803 Eng	32109908	6702 19th Ave., Brooklyn, NY	1123
Depa, Edward G.	192 Tank	36016369	717 N Pualina St., Chicago, IL	631
Derecola, Chris J.	724 ORD	33050102	366 Cherry St., Pottstown, PA	1441
Dickinson, J.	Loyals	Pfc	Radcliffe, Manchester, England	1188*
Dickson, Truman M.	USMC	276706	Thermopolis, WY	544
Dieball, Chas. W.	USMC	280450	Box 76, Nipomo, CA	611
Diemert, William A.	USMC	276707	12558 27th Ave. NE, Seattle, WA	719
Dietz, Herman G.	USN	3808894	641 Bradshaw Ave., Los Angeles, CA	526
Diez, Fernando B.	3 Pursuit	16005068	541 W MitchellSt., Milwaukee, WI	953
Dillard, C.F.	24 Pursuit	6937090	Box 624, Wardell, MO	156
Dillard, Erskino R.	59 CA	17016216	Nedleton, AR	1339
Dillon, J.D.	USMC	264944	1746 Geneva St., Aurora, CO	1119
Dinapas, Jos. B.	USMC	275658	3735 Deodar St., East Chicago,IL	506
Ditewig, Milton W.	USAFFE	36008321	4228 N Ridgewood Ave., Chicago, IL	1045
Doherty, Ahan H.	FEASC	6274123	Omaha, NE	966
Dolsen, John C.	USMC	xxx	320 W 12th St., Traverse City, MI	1140
Donelson, William	60 CA	6559733	311 N Broadway, Princeton, MO	900
Dorr, Samuel H.	MD	18046438	117 NW St., Anaheim, CA	1386
Dowland, W.	RAMC	Pfc	Murrumbeena, S.E., Victoria, Australia	1198*
Downing, Carl E.	USMC	274572	230 S. Covington St., Hillsboro, TX	262
Downs, George R.	QMC	19054518	St. Ignatius, MT	582
Doyle, M.L.	L/Mt	Pfc	Lanchfield Village, Australia	1196*
Dragich, Charles	19 AB	6911380	210 Norman Ave., Alliance, OH	226
Drexel, H.H.	AIF	Pfc	Newton, Sidney, N.S.W., Australia	1215*
Driggers, Jessie J.	803 Eng	19000101	Mamers, NC	260
Driver, Francis M.	USN	4143659	2315 7th Ave., Milwaukee, OR	694
Dugan, Leonard M.	60 CA	14042343	Shuqualak, MI	1038
Dunakey, Ben B.	31 Inf	17016372	Route 4, Sullivan, MO	408
Dunlavy, Harry G.	USMC	270544	Route 9, Box 350, Fresno, CA	672
Duran, Gilbert	60 CA	18016874	El Rito, NM	709
Duran, Gregory GD	60 CA	18016888	Box 53, Ortiz, CO	822

Auxden Roster - Original Group   11

Name	Unit	Number	Address	
Durand, Paul G.	QMC	19056817	Richmond, CA	521
Dusek, Milton	60 CA	18048932	Harlengen, TX	777
Dysinger, Richard W.	3 Sqdrn	6911570	524 Larrzlere Ave., Zanesville, OH	1323
Eagan, Mitchell W.	MD	6275782	2012 S Pheonix, Tulsa, OK	1309
Earhart, Ernest F.	803 Eng	35160842	Route 3, Crown Point, IN	1118
Earnest, Malcolm	27 Grp	6930009	617 Wall St., Shrevesport, LA	1368
Easeley, Robert C.	USN	3600888	Richard, TX	943
Eccles, T.	Loyals	Pfc	Bolton, England	1173*
Echols, Francis M.	28 Mat	6265778	Goose Creek, TX	1274
Eckardt, Arthur H.	59 CA	18048802	2414 Saunders Ave., San Antonio, TX	1420
Edlebrock, Melville J.	59 CA	18001669	226 7th Ave. N., St. Cloud, MN	1141
Edsall, Carlton E.	17 Sqdn	6838318	535 Ontario Ave., Renova, PA	1451
Edwards, George V.	USN	2583029	Grantsville, MD	252
Edwards, Randall S.,	USN	3164411	Ruskin, Nebraska	104
Eldridge, Paul O.	2nd Obs	6947288	11 Egyptian Ave., Christopher, IL	204
Elkins, Howard H.	59 CA	18046357	Ere, CO	283
Elliot, Jack E.	17 ORd	661273	1631 E. Weaver Road, Columbus, OH	344
Elliot, Leon A.	194 Tank	20900705	318 Church St., Salinas, CA	453
Elliot, Lewis H.	60 CA	19013469	Sunimersville, MO	186
Ellsworth, Earl E.	34 Pursuit	18003900	PO Box 343,Enid, OK	263
Embry, Billy M.	USN	2721951	19 Elizabeth St., Montgomery, AL	762
Emmard, Arthur D.	USN	4441958	Route 1, Box 149, Montesano, WA	1467
English, Merle L.	USN	3719782	54 Santa Clara Ave., Long Beach, CA	720
Epps, John R.	803 Eng	37056379	Harviel, MO	1028
Erler, Otto C.	USMC	267958	3422 Culver Ave., Dalla, TX	1446
Ervin, Rufus O.	7 Mat	R1492038	5392 Corner St., Riverside, CA	1266
Estel, B.J.	60 CA	xxx	xxx	1573
Etter, David R.	200 CA	20843318	Big Clifty, KY	1456
Evanczik, Joseph N.	MPC	6718748	144 Martin Road, Jamestown, NY	700
Evans, Chas. E.	USMC	xxx	1046 Orner St., Cartage, MO	862
Evans, David M.	803 Eng	33062330	Lonaconing, MD	457
Evans, Raymond G.	USN	2996941	236 N Ave. A, Clinton, IL	956
Evans, Robert L.	200 CA	20842683	1123 Forrester Ave., Albuquerque, NM	422
Ewing, Richard D.	200 CA	38012324	Box 72, Atoka, OK	1556
Farmer, K.L.	16 Bomb	7002784	Route 3, Wesson, MS	129
Farrant, B.H.	RE	L/Sgt	Great Yarmouth, Norfolk, England	1167*

Mukden Roster - Original Group　　12

Name	Unit	Serial	Address	No.
Fayal, Herman F.	60 CA	19053638	Mendicino, CA	257
Feeney, J.	Loyals	Cpl	Pendleton, Manchester, England	1229*
Feilzer, Fred. W.	USN	2232242	556 16th Ave., San Francisco, CA	1081
Ferneau, Willard L.	409 SC	19021224	202 Canal St., Bend, OR	1113
Ferrin, Kenneth R.	20 Bomb	Route 5,	Box 103, Pheonix, AZ	463
Fink, Nelson H.	USN	2795926	907 1/2 Wayne Ave., Dayton, OH	1344
Finley, Carl O.	59 CA	6297068	58 N St., Gennessee, NY	1546
Finnegan, David M.	60 CA	6993611	Cassandra, PA	595
Finnigan, Glen L.	3 Pursuit	15013371	Furnace St., Mineral Ridge, OR	952
Fipps, W.H.	34 Pursuit	18031289	San Gabriel, TX	133
Fite, James T.	27 Bomb	6928527	4 Allendale Road, Montgomery, AL	286
Fitzgerald, Donald L	MD	19053149	220 Castro, Mountain View, CA	1326
Fleming, J. W.	200 CA	20842945	410 S Girard St., Albuquerque, NM	692
Fleming, Robert W.	16 Bomb	11024240	684 Country Way, N. Scitukte, MA	448
Fletcher, Garth H.	27 Group	11000229	Enosburg Falls, VT	394
Fletcher, Pinex	200 CA	38012562	Dexter, NM	1046
Flowers, Daniel L.	31 Inf	17014694	Hoxie, AR	1554
Foley, G.	Loyals	Pfc	Newton Heath, Manchester, England	1193*
Forbes, Thomas J.	60 CA	15617503	109 7th St. West, New Philadelphia, OH	1470
Forehand, James M.	USN	2681253	Cochran, GA	704
Forehand, Julius C.	60 CA	6877613	Box 104, Del Ray Beach, FL	1131
Foster, John G.	803 Eng	34076738	Anacoco, LA	962
Fournier, Clarence D.	60 CA	18048704	230 Thompson Pl., San Antonio, TX	1372
Foust, Carl W.	USMC	271946	Route 2, Sandusky, OH	740
Fowler, Earl	194 Tank	26523453	Bergin, KY	811
Francis, James H.	59 CA	6259592	3005 Locke Lane, Houston, TX	843
Fredrick, Trevis P.	31 Inf	14042433	Route 1, Iuka, MS	1405
Freeman, Hubert E.	60 CA	15065693	Corbin, KY	896
Frising, Wm. A.	USMC	xxx	89-18 115th St., Richmond Hill, N.Y., NY	1414
Fromer, Sol	59 CA	19018310	335 Home St., Bronx, NY	659
Fuerst, Morris V.	USMC	xxx	Oakland, CA	1052
Fugazzi, Charles B.	59 CA	15065795	618 Lime St., Lexington, KY	1423
Fuller, C.N.	Loyals	Sgt	London, W.I., England	1211*
Funk, Leslie G.	59 CA	19020189	Snyder Road, Station E, St. Joseph, MO	883
Fyke, William L.	60 CA	16015549	80 Ineham Ave., Lackawana, NY	1511
Gagliano, Neil	803 Eng	33033801	Box 72, Hillsville, PA	266

Name	Unit	Service No.	Address	
Gagliardi, F.V.	24 Pursuit	6291425	DeLaqua, CO	143
Gagne, Roger H.	60 CA	11016520	2 Bowman St., Augusta, ME	1114
Gagnet, Thomas R.	803 Eng	34076399	516 Railroad Ave., Plagermine, LA	961
Gaines, Delmar	31 Inf	19021171	Route 3 Box 222, Hood River, OR	329
Galardi, Fred V.	60 CA	6013483	1033 Cooper St., Jackson, MI	652
Gale, Marvin	QMC	6550034	1908 NE Halsey St., Portland, OR	752
Gallagher	Loyals	Sgt	London, S.E., England	1240*
Gallagher, John T.	60 CA	16041134	833A 8th St., E. St. Louis. IL	588
Galler, Alfred H.	60 CA	18048860	Route 2, Rogers, TX	855
Galloway, Chas. H.	809 MP	19020918	Sand Lake, OR	494
Galloway, Herman L.	60 CA	6578908	Route 5, Boise, ID	753
Gamboa, Jacob S.	194 Tnk	20900661	211 Front St., Salinas, CA	1301
Garcia, Abel	MD	20842386	1401 S Broadway, Albuquerque, NM	1387
Garcia, Ernest	194 Tank	38054390	227 W. 17th St., Port Arthur, TX	461
Gardner, Lee J.	515 CA	20842507	Route 1, Rincon, NM	1102
Garland, Joseph M.	60 CA	15061807	914 N Belmont Ave., Indianapolis, IN	1418
Garrand, Stenis	60 CA	14042458	Route 1, Terry, MI	1370
Garrett, Alvin W.	200 CA	20842508	Box 294, Deming. NM	623
Garrow, Everett C.	USMC	296879	Marshall, MN	508
Gauntt, Clifford J.	60 CA	16017988	2620 Edward St., Alton, IL	793
Gavito, Valetin F.	59 CA	18048986	222 Jefferson St., Brownsville, TX	1026
Gazer, Jos. A.	17 ORD	36103409	9785 Kensington, Detroit, MI	1496
Gease, Thomas W.	803 Eng	35030854	73 Dakota Ave., Colombus, OH	214
Gebbers, George L.	60 CA	19014728	Pateros, WA	1013
Geerholt, R. E.	803 Eng	32092325	Route 4, Troy, NY	390
Genovese, John A.	515 CA	36106694	2652 Monroe St., Detroit, MI	830
Gentry, Walter J.	515 CA	20843937	19 Bennett St., Geneva, IL	651
Gerry, J.G.	FEAFC	11020414	12 Shenandoah St., Boston, MA	144
Ghebul, Joe R.	7 Mat	19050356	344 E Mercury St., Butte, MT	1348
Gibbs, Wayne	USN	3371107	Ina, IL	141
Giddings, Ralph E.	60 CA	12006752	52 Queens St., Jersey City, NJ	1461
Gilbert, A.	Loyals	Pfc	Ilkestone, Derbyshire, England	1222*
Gilbert, James A.	59 CA	6983531	Route 1, Elton Road, Alden, NY	273
Gilbert, Leslie A.	31 Inf	19017706	1401 S 18th Ave., Yakima, WA	904
Gilbert, Ross H.	USN	xxx	Box 554, Gatun Lock, Panama, C.Z.	591
Gildon, Oris J.	MD	6295320	Rodessa, LA	1488

Mukden Roster - Original Group   14

Name	Unit	Service No.	Address	No.
Gilliland, Howard M.	803 Eng	6579271	Star Route, Bend, OR	213
Gilman, Harold C.	200 CA	38012429	Belen, NM	488
Gilmet, John R.	21 Pursuit	6914200	423 N. Quincy St., Green Bay, WI	279
Gilmore, Clyde E.	48 Mat	6971590	Cordovo, AL	1430
Ginther, Merle E.	27 Mat	6274799	Atwood, KS	309
Gipp, John H.	200 CA	36106791	2757 W Euclid Ave., Detroit, MI	627
Gladden, Bryon G.	803 Eng	34080034	Route 2, Tallapoosa, GA	398
Glass, A.	Loyals	Pfc	London, S.E., London, England	1201*
Glodery, Alvin E.	USMC	301431	Britton, SD	1334
Goddard, John R.	200 CA	38012685	El Rito, NM	445
Gonzales, Joseph V.	USMC	xxx	219 Del Gado, Santa Fe, NM	590
Gooby, A. W.	Loyals	L/Sgt	West Hampton, W.I., England	1235*
Goode, William B.	USMC	289820	2137 S 76th St., West Allis, WI	1042
Goodson, James R.	31 Inf	18063234	Mount Vernon, TX	363
Gopenhauer, Allen J.	31 Inf	18049157	Route 2, Fairfax, OK	1381
Gordon, John P.	USMC	280703	736 Fisher St., Chicago, IL	1347
Gordon, Louis B.	698 ORD	7023400	606 High St., Petersburg, VA	948
Gordon, Marcus E.	AWSC	15065865	Madison, IN	807
Gozzo, Joseph S.	803 Eng	39233331	1021 S 25th St., Omaha, NE	1027
Grabski, H.J.	59 CA	16003943	4733 Hickory Ave., Hammond, IN	139
Graf, Albert J.	192 Tnk	36206245	Shell Lake, WI	1428
Graves, C. P.	19 AB	6822281	Traer, IA	191
Graves, DeWitt O.	USN	3602108	Box 64, LeCompte, LA	1076
Graves, Warren D.	200 CA	38011883	Nogal, NM	734
Grayson, Ben	60 CA	18050110	Route 2, Box 34, Broken Arrow, OK	554
Grayson, William F.	7 Mat	6575180	605 E 5th St., Port Angeles, WA	1548
Green, David J.	31 Inf	6842110	5202 Woodland Ave., Philadelphia, PA	483
Green, Harold B.	808 MP	12002557	22 Union St., Lockport, NY	1416
Greenman, Geo. E.	USMC	282791	824 N Ave., Aurora, IL	1073
Greig, L.A.M.,	RA	Lt.	Aukland, New Zealand	28
Griffin, A.B.	RA	Lt.	British Blenheim, New Zealand	30
Griffin, Ben T.	60 CA	xxx	426 S Main St., Logan, UT	773
Griffin, H.C.	60 CA	18042248	Route 3, Mullen, TX	166
Griffith, Ed F.	HDMSB	19050953	107 W. Elm St., Compton, CA	292
Griffith, Ralph E.	60 CA	17016381	1001 Broadway, Hannibal, MO	552
Grizzard, Herbert W	USN	2952423	1207 N 5th St., Nashville, TN	1088

Name	Unit	Service No.	Address	No.
Grobe, William O.	59 CA	R-208636	826 Kickapoo St., Leavenworth, KS	1061
Grokett, Russell A.	3 Pursuit	6262712	1020 Osage St., Neodeska, KS	319
Grooms, Hershell A.	515 CA	38012259	625 S Walter St., Albuquerque, NM	1532
Grounds, Edward A.	60 CA	6283005	Grapeland, TX	798
Grover, Theron E.	Eng	19052244	Sutter, CA	275
Groves, J.J.	AASC	Pfc	Stanmore, Sidney, N.S.W.,Australia	1216*
Grow, Neville L.,	CAC	0237525	2604 Ogden Ave., Ogden, UT	2
Gruber, Paul B.	809 MP	19000098	102 Florida Ave., San Bruno, CA	493
Grundy, Cody H	59 CA	17023623	Route 4, Box 291, Little Rock, AR	1037
Grundy, John T.	60 CA	17023627	Route 4, Box 291, Little Rock, AR	1036
Guess, Odell C.	USN	3561650	Millsap, TX	1019
Guidos, John C.	USN	2570899	129 E. 3rd St., Long Beach, CA	484
Guilfoil, John H.	17 Bomb	6920321	6239 N. Fairfield Ave., Chicago, IL	219
Gunnino, G.E.	RA	Pfc	xxx	1192*
Gussenhaven, Ray A.	USMC	267035	4605 Quitman, Denver, CO	731
Gust, George	60 CA	19020991	Box 1027, Beulah, ND	557
Gustafsen, C. P.	USMC	270355	2248 N. Springfield Ave., Chicago, IL	305
Guye, Earl W.	200 CA	38055882	1513 E. Alabama St., Houston, TX	181
Gwartney, James C.	USMC	xxx	319 SE 20th St., Oklahoma City,OK	313
Haase, Howard L.	USMC	301434	Steele, ND	999
Hafer, Rex N.	60 CA	17014191	Route 3, Lane City, AR	715
Haigwood, J.H. Jr.	60 CA	18015221	Box 503, Stephenville, Texas	111
Halford,William T.	USMC	280640	222 N. Congress St., Jackson, MS	459
Hall, Herman	19 Bomb	13035003	Democrate, KY	835
Hall, Wilson M.	31 Inf	37066983	Paragoud, AR	358
Hallmark, Kenneth L.	USMC	273593	1053 Pacific Blvd., San Diego, CA	577
Hamrich, Cecil	31 Inf	6649631	Blue Sulphur Springs, WV	926
Hand, James W.	60 CA	18038752	Route 2, Paducah, TX	1004
Handlin, Aubrey J.	60 CA	19020957	417 Rogers St., Hot Springs, AR	1000
Hankins, Stanley H.,	CAC	0278283	Frankfort, KY	1
Hankins, William L.	31 Inf	18021579	715 W Fruit St., Albuquerque, NM	1050
Hansen, Boyd S.,	SC	0406494	Malad, Idaho	7
Hansen, Carlos A.	3 Pursuit	6574296	Route 1, Trementon, UT	175
Hansen, D.P.	RAOC	Sgt	Wirswall, Whitchurch, Shropshire, Engl.	1181*
Harlan, Henry C.	60 CA	17014146	Truman, AR	901
Harland, Don W.	19 Bomb	6936110	Clarinda, IA	759

Mukden Roster - Original Group 16

Name	Unit	Number	Address	
Harless, Wiley L.	93 Bomb	14029568	905 Shorter Ave., Rome, GA	364
Harris, Chas. H.	60 CA	15061750	520 N 2nd St., Vincennes, IN	1041
Harris, James H.	USMC	275154	Route 1, Box 13, Coolodge, AZ	713
Harris, James R.	59 CA	18018204	Binger, OK	679
Harris, William N.	USMC	274608	Box 92, St. Louis, OK	758
Harriss, G.	AAOC	Pfc	N.S.W., Australia	1233*
Hartin, Robert T.	60 CA	17026179	724 19th Ave. S., Minneapolis, MN	288
Hartman, James R.	FEASC	6150533	Murphy's Lane, Shelton, CT	380
Hartman, Thomas J.	60 CA	17025097	529 Farrington St., St. Paul, MN	562
Haskill, Richard M.	17 Pursuit	16010667	Box 58 Weberville, MI	315
Hatch, Roy H.	60 CA	17014190	Route 3, Lake City, AR	729
Hayes, Otis N.	59 CA	18018248	Keota, OK	806
Hayes, Geo. W.	59 CA	19020889	605 North West St., Lima, OH	598
Hayman, Ralph M.	803 Eng	37064414	129 Velma, Lemay, MO	1383
Haysley, Louis A.	59 CA	15061733	Monda, IN	699
Hayton, Leroy C.	60 CA	16021838	Route 2, Tomahawk, WI	1011
Hearn, Chas. L.	803 Eng	15010318	Worthington, WV	616
Heaton, S.	Loyals	Pfc	Preston, Lanonshire, England	1189*
Hecimovich, John J.	31 Inf	17023975	404 Webb Location, Hibbing, MN	1411
Heck, Marion W.	515 CA	36050813	Gillespie, IL	1396
Hedemark, Earl O.	USMC	270045	Walnut Creek, CA	550
Hedges, Frank W.	31 Inf	17018687	Walthill, NE	1473
Hegoal, Joseph	24 Pursuit	6297000	PO Box 81, Borger, TX	622
Heiliger, H.B.	USMC	301137	218 E. Main, Madison, WI	136
Helchel, Warren W.W.	200 CA	20842600	805 N Tyler, Amarillo, TX	1394
Helfrich, James H.	803 Eng	35030937	328 Pearl St., Cresline, OH	1336
Helms, Walter A.	429 SC	19048842	Box 849, Maricopa, CA	927
Hembree, Huber L.	698 Ord	6230235	Oklahoma City, OK	306
Henderson, Jones R.	31 Inf	6385450	20 Crest St., Lyma, SC	1424
Henderson, Les T.	5 Int C	6286466	Route 1, May, TX	180
Hendrickson, W.E.	USMC	215237	4461 Connecticut Ave. NW, Washington, DC	1539
Henry, Pemberton D.	USN	3821025	RuLo, NE	994
Hensey, Donald F.	60 CA	20951809	1618 N 36th St., Seattle, WA	1519
Herbert, Robert C.	60 CA	18001657	Route 3, Golden, CO	1069
Herbert, Thomas	USMC	274831	Route 1, St. Martinville, LA	847
Herbert, Wayne H.	60 CA	15065667	38 West Riverside Dr., Newport, KY	361

Name	Unit	Serial	Address	No.
Herbon, Carl R.	USMC	234240	Eads, CO	890
Herbst, Mark G.,	MC	0419662	431 S. McKinley Ave., Canton, OH	3
Herring, Robert R.	27 Sqdn	6969898	233 Abercorn St., Savanah, GA	1426
Hewitt, M.G.	RAMC	Pfc	Highbury, London, N.I., England	1163*
Hewgley, William M.	34 Pursuit	6251383	110 Tremlett St., San Antonio, TX	223
Hicks, Leonard P.	QMC	36212102	371 W. Main St., Waukesha, WI	388
Hick, J.N.	RAMC	L/Cpl	Walton, Wakefield, Yorkshire, England	1162*
Hightower, P.T.	21 Pursuit	6241688	Gen. Del., Sequin, Tx	193
Hill, J.F.	Loyals	Pfc	Stainton, Cumberland, England	1186*
Hillard, Virgil	MD	1500839	Hagerstown, IN	1385
Hilton, Chas. M.	QMC	17014378	Delight, AR	663
Hitlon, J.	Loyals	Pfc	Catterton, Olkham, Lanconshire, England	1223*
Hinds, James D.	SC	15017608	122 Hughes Ave., Lima, OH	400
Histin, David S.	515 CA	38011258	Acomita, NM	542
Hitchcock, Raymond F.	803 Eng	35033409	Canal, Fulton, OH	667
Hnizdor, Nichlas	60 CA	16013590	1903 W Ohio St., Chicago, Il	637
Hoch, Elwell W.	19 Bomb	6978281	9 N. New Jersey Ave., Atlantic City, NJ	523
Hodge, Perry F.	60 CAC	16008689	Oakfield, WI	188
Hodgson, J.	RA	Pfc	Reccar, Yorkshire, England	1191*
Hoegert, Henry C.	60 CA	18048826	Robstown, TX	1360
Hogbe, William H.	HDMSB	7023311	Buckroe Beach, VA	472
Hogue, Dallas E.	USN	3466944	Box 937, Bakersfield, CA	706
Holliday, Frank N.	59 CAC	17008956	Marshfield, MO	145
Holton, Dexter J.	17 ORD	15047583	Mt. Sterling, KY	449
Holt, Aaron	60 CA	18036336	Chillicothe, TX	334
Holt, Edward W.	60 CA	19054264	Arlee, MT	524
Hoovman, Chas. W.	803 Eng	32063631	18 Union Ave., Clifton, NJ	271
Hopkins, W.H.	24 Pursuit	6555920	421 51st St., Long Beach, CA	295
Hopper, Aaron C.	194 Tank	35101735	Murray, KY	1017
Horner, R.B.	RA	Cpt	British Masterton, New Zealand	30
Hovarter, Maurice R.	27 Grp	15059076	Ashley, IN	1409
Howard, Berry	60 CA	18043816	Rush Springs, OK	776
Howard, Cecil	60 CA	18043819	Rush Springs, OK	775
Howard, Jean S.	59 CA	18017455	1611 W Errand Blvd., Detroit, MI	1009
Howard, William A.	USMC	301292	314 Gaines St., Little Rock, AR	1502
Howell, Clayton F.	200 CA	38012614	Clayton, NM	1509

Mukden Roster - Original Group   18

Name	Unit	Serial No.	Address	No.
Hubbard, Rob R.	197 Tank	20645214	308 S. Madison St., Ecansville, WI	353
Hudgens, S.R.	200 CA	38012314	203 West Len St., Hobbs, NM	150
Hudson, Chas.	60 CA	16013544	410 William St., Sturgis, MI	1012
Huebner, Arthur E.	60 CA	17025003	9509 Blase Dale Ave. S, Oxboro,MS	802
Huerta, Trino C.	200 CA	38031569	1411 San Fernando St., San Antonio, TX	548
Huff, Vernon G.	4 Sep Chem	19052637	Route 2, Blyville, AR	621
Huffman, Isaiah K.	60 CA	14037638	204 N.E. St., Kingston, NY	870
Hurd, Earl A.	60 CA	17027424	Route 1, Perry, IA	1525
Hurley, Walter S.	31 Inf	6536595	San Francisco, CA	489
Hutchinson, Stephen D.	59 CA	14013426	Milton, FL	1361
Hutton, Roy J.	200 CA	3801291	Box 296, Farmington, NM	1403
Ianozzi, Jos. J.	803 Eng	32033285	321 Campbell St., Rochester, NY	1495
Ireton, Carl V.	200 CA	3801245	515 N 5th St., Clinton, OK	958
Irvine, Wyatt H.	31 Inf	20932306	3916 E 2nd St., Long Beach, CA	593
Jackson, John R.	31 Inf	6379457	Box 186, Fairfax, OK	368
Jackson, Wendell R.	200 CA	36104992	8288 De Soto St., Detroit, MI	432
Jackson Robert G.	31 Inf	6386703	Box 105, Brinson, GA	452
Jacob, James H.	59 CA	6387701	3301 5th Ave., Columbus, GA	1020
Jagers, Wm.	803 Eng	6874489	350 Irving Ave., Bridgeton, NJ	1357
Janacek, Jack C.	USMC	xxx	Roanoke, IL	1018
Jemison, Edmund L.	ACWB	69820005	Basom, NY	253
Jenkins, J.T.	USMC	258017	608 S 4th St., McGhee, AR	671
Jenkins, Morgan E.	803 Eng	33076224	215 Schyler Ave., Kingston, PA	819
Jensen, Harold C.	USN	3823640	4437 Idaho St., San Diego, CA	1077
Jernigan, Carl	59 CA	18042242	Carrigan, TX	586
Jessop, J.J.	USMC	301363	1914 Arroyo Ave., San Carlos, CA	1566
Jette, Leon R.	HDMSB	19054363	Route 1, River Road, Missoula, MT	730
Jim, Glen	200 CA	38012463	Tohachi, NM	477
Jirasek, Norbert	4 CGAC	6442961	114 Paine Ave., Toledo, OH	629
Jobb, Thomas W.	60 CA	39000578	303 S. 3rd St.,Missoula, MT	246
Johler, Jacob J.	60 CA	12002558	456 Spring St., Buffalo, NY	564
Johngrass, Sam	HDMSB	6949857	Box 34, Hillvale, PA	735
Johns, E.N.U.	RASC	Pfc	Irymple, Victoria, Australia	1200*
Johnson, Amos	59 CA	6438587	585 Lloyd St., Barberton, OH	325
Johnson, Chas. T.	698 ORD	19044414	2384 Stockton Dr., San Diego, CA	1481
Johnson, Daniel W.	QMC	19012927	Fortuna, CA	501

Mukden Roster - Original Group   19

Name	Unit	Serial	Address	No.
Johnson, Ed W.	59 CA	37046659	Lawn Hill, IA	1497
Johnson, Erwin R.	48 Mat	14017289	1412 Alvar St., New Orleans, LA	277
Johnson, Francis A.	803 Eng	35160101	727 Perry St., St. Vincennes, IN	497
Johnson, Geo. A.,	20 Pursuit	6293958	Ramah, NM	121
Johnson, J.C.	RA	Captain	British Prospect, Bermuda	26
Johnson, Morris H.	USMC	297022	Route 3, Carthage, MO	675
Johnson, Orville A.	USN	3558213	321 E Cherry St., Enid, OK	1010
Johnson, Robert E.,	59 CA	18017444	53 Encanto Blvd., Pheonix, AZ	19
Johnson, Warren P.	60 CA	39010218	Uelino, NE	995
Johnson, Wendel C.	QMC	38023260	Box 475, Garber, OK	698
Johnson, William A.	60 CA	15061743	Route 1, Mt. Vernon, IN	884
Johnson, Willis A.	USMC	267444	Watson, IL	437
Johnson, Wilmer	USN	xxx	Box 726 Houma, LA	1329
Jolly, R.	Loyals	L/cpl 268238	West Houghton, Nr. Bolton, England	1231*
Jones, Harry E.	USMC	6274616	4421 Van Horn Ave., Los Angeles, CA	941
Jones, Louis C.	2 OBS	19015901	Dillon, MT	888
Jones, Melville T.	34 Pursuit	3371239	Nyssa, OR	951
Jones, Raphael O.	USN	6816513	203 Shelby St., Bevier, MO	1378
Jones, Robert H.	59 CA	xxx	Bentonville, AR	697
Jones, William B.	USN	6243898	2325 Ocean Front, Santa Monica, CA	946
Jordan, Murray G.	20 Pursuit	19054433	Route 3, Colorado, TX	247
Joslin, Frances L.	59 CA	Pfc	Missoula, MT	474
Joy, R.	RA	6132438	Beeston, Leeds, II, England	1178*
Joy, William J.	20 Pursuit	R1114757	31 Bradley St., Somerville, MA	207
Joyner, Charles	93 Bomb	18049938	1402 W Woodland Ave., San Antonio, TX	1503
Junk, P.G.	60 CA	6949515	Route 2, Tecumseh, OK	1528
Kachmar, Stephen A.	60 CA	37025333	Box 141, Borensboro, PA	560
Kachmarech, Lawernce D.	194 Tank	4143659	Route 3, Box 187, Foley, MN	456
Kane, John W.	USN	13017096	510 Delaware Ave., Wilmington, DE	693
Kane, William O.	24 Grp	301440	208 Minor St., Richmond, VA	1455
Karalinus, Peter B.	USMC	6578462	Firdale, Manitoba, Canada	1083
Karavos, George P.	ORD	6983395	223 Seneca Ave., San Francisco, CA	726
Karlson, Kennthe E.	59 CA	223466	508 Sheldon St., Norwich, NY	913
Karpin, Edward T. A.	USMC	6886161	743 Barard Ave., St. Paul, MN	912
Kasarda, George	803 Eng	6948945	606 Sanderson Ave., Throop, PA	541
Kazinetz, Isador	24 Grp		737 S 4th St., Philadelphia, PA	1462

Mukden Roster - Original Group   20

Name	Unit	Serial No.	Address	Page
Kearney, Earl	59 CA	15065704	Congleton, KY	683
Keever, Joseph W.	60 CA	6923564	York, SC	555
Keiffer, Joseph H.	USMC	257698	Grandview, WA	1395
Kiernan, Gerald M.	803 Eng	32116669	36 Yale St., Inwood, Long Island, NY	1067
Kilmer, Emmet L.	USN	3371089	Chesterfield, MO	724
Kimzey, J.W.	59 CAC	6951477	Route 2 Box 100, Hermleigh, TX	198
Kindell, William R.	192 Tank	2060448	1235 S. 20th Ave., Maywood, Il	466
King, Clarence J.	17 Pursuit	6772072	17605 Kentucky Ave., Detroit, MI	116
King, David L.	200 CA	38011828	420 S. Richmond St., Albuquerque, NM	405
King, Irvin R.	USMC	280834	745 Riverside Drive, New York, NY	1079
King, Jack W.	HDMSB	17023846	180 N Michigan Blvd., Chicago, IL	1346
King, Rollin O.	803 ENG	33084519	Box 186, Ford City, PA	558
King, Starling O.	31 Inf	18063208	Box 316, Gainesville, TX	1487
Kinney, Edward	808 MP	6942153	2021 E. Dauphin St., Philadelphia, PA	187
Kirk, Chas. D. Jr.	17 Bomb	14014439	Orlando, FL	172
Kirk, Mark	60 CA	19020990	Junction City, OR	1542
Kirshner, Max A.	SC	12057835	4044 Broadway, N.Y.,NY	21
Klein, Clayton C.	194 Tank	20935174	1604 Y Ave., La Grande, OR	782
Kline, Fred. W.	USAFFE	76345831	26 Anson St., Charleston, SC	1068
Kniffin, J.L.	HDNSB	18020638	General Delivery, Blackfoot, ID	162
Knight, Billy A.	808 MP	17025116	Marble, MN	1332
Knight, Jackson O.	60 CA	19056525	420 N Daisey, Pasedena, CA	540
Knight, Oscar O	USN	3932100	Wayside Inn, Tigard, OR	1075
Knight, Robert W.	803 Eng	32074001	Riverton, NJ	269
Knippenberg, Theod. R.	USN	2993538	37 Gov Espiritu, Cridad, Cavite, P.I.	559
Knisley, Donald P.	60 CA	15017071	Route 4, Marysville, CA	874
Knowles, Arlin D.	60 CA	18049865	Route 2, Shawnee, OK	502
Knowles, Jesse M.	27 Bomb	6970938	2112 1st St., Lake Charles, LA	194
Kobrinsky, Edward	60 CA	7021033	703 S. Phillip St., Philadelphia, PA	443
Kocevar, Mike J.	60 CA	?	501 S 4th St., Steelton, PA	779
Kocher, Paul D.	HDMSB	13000738	Route 1, Pottsville, PA	805
Kocsis, Bela	34 Pursuit	6716902	81 Dayton Ave., Passaic, NJ	640
Kocsis, Mitchell	MD	6655274	Box 151 Pearl Road, Bevea, OH	1384
Kodaj, Steve	192 Tank	20600413	4029 Anna Ave., Brookfield, MN	464
Koot, John S.	24 Pursuit	13002442	Route 1, Windber, PA	446
Kozakevitch, Felix	803 Eng	32120343	99 Jewel St., Brooklyn, NY	660

Name	Service No.	Address	Unit	Page
Kranc, Norbert J.	36106369	4633 Orleans St., Detroit, MI	200 CA	490
Krebs, John A.	19048951	Morro Bay, CA	60 CA	336
Kreiling, Daniel G.	17011274	Little Rock, AR	59 CA	1064
Kruczek, Michael	1300978	742 6th St., Donora, PA	59 CA	1093
Kucers, Robert L.	18048976	Route 1, Box 222, Edna, TX	59 CA	797
Kudel, Chas. L	6843605	188 West Ave., Lockport, NY	60 CA	584
Kudlac, Milton J.	6981860	36 Mygatt St., Binghamton, NY	60 CA	572
Kuhse, Melvin	17027431	2011 Birchwood Ave., Chicago, IL	60 CA	869
Kuntz, Edward G.	19019906	Wagner, MT	60 CA	810
La Heist, Vernon G.	3163574	4711 Cape May Ave., Ocean Beach, CA	USN	723
La Rue, Virgil	38012296	Sacorro, NM	200 CA	455
Lach, Peter J.,	17011044	4240 Jefferson St. NE., Minneapolis, MN	AMPS	20
Lacko, John W.	33070206	810 Colemont, Braddock, PA	803 Eng	1506
Ladd, David F.	36077434	814 6th St., Carrolown, IL	803 Eng	973
Lamarr, Arthur C.	14037630	Kernersvill, NC	59 CA	836
Lamm, Walter C.	33081923	937 Green St., Allentown, PA	803 Eng	122
Lanclos, H.P.	14014805	908 W. Simco St., LaFayette, LA	16 Bomb	128
Lane, Arthur V.	3803521	151 Rizal St., Olongapoo, P.I.	USN	741
Langdon, Berdette T.	6559310	Route 1, Box 157, Oswego, OR	31 Inf	496
Langevine, Hector J.	16013442	807 Elm St., Bay City, MI	60 CA	535
Langlois, Adlard	6689302	Norton Mills, UT	2 Sqdn	1464
Lankford, Paul H.	6972460	610 Polk St., Gadsden, AL	16 Sqdn	1440
Lanning, John L.	16005232	1944 5th St., Beliot, WI	MC	1080
Lapovsky, Lawrence P.	274876	5046 Damen, Ave., Chicago, IL	USMC	1469
Larkin, Ralph W.	33077147	Ceres, NY	803 Eng	615
Larrick, Cecil C.	6065967	Gove, VA	228 SC	754
Larson, Robert C.	19054362	Box 1335, Walkerville, MT	60 CA	1476
Laszko, Steve	32035831	417 Glenwood Ave., Buffalo, NY	803 Eng	636
Latoz, Sam J.	6798632	123 Nichols St., Westville, IL	20 Pursuit	248
Laughrun, Issac	20523499	Relief, NC	27 Mat	1029
Laursen, Eddy R.	19050430	428 Nevada Ave., El Monte, CA	93 Bomb	250
Lawson, Winston E.	11008307	21 Pleasant St., Orange, MA	27 Mat	617
Lay, Billy H.	15017092	Van, WV	59 CA	1568
Layson, James A.	14047081	Route 1, Monticello, GA	60 CA	1108
Le Grow, Silas B.	20500765	405 4th St., Toledo, OH	192 Tank	815
Leadly, Dale C.	17003454	Rolfe, IA	59 CA	796

Mukden Roster - Original Group   22

Name	Unit	Service No.	Address	No.
Leatherman, Dale	DEML	19019271	177 Simcox St., Wadsworth, OH	1398
Lee, A.	Loyals	Sgt	Stratford, London, England	1237*
Lee, Cleovis M.	200 CA	20843475	307 Reed St., Clovis, NM	118
Lee, Everett M.	59 CA	17023975	1509 10th Ave., Scottsbluff, NE	1413
Lee, Harold E.	194 Tnk	20900664	263 Maple St., Salinas, CA	1523
Lee, Jack B.	USN	3567031	Maud, OK	505
Leek, Warren H.	698 ORD	19056520	333 S Breesee Ave., Baldwin Park, CA	887
Legare, William B.	809 MP	6385718	214 Spring St., Charlestown, SC	979
Leggett, Marion K.	USMC	279861	Route 3, Newton, MA	367
Lehman, Paul C.	USN	3744474	Alemeda, CA	867
Leicester, P.	RA	Lt.	British Lensberg, Tennington, England	27*
Leininger, Fred J.	194 Tank	37026131	2421 Clinton Ave., S. Minneapolis, MN	465
Lemoine, Ernest M.	USN	xxx	Colfax, LA	914
Lemon, Albert L.	USMC	80244	2015 Hudson Ave., Norwood, OH	891
Lennartson, James E.	3 Sqdn	6976687	23 Center St., Jamestown, NY	1486
Leone, Donato	803 Eng	3204849	556 Manhattan St., Schenectady, NY	378
Lester, Kenneth C.	PE	19056886	3255 Monette Pl., Los Angeles, CA	1316
Levie, James K.	SC	0382883	511 Whitfoord Ave. N.E., Atlanta, GA.	12
Levrier, Alfredo	200 CA	38029820	1445 Van Buren St., Brownsville, TX	302
Lewis, Chax. J.	USN	3001122	1014 Summer St., Pekin, IL	686
Lewis, Corley B.	60 CA	xxx	Cutshin, KY	1574
Lidell, A. W.	RE	SQMS	Kentish Town, London, N.W., England	1151*
Lieb, Robert R.	60 CA	15017139	Route 6, Hillstop Station, Columbus, OH	978
Liebert, Harley E.	MD	19043540	120 State Line, Grand View, MO	1494
Lievy, David J.	680 ORD	39007376	1106 Stanyan St., San Francisco, CA	1054
Ligus, Thomas G.	28 Mat	6923836	Greensburg, PA	968
Lince, Clyde F.	60 CA	19016799	Selah, WA	834
Linsen, George	21 Sqdn	19015648	327 N Skidmore St., Portland, OR	1479
Lippard, John B.	USMC	273486	Seagrave, TX	578
Little, A.W.	RAMC	Sgt	Sunbury-on Thames, Middlesex, England	1153*
Littman, Morris	19 Bomb	6995757	768 South 4th, Philadelphia, PA	232
Locarnini, Peter R.	USN	xxx	Route 2, Diana, CA	743
Locke, H.	SAIF	Sgt	Mullimbimby, N.S.W., Australia	1239*
Lockhart, Estel E.	60 CA	5065804	Broadshaw, WV	479
Loftus, T.	Loyals	Pfc	xxx	1207*
Logsdon, Jeff T.	59 CA	18001712	Rye, CO	950

Mukden Roster - Original Group   23

Name	Unit	Serial	Address	No.
Lollar, Eugene M.	59 CA	18042181	Route 1, Box 69, Buffalo, TX	894
Loman, Louis E.	200 CA	20843754	Route 1, Box 109, Carlsbad, NM	653
Long, Carl N.	200 CA	36050907	Route 2, Manito, IL	680
Long, Geo. C.	60 CA	16013599	709 S Erie St., Bay City, MI	1272
Long, Martin S.	200 CA	36052689	Route 2, St. Elmo, IL	681
Long, Melton L.	59 CA	6250305	Burke, TX	907
Long, Roy J.	60 CA	6796346	310 Fremont St., Woodstock, IL	317
Long Donovan C.	34 Sqd	18018414	Austin, CO	1258
Longest, Russell B.	809 MP	6912656	Wilmington, IL	745
Lopez, Genaro B.	200 CA	20843145	619 Franklin St., Santa Fe, NM	426
Loux, Henry T.	31 Inf	6891519	103 Dagobert St., Wilesbarre, PA	462
Loverix, Campbell	USMC	xxx	1051 Dix Ave., Dearborn, MI	1557
Lowry, William A.	59 CA	15017287	533 Franklin Ave., Steubenville, OH	1110
Loy, Perley A.	60 CA	17023815	Route 1, Willard, MO	1129
Lucas, Frank J.	17 ORD	32041931	4 Berlin St., Binghamton, NY	594
Lucero, Alphonso M.	200 CA	20842748	1911 W.New York, Alberquerque, NM	264
Lucero, Felix D.	59 CA	19054517	Pompey's Pillar, MT	1135
Lurvey, Merle F.	USMC	178049	Santa Ana, CA	209
Lynch, William J.	USMC	256599	57 Victory Road, Dorchester, MA	607
Lyon, Marvin J.	194 Tank	20720213	2021 Washington Ave., St. Joseph, MO	308
Lyon, William J.	USN	2561560	29 Tejeros, San Pedro, Makati, P.P.	326
Mabry, Lonnie G.	USN	2658522	Big Four, WV	119
Macarovich, Walter	Chem	33033022	Box 7, Indianola, PA	634
MacLeod, Gordon A.	60 CA	18043755	Ajo, AZ	938
Magalich, John	59 CA	13002519	Lockport, PA	903
Majewski, Joseph	USN	3114842	425 Ingham St., Jackson, MI	1489
Makarovich, John	USMC	xxx	Route 2, Catawissa, PA	785
Malosek, Richard H.	724 ORD	19002286	6926 Woodrow Wilson Dr., Hollywood, CA	850
Maquire, Edward P.	803 Eng	33076255	150 Poplar St., Kingston, PA	547
Marchesini, Bruno	27 Mat	11020631	23 Sherman St., Peabody, MA	1342
Marcley, James I.	USN	4019751	5120 19th Ave., Brooklyn, NY	1243
Marion, Chas. E.	59 CA	12024813	Wellsburg, WV	790
Mark, Martin P.	803 Eng	xxx	Box 56, Plantersville, TX	1474
Markham, Roy H.	USMC	301445	Route 2, Petersburg, TN	703
Marlo, N.G.	RE	S/Sgt	Kettering, Norhants, England	1152*
Martin, Allen R.	59 CA	18001722	Fountain, CO	897

Mukden Roster - Original Group 24

Name	Unit	Number	Address	
Martin, Clarence N.	809 MP	6864647	Whiting, KS	737
Martin, Frank G.	200 CA	38012557	314 S Alamedo St., Carlsbad, NM	1139
Martin, Harvey L.	59 CA	16021847	Gresham, WI	864
Martin, Paul H.	75 ORD	65478473	Zenia, CA	612
Martin, Wm. G.	31 Inf	36075004	2130 Capitol Ave., Sacramento, CA	1432
Martiniz, Marcus	515 CA	38012348	Carlsbad, NM	1138
Mascavage, A.A.	USN	2435902	8 Garrahan St, Lynwood, Wilkes Barre, PA	153
Maselli, Leo J.	USMC	276212	385 N 13th St., San Jose, CA	1252
Mason, H.	Loyals	Pfc	Harwick, Bolton, England	1224*
Masser, Edmund J.	200 CA	36106749	804 N Frnaklin St., Staunton, IL	628
Massingill, R.H.	59 CA	6274928	Route 1, Evant, TX	998
Masterson, Norman J.	59 CA	17010553	Route 2, Lake City, AR	769
Mathews Thurman R.,	P.A.Inf	0890282	Weimer, TX	13
Mattern, Kenneth E.	803 Eng	33055720	Route 1, Klingerston, PA	820
Mayes, Chas. F.	MC	19050129	Route 2, Gadsden, AR	670
Mazelrod, Bane W.	59 CA	19020897	Box 575, Kalama, WA	929
Mc Creedy, O.C.	USN	3684663	N 27th Abbott, Billings, MT	1533
McCabe, John M.	75 ORD	18043901	306 S Girard St., Albuquerque, NM	1056
McCartney, Dan A.,	CAC	0413737	Deming, NM	8
McCavanaugh, Pat J.	USN	2147799	4673 Park Ave., New York, NY	922
McClelland, G. F.	27 Bomb	6967425	Weona, AR	282
McCoy, Rahmond J.	60 CA	16041120	126 N 5th St., E. St. Louis, IL	1035
McDonnell, C.F.	SC	13026972	242 E. Tioga St., Philadelphia, PA	414
McDowell, Jack W.	USMC	268997	1710 E 3rd St., Casper, WY	527
McFadden, H.W.	680 ORD	39079593	Route 3, Box 712, Fresno, CA	152
McGaha, Lem	59 CA	34044165	Route 1, Cosby, TN	801
McGee, James R.	USMC	xxx	Proctor, CO	918
McGhee, Darrell E.	USN	3374071	1411 E St. Louis St., W. Frankfort, IL	744
McGowan ,E.L.	19 Bomb	19002025	Route 9, Box 418A, Fresno, CA	151
McGowan, James W.	USN	3208475	3203 E 8 St., Des Moines, IA	691
McGrath, T	Loyals	Pfc	Glencar C.O., Waterford, England	1227*
McKarson, Jack J.	698 AVORD	6583412	Box 182, Cross Roads, CA	654
McKenna, Linus F.	23 Prsut	6076637	66 Powerdly St., Carbondale, PA	1555
McKiddy, C.R.	28 Mat	6578687	Chowchilla, CA	171
McLain, Max	59 CA	15061794	Route 6, Kokom, IN	561
McLaughlin Egbert B.	200 CA	38011975	McAddo, NM	596

Name	Unit	Number	Address	Page
McMillen, William C.	60 CA	6892685	Craigsville, PA	511
McMinn, Edward Q.	59 CA	18001622	5th W Main St., Rexburg, ID	1062
McQuillen, Earl J.	59 CA	12012145	508 Orchard St., Portage, PA	369
McWilliams, Dale M.	200 CA	38007960	Delhi, CO	1505
Mead, Grant L.	USN	3051278	860 S Sheldon St., Richland Center, WI	1482
Mead, Martin C.	SC	11016385	Underhill, UT	1277
Means, Dale J.	31 Inf	16003871	4729 N. Winchester Ave., Chicago, IL	211
Meese, Harold L.	60 CA	15017324	337 St. Clair Ave., New Philadelphia, OH	1109
Mefford, Claude A.	USMC	286936	563 Penn St., Gary, In	1373
Meinhardt, Fred A.,	60 CA	1047800	019 Cherokee Rd., Louisville, KY	112
Menges, Leon	803 ENG	6278302	Italy, TX	147
Menzies, E.R.	AAOC	Pfc	Nedlands, W. Australia	1232*
Meringolo, Ferdinand	USN	2239900	570 E 2nd St., Brooklyn, NY	1125
Merkley, Richard C.	60 CA	13030159	Route 1, Durwenville, PA	1545
Merritt, Smith	803 Eng	36115774	215 St. Clair river Dr.,Algonic, MI	276
Merritt, Chas. A.	59 CA	R-148140	48 W. Government St., Pensacola, FL	316
Methrall, R.	RE	S/Sgt	London, England	1154*
Metras, Treffle E.	803 Eng	6906982	150 LaFayette, Chicopee Falls, MA	906
Meyer, Fred E.	17 Prsut	6914551	Route 2, Carthage, IL	1514
Micele, Joseph	USMC	262771	51-18 102nd St., Corona, Long Island, NY	1030
Micken, Edwin W.	59 CA	19013506	Strasburg, PA	1527
Middlebrooks, Ralph W.	60 CA	17014168	Tupelo, AR	751
Middleton, T.W.	803 Eng	34113469	Tuckaseigee, NC	402
Midgett, Darius T.	USN	2657594	Box 57, Buxton, NC	360
Mignardot, Fred	60 CA	18016351	817 S. 2nd St., Albuquerque, NM	391
Mihok, Joseph A.	17 ORD	31010559	194 Walnut St., Bridgeport, CT	117
Milardovich, P.	60 CA	18043778	1122 E Willets St., Pheonix, AR	1437
Milevneck, Carl J.	USED	6809253	2834 R St. SE, Washington, DC	421
Miller, Andrew J.	USN	3373081	La Grange, MO	878
Miller, Calvin U.	60 CA	18048835	1214 Fannin St., Luling, TX	427
Miller, Carl J.	USMC	301298	Guthrie, OK	849
Miller, Denn A.	59 CA	18000401	401 E. Prospect St., Fort Collins, Co	473
Miller, Don	69 CA	19045983	9465 S. Harvard Blvd., Los Angeles, CA.	113
Miller, Harry I.	228 SC	19003055	537 1/2 S St., Glendale, CA	1567
Miller, James S.	515 CA	20842441	Golden, CO	1522
Miller, Kenneth R.	59 CA	15047797	Route 4, Glasgow, KY	772

Mukden Roster - Original Group   26

Name	Unit	Number	Address	
Miller, Laddie	515 CA	38012580	710 Simpson St., Lafayette, CO	522
Miller, Robert L.	USMC	xxx	1320 Oak St., Klamath Falls, OR	233
Miller, Walter F.	60 CA	17025112	Hibbing, MN	1276
Miller, Wayne I.	AWSC	13026954	Route 1, Kutztown, PA	1066
Miller, W.R.	91 Bomb	6971480	PO Box 75, O'Brien, FL	195
Millholland, Bruce S.	2 Sqdn	6911402	Dayton, OH	1460
Milligan, Howard L.	USMC	274462	Roby, TX	1382
Milligan, Sam	515 CA	20842989	Albuquerque, NM	932
Mills, Lonnie F.	31 Inf	6267986	Marietta, OK	1262
Minier, John D.	192 Tank	20500766	214 Maple St., Port Clinton, OH	816
Minshahll, W.	Loyals	Pfc	Salford, Manchester, England	1228*
Minter, Glen C.	60 CA	1716358	Box 567, Esther, Mo	532
Mitchell, Robert E.	200 CA	38012122	Box 32, Bernalillo, NM	327
Mitchell, R.G.	L/Mt	Cpl	Perth, W. Australia	1194*
Mitchell, William B.	60 CA	6571541	1712 S 8th Ave., Maywood, IL	787
Mitchell, W. J.	20 Pursuit	6265808	143 Linares Ave., San Antonio, TX	619
Mock, John T.	7 Chem	34082937	Route 4, Fitzgerald, GA	971
Molaro, Louis	17 ORD	32006943	Crotonia Ave, Bronx, NY	644
Molena, Dwayne W.	59 CA	17003467	888 12th St. NE, Cedar Rapids, IA	458
Momberg, Arnold W.	USN	3204999	303 Richings St., Charles City, IA	1006
Monroe, Stanley R.	31 Inf	6558596	319 10th St., Alamosa, CO	1425
Monroe, William M.	HDMSB	13009461	Pleasantville, PA	933
Montgomery, Lee R.	515 CA	38029852	Bishop, TX	1261
Montoya, Earnest	515 CA	20842724	2700 S William St., Albuquerque, NM	886
Moodt, Geo. W.	17 ORD	3500686	Rome, OH	1442
Moore, Chas. A.	USN	3467209	Route 3, Box 11, Benton, AR	1313
Moore, James J.	60 CA	32058225	234 W 55 St., West New York, NY	1275
Moore, John J.,	60 CAC	11007541	328 Pleasant St., Dorchester, MA	109
Moran, James P.	USMC	238080	1276 10th Ave., San Francisco, CA	1485
Mores, John S.	60 CA	12007194	99 E 7th St., New York, NY	1008
Morey, Edward R.	USN	2015060	357 Malden St., Medford, MA	1022
Morgan, Jack B.	USMC	288714	Box 546, 1330 Calloway St., Dallas, TX	469
Morrell, Keith N.	USN	3421889	320 Western Ave., Beloit, KS	1033
Morris, Harry F.	HDMSB	19056628	916 E 2nd St., Clovis, NM	1289
Morris, Lawrence W.	HPD	14042528	Centreville, MI	1003
Morrison, Wm. B.	59 CA	6398770	Chuckey, TN	1410

Name	Unit	Service No./Rank	Address	Page
Morse, Elmer A.	60 CA	16003848	315 N Farraday St., Peoria, IL	964
Morse, Robert H.	19 Bomb	11013317	77 Union Ave., Old Orchard Beach, ME	618
Moseley, John J.	515 CA	38011968	Quantah, TX	972
Mosiman, William D.,	MC 192 Tnk	0418459	Morton, IL	34
Moss, Harry J.	93 Bomb	6298045	507 West 15th St., Ada, OK	120
Mott, Charles T.	USMC	282610	425 W Monroe St., Jacksonville, FL	1290
Moyes, Norman L.	60 CA	19020539	Route 2, Nyssa, OR	1070
Mucha, Frank J.	220 CA	38030842	Route 3, Caldwell, TX	416
Mullikin, T.R.	28 Mat	17014735	Redfield, AR	158
Mullins, Levi	2 Obs	6948285	Sandston, VA	203
Mullins, Noah	803 Eng	15043941	Mossy Bottom, KY	1014
Mundell Warren F.	698 Ord	19054381	General Delivery, Barada, CA	296
Muniz, Angel	USMC	281841	5 W 11th Ave., Gary, IN	987
Murdick, Floyd G.	60 CA	17016339	105 E Main St., Flat River, Mo	531
Murray, Wayne	17 ORD	35152180	512 Hill St., Connersville, IN	632
Murrell, Loye E.	200 CA	38012581	Marysville, TX	491
Myers, Elvin J.	24 Pursuit	6579727	Box 90 A, Route 1, Fullerton, NE	268
Myers, James H.	59 CA	18042332	Shelbyville, TX	728
Myers, L.E.	24 Pursuit	6579732	Route 1, Fullerton, NE	157
Nab, Daniel D.	59 CA	19011583	Route 1, Jerome, ID	808
Neal, A.	Loyals	Pfc	Stock Ferry, Norfolk, England	1219*
Neary, B.	Loyals	L/Cpl	Bury, Lanconshire, Engalnd	1221*
Neighbors, C.D.	28 Mat	6296911	124 S-W Ave., Chicago, IL	164
Neitling, Aloysius	228 SC	19020872	Route 1, Box 4, Sublimity, OR	140
Nelson, Glen W.	59 CA	18046437	Deira Route, Los Animas, CO	795
Nerron, Hermon A.	59 CA	18042183	Route 1, Honeyton, PA	818
Nesbitt, Mason H.	200 CA	33005025	108 S. 5th St., Hopewell, VA	285
Newkirk, Ross E.	60 CA	19013552	Route 2, Box 116, Henford, CA	1402
Newton, Clate	60 CA	14040417	Route 1, Greenville, AL	690
Nicholas, John J.	60 CA	18000434	Box 844, Seymour, TX	866
Nicholson, D.S.	RAMC	Sgt	Folwood, Sheffield, England	1157*
Nicholson, George W.	809 MP	18048800	310 Gough Ave., Booneville, IN	537
Nicolini, Vincent	60 CA	17014325	Route 1, Lake Village, AR	1072
Nocera, Anthony S.	60 CA	6150060	108 Tremont St., New Britain, CT	1490
Nokes, R.C.	RAMC	Pfc	New Denham, Oxford, Middlesex, England	1169*
Nolan, Robert C.	60 CA	15065709	Mt. Victory, Pulaski County, KY	682

Mukden Roster - Original Group   28

Name	Unit	Number	Address	Page
Norfolk, William A.	60 CAC	17019467	Route 2, Stoutsville, MO	146
Norris, Peter S.	USMC	xxx	Route 5, Marion, IL	1321
Null, H.T.	USN	2915609	2002 S. Meridian St., Marion, IN	154
Nunn, Chas. R.	200 CA	38011624	Hillsboro, NM	916
Nuttall, R.	Loyals	Pfc	Preston, England	1206*
Nye, Marvin D.	USMC	287543	Stanton, NE	1048
Obrien, Richard	24 Pursuit	6558517	807 N. Zangs Blvd., Dallas,TX	225
Oconner, James A.	USN	2280426	213 Beach 99th St., Rockaway Beach, NY	485
Odom, Lawrence	194 Tank	35100616	Eddyville, KY	392
Odonnel, James J.	USMC	267388	32 Linclon St., Salinville,OH	592
Odronic, Joseph	QMC	19048536	Route 1, Mineo Junction, OH	988
Olechno, Ray H.	USN	2998863	2534 N Monitor Ave., Chicago, IL	685
Olivotti, Livio	28 Mat	7032346	Route 2, Irma, WI	1380
Olslager, T.J.	17 Pursuit	11010295	25 Marston St., Hartford, CT	126
Onacki, Albert J.	17 ORD	6944768	1242 Loomis Ave., Scranton, PA	343
Oosting, William R.	19 Grp	6834344	49 Giddings Ave., Grand Rapids, MI	1311
Orme, D.L.	Loyals	Pfc	Grinsthorpe, Sheffield, Yorks, England	1203*
Ortega, Julius J.	60 CA	19053661	Route 1, Goleta, CA	1057
Orth, James H.	60 CA	19021106	Fort Klamath, OR	817
Ortiz, Parfrio	60 CA	18001731	Chamita, NM	442
Osborne, J.D.	USN	3719931	Route 1, Rockport, TX	841
Ostermiller, Leo G.	USMC	281081	Route 1, Nampa, ID	673
Ostrom, Robert P.	803 Eng	32036312	West Hartland St., Middleport, NY	231
Owen, Issac J.	31 Inf	15067878	902 W. 2nd St., Owensboro, KY	258
Owen, J.	Loyals	Pfc	Bethsda, Nr. Bangor, N. Wales, England	1214*
O'Dell, Chas. H.	SCAW	13015286	Route 1, Bristol, TN	199
O'Neal, John E.	Hqt 24 Prt	6894356	Middleton, VA	224
Pablo, Julian A.	60 CA	19019049	c/o Dixson Agency, Dixon, MT	875
Padilla, Leo J.	200 CA	20842964	Route 3, Box 1403, Albuquerque, NM	589
Padilla, O.F.	200 CA	20842329	Route 2, Box 394,Alburquerque, NM	149
Page, Charles D.	27 Bomb	14027422	Slater, FL	576
Page, C.L.	200 CA	20842948	Armijo Sub Station, Alburquerque, NM	155
Painter, Layton D.	19 Bomb	19015927	Lake City, CA	825
Paliotti, Victor	USMC	274301	23 Mathew St., Cranston, RI	444
Parchman, W. E.	200 CA	38012336	PO Box 117, Justiceburg, TX	396
Parker, Delbert L.	59 CA	19054594	419 Independence Ave., Independence, MO	280

Mukden Roster - Original Group 29

Name	Unit	Service No.	Address	No.
Parks, Frank J.	USMC	275162	210 NW 4th St., Oklahoma City, OK	1144
Parks, Kenneth M.	60 CA	6731521	Lake Village, IN	406
Parman, Chas. A.	24 Pursuit	xxx	Box 120, London, KY	215
Pasavetti, Thomas A.	USN	2236299	26-20 96th St., Jackson Hghts, L.I., NY	1253
Pascoe, Raymond F.	AMPS	16021778	212 Norfolk St., Ironwood, MI	1364
Pase, Joseph G.	SCAW	12013918	323 Market St., Georgetown, DE	321
Pashkewich, William	USN	2629944	3326 Camoen Ave., Lorain, OH	1248
Pate, Ralph E.	USN	2683830	Benning Park, Columbus, OH	982
Patrick, Edward N.	60 CA	6896634	211 Sarah St., Pittsburgh, PA	529
Patrick, Stanley	59 CA	7022770	1910 Wrights Way, Attsburd, PA	1015
Patterson, George S.	USN	3561411	3337 Montague St., Fort Worth, TX	324
Paul, Edward J.	AWSC	13003791	127 W 6th St., Bridgeport, PA	829
Pavone, Louis	59 CA	19030355	6021 18th Ave. S, Seattle, WA	1065
Peatty,R., Major	British		Winchester, Hants, England	24
Pekarich, Joseph F.	USMC	163010	409 E 71 St., New York, NY	919
Peloquin, Victor A.	16 Bomb	11024362	144 South St., Lynn, MA	412
Pena, Laurencio	515 CA	38031209	Box 393, Rio Grande City, TX	301
Penda, Raymond	48 Mat	11017337	324 Market St., Lawrence, MA	1433
Pennington, Irwin	59 CA	18011052	815 N Magdian St., San Angelo, TX	895
Peralta, L.G.	59 CA	19042059	15 E Sonora St., Stockton, CA	1351
Pernal, Edward J.	USN	2000076	Beecher St., Southington, CT	705
Perona, John J.	803 Eng	37044408	321 9th St. W., Des Moines, IA	976
Perron, Joe P.	60 CA	xxx	Box 811, Jerome, AZ	780
Perry, Curtis W.	17 S Plt	19032332	111 Forest Ave., Deadwood, SD	176
Perry, Wilbourne M.	60 CA	18038637	Route 3, Brownwood, TX	961
Petak, Joseph A.	228 SC	19052612	Box 205, Midland Park, NJ	695
Peters, Donald A.	USMC	301745	Box 411, Scott City, KS	716
Peterson, Issiac	28 Bomb	6744096	907 2nd Ave., Seattle, WA	161
Petrosky, Andrew P.	803 Eng	32010117	Box 112, Tuxedo Park, NY	267
Pettit, William R.	USMC	xxx	Route 1, Mission, TX	880
Peyton, James J.	MC	6890320	726 Parade St., Erie, PA	510
Phebus, William W.	515 CA	20842730	Route 1, Albuquerque, NM	1453
Phelps, Estill O.	3 Bomb	6298717	Route 1, San Augstine, TX	1086
Phillips, Glen N.	USMC	279458	1219 W 6th St., North Platte, NE	1325
Phillips, Wallace R.	200 CA	20843782	305 Chisom Ave., Artesie, NM	1051
Phipps, David K.	60 CA	18050106	Route 3, Geary, OK	1039

Mukden Roster - Original Group   30

Name	Unit	Serial	Address	Page
Piacum, Nicholas F.	USN	2744108	3037 Tulane Ave., New Orleans, LA	1330
Pickle, Sterling D.	USMC	268115	Sayre, OK	1292
Pifer, Clyde H.	28 Mat	6913954	434 W Jefferson St., Atkinson, WI	981
Pignata, John A.	803 Eng	32082103	101 Victoria Blvd., Staten Island, NY	977
Pigott, Edgar M.	803 Eng	35043478	Arram, FL	1350
Pinkson, Chas C.	808 MP	6266489	400 Tyler St., Cilmer, TX	639
Pinson, Bart F.	USN	3721360	732 W. Colorado Ave., Colorado Sps, CO	438
Pistole, A. E.	QMC	29624370	Route 7, Sparta, TN	478
Pitman, Leo	200 CA	38012436	Mexhoma, OK	179
Pitts, Enoch M. Jr.	3 Pursuit	6948652	104 W. 5th St., Tuscumbia, AL	196
Pitts, Ralph H.	60 CA	14046199	433 39th St., Wylam, Birmingham, AL	539
Platten, John J.	59 CA	6983664	31 Pardea St., Rochester, NY	676
Plummer, J.	Loyals	Pfc	Rishton, Blackburn, Lanconshire, England	1190*
Poindexter, D.D.	75 Ord	6296847	Route 2, Springtown, TX	298
Porch, Troy W.	USN	3600310	Big Springs, TX	1504
Porter, T.	Loyals	L/Cpl	Preston England	1212*
Poster, Joseph T.	803 Eng	33076121	403 South St., Pittstown, PA	664
Potter, Fred	60 CA	19050565	Minersville, UT	1399
Powers, Ernest L.	60 CA	17014299	Atkins, AR	1244
Powers, Maurice O.	USN	2873129	240 Roosevelt Ave., Ashland, KY	1379
Pozarich, Nick Jr.	19 Bomb	6337956	101 N. 7th Ave., Yakima, WA	208
Pressman, Aaron A.	Finance	13006134	623 New Market St., Philadelphia, PA	1016
Prevatt, Barden W.	USN	xxx	Webster, FL	1549
Prevuznak, Andrew	31 Inf	669934	1828 Henry Ave., Canton, OH	425
Prewitt, Earnest G.	60 CA	18038602	Box 150, Marshall, TX	538
Prichard, Ralph J.	60 CA	18038799	Wink, TX	1353
Privatsky, Ed E.	60 CA	19020656	1201 Woodbine St., Boise, ID	984
Procell, Clifton	USN	2745236	Route 1 Box 46, Noble, LA	872
Proensa, William S.	MD	19016670	1845 E 15th St., Oakland, CA	1393
Prohaska, Howard L.	QMC	39156722	Westington, SD	1480
Proulx, Thomas E.	DEML	19056892	820 E Palmer, Compton, CA	1044
Pruett, Jack N.	200 CA	38012547	Carlsbad, NM	964
Prukop, Joseph P.	28 Mat	6283513	Inez, TX	346
Pue, Alfred	200 CA	20842527	13320 Mountain Ave., El Paso, TX	520
Pugh, Ryan E.	91 Bomb	13023406	19 E. Braddock Road, Alexandria, VA	382
Pyle, Clarence F.	FEASC	6579798	4405 N Willis Blvd., Portland, OR	1510

Name	Original Group	Rank	Serial No.	Address	No.
Pyle, J.	RAOC	Pfc	7021000	xxx	1185*
Pysher, Norman S.	808 MP		6911338	Route 2, Williams Port, PA	1279
Quandt, Milton P.	2 Sqd		17014200	Ryder, ND	1340
Quick, Lee J.	31 Inf		3465811	Deepwater, MO	1491
Raines, Kirby N.	USN		20843369	1303 Main St., Pine Bluff, AR	1242
Ramirez, Dagoberto S.	200CA		7023359	407 W Wilson Ave., Gallup, NM	647
Ratcliff, John E.	59 CA		36115832	Pikeville, KY	492
Rau, Raymond E.	803 Eng		3756594	Rees, MI	1268
Ravin, Fredrick S.	USN		15058819	2907 NE Cough St., Portland, OR	517
Rayel, Earl D.	17 ORD		7030262	West Union, IL	765
Rea, Gerald E.	17 Pursuit		3002606	Hillman, MI	234
Reardon, Thomas J.	USN		6578712	29 Cliff St., Norwich, CT	1443
Rees, Walter E.	QMC		17017134	Route 1, Wauseon, OH	338
Reeson, R. R.	RAMC	Pfc	15017140	Surrey, England	1159*
Rekken, Oswald M.	60 CA		38011836	Box 139, Lansing, OH	1352
Requilez, Edward W.	60 CA		13004809	Taos Pueblo, NM	566
Reyna, Antonio	200 CA		17011159	Hilltown, Bucks County, PA	237
Rhos, Nicholas T.	59 CA		6556364	Route 1, Conway, MO	911
Rhoten, Ray R.	60 CA		18049874	2336 N. 9th St., Milwaukee, WI	910
Rice, Arthur	27 Mat		6249340	Box 482, Keifer, OK	376
Richards, Donald M.K.	59 CA		6295700	2004 W Madison, Pheonix, AZ	556
Richman, Sprague W.	MD		2873515	Greenville, TX	1407
Ridenour, Henry B.	19 Sqdn		14014587	2609 Garfield Ave., Ashland, KY	1412
Riggs, Selby B.	USN		204698	Route 1, Bloomsburg, TX	436
Riley, Summie B.	16 Bomb		20645272	Barrow On Furnace, Lancaster, England	340
Rimmer, X.	RA	Pvt	19020835	5338 73rd St., Maspeth, L.I. NY	33
Rind, Alfred T.	USMC		39377865	1416 Osborne Ave., Jonesville, WI	322
Rinehart, Orvis L.	192 Tank		xxx	Goldhill, OR	137
Ring, Melvin E.	59 CA		6718256	11720 17th St.N.E., Seattle, WA	630
Ripley, Joseph W.	194 Tank		xxx	Gypsum, KS	222
Roark, Louis R.	60 CA		11016110	518 N Liberty St., Webb City, MO	771
Roath, Melvin H.	59 CA		16003950	221 North Cushhing St., Olympia, WA	1551
Robbins, Ronald R.	60 CA			14 Church Court, Springfield, UT	852
Roberts, Daniel H.	5 Int Cmd			Leeds, Lanconshire, Engalnd	1483
Roberts, J.	RAMC	Sgt		513 Railroad Ave., Momenie, IL	1183*
Roberts, Victor J.	60 CA				1333

Mukden Roster - Original Group   32

Name	Unit	Serial	Address	Ref
Roberts, Wayne D.	200 CA	39012036	Flora, LA	423
Robertson, James L.	USMC	xxx	Route 1, Columbia, KY	844
Robertson, Virgil	USMC	310162	Leroy, IL	707
Robins, Dorothy L.	60 CA	6849638	85 Jackson St., Roanoke Rapids, NC	601
Robinson, Benjamin	16 Sqdn	6973332	Yankeeton, FL	1463
Robinson, E.	Loyals	Pfc	Thornton, Blackpool, England	1213*
Robinson, Geo. W.	60 CA	19056843	711 Bottalo St., Corpus Christie, TX	781
Robinson, Glen R.	60 CA	15061738	St. Croix, IN	813
Robinson, James A.	200 CA	38011650	Hillsboro, NM	274
Robinson, Milo W.	USMC	277789	Box 464, Mt. Ayr, IA	530
Robinson, Riley T.	HDMSB	14039306	Route 1, Mars Hill, NC	837
Robinson, Robert J.	91 Bomb	14032404	195 Pine NE, Atlanta, GA	460
Robinson, Robert L.	60 CA	18033905	Route 1, Fort Worth, TX	1408
Rocelski, Lucian P.	228 SC	12023622	15 Forest Ave., Springville, NY	1389
Roden, John J.	809 MP	6253933	Amarillo, TX	739
Rodriquez, Grgory	59 CA	18049877	501 S 8th St., Henryetta, OK	768
Roetschke, Ralph W.	60 CA	18033909	Route 1, Moshein, TX	575
Rogers, Albert	7 Chem	14037881	Highlands, NC	655
Rogers, Derill L.	59 CA	6646440	St. Charles, VA	1543
Rogers, Harold S.	19 AB	6911381	208 DeweySt., Pittsburg, PA	1376
Rogers, Leo L.	USMC	265686	115 Madison Ave., Macon, MO	783
Rogers Jack	SC	0364009	Warren, AZ	5
Rohrabaugh, Thomas C.	PB	20842942	1515 S Elm St., Albuquerque, NM	1355
Roland, Orville D.	3 Pursuit	6295702	4410 Henderson St., Greenville, TX	142
Romero, Emilio E.	515 CA	38012145	Trujillo, NM	1282
Romero, Frank	200 CA	20842734	Deming, NM	1358
Rose, Chas. A.	USN	3925835	Box 79, Folsom City, CA	1466
Rosendahl, R.D.	3 Pursuit	6930812	St. Hilare, MN	127
Ross, Herman R.	60 CA	18042345	Conroe, TX	403
Ross, Louis W.	808 MP	6744790	Savannah, NY	935
Rossi, Frank P.	803 Eng	32063747	513 25th St., Union City, NJ	533
Rosson, Robert B.	31 Inf	14037710	Ripley, MS	1343
Rowland, John E.	192 Tank	35000804	7010 Cleveland Ave., Westervill, OH	1047
Ruback, Joseph	17 Pursuit	6911990	1132 Wait St., Gary, IN	218
Rucker, August G.	698 ORD	19050409	Hogan Ave., Gresham, OR	948
Ruebush, Elbert L.	200 CA	20842462	212 S. Iron St., Deming, NM	212

Mukden Roster - Original Group   33

Name	Unit	Rank	Serial	Address	No.
Russell, J.W.	RAMC	Sgt	6898306	South Brisbane, Q., Australia	1164*
Russell, Malcolm	59 CA		14042475	906 Lincoln St., Milton, PA	643
Russell, Robert W.	60 CA		14042521	Sardis,MS	238
Russell, William L.	60 CA		xxx	Box 365, Koskiusko, MI	1002
Ryan, Mathew J.	USMC		17007337	Amite, LA	1084
Rydeen, Ernest A.	28 Mat		6574831	Box 88 Route 2, Clearbrook, MN	375
Ryerson, John P.	93 Bomb		13024637	1233 N. 9th St., Alberquerque, NM	244
Sabo, Alex J.	27 GRP		14038457	1611 W Fayette St., Baltimore, MD	1260
Sadler, Edward O.,	60 CAC	Pfc		Mt. Dora, FL.	18
Sady, J.C.	Loyals		20842463	xxx	1202*
Sakalares, Angelo H.	200 CA		18016875	302 Ruby Ave., Deming, NM	812
Salas, Elias	60 CA		19054517	311 Cromwell Ave., Albuquerque, NM	710
Salazar, John A.	6800RD		20700192	Box 348, Barstow, CA	1137
Samuelson, Walter H.	194 Tnk		20843005	521 S 9th St., Brainard, MN	1534
Sanchez, Joseph	59 CA		19011060	Bernalillo, NM	1133
Sandburg, Hyrum J.	724 ORD		17001742	Grantsville, UT	1457
Sandergaard, Albert	59 CA		35020364	Westbrook, MN	1291
Sandor, John	192 Tank		17004530	1655 Midland Ave., Youngstown, OH	417
Sanford, Bernard E.	59 CA		6885362	1114 Stone St., Fall City, NE	1299
Santak, John	19 ABAC		6838298	Route 2, Box 533C, Plottsville, PA	641
Satofsky, A.F.	803 Eng		16017885	602 Ruth Ave., Scranton, PA	328
Savage, Clark A.	60 CA		3283677	306 Goodwin St., Peoria, IL	609
Savoie, Victorian A.	USN		12007330	430 4th St., Faribault, MN	905
Scanlon, John F.	4 Sep Chem		19000856	1155 Decatur St., Brooklyn, NY	486
Scarcelli, Gene L.	USAFFE		xxx	234 11St., Spanks, NV	1271
Schanzbach, Donald J.	USMC		18048868	4203 Parytania St., New Orleans, LA	1537
Schisser, Joseph G.	60 CA		38048868	1802 Summer St., Houston, TX	441
Schlick, Emory C.	200 CA		38015532	Box 69, Pinecliff, CO	924
Schlicter, John F.	2 Ob		6801939	321 N. 9th St., E. St. Louis, IL	228
Schmitz, Eugene W.	200 CA		38012186	Mountainair, NM	1445
Schnieder, William T.	USN		3370756	Bureau of Navy, Washington, DC	1558
Scholl, J.A.	RAOC	L/Cpl	11010234	xxx	1184*
Schreiner, S.A.	17 Pursuit		15061742	88 Ellis St., New Britain, CT	124
Schrode, Harold J.	60 CA		xxx	Rockport, IN	839
Schrode, Richard R.	USMC		xxx	New England, ND	879
Schroeder, Walter J.	USMC		310917	105 E 9th St., Fond Du Lac, WI	1116

Mukden Roster - Original Group   34

Name	Unit	Serial	Address	
Schultz, Leslie C.	60 CA	19017091	Snoqualine, WA	983
Schultz, Merrell	MD	15067954	244 Glenwood St., Ludlow, KY	1492
Scobie, D.	RAMC	Pfc	Blackford, Perth. Scotland	1177*
Scott, Jefferson D.	803 Eng	7085175	773 Leonard St., Spartansboro, SC	990
Scott, J.A.	L/Mt	Cpl	Hamilton Hill, W. Australia	1197*
Scott, Robert B.	429 SC	19052848	2705 22nd St., San Francisco, CA	243
Seale, James W.	429 SC	19028470	519 Filmore St., Taft, CA	1550
Seales, B.	RAMC	Pfc	South Shields, Durham, England	1179*
Sears, Chester R.	2 OBS	6211970	1109 Chino St., Santa Barbara, CA	1256
Secrest, Oscar D.	59 CA	18001734	Route 2, Wilberton, OK	863
Sedlar, Joseph	21 Pursuit	6712917	36 Van Buren St., Passaic, NJ	192
Semic, David J.	454 ORD	33013123	2503 S 4 th St., Steelton, PA	648
Semler, Joseph W.	60 CA	12011208	69 Ewing St., Trenton, NJ	345
Senften, Daniel O.	USN	3684706	Castlewood, ID	1458
Serna, Fernando	60 CA	18048794	512 Iturbide St., Laredo, TX	1025
Settles, Thomas M.	59 CA	16017986	162 Ross St., Whitehall, IL	1127
Severston, Luther D.	USN	3758879	Box 595, Fortuna, CA	518
Sexton, Delmas	HQMSD	7023699	Millstone, KY	525
Shabart E.J.,	MC	0411352	1653 W. Division St., Chicago, IL	4
Sharp, Clifton L.	60 CA	6953264	Center Point, AR	1335
Sharp, Elmer	USN	3808095	871 0 St., Chino, CA	1544
Sharpe, Ralph	RE	Cpl	Guilford, Perth, W. Australia	1182*
Shaw, D.M.	20 Prsut	19038241	128 8th St., San Bernadino, CA	1501
Shed, Homer L.	USMC	268044	Route 1, Dorsey, MI	708
Shelton, Chas.	60 CA	18017448	Route 10, Pheonix, AZ	293
Sheppard, William F.	USN	2578686	McLean, VA	991
Sheppard, William J.	17 ORD	15061451	Route 2, Lyman, IN	1273
Sheridan, Emmet M.	USMC	269322	320 S 60th St., Nebraska City, NE	1293
Sheya, Melvin	USMC	xxx	1363 Bryan Ave., Salt Lake City, UT	1053
Shimsky, Leo R.	QMC	3621924	5500 Mead Ave., Dearborn, MI	1375
Shockey, Marian K.	QMC	6655531	Route 1, Box 61A, Mer Rouge, LA	1305
Shoobridge,R..,	RA	Austral	Bridgewater, Tasmania	32
Simmons, Harry C.	20 Bomb	6759683	PO Box 122, McCrory, AR	249
Simpson, Eugene E.	91 Sqdn	14006600	64 Stenor Ave., Shrevesport, LA	1500
Simpson, Judson D.	194 Tank	20523465	Harrodsburg, KY	332
Sims, Harry L.	USMC	301310	Leola, AR	1319

Mukden Roster - Original Group   35

Name	Unit	Serial No.	Address	No.
Skabicki, Leo	60 CA	6948892	Rte 1, Honesdale, PA	38
Skareas, James D.	59 CA	18035226	AGO, Washington, DC	889
Slater, John E.	60 CA	6978012	110 Grand St., Albany, NY	428
Slayton, Clarence	16 Bomb	6970940	Route 2 Calfax, LA	230
Sliger, Thomas E.	31 Inf	19044361	PO Box 38A, Holdenville, OK	318
Small, W.	RAMC	Cpl	Weat Croydon, Surrey, England	1161*
Smallwood, Thomas E.	USN	3807091	717 Huron Ave., San francisco, CA	1034
Smidt, William	QMC	17012174	506 S Hastings Ave., Hastings, NE	642
Smith, Chas.	75 ORD	R-127550	1024 Shunk St., Philadelphia, PA	407
Smith, Chas. H.	60 CA	14047104	Cowan, TN	135
Smith, Dean B.	USAFFE	18046315	Akron, OH	1032
Smith, Donald E.	27 Mat	11014166	Mattawamkeag, ME	115
Smith, George M.	16 Bomb	6112604	1001 Edenborn St., Pineville, LA	351
Smith, Granville D.	60 CA	19044254	Casa Grande, AZ	625
Smith, James H	60 CA	19011174	C/O NYCCRR, Utica, NY	569
Smith, J.	Loyals	Pfc	Lower Ter., Nr. Wigin, Lanconshire, Engl	1226*
Smith, J.H.	194 Tnk	20900757	926 Del Monte Ave., Salinas, CA	165
Smith, Mark F.	59 CA	6931450	Box 508, Lakeworth, FL	1285
Smith, Noble F. USMC	USMC	xxx	Chicago, IL	487
Smith, Raymond R.	59 CA	6386453	PO Box 34, Scott, GA	371
Smith, R.L.	USN	3757478	Box 506, Tracy, CA	1498
Smith, Sylvester A.	803 Eng	36115859	11470 13 Mile Road, Warren. MI	377
Smith, Walter A.	59 CA	13009821	Route 3, Pleasantville, PA	1547
Smolleck, Geo.	59 CA	7022777	Whitney, PA	1105
Snow, Arthur R.	USN	3562087	2233 SW 29th St., Oklahoma City, OK	467
Snyder, Arthur O.	USN	2916197	Route 2, Walton, IN	284
Snyder, Geo. A.	31 Inf	19017698	Van Horn, TX	1101
Snyder, Vernon, A.	515 CA	38055792	Grainola, OK	1284
Sohn, Wilfred F.	24 Pursuit	6938734	Farmington, MO	312
Sokalsky, John	803 Eng	33081938	719 N Front St., Allentown, PA	665
Solomon, Virlus V.	91 Bomb	16019093	821 S 8th St., Springfield, IL	1001
Spampanato, Vincent	803 Eng	32117693	95-08 65th Road, Forest Hills, NY	265

Mukden Roster - Original Group　36

Name	Unit	Number	Address	
Spangler, William E.	31 Inf	18050441	Webb. OK	1049
Sparks, Geo. W.	USMC	263060	Malaga, WA	1120
Sparks, Merma J.H.	USN	2500553	Route 2, Everett, Bedford Co., PA	757
Spencer, F.	Loyals	Pfc	Tonyfield, Bolton, Lanconshire, England	1187*
Sperr, Roy L.	20 Pursuit	6937832	Vienna, SD	202
Staats, Clarence	31 Inf	16017848	Hillview, IL	851
Stafford, Louis P.	59 CA	6288816	Route 1, Ponta, TX	1257
Stahl, John A.	USMC	224522	1781 E Arlington Ave., St. Paul, MN	1518
Standefer, Davis G.	60 CA	18038649	Hamilton, TX	985
Stanko, Joseph J.	14 Sqdn	6949809	440 6th St., Donora, PA	1397
Stanton, Geo. H.	60 CA	6583833	Missoula, MT	696
Stanton, Leonard	Loyals	Pvt	Cranbrook, Worthing, Sussex, England	31
Stauder, Rudolph E.	59 CA	15017327	Avon Lake, OH	270
Staufer, Weldon M.	19 Grp	6579599	167 Church St., Ashland, OR	1337
Staybrylla, John P.	200 CA	20843821	Mildred, PA	923
Steckel, Mathew	228 SC	19016135	844 Clinton Ave., Rochester, NY	365
Steed, James H.	31 Inf	6964393	2009 19th Ave. S, Nashville, TN	1450
Steeves, James A.	31Inf	17001685	Nalmo, MN	341
Steffanski, Edward	USMC	300768	1127 E. Walworth St., Milwaukee, WI	342
Steirheim, Herman J.	59 CA	16013676	304 W. St., Vassar, MI	573
Stemmer, Frank H.	USN	3806449	429 S. Orange Ave., Brea, CA	579
Stenzel, Gerald O.	2 Obs	17012175	Genoa, NE	1250
Stevens, Benjamin F.	803 Eng	33070134	Pheonixville, PA	746
Stevens, Dorris	515 CA	36106752	914 Lasher Road, Detroit, MI	110
Stevens, Joseph W.	30 Bomb	6273566	Munday, TX	949
Stevens, Lorenzo D.	USN	2874089	287 Julius Ave, Pikeville, KY	702
Stewart, Alvin E.	803 Eng	39001667	1017 Lenington St., Delano, CA	954
Stewart, Glenn E.	USMC	xxx	Route 3, Box 72, Brandon, MS	840
Stewart, Guy H.	409 Scout	19017496	Edmonds, WA	357
Stockwell, Byron B.	USMC	xxx	Route 5, Charlotte, MI	1300
Stom, Claude O.	60 CA	8038675	Route 3, Bowie, TX	959
Story, Willard C.	228 SC	14049778	Whitnel, NC	678

Appendix A

Name	Unit	Number	Address	Page
Stout, John I	60 CA	18049873	Route 1, Sulphur, OK	774
Stroscheim, V.K.	USN	3285531	Long Beach, CA	189
Stuckey, Francis	7 Mat	6397192	107 22nd Ave., Meridian, MS	761
Sturges, F.E.	19 Sqdn	xxx	Peru, IN	1571
Sturtz, Rodney J.,	60 CA	15017358	Bay Shore Road, E. Toledo. OH	17
St. Lauren, Jos. N.	27 Bomb	11014858	Epping, NH	413
Sullivan, Murray M.	MD	36106531	811 Smith St., Bay City, MI	1493
Summers, Verble L.	USN	xxx	ONeal, NE	418
Sumner, T.	Loyals	Cpl	Preston, Lanconshire. England	1172*
Suttle, Mervin H.	60 CA	18036248	502 N Russle St., Pampa, TX	908
Sutton, Billy S.	60 CA	6583589	1175 Getz St., Akron, OH	764
Swann, Berkley R.	USMC	279837	581 Front St., St. Paul, MN	1484
Swanson, Clayton I	60 CA	19030299	1206 Beliveau, Seattle, WA	254
Swiger, Ralph D.	59 CA	15017307	Clarksburg, WV	1377
Swisher, Morris D.	USN	3561111	Route 1, Tryon, OK	1089
Taylor, Alfred A.	454 ORD	6390218	Brinkley, AR	1338
Teach, Joseph	19 Bomb	33062889	242 Woodtic Rd., Waterbury, CT	567
Tellez, David O.	200 CA	38012280	Box 98, La Mesa, NM	799
Temple, William J.	AWSC	6888702	729 Penn St., Pittsburgh, PA	1082
Templeton, Bill D.	19 Bomb	6938084	5 N. 5th Ave., Marshalltown, IA	174
Templin, Fred G.	19 Grp	6914489	135 Schwab Road, Thornton, IL	1391
Theriac, Regis M.	17 ORD	15061417	Route 2, Vincennes, IN	809
Thibeau, Frank E.	31 Inf	16046170	114 W. River St., Chippewa Falls, WI	528
Thickpenny, J.W.	60 CA	16008524	Route 1, Brookland, WI	1512
Thomas, Henry L.	59 CA	18050003	Route 1, Dustin, OK	290
Thomas, William	SC	14042312	Route 1, Jackson, MI	1302
Thompson, Arthur R.	USN	1040250	438 1/2 N. Ave. 52, Los Angeles, CA	359
Thompson, A.	RA	Cpl	Bishopton, Stktn on Tees, Durham. Engl	1175*
Thompson, Francis E.	USMC	266216	Harrison Ave., Cinncinatti, OH	917
Thompson, M.	RA	Pfc	Walney Is., Barrow/Furness, Lancs., Engl	1176*
Thompson, S.	Loyals	Pfc	Preston, England	1225*
Thompson, Thomas R.	USMC	279751	Route 1, Columbia, MS	1298

Mukden Roster - Original Group   38

Name	Unit	Number	Address	
Thompson, Wayne E.	809 MP	xxx	2427 Clay St., Denver, CO	1314
Thompson, William D.,		0331140	1429 Princeton Ave., Salt Lake City, UT	9
Thorman, Walter E.	59 CA	18001743	Feather Falls, CA	272
Thornell, Geo. H.	MD	5859684	Box 777, Gulfport, MI	1447
Thornsbery, Jim M.	31 Inf	19010290	Castleford, ID	515
Thornton, Chas. H	17 Bomb	6971017	Box 83, Crystal Springs, MS	221
Thorson, Arnold	60 CA	16021763	Route 4, Mondovi, WI	766
Tilton, Delton L.	2 Sqdn	19018446	Route 2, Kalispel, MT	1478
Tobin, J.	Loyals	Pfc	Bolton, England	1205*
Toffling, William H.	QMC	12004301	Washington, DC	1115
Toler, Ruben K.	16 Bomb	6971038	Route 2, Long View, TX	235
Tomecko, Geo. W.	27 Mat	16028642	1015 Anderson Ave., Bronx, NY	885
Toone, douglas B.	60 CA	18050056	Route 2, Cowata, OK	767
Torrisi, Alfred F.	CWS	32024752	66 N. Fulton Ave., Mt. Vernon, NY	481
Touchet, Wilson	USMC	278624	Gueydan, LA	495
Tovar, Alex E.	200 CA	38011264	126 Zavala St., San Antonio, TX	1134
Towery, Roland K.	60 CA	18048698	218 E. Dittmar, San Antonio, CA	858
Trice, Blount C.	59 CA	6287757	Aline, OK	727
Trout, Ira R.	31 Inf	6290482	Box 3, Deertrail, CO	354
Trout, William	60 CA	6066062	1343 Lark Ave., Lakewood, OH	909
Trowbridge, Harry A.	USN	3369537	4562 N. Figueroa St., Los Angeles, CA	419
Trupiano, Michael A.	USMC	289837	3346 E Fort St., Detroit, MI	756
Tuck, Ronald V.	16 Bomb	6286085	421 E. 40th St., Savannah, GA	183
Tullock, P.S.	USN	3682494	1632 Mesa Ave., San Pedro, CA	1561
Tuneberg, Earl S.	17 Bomb	6920813	Cheneyville, LA	281
Turner, Barney E.	7 Mat	6246974	214 N. Maple St., Alburqureque, NM	216
Turner, David F.	3 Prsut	6911363	922 40th Place, Des Moines, IA	1516
Turner, John P.	60 CA	18060296	Gail, TX	857
Tyrrell, W. J	RAMC	Pfc	Saltly, Birmingham, England	1180*
Underwood, Eugene S.	60 CA	17016351	3657 Page Blvd., St. Louis, MO	1521
Unglaub, Arthur L.	ORD	R-356628	808 Livingston Road, Elizabeth, NJ	512
Upchurch, Walter M.	515 CA	20843929	512 Howell & George St., Silver City, NM	310

Mukden Roster - Original Group   39

Name	Unit	Serial	Address	No.
Uphoff, Charles F.	2 OBS	6833858	1315 S 26th St., Omaha, NE	1564
Urban, John S.	DEML	19052713	Route 1, Freehold, NJ	1559
Uthman, Millard,	60 CA	19056344	264 S. Lake Ave., Pasedena, CA	23
Van Agtmael, Joseph	27Mat	6763162	Acorn St., Muskeegan, MI	921
Vanderkamp, Burton L.	USN	4134722	47 N 14th St., San Jose, CA	1499
Vandiver, Cecil R.	192 Tank	20523499	Harrodsburg, KY	1031
Vater, Joseph A.	803 Eng	33084463	1466 Steuben St., Pittsburgh, PA	974
Vaughan, Julius H.	27 Bomb	6399374	Route 2, Heflin, AL	970
Vaughn, W.E.	RAMC	Pfc	Freemantle, S. Hampton, Hants, England	1170*
Verba, Geo. M.	192 Tank	35001272	Box 116, Barton, OH	668
Vess, Eugene E.	31 Inf	6888321	Waynesboro, VA	1367
Vest, Carl H.	17 ORD	6665524	Bloomfield, IN	352
Vice, Bernard L.	USN	2742540	117 Park Ave., Abbeville, LA	831
Vidra, Andrew G.	17 Bomb	6987477	14501 Jenne Ave., Cleveland, OH	220
Vinger, Homer E.	60 CA	18001664	Dove Creek, CO	184
Vinson, Edward F.	59 CA	18050026	Canute, OK	824
Vissaris, Christopher	USMC	xxx	417 E 70 St., New York, NY	1280
Volden, Richard P.	60 CA	17025017	502 6th St. S., Virginia, MN	1530
Volger, R.J.	17 Pursuit	6583228	106 N. New Hampshire Ave., Hollywood, CA	138
Voselovsky, John R.	60 CA	xxx	200 McKinley Ave., Vandergrigt,PA	1043
Wade, Coy L.	59 CA	18038606	Route 2, Texarkana, TX	1327
Wade, Dumaont F.	60 CA	18045741	444 S. Marine St., Prescott, AZ	838
Wade, Elbert E.	60 CA	2999998	Route 1, Box 200, Reedsburg, WI	570
Wagner, Harry A.	USN	3561813	Route 11, Box 157-A, Tulsa, OK	1021
Waldrep, John P.	USN	xxx	Garden City, TX	1328
Waldrum, E.R.	USMC	6395645	Graniteville, SC	320
Walker, Chas. O.	59 CA	20843564	Box 386, Clovis, NM	239
Walker, Dale W.	515 CA	280483	5339 8th Ave., Los Angeles CA	440
Walker, Joseph L.	USMC	2684479	Route 1, Ellaville, GA	245
Wall, Thomas E.	USN	7002914	Crystal Springs, MI	366
Wallace, Alvin L.	17 Bomb	38031097	Route 2, Leonard, TX	997
Wallace, Ira D.	515 CA			289

Mukden Roster - Original Group   40

Name	Unit	Service No.	Address	No.
Wallace, Thomas C.	7 Chem	34083042	2300 E 18th St., Chattanooga, TN	1359
Waller, Geo. R.	17 Bomb	6971085	Dodson, LA	471
Waller, Joseph D.	60 CA	14046063	Box 233, Verbena, AL	657
Walton, Bernard T.	19 Bomb	6980652	1604 River St., Olean, NY	936
Walsh, Paul A.	200 CA	38012018	Box 1630, Pheonix, AZ	519
Walter, Chales A.	698 ORD	18001656	604 Benton St., Harrisburg, PA	1401
Walter, Dean F.	60 CA	0393366	135 Main St., Littleton, CO	865
Walter, William E.,	SC	2384472	54 Florence Place, Mt. Lebanon, PA	10
Ward, John C.	USN		1143 Steuben St., Utica, NY	602
Ware, William L.	60 CA	14042441	Route 3, Mendenhall, MI	876
Warren, Jack	59 CA	17007448	Cape Girardeau, MO	882
Wasilewski, Kounstant	60 CA	13004781	24 E Grand St., Nanticoke, PA	1096
Watersey, Michael L.	60 CA	17017248	2725 Madison St., Omaha, NE	902
Watkins, Orin D.	MD	19003712	150 W 55th St., Los Angeles, CA	1390
Watson, Joseph	59 CA	2011188	280 E Circle Ave., Bristol, PA	1369
Wayne, Philip	USN	xxx	Box 278, Railroad St., Baltic, CT	981
Weaver, Lonnie M.	200 CA	20842465	Deming, NM	261
Weaver, Loyal R.	803 Eng	33084414	New Bethlehem, PA	430
Weaver, Roy M.	USMC	269362	Route 1, Ellensburg, WA	610
Webb, Chas. W.	21 Pursuit	6420319	Prarie Hill, TX	967
Weeks, Carl G.,	CA	0384879	36 Richfield St., Squantum, MA	11
Weeks, Garland K.	60 Ca	10842287	Pineland, TX	748
Weeks, Orie B.	200 CA	38055580	Route 2, Box 79, Port Arthur, TX	1419
Weems, Chas. M.	USMC	xxx	405 Stanford Ave., Redwood City, CA	845
Wehner, Henry B.	27 Mat	6936285	Ralston, NE	330
Welch, Orville	59 CA	6864494	Route 3, Clarksville, TX	738
Wells, Arthur	31 Inf	6978412	Route 1, Berlin Road, Haddon Field, NJ	871
Welsh, James M.	228 SC	19045744	2001 Longwood Ave., Los ANgeles, CA	1459
Welsh, Thomas G.	QMC	18044300	926 E Filmore St., Pheonix, AZ	1092
Wertenberger, J.R.	60 CA	15017361	Fern Dell Farm, Garrettsville, OH	197
Whatley, Milton M.	60 Ca	6924624	Route 1, Cloumbia, AL	747
Whatmough, J.	Loyals	Pfc	Bermonsley, London, England	1220*

Murden Koster - Original Group   41

Name	Unit	Number	Address	
Wheeler, Alvin F.,	CA	0890164	715 W,6th Street, Silver City, NM	15
Wheeling, Walter F.	2 OBS	6564336	Plaza, ND	1005
White, Archie E.	60 CA	35150754	Dublin, IN	1307
White, Jess K.	24 Grp	6296187	Colorado City, TX	1452
White, Walter L.	QMC	6296803	11 S 3rd St., Pheonix, AZ	605
Whitehead, Raymond	28 Bomb	622490	PO Box 35, Mt. Clemens, MI	241
Whitmer, Harold L.	200 CA	36008406	4943 Lake Park Ave., Chicago, Il	549
Wilbur, Chas. S.	4 Material	6974552	Route 2, Cayuga, NY	236
Wilcoxson, John J.	200 CA	20842743	1623 S Edith St., Albuquerque, NM	1363
Wilks, Zach E.	USN	xxx	Harrisonburg, LA	411
Willaims, Lawrence L.	803 Eng	35033251	338 S 4th St., Gallion, OH	827
Willard, J.J.	60 CA	6914116	Landrum, SC	185
Williams, Carl J.	31 Inf	6374254	Williamston, SC	1471
Williams, Geo. L.	60 CA	18048862	Mertzon, TX	859
Williams, Jack	SC	15061981	Cayuga, IN	434
Williams, James O.	60 CA	6931887	2212 S. 7th St., St. Joseph, MO	107
Willie, Wilson E.	200 CA	38012620	Moriarty, NM	814
Wills, Carl A.	Finance	13003417	635 Manor St., York, PA	848
Wilson, Charles L.R.	59 CA	19051825	Route 2, Box 75, Kieskie Ln., Reno, NV	546
Wilson, Chas. F.	USMC	266895	Farewell, TX	717
Wilson, Chas. W.	194 Tank	20918529	4211 Cover St., Riverside, CA	977
Wilson, John P.	28 Bomb	6379075	246 4th St., Calexico, CA	314
Wilson, Leroy A.	USN	3420088	226 S. Ferce St., Kansas City, KS	384
Wilson, Robert J.	60 CA	17010090	1003 N 13th St., Fort Smith, AR	536
Wilson, Vinton J.	QMC	6555790	Iona, OR	1063
Winnekens, Alvin A.	60 CA	16008694	Route 1, Denmark, WI	881
Winston, R.G.	60 CAC	17026201	Route 1, Box 344, Robertson, MO	168
Wise, Robert C.	27 Bomb	6970875	213 Weaston St., Savannah, GA	242
Withrow, Lewis W	7 Chem	34083064	1016 Albany St., Brunswick, GA	177
Witter, William L.	USN	3207202	1711 Appleton St., LOng Beach, CA	701
Wohlferd, Glenn L.	60 CA	19051631	Pepin, WI	861
Wolfe, H.W.	USN	2830602	519 Columbus Ave., Canton, OH	1513

Mukden Roster - Original Group   42

Name	Unit	Service No.	Address	No.
Wolfers, R. L.	16 Bomb	6915748	811 Main St., Windber, PA	229
Wood, A.O.	60 CA	16017948	2716 N. Adams St., Peoria, IL	159
Wood, Kenneth C.	USN	xxx	55 Randolph St., Napa, CA	1060
Wood, Leoanard D.	59 CA	15061800	206 E Bronson St., South Bend, IN	750
Wood, Loyd H.	USN	3561146	810 Monte Vista Drive, Dallas, TX	1254
Woodfin, John E.	60 CA	18042270	Route 2, Timpson, TX	853
Woolham, W.	Loyals	L/Sgt	Manchester, England	1238*
Wooten, Curtis I.	60 CA	15065714	Wooten, KY	1304
Wooten, Gene W.	60 CA	19052041	Route 1, Marysville, CA	854
Worrick, Geo. J.	USMC	280628	123 Main St., Hicksville, OH	1331
Worthington,	Loyals	Pfc	Southport, England	1171*
Wright, Allen L.	59 CA	18049797	515 W 17th St., Ada, OK	662
Wright, Hurcell L.	59 CA	18018836	Brashear,TX	788
Wuttke, Wm. G.	803 Eng	30018640	21 St Lukes Pl., Balwin, L.I., NY	1475
Yahnozha, Homer	200 CA	38012084	Mescalero, NM	251
Yancik, John	803 Eng	33070124	353 Cherry St., Pottstown, PA	989
Yancy, Byron O.	59 CA	14043862	3371 Colbville Ave., Hopeville, GA	1406
Yarrow, Richard A.	USMC	236599	1613 Queen Anne Ave., Seattle, WA	1404
Yates, D.S.	RA	Sgt	Leeds, Yorkshire, England	1156*
Yeager, Harlow R.	60 CA	18017427	703 Van Buren St., Litchfield, IL	534
Yeast, Claude L.	194 Tank	20523466	Harrodsburg, KY	393
Young, Chas. W.	803 Eng	R274583	Route 1, Alexander, VA	1388
Young, E.S.	17 Bomb	R-715191	1540 Herring Ave., Waco, TX	131
Young, Thomas W.	USN	2623270	Route 2, Durham, NC	1143
Zech, Peter F.	USN	3049965	Camp John Hay, Baguio, P.I.	649
Zellers, R.E.	59 CA	19054271	517 N. Jersey St., Bicknell, IN	160
Zenda, John F.	20 Pursuit	6923834	2066 Bath Ave., Brooklyn, NY	424
Zettner, Francis F.	59 CA	15017363	Bay Shore Road, E Toledo, OH	658
Zills, Clyde D.	808 MP	6921941	New Market. TN	240
Zubrzycki, John S.	31 Inf	6983553	80 Ineham Ave., Lackawanna, NY	433

Mukden Roster - Original Group   43

John C. Ward, Mukden POW 602, US Navy, originally from Utica, NY, documented this list of the Allied POWs evidently with the assistance of some of his friends. The data has been reformatted and alphabetized.

The xxx designates that the information is unavailable. The * indicates British, Australian or New Zealand. The right hand column lists the POW number issued by the Japs.

This list is comprised of the original contingent of POWs that arrived in November of 1942, or soon thereafter, at the old Chinese Army Camp. The men assigned numbers 1495 to 1574 died either enroute to Mukden (Hoten) or soon thereafter.

The information on addresses is the best available.

SZSORTE

Mukden Roster 1945 Contingent 1

Name	Unit	Rank	Address	No.
Adams, G.P.	RASC	Lt	Lyle, Stoebridge, Worcester, England	2100*
Allen, Chas. D.	43 Inf	0890384	102 E Davis St.,Hearne, TX	2005
Allen, John H.	Tnk	9890115	225 Charles St., St. Paul, MN	1999
Allen, Lloyd C.	USA	0278831	Stuart, IA	1926
Allison, F.W.	Med Ser	Major	Park Lane, Alford, Lincolnshire, England	2048*
Altpress, H.V.	AA	Col.	North St., Brighton, Sussex, England	1749*
Andrews, Levinge	ADS&T	Col.	4 Eversley Park, Chester, England	1770*
Archer, Derek R.	RABA	Capt.	Beckenham, England	2090*
Aronds, T.E.	Dutch Inf	Lt	Bangdoeng, Java	2136*
Aulsmus, Delbert	USA	Col.	510 Mohawk Ave., Scotia, NY	1624
Backhouse, E.H.W.	54th Inf	Brig.	Bevy St., Edmonds, Suffolk, England	xxxx*
Bakkers, Rudolph	Dutch	Maj Gen	Bandoeng, Java	1608*
Balfanz, A.W.	AC	0413560	766 Peach, Abilene, TX	2002
Ball, C. H.	Brdr Reg	Corp	60 Bidder St., Islington, Liverpool, England	1862*
Ballentine, G.C.	India Brig	Brig	London, S.W., England	xxxx*
Bax, F.R.	Dutch	Sub LT	107 Tamaten Strazt, De Hague, Holland	2134*
Beale, Arthur G.	USN	Ensign	42 Bunnell St., Bridgeport, CN	1987
Beck, Chas. D.	AC	0417790	Oklaunion, TX	1990
Beckwith, C.V.	31 Inf	Pfc	San Francisco, CA	1841
Beebe, Lewis C.	4th Army	Br Gen	Ft. Sam Houston, TX	1603
Bell, Gilmer M.	USA	Col.	Box 274, Hopkinsville, KY	1626
Bennett, Chas. H.	USA	1st Lt	Route 2, Belle Vernon, PA	1952
Berry, K. L.	USA	Col.	415 W 4 St., Austin, TX	1627
Bethard, Alvin J.	USA	Capt.	31D E North St., Opelousas, LA	1936
Bishop, Allan G.	RAF	Capt.	London, England	1765*
Bittner, Robert D.	3rd Pursuit	Sgt.	Route 2, Boswell, PA	1820
Biykerk, Reins	Dutch	Corp.	Steenwyck, Holland	1867*
Blackburn, Arthur S.	Australia	Brig.	5 Salisbury Terrace, Collinswood, S. Australia	1620*
Bland, A.J.	3rd Pursuit	Sgt.	115 W Park Ave., Pleasnatville, NJ	1819
Bodie, Thos. M.	USA	1st Lt.	2020 S 24th St., Lincoln, NE	1966
Bonham, Roscoe	USA	Col.	2934 S E 34th St., Portland, OR	1629
Booth, Maynard B.	USA	1st Lt.	Ridgeview, SD	1958
Boudreau, Napolean	USA	Col.	Route 1, Box 219, Astoria, OR	1725
Bouma, W.	Dutch	Capt.	Bandoeng, Java	2175*
Bowen, J.V.	RNF	Lt.	Birmingham, England	2099**
Bowler, Louis J.	CAC	Col.	Middletown CA	1630
Boyle, James	RE	Major	London, England	2040*

Mukden Roster 1945 Contingent   2

Name	Unit	Rank	Address	No.
Bozua, Gerard G.	Dutch	Capt.	Hedler, Holland	1779*
Braddock, Wm. H.	MC	Col.	Washington, DC	1726
Braley, Wm. C.	HDMSB	Col.	Route 2, Box 1972, Lafayette, CA	1631
Brawner, Penbroke A.	USA	Col.	San Francisco, CA	1632
Bridge, Robert P.	RA	Capt.	12 George's Place, York, England	1752*
Bristow, Harry C.	Sigs	1st Lt.	Medehanpsted, Petersboough, England	2051*
Britt, Chester K.	USA	Br Gen	1508 Wood St., LaCrosse., WI	1957
Brougher, Wm. E.	USA	Major	Ft. McClellan, AL	1599
Brown, Burton R.	CAC	Capt.	225 E 31st St., Erie, PA	1901
Brown, Chas. M.	CAC	Capt.	710 S Zinc, Deming, NM	1918
Brown, Ernest L.	Inf	Sgt.	Lebanon, TN	1924
Brown, J.T.	RA	Lt.	250 Morden Rd., London, SW 19, England	1860*
Brown, W.N.G.	RA	Col.	London, England	2091*
Browne, E. H.	USA	Pfc	321 Marshall Ave., St. Paul, MN	1633
Browning, Harry R.	MD	Capt.	Pupeio, AR	1837
Bruns, Stockton D.	CAC	Lt.	Louise, TX	1944
Bryan, Wm. C.	USA	Pvt.	320 E Adams Ave., McAlester, OK	1961
Bunk, Alexander	Dutch	Pfc.	31 H.B.S. Straat, Soerabaya, Java	1868*
Burdette, Karl	803 Eng	Mj Gen	1206 6th Ave., Ford City, PA	1836
Callaghan, Cecil A.	Australia	Col.	Gordon Sydney, New South Wales, Australia	1616*
Callaghan, James W.	USA	Col.	2476 Nixon St., Eugene, OR	1634
Campbell, Alex H.	AWS SC	Capt.	3133 Connecticut Ave., Washington, DC	1635
Campbell, Leveson	RN	Col.	Travelane St., Wade Bridge, Cornwall, England	1776*
Carter, James D.	92nd Inf	Lt.	16 Elm Ave., Kentfield, CA	1636
Chalek, Wm. D.	USA	Brig	139 N. Atlanta Place, Tulsa, OK	1962
Challen, Bernard S.	Ind Brig	Lt.	S.W.I. England	1564*
Chamberlain, Geo. E.	USA	Major	1575 Perkins Rd., Baton Rouge, LA	1971
Chandler, E.M.E.	USA	Capt.	Ft. Leavenworth, KS	1908
Chapman, Melrose W.	Punj Rgmt	Capt.	London, England	2084*
Chapman, Rowland P.	RN	Col.	Army and Navy Club, London, England	1763*
Chase, Theo. M.	HDMSB	Col.	Washington, DC	1637
Chastain, Ben Hur	USA	Col.	344 Jefferson Dr., Mt. Lebanon, PA	1727
Christie, A.S.	USA	Lt.	Washington, DC	1728
Christie, Chas. P.	RN	Comm.	43 Meachom St., Williamstown, MA	1998
Chubb, E.J.	USA	Col.	3 Victoria Villas, Plymouth, S. Devon, England	2045*
Churchill, Lawrence S.	USA	Sgt.	914 N. Broad St., Rome, GA	1643
Churchyard, Geo. H.	USA	Col.	Box 21, Yerrington, NV	1818
Chynoweth, Bradford D.	USA	Br Gen	832 San Luis Rd., Berkeley, CA	1604

Mukden Roster 1945 Contingent 3

Name	Service	Rank	Address	Number
Cikot, Petru J.M.	Dutch	Comm	Hautmanstraat, 35 Bandoeng, Java	1781*
Clarke, Alfred J.	RAAA	Sgt.	26 Mozart St., London, England	1852*
Clifford, Esmond H.	RA	Col.	Army and Navy Club, London, England	1771*
Coe, Sheldon S.	USA	Capt.	418 Maple Ave., Rapid City, SD	1913
Coggle, C.K.J.	RA	Capt.	Chicester, Sussex, England	1766*
Collier, James V.	USA	Col.	155 Harrington Court, SAn Antonio, TX	1638
Collinson, Alfred C.	RN	Comm.	c/o Admiralty, London, England	1591*
Cook, John D.	USA	Col.	236 Corona Ave., Long Beach, CA	1729
Cooper, Wibb E.	USFIP	Col.	1503 Acklen Ave., Nashville, TN	1639
Corkhill, Wm. E.	USA	Col.	1216 NW 22nd St., Oktahima City, OK	1641
Cornell, Theo. M.	USA	Col.	1020 W 71st Terrace, Kansas City, MO	1730
Cottrell, Joseph F.	USA	Col.	Box 203 Danville, PA	1642
Cox, Jan H.	Dutch	Col.	Nangkalaan 14, Bandoeng, Java	1782*
Cox, Pierre A.	Dutch	Mj Gen	Twee, Molentieskade, Holland	1609*
Cranfield, P. G.	RN	Lt.	London, England	2096*
Crawford, Ben B.S.	RA	Brig.	London, England	xxxx*
Crenshaw, Harvey L.	60 CA	Corp.	Dawson, TX	xxxx
Creusere, Melville S.	USA	Col.	44 Bell Ave., San Rafael, CA	1731
Crews, Leonard R.	HDMSB	Comm.	2395 Francisco St., San Francisco, CA	1644
Curtis, Arthur D.	RA	Maj.	c/o Lloyd's Bank, London, England	xxxx*
Curtis, John	USA	Col.	197 Puritan Ave., Forest Hills, NY	1907
Dalley, John D.	Australia	Col.	Melbourne, Australia	2027*
Dalton, Wm. F.	USA	xx	Madison, WI	1732
Danielson, D. C.	USN	Col.	Bronson, KS	1848
De Carre, Octave	92 CA	Capt.	618 19th St., NW, Washington, DC	1645
De Jong, Wm. A.	Dutch	Maj.	Bandeong, Java	1783*
Delme, Radcliffe	RA	Col.	c/o Lloyd's Bank, London, England	2050*
Dequant, Carolus H.	Dutch	xxx	Bandeong, Java	1784*
Derham, Alfred P.	Australia	Maj.	18 Studley Park Rd., Kein, Melbourne, Australia	1810*
Derham, Tom P.	Australia	Col.	10 Studley Park Rd., Kein, Melbourne, Australia	1872*
Dinwiddie, Ronald R.	RA	Maj.	London, England	2044*
Doane, Irvin E.	USA	Col.	15 Morning St., Portland, ME	1646
Dobbin, Robert W.	RA	Col.	c/o Lloyd's Bank, London, England	2029*
Dodson, Thos. H.	USA	Capt.	751 9th Ave., Ft. Worth, TX	1942
Donaldson, Walter	USA	Capt.	701 S Pine, Deming, NM	1920
Dooley, Thomas O.	USA	Maj.	1103 W Lamar St., McKinney, TX	1900
Doran, Roy E.	USA	Maj.	754 Fulton Ave., San Antonio, TX	1906
Dougherty, Louis R.	USA	Col.	533 26th St., Santa Monica, CA	1647

Mukden Roster 1945 Contingent   4

Name		Rank	Address	No.
Drake, Chas. C.	USA	Br Gen	Cabin John, MD	1600
Duffy, John E.	USA	Maj.	2544 Parkwood Ave., Toledo, OH	1895
Duke, Cecil L.B.	RA	Brig	c/o Lloyd's Bank, London, England	xxxx*
Dumas, Hugh A.	USA	Col.	New Orleans, LA	1648
Eagan, P.	RA	Lt.	London, England	2101*
Eckles, A.R.	409 SC	Corp	Hopkinsville, KY	1831
Elmes, Chester H.	HDMSB	Col.	San Francisco, CA	1649
Enos, Wm. A.	USA	Col.	San Antonio, TX	1733
Erickson, Albert	USA	Capt.	Box 533, Spearfish, SD	1923
Esatow, Theo. R.	USA	LT.	114 Ivey St., Kearny, NJ	1951
Evans, Leonard N.	USA	Pvt.	Coleman, TX	1839
Evelegh, Geo. C.	RA	Brig.	c/o Lloyd's Bank, London, England	1568*
Fairbairn, John E.	RA	Capt.	Lloyd's Bank, Littlehampton, Sussex, England	2054*
Farrell, Harold M.	USMC	Warrant	817 W 1033rd St., Hawthorne, CA	2007
Farrell, Walter N.	USA	Lt.	Washington, DC	2004
Fasson, James C.H.	RA	Col.	Lanton Nr., Jeddburgh, Scotland	2033*
Faulkner, Geo.C.	USA	Lt.	1306 Hobart Bldg., San Francisco, CA	2003
Fennell, Geoffrey W.P.	RA	Maj.	Barclay's Bank, Hammersmith, London, England	2034*
Ferrey, James P.	USA	Lt.	Port Nelson, Ontario, Canada	1970
Firth, Leslie J.B.	RA	Capt.	Haywards Heath, Sussex, England	2056*
Fleisher, Johan A.	Dutch	Col.	Vermerlaan, Bandeong, Java	1785*
Forde, Noel	RA	Col.	Whitehall, London, England	1772*
Fortier, Malcolm V.	USA	Col.	Opportunity, WI	1650
Foster, Johnny M.	USA	Pvt.	311 North 1st St., Durant, Ok	1834
Foster, Valentine D.	USA	Col.	1401 Florabunda Ave., Burlingame, CA	1651
Fraleigh, Claud M.	USN	Lt.	Gulport, MS	1930
Frances, Charles M.	USA	Lt.	Box 263 T, Menlo Park, CA	1974
Frances, Gus C.	USA	Capt.	Santa Fe, NM	1917
Fraser, Francis H.	RA	Brig.	Culduthel, Weeke, Winchester Hants, England	xxxx*
Frissell, Howard N.	USA	Col.	Horseshoe Dr., Alexandria, LA	1734
Fry, Philipp T.	USA	Col.	228 15th St., N.E., Atlanta, GA	1652
Fullerton, Albert L.	USA	Capt.	23 Union Place, Yonkers, NY	1928
Funk, Arnold J.	USA	Br Gen	Ft. Sam Houston, TX	1602
Fuhrimaan, Royce J.	USA	Sgt.	Franklin, ID	1824
Gaffney, Peter M.	USA	Lt.	604 Temperance St., Covington, LA	1975
Galbraith, Nicoll F.	USA	Col.	1290 Mesa Ave., Colorado Springs, CO	1653
Garfinkle, Abe	USA	Col.	2500 W Wisconsin Ave., N.W. Washington, DC	1654
Gebow, Ben R.	USA	Sgt.	Porac, Pampanga, P.I.	1827

Mukden Roster 1945 Contingent   5

Name	Country	Rank	Address	Number
George, Albert M.	USA	Capt.	1816 Richland Ave., Aiken, SC	1949
Giblin, Roland G.L.	RA	Col.	Lloyd's Bank, London, England	1753*
Gibson, L.A.	Australia	Lt.	Melbourne, Australia	2116*
Gillespie, James O.	USA	Col.	645 Clarkson St., Denver, CO	1735
Gitshom, Alex J.	USA	Pvt.	14 Whitehall Mansion, London, England	1850*
Glover, J.A.	RA	Capt.	Lloyd's Bank, Leamington, Warwickshire, England	2078*
Goodman, Eric W.	RA	Brig	Lloyd's Bank, London, England	xxxx*
Goodman, Joseph	USA	Lt.	6230 Old York Rd., Philadelphia, PA	1985
Goudswaard, Adr. D.R.	Dutch	Col.	Bandoeng, Java	1786*
Grameme, Wm. J.	RA	Col.	440 Strand, London, England	1754*
Grant, Peter C.	RA	Maj.	Hurtsbourne Priors, Whitechurch Hants, England	2043*
Greeman, Gerald B.	USA	Capt.	709 S Tin St., Deming, NM	1921
Greenleaf, Harry B.	USA	Pfc.	Box 1415, Billings, MT	1838
Grimwood, Francis R.	RA	Col.	3 Granville St., Helensburg, Scotland	1755*
Hadley, Alvin C.	USA	Lt.	1420 E 8th St., Okbulgee, OK	1967
Hall, Australia H.	Australia	Corp.	190 Lewis St., Mudgee, NSW, Australia	1871*
Halstead, Earl T.	USA	Col.	2248 Union Ave., Memphis, TN	1893
Hamilton, Stuart A.	USA	Col.	3726 Connecticut Ave., NW, Washington, DC	1655
Hamilton, Wm. A.	USA	Lt.	5551 Monticello, Dallas, TX	1983
Harris, R.H.	USA	Pfc.	Fife, TX	1842
Harrelson, Banard T.	USA	LT.	Crossville, ME	1989
Harrison, Alfred M.L.	Australia	Pfc.	Bruarong, Frankston, Victoria, Australia	1756*
Hicker, Eugene S.	USA	Maj.	1933 Harvard N., Seattle, WA	1905
Hickley, J.A.V.	RN	Lt.	c/o Admiralty, London, England	2085*
Hilsman, Roger	USA	Col.	c/o AGO Washington, DC	1736
Hilton, Donald B.	USA	Col.	3922 W Holly St., Seattle, WA	1656
Hilton, Roy C.	USA	Col.	Laurens, SC	1657
Hirsch, Geo. W.	USA	Col.	Philadelphia, PA	1658
Heard, H.	RA	Maj.	c/o Lloyd's Bank, London, England	2042*
Heinzel, Jack H.	USA	Lt.	4204 La Luz, El Paso, TX	1991
Hennessey, Dudley M.	RA	Col.	c/o Lloyd's Bank, Calcutta, India	2031*
Hersee, Philip O.	RA	Pvt.	Shirley Dr., Baldslow, Sussex, England	1856*
Heymans, W.E.C.	Dutch	Pvt.	Batavia, Java	1870*
Hoeffel, Ken M.	USN	Capt.	3150 16th St. N.W., Washington, DC	1718
Hoffman, Robert G.	USA	Col.	16543 Glastenbury Rd., Detroit, MI	1659
Hopkins, Gilbert R.	RA	Col.	c/o Barclay Bank, Berkshire, England	1773*
Hope, J. Percy W.	RA	Capt.	Tamarisk, Broadmore Way, Surrey, England	2058*
Horan, John P.	USA	Col.	1203 Barbee St., Houston, TX	1744

Mukden Roster 1945 Contingent   6

Name	Service	Rank	Address	No.
Horigan, Wm. R.	USA	Maj.	403 Laurel, Texarkana, AR	1909
Howard, Sam L.	USMC	Br Gen	4530 Cathedral Ave., Washington, DC	1719
Howe, Kingsley J.A.	RA	Maj.	Valencia Island, Ireland	2035*
Hoyer, P.A.	Dutch	Lt.	Bandoeng, Java	2135*
Hughes, James C.	USA	Col.	c/o AGO Washington, DC	1660
Hughes, Kent W.S.	Australia	Col.	129 King St., Melbourne, Australia	1811*
Humphreys, Brian B.	RA	Capt.	Madras, India	2075*
Hundley, Wm. F.	USA	Sgt.	214 AnnSt., Lebanon, IN	1828
Hunt, Cecil	RA	Col.	Burton on Trent, Staffs, England	1757*
Ilgen, Gustav A.	Dutch	Mj Gen	Buurtweg 10, Wassenaar, Holland	1610*
Inglis, Wilford T.	RA	xxx	93 Hoppers Rd., Wichmoor Hill,London, England	1857*
Irey, James E.	USN	Seaman	2703 Norman Smith Dr., San Diego, CA	1849
Ives, Albert R.	USA	Col.	Harvey Cedars, NJ	1661
Jacobs, Eugene C.	USA	Maj.	2000 Connecticut Ave., Washington, DC	1897
Jephson, E.W.F.	RA	Col.	c/o Grindley & Co., Bankers, London, England	2023*
Jessup, J.J.	USMC	Corp	1914 Arroyo Ave., San Carlos, CA	1566
Joel, Henry F.	Dutch	Civil.	Flat Mourdwyk, Batavia	1809*
Johnson, A.J.	USA	Sgt.	Box 477, Kennard, NE	1826
Johnson, Edwin H.	USA	Col.	419 Harrisburg St., Gettysburg, PA	1662
Johnson, Lonnie M.	USA	Pvt.	AGO Wahington, DC	2018
Kamps, Hubert J.A.	Dutch	Col.	Bengawanlaan 38, Bandoeng, Java	1787*
Kasler, Chas.	USA	Lt.	Kings Park, Long Island, NY	1977
Kazerski, Frank A.	USA	Sgt.	737 S 4th St., Philadelphia, PA	1823
Kelly, L.L.	USA	Pfc.	Route 3, Leavenworth, KS	1816
Keltner, E.H.	USA	Col.	417 Weatherston St., Cleburne, TX	1663
Kengen, Emile T.	Dutch	Col.	Buderdykstraat 116, Bandoeng, Java	1788*
Key, Berthold W.	RA	Mj Gen	c/o Brindlay, 54 Parliment St., London, England	1557
Killen, Wade D.	USA	Col.	Northfield, VA	1737
King, Thomas	RA	Lt.	Ivy House, Clphill, Beds., England	2032*
Konik, E.D.P.	USA	Lt.	508 High St., New Britain, CT	1988
Koppen, Ernst T.	Dutch	Col.	Mohr-Heveawig 19, Djatinnegara, Java	1787*
Korthout, E.H.L.	Dutch	Corp	Batavia, Java	1866*
Kuhn, Francis A.	Dutch	Capt.	Coen Blvd 132,Trestes, Java	1790*
Lane, Chas. M.	RA	Col.	c/o Grindlay, Bank of Bombay, India	1767*
Langdon, B.B.	USN	Lt.	2480 16th St., Washington, DC	1931
Lathrop, Leslie T.	USA	Col.	4935 Stanford Ave.NE, Seattle, WA	1665
Laughinhouse, N. R.	USA	Col.	Kelly Field, TX	1666
Lawlor, Robert J.	USA	Capt.	791 Neil Ave., Colombus, OH	1914

Mukden Roster 1945 Contingent 7

Name		Rank	Address	Number
Lawrence, Chas. L.	USA	Col.	9152 S. Ada St., Chicago, IL	1567
Lay, Wm. O.	RA	Brig	Bentley Heath,Barnet Hearts, England	1571*
Lester, John E.	USA	Capt.	806 Turner St., Dallas, TX	1938
Levitt, Herbert A.	USN	Ensign	165 E Mosholu Pkwy., New York, NY	1986
Lilly, E.J.	USA	Col.	Fort McClellan, AL	1668
Locke, W.	Australia	Maj.	37 Cecil St., Gordon, NSW, Australia	2105*
Longmire, Richard L.	USA	Pfc.	524 E Canon Perdido St., Santa Barbara, CA	1847
Lough, Maxon S.	USA	Br Gen	66 Farrand Park, Highland Park, MI	1596
Lowman, Ken E.	USN	Capt.	1634 6th St.,, Coronado, CA	1720
Lucas, Hubert F.	RA	Brig	c/o Lloyd's Bank, London, England	xxxx*
Lyhene, D.J.	USA	Sgt.	Billings, MT	1825
Lynch, Thos. A.	USA	Col.	1751 E 73rd Place, Chicago, IL	1669
MacDonald, Stuart C.	USA	Col	207 Southwest 6th Ave. Mineral Wells, TX	1670
Maher, Wm.F.	USA	Col.	168 W Hudson Ave., Englewood, NJ	1672
Malevich, Steven S.	USA	Maj.	Box 336, Coverdale, PA	1899
Mallonee, Richard C.	USA	Col.	7711 Lookout Dr., La Jolla, CA	1673
Maltby, C.M.	RA	Mj Gen	c/o Lloyd's Bank, London, England	xxxx*
Mamerow, John R.	USA	Maj.	109 E bannock St., Boise, ID	1910
Manees, James R.	USA	Col.	276 Ila St., Fayetteville, AR	1674
Mangall, T.B.	RA	Capt.	30 N Promenade St., Lancashire, England	2082*
Martino, John	USN	Chief	639 Congress Ave., Waterbury, CT	1829
Mason, E.R.	USA	Maj.	535 Gadson Court, Spartanburg, SC	1902
Mason, N.A.K.	RA	Brig	Rose Cottage, Buckinghamshire, England	2081*
Makwell, Duncan S.	Australia	Col.	Imperial Service Club, Sydney, Australia	1619*
McCafferty, Gratton H.	USA	Lt.	95 Delafield Ave., Staten Island, NY	1671
McEntee, James N.	USA	Ensign	117 Bedford Ave., Freeport, NY	1950
McGrath, James M.	USN	Maj.	Box 360, San Luis Obispo, CA	1979
McIntosh, Ian R.	RA	Col.	Minley Manor, Chamberley, England	2046*
McLennan, Carter R.	USA	Brig	Cuba, NY	1738*
McLeod, Torquil	RA	Capt.	c/o Lloyd's Bank, London, England	1588*
McMinn, James	USA	Col.	Box 885, Carlsbad, NM	1919
Mead, C.A.	RA	Col.	c/o Lloyd's Bank, London, England	2028*
Mead, Everett V.	USA	Capt.	1508 Washington St., Hamburg, IA	1940
Mead, Wallace E.	USA	Col.	2425 Franklin St., San Francisco, CA	1676
Menzie, James T.	USA	Col.	Caladonia, NY	1677
Merritt, Chas.A.	USA	Sgt.	430 W Government St., Pensacola, FL	xxxx
Merryfield, Jaques V.	USA	Lt.	404 W Main, Urbana, IL	1980

Mukden Roster 1945 Contingent   8

Name	Nationality	Rank	Address	Number
Michel, John J.A.	USN	Lt.	126 E 93rd St., New York, NY	1956
Michie, Robert E.L.	USA	Lt.	Lubbock, TX	2001
Mielenz, Lloyd E.	USA	Col.	909 Orange St., Macon, GA	1678
Mihailov, Nicholas N.	USA	Lt.	5722 25th Ave. NE, Seattle, WA	1965
Miller, Wm.R.	USA	Corp	O'Brien, Fl	1950
Miner, Wm. D.	USA	Capt.	Vermont, IL	1915
Mitchell, Eugene H.	USA	Col.	4502 Shermqn Blvd., Galveston, TX	1745
Mitchell, John M.	RA	Col.	c/o Grindlay, 34 Parliment St., London, England	1758*
Mixson, Archibald M.	USA	Comdr	AGO, Washington, DC	1739
Modin, Chas. O.F.	RA	Maj.	c/o RAF Club,128 Picadilly, London, England	1585*
Moffat, M.G.F.	RA	Brig	251 Old Dover Rd., Canterbury, Kent, England	2036*
Moir, Robert G.	RA	Maj.	36 Wilton Crescent, London, England	xxxx*
Montresor, J.	RA	Col.	Alverstroke Hants, England	2037*
Moor, Arthur P.	USA	Capt.	25 Catherine St., Newport, RI	1680
Moore, Geo. B.	USA	Maj.	5807 Cornelia Ave., Chicago, IL	1935
Moore, Thos. M.	RA	Capt.	46 Holland Park, W.N.	2039*
Moss, John C.	USA	Maj.	Nutwood Cottage, Godalming, Surrey, England	2052*
Mullins, Jimmie	USN	Ensign	232 E 21st St., Jacksonville, FL	1996
Murphy, Dennis P.	USA	Col.	Fort Lewis, WA	1681
Napier, William E.S.	RA	Lt.	Kerfield, Peebles, Scotland	2024*
Nash, David	USN	Lt.	Indianapolis, IN	1933
Naylor, L.	RA	Lt.	20 Clarence Rd., Grancesend, England	2087*
Nelson, Frank	USA	Col.	3 Park Place, Keokuk, IA	1682
Newbigging, Tom K.	RA	Brig	The Lodge, Weeley, Essex, England	1575*
Nichols, Murl E.	USA	Pfc.	Route, Box 446-N, Traverse City, MI	1843
Nicholson, Dean	USA	Lt.	319 Cobb Bldg., Seattle, WA	1972
Nicholson, John L.	RA	Maj.	Staffield-Warminister, Wilts, England	2038*
Nicholetts, G.E.	RA	Capt.	RAF Claub, 128 Picadilly, London, England	1768*
Noble, C.H.	Australia	Capt.	368 Collins St., Melbourne, Victoria, Australia	1778*
Nugent, Dan H.	USA	Corp.	Hawesville, KY	1830
O'Connor, Edwin	USA	Col.	Box 263, Lindsay, OK	1683
O Day, Ray M.	USA	Col.	5224 39th Ave., Seattle, WA	1684
Packman, C. L.	Australia	Capt.	Wagga Wagga, New South Wales, Australia	2107*
Painter, G.W. A.	RA	Brig	c/o Lloyd's Bank, London, England	1576*
Parker, Geo. M.	USA	Mj Gen	2396 SW Cedar St., Portland, OR	1593
Parks, Comer L.	USA	Pfc.	Box 225, Chatauqua, KS	1844
Parks, Robert E.	USA	Lt.	1315 S 6thSt., Salt Lake City, UT	1955
Parks, Wm. R.	USA	Lt.	601 Thorn St., Marion, IL	1992

Mukden Roster 1945 Contingent 9

Name	Unit	Rank	Address	No.
Parsons, John E.	803 Eng	Pvt.	22 Everett Ave., Glen Falls, NY	1846
Parsons, Wm. A.	USA	Lt.	2313 W 2nd St., Wichita, KS	1964
Peake, Brian D.	RA	Col.	Orchard Cottage, Farnham, Surrey, England	1759*
Pearson, Richard A.	RA	Capt.	Crewdson, Helms Lodge, Kendal, England	2155*
Pearson, Sam R.	RA	Brig	Little Manton, Marlborough, Wilts, England	1586*
Pechek, Frank A.	USA	Sgt.	1123 Eagan Ave., Pueblo, CO	1822
Peck, A.L.	USA	Maj.	608 Michigan St., Pullman, WA	1904
Peck, Harry M.	USA	Col.	514 W Fruit Ave., Albuquerque, NM	1685
Pederson, Haakon A.	US Civ. MM	Capt.	9701 Shore Rd., Brooklyn, NY	1748
Peffers, Andrew	RA	Brig	c/o Lloyd's Bank, London, England	1589*
Pemberton, Chas. K.	RA	xxx	43 Crescent, Durham, England	1853*
Perkins, Robert M.	USA	Lt.	49 1/2 3rd Ave., Huntington, WV	2000
Pesman, Jacob J.	Dutch	Mj Gen	Uhoutenloan 8A, Holpman, Groningen, Holland	1611*
Peterson, Arthur C.	USA	Maj.	100 Lake St., San Francisco, CA	1896
Phillips, Paul D.	USA	Maj.	2360 Erdman Ave., Baltimore, MD	1903
Pierce, Clinton A.	USA	Br Gen	Fort Riley, KS	1601
Pilet, Nunez C.	USA	Col.	422 N Eye St., Tacoma WA	1687
Pitch, G.F.	RA	Pvt.	26 Huntington Rd., York Yorkshire, England	1863*
Plummer, James E.	USA	Pfc.	Route 2, Lawrence, KS	1845
Porter, Wm.	USA	Capt.	3201 Piedmont St., El Paso, TX	1922
Prickett, Wm. F.	USA	Capt.	1130 Lewis St., Belmead, TX	1947
Priest, Walter J.	RA	Capt.	c/o Lloyd's Bank, Bombay, India	2166*
Pugh, John R.	USA	Col.	2310 South St., NW, Washington, DC	1892
Quesenberry, Marshall	USA	Col.	531 Morley Ave., Nogales, AZ	1688
Quinn, Michael A.	USA	Col.	22 W 5th St., Kansas City, MO	1689
Quintard, Alec S.	USA	Col.	Fine Creek Mills, VA	1690
Ramsey, Kenneth W.	USA	Lt.	1324 Garfield, Glendale, CA	1973
Ramwell, B.T.	RA	Corp.	The Birches, Hayfield, Deryshire, England	1861*
Raulston, John W.	USA	Maj.	Richard City, TN	1898
Rawitser, Emil C.	USA	Col.	Memphis, TN	1691
Reed, Geo. A.	USA	Lt.	Hillcrest, Ft. Smith, AR	1953
Rendle, D.A.	RA	Col.	c/o Lloyd's bank, London, England	2026*
Retallick, Henry T.	Australia	Pvt.	Holloway Rd., Cheltenham, Victoria, Australia	1873*
Richards, Claude W.	RA	Brig	c/o Barclay's Bank, London, England	1577*
Richards, Grover C.	USA	Capt.	Box 503, Donaphin, MO	1912
Richardson, James D.	USA	Capt.	812 Berkley Rd., Wilmington, DE	1925
Ridgway, Michael C.W.	RA	Capt.	Westmister Bank, London, England	1769*
Riley, Frank E.	USA	Lt.	629 Vernon Ave., Venice, CA	1982

Mukden Roster 1945 Contingent   10

Name	Service	Rank	Address	No.
Roberts, Lyle J.	USN	Capt.	Astoria, OR	1721
Rogers, Richard G.	USA	Col.	5503 Huntington Prkwy., Bethesda, MD	1694
Rodman, John H.	USA	Col.	6940 S Stevens St., Tacoma, WA	1693
Romaine, Owen W.	USA	Lt.	9 Taylor Ave., Fort Thomas, KY	1997
Roper, Robert L.	RA	Col.	9 Deans Wag., Chippenham, Wilts, England	1760*
Rose, Henry B.	RA	Col.	8 Carew Rd., Wallinton Surrey, England	1774*
Routledge, Joseph S.	RA	Capt.	10 Greenwood Ave., Middlesboro, Yaks., England	2073*
Russell, Andrey G.	USA	Capt.	Humble, TX	1945
Russell, Robert E.	USN	Ensign	201 S Grand, Bozeman, TX	1995
Rusher, Arthur E.	RA	Brig	Park, Newqual, Cornwall, England	1578*
Rushing, N.L.	USA	Sgt.	810 W Grand, Ponca City, OK	1821
Rutherford, Dorsey J.	USA	Col.	227 Ravena Ave., Palo Alto, CA	1724
Rutherford, F.D.	Australia	Lt.	142 Kennedy Terr., W-I, Brisbane, Australia	2115*
Saalam, Paul E.	USA	Lt.	914 G Ave., Lawton, OH	1968
Sage, Chas. G.	USA	Col.	333 Tin Ave., Deming, NM	1695
Sanderson, Gerald B.	RA	Maj.	High Trees, Crammond Brdg., Edinburgh, Scotland	2047*
Savage, Columbus	USA	Lt.	Kennedy, AL	1993
Scardon, Beverly N.	USA	Capt.	Waterboro, SC	1911
Schilling, Wybrandos	Dutch	Mj Gen	Windoestratt 16 Karees, Bandeong, Java	1612*
Scholey, Geo. T.	USA	Capt.	321 Park Ave., Prescott, AZ	1941
Scholten, Pieter	Dutch	Col.	Bandeong, Java	1791*
Scudder, Irvine S.	USA	Col.	Irvine Road, Lexington, KY	1741
Seals, Carl H.	USA	Brg Gen	325 Riverside Dr., Ormond Beach, FL	1605
Searle, A.C.	USA	Col.	Woonsocket, RI	1747
Seidl, Francis X.	USA	Corp.	323 E 88th St., New York, NY	1832
Selby, Wallace	RA	Brig.	Epsom Rd., Guilford, Surrey, England	1579*
Selleck, Clyde A.	USA	Col.	1528 Mt. Eagle Pl., Alexandria, VA	1696
Servaes, H.C.	RA	Brig.	Beechfielf, Brassendale, Liverpool, England	1580*
Sewell, E.R.H.	RA	Capt.	c/o Barclay Bank, Herts, England	2071*
Simson, Ivan	RA	Brig.	c/o Llyod's Bank, London, England	1581*
Simson, John T.	RA	Col.	c/o Glenn Mills, Whitehall, London, England	1775*
Sitwell, Hervey D.W.	Dutch	Mj Gen	c/o Lloyd's Bank, London, England	1560*
Skarda, Cash T.	USA	Capt.	Clovis, NM	1916
Skerry, Harry A.	USA	Col.	2855 SW Champlain Dr., Portland, OR	1697
Sledge, Teo. J.	USA	Col.	Monticello, FL	1698
Slone, Wm. R.	USA	Lt.	517 Grand Ave., Abilene, TX	1960
Sharp, Wm. F.	USA	Mj Gen	Monkton, MD	1595
Sherwood, Llyod E.	USA	Lt.	219 Waverly St., Palo Alto, CA	1969

Mukden Roster 1945 Contingent   11

Name	Country	Rank	Address	Number
Smith, Carey M.	USN	Col.	4709 Edgeware Rd., San Diego, CA	1891
Smith, Hash	USA	Pvt.	30 1st Ave., D, Salt Lake City, UT	xxx
Solkesz, Jan H.	Dutch	Capt.	Soerabaja, Java	1808*
Solomon, P.E.	USA	Lt.	Temple, TX	1984
Speck, Jefferson W.	USA	Capt.	Frenchman's Bayou, AR	1948
Spier, Marcus	Dutch	Col.	Malabarweg 5, Malang, Java	1792*
Spurgeon, C.H.	Australia	Lt.	136 Victoria Rd., Hawthorne, E Melbourne, Aust.	2109**
Stansell, Joshua A.	USA	Col.	Elko, SC	1699
Statius, Muller	Dutch	Mj Gen	20 Goentoertaan, Bandeong, Java	1614*
Staton, Wm. E.	RA	Cmdr	7 Mear Park Rd., Northwood, Middlesex, England	xxx *
Steele, Charles L.	USA	Col.	Davidson, NC	1700
Steins, Anton P.	Dutch	Sgt.	Woman's Camp, Soerabaja	1865*
Stempin, Harry J.	USA	Lt.	South St., Milwakee, WI	1963
Stevens, L.R.	USA	Bg Gen	AGO, Washington, DC	1607
Stewart, George Murray	RA	Mjr.	5 William Gardens, Glasgow, NW, Scotland	2049*
Stickney, Henry H.	USA	Col.	Taylor's Island, MD	1701
Stiles, Lee M.	USA	Lt.	315 W Ninth St., Los Angeles, CA	1981
Stonor, Ian W.	RA	Lt.	26 Buckingham Ave., Shoreham/Sea, Sussex, Eng.	2089**
Stowell, Allen L.	USA	Col.	434 Russell Ave., Fort Monmouth, NJ	1702
Straughan, Millet A.	USA	Lt.	2222 Edison Dr., San Antonio, TX	1976
Street, J.S.	RA	Capt.	Chalo, Nyasaland, E. Africa	2057*
Stringer, Chas. H.	RA	Brig	c/o Glen Mills, Whitehall, S.W.I. England	1582*
Strybosch, J.H.	Dutch	Lt.	c/o KPM, Royal Packet Navigation, Batavia	2132*
Stryvenberg, Albert C.	Dutch	Col.	Batavia, Waterloopein, West	1793*
Swanton, Donovan	USA	Capt.	71 W 12th St., New York, NY	1703
Tabeart, Chas. F.	RA	Col.	Ashdowne, Ely Rd., Littleport, Cambs., England	2064*
Tarkington, Hiram W.	USA	Col.	1517 Tanglewood Rd., Columbia, SC	1764
Tarpley, Thos. M.	USA	Col.	22 Gramercy Park, New York, NY	1890
Taylor, Harold B.	Australia	Brig	Merriwa Wood St., Manly, Sidney, Australia	1617*
Taylor, Marion W.	USN	Lt.	1821 S Preston, Louisville, KY	1934
Taylor, Robert P.	USA	Capt.	2390 Chestnut Ave., San Francisco, CA	1929
Teague, Theo. J.	USA	Col	77 N Bedsford Dr., Beverly Hills, CA	1704
Thompson, John W.	USA	Col.	312 St. Lawrence Ave., Beloit, WI	1742
Thurgood, Lawrence	Australia	Lt.	33 Elmwood St., Melbourne, Australia	2097*
Thyer, James H.	Australia	Col.	4 MacDougal St., Kirivilli, N.S.W., Australia	1815*
Tisdelle, Achilee C.	USA	Capt.	xxx	1946
Toorop, Chas. G.	Dutch	Col.	Bandeong, Java	1794*
Torrence, Ken S.	RA	Brig	165 Teddington Pike, Toroanto, Canada	1592*

Mukden Roster 1945 Contingent   12

Name	Country	Rank	Address	Number
Townsend, Glen R.	USA	Col.	750 Byron Place, St. Louis, MO	1705
Trapnell, Thos. J.	USA	Col.	12 Mt. Vernon St., Newport, Ri	1889
Traywick, Jesse T.	USA	Col.	St. Simon Island, GA	1706
Trott, W.A.	Australia	Brig	c/o Bank of Adelaide, Adelaide, South Australia	1618*
Tulfer, Henricus J.	Dutch	Col.	Bandoeng, Java	1795*
Tweedie, M.W.F.	RA	xxx	Oakbank Rye, Sussex, England	2102*
Ulanowicz, Emil M.	USA	Lt.	2229 Bank St.,, Baltimore, MD	1978
Uhl, Johan H.	Dutch	Mj Gen	Ramboetanian I, Bandeong, Java	1613*
Uhrig, Jacob E.	USA	Col.	148 S Polar St., Spokane, WA	1707
Urquhart, Alex A.	RA	Col.	USC, 6 Charles St., St. James, London, England	1761*
Vachon, Jos. P.	USA	Bg Gen	Westbrook, ME	1606
Vandersteen, Pieter H.	Dutch	Col.	Tjelaket 37, Malang, Java	1796*
Van Dyk, Adrianus M.	Dutch	Col.	Ambaramacamp, Senarang, Java	1797*
Vance, Jack R.	USA	Col.	2022 Columbia Rd. NW, Washington, DC	1708
Vance, Lee C.	USA	Col.	Fort Riley, TX	1709
Van Leeuwen, Frank	Dutch	xxx	Bandeong, Java	1800*
Van Gregten, Jan G.	Dutch	Capt.	Bandeong, Java	1798*
Van Kuilenburg, Willem	Dutch	Col.	Bandeong, Java	1799*
Van Kanen, Sipke E.	Dutch	xxx	Djakarta, Java	1801*
Van Oortmerssen, T.C.	Dutch	LT.	D.E.I. Java	2131*
Van Oosten, Adrianus	USA	Maj.	Addison, IL	1894
Van Rekum, Lowys	Dutch	Col.	Bandeong, Java	1802*
Van Rhee, Willem A.	Dutch	Pvt.	Batavia , Java	1869*
Van Stavern, Marius T.	Dutch	Col.	Bandeong, Java	1803*
Van Veen, Willem P.	Dutch	Col.	Bandeong, Java	1804*
Vande, Velde J.	USA	Capt.	1296 W 116th St., Cleveland, OH	1943
Vennik, Henry N.E.	Dutch	Col.	Bandoeng, Java	1805*
Verkerk, Maarten	Dutch	Sgt.	Brayan, Medan, Sumatra	1864*
Vromans, Abraham G.	Dutch	Capt.	Beschermingskamp, Batavia	1806*
Waal, Corneilus H.C.	Dutch	Col.	Bandeong, Java	1807*
Wade, H.	RA	Lt.	c/o War Office, London, England	2198*
Wake, Custer E.	USA	Lt.	2219 Broadway North, Seattle, WA	1944
Walker, Jack K.	USA	Capt.	924 College Ave., Ft. Worth, TX	1937
Walter, J.W.	RA	Pvt.	80 Plymstock Rd., Welling, Kent, England	1851*
Wallis, Cedric	RA	Brig	c/o Eastern Bank, Bishopgate, London, England	1590*
Ward, Fred A.	USA	Col.	Horseheads, NY	1710
Wardle, Valentine H.	RA	Col.	Thornfield, Bishop, Aukland, Durham, England	1762*
Weaver, James R.N.	USA	Bg Gen	Ft. Ord, CA	1598

Mukden Roster 1945 Contingent   13

Name	Service	Rank	Address	No.
Webb, Wm. E.	USA	Capt.	2130 NE 19th St., Oklahoma City, OK	1932
Webb, Ralph B.	Australia	Civil	Grandview Terrace Kew, Melbourne, Australia	1815*
Wehrkamp, Roy V.	USA	Pfc.	317 SE 24th Ave., Portland, OR	1835
Weitzner, Dan N.	USA	Pvt.	Newhaven, CT	2020
Wermuth, Arthur W.	USA	Capt.	Travers City, MI	1939
Wetherby, Loren A.	USA	Col.	4337 15th Ave., NE, Seattle, WA	1711
Whitcombe, Arthur J.	RA	Lt.	Peachhaven, Worcestershire, England	2085*
Whitcomb, Harold J.	USA	Lt.	200 Buchanan St., Fremont, OH	1954
White, Cyril H.	RA	xxx	14 Whitehall Mansion, Archway Rd., London, Eng.	1854*
White, E.R.	Australia	Col.	Melbourne, Australia	1814*
Whitehurst, Mathew S.	803 Eng	Sgt.	2308 Hall St., Richmond, VA	1817
Wildey, Alec W.G.	RA	Brig	c/o Lloyd's Bank, London, Engkand	1583*
Wildy, John P.A.	RA	Capt.	c/o Imperial Bank of India, Puna, India	2061
Williams, Everett C.	USA	Col.	335 Elsmere Rd., Shawer Heights, OH	1712
Wilson, Ovid O.	USA	Col.	233 Howard St., San Antonio, TX	1888
Wilterdink, Wm. H.	USN	Capt.	917 Anselmo Ave., San Anselmo, CA	1722
Wood, Stuart	USA	Col.	55 S Ash St., Southern Pines, NC	1713
Worthington, Joseph W.	USA	Col.	Box 525, 1351 Lakeside Blvd., Brownsville, TX	1714
Wurest, Edwin A.	USMC	Corp.	6439 N Hamilton, Chicago, IL	1833
Yankey, Lucian F.	USA	Pvt.	Perryville, KY	1840
Young, Adlai C.	USA	Col.	1130 N 2nd Ave., Tuscon, Az	1715

Supplementary List.

Name	Service	Rank	Address	No.
Bakker, T.	Dutch	Lt Gen	Bandeong, Java	0050*
Beatton, Cecil	Australia	Gunner	2 Invery St., Concord, NSW, Australia	0060*
Chester, David	RA	Pvt.	Shawlands, Glasgow, Scotland	0052*
Dam, Ruth	Dutch	Pvt.	Kore, Mart 10, Tie, Holland	0059**
Drew, J.W.	RA	Pvt.	Pawlton's Park, Ramsay Hants, England	0062*
Fisher, Fred. C.	RA	Pvt.	35 Tunis St., Sculaates, Hull, England	0078*
Gielkins, J.	Dutch	Corp.	Bandeong, Java	0065*
Gonzales, Gordon B.	USA	Sgt.	Evanston, IL	0063
King, Rollin G.	803 Eng	Pvt.	Box 186, Ford City, PA	0058
Krieze, J.H.	Dutch	Pvt.	Bandeong, Java	0064*
Lay, Billy H.	59 CA	Corp	Van, WV	0100
Peto, Fredrick	RA	Corp.	43 St. Thomas Rd., Hastings, England	0051*
Smith, C.R.	Gov. N. Borneo	Pvt.	Royal Empire Society, London, England	0039*
Speekenbrink, J.C.	Dutch	Pvt.	New York, NY	0058*
Spitts, A.I.	Gov. Sumatra		Medan, Sumatra	0049*

Mukden Roster 1945 Contingent   14

Stewart, Alvin	USA	Sgt.	1115 Lexington, Delano, CA	0095
Tanner, Graham F.	RA	Pvt.	Shannak Rd., Bristol, England	0054*
Ter, Poorten H.	Dutch	Cmdr.	Bandeong, Java	0046*
Uphoff, Chas. F.	USA	Sgt.	xxx	0097
Van Rees, T.	Dutch	Mj Gen	Riouwstraat, N.I. Java	0047*
Yeager, Harlow A.	USA	Corp	Flagstaff, AZ	0053
Young, Sir Mark A.	Gov. Hongkong		Downing St., London, England	0038*

These were the men who were brought in by the Japanese in April and May of 1945. They had been in the Philippines and Formosa until as late as December of 1944. Many of these men were survivors of the ships that had been bombed in the Philippines by American forces.

This supplementary list is somewhat questionable. It is presented here as information only.

The numbers in the last column are the POW numbers assigned by the Japanese in the Mukden (Hoten) camp in Mukden, Manchuria.

* Indicates a member of another Allied Power.

The information in the National and Organization columns refers to the US, British and the Dutch military. Further details are not available.

The data presented here is as best as could be compiled from records that are available. This data is presented as a historical record. It is of particular interest to the men who were in this Prison Camp. It provides a record that has never been made public in the telling of the story of the Mukden POWs. There are 2052 men listed in the original contingent and the May 1945 contingent.

There were men who were in the Mukden Camp that are not listed because the records available are incomplete. There are many numbers unaccounted for.

The survivors of the B29s that bombed Mukden on December 7, 1944 were held in a small compound southeast of the main camp. These men are not in either of the lists published here. Data from Colonel Fortier's book helped to compose this list. Thanks to the Colonel.

Mukden - Remember Those Who Died.

1

Name	Date	No.	Name	Date	No.
Abraham, Ned L.	1/19/43	931	Buck, William E.	12/7/44	624+
Aitken, T.L.	11/?/42	1570	Bush, Ray J.	12/29/42	1374
Alexandrowicz, Casimir E.	12/22/42	509	Bushman, Francis S.	1/16/43	498
Allen, Fred J.	12/9/42	1535	Campbell, Virgil E.	3/27/43	504
Althaus, Rubin M.	12/4/42	1529	Capes, Carl R.	5/11/43	311
Alvis, William B.	2/4/43	1303	Carpenter, Morton E.	12/6/42	1318
Ammons, N.J.	12/10/42	1540	Carr, Ulussis B.	12/7/44	370+
Anderson, James C.	11/22/42	1515	Carver, A.J.	12/27/43	323
Anderson, Leonard V.	1/4/43	666	Casey, Geo. R.	11/26/42	1517
Anderson, Milan E.	11/7/42	1560	Cast, Ellie L.	12/9/42	1322
Armour, LaFaye	11/15/42	1507	Catt. Boyo	12/24/42	1071
Armstrong, Ralph E.	12/20/42	1078	Chandler, Paul B.	1/6/43	1552
Asher, Preston H.	12/18/42	210	Chastain, Joe B.	7/31/43	516X
Atchison,Earnest D.	12/1/42	1524	Cigoi, Walter F.	11/3/42	1565
Aulds, James V.	10/18/42	1563	Cisnneros, Luz R.	4/13/43	603
Baca, Ignacio	12/21/42	1283	Clymer, Milton I.	11/27/43	500
Baffo, Victor	12/9/42	1541	Compton, Bobbie B.	7/14/44	733
Baine, Harry M.	1/12 43	608	Cordoxa, Robert R.	11/23/42	514
Barkowski, J.J.	12/20/42	201	Corley, Richard C.	1/5/43	1366
Beauchat, Eugene P.	12/22/42	551	Cotton, Harry F.	12/8/42	1536
Bell, R.K.	12/6/42	1531	Davidson, Roy L.	1/1/43	792
Bertram, W.P.	12/6/42	1579	Dean, Ben J.	10/28/42	1572
Besserra, Julio T.	5/13/44	447	Deck, Leonard J.	1/4/43	1356
Bidgood, Clyde E.	12/19/42	1286	DeKoch, Edward	12/19/42	1341
Bishoff, David	1/27/43	1477	Delmuth, W.F.	1/7/43	1553
Bond, Duane G.	11/30/42	1526	Dillard, Ersking R.	12/18/42	1339
Branchaud, F.E.	11/17/42	1508	Dysinger, Richard W.	11/17/42	1323
Bressie, Jesse A.	12/10/42	1538	Eagan, Michael W.	1/5/43	1309
Brink, Ralph S.	1/10/43	597	Eckardt, Arthur H.	2/5/43	1420
Brister, Thomas H.	2/23/44	898	Edelbrock, Melville J.	1/24/43	1141
Britton, Albert E.	12/17/42	614	Estel, B.J.	10/28/42	1573
Bronley, Andrew T.	2/10/45	372	Evans, Raymond G.	12/9/42	956
Brookens, James O.	11/29/42	1349	Ewing, Richard D.	2/7/43	1556
Brown, G.J.	11/9/42	1562	Finley, Carl O.	12/22/42	1546
Bruce, Geo. D.	11/27/42	1520	Finnegan, David M.	12/22/42	595
Bryant, Chas. J.	11/29/42	828	Fleming, J.W.	12/7/44	692+

Name	Date	No.
Fleming, Robert W.	1/7/43	448
Fletcher, Garth H.	12/12/42	394
Flowers, Daniel L.	1/10/43	1554
Forbes, Thomas J.	1/23/43	1470
Foster, John G.	1/11/43	962
Francis, James H.	12/27/42	843
Fyke, William L.	11/14/42	1511
Gale, Marvin	1/4/43	752
Galloway, Chas. H.	12/12/42	494
Geerholt, R.E.	11/24/42	390
Giddings, Ralph E.	1/8/43	1461
Gipp, John H.	11/29/42	627
Gooby, A.W.	12/7/44	1235+B
Graves, DeWitt O.	3/4/43	1076
Grayson, William F.	12/25/42	1548
Grizzard, Herbert W.	12/7/44	1088+
Grooms, Hershell A.	12/6/42	1532
Grounds, Edward A.	12/14/42	798
Gussenhaven, Raymond A.	1/19/43	731
Hall, Wilson M.	1/2/43	358
Hanson, Carlos A.	2/19/43	175
Harland, Don W.	7/9/44	759
Harris, Chas. H.	12/9/42	1041
Harshbarger, Raymond H.	3/16/43	1320
Hayes, Geo. W.	11/26/43	598
Headabrand, Howard R.	11/30/42	1265
Heltrich, James H.	12/22/42	1336
Hendrickson, W.E.	12/10/42	1539
Hensey, Donald F.	11/27/42	1519
Henson, James C.	12/20/42	1267
Hoch, Elwell W.	11/12/43	523
Hodge, Perry F.	12/17/42	188
Holliday, Louis T.	12/7/42	1308
Hoovman, Chas. W.	12/20/42	271
Hovarter, Maurice R.	12/29/42	1409
Howard, William A.	11/8/42	1502
Howell, Clayton F.	11/17/42	1509
Hubbard, Robert R.	1/31/43	353
Hurd, Earl A.	12/2/42	1525
Hutton, Roy J.	1/29/43	1403
Jackson, Wendell R.	2/4/43	432
Jessop, J.J.	10/2/42	1566
Jette, Leon R.	12/7/44	730+
Jobb, Thomas W.	12/18/42	246
Johnson, Irvine E.	7/9/43	1255
Johnson, Wendel C.	1/20/43	698
Jones, Harry E.	1/4/43	941
Jones, Robert H.	11/16/42	697
Jones, William B.	11/20/43	946
Joyner, Charles	11/12/42	1503
Junk, P.G.	12/4/42	1528
Kachmar, Stephen A.	1/22/43	560
Karavos, George P.	11/30/42	726
Karlson, Kenneth E.	1/4/43	913
Kirk, Mark	12/13/42	1542
Knight, Billy A.	1/1/43	1332
Knight, Jackson O.	12/6/42	540
Knight, Robert W.	3/5/43	269
Knisley, Donald P.	12/23/42	874
Kuntz, Edward G.	12/27/43	810
Lacko, John W.	11/14/42	1506
Lamarr, Arthur C.	6/20/43	836
Lane, Aurthur V.	12/7/44	741+
Langevine, Hector J.	2/15/43	535
Lapowsky, Lawrence P.	6/14/43	1469
Lay, Billy H.	10/31/42	1568
Lee, Harold E.	11/29/42	1523
Lennartson, James E.	2/26/43	1486
Lester, Kenneth C.	1/9/43	1316
Lewis, Corley B.	10/28/42	1574
Lieb, Robert R.	1/5/43	978
Lollar, Eugen M.	2/27/43	894

3

Mukden - Remember Those Who Died.

Name	Date	No.
Long, Roy J.	12/7/44	317+
Loverix, Campbell	11/21/42	1557
Lurvey, Merle F.	12/20/42	209
Mabry, Lonnie G.	12/7/44	119+
Mc Creedy, O.C.	12/6/42	1533
McCabe, John M.	12/27/42	1056
McDonell, C.-F.	9/30/43	414
McKenna, Linus F.	12/24/42	1555
McWilliams, Dale M.	11/14/42	1505
Mead, Martin C.	3/20/43	1277
Menges, Leone	2/5/43	147
Meringolo, Ferdinand F.	7/31/43	1125X
Merkley, Richard C.	12/9/42	1545
Meyer, Fred E.	11/15/42	1514
Micken, Edwin W.	12/4/42	1527
Midgett, Darius T.	1/23/43	360
Miller, Calvin U.	2/26/43	427
Miller, Carl J.	12/7/42	849
Miller, Harry I.	11/3/42	1567
Miller, James S.	11/29/42	1522
Mitchell, Robert E.	12/7/44	327+
Mock, Martin P.	12/27/42	1474
Morrell, Keith N.	3/19/43	1033
Norris, Peter C.	1/3/43	1321
Page, C.L.	2/28/43	155
Paliotti, Victor	7/31/43	444X
Parker, Delbert L.	4/5/43	280
Pashkewich, William	5/21/43	1248
Piacum, Nichols F.	3/4/43	1330
Pickle, Sterling D.	12/26/42	1292
Pignata, John A.	1/21/43	976
Pigott, Edgar M.	12/16/42	1350
Pinkson, Chas. C.	12/9/42	639
Pitman, Leo	12/3/42	179
Poindexter, D.D.	12/18/42	298
Porch, Troy W.	11/12/42	1504
Pressman, Aaron A.	2/15/43	1016
Prevatt, Barden W.	12/28/42	1549
Privatsky, Ed E.	12/7/44	984+
Proensa, William S.	12/29/42	1393
Pyle, Clarence F.	11/21/42	1510
Quandt, Milton P.	12/4/42	1340
Ravin, Fredrick S.	12/7/44	517+
Ring, Melvin E.	1/3/43	630
Ripley, Joseph W.	1/1/43	222
Roath, Melvin H.	12/29/42	1551
Roetschke, Ralph W.	12/7/44	575+
Rogers, Albert	2/8/43	655
Rogers, Derill L.	12/13/42	1543
Rohrabaugh, Thomas C.	1/19/43	1355
Ruebush, Elbert L.	1/14/43	212
Rydeen, Ernest A.	3/22/43	375
Sabo, Alex J.	12/7/44	1260+
Samuelson, Walter H.	12/7/42	1534
Sanford, Bernard E.	12/30/42	1299
Savage, Clark A.	12/24/42	609
Schanzbach, Donald J.	12/9/42	1537
Schnieder, William T.	12/27/42	1558
Scholl, J.A.	12/7/44	1184+B
Seale, James W.	12/28/42	1550
Sears, Chester R.	3/8/43	1256
Semic, David J.	11/21/42	648
Sharp, Elmer	12/14/42	1544
Shaw, D.M.	11/8/42	1501
Sheridan, Emmet M.	1/21/43	1293
Simpson, Eugene E.	11/7/42	1500
Skareas, Jim D.	11/28/42	889
Sliger, Thomas E.	12/31/42	318
Smith, Walter A.	12/24/42	1547
Sparks, Mirma J.H.	12/20/42	757
Stafford, Louis P.	2/16/43	1257
Stahl, John A.	11/25/42	1518

Mukden - Remember Those Who Died.

4

Standefer, David G.	4/25/43	985
Steeves, James A.	11/26/42	341
Stenzel, Gerald O.	11/19/42	1250
Sturges, F.E.	10/28/42	1571
St. Lauren, Jos. N.	12/28/42	413
Sutton, Billy S.	12/7/44	764+
Teach, Joseph	12/3/42	567
Thickpenny, J.W.	11/22/42	1512
Thompson, Wayne E.	11/15/42	1314
Tilton, Delton L.	1/6/43	1478
Tutlock, P.S.	11/20/42	1561
Turner, David F.	11/26/42	1516
Underwood, Eugene S.	11/28/42	1521
Unglaub, Arthur L.	12/14/42	512
Uphoff, Charles F.	11/7/42	1564
Urban, John S.	10/14/42	1559
Van Agtmael, Joseph	3/3/43	921
Volden, Richard P.	12/5/42	1530
Wall, Thomas E.	12/7/44	366+
Waller, Geo. R.	1/9/43	471
Walsh, Paul A.	11/27/42	519
Warrick, Geo. J.	1/7/43	1331
Watson, Joseph	11/11/42	1369
White, Archie E.	12/16/42	1307
Wilbur, Chas. S.	12/28/42	236
Wilcoxson, John J.	12/4/42	1363
Williams, Carl J.	8/4/43	1471
Wilson, Chas. W.	1/20/43	977
Witter, Willim L.	2/10/43	701
Wolfe, H.W.	11/23/42	1513
Wood, Kenneth C.	12/7/44	1060+
Wood, Lloyd H.	12/26/42	1254
Yancy, Byron O.	12/31/42	1406
Yarrow, Richard A.	12/4/42	1404
Young, E.S.	2/5/43	131

The symbols beside the numbers indicate the following:

(X) Excuted after escaping from the prison camp and recaptured. These men were accused of having killed a Manchurian policeman. This could not be verified after the war ended.

(+) These men were the unfortunates that were killed when the American Air Corp bomb Mukden on December 7, 1944.

(B) British military personnel.

THE MUKDEN RAID OF DECEMBER 7, 1944

I started to research the bombing raid of December 7, 1944 in September of 1991 after I met Charlie Phillips at March Air Force Base, in Southern California during the POW MIA affair. He mentioned John Misterly who had been on one of the B-29s that had bombed Mukden on the 7th. John put me in touch with Denny Pidhayny and Harry Changnon. Harry had flown on the Mukden Raid. The following story about the Mukden Raid was extracted from information provided by Harry Changnon and John Misterly.

The Mukden Mission was launched from the Chengtu area, in the province of Szechwan, about a hundred and sixty-five miles northwest of Chungching. The distance is about thirteen hundred miles, although the bombers flew a little over three thousand miles on the round trip. The raid on Mukden was to be a maximum effort daylight attack on the 7th of December which was the third anniversary of the attack on Pearl Harbor. The 58th Wing of the 20th Air Force was assigned the mission. It was one of the first flights for the B-29s under the weather conditions where they encountered subzero temperatures of more than fifty below zero at an altitude of twenty-two thousand feet.

There were no defrosters on the aircraft, this caused visibility problems because the windshields froze and the pilots and crew members could not see where they were going. The cold temperatures also caused some guns to freeze.

A much better account of the air raid on Mukden is provided by the excerpts from Harry Changnon's unpublished book, B-29 Eddie Allen Story, 1985. These are printed with Harry's permission.

Mission No. 6 - MUKDEN, MANCHURIA

The XX Bomber Command's (XXBC) 19th Mission was on December 7, 1944, the third anniversary of the Pearl Harbor, and was a maximum effort daylight attack by all four Groups of the 58th Wing against the Manchurian Airplane Manufacturing Company plant at Mukden, Manchuria (Target # 177). This was a medium size aircraft assembly plant believed to be producing final-stage training aircraft, similar to Kate. Aircraft engines might also be produced there, or modifications made there on engines from the Mukden Arsenal factories. Buildings contained machine tools, presses, and jigs. Its destruction could delay production six months.

The secondary target was the Drydocks and the Shipping installations at Dairen, Manchuria which could handle ships up to 10,000 tons at the three drydocks. Construction and repair of ship engines and machinery were made there with numerous support shops for welding, boilers, electrical and pneumatic work, and a foundry.

The Last Resort Target was the Chenghsein Yards for the Peking-Hankow Railroad. This was possibly a bottleneck in providing the Japanese an alternate supply route to traffic on the Yangtze River.

A briefing was held during the afternoon of December 3rd at A-1 at which time the PT was announced as being the aircraft factory at Omura, Japan. The weather conditions at the time were questionable. After we had eaten supper and gone to bed for a few hours of sleep before takeoff time, word was sent through the Hostels that the mission had been called off. On the following two consecutive nights the weather forecast at the last minute indicated that Omura would be overcast and unsuitable for daylight precision bombing. On each occasion the mission was postponed just before they were to awaken us for breakfast.

The 20th AF in Washington concurred with XXBC and LeMay a few hours prior to the take-off on December 6th to hit the Mukden targets with the same bomb and gas loads already on the ships. It was planned that planes with new center-section wing tanks would carry a minimum of ten 500# GP bombs while older models took eight 500 pounders. These numbers were increased to achieve more tonnage. In the 45th Squadron of the 40th BG, Harry Changnon flew this mission in #276, one of the original planes, with Lt. Bob Winters and the original Landreth crew. They carried three bomb bay tanks and 15 bombs.On our trip over the hump we had flown in formation to get as much needed practice on that facet of bombing techniques.

We were down on the line with our plane by 2:00. As we, Winters crew, were not amongst the early ones, we didn't start engines until 2:30CST (061930Z) when we saw the first plane taking off. At the time we had a local overcast at 7000 feet with visibility limited to a mile by haze and dust. When we started climbing to altitude we ran into real problems as the glass on our nose kept freezing over despite all of our effort and methods. It was minus 54 degrees below zero at 20,000 feet. Some of us decided to depressurize and go on oxygen as we failed to be able to scrape a hole to see through. Most of us pilots flew with our windows open and a breeze further lowered the wind chill factor. It was miserable, but we had to go on.

Some bombadiers could not keep even a small hole open to look for the target or to keep an eye out for enemy fighters. In the 45th Squadron, Lt. Shorty Norton, flying in #579 kept a small hole, 3"x6", scraped clean in order to be able to see the bombs from the lead plane drop. The cold clear sky was good for formation flying and precision bombing as opposed to flying through clouds. It even helped the gunners spot the fighters coming out of the sun by watching their condensation trails. However, if the blister was frozen over, as most were, a gunner had to guess where fighters might attack. Many guns froze up in the extreme cold and were useless. This was caused by only a trace of moisture or oil on them.

Since we were on the left wing of Major Moss in #407 after we got into formation, Harry Changnon, the author, flew most of the time looking out of the open pilot's window of #276. As we neared Mukden and our bomb run, we put on our cumbersome flak jackets over our Mae Wests, parachutes, and electric flying suits. When I tossed my heavy shielding over my head,part of it bumped the electric suit heat control switch. It went to the "full hot" position. We had to work hard to stay in formation and I was sweating like crazy. Unlike me, everyone else was freezing in the minus 54 degree temperature which caused many cases of frostbite.

As we neared Anshan, where the Japanese expected us to hit the steel plant which had been our PT (Primary Target) on earlier missions, a black smoke screen (probably from oil) covered the entire mill area and most of the adjacent city. The surface winds from the west helped spread the smoke from the smudge pots. The fighters came up to meet us, but did not attack at that time, but flew at our elevations giving information to their gun crews on the ground.

Twenty-three of our 27 40th Group planes reached the PT in two formations. The first bombed from 22,000 feet at 8:27 CST (0127Z) with good observed results (recon photos taken several days later revealed considerable damage to the southern edge of the target area and to the hangar line of the adjacent airfield). An effective smoke screen quickly spread and blanketed the entire area of the aircraft factory, Mukden Arsenal to the west, and the airfield to the south. This formation was led by Major Ernest Turner and the crew in #225 with Lt. Thomas Sample as bombardier. They were preceded five minutes earlier by an 11 plane formation from the 462nd Group and followed by five more XXBC formations as the 80 B-29s hit the Primary, dropping 734 of the 500# GP demolition and 316 incendiary 500#ers during a 53 minute period.

The EDDIE ALLEN, #579, was in #2 position of this 14 plane

formation and was flown by Major Ira Matthews with the same crew members that had flown the recent Omura (Kyushu, Japan).

Harry Changnon was in the 5th formation of 11 planes which was led by Major Jack Eigenmann in #582. We were in our bomb run with our bomb doors open when there was an accidental release of the bombs by the deputy leader in #729. During the heavy fighter attack,the bombardier bumped the salvo switch (the safety cover had been removed at the start of the bomb run) as he swung his guns around to shoot at an approaching fighter. The rest of our formation, looking out holes in the frosted windows, quickly dropped our bombs when we saw the other bombs falling. I remember yelling at Harry Polansky, our bombardier, to drop our bombs. We were about three minutes early and nine miles short of the target. The bombs landed in the Su Hu Ton Railroad Yard and did some damage to rolling stock and tracks, but this was minor damage to the Japanese as compared to what the bombs might have done on the PT. Our lead bombardier, Lt. Jesse Ohr, in #582, continued on and dropped into the smoke screen in the target area as did three other aircraft.

Enemy AA fire over Mukden was moderate with flak consisting of black or white bursts in contrast to multi-colors we saw over Japan. However, the fighter opposition was far heavier than expected. At the briefing Major Louis Scherck, our S-2 officer, had told us that we would see mostly training planes and not many fighters up there in Manchuria. Evidently the Japanese had increased the number of planes to better defend against our raids in that area. Most of these pilots were better trained and much more aggressive than normal. One time I had to quickly lift the left wing as a twin-engined NICK flashed through our formation, barely missing all of us. We did notice one band of planes whose pilots appeared green and inexperienced. They were flying TOJOs which were fresh off of the production line which were not camouflaged and didn't even have the usual oil streaks on them.

Two of our Superfortresses were rammed by the Japanese and went down over Mukden. One may have been by accident. Only four parachutes were seen coming out of the two planes. Some of these unlucky fliers became POWs and were held there in the Mukden POW Camp which had a bad reputation. The Japanese did experiments on some of their prisoners that were against all Geneva Pact Rules. Some of the POWs held at Mukden were brought from the Philippines and the Bataan Death March and included the famous General Jonathan Wainwright.

When we landed there was alight rain and snow conditions. Some of our crew had to go to the hospital for treatment of frostbitten hands or faces due to the long exposure at sub-zero temperatures.

Interesting statistics for the Mukden Mission were that we averaged 13:20 hours for the 3,200 mile trip with only 5:42 (hours) spent on the way to the target.

In general, the bombing results were not as good as expected because bombs which had been dropped into the smoking target area were scattered. The heaviest damage was done immediately west and adjacent to the Aircraft factory. Of the eight formations attacking, only one really hit the factory itself; three obtained hits in the Arsenal area; one dropped in an area of barracks and administrative buildings south of the Arsenal; one dropped on the edge of the airfield over a mile from the target; and one dropped two miles north of the target when the bombs would not release on time from the lead plane (the few seconds it lost before salvoing them on the second release caused them to overshoot); * and finally there was the formation that we flew in which dropped two minutes early and except for the lead planes mostly wasted our bombs.

It made us sick to think that we had flown all that distance in freezing conditions and real danger to inflict such small damage to the aircraft plant. We were all aware that it meant that we would have to go back and do the job another time with probable more losses of men and planes. At that time, we men that did the flying, didn't appreciate how hard it was for General LeMay and the XXBC to send such poor results on to Washington and the Chiefs there.

The official XXBC report for Mission #19 listed 40th Group results this way:

2nd Formation 0128Z, 40th Bomb Group, 14 aircraft.

"The pattern obtained by the 2nd formation was centered approximately 1500 feet south of the A.P. Several hits or near misses were scored on the long flight hangar at the south edge of the works and several aircraft may also have been damaged. Each of the two propeller-mounting hangars appear to have received at least two hits and the large final assembly building in the northeast section of the plant was also hit, and a number of hits were scored in the barracks and administrative area south and east of the target."

5th Formation 0147Z, 40th Bomb Group, 11 aircraft.

"Due to an early release by one aircraft in the forward part of the formation (aircraft was hit by fighters, lost an engine, salvoed bombs in order to stay in formation) all aircraft except the leader dropped approximately 9 miles southwest of Mukden. About 40 of the bombs fell in the Su Hu Ton Railway Yards, scoring hits on trackage and rolling stock. The formation continued over the aircraft factory where the leader dropped his bombs. Impact was not identified because of smoke, but it is thought these bombs fell in the east part of the Arsenal."

Note the asterisk (*) on the previous page. I remember that a discussion that was held after the raid. I stated that I thought that the reason the two bombs hit us was because of hung bombs. I am reasonably sure that these were the bombs that landed in our prison camp.

Colonel Matsuda, the camp commander, with